Palgrave Handbooks in German Idealism

**Series Editor**
Matthew C. Altman
Philosophy & Religious Studies
Central Washington University
Ellensburg, WA, USA

Palgrave Handbooks in German Idealism is a series of comprehensive and authoritative edited volumes on the major German Idealist philosophers and their critics. Underpinning the series is the successful *Palgrave Handbook of German Idealism* (2014), edited by Matthew C. Altman, which provides an overview of the period, its greatest philosophers, and its historical and philosophical importance.

Individual volumes focus on specific philosophers and major themes, offering a more detailed treatment of the many facets of their work in metaphysics, epistemology, logic, ethics, aesthetics, political philosophy, and several other areas. Each volume is edited by one or more internationally recognized experts in the subject, and contributors include both established figures and younger scholars with innovative readings. The series offers a wide-ranging and authoritative insight into German Idealism, appropriate for both students and specialists.

More information about this series at
http://www.palgrave.com/gp/series/14696

Elizabeth Millán Brusslan
Editor

# The Palgrave Handbook of German Romantic Philosophy

*Editor*
Elizabeth Millán Brusslan
Department of Philosophy
DePaul University
Chicago, IL, USA

ISSN 2634-6230     ISSN 2634-6249 (electronic)
Palgrave Handbooks in German Idealism
ISBN 978-3-030-53566-7     ISBN 978-3-030-53567-4 (eBook)
https://doi.org/10.1007/978-3-030-53567-4

© The Editor(s) (if applicable) and The Author(s) 2020
This work is subject to copyright. All rights are solely and exclusively licensed by the Publisher, whether the whole or part of the material is concerned, specifically the rights of translation, reprinting, reuse of illustrations, recitation, broadcasting, reproduction on microfilms or in any other physical way, and transmission or information storage and retrieval, electronic adaptation, computer software, or by similar or dissimilar methodology now known or hereafter developed.
The use of general descriptive names, registered names, trademarks, service marks, etc. in this publication does not imply, even in the absence of a specific statement, that such names are exempt from the relevant protective laws and regulations and therefore free for general use.
The publisher, the authors and the editors are safe to assume that the advice and information in this book are believed to be true and accurate at the date of publication. Neither the publisher nor the authors or the editors give a warranty, expressed or implied, with respect to the material contained herein or for any errors or omissions that may have been made. The publisher remains neutral with regard to jurisdictional claims in published maps and institutional affiliations.

Cover illustration: Italian landscape with umbrella pines, Hendrik Voogd, 1807

This Palgrave Macmillan imprint is published by the registered company Springer Nature Switzerland AG.
The registered company address is: Gewerbestrasse 11, 6330 Cham, Switzerland

*In loving memory of Michael Mack (8/23/1969-8/21/2020),
who left us far too soon.*

# Palgrave Handbooks in German Idealism Series

*Series Editor:*
Matthew C. Altman, Central Washington University, Ellensburg, WA, USA
*The Palgrave Kant Handbook*
    Edited by Matthew C. Altman
*The Palgrave Schopenhauer Handbook*
    Edited by Sandra Shapshay
*The Palgrave Fichte Handbook*
    Edited by Steven Hoeltzel
*The Palgrave Hegel Handbook*
    Edited by Marina F. Bykova and Kenneth R. Westphal
*The Palgrave Handbook of German Idealism and Existentialism*
    Edited by Jon Stewart
*The Palgrave Handbook of German Romantic Philosophy*
    Edited by Elizabeth Millán Brusslan
*The Palgrave Schelling Handbook* (forthcoming)
    Edited by Sean J. McGrath & Kyla Bruff
*The Palgrave Handbook of German Idealism and Feminist Philosophy* (forthcoming)
    Edited by Susanne Lettow and Tuija Pulkkinen
*The Palgrave Handbook of German Idealism and Phenomenology* (forthcoming)
    Edited by Cynthia D. Coe
*The Palgrave Tillich Handbook* (forthcoming)
    Edited by Russell Re Manning & Harald Matern
*Palgrave Handbook of German Idealism and Analytic Philosophy* (forthcoming)

# Series Editor's Preface

The era of German Idealism stands alongside ancient Greece and the French Enlightenment as one of the most fruitful and influential periods in the history of philosophy. Beginning with the publication of Kant's *Critique of Pure Reason* in 1781 and ending about ten years after Hegel's death in 1831, the period of "classical German philosophy" transformed whole fields of philosophical endeavor. The intellectual energy of this movement is still very much alive in contemporary philosophy; the philosophers of that period continue to inform our thinking and spark debates of interpretation.

After a period of neglect as a result of the early analytic philosophers' rejection of idealism, interest in the field has grown exponentially in recent years. Indeed, the study of German Idealism has perhaps never been more active in the English-speaking world than it is today. Many books appear every year that offer historical/interpretive approaches to understanding the work of the German Idealists, and many others adopt and develop their insights and apply them to contemporary issues in epistemology, metaphysics, ethics, politics, and aesthetics, among other fields. In addition, a number of international journals are devoted to idealism as a whole and to specific idealist philosophers, and journals in both the history of philosophy and contemporary philosophies have regular contributions on the German Idealists. In numerous countries, there are regular conferences and study groups run by philosophical associations that focus on this period and its key figures, especially Kant, Fichte, Schelling, Hegel, and Schopenhauer.

As part of this growing discussion, the volumes in the *Palgrave Handbooks in German Idealism* series are designed to provide overviews of the major figures and movements in German Idealism, with a breadth and depth of coverage that distinguishes them from other anthologies. Chapters have been specially commissioned for this series, and they are written by established and emerging scholars from throughout the world. Contributors not only provide overviews of their subject matter but also explore the cutting edge of the field by advancing original theses. Some authors develop or revise positions that they have taken in their other publications, and some take novel approaches that challenge existing paradigms. The *Palgrave Handbooks in German Idealism* thus give students a natural starting point from which to begin their study of German Idealism, and they serve as a resource for advanced scholars to engage in meaningful discussions about the movement's philosophical and historical importance.

In short, the *Palgrave Handbooks in German Idealism* have comprehensiveness, accessibility, depth, and philosophical rigor as their overriding goals. These are challenging aims, to be sure, especially when held simultaneously, but that is the task that the excellent scholars who are editing and contributing to these volumes have set for themselves.

Ellensburg, WA, USA                                                                      Matthew C. Altman

# Acknowledgments

This volume is the result of a rich network of collaboration, of *Symphilosophie*, and I feel lucky to be indebted to so many intelligent, generous people. I am grateful to each and every one of the contributors to this volume, who made working on such a large project a true pleasure and a most rewarding intellectual endeavor. The volume would not have taken its final form without the generosity, patience, and wisdom of the editors at Palgrave, especially Lauriane Piette, who were so supportive and helpful during all stages of this project. Matthew Altman, the series editor of the *Palgrave Handbooks in German Idealism*, gave me the wonderful opportunity to reflect upon new aspects of German Romantic Philosophy when he invited me to join first as a contributor to his volume on German Idealism and then as an editor of the present volume. His outstanding work is a model that guided me in my labors. I was a part of the *Palgrave Schopenhauer Handbook*, edited by Sandra Shapshay, and her volume was a bright light of orientation for me as I worked on this handbook. George di Giovanni was not able to contribute to the present volume, but he was generous enough to recommend Paolo Livieri and Anna Ezekiel, two excellent scholars, and their work has strengthened this handbook. While neither Karl Ameriks nor Rachel Zuckert have essays in the present volume, their work and steadfast support helped bring the handbook to life. My own beginning with *Frühromantik* began in Tübingen with Manfred Frank, whose work continues to shape the field and whose intellectual generosity was and remains a great gift. DePaul University has supported my work in so many ways over the last 20 years, as have my excellent colleagues and students in the Department of Philosophy. Jamie and Michael Brusslan make my life so beautiful and fun; they are my inspiration for just about everything.

# Contents

1 The Meaning of German Romanticism for the Philosopher     1
  *Elizabeth Millán Brusslan*

**Part I    Historical Context**     17

2 The Poem of the Understanding: Kant, Novalis, and Early
  German Romantic Philosophy     19
  *Jane Kneller*

3 F.H. Jacobi on Reason and Nihilism in Romanticism     41
  *Paolo Livieri*

4 Spinoza and Romanticism     65
  *Michael Mack*

5 Religion and Early German Romanticism     95
  *Jacqueline Mariña*

6 Femininity and the Salon     119
  *Anne Pollok*

7 Fichte's Subject and Its Romantic Transformations     141
  *Andrew J. Mitchell*

8  Friedrich Schiller and the Aestheticization of Ethics  157
   *Marina F. Bykova*

9  Johann Gottfried Herder: Misunderstood Romantic?  177
   *Johannes Schmidt*

10 Hermeneutics and Orientation: Retracing the 'Sciences of the Spirit' (*Geisteswissenschaften*) in the Education-Related Writings of Fichte, Schleiermacher and Novalis  205
   *John G. Moore*

## Part II  Aesthetics and Romanticism  231

11 Philosophical Critique and Literary Criticism in German Romanticism  233
   *J. Colin McQuillan*

12 Romantic Irony  255
   *Karolin Mirzakhan*

13 The Role of the Fragment in German Romantic Philosophy and Nietzsche  271
   *Guy Elgat*

14 Early German Romanticism and Literature: Goethe, Schlegel, Novalis and the New Philosophical Importance of the Novel  297
   *Allen Speight*

15 The Cinematic Afterlife of German Romanticism  317
   *Laurie Johnson*

## Part III  Romanticism and the Sciences  345

16 Romantic Biology: Carl Gustav Carus at the Edge of the Modern  347
   *Robert J. Richards*

| | | |
|---|---|---|
| 17 | Goethe's Philosophy of Nature<br>*Tim Mehigan and Peter Banki* | 375 |
| 18 | Romantic Acts of Generation<br>*Jocelyn Holland* | 399 |
| 19 | Arts of Unconditioning: On Romantic Science and Poetry<br>*Gabriel Trop* | 421 |
| 20 | Romantic Conceptions of Life<br>*Leif Weatherby* | 449 |

## Part IV  Legacy  473

| | | |
|---|---|---|
| 21 | Women, Women Writers, and Early German Romanticism<br>*Anna Ezekiel* | 475 |
| 22 | Romantic Philosophy as Anthropology<br>*Carl Niekerk* | 511 |
| 23 | From the Pantheism Panic to Modern Anxiety: Friedrich Schelling's Invention of the Philosophy of "Angst"<br>*Jeffrey S. Librett* | 535 |
| 24 | Romanticism and Pessimism<br>*Frederick Beiser* | 573 |
| 25 | Romanticism as Modernism: Richard Wagner's "Artwork of the Future"<br>*Günter Zöller* | 587 |
| 26 | Between Appropriation and Transmission: The Romantic Thread in Heidegger's Existential Notion of Understanding<br>*Pol Vandevelde* | 607 |

27 Sensibility, Reflection, and Play: Early German Romanticism
and Its Legacy in Contemporary Continental Philosophy        631
*Elaine P. Miller*

28 'The Concept of Critique': Between Early German
Romanticism and Early Critical Theory        661
*Nathan Ross*

29 Romanticism, Anarchism, and Critical Theory        683
*Fred Rush*

30 Conclusion: Romantic Currents of Thought: An Open Ending   705
*Elizabeth Millán Brusslan*

Index        711

# Abbreviations

NS.   *Novalis. Schriften*, in three volumes, ed., Richard Samuel, Hans-Joachim Mähl and Gerhard Schulz (Darmstadt: Wissenschaftliche Buchgesellschaft, 1965).

KFSA   Friedrich Schlegel, *Kritische Ausgabe*, 35 volumes, ed., Ernst Behler (in collaboration with Jean-Jacques Anstett, Jakob Baxa, Ursula Behler, Liselotte Dieckmann, Hans Eichner, Raymond Immerwahr, Robert L. Kahn, Eugene Susini, Bertold Sutter, A. Leslie Wilson, and others) (Paderborn: Ferdinand Schöningh, 1958ff.).

# Notes on Contributors

**Peter Banki** is an associate member of the Philosophy Research Initiative at Western Sydney University, Australia. He is the author of *The Forgiveness To Come: the Holocaust and the Hyper-Ethical* (2017). He has also published in the fields of German Romanticism, post-structuralism, and the philosophy of sexuality.

**Frederick Beiser** is Professor of Philosophy at Syracuse University. He works on the history of modern philosophy, especially the history of German philosophy (Kant and German Idealism) and the English Enlightenment. Publications include *The Fate of Reason: German Philosophy from Kant to Fichte* (1987), *German Idealism. The Struggle against Subjectivism 1781–1801* (2002), *The Romantic Imperative. The Concept of Early German Romanticism* (2003), *Diotima's Children. German Aesthetic Rationalism from Leibniz to Lessing* (2009), and *Weltschmerz: Pessimism in German Philosophy 1860–1900* (2016).

**Marina F. Bykova** is Professor of Philosophy at North Carolina State University. She is the author of *The Mystery of Logic and the Secret of Subjectivity* (1996), *Hegel's Interpretation of Thinking* (1990), and the co-author of *Absolute Idea and Absolute Spirit in Hegel's Philosophy* (1993). She has edited Russian translation of Hegel's *Phenomenology of Spirit* (2000) and, most recently, *Hegel's Philosophy of Spirit: A Critical Guide* (2019), *The Palgrave Hegel Handbook* (with Kenneth R. Westphal; 2019), and *The German Idealism Reader: Ideas, Responses and Legacy* (2020, forthcoming).

**Guy Elgat** teaches at the School of the Art Institute of Chicago. He has written articles on the thought of Friedrich Nietzsche in various journals and is the author of *Nietzsche's Psychology of Ressentiment* (2017). He is working on a book on guilt in German philosophy.

**Anna Ezekiel** is an independent scholar working on feminist history of philosophy. In addition to publishing papers on the philosophy of Romantic writer Karoline von Günderrode, she is the translator of Günderrode's *Poetic Fragments* (2016); a collection of Günderrode's philosophical writings (*Philosophical Fragments*, forthcoming); and the German texts for *Women Philosophers of the Long 19th Century*, ed. Gjesdal and Nassar (forthcoming).

**Jocelyn Holland** is Professor of Comparative Literature at the California Institute of Technology. She is the author of *German Romanticism and Science* (2009), *Key Texts of Johann Wilhelm Ritter on the Science and Art of Nature* (2010), and *The Lever as Instrument of Reason* (2019). Co-edited projects include the aesthetics of the tool, theories of time-keeping, the Archimedean point in modernity, the role of equilibrium circa 1800, and most recently, the concept of the anomaly.

**Laurie Johnson** is Professor of German, Comparative and World Literature, and Criticism and Interpretive Theory at the University of Illinois at Urbana-Champaign. She is the author of *Forgotten Dreams: Revisiting Romanticism in the Cinema of Werner Herzog* (2016; paperback 2019), *Aesthetic Anxiety* (2010), and *The Art of Recollection in Jena Romanticism* (2002) as well as numerous articles.

**Jane Kneller** is Professor Emerita at Colorado State University. She is the author of *Kant and the Power of Imagination* (2007) and the editor and translator of *Novalis: Fichte Studies*, (2003). She is also the author of numerous articles on Kantian aesthetics, Novalis and early German Romanticism, and feminist critiques of Kant.

**Jeffrey S. Librett** is Professor of German at the University of Oregon and a psychoanalyst in private practice. He is the author of *The Rhetoric of Cultural Dialogue: Jews and Germans from Moses Mendelssohn to Richard Wagner and Beyond* (2000), and *Orientalism and the Figure of the Jew* (2015), and numerous essays. He is working on a genealogy of anxiety.

**Paolo Livieri** is JSPS Fellow at Hosei University, Tokyo. He is the author of *The Thought of the Object: Genesis and Structure of Section "Objectivity" in Hegel's Wissenschaft der Logik* (2012). He is working on the English edition of F.H. Jacobi's *Von den göttlichen Dingen und Ihre Offenbarung*.

**Michael Mack** was Associate Professor of English at Durham University. He is the author of *Contaminations: Beyond Dialectics in Modern Literature, Science and Film* (2016), *Philosophy and Literature in Times of Crisis: Challenging our Infatuation with Numbers* (2014), *How Literature Changes the Way we Think* (2012), *Spinoza and the Specters of Modernity: the hidden Enlightenment of Diversity from Spinoza to Freud* (2010), *German Idealism and the Jew: The Inner Antisemitism of Philosophy and German Jewish Responses* (2003) and *Anthropology as Memory: Elias Canetti's and Franz Baermann Steiner's Responses to the Shoah* (2001). He co-edited *The Palgrave Handbook of Philosophy and Literature* (2018) and wrote over fifty articles in peer-reviewed journals and books.

**Jacqueline Mariña** is Professor of Philosophy at Purdue University. She is the author of *Transformation of the Self in the Thought of Friedrich Schleiermacher* (2008). She edited the *Cambridge companion to Friedrich Schleiermacher* (2005) and is the author of numerous papers on Kant and in the history of philosophy more broadly. She is currently finishing a book on Kant, *Freedom and Insight*.

**J. Colin McQuillan** is Associate Professor of Philosophy at St. Mary's University in San Antonio, TX. He is the author of *Early Modern Aesthetics* (2015) and *Immanuel Kant: The Very Idea of a Critique of Pure Reason* (2016). He is also the editor (with Joseph Tanke) of *The Bloomsbury Anthology of Aesthetics* (2012) and (with María del Rosario Acosta López) *Critique in German Philosophy* (2020).

**Tim Mehigan** is Professor of German at the University of Queensland, Australia. He is the author of *Robert Musil and the Question of Science* (2020) and *Heinrich von Kleist: Writing after Kant* (2011). With Barry Empson he provided the first English translation of K.L. Reinhold's *Essay on a New Theory of the Human Capacity for Representation* (2011).

**Elizabeth Millán Brusslan** is Professor of Philosophy at DePaul University. Her research focuses on aesthetics, German Idealism/Romanticism and Latin American philosophy. Her previous publications include *Friedrich Schlegel and the Emergence of Romantic Philosophy* (2007), (with Bärbel Frischmann) *Das neue Licht der Frühromantik/ The New Light of German Romanticism* (2008), and (with Judith Norman) *Brill's Companion to German Romantic Philosophy* (2019). In addition, she contributed "Borderline Philosophy? Incompleteness, Incomprehension, and the Romantic Transformation of Philosophy" to the *International Yearbook of German Idealism*, Vol. 6 (2009) and has published many articles on the relation between German Idealism and the development of early German romantic philosophy.

**Elaine P. Miller** is Professor of Philosophy at Miami University. She researches and teaches nineteenth-century German philosophy and contemporary European feminist theory, particularly aesthetics and the philosophy of nature. Her books include *Head Cases: Julia Kristeva on Philosophy and Art in Depressed Times* (2014), *The Vegetative Soul: From Philosophy of Nature to Subjectivity in the Feminine* (2002), and an edited collection, *Returning to Irigaray: Feminist Philosophy, Politics, and the Question of Unity* (2006). She has also written articles in *Idealistic Studies*, *The Journal of Nietzsche Studies*, and *Oxford Literary Review*, among others.

**Karolin Mirzakhan** is a Lecturer of Philosophy at Kennesaw State University (Atlanta, Georgia). She earned her PhD from DePaul University (Chicago, Illinois). Her doctoral research focused on comedy and irony in G.W.F. Hegel and Friedrich Schlegel, respectively. Her forthcoming monograph, *An Ironic Approach to the Absolute: Schlegel's Poetic Mysticism*, brings Schlegelian irony in conversation with ancient and contemporary texts in an effort to uncover how irony reveals the Absolute to its readers.

**Andrew J. Mitchell** is Winship Distinguished Research Professor of Philosophy at Emory University specializing in nineteenth and twentieth centuries German philosophy (romanticism, Nietzsche, phenomenology). He is the author of *The Fourfold: Reading the Late Heidegger* (2015) and *Heidegger Among the Sculptors: Body, Space, and the Art of Dwelling* (2010).

**John G. Moore** is Professor of Philosophy at Lander University, where he has taught basic courses in undergraduate philosophy to first-generation college students for the last twenty-one years. He earned his doctorate in philosophy from Emory University, after completing a D.A.A.D. dissertation fellowship at the Rühr-Universität in Germany. In recent years, he has presented papers on diverse philosophical topics at international conferences in Japan, Finland, England, Italy, and the Netherlands. He is working on a book-length study about the role of hermeneutics in German universities, the Berlin-diaspora, and the German-American dialogue.

**Carl Niekerk** is Professor of German, Comparative and World Literature, and Jewish Studies at the University of Illinois at Urbana-Champaign. He is the author of *Reading Mahler: German Culture and Jewish Identity in Fin-de-siècle Vienna* (2010/13), and he recently edited *The Radical Enlightenment in Germany: A Cultural Perspective* (2018). He currently serves as the editor of the *German Quarterly* and the *Lessing Yearbook*.

**Anne Pollok** is Wissenschaftliche Mitarbeiterin at Johannes Gutenberg Universität, Mainz, Germany. She is author of *Facetten des Menschen. Zur Anthropologie Moses Mendelssohns* (2010) and of numerous articles on eighteenth-century aesthetics and anthropology, Ernst Cassirer, and women philosophers in the eighteenth and nineteenth centuries. She is co-editor of *The Method of Culture. Ernst Cassirer's Philosophy of Symbolic Forms* and the *Bloomsbury Series in Early German Philosophy*.

**Robert J. Richards** is the Morris Fishbein Distinguished Service Professor of the History of Science at the University of Chicago. His area of research is German Romanticism and the history of evolutionary theory. He is the author of several books, including *The Romantic Conception of Life: Science and Philosophy in the Age of Goethe* (2002); *The Tragic Sense of Life: Ernst Haeckel and the Struggle over Evolutionary Thought* (2008); and with Michael Ruse, *Debating Darwin* (2016). He is writing an intellectual biography of Carl Gustav Carus.

**Nathan Ross** is Assistant Director of the Faculty Center for Professional Excellence at Adelphi University. He is the author of *The Philosophy and Politics of Aesthetic Experience: German Romanticism and Critical Theory* (2017) and *On Mechanism in Hegel's Social and Political Philosophy* (2008). He edited *The Aesthetic Ground of Critical Theory: New Readings of Benjamin and Adorno* (2015).

**Fred Rush** is Professor of Philosophy at the University of Notre Dame. He is the author of *Irony and Idealism* (2016) and *On Architecture* (2009). He edited *The Cambridge Companion to Critical Theory* (2004) and for several years co-edited the *Internationales Jahrbuch des Deutschen Idealismus*.

**Johannes Schmidt** is Professor of German at Clemson University. His recent publications include "'I do desire no free will': G.E. Lessing's Peculiar View on Human Freedom" (*Eighteenth-Century Studies* 52,3) and "Herder's Religious Anthropology in His Later Writings" (Nigel DeSouza, Anik Waldow (eds.): *Herder. Philosophy and Anthropology* (2017)). He co-edits the *Herder Yearbook* and was co-editor of *Herder and Religion* (2016).

**Allen Speight,** PhD, University of Chicago, is Associate Professor of Philosophy at Boston University. A recipient of Fulbright, DAAD and Berlin Prize Fellowships, he is the author of *Hegel, Literature and the Problem of*

*Agency* (2001); *The Philosophy of Hegel* (2008); co-editor/translator of *Hegel's Heidelberg Writings* (2009); and editor of *Philosophy, Narrative and Life* (2015).

**Gabriel Trop** is Associate Professor of German at the University of North Carolina in Chapel Hill. He is the author of *Poetry as a Way of Life: Aesthetics and Askesis in the German Eighteenth Century* (2015) and co-edited the volume *Posthumanism in the Age of Humanism: Mind, Matter, and the Life Sciences after Kant* with Edgar Landgraf and Leif Weatherby (2018).

**Pol Vandevelde** (PhD Université de Louvain) is Professor of Philosophy at Marquette University. He is the author of *Être et Discours: La question du langage dans l'itinéraire de Heidegger (1927–1938)* (1994), *The Task of the Interpreter: Text, Meaning, and Negotiation* (2005); and *Heidegger and the Romantics: The Literary Invention of Meaning* (2012). He is also a translator and the co-editor of *Études phénoménologiques—Phenomenological Studies*.

**Leif Weatherby** is Associate Professor of German and the Director of the Digital Theory Lab at NYU. He is the author of *Transplanting the Metaphysical Organ: German Romanticism between Leibniz and Marx* (2016). He writes about German Romanticism and Idealism, digital media, and political economy.

**Günter Zöller** is Professor of Philosophy at the University of Munich. He is the author of *Objective Reference in Kant* (1984), *Fichte's Transcendental Philosophy* (1998), *Reading Fichte* (2013), *Res Publica* (2015), and *Philosophy of the 19th Century* (C. H. Beck, 2018). He edited *The State As a Means to an End* (2011) and co-edited *The Cambridge Companion to Fichte* (2016).

# List of Figures

| | | |
|---|---|---|
| Fig. 16.1 | Carl Gustav Carus (1789–1869), at about age 35; portrait (1824) by Carl Rössler | 356 |
| Fig. 16.2 | (a) Caspar David Friedrich, *Mondaufgang am Meer* (1822). (b) Carl Gustav Carus, *Blick auf Dresden bei Sonnenuntergang* (1822) | 357 |
| Fig. 16.3 | Johann Wolfgang von Goethe (1749–1832). (Portrait [1828] by Joseph Karl Stieler) | 360 |
| Fig. 16.4 | (a and b) The lower plate illustrates a human skull (lower image) and skull of a dog, with six skull bones marked in Roman numerals; the upper plate illustrates a teleost fish, a Jawless fish (fig. 2), a vertebra (fig. 3), and the "simplest schema" (fig. 1), or the archetype, all with the six anterior skull bones identified. Other plates trace the six skull bones in many other animals. From Carus's Von den Ur-Theilen des Knochen-und Schalengerütes (1828) | 364 |
| Fig. 16.5 | On the left, Carus's image of the archetype and two fish, from his *Von den Ur-Theilen und den Knochen-und Schalengerüstes* (1828); on the right, Owen's image of the archetype (top) and a fish, from his *On the Archetype and the Homologies of the Vertebrate Skeleton* (1848) | 367 |

# 1

# The Meaning of German Romanticism for the Philosopher

## Elizabeth Millán Brusslan

In 1941, when A.O. Lovejoy addressed the meaning of Romanticism for the historian of ideas, he lamented the trouble with coming to clarity regarding this term. In answering the question, "what is the meaning of Romanticism," Lovejoy wrote, "one's answer would express a judgment about what chiefly makes the historical thing called 'Romanticism' if there is any such thing—'important' what aspect or what effects of it are most noteworthy or momentous."[1] In the past decades, any doubt concerning whether Romanticism exists has vanished, and more and more work has illuminated its enduring importance not only for literary scholars but also for philosophers and historians of science. With this volume, I seek to offer a broad picture of early German Romanticism and of its philosophical importance. The volume is dedicated to a careful investigation of the meaning of early German Romanticism/*Frühromantik* for philosophers. Investigation into the meaning of Romanticism for philosophers has been an ongoing one for me. In 2005, upon the invitation of my colleague David Pellauer, I prepared a review article for *Philosophy Today* in order to explore what I dubbed "The Revival of *Frühromantik* in the Anglophone World."[2] Since 2005, the revival has continued, indeed morphed into a kind of romantic renaissance, and the volume of

---

A riff on A.O. Lovejoy's, "The Meaning of Romanticism for the Historian of Ideas," in *Journal of the History of Ideas*, Volume 2, No. 3 (June, 1941): 257–278.

---

E. Millán Brusslan (✉)
Department of Philosophy, DePaul University, Chicago, IL, USA

© The Author(s) 2020
E. Millán Brusslan (ed.), *The Palgrave Handbook of German Romantic Philosophy*, Palgrave Handbooks in German Idealism, https://doi.org/10.1007/978-3-030-53567-4_1

scholarly work on the philosophical dimensions of early German Romanticism has increased in exciting new directions.[3] One of the main aims of the *Palgrave Handbook of German Romantic Philosophy* is to provide advanced undergraduate students, graduate students, and scholars in philosophy, intellectual history, literature, science, and the arts a comprehensive view of German Romanticism, one that will enable new connections to be made between the fields of philosophy, literature, history, and science.

Early German Romanticism was unique for many reasons. The early German Romantics were interested in languages and cultures different from their own. For example, they were some of the first to translate Shakespeare and Cervantes into German. The German Romantics were some of the first European thinkers to break from the Eurocentric gaze that held many of their contemporaries hostage. They looked East and helped to develop the field of Sinology in German-speaking lands. They were also among the first to call for the inclusion of women in philosophy. The German Romantics were also most decidedly not deferential when it came to receiving the canonical figures of the period, and their trenchant critiques of figures such as Kant, Jacobi, and Fichte helped to open the post-Kantian period in fruitful ways. The early German Romantics were also some of the first truly interdisciplinary thinkers, and centuries after their call to unite the fields of poetry, philosophy, and science, we are far from heeding and acting on that call. In the spirit of romantic interdisciplinarity, this collection includes the work of philosophers, Germanists, historians, and literary scholars. The following 28 chapters explore several facets of early German Romantic philosophy. In Part I, the historical context of the period is discussed. In Part II, the contributions to aesthetics are the focus, as issues of irony, the fragment, the romantic conception of critique and of the novel, as well the cinematic afterlife of German Romantics, are explored. In Part III, the connections between Romanticism and the sciences are addressed. And in Part IV, the rich legacy of romantic thought is discussed, with a special emphasis on the inclusion of new voices, and the connections between early German Romanticism and both critical theory and continental philosophy are addressed. The collection thus offers accounts of the controversies that shaped the romantic period, while also addressing themes that formed the core set of issues of the period; issues not only of the post-Kantian period, for example, the issues of how German Romanticism relates to classical German Idealism, but also how later developments in modernism and critical theory were shaped by early German Romanticism.

The early German Romantics questioned the power of philosophy to solve problems in isolation from the other disciplines. They also pushed away from the model of the lone thinker working in isolation from the happenings of the world and the collaboration of other people. *Symphilosophie* was not merely a catchword for the early German Romantics; the thinkers of early German Romanticism saw collaboration, community, and friendship as part of the tapestry of their approach to philosophy, an approach that changed the conception of philosophy itself. In place of hierarchies of authority, we find a horizon of voices, each with authority and each contributing to the romantic dialogue. The call to fuse disciplines is resolutely sounded in Schlegel's Critical Fragment Nr. 115, where he claims that "[t]he whole history of modern poetry is a running commentary on the following brief philosophical text: all art should become science and all science art; poetry and philosophy should be made one."[4] A fusion of disciplines led to the development of a new form of expression, one that challenged readers. Adding to the problem of comprehensibility (and incomprehensibility) were the difficult philosophical, political, and social issues addressed by the early German Romantics: questions of the limits of reason, questions of reason and faith, and charges of nihilism all contributed to the intellectual soil of early German Romanticism. The French Revolution ushered in cultural and political changes and the early German Romantics responded to the erosion of political, cultural, and philosophical certainties. The philosophy of the early German Romantics is steeped in the fraught historical circumstances of their time, and the romantic thinkers did not shy away from a direct engagement with divisive cultural and political issues. Both the form and the context of German Romantic philosophy are incredibly diverse and complicated. The new literary forms and the unconventional content of romantic philosophy challenged readers of the late 1700s and continues to hinder reception of the early German Romantic Movement.

## 1 *Frühromantik* and Its Reception

Early German Romanticism flourished in two cities, Berlin and Jena, between the years of 1794 and 1808. Leading figures include the Schlegel brothers (Friedrich and August Wilhelm), Caroline (*née* Bohmer) Schlegel Schelling, Dorothea (*née* Mendelssohn) Veit Schlegel, Friedrich Daniel Ernst Schleiermacher, Friedrich von Hardenberg (Novalis), Wilhelm H. Ludwig and Sophie Tieck, and Wilhelm Wackenroder. The movement was short-lived, lamentably, due in part to the short lives of some of its members: Wackenroder died in 1798, Novalis in 1801. After having been active in Jena and Berlin, in 1802, Friedrich and Dorothea Schlegel left for Paris.[5] So brief was the burst of activity that one of the period's leading scholars, Theodore

Ziolkowski, has located the heart of an already brief intellectual movement in one year, 1794–1795, which he calls *the Wunderjahr* of early German Romanticism.[6]

A few years after the *Wunderjahr*, in 1798, after having left Jena for Berlin, Friedrich Schlegel and his brother founded *Das Athenäum*, a journal dedicated to pushing the boundary between philosophy and poetry and pushing its readers' hermeneutical limits. The journal, like so many aspects of early German Romanticism, was also short-lived, published only between 1798 and 1800. It was a reaction to the conservatism of some of the other journals of the period. As Schlegel put it, the journal would welcome contributions that were "sublimely impudent" (displaying "erhabene Frechheit"), that is, all contributions that were "too good" for other journals.[7] With such a goal, the seeds were sown for a disastrous reception on the part of the reading public, which all too often misunderstood the impudent romantic wink of irony, and found the contents of the journal not only offensive but also incomprehensible.[8] But seen in another, more charitable way, the romantic texts, in their refusal of finitude, of final words, or of closure, were meant to unsettle readers, to keep the process of understanding open and infinite. After all, for Schlegel, one could not *be* a philosopher, but only become one, and to stop the striving after the goal would be tantamount to relinquishing the goal. Alas, incompleteness, a romantic trope, has been (and for some remains) a perennial source of misunderstanding of the work of the early German Romantics. The chapters of this volume open many new paths for approaching and comprehending the work of the early German Romantics.

The contributors of this volume include Germanists, philosophers, and literary scholars, and each of the contributors brings the intellectual value of the early German Romantic Movement into sharp focus. Some of the contributors take paths that intersect with the disciplines of literature or science, but all of the paths converge on philosophy, which provides a vantage point crucial for an accurate assessment of the movement's contributions and an understanding of what the meaning of Romanticism for philosophy is.

## 2   Overview

Each of the four parts of the Handbook will contribute to the creation of fuller presentation of the philosophical contributions of early German Romanticism. The nine chapters of Part I, *Historical Context*, bring German Romantic philosophy into conversation with key figures and problems of the late eighteenth century/early nineteenth century. In this section, Spinoza,

Kant, Jacobi, Fichte, Schiller, and Herder figure prominently as issues of the limits of reason, religion, salon culture, and hermeneutics are explored through the lens of early German Romanticism.

In Chap. 2, *The Poem of the Understanding: Kant, Novalis, and Early German Romantic Philosophy*, Jane Kneller argues that in order to fully appreciate the contributions of early German Romanticism, it is necessary to recognize the important metaphysical and social commitments that this movement shared with Kant. Her focus is on one of the leading philosophers of the early German Romantic Movement, Friedrich von Hardenberg, known as Novalis. After briefly discussing both the philosophical milieu and personal circumstances of Novalis' defining contribution to early German Romanticism, Novalis' reception of Kant's work is examined and the case is made for the profound influence of Kant on Novalis' philosophical development. The chapter closes with a discussion of how Novalis' adoption of Kant's transcendental constraints on human knowledge provided the space for a profoundly new conception of the possibilities of human cognitive and social development.

As Kneller convincingly demonstrates, many paths the early German Romantics forged were opened by Kant. Kant was not the only prominent thinker in the orbit of early German Romanticism. Spinoza, Jacobi, Schiller, and Fichte loom large as well. In Chap. 3, *F.H. Jacobi on Reason and Nihilism in Romanticism*, Paolo Livieri presents the tensions between Jacobi and Fichte and offers an account of the consequences of these tensions for the development of romantic thought. Livieri presents an account of Jacobi's view that the system of reason, especially in the *Wissenschaftslehre*, amounted to the annihilation of the notion of God, which eventually leads to the negation of existence in general. Jacobi interpreted Fichte's rational system as the total annihilation of true Being. Livieri presents Jacobi's portrait of reason as one that denies neither God nor existence. In this chapter, we see that Jacobi's dispute with Fichte evolved into an examination of the limits of reason and a study of Being. Jacobi's *Letter to Fichte* (1799) brought the *Atheismusstreit* to a climax, and Livieri presents it as an essential element for an understanding of both Jacobi's thought and the history of post-Kantian philosophy. In Livieri's chapter, the nuances and implications of Jacobi's *Letter to Fichte* are given in vivid detail. Livieri's careful historical analysis of Jacobi's reading of Fichte and Jacobi's alternative to the dead end of rationalism he diagnosed in Fichte's thought opens us to a host of issues surrounding the limits of reason and the reach of faith, issues that shaped the development of romantic philosophy.

In Chap. 4, *Spinoza and Romanticism*, Michael Mack reveals another important historical dimension of the roots of Romanticism by taking us to the work of Spinoza. In his chapter, Mack first explores how Spinoza's heritage in Romanticism is the loss of one single, teleological line of thought. He then argues that rather than being isolated or alone, the romantic vision fuses or contaminates what traditional conceptions have separated as mutually exclusive opposites. This contamination of what is purportedly non-compatible diminishes the force implicit in one-dimensional, aprioristic conceptions of the universe as being teleological. In the second part of his chapter, Mack discusses how romantic poetry renders fictive and diminutive such grand schemes of teleology. Mack also illuminates some of the affinities between German Romanticism and English Romanticism. The chapter ends with an account of how the Spinozist heritage in Romanticism shapes contemporary science and how Spinoza's diminutive and at the same time contaminating rationalism gives rise to a sense of sadness in Romanticism and later on in modernism as well as postmodernism.

Having seen some of the ways in which the limits of reason and new attempts to grapple with Being and God were discussed in the period, in Chap. 5, *Religion and Early German Romanticism*, Jacqueline Mariña explores the reception of Kant's understanding of consciousness by both German Romantics and Idealists from 1785 to 1799, tracing its impact on the theory of religion. Kant's understanding of consciousness as developed in the first *Critique* is analyzed, and two fundamental strategies in the reception of Kant regarding his understanding of consciousness and its relation to the Absolute are examined. The first is that of the early German Romantics: Novalis, Schlegel, Schleiermacher, and Hölderlin, for whom the Absolute exceeds all possibility of conceptualization. The second is that of the German idealists: Fichte, Schelling, and Hegel, for whom the logic that makes possibility intelligible precedes actuality and thereby conditions the ground of Being itself. Lastly, the development of the first strategy by Friedrich Schleiermacher is explored.

As the chapters of Part I nicely illustrate, the early German Romantics were absorbing a set of disputes and problems that shaped their thought. They were influenced by Spinoza, Kant, Jacobi, and Fichte, but hardly deferential followers of those thinkers. Indeed, they were working to reform the very fabric of philosophy itself, by bringing it closer to poetry and to science. They were also interested in making the field much more inclusive than it had hitherto been. In Chap. 6, *Femininity and the Salon*, Anne Pollok presents a detailed account of salon culture and its role as a distributor of philosophy at the beginning of the nineteenth century, as a space for the mostly unacknowledged female thinkers of the period. Pollok presents the salon as the space between the private and the public domain in which the participants could try out new roles and change old ones. Pollok shows that the establishment of sentimental circles such as the *Tugendbund* around Henriette Herz, the extensive network of communication and representation established by Rahel Varnhagen, the opportunity to publish under either pseudonyms or hidden behind a male editorship used by writers such as Dorothea Schlegel, may all be seen as first attempts by women to take on roles as salient members of an enlightened community—moves that enabled them not only to be seen but to be able to see themselves. Pollok argues that the salon thus became an important stage for individual character development, enabling women to make their new roles visible to society and to themselves. The salon illuminated women in new, empowering ways and so contributed to a new understanding of German citizenship.

Innovation was part of the fabric of romantic philosophy, and romantic innovation had the effect of opening philosophy to new voices and of leading us to see the work of mainstream figures in a new light. In Chap. 7, *Fichte's Subject and Its Romantic Transformations*, Andrew Mitchell explores Fichte's influence on German Romantic literary theory and composition in the work of Novalis and Friedrich Schlegel. Stepping away from some of the more common readings of Fichte's foundationalism and Schlegel and Novalis' critique of that foundationalism, Mitchell argues that the key moment in Fichte that gets taken up by Novalis and Schlegel is the idea that the subject must posit itself. For Novalis, such self-positing is always a matter of self-representation, and thus an aesthetic act. According to Mitchell's reading, Schlegel adds to this by showing that such self-positing is never certain of success, that one can never truly possess oneself fully. Both Novalis and Schlegel begin from a Fichtean position not in order to show its limitations but rather to demonstrate its primacy for aesthetic creation. In Mitchell's account, we find a strong aesthetic bond connecting Fichte to the early German Romantics.

Marina Bykova continues the investigation of the aesthetic legacy in early German Romanticism. Bykova's Chap. 8, *Friedrich Schiller and the Aestheticization of Ethics*, explores the connections between early German Romanticism and the thought of a figure who shaped the movement in important ways, Friedrich Schiller. Bykova shows that at the very core of Schiller's ethical theory lies a notion of the aesthetic that becomes a specific experience of freedom and thus an essential accompaniment of morality itself. Bykova situates Schiller between Kant and the early German Romantics and reveals how Schiller's aesthetics assigns a distinctive place for the development of general moral sentiments and permits the cultivation of the human toward the free and truly moral individual.

In Chap. 9, *Johann Gottfried Herder: Misunderstood Romantic?*, Johannes Schmidt places Johann Gottfried Herder between German Enlightenment, Classicism, and Romanticism, as a unique and unconventional philosopher.

The chapter illustrates how Herder's anthropology shaped his philosophical thought. To illustrate Herder's notion of the human being as the middle point, Schmidt discusses Herder's *Sculpture* essay (1770/1778) and situates some of Herder's appeal to the early German Romantics in this work. Herder's far-reaching thoughts on sympathy and the sensation of touch provided the theoretical groundwork for romantic philosophical ideas to be developed further, whether in terms of human history, artistic expressions of the self, or social or political matters. The chapter concludes with a discussion of Herder's influences on the early German Romantics as well as their reluctance to openly recognize his impact. Herder's style of philosophy and the broad reach of this writings held great appeal for the early German Romantics, and Schmidt explores both the appeal and the distance that nevertheless endured between Herder and the early German Romantics.

In Chap. 10, *Hermeneutics and Orientation: Retracing the 'Sciences of the Spirit' (Geisteswissenschaften) in the Education-Related Writings of Fichte, Schleiermacher and Novalis*, John G. Moore takes up Fichte and Schleiermacher's rival submissions for the founding of the University of Berlin and makes them the subject of a brief comparative analysis. He begins by tracing out the effective history of their respective views on optimal program design, the nature of academic disciplines, and such hallmarks of Berlin's educational philosophy, as academic freedom and the autonomy of research. Moore then questions whether later readings, from the hermeneutical traditions of the early twentieth century, readings that indicate the human sciences, or humanities were first mobilized as a distinctive part of the University of Berlin's break with older traditions, occurred at the same time that hermeneutics was being expanded into the Berlin-theology curriculum during Schleiermacher's tenure there. Moore suggests that Schleiermacher's turn toward hermeneutics, in his own symposia-like seminars, acknowledges the unique problems faced by grounding the university in a time of cultural recession and foreign occupation, and that academic philosophy at the University of Berlin in its first turbulent decade had more to do with the socio-political problems of cultural orientation in occupied Prussia, than with refining pedagogical methods in the classroom.

The five chapters of Part II, *Aesthetics and Romanticism*, address central aesthetic issues that shaped the early German Romantic Movement, while they also make connections to contemporary work in the field of literary form, critique, film, and literature. The chapters of this section present romantic critique, romantic irony, and the romantic fragment and explore the notion of literature operative in the romantic period; there is also a careful look at the influence of early German Romanticism on later developments in cinema. In

Chap. 11, *Philosophical Critique and Literary Criticism in German Romanticism*, Colin McQuillan takes us to Kant and the "Preface" to the first edition of the *Critique of Pure Reason*, where Kant declared his time to be "the genuine age of criticism." McQuillan then gives a detailed account of the criticism that flourished in the decades that followed. McQuillan argues that the early German Romantics were at the center of the development of a conception of critique that began with Kant, but took a decidedly unique turn with the early German Romantics. In this chapter, we learn of the important contributions to debates about the nature of philosophical critique and literary criticism during the 1790s and early 1800s. It is through these new conceptions of philosophical critique and literary criticism that the early German Romantics were able to bridge the divide between history, philology, philosophy, and poetry in the early nineteenth century.

In Chap. 12, *Romantic Irony*, Karolin Mirzakhan offers an interpretation of the fragmentary writings of Friedrich Schlegel and Novalis, maintaining that irony is integral to their romantic method. Mirzakhan argues that the phrase "romantic irony," a statement of the method for the early German Romantics, is itself an ironic utterance; that is, this phrase joins the endless yearning to know the Absolute with the very force that threatens to undercut that striving. Taken together, the disruptive quality of irony combined with the progressive and universal quality of romantic striving transforms into "romantic irony": the playful, continuous activity of joining opposites that performs the striving for the Absolute, which is the essence of romantic philosophy. In order to support this reading of romantic irony, Mirzakhan makes reference to Schlegel's *Athenaeum* fragments and Novalis' *Romantic Encyclopaedia*, a poetic-scientific work that accomplishes the romantic imperative to join philosophy with poetry and science.

In Chap. 13, *The Role of the Fragment in German Romantic Philosophy and Nietzsche*, Guy Elgat explores the philosophical role of the fragment in early German Romantic philosophy, specifically in the thought of Friedrich Schlegel and Novalis. Elgat first provides a general account of the fragmentary form and then explains how its use by the Romantics could be seen as undergirded by a conception of the metaphysical importance of aesthetics as enabling access to the Absolute. The chapter then turns to compare Nietzsche with the Romantics and argues that while there are a number of illuminating similarities between the early Romantics and Nietzsche both in general and with respect to the aphoristic and fragmentary form, it is with Nietzsche that that the fragmentary form is realized to a fuller extent.

In Chap. 14, *Early German Romanticism and Literature: Goethe, Schlegel, Novalis and the New Philosophical Importance of the Novel*, Allen Speight explores competing idealist and romantic typologies of the romantic novel by examining three novelistic works of particular importance to the Romantic Movement: Goethe's *Wilhelm Meister's Apprenticeship*, which Friedrich Schlegel famously described as one of the "tendencies" of the age; as well as two works which look to Goethe's novel as a model or counter-model: Schlegel's own *Lucinde* and Novalis' *Heinrich von Ofterdingen*.

In Chap. 15, *The Cinematic Afterlife of German Romanticism*, Laurie Johnson takes us to another aspect of the aesthetic contributions made by the early German Romantics. In this chapter, Johnson pursues two arguments: (1) that German Romantic philosophy has echoes in contemporary film and (2) that contemporary film creatively alters central concepts of romantic philosophy, thus contributing to an "afterlife" of Romanticism that remembers the past while conforming to present aesthetic and philosophical expectations. The films analyzed in this chapter re-represent and cinematically transform elements of early, or Jena, romantic philosophy in particular. Johnson examines two films by German-speaking directors: Werner Herzog's, *The Dark Glow of the Mountains* (1984) and Joseph Vilsmaier's, *Nanga Parbat* (2010). Johnson argues that these films both echo and alter characteristics of romantic philosophy and thus contribute to Romanticism's cinematic afterlife.

As Schlegel pushed for new borders between philosophy and poetry, a new set of aesthetic possibilities were opened for philosophy. The disciplinary flexibility endorsed by the early German Romantics also pushed for new connections between philosophy, poetry, and science, which ushered in fascinating, innovative work in the field of the natural sciences. The five chapters of Part III, *Romanticism and the Sciences*, each address one of the divides that the early German Romantics sought to overcome, namely, the divide between the sciences and the humanities. In the work presented here, various aspects of how the Romantics dealt with issues of nature, generation, and the notion of life are analyzed. The five chapters in this section take us to an investigation of figures such as Karl Gustav Carus and Goethe to illuminate the new conception of nature that emerges under the romantic lens. In Chap. 16, *Romantic Biology: Carl Gustav Carus at the Edge of the Modern*, Robert J. Richards describes the contributions of romantic naturalists to the mainstream of late-nineteenth-century biology. He uses the work of Carl Gustav Carus, a disciple of Oken and Schelling, and a protégé of Goethe, as a prime example of the romantic naturalist's work. Carus was a leading romantic artist and anatomist who empirically demonstrated the vertebral theory of the skull. Carus' life and major works reveal an extraordinary scientist, whose ideas quietly flowed into the main currents of modern biology. As we learn in Richards' compelling account, Carus' conception of the archetype was appropriated by Richard

Owen, without attribution, and became integral to the theory of homology. Carus' notion of the unity of type also served as a pillar of Darwinian evolution. Yet, Carus himself could not endorse Darwin's theory—for aesthetic reasons.

In the work of the early German Romantics, the aesthetic often flows into the ethical. In Chap. 17, *Goethe's Philosophy of Nature*, Tim Mehigan and Peter Banki examine the most important features of Goethe's nature philosophy. As they contend, Goethe's thought, though highly reflective, eschews the directly philosophical in its desire to penetrate more deeply into nature than had been possible in any previous philosophy or organized form of thought. Thus, while Goethe's outlook has Platonic, Spinozistic, romantic, and even Kantian associations, in truth it must be seen as its own thing: a radical attempt to postulate and make palpable a vast cosmic ecology in which there is no separation between nature and culture and where the real source of human knowledge emerges from—and instantiates—the ethical.

As Goethe's exploration of nature takes us to the ethical, romantic investigations of nature also have far-reaching consequences for our understanding of the self and its relation to the world. In Chap. 18, *Romantic Acts of Generation*, Jocelyn Holland explores the broad spectrum of German Romantic thinking about generation, one which extends from the organic realm to the intellectual, and even the technological. The chapter also closely examines the topography of a discursive landscape whose primary characteristic is change and raises the question: what implications does a state of constant change have for creative subjects, their products, and the very instruments of production? Through a focus on the writings of Schlegel and Novalis, Holland argues that the multitude of perspectives on generation suggests an alternative to a conventional, centralized model of the self: one that allows for all manner of creative extensions, projections, and dislocations, all under the auspices of generation.

A new conception of science emerges from the work of the early German Romantic thinkers, as disciplines fuse in new ways. In Chap. 19, *Arts of Unconditioning: On Romantic Science and Poetry*, Gabriel Trop explores the romantic concept of a "new mythology" as developed by Schlegel, Novalis, and Schelling, presenting this as a repository for semiotic and imaginative operations framing romantic poetry and science as two distinctive strategic sites in a common romantic project. According to Trop, this common project seeks to "uncondition" Kantian transcendental operations that normally seek to secure knowledge, morality, and judgment through finding and articulating their conditions of possibility. In some important texts of romantic poetry and science, the operations of an Absolute of nature beyond human intelligibility flow into human practices and allow romantic thinkers and poets to reposition aesthetic, epistemological, scientific, and political commitments. As Trop indicates, romantic poetry can also call into question the emancipatory potential of such operations, as in the work of Karoline von Günderrode.

The repositioning that comes into focus as a legacy of romantic thought has implications even today. In Chap. 20, *Romantic Conceptions of Life*, Leif Weatherby argues that the early German Romantics brought life and semiotics into an influential proximity. Assessing the current scholarship as driven by the question of the "organic," Weatherby shows how force and meaning—always mediated by sign-giving—were set on a historical collision course during the Enlightenment that issued in their near identity in the works of Schelling, Johann Wilhelm Ritter, and Novalis. The chapter concludes with the suggestion that the role that electricity played in this association of life and signs makes the romantic philosophy of life an important predecessor of media theory and the philosophy of technology.

Early German Romanticism continues to exert an influence on how we think about nature, science, and the relation between disciplines. The nine chapters of Part IV, *Legacy*, present views of the ways in which romantic philosophy has shaped the thought that developed in its wake. Themes explored in the eight chapters of this section include the new paths for women that were opened in the romantic period, the influence of early German Romanticism upon Wagner's modernism, and Heidegger's relation to early German Romanticism. Highlighted in the chapters of this section are the existential dimensions of early German Romanticism, which too often was read rather superficially as a sentiment-infused, optimistic movement. The connections between early German Romanticism and the notions of *Angst*, pessimism, modernism, anarchism, critical theory, and contemporary continental philosophy are also analyzed. Some of the uncomfortable relations between Nazism and early German Romanticism are also discussed.

In Chap. 21, *Women, Women Writers, and Early German Romanticism*, Anna Ezekiel considers how women and gender are conceptualized within early German Romanticism and argues that work by early German Romantic women should be addressed in scholarship on this movement. The chapter addresses feminist critiques of early German Romanticism as exemplified by the work of Schlegel and Novalis, concluding that an essentialist view of traditional gender characteristics informs central aspects of these writers' work, including their view of the relationship between human beings and nature and their theories of language and poetry. Ezekiel argues that a thoroughgoing critique of gender categories and development of the implications of this critique are found in the early German Romantic writings, though not in the work of the male thinkers, Friedrich Schlegel and Novalis, but rather in the women of the movement, Dorothea Veit Schlegel and Karoline von Günderrode, upon whom Ezekiel focusses in her richly detailed chapter.

The early German Romantics were progressive thinkers, and new spaces for women were opened, as well as a deeper acceptance of non-European cultures, yet ominous shadows still lurked: the path to progress was not without its setbacks. In Chap. 22, *Romantic Philosophy as Anthropology*, Carl Niekerk looks at the reception of the new discipline of anthropology, which since the 1770s had gradually gained in popularity throughout Europe, among German romantic philosophers and authors. An analysis of texts by Kant, Herder, Achim von Arnim, Schlegel, and Alexander von Humboldt demonstrates an interest in understanding other, non-European cultures among these romantic philosophers and their immediate predecessors. However, Niekerk also shows that this interest is a highly contradictory one. Romantic anthropology connects culture to territory and, on the basis of this, privileges sedentary over non-sedentary and nomadic cultures, leading to a rejection of cultural mobility. This explains why Romanticism is associated with an interest in other cultures and simultaneously also fostered nationalism and anti-Semitism.

While Romanticism is often associated with optimism, there are roots of a darker existential awakening in the movement. In Chap. 23, *From the Pantheism Panic to Modern Anxiety: Friedrich Schelling's Invention of the Philosophy of "Angst"*, Jeffrey S. Librett examines Schelling's treatise, *On the Essence of Human Freedom* (1809), and his *Ages of the World* (1815) to trace therein Schelling's invention of the modern philosophy of anxiety. Librett shows how Schelling's response to the pantheism controversy in the *Freedom* text, his attempt to mediate between Spinozistic naturalism and Christian theism, issues in an articulation of human freedom as ineluctably marked by a vertiginous anxiety induced by the irresolvable contradiction between the universal and the particular aspects of the will. He then traces Schelling's much more extensive elaboration of the theme of anxiety in *Ages of the World*, where anxiety comes to affect God himself, in the moment of his creative self-actualization, to the point of divine madness. The romantic encounter with nature as a threatening force becomes the anxiety of the world-creating God. Librett's chapter leaves us with Kierkegaard picking up the relay, while Heidegger and Freud are not far off.

Is the *Angst* that Librett traces to Schelling connected to a kind of romantic pessimism? In Chap. 24, *Romanticism and Pessimism*, Frederick Beiser discusses the complicated relation between Schelling, the "prince of the romantics," and Schopenhauer, the father of pessimism. Beiser's detailed historical account of the relation between these two thinkers leads to a more accurate view of the relations between Romanticism and pessimism and of the influence that Schelling's work had on Schopenhauer. Beiser's comparison of Schelling and Schopenhauer reveals that pessimism is not just bad or sad Romanticism, but rather the very antithesis of Romanticism.

In Chap. 25, *Romanticism as Modernism. Richard Wagner's "Artwork of the Future,"* Günter Zöller argues for German Romanticism's preparatory and anticipatory relation to modernism by drawing on the works of the composer, writer, and theater practitioner, Richard Wagner (1813–1883). Zöller first addresses the special status of music, especially Austro-German music, in European Romanticism. He then places Romanticism in general and musical Romanticism in particular into the wider context of the early modern debate about the respective merits and demerits of ancient and modern art and culture. Zöller presents Wagner as an innovative theoretician and practitioner of romantic-era music theater, and then he argues that Wagner's main operatic works are manifestations of a modernism in romantic guise. Throughout this chapter, the focus is on Wagner's critical reception of ancient, classical theater and modern, romantic opera. In methodological terms, the chapter seeks to provide a comparative and contrastive morphology of Romanticism in order to exhibit the latter's affinities with modern art in general and with modern music theater in particular.

Existential themes are further developed in Chap. 26, *Between Appropriation and Transmission: The Romantic Thread in Heidegger's Existential Notion of Understanding*, where Pol Vandevelde examines the place of Martin Heidegger in the reception and transmission of the ideas of early German Romanticism. Vandevelde uses the key notion of "understanding" and brings out three points of contact between Heidegger and the early German Romantics, which can be supported by textual evidence: (1) understanding as an ontological historical condition, (2) understanding as the element in which work, author, and interpreter find their identity, and (3) understanding as a carving out of the world into specific entities. In addition, he shows how romantic ideas fill an explanatory gap in Heidegger's development, making us understand more clearly how the philosophy of life of the early Heidegger could become an analytic of existence in *Being and Time* and a "history of being" in the 1930s.

In addition to shaping aspects of Heidegger's thought, there is an important line of romantic legacy to be found in the development of contemporary continental philosophy. In Chap. 27, *Sensibility, Reflection, and Play: Early German Romanticism and Its Legacy in Contemporary Continental Philosophy*, Elaine Miller considers early German Romanticism's influence on contemporary continental philosophy, in particular that of Walter Benjamin and Jacques

Rancière. The chapter outlines the distinctive ways in which Schiller, Novalis, and Schlegel transformed the Kantian concept of aesthetic reflection, which Benjamin called the foundation of early romantic philosophy, into an ontological phenomenon. In so doing, the purely subjective reflective judgment described by Kant as the experience of the spectator becomes the objective activity of the artwork itself. For Benjamin and Rancière, this transformation has political implications, as the emphasis of aesthetics shifts from symbolizing morality through an indirect reference to the supersensible, to the expression of the materiality of embodied existence and the fragmentary and often exclusionary ways in which humans perceive the world.

The intersection of Romanticism with critique and critical theory is presented by Nathan Ross in Chap. 28, *'The Concept of Critique': Between Early German Romanticism and Early Critical Theory*. Ross claims that the early German Romantics more than any other group of thinkers were gifted with an insight into the life of literary works—an insight for which translation provides the highest testimony. To be sure, they hardly recognized translation in this sense, but devoted their entire attention to criticism—another if lesser factor in the continued life of works. Ross then connects the critical work of the early German Romantics to the work of Benjamin. The chapter presents Benjamin's, *Concept of Critique*, as a crucial point of contact between early critical theory and early German Romanticism.

The early German Romantics and Benjamin shared a view not only of critique but also a marked apprehension of closed systems. Hence, it should come as no surprise that there would be connections between early German Romanticism and the development of anarchism. In Chap. 29, *Romanticism, Anarchism, and Critical Theory*, Fred Rush notices an absence in the history of philosophy, claiming that it is striking that critical theory is not more engaged with German anarchist writings, given the importance of the anarchists to the revolutions that took place at the outset of the Weimar era. Rush explores the overlooked conceptual connections between early German Romanticism, early critical theory, and German anarchism. Theodor Adorno, Max Horkheimer, and Herbert Marcuse provided a conduit to Romanticism through the work of Benjamin, who was especially important to Adorno's development. Rush argues both that there is a great deal of conceptual commonality between Benjamin and the anarchist Gustav Landauer and that a great deal of the overlap stems from their critical appropriation of German Romanticism. Particularly striking are similarities in their accounts of temporality, historicity, and political revolution. Pairing Benjamin and Landauer highlights the conceptual resources that anarchism makes available to critical theory by way of Romanticism.

The chapters of the collection help us to more deeply appreciate the vast philosophical territory opened by the work of the early German Romantics—territory connected to the work of those who came before them and territory that helped to clear space for the thinkers who came after them.

## Notes

1. Arthur O. Lovejoy, "The Meaning of Romanticism for the Historian of Ideas," in *Journal of the History of Ideas*, Volume 2, No. 3 (June, 1941): 257–278, here 258.
2. See Elizabeth Millán, "The Revival of *Frühromantik* in the Anglophone World," *Philosophy Today* (Spring 2005): 96–117.
3. In the conclusion to this volume, I will discuss some of that recent work in more detail.
4. *KFSA 2, Kritische Fragment Nr. 115*/Firchow, 14. The *Athenäum Fragments*, as well as the *Critical Fragments*, and *Ideas* have been translated by Peter Firchow in *Friedrich Schlegel. Philosophical Fragments* (Minneapolis: University of Minnesota Press, 1991). Reference to Schlegel's original work is to *Friedrich Schlegel Kritische Ausgabe* (*KFSA*), in 35 volumes, ed. Ernst Behler et al. (Paderborn: Ferdinand Schöningh, 1958ff.).
5. For a fuller account of the historical details of the movement, see Elizabeth Millán-Zaibert, *Friedrich Schlegel and the Emergence of Romantic Philosophy* (Albany: State University of New York Press, 2007).
6. Theodore Ziolkowski, *Das Wunderjahr in Jena. Geist und Gesellschaft 1794–94* (Stuttgart: Klett-Cotta, 1998).
7. KFSA 2, xlii.
8. For an excellent account of the fraught relation between author and reading public during the period, see Nicholas Saul, "Aesthetic Humanism (1790–1830)" in Helen Watanabe-O'Kelly, ed., *The Cambridge History of German Literature* (Cambridge: Cambridge University Press, 1997), 202–271.

# Part I

Historical Context

# 2

# The Poem of the Understanding: Kant, Novalis, and Early German Romantic Philosophy

Jane Kneller

Early German Romanticism professed a view of philosophy that gave voice to a radical new understanding of philosophy, challenging not only its own forebearers but also academic philosophical contemporaries. It decried a fixation with first principles and what it saw as a misguided commitment to closure and completeness, thereby breaking with the Kant's defenders who undertook to expand and transform the "transcendental philosophy" as they understood it. In what follows I will argue that it was in fact the early German Romantics, and especially the philosophical work of Novalis, that better represented Kant's critical views of metaphysics and his defense of human freedom, albeit in a surprising new form. The main goal of this chapter is to explore their ingenious development of Kant's central philosophical insight.

For the early German Romantics, philosophy is an activity that takes place in the midst of life, is social to its very core, and is eclectic in its choice of subject matter and expression. On this view, philosophy is a quintessentially ordinary human activity that occasionally makes extraordinary progress, and is by its very nature non-dogmatic and unfettered by academic schools of thought. Their approach to philosophizing includes nontraditional modes such as poetry and aphorism—even fairy tales. On the surface of it, early German Romantic philosophy appears far removed from the spirit and letter of Immanuel Kant's philosophy, and it is hardly surprising that contemporary

---

J. Kneller (✉)
Colorado State University, Fort Collins, CO, USA
e-mail: jane.kneller@colostate.edu

Kant scholars, if they discuss the early German Romantics at all, usually characterize them as fundamentally *anti-Kantian*: mystical, dreamy, and irrational aesthetes.[1] Yet this characterization depends on viewing both the early German Romantics and Kant himself through a lens that ignores or downplays important shared conceptual and social commitments at the heart of both philosophies.

In the space of one chapter not every one of these mischaracterizations can be explored. Here I focus on the reception of Kant's *Critique of Pure Reason* by Friedrich von Hardenberg (known by his pen name Novalis) and the inspiration Novalis derived from it for his own philosophical enterprise. This focus is in no way intended to deny the importance of the collaboration of Novalis and Friedrich Schlegel whose joint efforts unquestionably defined both the literary tone and the central tenants of the practice of early German Romanticism. To be sure, Hardenberg and Schlegel jointly coined the term "Romanticism" to describe the literary-philosophical project that they and their cohort carried out over the course of a few intensely fruitful and innovative years in the mid-1790s. Yet, while Schlegel was the brilliant literary critic of the pair, he fondly deferred to Novalis as the philosopher. They called their many literary/philosophical exchanges "symphilosophizing".[2] Somewhat later, Friedrich Schleiermacher contributed to their conversation as well. Both Schlegel and Schleiermacher were major figures in the development of hermeneutics as a philosophical enterprise, and both made important contributions to early German Romanticism's theory of sociability.[3] Yet as Schlegel himself points out, it was Novalis who dedicated himself to a lifelong study of philosophy. This included his *Fichte Studies*, a sweeping and insightful philosophical critique of J. G. Fichte's *Wissenschaftslehre* that one leading scholar has recently called "the most important philosophical contribution of early German Romanticism".[4] Immediately following his study of Fichte, Novalis turned to a study of Kant that set the stage for a transformational new understanding of philosophy in German Romanticism.

In what follows, Sect. 1 sets the stage for this task with a very brief introductory summary of the transformation of philosophical ground after Kant, as well as a brief biographical account of Novalis' road from his initial Kant studies as a student in Jena with Reinhold through his year-long study and critique of Fichte, and thereafter to his re-engagement with Kant. Section 2 provides a brief overview of the central issues raised by Novalis in his re-reading of Kant, especially of the Preface and Introduction to the *Critique of Pure Reason*, followed in Sect. 3 by a more detailed account of Novalis' remarkable, conflicted reception of Kant's ground-breaking account of human understanding. Section 4 outlines Novalis' genuinely new philosophical contributions and argues that they remain, after all, still very much within the spirit and even the letter of Kant's original transcendental insight. My overall aim will be to bring into focus the degree to which Novalis' re-reading of Kant following his critique of Fichte clearly influenced his own philosophical activity and with it the heart of early German Romantic philosophy itself.

## 1   Novalis' Path to Kant

Early in 1792, Friedrich Schlegel wrote a letter to his older brother August Wilhelm, in which he described a remarkable new friendship:

> Fate has presented to me a young man capable of becoming anything … He appealed to me very much, and I befriended him … The study of philosophy has given him abundant ease in forming beautiful philosophical thoughts—he moves not towards the true but towards the beautiful—His favorite writers are Plato and Hemsterhuys.[5]

Schlegel's new young friend (who was barely two months younger—both were 20 years old at the time) was Georg Phillip Friedrich von Hardenberg, later known as Novalis. From the very start of their relationship, Friedrich Schlegel recognized Hardenberg as a brilliant philosophical thinker. Their friendship began the collaborative philosophical and artistic project that came to define early German Romanticism, and they introduced the term "Romanticism" to capture the spirit of the movement they hoped would usher in a new era of social, scientific, and artistic collaborations of all sorts.

Indeed, Schlegel was not exaggerating: his new friend's philosophical studies already at this young age were quite impressive: in addition to Plato and Hemsterhuis, in 1790–91, he had studied Kant's philosophy in Jena under Karl Leonhard Reinhold, the preeminent advocate and popularizer of Kantianism at that time. Reinhold at first focused on espousing Kant's moral theory and his views on religion, but went on to develop his own philosophical system with the intention of unifying, in a system based on a single first principle, Kant's account of morality with his account of the transcendental conditions of knowledge. Hardenberg studied Kant under Reinhold at precisely the time that Reinhold was both defending Kant and also publishing his own revisionist Kantian system, which relied on a single, self-evident "principle of consciousness" upon which, he argued, the entirety of Kantian philosophy could be founded.[6]

Over a decade after publishing the first edition of the *Critique of Pure Reason*, Kant's radical new approach to traditional metaphysics was well-entrenched, very much discussed, and both admired and hotly contested. By limiting the scope of knowledge of nature to the *a priori* conditions of human cognition, Kant claimed thereby to have also left open a separate, discontinuous realm for the idea of the moral law and human freedom. Human nature, he argued, is not limited to what we can know about the world around us. For practical moral purposes, human beings must recognize and honor their own ability to let reason determine their choice of action and to act according to a law that transcends natural impulses, namely, the moral law. On Kant's view, belief in our autonomy—the ability to be our own law-givers—is not merely possible; it is a necessary condition for the possibility of practical reasoning: human nature is therefore two-sided. Because of (not *in spite of*) the fact that human reason is both cognitive (causally determined) and also self-determined by a moral imperative that demands recognition of our equal standing vis-a-vis other rational beings, Kant's Critical philosophy upheld the legitimacy of both causal and moral necessity.

In the wake of Kant's momentous restructuring of the domain of philosophy, philosophers in the Germanic academy were at pains to situate their own approaches either in opposition to, or as improvements upon, his work. As we saw, Hardenberg had studied under Karl Leonhard Reinhold, Kant's foremost advocate, at the time when Reinhold was developing his own philosophy in an attempt to "save" the Kantian system from what Kant himself took to be his signature achievement: drawing a sharp divide between two systems of philosophical study, namely, on the one hand, the study of the conditions that determine nature (the world around us, including human nature) and, on the other, the study of human freedom and the unconditional command of morality. Reinhold aimed to bring both together again under a single, unitary principle. Kant was initially respectful of both, but in the end renounced their revisions of his work. He held firm to his two-sided account of human nature: with respect to nature, human beings are subject to causal determination. There is no legitimate science of nature that extends its analysis outside the bounds of human sensibility, and yet with respect to their power to choose to act purely for moral reasons, they show themselves to be capable of heeding a "super-sensible" calling. To understand what is truly *human* nature, this strict division must hold, and the domains of sense and of freedom must simply "coexist".7

Hardenberg's philosophical education began in the midst of this scramble among academic philosophers to reorient themselves. At the time when Hardenberg studied with him, Reinhold was concerned to avoid Kant's relativized account of nature to explain the universality of causal determination, on the one hand, and the move (or, as Reinhold saw it, the leap) from this to the legitimacy of the postulation of human moral freedom, on the other. He introduced a version of Kant's philosophy that undercut its very foundation by proposing a self-evident first principle of consciousness that would ground a single systematic account of nature continuous with human morality. But in the years that followed his Kant studies under Reinhold in Jena, Hardenberg continued to study philosophy, especially the work of Johann Gottlieb Fichte. Fichte was sympathetic to Reinhold's remaking of Kantianism in terms of an original first principle to anchor the transcendental system, but Fichte himself sought an even deeper substructure for an account of self-consciousness. This led him to his famous account of an ur-activity of the mind, namely, the notion of a "Tathandlung" ("deed-act" or "fact-act") as the original source of human consciousness. Hardenberg dedicated a year of philosophical study and comment to Fichte's notion of an "I" that spontaneously brings itself into being, but in the end, he rejected Fichte's account. It is this rejection that sent him back to a study of Kant. In 1795, Hardenberg met Fichte in Jena and began a serious study of Fichte's *Wissenschaftslehre (Science of Knowledge)* in the Fall. This study lasted over a year, until the end of 1796, and is now known simply as the *Fichte Studies*.[8] In these *Fichte Studies*, Hardenberg characterized Fichte's work as one step further down the Kantian path after Reinhold's adaptation of it.[9] Nevertheless, Hardenberg was quite critical of Fichte's argument, and, as we will see, his issues with Fichte were based on what were fundamentally Kantian scruples.

* * *

Meanwhile, in the midst of his *Fichte studies*, Hardenberg had fallen in love and became engaged to the very young Sophie von Kühn, famously writing to Schlegel that "the study dearest to me is basically named the same as my fiancée: It is called philosophy—philosophy is the soul of my life and the key to my real self." The *Fichte Studies* marks the beginnings of his own search for the meaning and nature of the "real self" upon which Fichte built his theory, and his critique of Fichte's conception of the nature of this "I" manifested, among other things, the philosophical expression of his recognition of the deep-seated human need to be able to connect with others: for while he was working on his Fichte critique, Sophie fell gravely ill. She was sent to Jena where she endured a series of excruciatingly painful operations that only worsened her condition. Distraught, Hardenberg, soon to become "Novalis", left off work on the *Fichte studies* in the Fall of 1796. Sophie died in March 1797. His beloved brother Erasmus died a month later. Their sufferings and his loss shook the young Hardenberg to the core. Through it all, philosophy provided the source of his greatest consolation and inspiration. It was during this time of grief and despair that Novalis returned to a dedicated study of Kant.

## 2 Kant's Impact on Novalis

Exactly what Novalis read of Kant during this period is not entirely clear. The full set of notes appears to have been lost. The remainder, now labeled the "Kant Studies", contains notes and comments on the second edition Preface and Introduction to the *Critique of Pure Reason*, the *Metaphysical Foundations of Natural Science,* and the *Metaphysics of Morals*.[10] What is clear is that Novalis already had a strong familiarity with the basics of the first *Critique* based on his prior studies with Reinhold and his references to aspects of Kant's work throughout the "Fichte Studies", which he completed just prior to his return to Kant. It is also clear that Novalis kept up with Kant's more recent writings, as is evidenced by Novalis' notes from this period on Samuel Thomas Sömmering's book, *Über das Organ der Seele nebst einem Schreiben von I. Kant (On the Organ of the Soul with a comment by I. Kant)*.[11] In it, Kant had argued that to locate a place where the soul is would require the ability to turn one's own self-intuition into something that can be grasped spatially, which would require that we "transpose the self outside itself, which is a contradiction".[12] Clearly, in returning to the Preface and Introduction to the *Critique of Pure Reason*, Novalis was now fully prepared to assess for himself the character and values of Kant's critical theory.

To fully appreciate Novalis' comments in his "Kant Studien", it is important briefly to review some of the central points of the texts at issue for Novalis, especially those in which Kant presents a summary of his own philosophical achievement in the first *Critique*. In *the Preface* to the *Critique of Pure Reason*, Kant proposes that he will approach problems in metaphysics by the same path of systematic investigation that led to the great success of the natural sciences in the modern era. That path, he says, was illuminated by the likes of Francis Bacon and Galileo because they recognized that they must let *reason* lead the way, and "they comprehended that reason has insight only into what it itself produces according to its own design".[13] Kant explains that in the *Critique of Pure Reason*, he aims to do the same for the science of metaphysics. The fundamental assumptions of metaphysics (e.g., the causal principle that every event has a cause) can justify their claims to universality only from within the framework of human reason. The *Critique* thus aims to examine the hypothesis that all human cognition is determined *a priori* by conditions of thought—*certain conceptual constraints*—that hold universally for rational beings for whom understanding the world around them necessarily takes place within a certain kind of sensibility, namely, a spatio-temporal one. Rather than assuming that these constraints simply mirror the way the world is "in itself", Kant famously invokes Copernicus' heliocentric hypothesis.[14] That is, instead of assuming that "cognition must conform to objects", Kant famously suggests that his solution might be the best explanation of the way the world appears to us:

> Let us once try whether we do not get farther with the problems of metaphysics by assuming that the objects must conform to our cognition of them ... This would be just like the first thoughts of Copernicus, who, when he did not make good progress in the explanation of the celestial motions if he assumed that the entire celestial host revolves around the observer, tried to see if he might not have greater success if he made the observer revolve and left the stars at rest.[15]

If certain fundamental concepts can be discovered that are *necessary for the very possibility of our cognition of objects in general*, then those functions of thought will define the very nature of all human *experience*.[16] Just as, on Copernicus' hypothesis, the observer's own spatial situatedness accounts for their visual experience of the motions of the stars and planets, so, Kant argues, characteristics of the human mind must account for our experience of the world around us. The mind, he says,

> experiences itself is a kind of cognition requiring the understanding whose rule I have to presuppose in myself before any object is given to me, hence *a priori*, which rule is expressed in concepts *a priori*, to which all objects of experience must therefore necessarily conform, and with which they must agree.[17]

At the heart of the *Critique of Pure Reason* is the premise that our situation is that of creatures endowed with an *active* reasoning capacity together with a sensibility that is our interface with the natural world and objects and beings in it. Kant understood sensibility to be human beings' way of receiving input ("intuiting" from the Latin ("in, on") + tueri ("to see, observe")). In human beings, intuition is sensory: we take the world "in" as spatial and temporal, while the understanding acts to structure it according to rules that we are equipped with prior to all experience.

In the *Introduction* to the *Critique of Pure Reason*, Kant claims to have produced a systematic account of the *a priori* concepts of objects in general.[18] As he explains it here, he is giving an account that deals not with the nature of the *actual* objects of human experience but rather with the conditions of their very *possibility*. What he is calling his *critique*, in other words, amounts to an explanation of the rules of mental functioning that are necessary for making our actual experiences *possible* in the first place. However, the *further* task of providing a complete systematic analysis of these rules and further rules derived from them he called the task of "transcendental philosophy": a task for future philosophers, and for which his *Critique* would lay the groundwork. Their task, he argues,

> should not be too great in scope for us to hope to be able entirely to complete it, [and] can be assessed in advance from the fact that our object is not the nature of things, which is inexhaustible, but the understanding which judges about the nature of things, and this in turn only in regard to its *a priori* cognition, the supply of which, since we do not have to search for it externally, cannot remain hidden from us … (A12/B27).[19]

Kant believed his own task was completed by the *Critique of Pure Reason*. *Total* completion of Kantianism amounted to filling in the details of this system of principles by future Kantians.[20] As we saw, Reinhold and Fichte were not content to simply work out the consequences of Kant's system—they wanted to fundamentally change it, by substituting a theory of human consciousness based on a single original principle for Kant's theory of a divided consciousness. They were not, then, in Kant's own sense of the term, "transcendental philosophers". In what follows I want to suggest that in a certain sense, Novalis and his cohort took up the post-Kantian enterprise by accepting Kant's fundamental metaphysics of human consciousness, dualism, and all, and to this extent, their enterprise could more properly be seen as a version of "transcendental" philosophy, than either Fichte's or Reinhold's.

## 3    Novalis' Reception of Kant in the *Kant Studies*

Novalis returned to Kant precisely because having completed his study and critique of Fichte, he was not only convinced that Fichte had failed to capture the true nature of consciousness—of the "I" as it is in itself—but also doubted that *any* such account was possible. Fichte had without warrant, he said, "arbitrarily packed everything into the I" in his very definition of it.[21] For Novalis, Fichte's move was basically a sleight of hand, like pulling the proverbial rabbit out of a hat. The problem came down to having failed to recognize what is, for human knowledge, ultimately ineffable, namely, the nature of human "being". The fact is, says Novalis,

> we are not aware of the first act (Fichte's *Tathandlung*) because it first makes awareness possible, and consequently lies *within* the sphere of the first act—the act of coming to awareness can therefore not go outside its sphere and hope to grasp the mothersphere.

For Novalis, knowledge of the self is never graspable purely and simply. It occurs within "mere-being" as "an image of being within being" that we can grasp only as a feeling, never as knowledge:[22]

> No modification—no concept—clings to mere-being—One cannot posit anything in opposition to it—except to say 'not-being'. But this verbalization [i.e., not-being] is just a little connecting hook for hanging things on pro forma—it only appears to connect things. *It just grasps a handful of darkness.* (emphasis added)[23]

This rejection of Fichte's claim to have fully explained the nature and origins of self-consciousness prompted Novalis to have another look at Kant, and Novalis' ensuing notes and comments signaled his readiness to remain within the boundaries of transcendental philosophy. He accepted Kant's basic claim that human experience could never be capable of grasping nature, including human nature, as it is "in itself". Indeed, the "Kant Studies" makes clear that Novalis agreed with and, indeed, took *as a given* Kant's account of human limitation and the impossibility of ever fully *understanding* anything as it is "in itself".

Of course, this does not prevent Novalis from making important criticisms of Kant's project. At the end of his notes and responses to Kant's Introduction to the *Critique of Pure Reason*, Novalis comments that most great philosophical works have a polemical side aimed at defending their theory against misplaced objections and that these objections, from the perspective of later generations, often seem hardly worthy of mention:

> In most philosophical systems one must distinguish between their polemical sides, which are directed at obvious and commonly occurring errors, and their pure material. In later times the effort wasted on refuting and repudiating what

now appear to be insignificant, crazy opinions (*Wahnmeinungen*) now seems like wasted effort, and so for instance, the Kantian proof against things in themselves already seems unnecessary and tiresome to thinkers unfamiliar with the philosophical history of modern times. (NS 2, 392, #49)

He then continues:

> This kind of polemic is really a self-struggle—in that the thinker who has outgrown his time continues to be unsettled by prejudices of his apprentice years,—a worry that subsequent and better educated generations cannot comprehend, and so they also fail to understand and feel the need to defend against such things.[24]

Again, Novalis' point here leaves no doubt that he fully embraced Kant's Copernican starting point. It is therefore all the more interesting that in the note immediately following these passages Novalis adds the following highly critical comment followed in the same breath by high praise:

> The whole Kantian method—the whole Kantian way of philosophizing is one-sided—and it would perhaps not be unjust to call it *Scholasticism*. Of course, it is a maximum of its kind—one of the most remarkable phenomena of the human spirit.[25]

Setting aside for the moment the accusation of "scholastic one-sidedness", it is important to emphasize that Novalis hastens to reaffirm Kant's transcendental hypothesis in the Preface and Introduction to the first *Critique*: for Novalis, Kant's argument for the empirical *unknowability* of things in themselves was so obvious as to be superfluous (*überflüssig*) and tiresome (*ermüdend*). Kant's Copernican method was for Novalis the *only* appropriate way to proceed and no longer worthy of more than a passing mention. With all the audacity of his 27 years, Novalis is here basically claiming that of *course* human knowledge is conditioned by the kind of minds we human beings have, and thus there is no need to belabor the point, then he generously forgives Kant for doing so, by reminding himself that it was after all not so very long ago that this point was not at all obvious.

Taking Novalis at his word here puts into perspective his great admiration for the "objective" idealism of Plato and Novalis' neo-Platonic favorite, Hemsterhuis. Their contributions continue to play a role in Novalis' philosophical enterprise, but always with the implicit understanding that they are not to be read "dogmatically" in Kant's sense. That is, their claims can never be taken as true metaphysical statements of how things really are, "in themselves". For Novalis, the beauty and power of these philosophers' metaphysics must be understood non-dogmatically as taking place always already within the context of human understanding and judgment. The search for the unconditioned or "absolute" drives us beyond the boundaries of the phenomenal world, or "out of ourselves", as Novalis says in his paraphrase of Kant: "In dogmatism the unconditioned cannot be conceived without contradiction—however in *relative idealism* the contradiction disappears."

This is an extremely important point in Novalis' development: Novalis introduces his own term, "*relative idealism*", for Kant's philosophy. Kant's philosophical, non-dogmatic, *relative* idealism ties human experience to mental activity *determined a priori* by human categories of experience. This leaves the rationalist, "objective" idealist notion of the absolute for the realm of *practical* reason. Novalis paraphrases Kant "the determination of the rational concept of the unconditioned remains only insofar as it is given over to practical reason", and he adds his own comment:

> We cognize (*erkennen*) something only insofar as we bring it into reality. ("*es realisiren*") [26]

To sum up, Novalis' "Kant Studies" makes clear that for Novalis, the Copernican revolution was complete and there was no question of leaving it behind. Certainly, there were philosophers who deeply inspired him and who, it is probably fair to say, he *loved* more than Kant: Plato, Hemsterhuis, and also Spinoza. Still, their insights were, for Novalis, always embedded in Kant's critical perspective, and to be implemented "on the ground", in the realm of empirical knowledge as limited by the *a priori* conditions of human understanding. Novalis was not an "objective" idealist because he no longer accepted the substance metaphysics of Platonism and pre-Kantian German rationalism or, for that matter, of Spinoza's neutral monism.[27] Nor was he a subjective idealist à la Fichte. He simply accepted the obvious: philosophy must begin by recognizing its own *a priori* limits—the limits of pure reason. We can only know ourselves based on the kinds of minds we have. Kant's "relative" idealism is a kind of naturalizing move, on Novalis' reading, because it begins *in medias res*—in the middle of things—which is always to say, within the limits of human reason *a priori*. As he puts in his last sustained philosophical work, the *Allgemeine Brouillon*, "philosophy disengages everything—relativizes the universe—And like the Copernican system, eliminates the *fixed* points".[28]

## 4 Philosophy, Post-Critique: Novalis' Enchanted Naturalism

Of course, none of this is to say that Novalis' Kantianism followed Kant's own marching orders for future transcendental philosophizing. Far from it, Novalis had no desire whatsoever to be a "transcendental philosopher" in Kant's sense of the term (a mere acolyte), and the future of philosophy after Kant was for Novalis never going to be a matter of producing ever more fine-grained, technical analyses of the *a priori* conditions of human cognition. That would only amount to the old "scholastic" approach of staying close to the great teacher's original ground, failing to recognize—or unable to imagine—the creative possibilities that his system opened by denying knowledge in order to make room for belief. To be sure, Novalis also believed that Kant's standpoint is the only place to start, and that its remarkable achievement was that transcendental critique itself opens the intellectual and moral space for its own continued expansion. "The *Critique*", Novalis says, "already contains the transcendental standpoint of the system—It is already above the system. It is philosophy of philosophy." He then muses, "Is there a pre- and post-critique?"[29] In posing this question, Novalis no doubt was positioning his own developing philosophy as "a post-critique", that is, a way of doing the philosophical work that needed to be carried out in real time, within the bounds of ordinary human experience described by Kant.

While his *Kant Studies* were Novalis' homage to Kant's philosophical achievement, they were also the starting point for his and Friedrich Schlegel's budding new project. He saw in Kant the groundwork for an exploration and actual expansion of the constructive power of human reason: a "post-critique" that would bring the abstract, pure concepts of the understanding to life by exploring new possibilities for enacting them in space and time. Kant's categories of pure understanding are, after all, formulae for engaging an active, creative reason: in Novalis words, "apriori judgments are functions of the absolutely independent self-affecting sense—of the 'I'—that affects itself after every single impulse".[30]

In his introduction to the "Kant Studies" in the historical-critical edition of Novalis' writings, Hans-Joachim Mähl describes them as the pivotal point where Novalis turns decisively away from Fichte's project of discovering the "pure I" and instead adapts Kant's famous question "How are synthetic judgments possible *a priori*?" to his own philosophical project.[31] Specifically, Mähl argues that in the "Kant Studies", Novalis moved beyond Fichte toward his own signature concept of genius:

It is no accident that from then on, Kant's "famous question" became for Novalis a question of the possibility and method of construction of philosophical genius. The presupposition for it, as we can now recognize, is provided in the "Kant Studies". Novalis had never given up this relationship to Kantian philosophy, and also later emphasized that the actual starting point for working out his concept of genius was not Fichte, but was thanks to his renewed working through of Kant's *Critique of Pure Reason*.[32]

Certainly, Novalis' key idea of genius, what Mähl calls his "principle of creative observation of the world" [*Prinzip der schöpferischen Weltbetrachtung*], has roots in the famous Kantian passage: "We can cognize of things *a priori* only what *we* ourselves have put *into* them", which Novalis paraphrases as, "We cognize (*erkennen*) something only insofar as we bring it into reality (*es realisiren*)".[33] Novalis' return to Kant led him to the view that all genuine cognition is in an important sense an act of willful creativity, or as Novalis expresses it later in his *Novices of Sais*, it is "the most marvelous alternating between bringing forth [something] and knowledge [of it]".[34] The reference to alternating also has Fichtean overtones, but the difference lies, as we saw, in Novalis' rejection of Fichte's notion of an original first act that literally brings consciousness into being. For Novalis, as for Kant, it is the actual, spontaneous application of functions of human judgment that give rise to our coherent experience, and this experience is therefore a *creative activity*. It occurs in time and space, in the midst of life, and may be replicated intentionally in the interplay of reflection and artistic production.

The question then is: What does philosophy become for Novalis, after Kant? In the *Fichte Studies*, he had already been struggling with the question of what philosophy can really accomplish in terms of explaining consciousness, or the "self". Under the heading "Deduction of the Categories", Novalis claims that "the Categories must be *free* procedures or forms of thinking" and "it is only by being applied that they can be found".[35] He calls them "necessary free effects of *life* on the *something* in the I".[36] "Philosophy must not answer more than it is asked", he says. "It can generate nothing. Something has to be given to it."[37] It cannot simply be a matter of introspection or "self-observation" (the self "eavesdropping on itself").[38] At bottom, he argues, it comes down to this:

> Philosophy is *originally* a feeling. The philosophical sciences conceptualize the intuitions of this feeling. It must be a feeling of inner, necessary free relations. Thus philosophy always needs something given … Philosophy does not admit of construction. The borders of feeling are the borders of philosophy (my emphasis).[39]

Later, near the end of the *Fichte Studies*, he expands on this to argue that philosophy is an *activity* of intelligence, it is *philosophizing*, and "a unique kind of thinking": it is reflectively striving for a ground, that is, a final, absolute starting point from which everything follows. But he says, if it were to turn out (as he believes it does) that this absolute is unreachable, then the drive (the feeling and desire for philosophy) still remains. This is the essence of philosophical reflection—but it is a drive without end. For Novalis, it is possible to embrace this activity while also "freely renouncing" the existence of a final or absolute end. In that case, the only "absolute" of philosophy must be the free renunciation of an absolute:

> Philosophizing must be a unique kind of thinking ... Unending free activity in us arises through the free renunciation of the absolute—the only possible absolute that can be given us and that we only find through our inability to attain and know an absolute ... [U]understanding extended through imagination/striving for freedom would thus be that striving to philosophize ... Philosophy, the result of philosophizing, arises accordingly through interruption of the drive toward knowledge of the ground—through standing still at the point where one is. [40]

Here we see Novalis rebelling against Kant's own vision for the future of "transcendental philosophy", even as he embraces Kant's relativization of knowledge to the human condition. For Novalis, the beauty and promise of philosophizing, what makes it the quintessentially *human* activity, is that it is most alive when it is actually happening, in the real world, in the midst of life. The beauty of Kant's philosophy, for Novalis, was that Kant recognized the living nature of human thought, from the most simple to the most reflective, as the enactment at every moment of the *a priori* conditions of human understanding. The problem with Kant was that he was still mired in the paradigms of the past, still too anxious to defend his revolutionary approach against the narrow view of prior metaphysics, and also, when all was said and done, too willing to rest on his laurels. The moment philosophers claim their job is done and leave the filling in of the details to others, they are no longer philosophizing. When Kant left "Transcendental Philosophy" to others, he stopped philosophizing and stood still at the point where he was, unable to imagine anything else. And this, in the eyes of Novalis and his cohort, made him a one-sided old scholastic.

\* \* \*

Thus, in a remarkable turning of Kant's own insight back upon itself, Novalis took the critical philosophy into completely uncharted new territory. He took Kant's own claims very seriously: human reason can only know that aspect of nature which conforms to reason's own plan. But if pure practical reason is capable of freely choosing to change human nature for the better, then surely this productive power can be exercised in nature at large. It is worth noting that Kant himself struggled, in both the second and third *Critiques*, with the problem of how the moral law can possibly be enacted in the world of nature, and—long story short—he argued that it must be possible to *believe* that we are capable of bringing about what morality demands, namely, moral character in ourselves and justice in our social relations. For Novalis, however, this was not just a matter of postulating the existence of God and of human immortality to support our belief in the possibility of bringing about true virtue and justice. It was a matter of actively *developing* what is given to us in our empirical, natural selves to our inner sensibility. Enacting moral change in ourselves and social change in our world requires the development of moral and social feelings, along with an effort of reflection and imaginative creativity to model the change needed to replace a hostile environment.

Throughout the "Kant Studies", we see Novalis reflecting on the potential for using reflective imagination to breathe life into this aspect of Kant's philosophy. So, for example, in response to Kant's claim that philosophy needs a science that "determines the possibility, the original principles and extent of all knowledge *a priori*", Novalis suggests that philosophizing *is* doing science, namely, the activity of recognizing knowledge through scientific and, he adds, through *poetic* means—the poetic may be considered a species of practical reason. Since practical reason is granted its own realm of freedom and the power of moral reasoning, Novalis is suggesting, why not consider the possibility that practical reason can be enacted in the world of sense experience, via the poetic arts, so that just as scientific experiment yields new understanding and reshapes the way in which we think of objects and occurrences, art in its various forms can do the same?:

> Philosophy is nothing else but doing science, the thinking through of thoughts, recognizing knowledge—treating the sciences scientifically and *poetically*. Are the *practical* and poetical the same—and does the latter signify absolutely practical *in particular*?[41]

Novalis plays with the thought that just as mathematics and the pure natural sciences allow us real knowledge of the outer world, there must be a "science that relates to the forms of inner sensibility", that is, a science that would involve both feeling and imagination.[42] He then opens up a very unorthodox set of issues by asking:

> Is there furthermore such a thing as *extra-sensory* knowledge? Is there perhaps another path available to go outside oneself and to reach other beings, or to become affected by them?[43]

As we saw, Novalis had read Kant's published comments on Thomas Sömmering's *On the Organ of the Soul* and was well aware, while re-reading the first and second introductions to the first *Critique*, of Kant's deflationary response to the question of the location of the soul: it is incoherent to try to "set oneself outside oneself". Yet, although the term "extrasensory" sounds mystical to our ears, Novalis soon makes clear that he is speaking here of something within the realm of nature that is neither paradoxical nor rare: "The seat of the soul is there, where the inner and outer world touch [*berühren*], it is in every part of the permeating each other [*sich durchdringen*]."[44] He later claims that "it is the most arbitrary of prejudices to deny humanity the capacity to be *outside oneself*, to be conscious beyond the senses. One is able to be an extra-sensory being at any moment." He also argues that it is not easy to notice it because it requires calmness to find ourselves in this kind of consciousness in the bustle of everyday life. But once we get used to this condition, it becomes easier and we see, hear, and feel it mostly in momentary experiences of certainty and clarity, and occasionally in a lasting sense of revelation.[45]

A passage from his combined philosophy/prose/poetry work, *Die Lehrlinge zu Sais*, represents his answer to the question of whether we can "get outside ourselves to reach other beings" and also the kernel of his own philosophy: creative thinking is what makes the world what it is for us. We can be outside ourselves because "reflection" is not simply a mirror but a creative act of understanding the world that expands and transforms us in the process:

> The thinking person turns to the original function of his being, to the creating (*schaffenden*) observation, back to that point where producing and knowing stand in the most marvelous alternation between bringing forth and knowing.[46]

This naturalizing of the supersensible moments that human beings do occasionally feel is a move that for Novalis is not at all materialist, neither reductive nor determinist. Novalis views philosophy as both making the world more ordinary and understandable, on the one hand, and more fascinating and mysterious, on the other. For Novalis, Kant's deflationary metaphysics, far from disenchanting the universe, opens up a whole new field of possibility for experiencing what is beyond or outside our individual selves. Within the bounds of reason and feeling, it uncovers the human capacity for enacting a self that is in touch with "others" in the world of nature that surrounds it. The seat of the soul for Novalis, then, is to be found wherever/whenever we are able, in reflection and imagination, to let this happen. Novalis' philosophical and literary achievement is to describe and invoke through poetic means the realm of interpersonal community that Kant had only hinted at in his final *Critique*: that is, a realm in which an enlightened community is able to improve its own nature in order to progress from what he earlier called "unsocial sociability" to a more free and open cosmopolis.[47]

* * *

When Novalis and Friedrich Schlegel invented and defined "Romanticism", they defined it as a verb: "romantizieren"—"to romanticize":

> The world must be romanticized. In this way one rediscovers the original meaning. Romanticizing is nothing but a qualitative raising to a higher power. The lower self becomes identified with a better self … Insofar as I give the commonplace a higher meaning, the ordinary a mysterious countenance, the known the dignity of the unknown, the finite an appearance of infinity, I romanticize it. The relation is precisely the opposite for the higher, unknown, mystical and infinite—these are logarithmized by this connection—they become common expressions.

Novalis' understanding of philosophy is a romantic project by their definition: unending free renunciation of the absolute, permanently seeking and producing knowledge, criticizing, seeking and finding again, and, in the process, expanding what it means to be human. Reason and imagination unite in the process, to merge science and poetry:

> The poem of the understanding is philosophy—it is the highest impulse that reason gives itself about itself.—Unity of Reason and Imagination. Without philosophy human beings remain divided in their essential powers—There are two persons—one a reasoner—the other a poet. Without philosophy, incomplete poet—without philosophy, incomplete thinker—a judge.[48]

True philosophy is ultimately social, it takes us outside ourselves, and it elevates and transforms us. It pushes us to expand the horizons of our understanding and our science, to understand others, both human and nonhuman beings, and nature itself. In the process of expanding us, the "poem of the understanding" broadens our prior sense of ourselves and our theories, and pushes us to evolve further.

Kant may have been surprised to find his germinal, transcendental insight being turned into a form of poetry, and yet, that very insight led him ultimately, in his final *Critique*, to call for the collaboration of reason and imagination to construct a vision of sociability that is "appropriate to humankind by means of which it distinguishes itself."[49] Novalis' philosophy and the literature that embodied it simply took it upon themselves to do just that.

## Notes

1. To be sure, not all Kantians embrace all these stereotypes, but they are still very common among many, and this view prevails among historians of modern European philosophy in general.
2. These were published at the time in the *Athenäum*, KFSA 2/ *Friedrich Schlegel: Philosophical Fragments*, ed./trans. Peter Firchow (University of Minnesota Press: Minneapolis, 1991).
3. I have addressed these contributions more fully in "Sociability and the Conduct of Philosophy: What We Can Learn from Early German Romanticism" in *The Relevance of Romanticism Essays on German Romantic Philosophy*, ed., Dalia Nassar (Oxford: Oxford University Press, 2014), 110–126.
4. Manfred Frank, *Einführung in die Frühromantische Ästhetik: Vorlesungen* (Surkamp Verlag, Frankfurt: 1989), 248, Lecture 15. Frank is referring here to Novalis collections of notes, comments, and criticisms of *Fichte's Wissenschaftslehre*, known as the *Fichte Studies*. In *Novalis: Schriften, 1981–1988*, ed. Richard Samuel with Hans-Joachim Mähl and Gerhard Schulz (Stuttgart: Kohlhammer, 1960–88).
5. NS, 571–572. In addition to mentioning his new friends' youth three times and emphasizing his love of philosophy, he also remarks on his friends' poetry (which he describes as still immature). Friedrich Schlegel promises to send August an earlier poem written by his friend that was inspired by August's own well-established poetic abilities. Schlegel begs his brother not to judge the youthful work too harshly, assuring him that his new friend has the makings of "a good, perhaps great, poet—an original and beautiful sensitivity and a receptivity to all shades (literally: 'tones') of sentiment".
6. Reinhold's original first principle, the "principle of consciousness" that precedes all other principles in the transcendental system and from which they are derived. For an excellent brief introduction to Reinhold's work, see Dan Breazeale's article, "Karl Leonhard Reinhold", in *The Stanford Encyclopedia of*

*Philosophy*, ed., Edward N. Zalta (Spring, 2018), URL = https://plato.stanford.edu/archives/spr2018/entries/karl-reinhold/.
7. See the *Critique of the Power of Judgment*, Introduction (2nd), AK:174 ff. The virtue of this separation, for Kant, was that it restrains human reason's tendency to arrogant overreach, that is, to claim knowledge that exceeds the limits of human understanding. Theoretical completeness, Kant insisted, can only be attained if the arrogance of reason is held in check by knowledge of the limitations of its conceptual possibilities. Only then can it be said that "a system of pure philosophy under the general title of metaphysics is … both possible and of the utmost importance for our use of reason in all contexts". Similarly, a philosophy of morality and human freedom can be possible only in the completely separate context of the claims of pure practical reason where the necessity of the moral law maintains its grip on human conscience.
8. He also undertook a study of Spinoza and the social and religious reformer Zinzendorf at that time.
9. "Kant established the possibility, Reinhold the actuality, Fichte the necessity of philosophy." NS 2, 143 #69, English edition *Novalis: Fichte Studies*, ed./trans., Jane Kneller (Cambridge University Press, 2003), 41.
10. See NS, 2, "Kant und Eschenmayer Studien", 379–394. Translated by David Wood as "Novalis: Kant Studies (1797)" in *The Philosophical Forum*, Volume XXXII, No. 4 (Winter 2001): 323–338, at 325 fn7, fn8. See David Wood, *op. cit.*, 325, and fn. 7, and, also Hans-Joachim Mähl's introduction to the *Kant Studien*, NS 2, 334ff, for further analysis of what Novalis had already read and why he returned to Kant after his *Fichte Studies*. Mähl makes a point of noting that Novalis continued to follow Kant's most recent work as it appeared in print in the 1790s.
11. Hans-Joachim Mähl, NS 2, 380.
12. Ibid., 331.
13. Immanuel Kant, *Critique of Pure Reason*, ed./trans., Paul Guyer and Allen W. Wood (Cambridge University Press, 1998), 109.
14. Copernicus, of course, had tested the hypothesis that the earth rotated around the sun to explain perceived anomalies on the old Ptolemaic view that all the celestial bodies revolve around the sun.
15. Immanuel Kant, *Critique of Pure Reason*, ed./trans. Paul Guyer and Allen W. Wood (Cambridge University Press, 1998), 110, B, xvi.
16. Ibid., 111, B, xvii.
17. Ibid., 111, B, xviii.
18. *Critique of Pure Reason, op. cit.* Ak. A12–13/B25–26, 133.
19. "I call all cognition transcendental that is occupied not so much with objects but rather with our mode of cognition of objects insofar as this is to be possible *a priori*. A *system* of such concepts would be called *transcendental philosophy.*" *Critique of Pure Reason*, A11/B25, 150, ed./trans. Paul Guyer and Allen W. Wood (Cambridge University Press, Cambridge: 1998), 133 and 149, A

and B editions, respectively. Novalis' "Kant Studies" were based on his reading of the B edition of 1787. All references to Kant's work are the Prussian Academy Edition of his complete works.

20. Of course, he then turned from critique of the theoretical cognition of nature to produce two further critiques that would examine the *a priori* conditions of moral reason (human freedom and the absolute command of moral reason) and finally a critique of the fundamental conditions of reflective judgment.
21. *Fichte Studies*, #5, NS 2, 107.
22. He makes the same claim here, less clearly but in a more quotable form: "Consciousness is a being outside of being that is within being", *Fichte Studies*, #2, NS, 106 (Kneller trans., 5).
23. *Op. cit.*, *Fichte Studies*, *#3*, NS 2, 106 (Kneller trans., 6).
24. NS 2, 392, David Wood translation, "Novalis: Kant Studies (1797) in *The Philosophical Forum*, Volume XXXII, No. 4 (Winter 2001), 323–338, at 337, Note #49.
25. Ibid.
26. This echoes his Hemsterhuis studies from the same period, wherein he noted, we know (*wissen*) insofar as we make. Novalis then makes a move that I believe typifies his philosophical stance both as fundamentally Kantian in its framework but genuinely new and unique in its application. He personalizes and naturalizes Kant's analogy between chemical reduction and synthesis with his "experiment" of separating things as they appear and things in themselves: appearances are "things in relation or in contact with me", and things in themselves are things having *no contact with me*. Kant Studies *op. cit.*, 386–387.
27. This constitutes my response to Frederick Beiser's claim, directed primarily at Manfred Frank's reading of Novalis, that Novalis (along with his cohort) was not a subjective idealist, but rather, he became an absolute or "objective" idealist. I see a third way between Frank and Beiser on this. There is no reason to Kant a subjective idealist, since that would put him in the camp of Berkeley, for whom physical objects are literally "congeries" of ideas—a sort of three-dimensional pictographic language used by God to speak to human beings. Kant, of course, is at pains to reject any such extreme subjectivism, and his position is altogether different. Novalis' use of the label "relative idealism" is an extremely helpful way of reminding us that the Kantian method marks the end of traditional substance metaphysics in the modern era of philosophy.
28. NS 3, #622, 111.
29. "Kant Studies", NS 2, 387 (Wood, 331–332).
30. Ibid., 389 (Wood, 334).
31. Mähl, in *Novalis Schriften*, 2, 337–340. This suggests a change in his views after the *Fichte Studien*, where Novalis had at one point suggested that Fichte and Kant were pursuing the same question: see Novalis comment in FS: #39:

"Is there a pure I, or are synthetic judgments possible a priori! Is One [and the same] question."
32. *Op. cit.* 340. In support of this, Mähl cites the following passages from Novalis last major work *Allgemeine Brouillon* # 457, #650, #775, NS 3, 333, 388, 418-19.
33. The original text from Kant in the Preface to the *Critique of Pure Reason* that Novalis is commenting on is Bxviii.
34. Ibid., 337–338. Novalis citation from *Novalis Schriften*, 1, 101.
35. *Fichte Studies*, #12, NS 2., 112 (Kneller translation, 11).
36. *Fichte Studies*, #13, NS 2, 112 (Kneller translation, 12).
37. Ibid.
38. Ibid.
39. Fichte Studies, #15, NS 2, 113 ff/Kneller translation, 12 ff.
40. Here is the entire quote from the *Fichte Studies* (Kneller translation, #566, 167–168): "Philosophizing must be a unique kind of thinking. What do I do when I philosophize? I reflect upon a ground. The ground of philosophizing [i.e., of this activity] is thus a striving after the thought of a ground. Ground is not, however, a cause in the literal sense—but rather a constitution—connection with the whole. All philosophizing must therefore end in an absolute ground. Now if this were not given, if this concept contained an impossibility—the drive to philosophize would be an unending activity, and without end because there would be an eternal urge for an absolute ground that can be satisfied only relatively—and that would never cease. Unending free activity in us arises through the free renunciation of the absolute—the only possible absolute that can be given us and that we only find through our inability to attain and know an absolute … understanding extended through imagination/striving for freedom would thus be that striving to philosophize … Philosophy, the result of philosophizing, arises accordingly through interruption of the drive toward knowledge of the ground—through standing still at the point where one is."
41. "Kant Studies", #45, NS 2, 390 (Wood, 334–335).
42. "Kant Studies", #46, NS 2, 390 (Wood, 335).
43. Ibid.
44. "Vermischte Bemerkungen", #20, NS 2, 418.
45. Ibid., #23, 420.
46. NS, 1, 101.
47. Kant, *Critique of the Power of Judgment, op. cit.*, 228–230. For a discussion of how Kant sees this as in no small part a task for aesthetic reflective judgment, see my ""Nur ein Gedanke". Eing Commentar zum Dritten and Vierten Satz von Kant's *Idee*" in *Immanuel Kant: Schriften zur Geschichtsphilosophie*, ed. Otfried Höffe (Berlin: Akademie Verlag, 2011), 45–62.
48. Logologische Fragmente, NS, 2, 531.
49. *Critique of Pure Reason* V: 355 (Guyer and Wood, 229).

# 3

## F.H. Jacobi on Reason and Nihilism in Romanticism

Paolo Livieri

Friedrich Heinrich Jacobi (1743–1819) was a peculiar literary figure and one of the most influential German intellectuals of the second half of the eighteenth century. As a seminal polemicist, Jacobi was a vocal critic of German late Enlightenment thought, Kant's transcendental idealism, Fichte's doctrine of knowledge, and eventually of Schelling's early philosophy. Had he lived longer, he would certainly have tackled Hegel's system of philosophy, thanks to the acute insight he so often proved to possess. Unfortunately, although Hegel himself eventually recognized the strength of Jacobi's intuitions and discussed his theses in the introductory paragraphs of his *Encyclopaedia* (1830) alongside Aristotle's, Kant's, and Descartes', this last battle did not occur.[1]

Jacobi was certainly not naïve, but he definitely was not interested in polemic *per se*. On the contrary, he was an affectionate friend and perceptive companion. He was either acquainted or in contact with Kant, Fichte, Reinhold, Goethe, Klopstock, Friedrich Schlegel, Wieland, Mendelssohn, Lavater, Hemsterhuis, Lessing, Matthias Claudius, Schelling, Hamann, Alexander and Wilhelm von Humboldt, Schiller, Madame de Stael, and Herder, to name only a few. Mirroring his cultural fervor, this network also shows the wide range of debates that he was able to engage and even promote. A good survey of eighteenth- and nineteenth-century philosophy cannot but

P. Livieri (✉)
Hosei University, Tokyo, Japan
e-mail: paolo.livieri.22@hosei.ac.jp

© The Author(s) 2020
E. Millán Brusslan (ed.), *The Palgrave Handbook of German Romantic Philosophy*, Palgrave Handbooks in German Idealism, https://doi.org/10.1007/978-3-030-53567-4_3

mention the influence Jacobi had on major German philosophers, considering that Jacobi started (or defined) the main philosophical controversies of his age: the Pantheism Controversy (*Pantheismusstreit*), the Atheism Controversy (*Atheismusstreit*), and the Theism Controversy (*Theismusstreit*). Somehow, this stream of disputes derived from his bringing Spinoza back to the main stage of philosophical debates while showing that even the Kantian emancipation of subjectivity had fallen victim to sheer pantheism. In Jacobi's eyes, the transcendental system of reason was both the cradle of moral oppression and the ultimate assault on a personal God.

As a passionate champion of a kind of liberal individualism, Jacobi claimed that the negation of personal singularity was grounded on a theory of the I deprived of all substance and existence. On his view, the history of modern thought had obliterated the true I, true reality, and true God in the name of an enthusiasm for explanations. So, in the midst of one of the richest philosophical periods, Jacobi courageously denounced how philosophy had led to a total annihilation of the true for the sake of a dangerous illusion.

In order to assess the nature of such an illusion, this chapter will offer a few remarks on one of F.H. Jacobi's most famous texts, the *Letter to Fichte* (1799). This text is crucial not only for understanding Jacobi's thought in general—regardless of its evolution—but also for understanding early German Romanticism as it marks a turning point in its development.[2] As we will see, the *Letter to Fichte* affirms that systematic knowledge (perfectly exemplified by Fichte's *Wissenschaftslehre*) is incapable of countenancing both the individual being and a personal God.[3] Moreover, on the basis of Jacobi's analysis of transcendental philosophy, the epoch-making equation between philosophy and nihilism is introduced for the first time in history, providing the first account of a concern that will haunt European culture for centuries.

With this backdrop in mind, we need to acknowledge that the more unequivocal and self-proclaimed German Romantics are listed in this *Handbook*; Jacobi, in contrast, belongs to an older generation of German intellectuals of a foregone age. Jacobi started publishing philosophical essays and prose in the 1770s, before the advent of the early German Romantic Movement.[4] But, in a way that associates him with early German Romanticism, he devoted a large part of his works to the identification of true rationality.[5] His tense distrust of an all-encompassing system of knowledge did not result in the worship of irrationalism; rather, it aimed to clear the way for an authentic apprehension of the true, the beautiful, and the good.[6] As it is evident and often overtly proclaimed, the common trait among romantic philosophers, theologians, poets, and artists consists in the rejection of systematic philosophy, but such a rejection, at least in Jacobi's case, reflects anything but a different rational conception of reality.[7]

## 1   *Atheismusstreit*

Notoriously, in the second issue of the first volume of the *Athenaeum*, Friedrich Schlegel proclaimed the three paradigms of his era: the French Revolution, Goethe's *Wilhelm Meister*, and Fichte's *Wissenschaftslehre*.[8] Notwithstanding this honorific salutation, the early German Romantics developed quite a bitter dissatisfaction with Fichte's *Wissenschaftslehre*. At first, Fichte's moral and political ideas inflamed intellectuals' enthusiasm; his elaboration of Kantian spontaneity connects freedom and necessity under a defined principle: the I. Yet, Fichte's doctrine of knowledge conflicted with the ethical, aesthetic, and religious ardor of early German Romanticism. The early German Romantics were dismayed by the fact that Fichte's philosophy promoted a rational system dominated by the mechanical lawfulness of the I, which reduced to nothingness any otherness.[9] Fichte erected a system in which concrete otherness (the non-I) is unquestionably banished: "I discover myself to be free of any influence from the sensible world, absolutely active in and through myself," and he continues, "and thus I discover myself to be a power elevated above everything sensible."[10] Eventually, on the basis of the conceptual self-sufficiency of the I, the distance between Fichte and the romantics quickly grew, finding in the so-called Atheism Controversy its climax—though surely not its conclusion.[11]

The Atheism Controversy started over two essays—one authored by Fichte himself and the other by F.K. Forberg—that appeared in 1798 in the *Philosophical Journal*, a periodical that Fichte co-edited with F.P.I. Niethammer. Fichte's "On the basis of our belief in a divine governance of the world" serves as a reply and an introduction to Forberg's "Development of the idea of religion" and provides an explanation of both points of agreement and disagreement with the latter. But, more importantly, Fichte also had the opportunity to explain his "thoughts on this topic" that indeed "follow from his own philosophical views."

The somehow simplistic contribution of Forberg has the merit of stating in clear terms a critical idea that was growing in popularity: "religion is neither a product of experience nor a discovery of speculation, but rather merely and only the fruit of a morally good heart" which wishes to "maintain the upper hand over the evil in the world."[12] Consequently, the only concept of deity admissible is "the sublime spirit who governs the world in accordance with moral laws."[13] In this thesis one may recognize a rather unscrupulous rendering of Kant's moral doctrine, and despite its laxity, it surely raises issues with which Fichte himself was familiar. Only a few years before, in the most popular of his writings, the *Foundation of the Entire Wissenschaftslehre* (1794–1795), Fichte clearly maintains that the idea of a deity is unthinkable.[14] Moreover, in the acclaimed *Attempt at a Critique of All Revelation* (1792), he states—following the precepts of Kant's philosophy—that the idea of God is "based on an alienation (*Entäusserung*) of what is ours"[15] and that religion develops from this alienation. What Fichte writes in his "On the basis of our belief in a divine governance of the world" is, therefore, congruent with this very general framework: "the living and efficaciously acting moral order is itself God. We require no other God, nor can we grasp any other."[16]

After the publication of the journal, political and academic agitation arose. This was witnessed in the circulation of an anonymous pamphlet entitled, *A Father's letter to his son, studying at the University, concerning the Atheism of Fichte and Forberg*, the arraignment by the theologian—and Fichte's friend—F.V. Reinhardt on behalf of the Grand Duke Charles August, and Reinhold's own letter, to mention only but a few examples.[17] With very few exceptions—for example, H. Paulus and F. Bouterwek—Fichte appeared to be abandoned by his colleagues, old friends, and allies. Turmoil around Fichte's public activities was not new: as early as his essay in defense of the French Revolution (1793), Fichte had already suffered a number of public and private attacks because of his alleged political Jacobinism, religious impiety, and moral intransigence. But nothing was comparable to what he suffered during the Atheism Controversy.[18]

As could be expected of Fichte, he wrote a hasty, direct response to his critics. As a result, the situation worsened. Fichte published the famous *Doctors und Ordentlichen Professors zu Jena Appellation an das Publikum über die durch ein Kurf. Sächs. Confiscationsresccript ihm Beigemessenen Atheistischen Aeusserungen* (1799)[19] soliciting Jacobi's intervention in the name of the shared view according to which "belief or faith is the element of all certainty."[20] At that time, he did not expect the coming disappointment. Following Lavater's advice, Jacobi replied with the famous open letter, which was published with both Fichte's and Reinhold's agreement.[21]

## 2    Jacobi's Letter: The Rise of Nihilism

The *Letter to Fichte* is a manifesto of dissatisfaction; it is both a critique against the ambitions of systematic thinking and an exposition of the true destiny of speculation. The dissatisfaction with the systematicity of Fichte's philosophy is expressed, however, in light of the indubitable obligation that Jacobi—and all the early German Romantics—felt to Fichtean principles of science, to the indomitable practical will located at the origin of his doctrine, and to his descent into the conundrum of the dialectical principle of reality.[22]

The *Letter to Fichte* represents the center of the tension between two conceptions of thought whose conflicting paradigms grew stronger to each other's benefit: the more the Fichtean system of reason appeared as the ultimate, the stronger the Jacobian retaliation of individuality grew.

Jacobi's analysis of the concept of system appears right at the beginning of the Preface of the letter: "I am bound to be pleased with Kant that he preferred to sin against the system rather than against the majesty of the place."[23] In this context, the term system refers to the notion of *system of reason*. This implies that the founding principle of science is formally homogeneous with the objects of that same science. As a consequence, the form of the objects of science is exactly the expression of the principle of science. A further explanation of the kind of systematic unity that Fichte's doctrine offers, according to Jacobi, can be obtained from the last edition of *Concerning the Doctrine of Spinoza in Letters to Herr Moses Mendelssohn*, with particular reference to the section dedicated to the reply to M. Mendelssohn's *Memoranda*. In proposition *XXXIX*, Jacobi states, "All individual things mutually presuppose one another and refer to one another so that none of them can either be or be thought of without the rest, or the rest without it." The necessary conclusion arrives in proposition *XLI*: "The absolutely indivisible essence, in which all concepts exist together, is the infinite and absolute thought."

At first, this last reference to Spinoza can be seen as an unorthodox form of Fichte's doctrine of knowledge, which clearly promotes subjectivity as the origin and justification of every "individual thing." Yet in light of Fichte's success in deriving the whole reality from the activity of the I, Jacobi regards the comparison between Fichte's I and the Spinozian *natura* as thoroughly justified:

> Little was lacking for this transfiguration of materialism into idealism to have already been realized through Spinoza. His substance, which underlies extended and thinking being, equally and inseparably binds them together; it is nothing but the invisible identity of object and subject (demonstrable only through

inferences) upon which the system of the new philosophy is grounded, i.e. the system of *the autonomous philosophy of intelligence.*[24]

This new philosophy of intelligence shows a coherent development of Spinoza's materialism because what is *conceivable* appears according to the form of the *self-generation of a principle*. Both Spinoza's substance and Fichte's I imply that what really *is* is that which is conceived per se; everything else arises within this unity.[25] Yet, the exposition of this thesis—that was to be discussed for years to come—is preparatory for Jacobi's own critique.[26] In fact, the philosophical core of the *Letter* comes to light when Jacobi starts to assess the *completeness* of the science of knowledge.

In accordance with its purity, science—namely, Fichte's philosophy—is "this very production *in thoughts*," "an inner activity" that "consists in the autonomous production of its object."[27] Science is complete because it translates what is other-than-itself into itself and makes the very possibility of otherness disappear. In other words, science concerns itself only with objects that its principle defines so that the products of science represent the only objects that should be regarded as knowable. As a result, everything that is conceived is known precisely because it is the product of that principle which makes everything conceivable.

The character of science is thus grounded on the production of both ethical and epistemological values, whose justification rejects any form of correspondence theory: there is not a world of facts or values to correspond to because everything is a product of the "intelligence" of the I. Consequently, Fichte's doctrine presents a magnificent achievement of abstract thinking: the principle of the Doctrine of Science—the I—defines lawfulness for ethics and truthfulness for epistemology. Fichte makes explicit the conversion from "form alone into the substance":[28] all what is, is posited by the I and what is not posited by the I, is not. The crucial *opus* of idealism consists in this transition, which replaces substance with form. Even more than geometry and arithmetic, Fichte's *Wissenschaftslehre* shows the principle that stands for the "*element of unity* in all sciences" and that divests reality of its independence.

But, Jacobi maintains that a single crucial problem arises: the principle of science fashions concepts which lack the "true."[29] The purity of science depends on the fact that the truth lies in the science itself, whereas Jacobi is committed to showing that the foundation of all knowledge lies outside of both science and thinking in general. Put simply, Jacobi is committed to showing that an independent world of substances exists outside the perimeter of science. The real problem for Jacobi will be defining a way of knowing this world without turning it into a mere product of science, as idealism does.

Despite his criticism, Jacobi assumes the definition of science that Fichte introduces: Jacobi admits that there cannot be scientific knowledge of substance because every element of science is a product of thought. Therefore, substance must be the object of a non-scientific knowledge, but this does not imply that the apprehension of substance falls into irrationalism. On the contrary, Jacobi aims to propose a theory of substance that should enrich our notion of rationality. The issues at stake are twofold: (a) the demonstration of the incompleteness of the abovementioned *philosophy of intelligence* and (b) the possibility for reason to be defined as the faculty to apprehend what falls outside the mere production of the I.

Jacobi's critique starts by affirming that the "being given" of an object represents the only access to science; if a "being" is not "given" to our understanding, then what we call "thing" is a mere product of the I, it is mere form (*Gestalt*). And *Gestalt* is nothing at all.[30]

In Jacobi's eyes, what makes Kant's philosophy as problematic as it is revelatory is the assumption that knowledge involves abstraction from a being that is not a product of our thought, but a "given." On the contrary, Fichte's Doctrine of Science annihilates that external-to-thought source of knowledge to the advantage of an abstract architecture of forms, which are intertwined, self-contained, and self-directed.[31] If Kant assumes that our knowledge refers to objects that lie outside of our thought, Fichte provides arguments to reject this thesis and build a system of mere *Gestalten*. Fichtean science becomes the display of the power of the I to produce the truth and obliterates the "realm of beings."[32] This represents a momentous turn in the history of Western thought: the science of *truth* comes to oppose the knowledge of *being* Jacobi tries to debunk the "naked logical enthusiasm" that turns perception of being into "necessary imaging,"[33] but he can only witness this crucial turn of philosophy into sheer contemplation of the Self: once we accept that only logical explanations can contribute to the definition of objects, we have fallen victim to the logical enthusiasm that blinds our senses.

In the wake of the success of Fichte's system of knowledge, drama ensued: "I invoke Annihilation, like a divinity, against such a Danaidic, such an Ixionic bliss."[34] As mentioned above, despite the dramatic utterance, Jacobi does not locate the knowledge of being in an irrational realm, nor does he aim to give rise to a counter-Enlightenment movement of fideistic flavor. On the contrary, Jacobi appears committed to a critique of thinking in the same way as Kant devoted his efforts to a critique of reason.[35]

After his concise analysis of the consequences of Fichte's endeavor, Jacobi denounces the ultimate result of the Doctrine of Science, yet he emphasizes that Fichte's philosophy does not amount to atheism. Like arithmetic or geometry, Fichte's philosophy forgets being and plays with images; in that realm of images, true God never disappears because he never came into being.[36]

What Fichte calls God in his essay "On the grounds of our belief in a divine government of the universe" is only a product of thinking. He posits that God is caused: it is a creation of the I—the *Gestalt* of the moral world—and therefore it is a non-entity. In the end, God becomes an icon of our actions. But still, states Jacobi, this is not atheism. Rather, it is the emergence of a phenomenon that will become crucial to the history of philosophy: nihilism. Contrary to what might be perceived, true nihilism is a human project that creates a new God. This human creation implies the annihilation of true being while it poses a major threat to the Romantic Age: the creation of a God that has no being.

The last few pages of the *Letter* are dedicated to defining this opposition to science, that is, the realm of beings. Confronting the light of science, Jacobi's exploration seeks being where that light reduces its power and is shrouded by darkness. As Kant had summarized in his essayWhat does it mean to orient oneself in thinking": "through the mere concept, nothing is settled in respect of the existence of this object and its actual connection with the world (the sum total of all objects of possible existence). But now there enters *the right* of reason's *need*, as a subjective ground for presupposing and assuming something which reason may not presume to know through objective grounds; and consequently to orient itself in thinking, solely through reason's own need, in the immensurable space of the supersensible, which for us is filled with dark night.[37]

Advancing from where he left 15 years before in the *Spinozabriefe* and hinting at Kant's systematic analysis of reason, Jacobi appeals to reason to assume and develop its proper function, which makes it the "faculty of presupposing the true."[38]

To be sure, Jacobi's motives and concern are consonant with a debate that involved other authors during the nineties of the eighteenth century like, for instance, the young Schelling and Fr. Schlegel, and that coagulated around the possibility of an escape from such a nihilistic objectification of reality. While Schelling pursued this idea by following Fichte's project of countering the anti-foundationalist interpretation of Kant's transcendental philosophy and developing a systemic comprehension of the principle of reality (as it is evident ever since his *On the Possibility of a Form of Philosophy in General*, 1794), Fr. Schlegel felt the urgency of a revolution—a term that often appears in his writings of this period—based on untouched spiritual sources of human nature. Schlegel's as well as Novalis' philosophical studies might even be associated with Jacobi's inquiry into the danger of an all-positing I. In this regard, it suffices to recall how Schlegel in his famous *On the Study of Greek Poetry* (finished 1795, published 1797) theorizes the necessity to go past science and retrieve a "perfect intuition" that gives infinite content to an otherwise empty scientific law.[39] Nevertheless, contrary to Schlegel's confident cultural enterprise, Jacobi's metaphysical problem seems to capture the atmosphere that subsequent history of philosophy will eventually betray. Jacobi's idea of reason—whose evolution cannot be treated here—unveils a noetic activity that, while being rational, is not discursive. As a consequence, Jacobi's notion of presupposing the true seems to identify a real problem for, with, and in transcendental idealism.

## 3 Faculty of Reason

In search of a more precise interpretation of Jacobi's insight, this section will delve into his notion of reason as it appears in the *Letter* and see in what sense he proclaimed that Kant committed a sin against system. In Jacobi's eyes "sin" was committed not against but in compliance with reason's own power. His account of reason—as it appears in the *Letter*—must be carefully reconstructed with some help from Kant's account. Surely, we cannot detail Kant's articulate notion of reason, but we can collect some introductory elements that will guide our understanding of Jacobi's trajectory.

On the one hand, Jacobi regards reason as the faculty of being inasmuch as it perceives what is "prior to" and "outside" knowledge; therefore, reason is crucial to knowledge because it is concerned with what knowledge necessarily refers to. On the other hand, reason is also the faculty of systematic truth "endowed with *reflection* and *purpose*" that follows "regulative perception."[40] Jacobi seems to give two distinct assessments of reason: one concerns its capacity of perceiving what is outside subject's knowledge, the other concerns its capacity of giving shape to knowledge. Nevertheless, these two aspects are discrete formulations of a dual function that reason singly performs. This dual function, in fact, shows the real faculty of being insofar as reason refers both to the supersensible and sensible levels. We believe that Jacobi alludes to the complex significance that the term "reason" assumes in Kant's lexicon and that Jacobi seems to inherit in light of his need to explain the connection between objective knowledge and true being. We can lay out this legacy in a very general summary that points directly to the core of the theme, leaving aside an otherwise necessary exegesis of Kant's vocabulary.

To shed light on Jacobi's text, we need to remember that the aforementioned distinction between different formulations of the notion of reason relates to some introductory notes of Kant's transcendental distinction between *logical* and *pure* use of reason. In its *logical* use, reason refers to the faculty of inference that abstracts from any content of knowledge, while in its *pure* use, it refers to itself as the origin of some transcendent principles, which at first Kant does not specify.

The *logical* use of reason gives a syllogistic order to knowledge without any addition in content. In fact, the *logical* use of reason pertains only to the form of knowledge: it gives systematicity to the whole body of propositions that knowledge collects. Through reason we produce the highest unity of knowledge from the manifold of cognition giving systematic unity to our apprehension of reality. The *logical* use of reason makes explicit the condition of the cognition and guides our thinking to define where the unconditioned—of conditioned cognition—is to be sought.[41] By contrast, the *pure* use of reason provides the foundation for transcendent principles.[42] The *pure* use of reason entails a specific synthetic tendency to the unconditioned, where thought is independent of the empirical world. Assuming, for our purpose, Jacobi's terminology: if the *logical* use of reason identifies how unconditioned being relates to scientific knowledge, the *purity* of reason identifies how being should be defined according to this non-scientific knowledge. In fact, the *pure* use of reason refers to the ability to apprehend purely.

On this account, we maintain that reason is purely "passive" only because it perceives the pure character of being beyond reason's "active" constitution of knowledge. From the point of view of the development of the critique of pure reason, this reflection on the system prepares the stage for the dialectic of reason, where Jacobi finds proof for the dependence of knowledge on what is extra-objective. Eventually, in this double function (logical and pure) of reason, Jacobi finds material for his criticism of the system of knowledge. Reason becomes the faculty that can disclose *Gestalt*'s dependence on being.

The first disclosure of this dependence is shown in the paradigm of Jacobi's ontology: "my reason instinctively teaches me: God."[43] Against Fichte's legalistic morality, Jacobi opposes the intimation of the person of God. But nothing is settled: for only reason's need for God has raised its voice over thunderous nihilism. Now that the rationality of the need for being has been intimated, Jacobi approaches the real problem for his epistemology: how to define being? To this purpose, Jacobi adds further elements to his ontological inquiry, but this time he proceeds *via negativa*.

In the process of defining being, he takes a polemical step that should cast doubts on a possible convergence between his idea of being and Kant's postulates of practical reason.[44] In fact, he maintains that Kant's notion of moral law does not unfold one of the manifestations of true being: a free man. Moral law is "barren, desolate and empty" and cannot fulfill the function of manifesting the essence of a free agent. In Jacobi's terminology, moral law cannot become the heart of a man.[45] In the end, Kant's and Fichte's moral agent does not belong to what Jacobi calls "being"; the moral agent is, in fact, contrary to being. In the more emphatic terms that Jacobi employs, transcendental moral law generates the "utterly void," an infinite, lawful universe which promotes the "nothing, the absolutely indeterminate."[46] Using Jacobi's words, the moral God is a non-entity that produces non-entities. But such is the God of the worshipers of science, a God that rules over a world of "chemical, organic, and psychological, modes of production."[47]

## 4 Understanding a Modal Category

If we consider the inception of Romanticism to be shaped around the theoretical efforts of post-Kantian philosophies such as Reinhold's and Fichte's, one may consider 1799 as the year in which this philosophical initial phase of Romanticism begins to show its epilogue, but Jacobi's prophetic emphasis about the danger of a world of "production" conveys, even today, a concern that we should not comfortably dispel or store in the dusty shelves of the history of philosophy. Against this world of production, Jacobi does not oppose pure contemplation to earn authentic access to being; rather, he opposes a different ethics which unveils the true essence of it. In fact, in the *Letter*, being is portrayed by means of a special kind of ethics: Jacobi portrays being that is active, namely, being that *is* insofar as it *acts*. This trait is not uncommon among the romantics: the propulsion toward ethical or aesthetic activity in the pursuit of concrete, true life can easily be recognized in Hegel's early writings, in Goethe's *Wilhelm Meister*, or in Novalis' poetry. And both Schlegel and Novalis, in their philosophical work, emphasize the centrality of moral and aesthetic agency. Jacobi, for his part, affirms that the homology between action and being discloses the truth about the "heart of man."

In order to have a better grasp of what this means, we need to look into how the difference between the activity of being and the activity of the modes of production is articulated. The answer lies in methodology. Jacobi needs to build a theory of being that should have a rational language beyond systematicity: the language of the theory of being must not stem from a founding principle like the Fichtean "I." To solve the *Rätsel des Seins* (the enigma of being), Jacobi promotes an ontology that moves polemically from the annihilation of being operative in Fichte's *Wissenschaftslehre* and focuses on the notion of action. But what kind of action?

We must concede that if Jacobi's *Letter* seems successful in presenting why reason is in *need* of being, it remains quite vague when it comes to the understanding of being. How can we look into being? How does being manifest itself? What is being, if it is not a represented object, viz. an object of science? How does it act? These are the questions that Jacobi only partially answers in his text. Perhaps we may ask Kant for help in the same way Jacobi did when he turned to Kant's *The Only Possible Argument in Support of a Demonstration of the Existence of God* to start his philosophical endeavor.

First, for Jacobi being entails existence: Being is not abstract or ideal; it is not subjective. Instead, being is that which *exists*. Following Kant's teaching, Jacobi maintains that existence is not a predicate or a determination, it is rather an "absolute position," wholly simple.[48] In other words, existence cannot be produced but is given to experience before any determination or representation.[49] This makes existence congruent with the preeminent non-representational quality of Jacobi's notion of being. But it is still not entirely clear how the relation between activity and existence should be defined.

A further determination of existence arises when we think that being is not merely the possibility of a concept, but rather refers to substantive existence. In other terms—less abstract than the former— being is not just what is or exists, for being is the actual (*Wirklich*). This helps us formulate the next, more precise question: what is the special activity of the actual (*Wirklich*) that makes it be a non-object of our experience? What is the absolutely simple activity that, not listed among the modes of production, is the fundament of concrete existence?

If we were to unravel the special activity of the actual (*Wirklich*) in Kantian terms, we should move into the realm of assertoric judgments that, according to the *Critique of pure Reason*, are those by means of which the actual is defined. In the form of the assertoric judgment, thought must be seen neither as a function of the understanding nor as a function of the reason, but rather properly as a function of the "faculty of judgment."[50] According to the faculty of judgment, the truthfulness of a judgment is given—originally—by sensibility. Hence, the activity of being is not the activity of an abstract principle or a rule. It is closer to the activity of a perceivable element. Yet, this perceivable element is not an object of synthesis; otherwise—according to Jacobi's criticism—it would become a product of the I. A striking paradox arises: being is unity without synthesis or, more precisely, being is the absolute position of the actual (*Wirklich*) whose identity is maintained because not represented.

But how is this active unity possible without synthesis? No definitive answer comes from the *Letter*. Or, better said, the answer is not as clear as one would expect. If one considers Jacobi's text, the hardship in defining being is unexpected since the identity of being looks very close to us, for it lies in the "heart of man." Perhaps Jacobi would endorse the first of Novalis' Hymns: "More heavenly than these flashing stars seem to us the infinite eyes which the Night has opened within us." The darkness of the night welcomes—as it happens in Kant's "What does it mean to orient oneself in thinking"—our attempts to grasp true existence, but those same eyes that Novalis sees in his heart, Jacobi has opened in his reason. As the poet continues, "They see further than the palest of those countless hosts; without need of the Light they penetrate the depths of a loving heart, a feat which fills a higher realm with unutterable delight."[51]

This hardship with the notion of actuality is not a surprise. Actuality is a category that belongs to modality and does not add anything to knowledge of the object. Kant says, "when I think a thing, through whichever and however many predicates I like (even in its thoroughgoing determination), not the least bit gets added to the thing when I posit in addition that this thing *is*. For otherwise what would exist would not be the same as what I had thought in my concept, but more than that, and I could not say that the very object of my concept exists."[52] With regard to the category of actuality, we find Jacobi in profound agreement with Kant: the actual is epistemologically "transparent" to synthesis. Unity without synthesis implies that being refers to an aesthetic dimension that is not contained in the predicates of the objects, and yet being pertains to the "given." Being must be thought of as existence; therefore, existence must be perceivable, active, absolutely simple, and non-synthetic.

Although it may look like a game of taxonomy, this brief examination of the outcome of Jacobi's *Letter to Fichte* through Kant's lexicon is not peripheral to the question at hand. On the contrary, it helps us understand the care with which Jacobi chooses the characteristics of existence. He seems to draw those characteristics from the tradition of transcendental philosophy that he accepts. Certainly, this knowledge of existence is introduced only via "intimation." Jacobi himself admits that he provides a full elaboration of this "intimation" only in his essay "On Divine Things and Their Revelation" (1811),[53] but the direction of Jacobi's trajectory has now become clear: existence is unity without synthesis, identity without discursive content. These are the traits that represent the basis of the *Wirklich* (active and true). Eventually, this peculiar definition of existence shows the traits of a *Person*, of the "I" before the "Thou."[54] A *person* cannot be known via synthesis because it is not a product of a scientific knowledge, nor can its identity be expressed via discursive explanation because it cannot be analyzed. And yet it is absolutely simple and given, and in need of a different lexicon to be discussed and determined.[55]

The traits of a person appear surrounded by the Kantian "night," so it is fairly easy to imagine that Jacobi would be pleased by Novalis' verse: "I wake now, for I am thine and mine: thou hast proclaimed to me the Night as life and made me human."[56]

## 5   On Death and Dying

A different text may help us assess the mark impressed on our personal life by the progressive inability of science to speak the truth about being. If being reveals its true nature in the moment in which we assume that existence discriminates between a *person* and an usual represented object, then considering the limit of existence—its finitude—may help us progress in revealing the unchanging truth about being. So far, we have seen that to think properly involves thinking about true being, as if to say that a different object of thinking implies a different form of thinking. A specific dialogue by Plato connects the problem of finding the proper form of thinking with the definition of the proper object of thinking. Moreover, the same dialogue asserts that the true form of thinking emerges only when we interrogate ourselves about human existence. We could go even further and argue that Jacobi's critique of reason echoes Socrates' dissatisfaction with Anaxagoras' teaching, as it is portrayed in Plato's *Phaedo*.[57] To be sure, it is not a surprise that we find aspects of Jacobi's concern in one of the most eminent discourses on transcendent forms of truth.

Both Plato's and Jacobi's critiques of systematic thinking aim to acquire an access to truth that does not rely on discursive description of the composition of truth. Rather, they both provide access to truth by means of unveiling its principle. Notwithstanding the many differences, they both intend to save human personality from its dissolution at the hands of a lawful oppression. They both give to life—the special activity that we are—the quality of stolid defiance against the petitions of lawful thinking. But how does this activity manifest itself when systematic thinking seems to reduce the true to silence? The solution emerges when ruin hits. The personal tragedy Socrates is suffering in the dialogue mirrors the struggle that thinking endures when it is asked to define its own nature: in that moment, thinking is deprived of any firm support and holds itself only on its motility. As in the case of Jacobi's *Letter*, the meaning of existence manifests itself only when the thinking confronts its hesitation to define the distinct motility (*Wirklichkeit*) that existence is.

As it appears in the case of the *Phaedo*, the idea of dying invades the dominion of our identity with imperative potency. Death inspires decisions, motivates attitudes, and influences both the evolution and manifestation of our character. On the contrary, birth does not exercise the same leverage on our moral life; it merely shows a commencement without conscious content; it is a bare yet-to-be. But, notwithstanding death's potency upon our moral identity, one aspect of our identity may partially divest death of its authority. In opposition to the mortality of our body, it seems that our theoretical achievements are not destined to die with us. The finitude of our existence seems to contrast with our connection to true knowledge, which aims to be universal not only because it evades solipsistic fixation to become the universal language but also because it claims to be untouched by the burden of dissolution. In other words, what is true, is true forever. This continuity appears to be fundamental to rational beings because it defines their rational nature; nevertheless, the very act of bearing forms of true knowledge seems to disregard the end of their bearer's existence. It appears that only in the name of this rational faculty can humans be likened to a bridge between two worlds, the mortal and the immortal.

Contrary to the common view, existence does not deny the human connection to the eternal. Plato suggests that the foundation of our connection to true forms explicitly refers to and emerges out of the question about existence. The famous outset of the theory of the ideas in Plato's *Phaedo* springs from his efforts to explain the essence of existence. While describing his first wandering in search of the truth, Socrates admits a bitter discontent with Anaxagoras' philosophy: his early esteem of Anaxagoras' systematic approach to the question about "why one or anything else is generated or destroyed or is at all" turns into suspicion and criticism against the method that Anaxagoras adopts to investigate existence.[58] Before introducing the need for a theory of forms, Socrates appears satisfied with Anaxagoras' teaching that the mind is the true cause of existence, only to discover afterward that Anaxagoras explains actions and events without any mention of their cause but only by reference to the corporeal elements of those same items. To explain existence, maintains Socrates, we must differentiate between the cause of a thing and its composition: only the former, the cause, expresses the reason of the motility in which existence consists.[59] Instead of turning toward the conditions of material existence, Socrates looks at the ideas as a way to understand the "workings" in which existence consists.[60] Ideas are principles of explanation that appears to be the strongest as they refer not to the condition or composition of a certain thing, but to the proper essence of the thing, which defines the cause of its existence.[61] Contrary to the composition of the thing, its essence is grasped "aute kath auten,"[62] by means of itself: the coming to be, ceasing to be, and existing in general are known directly through the simple apprehension of the special activity, the motility, that existence is.[63] Thus, Socrates suggests, if we want to know existence in general, we have to be careful not to mix the principle of a thing with its composition, which is the usual mistake that the *antilogikoi* make when they confuse the knowledge of a principle with the knowledge of its consequences.[64]

In the end, the *logos* does not spell out reality piece by piece in search of the complete chain of conditions that bring about objects, but makes explicit the form of existence, which lies in the special activity that those objects are. This explanation does not fall prey to dissolution; rather, it remains unaltered in the dimension of thought in virtue of its unconditional nature. In that very dimension of pure thinking, the special activity that we are is the only thing that withstands a vanishing world trapped in a restless dialectic of negating-and-determining.

As in the case of Jacobi's criticism of Fichte's *Wissenschaftslehre*, the direct vision of the thing in itself entails directing our attention toward true knowledge. But since knowledge can take many forms, we need to pay attention to the principle of it: if the principle does not yield "aute kath auten," it means that we compute composition, condition, or material content of things—but not their essence. Only when we look at what defines the existence of things do we evade the grasp of what is corruptible and conditional to see the unconditional nature. The preeminence of the principle of existence over other principles of knowing turns Jacobi's theory of personhood into a general methodology of knowledge, which oversees different kinds of knowledge, none of which pertains to being, except his special ethics.

## Notes

1. Hegel's interpretation of Jacobi's thought evolved throughout the years: from the negative critique published in *Faith and Knowledge* to the subtle analysis that appears in the *Encyclopaedia* 1830 (§§ 61–78). For a first orientation see, Jean-Michel Buée, *Savoir immédiat et savoir absolu La lecture de Jacobi par Hegel* (Paris: Classiques Garnier, 2012); Paul Franks, "All or Nothing: Systematicity and Nihilism in Jacobi, Reinhold, and Maimon," in *The Cambridge Companion to German Idealism*, ed. Karl Ameriks (Cambridge University Press, 2000), 95–116. Christoph Halbig, "The Philosopher as

Polyphemus? Philosophy & Common Sense in Hegel and Jacobi," in *Internationales Jahrbuch Des Deutschen Idealismus*, ed. Jürgen Stolzenberg and Karl Ameriks (Berlin: De Gruyter, 2005), 261–82, Birgit Sandkaulen, "System und Zeitlichkeit. Jacobi im Streit mit Hegel und Schelling," in Birgit Sandkaulen, *Jacobis Philosophie* (Hamburg: Meiner, 2019), 271-288, and Birgit Sandkaulen, "Dritte Stellung des Gedankens zur Objektivität: Das unmittelbare Wissen," in Birgit Sandkaulen, *Jacobis Philosophie* (Hamburg: Meiner, 2019), 289–316.
2. Friedrich Henrich Jacobi, "Letter to Fichte," in Friedrich Henrich Jacobi, *The Main Philosophical Writings and the Novel Allwill*, ed. George di Giovanni (Montréal: McGill-Queen University Press, 1994), (henceforth: *Letter to Fichte*), 497–536.
3. George di Giovanni, "Introduction: The Unfinished Philosophy of Friedrich Henrich Jacobi," in Friedrich Henrich Jacobi, *The Main Philosophical Writings and the Novel* Allwill, ed. George di Giovanni (Montréal: McGill-Queen University Press, 1994), 3–167 (pp. 67–116). See Birgit Sandkaulen, "Ichheit und Person. Zur Aporie der Wissenschaftslehre in der Debatte zwischen Fichte und Jacobi," in *System und Systemkritik um 1800*, ed. Christian Danz and Jürgen Stolzenberg (Hamburg: Felix Meiner Verlag, 2011), 45–68, and Birgit Sandkaulen, "Daß, was oder wer. Jacobi im Diskurs über Personen," in *Friedrich Heinrich Jacobi. Ein Wendepunkt der geistigen Bildung der Zeit*, ed. Walter Jaeschke and Birgit Sandkaulen (Hamburg: Felix Meiner, 2004), 217–237, and Birgit Sandkaulen, "System und Systemkritik. Überlegungen zur gegenwärtigen Bedeutung eines fundamentalen Problemzusammenhangs," in *System und Systemkritik. Beiträge zu einem Grundproblem der klassischen deutschen Philosophie*, ed. Birgit Sandkaulen (Würzburg: Königshausen u. Neumann, 2006), 11–34.
4. Jacobi starts publishing philosophical essays and prose in 1970s, a decade in which the systematical proportions of reality had just begun to be challenged by enlightened skepticism and the aesthetic of the *Sturm und Drang*. Rather than at Reinhold's or Fichte's re-foundation of a system of science, Jacobi looked at Spinoza's and Kant's ethics and epistemology to find the polemical source of his philosophical project.
5. To inquire into the origin of the term *Frühromantik*, see Ernst Behler, *Frühromantik* (Berlin: de Gruyter, 1992), 13–23. The text provides a general understanding of the overall movement and its chronology.
6. Friedrich Henrich Jacobi, "David Hume on Faith, or Idealismus and Realismus, A Dialogue: Preface and also Introduction to the Author's Collected Philosophical Works," in Friedrich Henrich Jacobi, *The Main Philosophical Writings and the Novel* Allwill, trans. George di Giovanni (Montréal: McGill-Queen University Press, 2009), 537–590.
7. See A.W. Wood, *Fichte's Ethical Thought* (New York: Oxford University Press, 2016), 12–22. Notoriously, defining the relationship that the romantics had

with the idea of system is not an easy task. Scholarship has long debated whether early German Romanticism had to be considered a reaction against systematic reason altogether. Lately, the debate has definitely evolved toward a more documented interpretation of different conceptions of systematicity that are distinctive of the early German Romanticism. On this, see Dieter Henrich, *Konstellationen. Probleme und Debatten am Ursprung der idealistischen Philosophie (1789–1795)*, (Stuttgart: Klett-Cotta, 1992). See also Manfred Frank, *»Unendliche Annäherung«—Die Anfänge der philosophischen Frühromantik* (Frankfurt am Main: Suhrkamp, 1997), and Frederick C. Beiser, *The Romantic Imperative. The Concept of Early German Romanticism* (Cambridge: Harvard University Press, 2006).

8. Friedrich Schlegel, "Athenaeum Fragments," *The early political writings of the German romantics*, ed. Frederick Beiser (Cambridge: Cambridge University Press, 1996), 118. On the debt that *Frühromantik* may have incurred with Fichte's philosophy, see the following groundbreaking texts: Rudolf Haym, *Die romantische Schule* (Berlin: Gaertner, 1882), Nicolai Hartmann, *Die Philosophie des deutschen Idealismus* (Berlin: de Gruyter, 1923), and Hermann August Korff, *Geist der Goethezeit* (Leipzig: Koehler und Amelang, 1964).

9. See Daniel Breazeale, "Introduction," in J.G. Fichte, *Early Writings*, ed. Daniel Breazeale (New York: Cornell University Press, 1988), 24.

10. Johann Gottlieb Fichte, "On the Basis of Our Belief in a Divine Governance of the World," in *Introductions to the Wissenschaftslehre and Other Writings (1797–1800)*, ed. Daniel Breazeale (Indianapolis: Hackett, 1994), 147.

11. On origin and consequences of the *Athesimusstreit*, please see *Fichtes Entlassung: der Atheismusstreit vor 200 Jahren*, ed. Klaus-M. Kodalle and Martin Ohst (Würzburg: Königshausen & Neumann, 1999). Many authors in the last decades have published valuable works on this topic, but for a first orientation on the complex history of early reception of Fichte's philosophy, see *Fichte und seine Zeit*, ed. Matteo Vincenzo d'Alfonso, Carla de Pascale, Erich Fuchs, and Marco Ivaldo (Fichte-Studien 43 and 44), (Leiden: Brill, 2016 and 2017); George di Giovanni, "The First Twenty Years of Critique: The Spinoza Connection," in *The Cambridge Companion to Kant*, ed. Paul Guyer (Cambridge: Cambridge University Press, 1995), 417–448; Elizabeth Millán-Zaibert, *Friedrich Schlegel and the Emergence of Earl German Romanticism* (New York: State University of New York Press, 2007), especially 53–94; Bernward Loheide, *Fichte und Novalis: Transzendentalphilosophisches Denken im romantisierenden Diskurs* (Amsterdam: Rodopoi, 2000).

12. Friedrich Karl Forberg, "Development of the Concept of Religion," in *J.G. Fichte and the Atheism Dispute (1798–1800)*, ed. Yolanda Estes and Curtis Bowman (Burlington: Ashgate Farnham, 2010), 39.

13. Friedrich Karl Forberg, "Development," 37.

14. See Johann Gottlieb Fichte, *Foundations of the Entire Science of Knowledge*, in Johann Gottlieb Fichte, *Science of Knowledge* (*Wissenschaftslehre*), ed. Peter

Heath and John Lachs (Cambridge: Cambridge University Press, 1982), 225. See also Johann Gottlieb Fichte, "On the Basis of Our Belief in a Divine Governance of the World," in *Introductions to the Wissenschaftslehre and Other Writings (1797–1800)*, ed. Daniel Breazeale (Indianapolis: Hackett, 1994), 149–151.

15. Johann Gottlieb Fichte, *Attempt at a Critique of All Revelation*, ed. G. Green (Cambridge: Cambridge University Press, 1978), 73.
16. Johann Gottlieb Fichte, "On the Basis of Our Belief in a Divine Governance of the World," in *Introductions to the Wissenschaftslehre and Other Writings (1797–1800)*, ed. Daniel Breazeale (Indianapolis: Hackett, 1994), 151. In a concise reconstruction of those events, A.W. Wood hints at Fichte's social solitude: in his writings, his political and philosophical radicalism was blended with religious symbols and terminology, so as to estrange both secular and religious movements. See A.W. Wood, *Fichte's Ethical Thought* (New York: Oxford University Press, 2016) 19. To be sure, Fichte thinks that God can be attained through knowledge; God does not show itself via analogy or as an "als-ob"; rather, it refers to the "starting point (*das absolut erste*) of all objective cognition." Johann Gottlieb Fichte, "On the Basis of Our Belief in a Divine Governance of the World," in *Introductions to the Wissenschaftslehre and Other Writings (1797–1800)*, ed. Daniel Breazeale (Indianapolis: Hackett, 1994), 151.
17. Karl Leonhard Reinhold, "Letter to Fichte," in *J.G. Fichte and the Atheism Dispute (1798–1800)*, ed. Yolanda Estes and Curtis Bowman (Burlington: Ashgate Farnham, 2010), 127–144.
18. As it is well known, Fichte's *Attempt at a Critique of All Revelation* was rejected by the Theological Faculty of Halle.
19. Johann Gottlieb Fichte, "Appeal to the Public," in *J. G. Fichte and the Atheism Dispute (1798–1800)*, ed. Yolanda Estes and Curtis Bowman (Burlington: Ashgate Farnham, 2010) 85–125. See also the more cautious "From a Private Letter," in *Introductions to the Wissenschaftslehre and Other Writings (1797–1800)*, ed. Daniel Breazeale (Indianapolis: Hackett, 1994), 155–176.
20. Johann Gottlieb Fichte, "On the Basis of Our Belief in a Divine Governance of the World," in *Introductions to the Wissenschaftslehre and Other Writings (1797–1800)*, ed. Daniel Breazeale (Indianapolis: Hackett, 1994), 147. For further considerations on Fichte's hope in Jacobi's help, one should take into consideration the notion of "göttliches Leben" mentioned by Fichte in his *Appellation*. Unfortunately, we cannot indulge in an analysis of this text.
21. For a general introduction to Jacobi's letter, please see Klaus Hammacher, "Jacobis Brief "An Fichte" (1799)," in *Transzendentalphilosophie und Spekulation. Der Streit um die Gestalt einer Ersten Philosophie (1799–1807)*, ed. Walter Jaeschke (Hamburg: Meiner Verlag, 1993), 72–84. See also Klaus Hammacher, ed. "Fichte und Jacobi, Tagung der Internationalen J.G. Fichte-Gesellshcaft." Special Issue, *Fichte Studien*, no. 14 (1998).

22. On the consonance of Fichte and Jacobi in their contrast against the Berliner *Aufklärer* in general and Nicolai in particular, see Stefan Schick, "Das Interesse der Aufklärung—Fichte, Jacobi und Nicolai im Disput über Bedingtheit und Unbebingtheit der Vernunft," *Fichte Studien*, no. 43 (2016), 106–127. On a more general overview on Fichte and early German Romanticism, please see *Fichte, German Idealism, and Early Romanticism*, ed. Daniel Breazeale and Tom Rockmore (Leiden: Brill, 2010).
23. *Letter to Fichte*, 499.
24. *Letter to Fichte*, 502.
25. On this see George di Giovanni, "Introduction: The Unfinished Philosophy of Friedrich Henrich Jacobi," in Friedrich Henrich Jacobi, *The Main Philosophical Writings and the Novel Allwill*, ed. George di Giovanni (Montréal: McGill-Queen University Press, 2009), 70 and ff., as well as Walter Jaeschke, "Der Messias der spekulativen Vernunft," in *Fichtes Entlassung: der Atheismusstreit vor 200 Jahren*, ed. Klaus-M. Kodalle, Martin Ohst (Würzburg: Königshausen & Neumann, 1999), 143–157 (pp. 149–150).
26. We need to stress that Jacobi's first reaction to Fichte's *Über den Begriff der Wissenschaftslehre* is not negative under many respects, as showed in Jacobi's letter to Goethe dated June 7th, 1794, see Friedrich Heinrich Jacobi, *Briefwechsel*, vol. 10 (Stuttgart-Bad Cannstatt: frommann-holzboog, 2015), 361–363. Jacobi's criticism grows as soon as he realizes that according to Fichte's doctrine we understand only that which we do. See his letter to Dohm of December 12th, 1797, in Friedrich Heinrich Jacobi, *Briefwechsel*, vol. 11 (Stuttgart-Bad Cannstatt: frommann-holzboog, 2017), 265–267. Cf. Klaus Hammacher, *Die Philosophie F.H. Jacobis* (München: Fink, 1969), 180 and ff.
27. *Letter to Fichte*, 505. See Klaus Hammacher, "Jacobis Brief "An Fichte" (1799)," in *Transzendentalphilosophie und Spekulation. Der Streit um die Gestalt einer Ersten Philosophie (1799–1807)*, ed. Walter Jaeschke (Hamburg: Meiner Verlag, 1993), 77.
28. *Letter to Fichte*, 504.
29. On Jacobi's critique to Fichte in the *Kladden*, see Klaus Hammacher, *Die Philosophie F.H. Jacobis* (München: Fink, 1969), especially the third chapter.
30. *Letter to Fichte*, 508.
31. *Letter to Fichte*, 509–510.
32. *Letter to Fichte*, 508.
33. *Letter to Fichte*, 510–511.
34. *Letter to Fichte*, 511.
35. Jacobi admired those *Aufklärer* such as Voltaire or Rousseau—see Friedrich Heinrich Jacobi, *Werke*, vol. 1,1, *Ueber die Lehre des Spinoza in Briefen an den Herrn Moses Mendelssohn* (Hamburg and Stuttgart-Bad Cannstatt: Meiner and frommann-holzboog, 1998), 20 and 47. On the contrary, Woldemar sees in the *Auklärung des Verstandes* the stumbling block for a development of the healthy heart, healthy man, and healthy understanding. See Friedrich

Heinrich Jacobi, *Werke*, vol. 7, 1, *Woldemar* (Hamburg and Stuttgart: Meiner and Frommann-Holzboog, 2007), 197. On this see Stefan Schick, "Die Vollendung des Deutschen Idealismus in Friedrich Heinrich Jacobis Sendschreiben an Fichte?", *Deutsche Zeitschrift für Philosophie*, no. 61 (2013), 21–41. Further reference may be found in Friedrich Heinrich Jacobi, *Werke*, vol. 5, *Fliegende Blätter* (Hamburg and Stuttgart: Meiner and frommann-holzboog, 2007), 403.

36. *Letter to Fichte*, 512. The comparison of this quasi-arithmetical order with Fichte's doctrine closes the distance between Fichte and the Berliner *Aufklärer*, whose methodology—in the words of Mendelssohn's "Über die Frage: was heißst aufklären?"—reproduces the rules of arithmetic. In the same vein, the critique against the metaphysics that lies in natural theology is what bods Jacobi with Kant. Fichte's moral theology, in this sense, represents the last chapter of natural theology. On this theme is interesting the epistolary between Jacobi and Reinhold in 1799.
37. Immanuel Kant, "What does it mean to orient oneself in thinking?", in *Religion and Rational Theology*, ed. Allen Wood and George di Giovanni (Cambridge: Cambridge University Press, 1996), 10. See also Immanuel Kant, *Critique of Pure Reason*, ed. Paul Guyer and Allen Wood (Cambridge: Cambridge University Press, 2009), 354 and ss.
38. See Birgit Sandkaulen, "Fürwahrhalten ohne Gründe. Eine Provokation philosophischen Denkens," *Deutsche Zeitschriftfür Philosophie* 57, no. 2 (2009): 259–272.
39. Cf. Friedrich Schlegel, *On the study of Greek poetry*, ed. Stuart Barnett (New York: SUNY Press, 2001), 47.
40. *Letter to Fichte*, 514.
41. Immanuel Kant, *Critique of Pure Reason*, ed. Paul Guyer and Allen Wood (Cambridge: Cambridge University Press, 2009), 391–392.
42. Immanuel Kant, *Critique of Pure Reason*, ed. Paul Guyer and Allen Wood (Cambridge: Cambridge University Press, 2009), 392.
43. *Letter to Fichte*, 515.
44. This polemical step is indeed relevant for the development of Jacobi's non-philosophy, which will later feed off an exploration of Kant's theory of postulates. For the sake of brevity, we need to follow the restrictions set by the text and assess only this negative reference to that theory. Nevertheless, it cannot be stressed enough that Jacobi has the merit to pinpoint both positive and negative consequences of the ethic-ontological identity of God that emerges out of the post-Kantian era.
45. *Letter to Fichte*, 517.
46. *Letter to Fichte*, 519.
47. *Letter to Fichte*, 528.

48. Immanuel Kant, "The Only Possible Argument in Support of a Demonstration of the Existence of God," in Immanuel Kant, *Theoretical Philosophy 1755–1770* (Cambridge: Cambridge University Press, 1992), 119–122.
49. Immanuel Kant, *Critique of Pure Reason*, ed. Paul Guyer and Allen Wood (Cambridge: Cambridge University Press, 2009), 297 and 324–325.
50. Immanuel Kant, *Critique of Pure Reason*, ed. Paul Guyer and Allen Wood (Cambridge: Cambridge University Press, 2009), 209–210.
51. Novalis, *Hymns to the Night*, in *Hymns to the Night and Other Selected Writings* (New York, The liberal Art Press, 1960), 4.
52. Immanuel Kant, *Critique of Pure Reason*, ed. Paul Guyer and Allen Wood (Cambridge: Cambridge University Press, 2009), 567–568 and 325–326.
53. *Letter to Fichte*, 512 (footnote 6).
54. *Letter to Fichte*, 524. In the work published in 1811 "On Divine Things and Their Revelation," Jacobi defines a Person (*Mensch*) as an "incomparable" (*Unvergleichbares*), "one for itself." F.H. Jacobi, "Von den göttlichen Dinge und Ihrer Offenbarung," in F.H. Jacobi, *Werke*, Bd. 3, ed. Klaus Hammacher and Walter Jaeschke (Hamburg: Meiner, 2000), 26 (I thank Majk Feldmeier for pointing that out). This essay does only point to some transcendental elements that are the source for the definition of concrete existence; it does not have the ambition to exhaust the topic, which would need to be analyzed according to the difference between human being and God with regard to freedom and time.
55. Birgit Sandkaulen, "Daß, was oder wer? Jacobi im Diskurs über Personen," in *Friedrich Heinrich Jacobi. Ein Wendepunkt der geistigen Bildung der Zeit*, ed. Walter Jaeschke and Birgit Sandkaulen (Hamburg: Meiner, 2004), 231. And Birgit Sandkaulen, "Ichheit und Person. Zur Aporie der Wissenschaftslehre in der Debatte zwischen Fichte und Jacobi," in *System und Systemkritik um 1800*, ed. Christian Danz and Jürgen Stolzenberg (Hamburg: Meiner, 2011), 50 and ss.
56. Novalis, *Hymns to the Night*, in *Hymns to the Night and Other Selected Writings* (New York, The Liberal Arts Press, 1960), 4.
57. Notably, in the second half of eighteenth century, a point of reference for the interpretation of Plato's *Pheado* was M. Mendelssohn's *Phädon, or on the Immortality of the Soul*. Yet, the aim of this conclusive paragraph is quite different from a metaphysical inquiry into rational psychology. Although Jacobi's *Letter to Fichte* might partially be read as a discourse about the soul, our final digression on the similarity between the *Letter* and Plato's dialogue wishes to stress Jacobi's effort to explain the function that the faculty of reason fulfills in our perception of the true. On a general understanding of a Platonic subtext of Jacobi's works, see the recent P.J. Brunel, *De Protée à Poliphème. Les Lumières platoniciennes de Friedrich Heinrich Jacobi* (Paris: PUPS, 2014).
58. Plato, "Phaedo," in Plato, *Complete Works*, ed. John J. Cooper (Indianapolis: Hackett, 1997), 85.

59. Plato, "Phaedo," in Plato, *Complete Works*, ed. John J. Cooper (Indianapolis: Hackett, 1997), 85.
60. Plato, "Phaedo," in Plato, *Complete Works*, ed. John J. Cooper (Indianapolis: Hackett, 1997), 86.
61. Plato, "Phaedo," in Plato, *Complete Works*, ed. John J. Cooper (Indianapolis: Hackett, 1997), 87–88.
62. Plato, "Phaedo," in Plato, *Complete Works*, ed. John J. Cooper (Indianapolis: Hackett, 1997), 57.
63. Plato, "Phaedo," in Plato, *Complete Works*, ed. John J. Cooper (Indianapolis: Hackett, 1997), 86.
64. Plato, "Phaedo," in Plato, *Complete Works*, ed. John J. Cooper (Indianapolis: Hackett, 1997), 87.

# 4

## Spinoza and Romanticism

Michael Mack

This chapter analyses Spinoza's legacy in early German Romanticism. The first section traces the ways in which Spinoza's reception by early German Romantic poets and philosophers was slightly distorted through the so-called pantheism controversy provoked by the publication of Friedrich Heinrich Jacobi's *On the Doctrine of Spinoza* towards the end of the eighteenth century. Albeit misleading in many ways, Jacobi's 'little book' associates the name Spinoza with progressive tendencies which immediately become demoted as regressive (Jacobi's charge of fatalism) and subversive (Jacobi's charge of atheism).

The unease with Spinoza from the late seventeenth to the late eighteenth centuries crystalizes in Jacobi's term 'spectre'. The spectre of Spinoza is that of an Enlightenment version of modernity that has done away with traditional notions of teleology and philosophical foundations: "Romanticism was anti-foundationalist through and through; and it was so in an attempt to capture the inherent incompleteness of philosophy and knowledge".[1] It may sound odd to discuss Spinoza's philosophy within the context of romantic incompleteness and fragmentation. However, the fragmentary and the incomplete is part of Spinoza's version of modernity. How so? While his notion of substance denotes completion, much of his philosophical endeavours in Spinoza's *Ethics* set out to render incomplete and limited various anthropocentric distortions of what substance truly is.

M. Mack (✉)
Durham University, Durham, UK
e-mail: Michael.mack@durham.ac.uk

© The Author(s) 2020
E. Millán Brusslan (ed.), *The Palgrave Handbook of German Romantic Philosophy*, Palgrave Handbooks in German Idealism, https://doi.org/10.1007/978-3-030-53567-4_4

Spinoza's critique of anthropomorphic and anthropocentric notions of substance in fact marks the meeting point of his scientific and literary acumen: he uncovers as fictions various pseudo-scientific representations of the universe in terms of teleology and first principles. Teleology does not denote natural laws or goals. Instead, first principles are what humanity anthropocentrically and anthropomorphically projects into its image of what the universe or nature is supposed to be. These representations are inadequate, are fictitious, because they use anthropocentric wishes and anthropomorphic projections for the vast, and, to our limited human understanding, incomplete and fragmentary universe.

We may thus discover in Spinoza the scientific and philosophical context for what would later become Schlegel's famous notion of romantic irony: "Irony is a sort of play that reveals the limitations of a view of reality that presumes to have the last word".[2] By uncovering representations of the universe in terms of teleology as being limited—because they are grounded in a one-sided anthropocentric perspective—Spinoza subjects grand, foundationalist claims of human knowledge to ironic treatment. Here, traditional philosophy no longer has the last word, and similarly "with the use of romantic irony, Schlegel showed that there was no last words".[3] Spinoza's deflation of purported keys to understanding the universe as anthropocentric and anthropomorphic deceptions or fictions feeds romantic philosophy's struggle with the foundationalism and the teleology that undergirds the knowledge claims of German idealism. Spinoza's scientific discovery of our limited and self-centred representation of substance or the universe provides the philosophical backbone for the romantic wariness and ultimate rejection of German idealism's claim "that the ultimate origin of Being is transparent".[4]

As I have shown elsewhere, the ghost of Spinoza evokes a hidden Enlightenment of diversity that deviates from the foundationalism and aprioristic paradigm of German idealism.[5] Due to his unsettling and persistent haunting, Spinoza's thought shaped not only Romanticism, scepticism and anti-foundationalism but also the early German Romantic's fascination with experiential science that is no longer grounded on the first principle of either teleology, the Cartesian cogito, Fichte's absolute *Ich* or the Kantian a priori. As will be discussed in the second section of this chapter, this non-teleological and anti-foundational heritage of Spinoza's approach to scientific inquiry might explain the unexpected modernity of Romanticism. In this respect, the following chapter will further develop recent work on Romanticism's modernism. As Frank has shown, the Nazis despised the early German Romantics for aesthetic as well as ideological reasons:

"In the authors of early German Romanticism, the Nazis saw—and rightly so—ground breakers of the literary avant-garde, whose irony was biting and whose sincerity was doubted, enemies of the bourgeoisie, friends and spouses of Jews, welcomed guests and discussion partners at the Jewish Berlin salons, aggressive proponents of 'the emancipation of the Jewry,' and finally 'subversive intellectuals' (a slogan which the Nazis used indifferently to refer to members of the political left, to Jews as a group, and to intellectuals)".[6]

As the following will show, next to the literary avant-garde quality of Romanticism, Spinoza's heritage also informs the fascination of the romantics with the philosophical and scientific implications of a modernity that has overcome the teleological foundations of traditional, representational methodologies, which Spinoza unmasked as anthropocentric and anthropomorphic fictions as will discussed and analysed in the course of this chapter.

## 1   Spinoza's Modernity and Romanticism

As has been intimated in the introduction, Spinoza's legacy in Romanticism could be somewhat reductively summarized by the term 'modernity'. The most striking aspect of Spinoza's modernity within Romanticism is the so-called pantheism controversy in Germany at the end of the eighteenth century. This intellectual event caused a huge upheaval not only in the German-speaking world, but the waves it set free swept over into England, as will be discussed in the concluding section to this chapter by mainly focusing on Coleridge's reception of the so-called pantheism controversy. As we will see, the word pantheism is actually a misnomer for Spinoza's philosophy and the true target of Friedrich Heinrich Jacobi's 1785 publication *On the Doctrine of Spinoza* is what he calls atheism and, more importantly for how Romanticism navigates its relationship with German idealism, fatalism: "Jacobi equated Spinozism to atheism and condemned the German Enlightenment thinkers for taking a path that led to fatalism and atheism".[7] As we shall see, from the late seventeenth to the early nineteenth centuries, the name Spinoza was a red flag signalling the atheistic dangers of a modern, secular age.

Jacobi's accusation of atheism refers to Spinoza as the symbol of the threatening, atheist force of modernity. Following Elizabeth Millán's complex perspective on Jacobi's multi-layered position, one could argue that he propounded a counter-modernity to the one outlined by Spinoza. Millán mentions fatalism as the second charge Jacobi advances in his immensely influential book of 1785. Jacobi accused Spinoza as founder of the Enlightenment of the twin evils linking atheism and fatalism and proposed a leap of faith as a modern anti-dote: Jacobi's "solution to the Enlightenment dead end was a leap of faith that would jump-start our epistemological enterprises and free us of atheism and fatalism, the twin evils of Spinozism".[8] The allegation of fatalism does not so much go back to the late seventeenth century but is contemporaneous with the age of German idealism and Romanticism.

One can trace this mutation of an atheist to a fatalist Spinoza in Hegel's development of Kant's idealist philosophy. In his *Religion with the Limits of Reason Alone* (1793), while hinting at an underlying charge of atheism (derived from the late seventeenth and early eighteenth centuries), Kant grounds his interpretation of Judaism in a reading of Spinoza, hypostasizing an atheist "religion without religion" wherein "the subjects remained attuned in their minds to no other incentive except the goods of this world and only wished, therefore to be ruled through rewards and punishments in this life".[9] Here Kant constructs what he calls a "Jewish theocracy"[10] on the basis of Spinoza's reading of the Hebrew Bible.[11]

At this point, the charge of a worldly quasi-atheist religion fuses with that of fatalism: Kant describes subjects who are fatalistically ruled exclusively by 'rewards and punishments in this life' and whose minds are passively attuned to 'no other incentives except the goods of this world'. Another word for such fatalist passivity is what Kant takes issue with under the term heteronomy, whereas autonomy names the free and active workings of human rationality.[12] In the ultimate footnote to chapter 1 of his *Hegel or Spinoza*, Pierre Macherey traces the image of Spinoza as fatalist and passive Oriental in Hegel's *Lectures on the History of Philosophy* to yet another source in Kant:

> The orientalist interpretation of Spinozism is a common link in German philosophy. One can read in the opuscule of Kant on *The End of All Things*: '[…] the pantheism of Tibetans and of other oriental peoples, then later through metaphysical sublimation, Spinozism: two doctrines closely affiliated to one of the oldest systems, that of emanation, according to which all the human spirits after having emerged from divinity finish by reentering and being reabsorbed by it'.[13]

This quote highlights how in the misleading term pantheism the charges of passivity, fatalism and being Oriental fuse with that of an atheist religion without religion (i.e. a religion that is not a proper religion but instead instantiates atheism). German idealists from Kant via Hegel to Fichte try to banish Spinoza's modernity by labelling it non-rational: a religion that is atheist without being properly religious but immanent-heteronomous—oriented towards the goods of this world—passive and hence fatalistic, fitting the prejudicial construction of a backward 'Oriental' Spinoza who also happens to be the biblical, expert interpreter of Judaism as a worldly religion without religion.

In a highly disturbing and yet fascinating way, Jacobi's allegations against Spinoza's version of the Enlightenment do not contradict but instead partake of a German idealist project to advance a notion of modernity that is aprioristic, does away with heteronomous (experience-based) evidence and hence relies on leaps of faith performed by the Kantian autonomy of the human mind. The highly derogatory term 'fatalism' thus actually denotes a scientific, experiential approach (at the mercy of unpredictable outcomes) to the analysis of our world. Hence, fatalism and realism are synonymous.

As Elizabeth Millán has clearly shown, for a romantic philosopher such as Friedrich Schlegel, Spinoza counterbalances the idealist disregard of contingency and a non-teleological understanding of nature with a realist—what Jacobi and Kant, Fichte and Hegel would label fatalist and atheist—awareness of things not going according to a grand plan: "Schlegel's critical philosophy was not a pure form of idealism at all; it was, rather, a unique antifoundational hybrid of idealism (à la Fichte) with realism (à la Spinoza) that was coherentist (and coherent) through and through".[14] As we shall see in the following section, what made Spinoza such a crucial thinker of the antifoundational, incomplete and contingent for Romanticism's struggle with idealism is exactly what has led to a scientific rediscovery of his work in the late twentieth and early twenty-first centuries, at a time, that is, when new neuroscientific and biophysical research—such as that of emergent forms of life that happen randomly rather than teleologically—has discredited a foundational and aprioristic methodology in the sciences.

Against this background, it is not surprising that perhaps the most radical of German idealists, Fichte, explicitly endorsed Jacobi's leap of faith as idealism's defence against Spinoza's purported passivity and heteronomy:

> Like Jacobi before him, Fichte sees in Spinoza's philosophy a model of the sort of determinism/fatalism that he finds threatening to the well-being of philosophy. For Fichte, Spinoza was a thinker focused upon things rather than the I, on substance rather than the active subject. In Spinoza's system, the I is posited merely as a mode of being, subject to the laws of nature, with no access to the supersensible realm, and thereby robbed of its freedom.[15]

Jacobi's charge of passivity in terms of fatalism permeates the whole of German idealism's philosophical vilification of Spinoza. The idealists cast their philosophy of an active and autonomous modernity—a *Tathandlung* as

Fichte put it—in stark opposition to what they rejected as the backward, 'Oriental' passivity and heteronomy, embodied in Spinoza substance.[16]

For the early German Romantics, Spinoza's name signalled a glaring contrast to the foundationalist, aprioristic approach that has shaped idealism from Descartes to Kant, Hegel and Fichte. As has been intimated above and as will be discussed with a close focus on Spinoza's non-teleological philosophy of mind and body in the following section, the early German Romantics sympathies with a Spinozist suspicion of an idealistic version of modernity that is one-dimensionally aprioristic by dismissing the (heteronomous) evidence of experience chime with a contemporary rediscovery of Spinoza in the natural sciences. Here, it is apposite to highlight how both modernist literature and contemporary sciences have rendered as regressive the purported progress story which partakes of the aprioristic foundationalism of Descartes and then the German idealist understanding of modernity and scientific advancements.

Contemporary scientific discoveries as well as a modernist abandonment of omniscience have called into question claims of all-encompassing comprehension that are grounded in the foundationalism of Fichte's radical development Kant's and Hegel's epistemological claims that render the autonomous human mind the foundation of absolute knowledge: "Because Fichte believes that philosophy begins from an absolute foundation, pure and certain comprehensibility is not only possible but demanded. Recall that he defines philosophy in terms of the 'absolute comprehensibility' of consciousness".[17] Schlegel's romantic philosophy of the incomplete and fragmentary balances claims of absolute comprehension with Spinoza's epistemological scepticism as regards self-centred, anthropocentric and anthropomorphic (mis-)representations of reality: Spinoza's notion of mind, nature and "form is not imposed on the body by the soul, as in Leibniz's model. Nor does it operate like an artificial machine, as in the Cartesian animal-machine, modelled on hydraulic or mechanical devices, in which a specific energy source, like an internal fire is needed to activate its parts. What is more, this form has no final causes and is not teleologically adapted to some function, unlike an artificial machine".[18] Spinoza abandons theologically conditioned aggrandizements of the human mind (theological as the image of God) and separates our environment from anthropocentric superimpositions such as mechanical functions serving human goals or end-points that advance humanity's role in the universe. In eliminating teleology and the mechanical apparatus serving an anthropocentric as well anthropomorphic conception of nature, Spinoza advances anti-foundational ways of thinking which provide support for romantic philosophy's critical engagement with idealism's claims of the human mind's all-comprehensive consciousness:

> Romantic philosophy does not rest on firm foundations from which it spins a deductive web of certainty. In place of a closed, grand deductive system that would provide the first and last word on the foundations of knowledge, the romantic conception of philosophy breaks with the view that philosophy must rest upon any foundation at all. In this conception of philosophy, there is no attempt to keep uncertainty out of the picture, but rather a humble acceptance of the provisional nature of all our claims to knowledge.[19]

As we shall see in the following section, while encouraging such epistemological humility, Spinoza's scepticism is not relativist insofar as he does not dispute notions of scientific truth. But neither does a romantic philosopher à la Schlegel.

At issue is thus *not* a relativist questioning of the existence of truth. Instead, a romantic conception of philosophy critically investigates the delusions and fictions in self-centred, anthropocentric and anthropomorphic notions of truth and reason which have become highly dubious in our contemporary age of the Anthropocene: "Prominent representatives of the modern European philosophical tradition such as Descartes and Fichte sought the foundation for philosophy in a lonely cogito or *Ich*, but Schlegel's rejects this move and any attempt to isolate a single, fixed principle (whether that principle is understood as an activity or as a fact) underlying all knowledge claims".[20] This rejection of a single, fixed foundation or principle deviates from the mainstream of European philosophy and re-connects to Spinoza's radical divergence from Descartes's cogito and the anthropocentricism of the Western philosophical and scientific tradition, which has recently been called into question with an emphasis on the destructiveness of idealist constructions of our environment that has rendered humanity a geographic force interfering with various eco-systems of our planet, with Ozone levels rising in the air and plastic overwhelming organic and inorganic maritime systems.

It is against the contemporary background of not only the socio-economic but also a planetary triumph of anthropocentric idealism (from Descartes's cogito to Fichte's absolute *Ich*) that we have come to see Romanticism's difference to a Western philosophical tradition.[21] That this difference is largely due to Spinoza's different, non-anthropocentric and non-teleological heritage within Romanticism, becomes apparent in the idealist vilification of his thought in the wake of the pantheism controversy that Jacobi's little book of 1785 provoked. As has been discussed in this section, the butt of such vilification was the equation of Spinoza's purported atheism with his assumed fatalism. Both atheism and fatalism are categories that function to vilify Spinoza's diminution of humanity's role in nature. Behind the charge of atheism is the aggrandizement of human achievements in the theological tradition of the West, wherein the human is famously the image of God. Fatalism is the logical consequence of such evisceration of the will as sanctioned by divine creation.

We are able to see a more nuanced perspective in which early German Romanticism and German idealism are not indistinguishable as has been claimed by Frederick Beiser following the line taken by Isaiah Berlin who subscribes to Fichte's denigration of "Spinoza's system"[22] as "at best [...] simply a rigid, logical unity in which there is no room for movement".[23] To be fair to Berlin, his lectures of 1965 were a courageous attempt to extricate Romanticism from the common post-WWII association with irrationalism or, worse still, fascism and Nazism.[24] Beiser has ceaselessly and admirably attempted to continue the rehabilitation of Romanticism as first attempted by Berlin five decades ago. However, as Elizabeth Millán-Zaibert has shown, there is an underlying tendency in Beiser's work (here clearly following Berlin) to render Romanticism acceptable by making it compatible with German idealism: Beiser "insists that the early German Romantics are absolute idealists".[25] This is in contrast to Manfred Frank's and Andrew Bowie's approach that sets out to show the ways in which Romanticism informs the breakdown of totality, certainty and omniscience in modern and postmodern writing and thought (see Bowie 1996 and Frank 1996). As should be clear by now, the line of argument of the current chapter is close to Frank's and Bowie's perspective and widens the scope of Romanticism's modernity and contemporaneity by delineating how Spinoza's romantic heritage resurfaces in recent scientific discoveries.

With his admirable scholarly expertise, Beiser has taken Berlin's open-minded approach towards the philosophical study of Romanticism much further and has shown how much the early German Romantics have learned from Spinoza's notion of nature whose monism diverges from the dualism that underlines various hierarchies—of nature and humanity, of body and mind, of autonomy and heteronomy—in idealist thought: "True to their anti-dualism, the romantics placed the self within nature, insisting that it is one mode of single infinite substance, one part of the universal organism. They were no less naturalistic than Spinoza: they too affirmed that everything is within nature, and that everything in nature conforms to law".[26] However, by rendering idealistic the Spinozism of the romantics, Beiser implicitly accepts Jacobi's misnomer of pantheism which has informed the long confusion of Spinoza's position with that of the German idealists, which, as we shall see in the concluding section of this chapter, also spills over into the English reception of the Dutch philosopher: "What the romantics admired in Spinoza was his synthesis of religion and science. Spinoza's pantheism seemed to resolve all the traditional conflicts between reason and faith. It had made a religion out of science by divinizing nature, and science out of religion by naturalizing the divine".[27] First of all, it is imperative to make clear that Spinoza was not a pantheist. Were Spinoza's thought pantheistic, it would render null and void his critique of various forms of anthropomorphism and anthropocentricism that forms a major part of his magnum opus, the *Ethics*. How does pantheism clash with Spinoza's elimination of anthropocentric teleology? Beiser accurately describes pantheistic deifications of nature (and perhaps science too), but this is precisely what Spinoza takes issue with: he deflates deified and inflated notions of nature, human nature included. As pantheist, Spinoza may well be compatible with Fichte's quasi-deification of human actions.

The distinctiveness of Spinoza's rationalism is that he precisely abstains from and, on the contrary, does away with deified notions of nature of which humanity partakes. That he equates God with nature does not mean that he deifies the latter. His notion of God denotes not a personal or impersonal deity but substance which is another word for all there is, for the universe in its (for us humans) immeasurable immensity. The most striking difference to any form of pantheism goes back to Spinoza's distinction between a 'naturing nature' (*natura naturans*) and nature as it appears to us (*natura naturata*). The former is the principle behind nature and the latter is its often deceptive formation and appearance which our senses tend to get wrong when, for example, we take the sun to be close to us, simply because it makes a strong or close impression on us (because it is a hot and sunny summer day).

Clearly, Spinoza's huge distance from any form of pantheism makes possible his critique of a quasi-divine teleology which we in our anthropocentrism impute into the workings of nature. Rather than endorsing human goals as part of the telos of a pantheistically conceived nature, Spinoza sets out to separate our particular endeavours from any grand scheme of God or Nature. Spinoza's outlook is sober and scientific, and he warns against any exuberant extolling of the natural and/or the human as supernatural or divine forces. As Stuart Hampshire has accurately argued, "Spinoza gives the strong impression of thinking like a biologist".[28] Spinoza's scientific way of thinking also cautions against making any hasty jumps that would reach deterministic conclusions about nature or positing laws within it.

Just as pantheism is a highly distortive label, the presumption that accurate science (rather than pretentious pseudo-science) 'discovers' the laws of nature (should there be any, Spinoza would immediately and doubtfully interpose) is a very misleading and, alas, popular misperception of what science is about and what scientists actually do. In the quote above, Beiser extolls both Spinoza and his romantic idealists as doing 'science' by working out the laws of nature. This is precisely what Spinoza's radically non-pantheistic deflation of anthropomorphic and anthropocentric conceptions of the universe calls strongly into question: he shows how any pseudo-scientific notions of determinism and final causes are the outcome of human delusion and fictions about Nature or God.

A deterministic conception of the world as predictable is the offspring of a teleology created by the fantasies of anthropomorphism and anthropocentricism. Contrary to common perceptions, Spinoza is not a determinist, as the term is commonly understood (as in the Beiser quote above). As Hampshire has shown, "a determinist, as this label is commonly understood, has the single idea that any human behaviour is to be explained by well-confirmed natural laws which, taken together with a statement of initial conditions, exhibit the behaviour, whatever it may be, as always in principle predictable. This is not the kind of understanding, and of self-understanding that is proposed by Spinoza".[29] Far from deifying science, as Beiser claims in the quote above, Spinoza's critique of the theological tradition is directed against the elevation of human teleology—be it as 'natural determinism' or as grand scheme of history's unfolding—into a quasi-divine sphere (i.e. what he calls anthropomorphism). As Hampshire has astutely pointed out, reflection, in contrast, "entails the suppression of egoism in our relation with the external world".[30] The issue at the heart of Spinoza's philosophy is not so much dualism and its purported overcoming—as we will see in the following section, Spinoza's strategy is at first dualistic so as to outdo various hierarchical command structures which presuppose forms of unity—but the deflation of teleology as a human fiction and delusion about humanity's place in the universe. Teleology is the driving force behind Descartes's cogito, Hegel's absolute spirit/intellect (*absoluter Geist*) and Fichte's absolute Ich. By idealizing Spinoza and the romantics, critics like Beiser only work into the hands of the idealists and undermine the difference of both Spinoza's and Romanticism's rationalism.

Until recently, however, the idealists have managed to brand—ironically with the help of Jacobi's leap of faith—Spinoza with the vilification of backwardness; be it 'Oriental' in Kant's and Hegel's discourse or 'pre-critical' as Slavoj Žižek has recently put it.[31] The early German Romantics were ideal place holders for Spinoza's exteriority to mainstream scientific and philosophical inquiry. Romanticism "has been interpreted as *at best* a literary movement with excessive emphasis on the irrational forces of human life, in the words of no less an icon of German literature than Goethe, a sick movement to be avoided by anyone with a healthy spirit, and at worst, a movement sowing the seeds of something as diabolical as National Socialism".[32] As we have seen, this highly dubious, threatening and even diabolic image surrounded the public perception of Spinoza from the late seventeenth century until Jacobi's *On the Doctrine of Spinoza* gave ammunition to the German idealist enterprise to turn the tables on a Spinozist radical Enlightenment by relegating it to backwardness, to what the term 'Orient' brought to mind as non-modern, non-Enlightened, non-rational and passively 'pantheistic' (which Spinoza's philosophy, as shown in the preceding paragraphs, clearly is not). Insidiously, 'the renegade Jew who gave us Modernity' (Rebecca Goldstein) here becomes a caricature taken out of the worst of racist, Orientalist stereotyping. Behind this act of 'philosophical' stereotyping is a strategy, a socio-political agenda: that of declaring 'irrational' and 'non-progressive' (backwardly 'Oriental') what has been seen as the diabolical threat of Spinoza's radical Enlightenment which does without the hierarchical as well as teleological structures that are part and parcel of idealist rationalism from Descartes to Hegel and Fichte and beyond (nowadays the 'progressive' teleology of Pippin on the liberal right and Žižek on the left).

Jacobi employs the word spectre to capture the all-pervasive danger of Spinoza's non-teleological and non-hierarchical philosophy. The politics of such haunting become more than apparent when one pays attention to the historical itinerary of such ghosting. Jacobi's phrasing as regards the spectre of Spinoza precisely reappears in Marx's Communist manifesto as the ghost which has been haunting Europe, that of Communism itself.[33] In Jacobi's *On the Doctrine of Spinoza*, this haunting is more geographically restricted to Germany rather than the whole of Europe as it is at the opening of Marx's *Communist Manifesto* (1848) where we encounter Jacobi's formulation almost verbatim—from 'A spectre is haunting Europe—the spectre of communism' to

> a Ghost [*Gespenst*] has recently been haunting Germany in various shapes (I wrote to Moses Mendelssohn) and it is held by the superstitious and by the atheists in equal reference [...] Perhaps we will witness someday that an argument will arise over the corpse of Spinoza equal to the one which arose between the archangels and Satan over the corpse of Moses.[34]

Jacobi makes clear that he endeavours to put an end to the haunting with which Spinoza's ghost seems to keep Germany and then later England and the whole Europe (by the time it seems to have mutated to what Marx calls communism in 1848) enthralled. Jacobi composes and publishes the writings gathered together in *On the Doctrine of Spinoza* to exorcise the persistent impact of a figure that appears to be an anti-Moses of sorts. As we shall see in the concluding section to this chapter, Jacobi's attempt at exorcism achieved the opposite result: it hugely increased the fascination with Spinoza to such an extent that the so-called pantheism controversy reached the rest of Europe, the shores of England included. The haunting of Spinoza is far from over by now. First, it re-emerged as Marx's spectre of communism in the nineteenth century. The romantic kernel of such haunting might well be its scientific scepticism and its avoidance of one-dimensional, teleological reductions of our world—as Coleridge puts it in his Spinozist poem 'Christabel':

> The maid, alas! Her thoughts are gone,
> She nothing sees—no sight but one!
> The maid, devoid of guile and sin,
> I know not how, in fearful wise,
> So deeply had she drunken in
> That look, those shrunken serpent eyes,
> That all her features were resigned
> To this sole image in her mind:
> And passively did imitate
> That look of dull and treacherous hate![35]

There might be no better presentation of Spinoza's raison d'être for his deflation of the one-dimensional fixation that accompanies the workings of teleology. These lines focus on the cruelty—hatred, to be more precise—that partakes of such seemingly innocent—'the maid, devoid of guile and sin'—reduction of nature's and humanity's multi-layered world to only one line which is that of teleology: 'To this sole image in her mind'. The next section will discuss Spinoza's contemporary scientific relevance, and the conclusion to this chapter will revisit the lines quoted above to show how these partake of the Spinozist heritage in English romantic poetry.

## 2    Spinoza or Romanticism's Spectral Modernity

As we have seen in the previous section, Spinoza is a spectral figure in the history of ideas. His legacy is multi-layered. From the seventeenth and early eighteenth centuries onwards, his name, however, first of all signified scandal:

most of all the outrage of having written a "book forged in hell".[36] The book in question is his *Theological-Political Treatise* of 1670. It made its author's name synonymous with that of the devil. What caused such strong invectives? Spinoza's treatise is indeed a breakthrough in a scandalous way because it is the first book to introduce its readers to the literary or secular study of religious texts. The Bible or, for that matter, any other form of holy script is not—as had been proclaimed at the time and in the centuries preceding the seventeenth and early eighteenth centuries—the word of God but an entirely human product. The Bible here turns into a fiction, into a work of literature. In his *Theological-Political Treatise* Spinoza thus stripped sacred texts of their transcendence. The philosopher here is both a philologist and literary critic, and he employs the skills of literary criticism in order to deflate inflated—fictional—notions of both sovereignty and transcendence. In his posthumously published *magnum opus*, *Ethics*, Spinoza radicalizes and further develops this new hybrid literary-philosophical approach and here not only as regards the theological and political sphere but as applies to the whole spectrum of human society and human knowledge. Spinoza uncovers as fiction what we have taken to be representations of truth not only in the sphere of religion but also in scientific and philosophical inquiry.

At this point another layer of Spinoza's spectral legacy appears: his scepticism as regards human epistemology: what we take to be God or nature—and their purported teleology—or for that matter good or evil (morality) might be nothing more than a product of our *figmenta*, our mental projections and wishes; in short, it might well be that it is our fictions and inventions rather than our epistemological achievements that shed light on the real constitution of God, nature, good and evil: teleological constructions about "all final causes are nothing but human fictions";[37] *omnes causas finales nihil, nisi humana esse figment*.[38] As I have shown elsewhere,[39] Spinoza does not set out to abolish these fictions. If he did, he would be hostile to diversity because it is exactly in the figuration of these *figmenta* that the imagination shapes the cultural formation of different ethnic groups. Instead, Spinoza critiques an inability to detect the fictional element that underpins human modes of reasoning.

By sceptically unmasking sacred and other truths of purported rational operations as fictions of the human mind, Spinoza is the first thinker who attempts to theorize narrative (*figmenta*, fictions) as the constitutive fabric of politics, identity, society, religion and the larger area that encompasses what goes under the rubric 'human knowledge'. Spinoza's hybrid literary-philosophical methodology is highly destabilizing: it unhinges the supposedly solid foundations of not only political theology—that is, sovereignty, religion and political order—but also of what has been taken to be unquestionable scientific insights, discoveries and sound (if not sacred) truths of purported rational inquiry. Spinoza's Enlightenment is radical to the point that it subjects to critical observation that which we have taken to be rational. Are our cerebral operations not also caught up in the realm of human wishes and desires and the various fictions to which they give rise? Spinoza encourages us to take a critical approach towards human claims to reason and truth.

It is nevertheless incumbent to qualify the term scepticism when applied to Spinoza's philosophy. He may be sceptical as regards what goes sometimes under the names of reason or truth, but he does not call truth or rationality as such into question. His scepticism regards categories and representations of reality, but it does not question the scientific investigation of our world. As Pierre Macherey has brilliantly shown, Spinoza uncovers the fictions that claim to be representations of truth which are then supposed to function as being representative of reason's operations. Macherey makes clear that Spinoza's break with Descartes's method results in a new understanding of science and rationality, one no longer premised on representations that "restore effects to their causes",[40] but one that is grounded in what I would call contamination and what Macherey as well as Atlan describe as simultaneity:

> It is on this precise point that Spinoza breaks absolutely with the Cartesian problematic of method. *The Meditations* restore effects to their causes: they go from the finite to the infinite, for example from the human soul to God, taking things in the inverse order to which they are actually produced, which goes necessarily from causes to effects. We understand from this point of view that knowledge is first determined as a representation, because it reflects the real in thought and from its point of view, confirming with criteria of validity that at the outset are given within it and that reproduce the order of the real by inverting it. For Spinoza, by contrast, an adequate knowledge, "explains" its object to the extent that it affirms itself as identical to it, not in the transparency of a conforming representation but in the likeness of the order of an equally necessary reality. This is the real order in which things were produced, and it must also be that of ideas: this is a generic order that goes from cause to effects, and it is this that precisely expresses the *more geometrico*.[41]

Spinoza's non-representational disruption of a Cartesian methodology which restores effects to their causes significantly structures the framework of modern and contemporary science as depicted in Thomas Pynchon's *Gravity's Rainbow*, a text which has come to epitomize postmodern literature.[42] The opening sentence of Pynchon's novel relates to the non-teleological methodology of modern science, which Spinoza's philosophy first delineated theoretically by breaking with the representational paradigm of Descartes's approach to science: "A screaming comes across the sky. It has happened before, but there is nothing to compare it to now. It is too late".[43] This is non-representational *in nuce*: 'It has happened before, but there is nothing to compare it to now', because each thing is identical to its idea and vice versa and thus cannot not be compared to or represented by anything else.

Effects here precede causes, and it is 'too late' to restore the former to the latter. Pynchon invents a word for such Spinozist reversal of the traditional, Cartesian paradigm of representation: "But among *Gravity Rainbow's* untimely traits, the most prominent is surely its obsession with hysteron proteron, the figure of reversal in which effect precedes cause, response anticipates stimulus, sequelae predate injury".[44] Precisely because the order of things is identical with the order of ideas, we no longer need a representational framework wherein one would be representative of the other. Spinoza does away with the hierarchical command centre of the mind that is supposed to control the movements of the body: likewise, the identity of the corporeal and the cerebral renders inoperative the hierarchy that is constitutive for a thinking grounded in representation: we no longer require the lowly sphere of matter to be representative of the higher sphere of the spirit; after all, the two are identical, are contaminated with each other or, in other words, are simultaneously one entity, through conceptually distinct.

How can we explain this strange meeting of romantic philosophy and a modernist as well as postmodernist sensibility à la Pynchon? As has been discussed at the opening of this section, Spinoza's thought is at once literary critical/philological and scientific. This explains why it attracts poets, writers and scientists as well as philosophers. Indeed, as has been argued above, Spinoza is fascinated by the concept of fiction, and significantly, he uses the term to question anthropocentric delusions about nature and the universe that claim to be scientific. In this way, Spinoza refers to literature as a way to correct inaccurate forms of science. In his study of romantic philosophy and science, Robert J. Richards has rightly revised Heinrich Heine: "Heinrich Heine called Goethe 'the Spinoza of poetry.' He could have added 'the Spinoza of science' as well".[45] Goethe's reading of Spinoza was shaped by that of his mentor, the romantic philosopher, literary critic and founder of the modern discipline of social anthropology, Johann Gottfried Herder. As I have shown elsewhere,[46] Goethe as well as Herder develop a non-teleological perspective on society and history (Herder's anthropological and historical writings) as well as on nature and the universe (Goethe's scientific and literary-theological work) that maintains the non-hierarchical and non-causal, non-representative interconnection of organic and inorganic being. As Richards has put it apropos Goethe, "an adequate idea would indicate why the individual had to exist; yet, he [i.e. Goethe] maintained, every individual is linked to every other, so that the conditions of the whole required the existence of each individual".[47] Herder's and Goethe's philosophy of diversity grows out Spinoza's notion of *conatus*. The *conatus* affirms each individual's and each state's and each moment's incomparable validity to exist within a non-teleological and non-hierarchical universe that is nevertheless interconnected (what Deleuze and Guattari would later call Rhizome).

As we have seen, in contrast to Descartes, Spinoza maintained that virtue was not superimposed on nature by reason, God or political power. Rather, the virtuous coincides with the joyful fulfilment of each individual's different natural potential. This appreciation of an infinite variety of different (but also subtly interconnected) forms of life makes for the *differentia specifica* of Spinoza's understanding of self-preservation (*conatus*) from that of Hobbes (Hobbes's political philosophy is based on a dualism between the state of nature and the politics of reason). Spinoza emphasizes radical difference (the incomparable and non-representational scream with which Pynchon's *Gravity Rainbow* opens) but also highlights how what differs interconnects in contaminated states of simultaneity—to neglect this contaminating element is to fall prey to the paranoia as presented in *Gravity's Rainbow* as the destruction and self-destruction of colonial violence and warfare.

A paranoid gaze intent on the destruction of the other also destroys the self. Any form of violence outdoes Spinoza's *conatus*. As in the lines quoted from Coleridge's poem 'Christabel' at the end of the last section, it fixates on one element but ignores the universe's interconnection ("That look, those shrunken serpent eyes,/That all her features were resigned/To this sole image in her mind:/And passively did imitate/That look of dull and treacherous hate!").[48] As in Spinoza's identity of body and mind, his conception of the *conatus* holds together at once two seemingly incompatible entities: it contaminates radical difference and intrinsic interconnection in ever-changing states of simultaneity. Spinoza's philosophy of simultaneity thus questions the hierarchical dualism of traditional science and philosophy where mind is in charge of body as well as various binary oppositions that structure one-dimensional ways of conceptualizing politics and society at large (as illustrated by the lines quoted from Coleridge's poem 'Christabel'). However, his thought certainly does not question the validity of science and rational inquiry. On the contrary, many of his philosophical insights anticipate cutting-edge scientific discoveries of the late twentieth and early twenty-first centuries, as will be discussed in the following paragraphs.

By abandoning the notion of representation, Spinoza inaugurates a scientific revolution that is so groundbreaking that it took centuries to be recognized as such by scientists such as Antonio Damasio and philosophers of science such as Hilary Putnam. What does Spinoza's rejection of representation entail then? An entirely new approach towards human knowledge that avoids hierarchical or representative models of truth such as Descartes's method or, much later, Hegel's dialectics. Instead of representing the spirit in matter or moving from the lowly sphere of the dialectical negative to the higher sphere of the positive—under which the negative becomes subsumed—Spinoza makes us see the identity of what we take to be hierarchically opposed entities. As Macherey has shown, Spinoza's notion of *adequatio* makes us see as contaminated—in other words, as being simultaneous—what the operations of representation as well as dialectics separate and temporally dilate as the distance marking off the merely embodied (dialectically, the negative) from the cerebral (dialectically, the positive) which the former is supposed to represent: "The essential function of the category of *adequatio* is to break with the concept of knowledge as representation that continues to dominate Cartesianism. To know, in the sense to represent, to re-present, is literally to reproduce, to repeat; the idea is thus nothing more than a double, and image of the thing, for which it provides a representation, which exists and subsists outside of it".[49] According to Descartes, the mind controls the body and renders the merely material a representation or reproduction of its mental concepts or sense of order (nature's purported order and hierarchy). Spinoza shows how representations are mental constructions and fictions. They do not illuminate the world but are merely reproduced images of our anthropocentric (human and self-centred) approach to our environment.

Spinoza's abandonment of representation profoundly informs and shapes various romantic critiques of anthropocentrism. As Macherey has shown, it not only counteracts the work of Spinoza's contemporary Descartes but also implicitly refutes the further development of Cartesian method in Hegel's dialectics:

> It is thus possible, at the risk of chronological violence, to talk about the refutation to which Spinoza himself subjects Hegel: what awaits this refutation is the idealist presence of the dialectic, which bases its universality on the presupposition that thought, by reason of its internal reflexivity, is the form par excellence of the real, of all the real: it is as such that it presents itself as an absolute rational order that gathers, and absorbs, all other orders, in the process of its own totalization. The Hegelian dialectic, which presents itself as a circle of circles, presupposes a relation of hierarchical subordination between all the elements that it reunites,

and this subordination is reflected through an ultimate term, from whose point of view the entirety of its progress can be understood, because it has a meaning. But it is exactly this presupposition that is immediately rejected by Spinoza, because he eliminates from his conception of the real, from substance, any idea of hierarchical subordination of elements.[50]

Hegel's dialectics with its unity grounded in hierarchical subordinations of its elements indeed further develops and radicalizes the Cartesian priority of thought. For Spinoza, by contrast, "thought is identical to everything and therefore has nothing above it, but the sequence through which it is realized poses, at the same time, its absolute equality with all other forms in which substance is also expressed, and these are infinite in number".[51] As we have seen in the preceding section, German idealists from Kant onwards orientalize Spinoza and equate the lack of hierarchy in his thought with passivity, which, according to the prejudices implicit in German idealism, becomes equated with the Orient (as hierarchically inferior to the idealism of the Occident).

This Orientalized figure shapes the famous Spinoza controversy which Friedrich Heinrich Jacobi provoked through the publication of his 1785 book *Concerning the Doctrine of Spinoza*. As Elizabeth Millán has shown, even though the controversy went under the name pantheism—because Spinoza was wrongly identified as a pantheist during Romanticism—the real issue at its core was the clash between reason and faith. On the surface, Jacobi claims to advocate the affirmations and tenants of faith. Elizabeth Millán-Zaibert has convincingly argued that Jacobi's first English translator, George di Giovanni, has a point in interpreting Jacobi's stance as that of Cartesian rationalist. She shows how di Giovanni "even goes so far as to compare 'the inner light' that Jacobi invokes, to Descartes' notion of reason"[52] and how di Giovanni's rationalist "reading of Jacobi cannot be ignored or easily dismissed".[53] Indeed, this kind of reading would prove right Macherey's contrast between the idealist rationalism of Descartes and Hegel and the striking anomaly of Spinoza.

It is this anomaly which German idealists—be it Kant, Fichte or Hegel—dismissively label passive and fatalist. Indeed no-one less than Hegel's absolute spirit appears in its true active and activated glory when configured as a stark contrast to the presumed 'Oriental' passivity of Spinoza's substance: "By contrast, Hegel thinks of Spirit as subject and as entirely within a perspective of eminence, which constrains and subordinates unto itself all that is produced as real and which would appear as its manifestation".[54] As has been discussed above, Spinoza's notion of the *conatus* establishes the simultaneity of the subjective and the objective; a subject—most prominently Hegel's absolute spirit itself—that sets out to subordinate its objective, 'merely material' environment would destroy not only that but also itself (it would be auto-immune, as Derrida would call it).

Indeed, the moot point in this context of subjectivity and objectivity, or spirit and matter, is Spinoza's prescient and scientifically accurate approach towards the mind-body divide. As Henri Atlan has recently shown, the American philosopher of science Hilary Putnam's notion of a "synthetic identity of properties"[55] is part and parcel of a scientific rediscovery of Spinoza. As Atlan explains, Putnam's notion of a *synthetic identity of properties*

> is from a study on 'mind and body' in which Putnam traces the history of theories of the identity of body and mind in modern philosophy, Spinoza's theory, and those of other authors, like Diderot, who were inspired by it, were not taken seriously until the second half of the twentieth century, because philosophers considered them to be a priori false. In the absence of empirical arguments for or against identity, it was untenable, because it was implausible and inadmissible *a priori* for rational thought. The situation changed when the philosophical mainstream stopped being *aprioristic* and actually become *anti-aprioristic*, under the effect of the blows dealt by the natural sciences to various rational axioms, such as Euclid's postulate, or the nature of physical magnitudes in the nineteenth and twentieth centuries.[56]

Spinoza's approach anticipates modern anti-aprioristic science that is grounded in experience.

Aprioristic procedures presuppose order, purity and teleology as foundation of our universe. Spinoza's scepticism apropos categorizations of rationality in terms of order and purity preconditions his experiential approach to science. Cutting-edge modern science has abandoned various notions of an a priori order or teleology and has shown that Spinoza was right: teleology is a fantasy of the human mind. Instead of a plan, there is chance and randomness. Animal and human behaviour only become intentional once there is a final outcome of a random, chance event that is then remembered and intentionally carried out. In his recent lecture, Atlan refers to apes learning from experience that they can harm another ape with a bone: first, the apes randomly play with the bone until one ape experientially realizes that the bone in question can be used as destructive tool or instrument to inflict harm on someone else. Like apes, we learn from experience and not from aprioristic notions that ignore truths gathered from the trial and error of chance encounters. Neurons and all other natural systems organize in a chance and random manner.⁵⁷ The body is the mind and the mind is the body. There is no control or causation between the two because the two are identical.

Against this background, Spinoza's spectral philosophy emerges as that of impurity. Spinoza is the thinker of the impure, the contaminated and contaminating. Related to the issue of impurity is that of destruction. Spinoza indeed engages in what Friedrich Schlegel calls "a negative, destructive system of highest knowledge" (*negativ vernichtendes System des höchsten Wissens*).⁵⁸ This is of course not the *Frühromantiker* but the Schlegel of 1828. However, the late Schlegel has a point here: there is a destructive or negative element in Spinoza's scientific methodology—one that fragments pseudo-scientific notions of the All or the Universe and makes us see their rather illusory and, for scientific purposes at least, rather disappointing proclivities for operating in the name of metaphysical and other ideological presuppositions, such as God.

It is precisely such impetus to destroy irreverently, unified structures that informs the early Schlegel's and Novalis's romantic genre of the fragment. Moreover, this is true not only of the German case but, as Jerome McGann has shown, of early Romanticism as a whole: "The earliest Romantic theories of Romanticism are always cast in polemical, incomplete, or exploratory forms".⁵⁹ The incomplete and explorative aspect of early Romanticism will then inform modernism's suspicion of totalizing attempts to unify our experience of the world. The fragment disrupts presumptions of completeness and totality. It renders inoperative the totalizing operations of Cartesian and, later on, Hegelian systems of human knowledge and science.

Spinoza introduces a certain destructive element that has become a driving force for the courage to engage the fragmentary and incomplete in Romanticism, modernism as well as postmodernism. Spinoza's destructive element demolishes not only the purity of religion but also that of science. What Descartes establishes as the autonomy of the mind and its control over the body, Spinoza contaminates with the often misleading work of the affects of which our rational workings are ineluctably a part. This is not as straightforward as it may first sound because Spinoza separates body and mind, perhaps most famously in his *Ethics*, Part III, Proposition 2 which states that "the body cannot determine the mind to thinking, and the mind cannot determine the body to motion, to rest, or to anything else (if there is anything else)".⁶⁰ This proposition is not meant to argue for a dualism of mind and body but rather to confound a Cartesian notion of an interaction between the two entities wherein the cerebral commands and controls corporal actions, a point with which Spinoza takes issue under Proposition 2 writing: "They are so firmly persuaded that the body now moves, now is at rest, solely from the mind's command, and that it does a great many things which depend only on the mind's will and its art of thinking".[61] While not being able to determine each other, the mind and the body are nevertheless (paradoxically) contaminated with each other. As Spinoza puts it, they are 'the same thing'.

We come to this state of contamination wherein body and mind are the same thing from what Spinoza describes as that which reason has learned from experience, namely that the mind, being ignorant of the causes by which it is conscious of its own actions, does not understand how it is prompted by the irrational sphere of appetites. The appetites are the unknown causes of consciousness, as Spinoza says in the following passage worth quoting in full:

> So experience itself, no less clearly than reason, teaches that men believe themselves free because they are conscious of their own actions, and ignorant of the causes by which they are determined, that the decisions of the mind are nothing but the appetites themselves, which therefore vary as the disposition of the body varies. For each governs everything from his affect; those who are torn by contrary affects do not know what they want, and those who are not moved by any affect are very easily driven here and there.[62]

Our consciousness of our own actions does not mean that we are free agents, because being conscious is not the same as being cognizant of the causes by which we are determined. The true cause of our action—of which we may well be aware but this awareness says little here—resides in the contamination of mind with appetites, with affects. Hence there is no parallelism but, as Henri Atlan has shown, an identity of body and mind: "In fact, Spinoza himself never uses the word 'parallelism' and explicitly refines his position as an ontological monism manifested in a conceptual dualism".[63] Or, as Spinoza puts in the paragraph following the one cited above:

> All these things, indeed, show clearly that both the decision of the mind and the appetite and the determination of the body by nature exist together—or rather are the same thing, which we call decision when it is considered under, and explained through, the attribute of thought, and which we call a determination when it is considered under the attribute of extension and deduced from the laws of motion and rest.[64]

Here we have not a parallelism, but something more far-reaching, an identity of body and mind. There is a simultaneity rather than a spread-out opposition between the two entities. I have advanced a notion of simultaneity through the figure of contamination in my recently published book *Contaminations:*

*Beyond Dialectics in Modern Literature, Science and Film*.[65] The figure of contamination instantiates simultaneity and thus moves beyond Hegel's paradigm of dialects which is still holding a firm grip on political and philosophical inquiry from Robert Pippin to Slavoj Žižek. The premise of Hegel's dialectics is a dualism that, as Henri Atlan has shown, has formed much of our scientific heritage. Atlan has analysed the ways in which Spinoza's thought differs from the mechanical and dualistic premises of philosophers of science that have shaped our understanding of what it means to be scientific, most notably Leibniz and Descartes:

> Spinoza's physics has nothing to do with mechanics. Unlike the physics of Descartes and Leibniz, it is not a theory of motion that can be judged in the light of modern physics. These statements in *Ethics* II, outlining a theory of simple and compound bodies are more relevant to what we would consider chemistry or biophysics; that is, they constitute a physical theory about the nature of compound entities, with no fundamental difference between the living and the non-living.[66]

Simultaneity defines the state of compound bodies. The simultaneity of the compounded emerges in the figure of contamination, where we come to see at once, what Hegelian dialectics spreads out over time in states of opposition.

The early German Romantic philosopher Novalis reads Spinoza in terms of this monistic simultaneity of what idealist thought separates: Spinoza contaminates nature with its purported opposite, namely, reason. In his letter of 20 January 1799 to Caroline Schlegel, Novalis maintains that in "Spinoza lives already this divine spark of nature's reason" (*in Spinoza lebt schon dieser göttliche Funken des Naturverstandes*).[67] Following and deflecting Spinoza's one substance monism, Novalis contaminates what idealist rationalism separates in opposition to each other: nature and reason. By contaminating reason with its purported opposite, nature, he declares as foolish the antagonism between realism and idealism. From the perspective of Spinoza's monism, oppositions are illusory and it is only thinking that makes them so: "All real conflict (*Streit*) is an illusion (*Schein*)—therefore the question of idealism and realism is so foolish, so *illusory* (*scheinbar*)".[68] Novalis argues that there is a methodology of correlation—what he calls an 'infinite idea of love'—in Spinoza's philosophy, which he misses in the idealist philosophy of Fichte:

> Spinoza [...] has grasped the infinite idea of love (*die unendliche Idee der Liebe*) and has adumbrated its method—to realize oneself for it and realize itself for oneself on this thread of dust (*Staubfaden*). It is a pity that I do not see any indication of this idea in Fichte and that there I do not feel the breath of creation.[69]

The idealism of Fichte and Hegel is from the romantics' perspective one-sided. Idealist cognition lives the illusion of taking one half—or one part of an opposition—to be the whole truth:

> The illusion (*Schein*) is always the half (*ist überall die Hälfte*)—the half of a whole is exactly illusion (*das Halbe eines Ganzen allein ist Schein*)—because everything, however, cannot simply be halved, we encounter illusion everywhere. The illusion of cognition originates in the elevation of the half to being the whole (*Der Schein unsrer Erkenntnis ensteht aus dem Erheben des Halben zum Ganzen*)—or, in the making half of what is inseparable, of that whose *mere existence consists* in its correlation (*oder aus dem Halbiren des Untheilbaren, desjenigen, des Wesen blos in der Zusammensetzung besteht*)—in the counter-natural (*widernatürlichen*) abbreviation or division of transcendence and immanence.[70]

Because Spinoza makes us see the world in correlated, contaminated ways as the monism of one substance, he is for Schlegel and Novalis not operating in the field of thought but that of love. Idealist thought, however, is "the art of illusion" (*Alles Denken ist also eine Kunst des Scheins*).[71] In their appreciation of the incomplete, unsystematic and the fragmentary, the early German Romantics implicitly engage Spinoza's critique of anthropocentricism that rejects as delusory claims to scientific knowledge that are merely reflections or representation of how our species tends to perceive the world (and hence how we are merely a tiny part but not the world in its entirety). Significantly, Novalis criticizes Fichte's notion of reason as a partial position, as that of the I (*Ich*), against the background of a Spinozist deflation of human knowledge as biased (ideologically anthropomorphic and anthropocentric).

We take God, the All and world as mere reflections of ourselves: "We think God as personal, in the same way as we think of ourselves as personal" (*Wir denken uns Gott persönlich, wie wir uns selbst persönlich Denken*).[72] Spinoza takes another path.

He depersonalizes and this is what Novalis perhaps rather misleadingly calls an inebriation filled with God or the World Soul: "Spinoza is a human filled with God to the point of inebriation" (*Spinoza ist ein gotttruckener Mensch*).[73] This is of course Spinoza's famously depersonalized God of nature, of biophysics, of the universe, which to us humans is ungraspable in its entirety.

Spinoza's intellectual love of God denotes the almost romantic longing of the incomplete, for understanding of the World and its soul in a, for us, unreachable state of completeness. Because each of us is fragmentary and incomplete, we rely on diversity, on interconnection and, in short, on a sense of community—and Spinoza's notion of love denotes this interconnectedness and interdependence of the universe's fragmentary parts (of which humanity partakes):

> This love toward God is the highest good which we can want from the dictate of reason and, is common to all men; we desire that all should enjoy it. And so it cannot be stained by any affect of envy, nor by an affect of jealousy.[74]

This is not the rationality of a complete system. Rather, the dictates of reason ask of us to understand our limitations. It is this epistemological humility that guards against hostility towards our environment as manifested in envy when the self wants to usurp the life of others or jealousy when someone does not endure the well-being of others. Far from being absolute, scientific knowledge here operates in a self-critical or ironic mode. It remains fragmentary and disappoints expectations of its dialectical transformation into a system of purported completeness. As will be discussed in the following concluding section, Spinoza's scientific notion of the simultaneity of purported opposites or contrasts constitutes what romantic poets and philosopher discuss as love, nature and the correlating force of the imagination—terms that here denote the contaminating chemistry that is romantic poetry.

## 3 Conclusion: Coleridge's Imagination and Other Contaminations of Spinoza's Rationalism

Much of this chapter has been dedicated to tracing the struggle between idealism and Romanticism as well as to delineating how Spinoza's rational, scientific thought has encouraged romantic thinkers and poets to embark on a non-foundational, non-teleological and non-aprioristic path of writing and thinking (prefiguring what Deleuze and Guttari would call the Rhizome in the twentieth century). As we have seen in the first section of this chapter, the romantic reception of Spinoza was preconditioned by Jacobi's theological and idealist charge of both fatalism (heteronomy and passivity) and atheism.

Jacobi's term 'pantheism' distorted how Coleridge, Hölderlin, Novalis and Schlegel potentially perceived Spinoza's conception of the simultaneity of self and other, of body and mind. Despite the misleading term of 'pantheism' which the romantics inherited from Jacobi's *On the Doctrine of Spinoza*, the contours of a philosophy of simultaneity and contamination emerged as an alternative to the teleological paradigm of the purity of the thinking subject

(Descartes' cogito, Kantian autonomy, and Fichte's absolute *Ich*). As Nicholas Halmi has recently pointed out, "Coleridge recognized in Spinoza's monism the only intellectually viable alternative to Kant' transcendental idealism".[75] Here we encounter the divergence between ontology and anthropology, realism and idealism, which has been discussed throughout this chapter. For the early German Romantics, Spinoza proffered a realist alternative to the idealist philosophy of Descartes's *cogito*. But this is not the whole story of Spinoza and Romanticism.

As I have shown in this chapter, there is more to Spinoza's heritage within Romanticism than this broad appeal as an avenue out of the aprioristic foundationalism of idealism. Critics who focus on the philosophical and theological issues only come to the conclusion that a romantic poet à la Coleridge finds Spinozist monism appealing while shying away from Spinoza's abandonment of a personal, transcendent God: "While satisfying what reason demanded, the dissolution of subject-object dualism, Spinozan monism, denied what morality required, a voluntaristic conception of God".[76] The spectre of Jacobi's atheistic Spinoza looms large here, and Coleridge seems indeed to have been torn by a purported conflict between religion and reason, between the heart and the head as he describes it in the *Biographia Literaria*: "For a long time indeed I could not reconcile personality with infinity; and my head was with Spinoza, though my whole heart remained with Paul and John".[77] Even though Spinoza eliminates both teleology and a personal, transcendent deity, his philosophy is not necessarily hostile to religion. As has been discussed in this chapter, he undermines anthropocentric and anthropomorphic conceptions of nature, god and the universe, but he does not dispute the ethical and moral role of religion.[78]

Rather than residing in the conflict between religion and reason, Coleridge's preoccupation with Spinoza springs from an underlying demand for a holding together what seem to be mutually exclusive entities or tendencies. Spinoza fascinated the romantics due to the figure of contamination that emerges from his ontologically monistic, though conceptually dualistic, philosophy. Paradoxes here no longer come across as they traditionally have done, as impasse, as aporetic. Spinoza's thought makes possible the insight into the ever-changing simultaneity of what seems otherwise mutually exclusive and diametrically opposed. This is why Goethe, Herder, Schlegel, Novalis, and Hölderlin associate Spinoza with a philosophy of love and in Coleridge's case, rather misleadingly, with mysticism. Halmi is justified in being astonished at Coleridge's fusion of Spinoza's rationalism with mysticism: "The differentiation of Spinozan monism from conventional pantheism figures in the *Biographia Literaria*, where Spinoza is unexpectedly aligned with the theosophist Jakob Böhme and the Quaker George Fox, 'mystics' whom Coleridge credits with having enabled him 'to skirt, without crossing, the sandy deserts of utter unbelief'".[79] Could it be that the figure of contamination implicit in Spinoza's philosophy allows us to hold in a state of simultaneity what has traditionally been rendered paradoxical and mutually exclusive or aporetic? As we have seen in this chapter, Spinoza is at once a dualist and a monist, affirming difference while at the same time insisting on the intrinsic interrelation of what differs. It is this contaminating paradigm of simultaneity which makes Coleridge compare Spinoza to the mystics. As regards the history of ideas, this is a misleading term for Spinoza who was of course a rationalist philosopher. But he was a rationalist with a difference, and it is this contaminating difference that Coleridge has in mind when he puts Spinoza in the company of Fox and Böhme: "For the writings of these mystics acted in no slight degree to prevent my mind from being imprisoned within the outline of any single dogmatic system".[80] In this avoidance of one exclusive perspective, we witness Spinoza's contaminating thought of simultaneity which holds together what traditional philosophy separates and opposes.

For Coleridge the romantic poet facilitates Spinoza's departure from a teleological, one-sided and anthropocentric misperception of our world: "He [i.e. Coleridge's poet] diffuses a tone and spirit of unity that blends and (as it were) fuses, each into each, by that syntactic power to which we have exclusively appropriated the name imaginations".[81] While defining the imagination by the term 'syntactic power', Coleridge employs the synthetic thought structure of Spinoza's *Ethics* which does not leave one term or vision separate from what might otherwise be conceived as its mutually exclusive opposite.

This is not only a philosophical issue. It informs much of romantic poetry from its warning visions of the Ancient Mariner's isolation at sea ("Alone, alone, all all alone/Alone on the wide wide sea"[82]) to the abhorrent prospect of a purity of vision which is that of violence and hatred in 'Christabel' ("That all her features were resigned/To this sole image in her mind:/And passively did imitate/That look of dull and treacherous hate!").[83] Spinoza's heritage in Romanticism is the loss of one single, teleological line of thought.

Critics who declare Romanticism to be part of idealism, do not do justice to a refusal of one single vision (be it idealist or realist) in romantic poetry and philosophy. McGann associates Coleridge's belief in ideas with the idealism of Hegel:

> First, Coleridge never ceased to believe that ideas shaped historical events—that thought always preceded and determined action rather than the other way round. Second, even as Coleridge (like Hegel) saw real human history flow unselfconsciously out of the precedent Idea, he lost his conviction that this pattern could be purely grasped, even unselfconsciously, in the single inspired

individual. The macrocosm was firmly fixed in the realm of transcendent Ideas, and its historical continuance could be counted on through the institutional forms. The more fundamental idea, however, of the determining primacy of the creative person, collapsed under the pressures which Coleridge's own mental pursuits placed upon it.[84]

This account of Romanticism assumes a 'firmly fixed' idealistic framework. It only collapses in the case of an individual poet's inability to determine the constancy of creative powers. This approach to romantic poetry and philosophy misses the important aspect of a Spinozan destructive element that refutes the primacy of a one-sided idealist perspective in the first place. It is this destructive element that dismantles idealist illusions of a world that resides in mutually opposed spheres (of body and mind, realism and idealism and so forth), which is Romanticism's moment of critique wherein we are free to avow disappointments: "The consequence is a new kind of poetic tale whose function is purely critical and disillusionary".[85] McGann notes such realist disillusionment in Coleridge's romantic poetry, but he does not establish its divergence from Hegel's idealism, which strikingly disavows disappointment by dialectically transmuting the negative into the positive.

Rather than being isolated or alone, the romantic vision fuses or contaminates what traditional conceptions have separated as mutually exclusive opposites. This contamination of what is purportedly non-compatible diminishes the force implicit in one-dimensional, aprioristic conceptions of the universe as being teleological. Romantic poetry renders fictive and diminutive such grand schemes of teleology. Byron's *Childe Harold* is "by pensive Sadness, not by Fiction led".[86] Spinoza renders fictitious traditional anthropocentric and anthropomorphic conceptions of nature, god and the universe. No wonder that his diminutive and at the same time contaminating rationalism gives rise to a sense of sadness in Romanticism and later on in modernism as well as postmodernism.

## Notes

1. Manfred Frank, *The Philosophical Foundations of Early German Romanticism*, ed./trans. Elizabeth Millán-Zaibert (Albany: State University of New York Press, 2004), 10. Hereafter *Philosophical Foundations*.
2. Elizabeth Millán-Zaibert, *Friedrich Schlegel and the Emergence of Romantic Philosophy* (Albany: State University of New York Press, 2007), 168. Hereafter, *Emergence of Romantic Philosophy*.
3. Ibid., 168.
4. Ibid., 32.

5. Michael Mack, *Spinoza and the Specters of Modernity: The Hidden Enlightenment of Diversity from Spinoza to Freud* (London: Bloomsbury, 2010). Hereafter, *Specters of Modernity*.
6. Frank, *Philosophical Foundations*, 25.
7. Elizabeth Millán-Zaibert, *Emergence of Romantic Philosophy*, 21.
8. Ibid.
9. Kant, *Schriften zur Ethik und Religionsphilosophie*. Volume 2, ed. Wilhelm Weischeidel (Frankfurt a. Main: Suhrkamp, 1964), 735.
10. Ibid., 735
11. For a detailed discussion of this point, see Mack, *German Idealism and the Jew* (Chicago: University of Chicago Press, 2003), 13–82.
12. Ibid., 73–89.
13. Pierre Macherey, *Hegel or Spinoza*, trans. Susan M. Ruddick (Minneapolis: University of Minnesota Press, 2011), 223.
14. Elizabeth Millán-Zaibert, *Emergence of Romantic Philosophy*, 87.
15. Ibid., 81.
16. Ibid., 74.
17. Ibid., 83.
18. Henri Atlan, *The Sparks of Randomness. Volume I: Spermatic Knowledge*, trans., Jenn L. Schramm (Stanford: Stanford University Press, 2010), 174.
19. Elizabeth Millán-Zaibert, *Emergence of Romantic Philosophy*, 147.
20. Ibid., 83.
21. See Timothy Morton, *Hyperobjects: Philosophy and the Ecology at the End of the World* (Minneapolis: University of Minnesota Press, 2013).
22. Isaiah Berlin, *The Roots of Romanticism*, ed., Henry Hardy (Princeton: Princeton University Press, 1999), 88.
23. Ibid.
24. See Millán-Zaibert, *Emergence of Romantic Philosophy* and Mack, *Specters of Modernity*.
25. Millán-Zaibert, *Emergence of Romantic Philosophy*, 37.
26. Frederick Beiser, *The Romantic Imperative. The Concept of Early German Romanticism* (Cambridge, MA: Harvard University Press, 2003), 15.
27. Ibid., 134.
28. Stuart Hampshire, *Spinoza and Spinozism* (Oxford: Clarendon Press, 2005), xlvii.
29. Ibid., 195.
30. Ibid., xxiii.
31. Slavoj Žižek *Less than Nothing: Hegel and the Shadow of Dialectical Materialism* (London: Verso, 2012), 720.
32. Millán-Zaibert, *Emergence of Romantic Philosophy*, 1.
33. Mack, *Specters of Modernity*, 4–10.
34. Bold in the German original. Friedrich Heinrich Jacobi, *Über die Lehre des Spinoza in Briefen an den Herrn Moses Mendelssohn* (Breslau: Gottlieb Löwe. 1785), 168.

35. Samuel Taylor Coleridge, *Poems*, ed., John Beer (London: Dent/Everyman, 1991), 276.
36. See Steven Nadler, *A Book Forged in Hell: Spinoza's Scandalous Treatise and the Birth of the Secular Age* (Princeton: Princeton University Press, 2011).
37. Baruch Spinoza (1996) *Ethics*, ed./trans. Edwin Curley with an introduction by Stuart Hampshire (Harmondsworth: Penguin, 1996), 27.
38. Baruch Spinoza, *Opera* Vol II, ed., Carl Gebhardt (Heidelberg: Carl Winter, 1925), 80.
39. Mack, *Specters of Modernity*, 11–47.
40. Pierre Macherey, *Hegel or Spinoza*, trans. Susan M. Ruddick (Minneapolis: University of Minnesota Press, 2011), 56.
41. Ibid., 56–57.
42. Brian McHale, "Period, Break, Interregnum" *Twentieth Century Literature* 57, Nrs. 3–4, Fall/Winter (2011): 328–340, 331; Edward Mendelson, "Gravity's Encyclopaedia", in *Mindful Pleasures: Essays on Thomas Pynchon*, eds., George Levine and David Levernz (Boston: Little, Brown and Company, 1976), 165.
43. Thomas Pynchon, *Gravity's Rainbow* (London: Ban Books/Picador, 1975), 3.
44. Paul K. Saint-Amour, *Tense Future: Modernism, Total War, Encyclopaedic Form* (Oxford: Oxford University Press, 2015), 309.
45. Robert J. Richards, *The Romantic Conception of Life: Science and Philosophy in the Age of Goethe* (Chicago: University of Chicago Press, 2002), 376.
46. Mack, *Specters of Modernity*, 138–167.
47. Richards, *Romantic Conception of Life*, 379.
48. Coleridge, *Biographia Literaria: Or Biographical Sketches of my Literary Life and Opinions*, ed., with an introduction, by George Watson (London: Dent/Everyman, 1991), 276.
49. Pierre Macherey, *Hegel or Spinoza*, trans. Susan M. Ruddick (Minneapolis: University of Minnesota Press, 2011), 60.
50. Ibid., 74.
51. Ibid., 74.
52. Millán-Zaibert, *Emergence of Romantic Philosophy*, 56.
53. Ibid.
54. Macherey, *Hegel or Spinoza*, 74.
55. Atlan, *The Sparks of Randomness. Volume I: Spermatic Knowledge*, trans., Jenn L. Schramm (Stanford: Stanford University Press, 2010), 176.
56. Ibid., 177 note 16.
57. This is based on a fascinating seminar Henri Atlan presented on "Spinoza and Biophysics" at the Institute of Advanced Studies, Durham University, on 16 May 2018.
58. Friedrich Schlegel, KFSA 9, 134.
59. Jerome J. McGann, *The Romantic Ideology: A Critical Investigation* (Chicago: University of Chicago Press, 1983), 47.
60. Spinoza, *Ethics*, 71.

61. Ibid.
62. Ibid., 73.
63. Atlan, *The Sparks of Randomness*, 170.
64. Spinoza, *Ethics*, 73.
65. Mack (2016).
66. Atlan, *The Sparks of Randomness*, 171.
67. NS I, 686.
68. NS II, 141.
69. NS I, 602.
70. NS II, 88.
71. NS II, 89.
72. NS II, 712.
73. NS II, 712.
74. Spinoza, *Ethics*, 170.
75. Nicholas Halmi, "Coleridge's Ecumenical Spinoza" in *Spinoza Beyond Philosophy*, ed., Beth Lord (Edinburgh: Edinburgh University Press, 2012), 196.
76. Ibid., 203.
77. Coleridge, *Biographia Literaria*, 112.
78. See also Mack, *Specters of Modernity*, 25–30.
79. Nicholas Halmi, "Coleridge's Ecumenical Spinoza" in *Spinoza Beyond Philosophy*, ed., Beth Lord (Edinburgh: Edinburgh University Press, 2012), 200.
80. Coleridge, *Poems*, 83.
81. Coleridge, *Biographia Literaria*, 174.
82. Coleridge, *Poems*, 228.
83. Ibid., 276.
84. McGann, *Romantic Ideology*, 104.
85. Ibid., 107.
86. Lord George Gordon Byron, *The Poetical Works of Byron*, revised and with a new introduction by Robert F. Gleckner (Boston: Houghton Mifflin Company, 1975), 25.

# References

Andrew Bowie, "Rethinking the History of the Subject: Jacobi, Schelling, and Heidegger," in *Deconstructive Subjetivities*, eds. Simon Critchley and Peter.
Dews (Albany: State University of New York Press, 1996): 105–26.
Mafred Frank, "Alle Wahrheit ist relativ, alles Wissen symbolisch--Motive der Grundsatz-Skepsis in der fruehen Jenaer Romantik (1796)," *Revue Internationale de. Philosophie* 50, no. 197 (1996): 403–36.
Michael Mack, *Contaminations: Beyond Dialectics in Modern Literature, Science, and Film* (Edinburgh: Edinburgh University Press, 2016).

# 5

# Religion and Early German Romanticism

Jacqueline Mariña

For the early German Romantics, religion must be understood in terms of consciousness, that is, in terms of what consciousness is and what it is not, namely, that which grounds consciousness but exceeds its capacity for self-reflection and, therefore, for knowledge. Prior to Kant, metaphysics and theology concerned themselves with ultimate objects such as God and the soul in a naïve sort of way, without taking into account the problem of how consciousness conditions our capacity to know such objects. With Kant and after him, the objects of religion become problematized precisely because they had to be understood in relation to consciousness, and the objects *of* consciousness are limited to the conditioned, phenomenal realm. Kant, as is well known, saved the objects of faith by making them necessary suppositions of practical reason: the person of good will, acting as she must in the context of finitude and its uncertainties, must hope that there is a God and think of her own existence as endless. Schleiermacher, a member of the Jena constellation of the early German Romantics, would complain that this relegated religion to a mess of "metaphysical and ethical crumbs."[1] Instead, he, and other important figures working out the reception of Kant, would understand religion in terms of an analysis of consciousness and its conditions, namely, in relation to the Absolute. Religious song, myth, and dogma are the result of the "outpourings of the inner fire"[2]; they are expressions of a feeling at the ground of the

J. Mariña (✉)
Purdue University, West Lafayette, IN, USA
e-mail: marina@purdue.edu

soul in which the self grasps itself in the infinite. Religious experience is an inchoate reflection of consciousness on itself and its origins. The reception of Kant's theory of consciousness and its relation to religion was marked by two fundamental strategies. The first was that of the early German Romantics: Novalis, Schlegel, Schleiermacher, and Hölderlin, for whom the Absolute exceeds all possibility of conceptualization. The other was of the German idealists, Fichte, the early Schelling, and Hegel, for whom possibility, and hence the logic that makes possibility intelligible, precedes actuality and thereby conditions the ground of Being itself. The import of the strategy of the early German Romantics can only be understood in relation to the approach of which they were deeply critical, an approach that would culminate in the absolute philosophy of Hegel.

# 1 Historical Preliminaries

Dieter Henrich has righty called the last two decades of the eighteenth century the classical age of German philosophy. The first edition of Kant's *Critique of Pure Reason* had appeared in 1781 and the second in 1787, the *Critique of Practical Reason* in 1788, and the *Critique of Judgment* in 1790. With the appearance of Kant's major works, philosophy was never the same. No serious philosopher could ignore it. Immediately controversies ensued on how it was to be received and interpreted, and figures such as Karl Leonhard Reinhold and Johann Gottlieb Fichte made important attempts to perfect Kant's transcendental idealism, making it more "scientific" and systematic by grounding it in a single self-evident first principle. Whether or not these efforts remained true to the critical philosophy (Kant himself thought they were not), they were undeniably inspired by it. As Henrich notes, between 1789 and 1798, "all the fundamental decisions crucial to ensuing developments had been made,"[3] that is, all points of departure stemming from Kant's insights and their trajectories had been mapped out. During this period, the University of Jena became a central hub for the dissemination of Kant's philosophy. Karl Reinhold and Carl Christian Erhard Schmid, both well-known expositors of Kant's work, taught there, and the *Jenaer Allgemeine Literaturzeitung*, an important journal whose purpose was to disseminate and discuss Kant's philosophy, was edited there as well.

In 1794, Fichte, himself impressed with Reinhold's call to systematize transcendental idealism, succeeded him in the chair devoted to Kant's philosophy. Such was the context of the Jena constellation of early Romanticism, a group of friends that included Novalis (Georg Friedrich von Hardenberg), Friedrich and Wilhelm Schlegel and Friedrich Schleiermacher, among others. They came together during the period between 1796 and 1800 in Jena and Berlin, often congregating at the house of the Schlegel brothers in Jena. The group engaged in lively philosophical conversations that included the topic of Kant's philosophy and the new attempts to systematize it. The result was a prodigious literary and philosophical production by many of its members. The group also produced the journal *Das Athenäum*, published between 1798 and 1800. Manfred Frank rightly expands the circle of early German Romantics to include Friedrich Hölderlin, even though he was only at Jena for six months in 1794–95, and that aside from a meeting in May with Novalis in the home of Niethammer, there seemed to have been little contact between Hölderlin and his friends and the Jena group. Nevertheless, there are striking similarities in their critical reactions to the philosophy of first principles as laid out by Reinhold in his *Attempt at a New Theory of the Human Faculty of Representation* (1789) and by Fichte in the first paragraphs of the Jena *Wissenschaftslehre*. As Frank notes, these common strategies criticizing the philosophy of first principles had their root in the discussions that took place among Reinhold's students beginning in 1792[4]; Jacobi's philosophy, especially as laid out in his second (1789) edition of *On the Doctrine of Spinoza*, was also particularly influential.[5]

The philosophical principles developed by the romantics not only concerned the ontological nature of consciousness and its metaphysical ground but also had important consequences for the theory of religion. The most important figure in this regard is Friedrich Schleiermacher (1768–1834), whose first edition of *On Religion* burst onto the scene in 1799 (the book was revised in 1806, 1821, and reissued in 1831) and who is best known for his magisterial systematic interpretation of Christian theology, *The Christian Faith* (*Glaubenslehre*), appearing in two editions, the first in 1821–22 and the second in 1830–31. In this chapter, I first discuss the most important philosophical principles of early German Romanticism, and I later detail the way these views were developed by Schleiermacher in his theory of religion and rethinking of the Christian faith.

## 2 The Reception of Kant's Groundbreaking Theory of Consciousness

Why did the early German Romantics resist the philosophy of first principles and the speculative idealism to which it led? In order to grasp what was at stake, we must first turn to the groundbreaking claims of Kant's *Critique of Pure Reason*. Famously, Kant had declared in §16 of the second edition, "the *I think* must *be able* to accompany all my representations, for otherwise something would be represented in me that could not be thought at all" (B 132). Since this *I think* must be able to accompany my representations, it is itself a *reflected* representation and must be distinguished from the original activity of consciousness.[6] In other words, this *I think* must be capable of being an intentional object of awareness: I must be able to become self-aware by having myself as an object of cognition if I am to be capable of knowing a representation as my own. In *The Christian Faith*, Schleiermacher would later refer to this as a "duplication of consciousness" and base his exposition of the nature of the immediate self-consciousness on an analysis of it.[7] We have then two elements of consciousness, each equally necessary for its possibility: the *reflecting* activity of consciousness and the *reflected* states through which it becomes aware of itself. With regard to these two elements, Kant notes,

> But how the I that I think is to differ from the I that intuits itself (for I can represent other kinds of intuition as at least possible) and yet be identical with the latter as the same subject, how therefore I can say that *I* as intelligence and *thinking* subject cognize myself as an object that is *thought*, insofar as I am also given to myself in intuition, only, like other phenomena, not as I am for the understanding but rather as I appear to myself, this is no more and no less difficult than how I can be an object for myself in general and indeed one of intuition and inner perceptions. (B155)[8]

This implies that there are two ways that the self is conscious of itself: one in which the self *appears* to itself in intuition and the second the self's original factical self-presence to itself in its activity of synthesis. Importantly, regarding the latter Kant claims, "in the transcendental synthesis of the manifold of representations in general, on the contrary, hence in the synthetic original unity of apperception, I am conscious of myself not as I appear to myself, nor as I am in myself, but only *that* I am" (B 157). It can be argued that part of the problem of the transcendental deduction was to show how the I think that can accompany my representation x (a reflected representation) can be thought to be identical with the activity of thinking that grounds all my representations: how do we identify the two? This is particularly a problem because Kant recognized, following Hume, that the I think has no content of its own.

Kant's followers, however, focused on another problem, namely, original consciousness itself and its relation to the reflected I. In his Jena *Wissenschaftslehre,* Fichte famously claimed that "the I posits itself as an I"; the claim, which stands as Fichte's first principle, has to do with the relation of original consciousness, namely, the activity of synthesis, to the reflected self. Through its activity, original consciousness reflects on itself and thereby posits and achieves itself. This is not a fact, but an act, a *Tathandlung* of which we are immediately existentially aware in the very act of reflective self-awareness. The *Tathandlung* is given through what he called an "intellectual intuition." Following Kant, he called it an intuition because it is immediate and not a reflected representation; it is, however, intellectual since it has to do with the synthetic *activity* of consciousness. But Fichte went even further than this, for he argued that this original consciousness must also be the source of the objects that are the counterpart of the subject's self-awareness. The I cannot reflect on itself as an I, and thereby posit itself, unless the non-I is also posited, for a subject is no subject without an object that is other than itself. Here he no doubt partially took inspiration from Reinhold's principle of consciousness. Consciousness is what it is through its activity of representing. But this implies that if a subject is to have a representation, this representation must not only be understood as a representation of the subject who has it, but equally must be referred to an intentional object.[9] However, Fichte conceived of representation through an added twist. He argued that "consciousness of the object is only a consciousness of my production of a presentation of the object" and therefore that "all consciousness is only ... a consciousness of myself."[10] Original consciousness is thereby the origin of *both* the subject and the world that stands in opposition to it, and as Fichte would claim, "in finding myself I find myself as subject and object, which, however, are immediately connected." This connection between subject and object is given at the origin of representation itself, that is, there is an original moment before the subject-object split that grounds both the subject's awareness of itself as having a representation (the representation as a mere content of consciousness) and the representation as referring to an intentional object. Fichte admits that consciousness of this identity is impossible, for "I am always conscious only on condition that *that which is conscious* and *that of which there is consciousness* appear distinct from each other" (48). Nevertheless, this original moment of unity must be presupposed.

We are now well on our way to absolute idealism, although there are still other crucial presuppositions needed to get there. But what is important here thus far is that with these moves Fichte believed he had decisively shown that access to all possible objects of experience lies in consciousness and that there is a pre-thetical unity to self and world. Totality, therefore, already lies at the ground of consciousness or at least is given in it in some way. It is given to that moment inaccessible to reflection where self and world are one, that is, in original consciousness. The early German Romantics would have followed Fichte this far. There will, however, be a serious bone of contention between the romantics and the German idealists, and it concerns the character of this original consciousness itself.

Highly influential in this debate were the views of Friedrich Heinrich Jacobi (1743–1819). His 1799 *Open Letter to Fichte*, in which he argued that Fichte's transcendental philosophy amounted to nihilism, put the last nails in the coffin of Fichte's reputation. This ultimately led to Fichte's forced resignation from his chair at Jena. Jacobi's first edition of *On the Doctrine of Spinoza*, in which Jacobi alleged Lessing had confessed to him that he was a Spinozist, had appeared in 1795 and caused an uproar. There Jacobi argued that Spinoza was the most consequent of philosophers and that the principle of sufficient reason inevitably leads to the annihilation of human individuality and freedom, and ultimately to atheism. In 1787, he published his book *David Hume on Faith, or Idealism and Realism*, attached to which was an appendix containing an influential critique of Kant, whose revised edition of the *Critique of Pure Reason* had just appeared. Important here, however, is that in the book Jacobi attempted to develop an iteration of transcendental philosophy that avoided the distasteful subjectivism he found in the Kantian version.[11] But a version of transcendental philosophy it was. He too was concerned with the nature of subjectivity, and he argued, against classical empiricism, that there can be no subject without an object. But for Jacobi subject and object are *immediately* given. As he notes in his *David Hume*:

> The internal consciousness and the external object, must be present both at once in the soul even in the most primordial and simple of perceptions—the two in one flash, in the same indivisible instant, without before or after, without any operation of the understanding—indeed without the remotest beginning of the generation of the concept of cause and effect in the understanding.[12]

Importantly, what this means for Jacobi is that the division between subject and object is not the *result* of reflection, but is given prior to it. Representation in a concept *presupposes* the immediate intuition of the object, and this means that the constitution of the object cannot depend on reflection. In fact, Jacobi claims, in this moment of immediacy there are no representations; rather, "they make their appearance only later on in reflection, as shadows of the things that were formerly present" (277). This constitutes his realism.

Just as important is Jacobi's theory of revelation. In his 1789 *On the Doctrine of Spinoza*, Jacobi declared "the greatest service an investigator can do is to uncover and *reveal* being (Dasein) … [italics mine]."[13] This revelation, he argued, must be given to us in unmediated cognition, that is, through feeling. Without it, our knowledge would be baseless, for each proposition would depend for its justification on another proposition, which would in turn require its own, and so on, in an endless regress. If the regress is to be stopped, and knowledge is to be possible, there must be a fact that is given to consciousness immediately and that is the immediate *factum* of our own existence and its dependence on the unconditioned. This is a groundless, unjustified cognition needing no justification. It is given in feeling (a kind of self-feeling) or what Jacobi also calls belief [*Glauben*]. While Kant took issue with Jacobi's equation of this self-feeling with *Glauben*, Jacobi certainly followed Kant in characterizing the original cognition in terms of feeling: the *Dasein* or existence of things can only be given through sensation, and not through a concept. Hence, Kant notes that "perception, which yields the material for a concept, is the sole characteristic of actuality" (A225/B272–3), and "I cognize existence through experience" (Reflexion 5710, AA 18: 332).[14] Yet, more to the point, regarding the self's awareness of itself, Kant explicitly notes, "the 'I think' is, as has already been said, an empirical proposition" (B422, note).[15] For his part, Jacobi referred the unmediated feeling of Being to Kant's "transcendental apperception,"[16] and noted, "of our existence (*Dasein*), we have only a feeling, but no concept."[17]

For Jacobi, Being is *revealed*, and in this revelation, faith is born. And while Jacobi might seem an irrationalist for all his talk of the "*salto mortale*" into the arms of the divine mercy, he did, in fact, have powerful arguments for his position. An important argument is closely related to the one noted above regarding the endless regress of propositions that depend upon others for their justification. Only if something is *given*, and given immediately with Cartesian certainty through *experience*, is the regress stopped and a foundation for knowledge achieved. The ideas are nicely presented in a letter he wrote to Mendelssohn, and which he reproduced in the book on Spinoza:

> We are all born in faith and must remain with this faith, just as we are all born in society and must remain within society … How can we strive for certainty when certainty is not known to us in advance; and how can it be known to us,

> other than through something that we already recognize with certainty? This leads to the concept of an unmediated certainty, which stands in no need of explanation (*Gründe*), but rather excludes all such explanation, and solely and alone is the corresponding representation itself of the represented thing. Conviction based on argument is secondhand conviction … The conviction which these bring about arises from a comparison and can never be totally certain or complete. If faith is an act of holding something to be true without relying upon argument, then the very security we place in arguments of reason must be rooted in faith (*Glaube*) and so arguments of reason must take their strength from faith.[18]

This is an extraordinary argument: our very capacity to trust our reason and our ability to carry out valid arguments must depend on an unmediated foundation whose certainty is beyond the need for argument, for through argument we cannot ascertain our capacity for valid argument. Rather, this certainty is given in unmediated self-feeling and its correlate, the unconditioned. Importantly, Jacobi also argues that with every conditioned the unconditioned is also given and that we have just as great a certainty of the unconditioned as we have of our own existence. In fact, we have an *even greater* certainty of the unconditioned![19] Importantly, it is in this certainty of the unconditioned that we know God.

> Since everything that lies outside the complex of the conditional, or the naturally mediated, also lies outside the sphere of our distinct cognition, and cannot be understood through concepts, the supernatural cannot be apprehended by us in any way except as it is given to us, namely, as fact—IT is! This Supernatural, this Being of all beings, all tongues proclaim *GOD*.[20]

Now, while we have a Cartesian certainty of God given in immediate experience, it also follows that due to this immediacy we can have no discursive understanding of Being. For it lies prior to reflection and as such "cannot be understood through concepts," which as such are always mediated by reflection. Reflection always presupposes Being, although it cannot penetrate it.

This means that for Jacobi actuality always precedes possibility, the latter of which can only be grasped through concepts. On this point, Jacobi was influenced by Kant's pre-critical essay from 1763, *The One Possible Basis for a Demonstration of the Existence of God*.[21] There Kant had argued that existence must precede possibility: "the phrase 'nothing exists' is synonymous with 'there is nothing at all;' and it would be pretty contradictory to add in spite of this that something would be possible" (AA 11:78). But if actuality precedes possibility, the actual cannot itself be comprehended in terms of the possible.

Our only access to it is a factical one: IT IS. We apprehend Being through the immediacy of feeling. And this is the revelation of Being that Jacobi sought to express. Being could not be proved through a series of inferences, it could in no way be known discursively, it could only be revealed.

This, as we shall see, was Jacobi's legacy to Romanticism, and from it much followed.[22] But right from the start, we can already glean how seriously Jacobi departs from Fichte's insights and why the dispute between them became a central contention of the period. Through his foundational starting point, "the I posits itself as an I," Fichte emphasized the *activity* of self-positing through which the self achieves its existence. This activity, moreover, had a definite structure, namely, the structure through which the I determines itself through reflection. The process of reflection therefore becomes the necessary condition of the achievement of the I. Jacobi, on the other hand, emphasized the factual quality of immediate consciousness: the self simply *finds* itself in existence, and this is an empirical proposition. Moreover, the self that is immediately encountered is a radically conditioned self, and in this immediate encounter, the self also encounters that upon which it is radically dependent. This is the foundation of Jacobi's realism, one that would also be adopted by Schleiermacher. All of this was not lost on Jacobi, who in his 1799 *Open Letter to Fichte* called him an inverted Spinozist: inverted because in his system reflection, and not substance, was the foundational principle of all reality, and a Spinozist, because this was, indeed, the *one* principle behind all reality. There could not have been a more apt characterization of Fichte's idealism than that which Jacobi reports as having occurred to him in a "mischievous moment." In the letter, Jacobi compares Fichte's idealism to a knitted stocking. The stocking "attained actuality through the mere back and forth movement of the thread." The flowers, borders, and figures woven into the stocking were "nothing but a product of the productive imagination of the fingers hovering between the I of the thread and the not I of the stitches." But, Jacobi emphasized, the stocking "is still only its thread," and the thread "only need return to its original identity by exposing the rows of its reflections in order to make it visibly apparent that that infinite manifold, and manifold infinity, was nothing but a empty weaving of its weaving, and that the one single reality is only itself with its self-initiated, self-contained, and self-directed activity."[23] And with such and an apt and witty metaphor, Jacobi sealed Fichte's fate. Fichte already stood accused of atheism. Jacobi's image not only made Fichte look ridiculous, it also exposed his system as portraying humanity as autonomously creating castles out of thin air, so to speak, through a "self-initiated, self-contained, and self-directed activity." This was certainly atheism or at the very least a philosophy with no need for God. To be sure, Jacobi had not been entirely fair to Fichte. In the *Wissenschaftslehre* Fichte had already argued that there must be a moment of immediacy grounding reflection. But the damage had been done, and Fichte's reputation would never completely recover.

Jacobi's arguments were decisive for early German Romanticism. His writings, and his *Open Letter* in particular, drew attention to Fichte's problematic claims for the self-sufficiency of self-consciousness. It was, however, the romantics who worked out the philosophical deficiencies of this view, as well as the implications of their metaphysical claim that self-consciousness depends on Being. Being or actuality cannot be known in terms of reflective judgment since it precedes it as its condition. As Frank so aptly notes,

> the basic conviction common to the early German Romantics … consists in the supposition that Being—as the simple seamless sameness (*Einerleiheit*), in contrast to the identity of the Kantian-Fichtean *cogito*—cannot be understood on the basis of the relations of judgment and reflection, all of which are occupied with reuniting original divisions and can always merely presuppose an original simple unity.[24]

This priority of Being (*Dasein*) over reflection constitutes the basic realism at the heart of German Romanticism. It amounts to, as Frank would put it, a "re-Kantianization"[25] of German philosophy, that is, Romanticism's insights were fundamentally more true to Kant's critical philosophy than the revisionary moves undertaken by Fichte and those who worked these out to their ultimate conclusions, culminating in Hegel's absolute philosophy. In what follows I sketch out the most powerful of the romantic critiques of the philosophy of first principles and their implications. These have to do with the following themes, all intrinsically connected: (1) the priority of Being over reflection; (2) the nature of identity; (3) epistemological modesty and the impossibility of an absolute philosophy of first principles. I begin with Hölderlin's famous fragment, written possibly as early as 1775,[26] "Judgment and Being" because it constitutes a singular and remarkable self-sustained argument making intelligible arguments by the other romantics, many of which can only be found in fragments.

In the fragment Hölderlin echoes important themes from both Jacobi and Kant, in particular Jacobi's insistence that actuality must precede possibility: "Actuality and possibility are distinguished, just as mediated and unmediated consciousness. If I think a thing as possible, then I only repeat the previous perception, through whose power it is actual. There is for us no thinkable possibility that was not actuality. For this reason the concept of possibility is not at all valid of the objects of reason."[27] Possibility is given only to mediated consciousness, that is, consciousness in which the self is conscious of itself, and can therefore reproduce perceptions and form concepts. As Kant made clear, concepts are always mediated representations, for they depend on the capacity of consciousness to make itself its own object, which is the condition of its capacity to grasp the multitude of intuitions that can fall under a concept as its own possible intuitions. We grasp the possible through concepts, and this means that our grasp of what is possible not only depends on the mediation of consciousness, but this grasp itself depends on the actuality of consciousness. Furthermore, here Hölderlin also echoes Jacobi's empiricist insistence that actuality must precede our capacity to represent: imagining the possible depends on our capacity to reproduce the material that has already been given to perception. But in his discussion of mediated and unmediated consciousness and of the conditions of the possibility of judgment, Hölderlin goes beyond mere empiricist principles. His claim that the concept of possibility "is not at all valid of the objects of reason" is of enormous significance. Here he lays out one of the paths forward stemming from Kant's critical philosophy and analysis of consciousness; the other path would find its ultimate expression in Hegel's absolute philosophy. Possibility depends on mediation, on the activity of consciousness, and therefore on its actuality. Hence Being (Dasein) precedes possibility, which is only intelligible in terms of mediated consciousness. And if this is the case, there is no path forward for a philosophy of the Absolute, that is, a philosophy that can grasp the inner workings and fate of the totality of existence. Reason cannot grasp this totality. For consciousness cannot penetrate the conditions of its own actuality. Our grasp of the conditions of determination is not applicable to it, and neither is the principle of sufficient reason. It *is*, pure and simple. Because it cannot be penetrated, it can only be an object of belief, not of knowledge. As Novalis would note, echoing Jacobi, "access to the unconditioned is given in Belief: what I don't know, but I feel, [...] I believe" (NS II: 105).[28] As we shall see, these ideas would become the basis of Schleiermacher's theology. For Fichte, the early Schelling, and then Hegel, on the contrary, the ontological conditions of the possibility of determination, which are purely logical, precede determination and, therefore, actuality. The I determines itself, and thereby achieves actuality, through opposition with the not-I; Hegel would expand this principle of the logical conditions of determination to one governing the inner possibility of the actualization not only of the I but also of absolute Mind itself. Being presupposes thought, and for this reason, logic must precede nature in Hegel's system.

The rest of Hölderlin's fragment engages the early Schelling. In a famous passage of the *Ich Schrift*, Schelling exclaimed, "I am! My I contains a Being that precedes all thinking and representing. It is insofar as it is thought, and it is thought because it is ... This, in turn, is precisely because it is and is thought only insofar as it thinks itself" (SW 1/1: 167).[29] For Schelling the Absolute I achieves existence precisely through its thinking of itself, and as such, conditions of the activity of thinking condition actuality. Hölderlin would take issue with this. Using Fichte's terminology, he calls original consciousness "intellectual intuition" and agrees with Fichte and Schelling that "subject and object are intimately united in intellectual intuition." All judgment depends on an original division "through which subject and object are first possible." Further, he argues, "in the concept of this division there already lies the concept of the relation of object and subject opposing one another, and the necessary presupposition of a whole, of which object and subject are parts." The issue, however, is how we are to think of this whole. Is this whole something that achieves itself through thinking?

Hölderlin continues, "I am I is the most fitting example of this judgment," that is, *self-consciousness* is achieved through an original judgment in which I recognize myself as the thinker of my thoughts. This original judgment makes all other judgments possible. But in what way is judgment an achievement of an I of original consciousness? What is it that is contained in original consciousness anyway? Here the problem Kant had recognized in the first *Critique*, but had glossed over (B 155), becomes the central issue dividing Romanticism from idealism:

> Where subject and object are absolutely, not merely partially unified, in such a way that no division could be presupposed without damaging the essence of that which is to be divided, there is no other way can we speak about absolute Being, as is the case in intellectual intuition.
>
> Yet this Being should not be confused with identity. If I say: I am I, then the subject (I) and the object (I) is not unified in such a way that no division could be presupposed without damaging that which is to be divided; on the contrary, the I is only possible through this division of the I from the I. How can I say I! without self-consciousness? How is then self-consciousness possible? It is possible through opposing myself to myself, dividing myself from myself, but in spite of this division I recognize myself in opposition as the same. But to what extent the same? I can, I must question this, for in another respect it [the self] is opposed to itself. Therefore identity is not a unification of subject and object that takes place absolutely, therefore identity is not = Absolute Being.[30]

Hölderlin's insightful critique of Schelling is that he has put the cart before the horse; he has presupposed what he has been trying to prove. Mere Absolute Being, given as it is pre-thetically, cannot be thought of in the same way as one would an object of consciousness. It cannot be thought of as having "parts" that are distinguishable from one another *prior* to the division that occurs through self-consciousness and then *later* identified with one another after the division; this would injure its absolute unity. Knowledge of the I, the capacity to make a judgment about it, is *dependent* on self-consciousness. And self-consciousness is dependent on original consciousness. In order to make the judgment I am I, I must already have identified original consciousness with the I. But any knowledge of an I depends on the original division that gives rise to self-consciousness, so original consciousness cannot be singled out as an Absolute I that is then somehow identified with the reflected I. The original unity is not the Absolute Being of an I; the unity between the I and the not-I is not a product of the activity of thinking and willing. It transcends it and is given in Being. Hence, the judgment of identity cannot lie at the heart of Being. Being remains dark to consciousness, an enigma.

Novalis, too, was deeply aware of the implications the differences between thetic and pre-thetic awareness had for a philosophy of Being. He begins his set of fragments entitled *Pollen* with the line "Everywhere we seek the unconditioned, but find only things."[31] All our knowledge is mediated through the reflected I of self-consciousness, which is conditioned not only by the not-I, but by original consciousness itself. Unconditioned Being can only be given in original consciousness, and as such cannot be accessed through concepts and judgment, and thus through knowledge. A related idea is expressed in his fragment, "We leave the identical in order to represent it" (NS II: 104, Nr. 1), that is, once consciousness has reflected upon itself, it has lost its identity, and in fact, there is never a complete identity between original consciousness and its successive reflections. Each reflection is only a partial snapshot of the activity of original consciousness and as such cannot capture it. Consciousness, argued Novalis, "is not what it represents, and does not represent what it is" (NS II: 226, Nr. 330).[32] Truth, then, can only be grasped through successive approximations, that is, through a synthesis of past moments of reflection with successive new ones. Each reflection encompasses self *and* world (I and not-I), for the world that is known is the world that is known *as* given to consciousness. And each reflection must be brought together with other ones in the temporal manifold. How do I know that a representation is valid of an object? Only if I can integrate it coherently with others that have been attributed to it. Since the world is given to consciousness through an infinite series of apprehensions of self and world, there can never be a definitive grasp of what is objectively true. Our understanding of the world must be infinitely revisable. Here we have the beginnings of a theory of truth that would be only fully worked through by Husserl.

Given these considerations, an absolute philosophy rooted in foundational first principles is out of the question. There is, furthermore, no absolute knowledge. There is only coherence and successive approximations. Since we cannot provide a foundation to philosophy on which all knowledge can be grounded *modo geometrico*, philosophy can only begin in the middle. Friedrich Schlegel eloquently noted that "our philosophy does not begin like the others with a first principle—where the first proposition is like the center or first ring of a comet—with the rest a long tail of mist—we depart from a small but living seed—our center lies in the middle."[33] Schleiermacher too noted the impossibility of beginning with first principles when he noted in his *Dialektik* "Beginning in the middle is unavoidable."[34] This middle is the actuality of human existence and its commitments; from them we argue backward and forward, from the *terminus a quo* to the *terminus ad quem*, never, however, completing the synthesis, but ever coming closer to it through successive approximations.

## 3 Schleiermacher and the Philosophy of Religion

It was Friedrich Schleiermacher who systematically worked through the important hints we found in the thought of Jacobi, Novalis, and Hölderlin for a systematic theory of religion and the fundamental principles of a Christian theology. Against idealism and the philosophy of first principles, Schleiermacher stands firmly on the side of the re-Kantianization of philosophy: original consciousness and its ground cannot be penetrated by thought. It is, in fact, cognized only through feeling. In his *Dialektik*, Schleiermacher asks, "How does it [the immediate self-consciousness] relate to the transcendental ground?" He answers, "We consider the latter to be the ground of the thinking being in regards to the identity of willing and thinking. The transcendental ground of thought precedes and succeeds all actual thinking in an atemporal manner, but never itself becomes thought."[35] Original, immediate consciousness can never become an object of thought; its operations are only partially reflected in the self's awareness of itself. The Absolute transcends consciousness so thoroughly that it "does not come to an appearance at any time." Moreover, consciousness of God is not given directly in the immediate self-consciousness. What is given directly is consciousness of the self *as* absolutely dependent. Co-posited along with this consciousness is the Absolute itself. Here, no doubt, we hear echoes of Jacobi, who had argued that along with the conditioned the unconditioned is always also co-posited. While there are no doubt significant differences between the two, Schleiermacher was significantly influenced by Jacobi. He had even toyed with dedicating the first edition of *Christian Faith* to him, but changed his mind when Jacobi died in 1819.[36]

Schleiermacher first brought these ideas to bear on the problem of religion in the first edition (1799) of his *On Religion: Speeches to its Cultured Despisers*. Contra both Kant and Fichte, he argued that religion was not ethics and was no mere ethical postulate; moreover, it cannot be based on the all-too-human enterprise of metaphysics. Kant's philosophy had made impossible a naïve speculation about the nature of things in themselves, and God cannot be an object of consciousness in opposition to a subject, for all objects of consciousness are finite and conditioned by the subject. Religion "does not wish to determine and explain the universe according to its nature as does metaphysics; it does not desire to continue the universe's development and perfect it by the power of freedom and the divine free choice of human being as does morals. Religion's essence is neither thinking nor acting, but intuition and feeling."[37] To think of religion merely in terms of the hopes of the morally committed individual, as Kant had done in his *Religion within the Limits of Reason Alone*, is to miss its fundamental character. Genuine religion can be found only at the heart of consciousness. We have already witnessed both Jacobi and Novalis referencing the feeling of Being given through the self's immediate awareness of itself: faith or belief is directed toward the ground of the self who cognizes its own existence immediately, through feeling. Schleiermacher would develop these ideas further in *Christian Faith*: we cannot know this ground, but we feel our conditioned existence and have faith in the unconditioned that sustains it.

In *On Religion* Schleiermacher makes a groundbreaking move for philosophy of religion and theology: he claims that the basis of all religion and theology is *religious experience*, and for this reason, the category of religion is *sui generis*. Schleiermacher notes the purpose of the *Speeches*: "I wish to lead you to the innermost depths from which religion first addresses the mind" (10). The journey to these depths will allow us to consider "religion from its center according to its inner essence" (12). The basis of religion is decidedly not an "objective revelation" whose significance can be codified in dogmatic propositions that must be accepted as a condition of salvation. Whatever revelation there is given along with the feeling of Being, that is, along with the immediate awareness of one's own finite and conditioned existence. Whoever does not have this experience will remain blind to the true nature of religion; religion is a "scandal or folly" for the individual who has not experienced it herself firsthand; "the matter of religion is so arranged and so rare that a person who expresses something about it must necessarily have had it" (9). The "spiritual material" for this experience "lies latent" in the soul of all individuals and develops from this material in the more advanced: "It springs necessarily and by itself from the interior of every better soul, it has its own province in the mind in which it reigns sovereign" (17).

What, then, is the nature of this experience? In his second speech, Schleiermacher famously notes that "praxis is an art, speculation is a science, religion is the sensibility and taste for the infinite" (23). That Schleiermacher connects religion to "sensibility and taste for the infinite," that is, with feeling is absolutely central, since it positions him along with the early German Romantics against Fichte, for whom the *activity* of consciousness was the first principle of philosophy. For Kant, let us remember, there are "two stems of human cognition, which may perhaps arise from a common but to us unknown root, namely, sensibility and understanding, through the first of which objects are given to us, but through the second of which they are thought" (A15/B29). We can think of the split between the romantics and the followers of Fichte as having to do with how to characterize original consciousness. What is most central to it, spontaneity or receptivity? Does it know its existence as it achieves itself through its own positing, or is there something yet more central through which the self simply recognizes its own facticity and its own absolutely conditioned character? If the latter, the self experiences an existence that has already been granted to it; the self does not simply achieve itself and is not its own ground. For Schleiermacher in *Christian Faith*, God is the "Whence of our passive and active existence" (*KGA* I.13,1, 39).[38] But how does the self cognize its own existence? Schleiermacher argues that the self has a direct and immediate awareness of itself in both its passivity and activity; this awareness is more central than the awareness the self has of itself in its reflected representations. According to Kant's terminology, because this is an *immediate* awareness of the self in its particularity and specificity, it is an *intuition*. Concepts, on the other hand, are merely reflected representations in principle applicable to an infinite number of individuals. And Kant had argued that for human beings all intuition is sensible, that is, because human beings cannot *produce* individual objects through thinking them, but can only achieve concepts of them, human cognition is incapable of intellectual intuition. Only God is capable of an intellectual intuition, producing that which God thinks. For finite human cognition, on the other hand, individuals are *given* directly to cognition, through sensation (and thereby not through a concept); they are intuited. As Schleiermacher notes, "Intuition is and always remains something individual, set apart, the immediate perception, nothing more" (*On Religion*, 26). The difference between Schleiermacher and Fichte in characterizing the cognition of original consciousness is therefore of great significance. For Fichte, we have an *intellectual* intuition of original consciousness. It is intellectual for we achieve ourselves in our very positing of ourselves, and it is an intuition for we know ourselves in our particularity through this very activity. For Schleiermacher, on the other hand, original consciousness is given through intuition and feeling. In *Christian Faith*, he would speak of the *feeling of absolute dependence*, an experience the self has of itself in its conditioned immediacy that is the jumping off point for faith.

The battle with Fichte stands front and center of Schleiermacher's characterization of religious experience in *On Religion*. He asks, "And how will the triumph of speculation, the completed and rounded idealism, fare if religion does not counterbalance it and allow it to glimpse a higher realism than that which it subordinates to itself so boldly and for such good reason." And echoing Jacobi, he answers, "Idealism will destroy the universe by appearing to fashion it; it will degrade it to a mere allegory, to an empty silhouette of our own limitedness" (24). In contrast to idealism and naïve empiricism, Schleiermacher advocates a "higher realism" based on the feeling of Being given to original consciousness. This is no naïve realism advocating the contradictory notion that things as they are in themselves might be given to consciousness; Schleiermacher's "higher realism" has to with the givenness of Being in original consciousness.

Schleiermacher's stress on the givenness of Being is nowhere more clearly evident than in his famous passage on the origin of the religious experience. It cannot be stressed enough that for Schleiermacher the ground of religion lies in the moment prior to the split between *intuition and feeling*. In this way Schleiermacher stresses our *receptivity* to what is given, namely, to the IT IS of existence. Religion does *not* have to do with spontaneity or the activity of thinking so stressed by Fichte. And so we find Schleiermacher speaking of the subject/object split key to the achievement of self-consciousness in terms of the split between *intuitions and feeling*, and not in terms of the activity of original consciousness positing itself. He mourns that he "cannot speak of both other than separately" and that "the finest spirit of religion is thereby lost" for his speech:

> But reflection necessarily separates both [intuition and feeling]; and who can speak about something that belongs to consciousness without first going through this medium? Not only when we communicate an inner action of the mind, but even when we merely turn it into material for contemplation within ourselves and wish to raise it lucid to consciousness, this unavoidable separation immediately occurs. This state of affairs intermingles with the original consciousness of our dual activity, what predominates and functions outward and

what is merely sketching and reproducing, which seems rather to serve things. Immediately upon this contact the simplest matter separates itself into two opposing elements, the one group combining into an image of an object, the other penetrating to the center of our being, there to effervesce with our original drives and to develop a transient feeling. (31)

While feelings have to do with how we have been affected and therefore with our own states, intuitions are referred to individual things distinct from ourselves; as Schleiermacher notes, they combine "into an image of an object." The idea is related to one already put forward by Kant in his discussion of the third analogy: each of our empirical representations must have a double reference (A189–90/B234–5). The first is to the subject of representation: each representation is a modification of the mind of the subject. The second is to the intentional object of representation: the representation is *of* an object and is attributed to it. Schleiermacher argues that in "the first stirring of the mind," there is a moment of unity before the split between feeling (referred to the subject) and intuition (referred to the object): "Intuition without feeling is nothing and can have neither the proper origin nor the proper force; feeling without intuition is also nothing; both are therefore something only when and because they are originally one and unseparated" (30). In this moment of original unity, subject and object are one; it is a moment prior to reflection, one in which the I and the not-I are not yet distinguished from one another and in which there is not yet consciousness of self:

> That first mysterious moment that occurs in every sensory perception, before intuition and feeling have separated, where sense and its objects have, as it were, flowed into one another and become one, before both turn back to their original position—I know how indescribable it is and how quickly it passes away … Even as the beloved and ever-sought for form fashions itself, my soul flees towards it; I embrace it, not as a shadow, but as the holy essence itself. I lie on the bosom of the infinite world. At this moment I am its soul, for I feel all its powers and its infinite life as my own; at this moment it is my body, for I penetrate its muscles and its limbs as my own, and its innermost nerves move according to my sense and my presentiment as my own … This moment is the highest flowering of religion. (Crouter 32)

While in original consciousness alone there is no *self-consciousness*, there is, nevertheless, consciousness. It is a consciousness of a feeling of Being in which there is only unity with all that is. The moment prior to reflection in which the mind is fully quiet and not yet full of itself is "the natal hour of everything living in religion" (32).

From this, several things follow. First, the infinite can only be given in the immediacy of original consciousness. The achievement of self-consciousness is always a limited one, and what is reflected in consciousness of self can never express the fullness of what is given in the immediacy of our active and receptive existence. Fichte's focus on the virtuosity of the I, on its activities and reflections, leads only to self-deception and self-destruction, for the self can never capture itself; it is always too great for its reflections: "Can we, advancing from one limited work to another, really exhaust our whole infinite energy? Will not, rather, the greater part of it lie unused, and consequently turn away and consume us? How many of you go to ruin simply because they are too great for themselves?" (47). How can this ruin be avoided? Only through resting in the passivity of original consciousness, in the fullness of Being and its ground.

Second, because religion is born in intuition and feeling, it resists systematization.[39] Systematization requires concepts, themselves depending upon reflection. But the moment reflection comes into the picture, the heart of religion has been covered over and its essence lost. Concepts are general representations, and they cannot capture the particular *qua* individual. The particular can only be given in the religious experience itself. Hence Schleiermacher argues that religion "stops with the immediate experience of the existence and action of the universe, with the individual intuitions and feeling." Religion knows nothing about "derivation and connection"; that is "what its nature most opposes," for everything in religion "is immediate and true for itself" (26). Once the drive to systematize has come upon the scene, we are left only with the "dead slag," which was "once the glowing outpouring of the inner fire that is contained in all religions" (99).

Third, the person who has had a genuine religious experience *knows* that it can never be adequately conceptualized or systematized. The religious experience is fleeting and has passed as soon as reflection sets in; the person who has lived religion is therefore very tolerant of the religious experiences and views of others: "Each person must be conscious that his religion is only part of the whole, that regarding the same objects that affect him religiously there are views just as pious and, nevertheless, completely different from his own, and that from other elements of religion intuitions and feelings flow, the sense for which he may be completely lacking" (27). Since religion is ultimately rooted in experience, there may be very different religious practices foreign to one's own that give rise to it in others. Recognition of the effectiveness and importance of those practices for others takes nothing away from the validity of one's own religious experience, which immediately validates itself.

Fourth, how the religious experience is *conceptualized* is not of supreme importance. What is important is the religious experience itself. Schleiermacher notes that "belief in God depends on the direction of the imagination" and that "the idea of God does not rank as high as you think" (53). Truly religious persons are content to live and let live; they have no need to force the idea of God upon anyone, for they rest in the quiet confidence of God's activity; hence "among truly religious persons there have never been zealots, enthusiasts or fanatics for the existence of God" (53). This insight contributes to our capacity to tolerate those with different religious views than our own, for what is important is not belief resting on ideas, but the experiential ground from which such ideas spring.

## 4 Concluding Remarks

Let me close with some final reflections. Fundamental differences in the reception of Kant between the romantics and idealists on the question of consciousness and its access to the Absolute came to a head in the differences between Hegel's absolute philosophy and philosophy of religion and Schleiermacher's *Christian Faith*. Hegel took Fichte's foundational insights on consciousness and applied them to Absolute Mind: the logic of Absolute Mind conditions its actualization. Since this logic is repeated in human consciousness, we are able to rationally plumb the depths of the Absolute and recognize ourselves as its expression and realization. There are no things in themselves, unknown and unknowable, and hidden from knowledge. This was an absolute and totalizing philosophy. The view was antithetical to Schleiermacher, who, along with the other romantics, had worked out a penetrating critique of Fichte's method. Once Hegel arrived at Berlin, the conflict between the two intensified: Harnack notes that Schleiermacher barred Hegel from the Berlin Academy of Sciences fearing "the despotism of the Hegelian philosophy."[40] Tensions between the two men gradually worsened and finally came to a head in 1822 when Hegel, in a preface to a book by Hinrichs, quipped that if religion is grounded in the feeling of absolute dependence, then "a dog would be the best Christian" (90–91). For Hegel religion must be superseded: it remains at the level of "picture thinking" and needs to be transcended by philosophy. For Schleiermacher, on the other hand, Being remains an enigma. What is given to us is consciousness of our conditioned character and radical finitude; this is the jumping off point for faith. In his 1802 letter to Reiner, Schleiermacher averred that he had "become a Herrnhuter again, but of a higher order."[41] This is reflected in his understanding of the feeling of absolute dependence, which *already* contains an expression of faith and piety. Our facticity confronts us as an enigma to ourselves. The feeling of absolute dependence is a response to this enigma; as Jacobi would put it, it is a jump into "the abyss of the divine mercy." Faith, and not knowledge, stands at the heart of Schleiermacher's method. This was the legacy of the early German Romantics to the theory of religion.

# Notes

1. Friedrich Schleiermacher, *On Religion: Speeches to its Cultured Despisers*, trans. John Oman (New York: Harper, 1958), 31. This is a translation of the 1821 (third edition) of the *Speeches*. However, for the most part, this essay will focus on the first (1799) edition of the *Speeches*, Friedrich Schleiermacher, *On Religion: Speeches to its Cultured Despisers*, ed./trans., Richard Crouter (Cambridge: Cambridge University Press, 1988, 1996). Henceforth, each edition will be indicated by the name of the translator.
2. *Speeches* (third edition, Oman translation) p. 216; first edition (Crouter translation), 99.
3. Dieter Henrich, *The Course of Remembrance and Other Essays on Hölderlin*, ed., Eckart Förster (Stanford: Stanford University Press, 1997), 93; cf., 73.
4. Manfred Frank, *The Philosophical Foundations of Early German Romanticism*, ed./trans., Elizabeth Millán-Zaibert (Albany: State University of New York, 2004), 26. Cf. Karl Ameriks, *Kant and the Fate of Autonomy* (Cambridge: Cambridge University Press, 2000), 64.
5. Frank, *Philosophical Foundations, op. cit.*, 55–75.
6. I discuss Kant's understanding of consciousness in significant depth in "Transcendental Arguments for Personal Identity in Kant's Transcendental Deduction," *Philo*, 14 no. 2 (Fall/Winter, 2011): 109–135.
7. For a more in-depth discussion of this point, see my "Where Have all the Monads Gone? Substance and Transcendental Freedom in Schleiermacher," *Journal of Religion*, Volume 95, No. 4 (October 2015): 477–505, especially 498–499.
8. Immanuel Kant, *Critique of Pure Reason*, ed./trans., Paul Guyer and Allen Wood (Cambridge: Cambridge University Press, 1999). All references to Kant's first *Critique* are to this translation; page references to the Academy edition pagination follow the citation.
9. So Reinhold, "in consciousness, the subject distinguishes the representation from the subject and the object and relates the representation to both." Karl Leonhard Reinhold, *Contributions Toward Correcting the Previous Misunderstandings of Philosophers*, Vol. I (1790) 167; cited from Dan Breazeale's article "Karl Leonhard Reinhold" in the *Stanford Encyclopedia of*

*Philosophy*. For an excellent discussion of Reinhold, see Karl Ameriks, *Kant and the Fate of Autonomy*, 81–160.

10. Johann Gottlieb Fichte, *The Vocation of Man*, trans. Peter Preuss (Indianapolis: Hackett: 1987), 44–45. While the book appeared in 1800, it was a defense and popularization of Fichte's already published views. For an up-to-date and accessible account of Fichte's views, see Allen W. Wood, *Fichte's Ethical Thought* (Oxford: Oxford University Press, 2016), as well as the discussion by Ameriks in *Kant and the Fate of Autonomy, op. cit.*, 187–264.
11. On this point, see George di Giovanni, *Freedom and Religion in Kant and his Immediate Successors* (Cambridge: Cambridge University Press, 2005), 77.
12. *Friedrich Heinrich Jacobi: The Main Philosophical Writings and the Novel*, Allwill, trans. George di Giovanni (Montreal: McGill-Queen's University Press, 1994), 277.
13. Jacobi, *On the Doctrine of Spinoza* (1789), 42; cited in Frank, 70.
14. Immanuel Kant, *Notes and Fragments*, trans., Curtis Bowman, Paul Guyer, and Frederick Rauscher (Cambridge: Cambridge University Press, 2005), 294.
15. On these points, see Frank, *Philosophical Foundations, op. cit.*, 63.
16. Cited in Frank, *Philosophical Foundations, op. cit.*, 64.
17. *On the Doctrine of Spinoza* (1789) 420, note; cited in Frank, *Philosophical Foundations*, 64; Giovanni, *Jacobi*, 374.
18. *On the Doctrine of Spinoza* (1789) 215f.; cited in Frank, 204.
19. *On the Doctrine of Spinoza* (1789) 423, Giovanni, *Jacobi*, 375.
20. *On the Doctrine of Spinoza* 427; Giovanni *Jacobi*, 376.
21. On this point, see Giovanni, *Freedom and Religion*, 85–86, and Frank 68.
22. The centrality of Jacobi's influences on Romanticism is documented by Frank in his chapter "The Unknowability of the Absolute," in *Philosophical Foundations*, 55–75.
23. Giovanni, *Jacobi*, 509.
24. Frank, *Philosophical Foundations, op. cit.*, 125.
25. Frank, *Philosophical Foundations, op. cit.*, 97.
26. On this point, see Henrich, "Hölderlin on Judgment and Being," 71–89, in Henrich, *The Course of Remembrance*.
27. Friedrich Hölderlin, *Sämtliche Werke*, Stuttgart: 1943–1985, Bd. 4, 216f. All translations of Hölderlin's fragment are my own.
28. Cited in Frank, *Philosophical Foundations, op. cit.*, 34.
29. Cited in Frank, *Philosophical Foundations, op. cit.*, 89.
30. Hölderlin, SW, 4. 216, translation mine.
31. *Novalis: Schriften*, Vol. II, ed., Paul Kluckhohn and Richard Samuel (Stuttgart: Kohnhammer, 1960 ff.), 412, Nr. 1. An English translation can be found in *Novalis: Philosophical Writings*, trans./ed. Margaret Mahony Stoljar (Albany: State University of New York Press, 1997), 23.

32. An English translation can be found in *Novalis: Fichte Studies*, trans./ed. Jane Kneller (Cambridge: Cambridge University Press, 2003), 123. On this point, see also Frank, *Philosophical Foundations*, 172ff.
33. Friedrich von Schlegel, *Kritische Ausgabe*, ed. Ernst Behler et al. (Paderborn: Schoeningh, 1958 ff.), KFSA 12, 328.
34. Friedrich Schleiermacher, *Dialektik (1814–15), Einleitung zur Dialektik (1833)*, ed. Andreas Arndt, Philosophische Bibliothek. Vol. 335 (Hamburg: Felix Meiner, 1988), 105.
35. Friedrich Schleiermacher, *Vorlesungen über die Dialektik, KGA*, II.10.2, 568.
36. On this point, as well as a discussion of the differences between Schleiermacher and Jacobi, see Richard Crouter, *Friedrich Schleiermacher: Between Enlightenment and Romanticism* (Cambridge: Cambridge University Press, 2005), 77–80.
37. Crouter, 22.
38. *Schleiermacher Kritische Gesamtausgabe*, ed. Berlin-Brandenburg Academy of Sciences (Berlin: de Gruyter, 1972–) (hereafter KGA, cited parenthetically in the text by division, volume, and page number).
39. For further discussion of these points, see my "Metaphysical Realism and Epistemological Modesty in Schleiermacher's Method," in *The Persistence of the Sacred in Modern Thought*, ed. Chris Firestone and Nathan A. Jacobs (Notre Dame: University of Notre Dame Press, 2012).
40. Cited in Crouter, *Between Enlightenment and Romanticism*, 88.
41. *Life of Schleiermacher*, ed./trans. Federica Rowan (London: Smith Elder and Co., 1860), I: 283–284.

# 6

## Femininity and the Salon

### Anne Pollok

The philosophical and literary world of the 'romantic era' is—hidden from the mainstream discussion—also an era of women intellectuals. Certainly, these intellectuals struggled to be accepted as thinkers in their own right. It is my contention that this is a hermeneutic issue: due to the lack of role-models, individual agents struggled to establish an exact outline of their own persona without losing contact to their surroundings. On the one hand, a woman broke the established distribution of social roles if she reached for the male field of agency, and thus was harder to 'read' or understand by her contemporaries—notes on the 'weird spinster' that either enraged or amused the (male) observers are numerous in almost any given time of Western history. On the other hand, women had to either see themselves as 'new males', or at least deny themselves the already acknowledged female persona in order to follow through with their intellectual interests. Having *accepted* role-models in their field of interest was incredibly rare; most woman intellectuals were seen—and tended to see themselves—as a notable exception to a generally male rule. The establishment of exclusive circles such as the *Tugendbund*, the exchange of letters, publishing under pseudonyms or hidden behind a male editorship may all count as first attempts to form such a role as salient members of the intellectual community—to not only be seen, but to be able to see themselves.[1]

A. Pollok (✉)
Johannes Gutenberg Universität, Mainz, Germany
e-mail: apollok@uni-mainz.de

However, the most important—and on an individual level[2] successful—strategy was the establishment of the salon as an intellectual meeting place. This opened up a social space which enabled women to fulfill a plethora of new roles, or re-define old ones. The salon helped women to make their new role *visible*, and thus contributed to a new understanding of what it meant to be an intellectual citizen. This chapter focuses on salon culture as a stage[3] for developing new roles in and facets of philosophy in nineteenth-century Germany.[4] In the context of German Romanticism's key ideas, the salon helps clarify the notion of *sociability*, as it is only through amicable exchange and mutual acceptance that such a novel form of character formation becomes possible.

# 1   What Is the Salon?

Since the salon itself is not a literary genre, but rather an intellectual space that opened dialogues for voices that were often excluded from academic and print culture, its traces must be uncovered through historical detective work that is different from the way we trace legacy through written texts. In what follows, my assessment of salon culture will build on the descriptions we find in letters and diaries,[5] which, though never without personal interest and a good portion of self-stylization, help us to reconstruct the mechanics and effects of salon culture on the individuals of the period.[6]

Much of the earliest attempts at a historical *reception* of the salon has been formed by the late nineteenth-century dream to create Germany as a culture and nation, done by and large by male scholars.[7] But we fail to understand the fluidity of this institution if we go with these rather biased accounts. Indirectly, though, these accounts make us realize that our assessment has to be sensitive to demarcations by gender, profession, or class: "Reading their work suggests that the experience of the romantic period was significantly different for women than it was for men. … [even though there might also be male writers writing about similar issues in similar ways.] Nonetheless, it is true that the dialectic of public and private and the complex subordination of letters to literature conspired to impede women authors and that the impediment affect the female voice".[8]

Fortunately, although contentious in its own rights, the path-breaking study by Arendt,[9] but mostly with the work done by scholars on both sides of the Atlantic in the 1980s,[10] and then, in a second wave starting in the 2000s,[11] we now have a more balanced account of this social phenomenon. Any assessment after 1989 rests on the results of Wilhelmy-Dollinger's important study, which she herself characterizes as a work in social and societal history.[12] I give the assessment of this phenomenon a systematic twist in that I consider more current and critical literature, and, heuristically, read the institution of the salon as a means of emancipation, and a motor of change in the understanding and character of the public sphere at large in the romantic era.[13] Thus, I systematically connect the concept of *sociability* with the concepts of *self-formation* and *dialogue*. I shall argue that the salon offers a social sphere for the exploration of new roles of and relations between the sexes.

One of the few works that reflected philosophically on the conditions of intersubjective exchange—and oriented itself on the social phenomenon of the salon—is Schleiermacher's fragment from 1799, *Toward a Theory of Sociable Conduct*.[14] Here, Schleiermacher develops a theory of sociability founded on the needs of educated people, who are compartmentalized in either their professions or the household.[15] His theory of personal development is egalitarian and dialogical—and even though the piece itself might not have been immensely influential, it does offer us a picture of the ideals that were sought in these social circles. It can thus be understood as a reliable reflection on the then current salon culture.[16] Schleiermacher argues that there should be a state-free realm of social interaction to bring the spheres of individuality[17] and society together most fruitfully. To him, women are supremely fit to offer a platform for this, since they are not limited by professions, and are less tempted to solve misunderstandings in a violent way.[18] Overall, it is the concept of a dialogical self that speaks most to the issue of the female agent of that time, in that it comprises both the possibility of self-expression, but also of genuine mutual exchange (*Wechselwirkung*).[19]

With his theory, Schleiermacher develops an ideal of society in which the different spheres of human life are not strictly separated, in particular not into the private realm of the house (usually the wife's domain) and the public sphere of business and politics (typically the male sphere). He advocates for a state in and through which both of these are complemented and completed (*ergänzt und erfüllt*). A state that "puts the sphere of the individual in a position in which it is as often as possible overlapping with the spheres of others, and that every of those overlapping areas allows the individual to peer into other and foreign worlds, so that, step by step, all aspects of mankind become known, and even the most foreign minds and conditions become amicable and neighborly. This task is solved through the free sociability among rational human beings who form and educate each other".[20] It is most noteworthy that Schleiermacher advocates for a form of education, or *Bildung*, through contrast, dialogue, and amicable exchange: in a similar manner as Schiller in his *Aesthetic Education*,[21] Schleiermacher seeks a middle ground between the extremes of the house and the profession—and finds it not in the experience of art, as his Classicist counterpart, but in *sociability*, which opens a semi-private, semi-public space where each person can come to herself, and autonomously submit to that universal—and, in Schleiermacher's understanding—*shared* law that she can understand as her own, and hence, feel genuinely part of a society of equals.

However fascinating Schleiermacher's theory is, he is very clear that it is still a work in progress—very similar to its object, the social space of the salon. The very *concept* of the salon preceded its *name* in Germany—most salonnières were hesitant to refer to their gatherings as a 'salon', mainly to stress the (somewhat imaginary) difference to the French original,[22] or, as Hahn argues,[23] to keep the project vague, but dynamic. Most rather referred to it as their 'circle', 'society' (*Gesellschaft*), 'open house', the particular day of the meeting ('*my Thursday*', '*jour fixe*', in particular in the 1820s), or to the refreshments served ('*Teegesellschaft*', around 1800). It is next to impossible to give an exact date of when the term 'salon' is used in the way to denote the social institution. First, because documentation is not dense enough, second, because 'salon' also denotes the place where the gatherings happen and is used ambivalently by hostesses, guests, and bickerers alike.[24] For Germany, the closest we get to this is with Karl August von Varnhagen's, *Der Salon der Frau von Varnhagen*, Berlin 1830. At the beginning of the nineteenth century, Germans tend to reference the French institution as a salon but stuck to the aforementioned nomenclature for the German counterpart. Later in the century, however, and ironically in particular when the institution is wavering, complaints about the over-use of the term arise. There is a certain air of nostalgia involved in the coining of the term.

Following Wilhelmy-Dollinger,[25] a salon can be defined according to the following criteria:

1. They center around a female hostess.[26] This is, on the one hand, a pragmatic decision, since it would make it otherwise nearly impossible to distinguish between this form of sociability and some 'learned circles', such as the gatherings around Marcus Herz. While it is wrong to think that female-led gatherings could not have covered scientific topics, the particular mixture of participants in a salon is much less restrictive in this regard—artists, politicians, nobility were also welcome. On the other hand, I also embrace this requirement to showcase the social, semi-private space in which woman intellectuals could find an expression—neither academia, the church, nor the workspace could offer this.
2. The salon is scheduled for a particular day of the week. Once invited, one was part of the circle, and in most cases even allowed to bring one's own guests.[27]

3. A salon is not a club, a society, or an association: there are no fixed lists of members, nor fees. Neither were these meetings intended to foster business relationships in the first place.
4. Salons have a high cultural attraction and influence. Being invited to an important salon could be a form of cultural knighting for aspiring artists or help them forge important connections to patrons or other, more established artists.

    Clever authors such as Goethe knew very well how to utilize the salon. He advertised his newest works to the enthusiastic salonnière, Sara Baronin von Grotthuß for example, about whose connections to the literary scene Karl Varnhagen begrudgingly wrote: "In her youth she received flattery from Lessing, later from Herder, and finally Mrs. von Genlis, the prince of Ligne, and Goethe were in the most amicable connection with her".[28] It did not hurt, either, that many salonnières were married to publishers (e.g. Minna Reimer, Sophie Sander, and Friederike Helene Unger). The Goethe-cult as a unifying feature for the most famous salons around Henriette Herz, Bettina von Arnim, Rahel Varnhagen, and many others.[29] "Listen to Goethe …. With tears I write the name of this mediator, in memory of my extreme distress … Read (him) as one reads the Bible in misfortune".[30]

5. Membership in a salon was not dependent on social status—ideally, anyone could join, and everybody was allowed to contribute to the discussions. This does not say, however, that in fact all salons were the epitome of social equality: most of the active and influential participants of the salon are white Christian males of the higher ranks.[31]
6. Although a salon lacks official or written protocol, it is not bohemian: it does not intend to break with the art of social conduct, but to improve it. In this regard, Schleiermacher's theory of sociability perfectly reflects its general spirit: everyone shall be concerned about everybody's comfort, and hence should not bring up issues that would make others feel uncomfortable.[32] We should add here, however, that this concern does not quite count for the later, political salon—in particular not Bettina von Arnim's.
7. Although salons lacked a rigid program, quite some of them are concentrated around a particular art, or style. The height of the 'musical salon' was between 1815 and 1830. The year 1816, for instance, saw the debut of Fürst Anton Radziwill's musical version of Goethe's *Faust*. The most important musical salons were led by Amalie Beer (the mother of Giacomo Meyerbeer), and Leah Mendelssohn-Bartholdy and her daughter Fanny Hensel, sister of Felix Mendelssohn-Bartholdy. The latter's *Sonntagsmusiken* were a special and important feature of Berlin city-life, and premiered many of the son/brother's compositions, as well as a thorough rediscovery

of Johann Sebastian Bach, thus marking him as the other national artist besides Goethe.

Whichever art it is that is practiced, shared, or adored, the food is always on the sideline, in particular during the earlier phase. Only the later salons offer more to the palate, sometimes effectively drowning out the more artistic aspects.

8. A salon offers freedom in many respects. Monetary, since it is not about representation of wealth, nor noble lineage, but of skills, knowledge, and the rare art of sociability and communication. Socially, in that it is not strictly bound to common social practices, or to class or religion. Jewish members of society found their place in the salons, at least as salonnières, as did women who considered themselves authors or artists, actors and poets. Even the overtly political salons were oriented toward an open discussion, not political gerrymandering. In its way, the salon is perfect for self-formation (or, more exactly, *Bildung*, the then-en-vogue idea in Germany, as developed by the Late Enlightenment), mutual acceptance, tolerance, respect, and support.

Overall, the salon is not just a physical meeting place,[33] but a space for artistic and intellectual exchange. It is supposed to offer entertainment, exchange, and relaxation from the demands of professional and domestic life. Such a place besides 'the real world' needs leading without stifling, and hence put high demands on—and thrived or shriveled under—its respective central lady, the salonnière, and her gift of bringing people together to form some lose kind of unity, connected by shifting common interests. After all, "[t]here is no greater proof of our common humanity besides the fact that we can communicate with and understand each other".[34]

Although it was mostly sought as an opportunity for relaxation and entertainment, the salon proved to be socially transformative. It helped re-establish groups and people (standing against the 'court') within a new society—this is particularly true for the more stratified and exclusive class system in Prussia and the German states than for the blossoming life of the salon in Paris of the middle of the eighteenth century. This less formal, not court-like structured, German version of the salon is a child of the German Enlightenment, prominently pre-formed by the Mendelssohn-family. Given that the *Urvater* of the salon, Moses Mendelssohn,[35] resisted this way of assimilation vehemently, it is quite ironic (and also telling for the lack of actualized tolerance) that this social event in the spirit of his understanding of interreligious interaction paved the way for many conversions. Historically, the salon was not necessarily a motor of social change that fostered a heightened acceptance of others.

Rather, it helped the pariahs to gain access to the core of society[36] and test out her social worth—in the end, though, this worth could only fully shine through assimilation. It remains questionable how much of a sign of progress this is.

The early salon itself is quite characteristic for the spirit of its first founders in their fondness of the blurring of demarcations—before the salon itself became a fixed dogma and succumbed mostly to the restorative forces of 1848, ultimately petering out at the beginning of the twentieth century. The early Salons around the turn of the century were led by educated Jewish women of the *Haskalah* (the experimental ones led by Henriette Herz and Rahel Levin, the French inspired ones led by Sara Levy and Amalie Beer, for instance, or the Vienna salons by Fanny von Arnstein and Cäcilie von Eskeles), or, a bit later, female representatives of the Christian bourgeoisie (*Bildungsbürgertum*) (Sophie Sander, for instance), or nobility (Princess Louise Radziwill) who were by and large politically liberal; first supporting, then disappointedly dismissing the French Revolution and turning all the stronger to literature and art instead of politics. Its prime values are still situated within the enlightenment tradition and its call for a shared humanity, even though the prevalent representatives of Enlightenment (and Classicism) were thoroughly mocked in particular among the circles of the early German Romantics (which are not completely equivalent to the salons, but share a great deal of personnel). Of great importance is also the adoration of art, and particular artists—most notably, of course, Goethe—in these houses. The old ideal of *Culture* and *Bildung*, first formulated in the Enlightenment, was clearly in need of a new expression—and the social space of the salon offered it. A first deep change occurred with the fall of neutral Prussia to Napoleon in 1806 after the lost battle of Jena, and, more forcefully even if under opposite forces, with the formation of the German Confederation in 1815. The latter in particular set back any attempts at political equality for Jews,[37] thus harming the Jewish salon. It also suppressed more liberal ideals by its deep aversion to middle class, it suppressed more liberal ideals. In this time of the *Vormärz*, we begin to see more salonnières from the nobility (e.g. Dorothea Herzogin von Kurland). However, in their self-conception, the values of *Bildung*, talent, and spirit (*Geist*) still rank above lineage.[38] This is also reflected in the prominent standing in such circles of leading or aspiring writers, notably Jean Paul[39] and Goethe. But generally, *Biedermeier* brought in conservative forces; "officialdom now came to the fore".[40] Brentano's and Arnim's[41] *Christlich-Deutsche Tischgesellschaft* (founded 1811) banned women and Jews (among others). Rahel, now as Frau Varnhagen von Ense, knew—and she was probably not the only one to sense this change—that she would not be able to rekindle the

*Dachstube*, which from now on served as a romanticized memory for her.[42] As restoratorative as they may have been, even these new forms of the salon offer a much-needed reprieve from normal life and still generate a space where freedom of speech and conscience are celebrated. Particularly noteworthy is Bettina von Arnim's salon, which lasts up to the period of restoration in 1848, and represents the political salon, but also showcases the transformative character of its salonnière and her impact on late Romanticism. In a way, even the later, more formal salons all represent the perfectly romantic idea of a utopia in the midst of bland reality. And, as suffused into daily or conventional routines as it got, this utopia actually enabled through its bold fantasy a change in reality—the attempt to achieve the impossible in the end enabled the possible:[43] a social change, later expressed in the various strands of the *Frauenbewegung*.[44]

## 2   The Early Days: Henriette Herz and Rahel Varnhagen

The salon of Henriette Herz is quite characteristic for the beginnings of the salon in Germany—in particular if seen in tandem with her counterpart, Rahel Varnhagen in her *Dachstube*.

As the sculptor Johann Gottfried Schadow described it retrospectively, Henriette Herz' salon was the pendant to her husband's, the eminent physician and philosopher Marcus Herz' *Gesellschaft* of learned men. While those, smoking and discussing, were presented with experiments by the host, the younger scholars with more literary interests chose Henriette's circle that mainly discussed the newest literature. Her salon flourished from the 1780s up to Marcus' death in 1803, but petered out in 1806. One important spin-off of the salon was Henriette's institution of the *Tugendbund*, a more exclusive circle of friends with the aim of the cultivation and ennoblement of the soul through quasi-amorous friendship, complete honesty, and mutual devotion. This version of sociability flourished for only a little while: complete honesty and equality is hard to sustain if all-too worldly affairs begin, and some members did not completely believe in the actual equality of all members in 'the real world'. For instance, Wilhelm von Humboldt's engagement with Caroline von Dacheröden got in the way of the *Tugendbund* and ultimately revealed it as a set of idealized rules of a merely imaginary world that they had built for themselves. This just made obvious that some members were reluctant to transition from mere play to reality—in particular, they seemed most unwilling to allow the female and Jewish participants as prominent a role as they sought to obtain themselves.

While Henriette was famous for her beauty and her pleasant attitude, the unmarried and highly intellectual Rahel Levin gave her salon a rather different flair. Her first salon, which she sometimes rather mockingly called her *Dachstube*[45] was one of the most important social circles of early German Romanticism in Berlin of the 1790s. Varnhagen was exceptionally gifted in giving all her visitors a stage.[46] Her salon, as far as we know, was not decidedly unconventional[47] in manners, but worked under the strict assumption of equality. Quite 'naturally',[48] she offered everyone, even Prince Louis Ferdinand, her *Dachstubenwahrheiten*.[49] This frankness needed to be paired with a good amount of politeness to keep the overall atmosphere friendly and constructive—a feat that Varnhagen achieved admirably. Among her guests were the brothers Humboldt, Friedrich Schlegel, Schleiermacher, the brothers Tieck, the aforementioned Prince Louis Ferdinand of Prussia, and his mistress, Pauline Wiesel (with whom Rahel had an interesting exchange of letters that is now edited in an excellent, historically sensitive volume).[50]

With the fall of Prussia, more patriotic salons were established, such as Luise Gräfin Voß's salon that even played with the idea of a Prussian revolution—its leading lady, as well as Fürstin Luise Radziwill were members of the new *Tugendbund*, a patriotic circle established to re-instantiate the Prussian reign.[51] As little as these circles actually did for such a goal, the influence on the salon era of that time is palpable, as most of them centered around the ideal of Prussia, and were more or less actively engaged in said re-establishment. As a side-effect, these salons tended to be relatively open to all classes and genders.[52] But with the rise of Metternich and *Biedermeier*, even the salon fell victim to the more restrictive times of the restauration.[53] Where it didn't degenerate into the populistic, but mediocre aesthetic *Teetisch*, it at least became less involved with current developments and focused more on literature (thus paving the way for a quite common conception that German *Bildung* is by and large apolitical, despite its political roots in the Enlightenment and Schiller's *Aesthetic Education*; see the salons of Elisabeth von Staegemann, Amalie von Helvig).

## 3   Varnhagen's Second Salon

After having been driven out of Berlin in the aftermath of the Prussian defeat of 1806, Rahel married Karl August Varnhagen in 1814,[54] and accompanied him on missions in Vienna and Karslruhe. In 1819 the Varnhagens returned to Berlin. Rahel did not enjoy her second salon as much as her first and felt that she gave more to the gatherings than she ever received back. But even though the salonnière was hesitant and, for good reasons, appalled by the reactionary politics of Prussia after 1815, her salon became a cult (which, in turn, might not have helped to endear it to her). Heinrich Heine, Alexander von Humboldt, Leopold von Ranke, and Friedrich Carl von Savigny were among her guests, whom Rahel wanted to educate in a better social language (the spoken word, but also the manner in which newest developments were relayed), to counteract the French and the church's dominance, and cultivate life as an artform.[55] Even Franz Grillparzer could attest that Rahel offered a perfect example of vivid and impressive speech. He admits to having been struck by a kind of 'stupor' (*Trunkenheit*) when he heard her speak: "She talked until midnight, and I don't recall whether they chased me away or whether I left on my own accord. Never in my life have I heard more interesting or better speech".[56]

The reason why her influence on female self-formation is so lasting, however, is not the salon as such, but its 'replacement' as edited by her husband after Rahel's death: the 1834 collection *Rahel—Ein Buch des Andenkens für ihre Freunde*. Of course, this fabricated volume might show a strong hand by her husband,[57] but we should remember that the first version of this book was already compiled in Rahel's lifetime. Be it as it may, the publication of letters was meant as the establishment of a memory, a statuesque memorial even, but, in Rahel's case, it was also meant to stylize a life. The 1830s were the time of important publications of letters, which also helped to set a memorial to those involved, signifying poetical and humane importance. *Rahel* took the publishing world by storm. It also immortalized her time (*Spätromantik, Freiheitskriege*) and her husband. His niece Ludmilla Assing continued his work—and, as Hahn argues,[58] the work is still continued today, lending the most famous representative of the salon a still vivid voice and influence.

When Varnhagen promises in his foreword that this collection (which also covers diaries and notes) should establish a picture of Rahel's personality and character, thereby showing us "her fate, her sense (*Sinn*), and her experiences (*Begegnisse*)",[59] this also tells us that snippets from her life are supposed to stand for its entirety, and that, most importantly, the dialogue with each 'friend' (as Varnhagen calls her readers) is not over yet. "It is an original story and poetic" wrote Rahel before her death,[60] and the readers of her time wanted to believe this. It is most telling not of Rahel herself, but of the changing times, that this stylized version of a memory now seems stilted and too artificial, and that we tend to view newer, historically 'correct', and 'authentic' critical editions, as the exchange of letters with her friend Pauline Wiesel, as more refreshing and relatable.[61] All these editions, however, make clear that Rahel incorporated the ideal of romantic self-reflection as an intense, detailed, and honest-but-artful account on one's inner life. Seen this way, even Arendt's 'biography' of Rahel, which does not stand the critical test of preserving the correct historical data,[62] might still reveal this ideal of self-criticism, in that it turns on this very axis: the assessment of Rahel's view of herself by herself.[63] And still, this self-assessment is oriented toward the other, it is essentially dialogical: Rahel needs her relation to the other to fully assess herself. She realizes the full insight as something that is indeed reflected in other people's minds and actions—as isolated and alone as she felt over long periods of her life, and which the salons only partly helped to alleviate, as little are her letters (that at times can be annoyingly self-centered) monologues. Instead, Rahel's letters breathe the air of her time: they are deeply introspective, realize the romantic self-understanding of the artist and poet, but they also invest in the other: Rahel's understanding of herself is reflected in and through the other—may it even be an imaginary other, a closeness she lacked for most of her life. Ironically, the mere making up for an absence became the thing itself, so that, philosophically speaking, the *mode* of self-formation is clear, even if the result appears somewhat diminished.

## 4 Later Developments, Alternative Formats, and Bettine von Arnim

The abovementioned *Tugendbund* by Henriette Herz and her husband's learned society were interesting and valiant alternatives to the salon in the early nineteenth century. In the later *Vormärz* era of the German Confederation we find many societies that excluded certain parts of society, mainly Jews and women—lending the new Germany the conservative air for which it is still infamous. There are still salons, but also literary 'reading circles' of various degrees of intellectual quality and 'learned circles' such as the famous *Wednesday Society* founded in the late eighteenth century by Ignatius Aurelius Feßler.[64] Schleiermacher describes the latter as an "exclusive society … in which people get together to read papers (*Aufsätze*) to each other, heed to works of the *belle lettres*, impart literary news, etc."[65] Here Schleiermacher met his best friend Schlegel; a friendship that proved decisive for the development of early German Romanticism.[66]

Later, there was also Arnim's aforementioned *Tischgesellschaft*.[67] Brentano, Heinrich von Kleist, Adam Müller, Savigny, Fichte, Zelter belonged to its members,[68] and there are some parallels to the salon, for instance the stress on literature and Goethe.[69] This should, however, not blind us to the fact that the *Tischgesellschaft* mainly strived to establish a new 'national consciousness'—and that this, no matter how amicable and peaceful as it seems, is a precursor of later institutions much more sinister.

Even though the height of the salon, in particular in Berlin, seemed to be over in the 1830s, there are still some interesting salonnières: Sara Levy (whom Wilhelmy-Dollinger describes now as a "phenomenon", "combining cultural conservatism with the ideas of political progress"[70]), Amalie Beer, Hedwig von Olfers, Johanna Schopenhauer in Weimar, and, indeed, Bettina von Arnim, who now enjoyed her 'third life'. The young Bettina knew the earlier salons,[71] and grew up close to leading artists, Goethe in particular, who had a fleeting love for her mother Maximiliane. Bettina married Achim von Arnim and lived the life of a more or less typical wife and mother from 1810 to 1835, bringing up seven children (espousing her own view on health, quite successfully), and having a distant, but not estranged relationship with her husband. But after his and Schleiermacher's death, Bettina decided to return to Berlin, started to write, became famous with her 1835 *Goethes Briefwechsel mit einem Kinde*, and steadily moved on to more and more serious materials, ultimately defending the rights of Jews, as well as of the poor laborer against royal gain. Her radiant intellect, but also her unconventional manner—Caroline von Schlegel sharply remarked that one is more likely to converse with Bettina sitting on the table or having her feet on a chair rather than sitting on it properly—made her a noteworthy and notorious figure in the 1830 and 40s; even though she finally came to understand, bitterly,[72] that her literary influence on the throne did not include political aspects as well.

## 5 Concluding Remarks

Overall, the salon factors as a stage to try out and present different versions of oneself, in a semi-public realm that the subsequent generations can only explore indirectly, when we delve into letters, diaries, and other forms of self-conscious note-taking (and, in turn, self-presentation). Such a multitude of dimensions of self-stylization befitted the main representatives of the German intelligentsia of the nineteenth century—even though an actual change of society was rather slow in the making. The salon is a respite, and it offers its leading ladies a forum to try out roles, indeed. But in the end more traditional social forces proved to be stronger, and suppressed what was achieved for several decades. In a way, the stage also proved to be confining: here differences are suspended, but only to be reaffirmed in other spheres such as professional life or artistry. The fate—and self-image—of strong romantic women like Dorothea Schlegel proves this more cautious and negative result.[73]

According to Schleiermacher's theory, not social forces, but the uncommunicable residue of the I is the reason for the failure of perfect sociability: in every communication there is a residue that throws one back onto oneself. Ultimately, communication exposes the *limits* of complete harmony, instead of surpassing those limits.[74] Every communication inherently also communicates its own limitation—thus, complete freedom and complete openness in exchange remain ultimately impossible. However, our *awareness* of this is liberating. Sociability is as close as we can get to the goal of humanization and perfection of society. It is thus not surprising that the sociability which the salon of late eighteenth, early nineteenth century stands for, is still very much alive. Maybe not in the indifferent and non-differentiating social media that rather obscure any genuine communication, but in the counter-movements that are not afraid of technology. That an online forum can still be called—and taken to be—'the philosophical salon' (see, for instance, the forum edited by Michael Marder and Patricia Vieira for the Los Angeles Review of Books, and many similar sources), just show our continued need for such spaces. We are still not able, and will never be, to transcend the limits of our respective individualities. But maybe the stage of a salon can help us to play with them.

## Notes

1. In a way, I end up arguing against Lokke who holds that "an idealist and spiritualized understanding of the woman artist's role in historical process made this emancipatory movement [from the self-destructive emotional excess of Staël's *Corinne* to the inspired artistic freedom of Sand's *Consuelo*] possible." It is no question that the artistic transformation of these processes in writing constitute a form of 'spiritualization'. However, taking the salon into consideration changes this idealized picture and highlights the social reality of this process of 'emancipation'. Just a few paragraphs later Lokke herself also highlights the individualistic streak of the male conceptions of *Bildungs*—and *Künstlerroman* of the same period—so, we are still on shared ground here: the 'spiritualization' should then be understood much less as a retraction from the public, but as a deeper understanding of it, encompassing a heightened awareness of political and historical forces as well. See Kari Lokke, *Tracing Women's Romanticism: Gender, History, and Transcendence* (London: Routledge, 2004).
2. This is Becker-Cantarino's main contention: the salon did not, in the end, change society so that it became more accepting of female agents, but it did

help some salonnières to improve their respective position (Barbara Becker-Cantarino, *Schriftstellerinnen der Romantik: Epoche—Werke—Wirkung* (Munich: C. H. Beck, 2000), 197).
3. Schleiermacher calls the salon the "little stage" (*kleine Bühne*), see Friedrich Daniel Ernst Schleiermacher, *Versuch einer Theorie des geselligen Betragens* (1799/1800), ed. Hermann Nohl, in Schleiermacher, *Werke, Auswahl in vier Bänden*, ed. Otto Braun, Vol. 2 (Leipzig 1913), 1–32, here 26. See also Petra Wilhelmy-Dollinger, *Die Berliner Salons: Mit historisch- literarischen Spaziergängen* (Berlin: Walter de Gruyter, 2000, 15). Hannah Arendt (in her biography *Rahel Varnhagen. The Life of a Jewess*, ed. Liliane Weissberg, trans., Richard and Clara Winston (Baltimore, London: Johns Hopkins University Press, 1997) (from the 1st ed. 1957), here 127–128) seems to relate to this in her assessment of the new 'players' in German society of the early nineteenth century, the Jew and the actor.
4. However, a study with more breadth on the international aspect of the Salon culture is *Europa—ein Salon? Beiträge zur Internationalität des literarischen Salons*, ed., Roberto Simanowski, Horst Turk, and Thomas Schmidt (Göttingen: 1999), and Verena von der Heyden-Rynsch, *Europäische Salons. Höhepunkte einer versunkenen weiblichen Kultur* (München: Artemis&Winkler, 1992).
5. See Manuel Bauer, "Geselligkeit in 'sehr gemischten Kreisen'. Der literarische Salon der Romantik" *in Romantische Frauen. Die Frau als Autorin und als Motiv von der Romantik bis zur romantic Fantasie, Europa—ein Salon? Beiträge zur Internationalität des literarischen Salons,* ed., Thomas Le Blanc and Bettina Twrsnick (Schriftenreihe und Materialien der Phantastischen Bibliothek Wetzlar, Bd. 105) (Wetzlar, 2011): 178–189, at 180. Interesting is also his later reference to the tight connections between the Berlin Salons and the *Jenaer Frühromantik*, the famous group around the brothers Schlegel and their rather unconventional partners. The utopia of individual perfection through harmonious exchange with friends lived in both circles, and, as Bauer puts it, still fascinates us (see p. 187).
6. These media also supported the shift in interests and helped the newly discovered values of individualism, personality cult, culture of intellect (*Geisteskultur*), and *Bildung* as a development of the whole person as a cultured and politically autonomous agent. Wilhelmy-Dollinger calls diaries, letters, and the salon accordingly "media of individual self-realization" (*op. cit.*, 8). That Madame de Staël's assessment of it in her massively influential *On Germany* is to be taken with caution goes without saying, as the pointed contemporaneous replies to it already make abundantly clear (see Becker-Cantarino 2000, *op., cit.*, 187).
7. See Ruth Whittle, *Gender, Canon, and Literary History. The Changing Place of Nineteenth-Century German Woman Writers (1835–1918)* (Berlin, Boston: de Gruyter, 2013), Chapter 2, where Alexander von Gleichen-Rußwurm, *Geselligkeit. Sitten und Gebräuche der europäischen Welt 1789–1900* (Stuttgart:

1909) is mentioned. For the salons in Berlin cf., 79–93, 197–202, 339–352. Whittle discusses mainly Gervinus, Vilmar, and Gottschell. The English reception started off on a better foot, see the first book-length publication on the issue by Bertha Meyer, *Salon Sketches. Biographical Studies of Berlin Salons of the Emancipation* (New York: 1938). It is true that scholarship was also rich in the late nineteenth century up to the 1930s. I contest, however, that the prevalent perception of scholarship from that period is dominated by the male scholars who were still reading during the 1940s and 1950s. Unfortunately, the Nazi indoctrination lasted much longer than is generally admitted.

8. Margaretmary Daley, *Women of Letters. A Study of Self and Genre in the Personal Writings of Caroline Schlegel-Schelling, Rahel Levin Varnhagen, and Bettina von Arnim* (Rochester: Camden House, 1998), 106.

9. Arendt's biography of Rahel Varnhagen should always be read together with Deborah Hertz' and Seyla Benhabib's critical assessments ("The Pariah and her Shadow: Hannah Arendt's Biography of Rahel Varnhagen", *Political Theory* 23.1 (1995), 5–24, and D.H., Deborah, *Jewish High Society in Old Regime Berlin* (New Haven, London: 1988). (Revised edition of: *The Literary Salon in Berlin, 1780–1806: The Social History of an Intellectual Institution.* Phil. Diss. University of Minnesota 1979, Ann Arbor, Michigan: 1979), and her "Salonnières and Literary Women in Late Eighteenth Century Berlin", in: *New German Critique* 14 (1978), 97–108).

10. See, for instance, *German Women in the 19$^{th}$ Century*, ed., John Fout (New York, 1984); *Berlin zwischen 1789 und 1848. Facette einer Epoche*, ed. Barbara Volkmann (Berlin: Akademie-Verlag, 1981); *"Der Geist muß Freiheit genießen…!" Studien zu Werk und Bildungsprogramm Bettine von Arnims*, ed. Walter Schmitz and Sybille von Steinsdorff (Berlin: Saint Albin, 1989), Silvia Bovenschen, *Die imaginierte Weiblichkeit: Exemplarische Untersuchungen zu kulturgeschichtlichen und literarischen Präsentationsformen des Weiblichen* (Frankfurt/Main: 1979), *Rahel Levin Varnhagen. Die Wiederentdeckung einer Schriftstellerin*, ed. Barbara Hahn, Ursula Isselstein (Göttingen: Vandenhoeck and Ruprecht, 1987), and in general the works in particular by Barbara Hahn, Konstanze Bäumer, and Konrad Feilchenfeldt.

11. Wilhelmy-Dollinger, Becker-Cantarino, Whittle, among others. For the discussion in Germany in the 1990s see for instance Peter Seibert, *Der literarische Salon: Literatur und Geselligkeit zwischen Aufklärung und Vormärz* (Stuttgart: Metzler, 1993); and *Salons der Romantik. Beiträge eines Wiepersdorfer Kolloquiums zu Theorie und Geschichte des Salons*, ed., Hartwig Schulz (Berlin, New York: 1997).

12. First published under Petra Wilhelmy, *Der Berliner Salon im 19. Jahrhundert (1780–1914)* (Berlin/New York: de Gruyter, 1989) (=*Veröffentlichungen der Historischen Kommission zu Berlin, Vol. 73*). Ten years later, the study (without the extensive Bibliography and the 'catalogue of salonnières') appeared in sec-

ond edition as *Die Berliner Salons. Mit kulturhistorischen Spaziergängen* (Berlin/New York: de Gruyter, 2000), here, 5.

13. As Wilhelmy-Dollinger stresses (*op. cit.*, 2), this requires change from the female side (the hunger for education and proper participation in public affairs) as well as the male side (the longing for a more humane and encompassing semi-public sphere that offered reprieve from the strict rules of professional life). In his book on Early Romanticism, *Frühromantik. Epoche—Werk—Wirkung* (München: Beck, 2000), Pikulik survives mostly without even mentioning the female contributors (nor researchers). Whether the salon had any influence on Romantic theory "cannot be proven, or has at least to far not been thoroughly investigated" (Pikulik, ibid., 65), even though both have a common "social-historical denominator: that they—in contrast to the mainly bourgeois tradition—elevate and revalue the role of the woman" (ibid., but without reference to Wilhelmy-Dollinger's work).

14. Anonymously published in the renowed *Berlinisches Archiv der Zeit und ihres Geschmacks*. Schleiermacher's authorship was only rediscovered in 1909. For more of Schleiermacher's influence on the theory of the salon Becker-Cantarino (2000), *op. cit.*, 189, and, less skeptical, Andreas Arndt, "Geselligkeit und Gesellschaft", in *Salons der Romantik. Beiträge eines Wiepersdorfer Kolloquiums zu Theorie und Geschichte des Salons*, ed. Hartwig Schultz (Berlin, New York: de Gruyter, 1997), 45–61, here 47. Arndt's comparison of Schiller's *Aesthetic Education* with Schleiermacher's text is most instructive (see 54–58), in that he reconstructs the Enlightenment basis in both of their argumentation. We should, of course, also consider the fact that many ideas Schleiermacher deals with here are also included in his *Ethics*, for instance §§100–8 (version 1812/13), which discusses Sociability as the medium in which genuine exchange is possible (Schleiermacher Werke 2, 293–294, and Konrad Feilchenfeldt, "Rahel Varnhagens 'Geselligkeit' aus der Sicht Varnhagens", in: Schultz, *op. cit.*, 147–169, here 160–165).

15. *Rahel Bibliothek* (Rahel Varnhagen, *Gesammelte Werke*, ed. K. Feilchenfeldt, U. Schweikert, R. Steiner (München: Matthes & Seitz, 1983), Vol 10, 253).

16. Becker-Cantario (2000), *op. cit.*, 189 observes that even though Schleiermacher was good friends with central figures of the salon, his piece remained anonymous and left "no traces in the letters of the time". This may very well be true. However, the piece itself mentions the salon rather explicitly for it to be just some "attempt of grounding a society of individuals on an ethical foundation" (190). As Stefan Nienhaus, *Gechichte der deutschen Tischgesellschaft* (Tübingen: Niemeyer, 2003) argues, Schleiermacher's treatise is somewhat visible in the statutes of the *Tischgesellschaft* and similar societies. That nobody outright cited Schleiermacher does not necessarily indicate that people were not aware of him. It was rather a common usage of the time, as lamentable as this is for historians (see ibid., 41).

By the way: Schleiermacher, in contrast to many others (here it is Friederike Helene Unger), does not lose his head over the predominance of Jewish salonnières. "Daß junge Gelehrte und Elegants die hiesigen großen jüdischen Häuser fleißig besuchen, ist sehr natürlich, denn es sind bei weitem die reichsten bürgerlichen Familien hier, fast die einzigen, die ein öffentliches Haus halten, und bei denen man wegen ihrer ausgebreiteten Verbindungen in allen Längern Fremde von allen Ständen antrifft. Wer also auf eine recht ungenierte Art gute Gesellschaft sehen will, läßt sich in solchen Häusern einführen, wo natürlich jeder Mensch von Talenten, wenn es auch nur gesellige Talente sind, gern gesehen wird und sich auch gewiß amüsiert, weil die jüdiscchen Frauen—die Männer werden zu früh in den Handel gestürzt—sehr gebildet sind, von allem zu sprechen wissen und gewöhnlich eine oder die andere schöne Kunst in einem hohen Grade besitzen" (*Henriette Herz, Ihr Leben und ihre Zeit*, ed. Hans Landsberg (Weimar: Kiepenheuer 1913/reprint Frankfurt: Klotz, 2000), 15). It is marvelous how diplomatically Schleiermacher covers all bases of concern and then explains them in a reasonable way: (a) these are the only open houses, (b) they offer all sorts of important connections (also for business people), but also (c) high-class relaxation, and may be led by women, but that is (d) just because the men are busy making money.

17. "Jeder Mensch hat als endliches Wesen seine bestimmte Sphäre, innerhalb der er allein denken und handeln, und also sich auch mittheilen kann. Die Sphäre des Einen ist nicht völlig die des Andern, so gewiß er nicht selbst der andre ist, und jeder—dies geht durch alle Mitglieder einer Gesellschaft hindurch—hat in der einen etwas, was nicht in der andern liegt." (Schleiermacher 1799, in Landsberg, *op. cit.*, 171).
18. See also his "Brouillon zur Ethik", 34. Stunde, in: Werke 2, 59–60.
19. Aus Schleiermachers Tagebuch, in: Werke 2, xxv, here xxvii.
20. Werke 2, here 3–4, my translation. "Ein Zustand der diese beiden [Sphären des privaten und öffentlichen] ergänzt, der die Sphäre eines Individui in die Lage bringt, dass sie von den Sphären Anderer so mannigfaltig als möglich durchschnitten werde, und jeder seiner eigenen Grenzpunkte ihm die Aussicht in eine andere und fremde Welt gewähre, so daß alle Erscheinungen der Menschheit ihm nach und nach bekannt, und auch die fremdesten Gemüter und Verhältnisse ihm befreundett und gleichsam nachbarlich werden können. Diese Aufgabe wird durch den freien Umgang vernünftiger sich untereinander bildender Menschen gelöst."
21. See also Arndt (1997), *op. cit.*, 54–56. Although we lack proof that Schleiermacher knew Schiller's work, it had been famous enough in his time to assume some influence.
22. Although the Germans strained to break themselves free of their fascination with their neighbor, not even avoiding the term salon could—surprisingly—achieve this aim. Quite the opposite, since they ended up comparing "their" salonnières with the French counter pieces, calling Franziska/Fanny von

Arnstein the "Madame de Staël of Vienna", Rahel Varnhagen as the secret Lespinasse, and Henriette Herz as Madame Récamier (*Henriette Herz, Ihr Leben und ihre Zeit*, ed. Hans Landsberg (Weimar: Kiepenheuer 1913/reprint Frankfurt: Klotz, 2000), 35). The 'Ur-salon' led by the Marquise de Rambouillet (Wilhelmy-Dollinger, *op. cit.*, 25–27), by the way, matches the ideals of the early nineteenth century exactly: spirit and personality ranked above nobility, and the discussion was expected to foster reason and 'urbanité', sophistication and inner nobility. Some salons in France might be more focused on the courting of the aristocracy, but that holds true for some German salons as well—the difference is in the respective detail of each salon, not in the nationality.

23. Barbara Hahn, "Der Mythos vom Salon. 'Rahels Dachstube' als historische Fiktion", in *Salons der Romantik. Beiträge eines Wiepersdorfer Kolloquiums zu Theorie und Geschichte des Salons*, ed., Hartwig Schultz (Berlin, New York: de Gruyter, 1997), 213–234, here 232.
24. Wilhelmy-Dollinger, *op. cit.*, 30, who also notes that the term really only settled when its institution was degenerating—and the term salon became a symbol of longing and remembrance.
25. See also, Becker-Cantarino's concise summary of it in Becker-Cantarino (2000), *op. cit.*, 191.
26. Wilhelmy-Dollinger *op. cit.*, 2: *schöngeistig* or political, centered around a mostly female, inspiring person. For Wilhelmy-Dollinger, these "*echte Salons*" were quasi-public institutions, which were discussed in public media (newspapers, journals), as well as in memoirs and letters of its constituents.
27. Hartwig Schultz, *Unsre Lieb aber ist außerkohren Die Geschichte der Geschwister Clemens und Bettine Brentano* (Frankfurt/Main: Insel Verlag, 2004), 266. "Es gehörte zum Prinzip des literarischen Salons, dass formelle Einladungen nicht ausgesprochen oder verschickt wurden."
28. Karl August Varnhagen von Ense, *Denkwürdigkeiten und vermischte Schriften*, Bd. 4, 2. Aufl. (Leipzig 1843), 636. "Sie hörte in ihrer Jugend Schmeicheleien von Lessing, in späterer Zeit von Herder, dann standen Frau von Genlis, der Fürst von Ligne und Goethe mit ihr im freundlichsten Verkehr."
29. See Ruth Whittle, *Gender, Canon, and Literary History. The Changing Place of Nineteenth-Century German Woman Writers (1835–1918)* (Berlin, Boston: de Gruyter, 2013), 62.
30. Hannah Arendt, *Rahel Varnhagen. The Life of a Jewess*, ed., Liliane Weissberg, trans., Richard and Clara Winston (Baltimore, London: Johns Hopkins University Press, 1997) (from the 1st ed. 1957), 108, letter to R. Friedländer from 28 March 1808.
31. Becker-Cantarino (2000), *op. cit.*, 192. See also Landsberg *op. cit.*, 18, who observes that the need of the Jewish salonnières to shine necessitated the marginalization of male Jews, with the exception of artists such as Michael Beer and Giacomo Meyerbeer.

32. Schleiermacher, *Versuch*, 11–12. It should be noted, though, that this restriction somewhat clashes with the next requirement, namely, that sociability is aimed at the "whole human being" (*den ganzen Menschen*, ibid., 13). Only from the standpoint of the ideal society (and the ideal human being) are both aspects not mutually exclusive.
33. But speaking of physical place: The center of the Salon was without question Berlin, but there were also important circles in Weimar, Dresden, Heidelberg, and Jena—all, quite incidentally, also centers of German Romanticism. Some of these circles moved with their hosts, and as such we see a version of the salon pop up around the Schlegels in Italy, or the Tiecks wherever they went. See Ina Hundt, "Geselligkeit im Kreise von Dorothea und Friedrich Schlegel in Paris in den Jahren 1802–1804", in Hartwig Schultz, ed., *Salons der Romantik. Beiträge eines Wiepersdorfer Kolloquiums zu Theorie und Geschichte des Salons* (Berlin, New York: de Gruyter, 1997), 83–133, here 83–85.
34. Benhabib, "The Pariah and her Shadow: Hannah Arendt's Biography of Rahel Varnhagen", *Political Theory* 23.1 (1995), 5–24, here 17.
35. Wilhelmy-Dollinger (2000), *op. cit.*, 44–45: his translations as a starting point for assimilation, the open sociability (*Geselligkeit*) of his house as a model for the later salon. Mendelssohn was not only Dorothea Schlegel's father, but also the mentor of Sara von Grotthuß, and introduced her to Shaftesbury's works, see her *Briefe an Goethe*, ed. L. Geiger, in: *Goethe Jahrbuch* 14 (1893), 27–142, here 52.
36. "The Jewish salon, the recurrently dreamed idyll of a mixed society, was the product of a chance constellation in an era of social transition. The Jews became stop-gaps between a declining and an as yet not stabilized social group: the nobility and the actors; both stood outside the bourgeois society—like the Jews—and both were accustomed to playing a part, to represent something, to expressing themselves, to displaying 'what they were' rather than 'showing what they had'; in the Jewish houses of homeless middle class intellectuals they found solid ground and an echo which they could not hope to find anywhere else. In the loosened framework of conventions of this period Jews were socially acceptable in the same way as actors: the nobility reassured both that they were socially acceptable." (Arendt, *op. cit.*, 127, see also Benhabib, *op. cit.*, 17)
37. After all, the 1812 decree of emancipation suffered from the get-go from unequal realization and too many 'exceptions', but it was positively killed by 1815.
38. Wilhelmy-Dollinger (2000), *op. cit.*, 77.
39. Who described the hype around his persona as the hare who is encircled by the hunter in ever closer circles, see Landsberg, *op. cit.*, 24 (citing a letter to Otto from 1800).
40. Arendt, *Rahel Varnhagen. The Life of a Jewess, op. cit.*, 177.

41. Schultz (2004), *op. cit.*, 265, notes that Bettine does not exhibit any anti-Semitic tendencies, and keeps visiting the Berlin Salons of Jewish women such as Sara Levy and Fanny Lewald. On Bettina's attitudes toward Jewish citizens see also Bäumer/Schultz (1995, 129–136).
42. See Seibert (1993, 164). Interesting account overall on the difference between first and second salon, the more consumerist nature of the second, p. 165. We should also take Hahn's criticism to heart, namely that *Dachstube* is not only Rahel's romanticized memory, but that of many contemporary researchers as well. However, as Hahn seems to overlook in the final pages that Rahel calls her memory one that cannot easily be taken seriously—given the somber note of all her memories, this only indicates her intent to color this memory in a particular—romantic—way. See Rahel Levin Varnhagen: *Briefwechsel mit Pauline Wiesel*, ed., Barbara Hahn (München: C.H. Beck, 1997), esp., 233–234.
43. Wilhelmy-Dollinger (2000, 11).
44. Wilhelmy-Dollinger (2000, 17), see also her "Die Berliner Salons und der Verein der Künstlerinnen und Kunstfreundinnen zu Berlin". In *Profession ohne Tradition. 125 Jahre Verein der Berliner Künstlerinnen*, ed. by the Berlinische Galerie […] in cooperation with the Verein der Berliner Künstlerinnen, Berlin: 1992, 339–352.
45. Landsberg, *op. cit.*, 24, citing a letter to Gustav von Brinckmann, Mai 1800. See also Hahn (1997).
46. "Rahel acquired to the point of mastery the art of representing her own life: the point was not to tell the truth, but to display herself; not always to say the same thing to everyone, but to each what was appropriate for him" (Arendt, *op. cit.*, 173).
47. See Wilhelmy-Dollinger (2000, 85).
48. The Mignon-parallel that was also used to characterize Bettina. In her correspondence with Pauline Wiesel, Rahel (Ralle) and Pauline (Pölle) referenced their preferences of the natural life as "loving green things"—note that this is a highly romanticized version of nature. Heidi Thomann Tewarson, *Rahel Levin Varnhagen. The Life and Work of a German Jewish Intellectual* (Lincoln: University of Nebraska Press, 1998), 106.
49. See Wilhelmy-Dollinger, *op. cit.*, 85; Daley, *Women of Letters. A Study of Self and Genre in the Personal Writings of Caroline Schlegel-Schelling, Rahel Levin Varnhagen, and Bettina von Arnim*, *op. cit.*, 49; Rahel Levin Varnhagen: *Briefwechsel mit Pauline Wiesel*, ed., Barbara Hahn (München: C.H. Beck, 1997), 213–223.
50. Rahel Levin Varnhagen: *Briefwechsel mit Pauline Wiesel*, ed. Barbara Hahn (München: C.H. Beck, 1997).
51. See Wilhelmy-Dollinger, *op. cit.*, 108.
52. Ibid., 113.

53. During the Napoleonic wars, in particular 1813/14, most salons were on halt, anyways.
54. When she married, she had to take up a Christian surname. Rahel chose Friederike Antonie Varnhagen von Ense, signing all letters like this ever since. However, for her old friends, she remained "Rahel": "The stroke 'R' remains my coat of arms", cit. in Tewarson, *Rahel Levin Varnhagen. The Life and Work of a German Jewish Intellectual*, op. cit., 139.
55. See Wilhelmy-Dollinger, *op. cit.*, 140.
56. Ibid., 14.
57. See Arendt, *Rahel Varnhagen. The Life of a Jewess*, op. cit., with some rather unfair charges; Whittle, *Gender, Canon, and Literary History*, op. cit.; Tewarson, *Rahel Levin Varnhagen. The Life and Work of a German Jewish Intellectual*, op. cit.; Konrad Feilchenfeldt, "Rahel Varnhagens 'Geselligkeit' aus der Sicht Varnhagens", in Schultz, *op. cit.*,, 147–169, here 147; and Hahn (2004, 553) with better judgment (also informed by findings in the library of Krakow) on the issue.
58. See Hahn (2004, 553–555), calling it a collective, ongoing effort. Hahn (1997, 102): the letters as an echoing structure (*Echostruktur*).
59. *Rahel Bibliothek* I, foreword.
60. *Rahel Bibliothek* I, 208.
61. The letters have been rediscovered in the 1980s, and the scholarly interest arose again when the lost collection Varnhagen reappeared in Krakow (see Becker-Cantarino *op. cit.,* 161).
62. See Endnote 9.
63. Curiously, Arendt claims not to write objective history, but rather to offer an account of "how Rahel herself" would have written about it (Arendt, *Rahel Varnhagen. The Life of a Jewess*, op cit., xv–xvi). See also Benhabib, *op. cit.*, 8–10.
64. Who, together with Fichte was one of the rejuvenators of the *Freimaurergesellschaft*.
65. Eine "geschlossene Gesellschaft… wo man zusammenkommt, um sich Aufsätze vorzulesen, schöne Schriftstellerische Werke zu beherzigen, literarische Neuigkeiten mitzutheilen u.s.w. " (Landsberg, *op. cit.*, 252, letter to his sister from 22 October 1797).
66. See in particular Manuel Bauer, *Schlegel und Schleiermacher. Frühromantische Kunstkritik und Hermeneutik* (Paderborn: Schöningh, 2011).
67. "Arnim ist der Stifter einer Eßgsellschaft, welche sich die christlich-deutsche nennt und keine Juden, keine Franzosen und keine Philister duldet. Ich habe neulich auch darin gegessen, und es geht recht animisch darin zu" (cited in Landsberg, *op. cit.*, 17).
68. See in particular Stefan Nienhaus, *Gechichte der deutschen Tischgesellschaft* (Tübingen: Niemeyer, 2003). Nienhaus situates the Tischgesellschaft as a "private public space" and concentrates on its political implications, not with-

out also touching on the importance of wit and satire—but also the chauvinism and questionable nationalism of such *Vereine*.
69. See ibid., 34–35.
70. https://jwa.org/encyclopedia/article/berlin-salons-late-eighteenth-to-early-twentieth-century%20. It should also be noted that Levy supported her great-nephew Felix Mendelssohn-Bartholdy in his rediscovery of Johann Sebastian Bach, as Wilhelmy-Dollinger also points out that Sara Levy and the (at this point quite elderly) Henriette Herz were sources of inspiration of the feminist and salonnière Fanny Lewald.
71. Particularly noteworthy is her hilarious report of Madame de Staël's entrance in Bethmann-Schaaf's salon in Frankfurt, dressed as "Corinna" (i.e. the heroine of her most famous novel), in an obviously tight dress that she—"unfortunately", as Bettina slyly notices—gathers in the front, not the back, so that the guests are treated to a good look on her thighs when she descends four flights of stairs to greet the other guests. That Bettina also gets into an argument with Frau Rath concerning who—de Staël or she, Bettina—are more apt philosophical partners for Goethe, gives Bettina the opportunity to once more advance on Goethe himself: if he really just 'plays' with her as with a doll, she asks him in the 'letter'/novel, thus, in combination with the aforementioned, unflattering description of her rival, cementing her position as an infatuated equal (see *Goethes Briefwechsel mit einem Kinde* (Berlin: Aufbau, 1986), 200–203).
72. Konstanze Bäumer and Hartwig Schultz, *Bettina von Arnim* (Stuttgart: Metzler, 1995), 124–125.
73. See Carola Stern, *"Ich möchte mir Flügel wünschen." Das Leben der Dorothea Schlegel* (Reinbeck: Rowohlt, 1990); Irina Hundt, "Geselligkeit im Kreise von Dorothea und Friedrich Schlegel", in *Salons der Romantik. Beiträge eines Wiepersdorfer Kolloquiums zu Theorie und Geschichte des Salons*, ed., Hartwig Schultz (Berlin: de Gruyter, 1997), 83–133, here 102, 132, also Becker-Cantarino, "'Feminismus' und 'Emanzipation'? Zum Geschlechterdiskurs in der deutschen Romantik am Beispiel der *Lucinde* und ihrer Rezeption" in: Schultz, *op. cit.*, 21–44, and Anne Pollok, "On Self-Formation through Writing and Sociability: Henriette Herz, Rahel Levin Varnhagen, Dorothea Schlegel, Bettina von Arnim", in *Women and Philosophy in 18th Century Germany*, ed., Corey W. Dyck (Oxford: Oxford University Press: 2020).
74. Arndt (1997), *op. cit.*, 50, citing from Schleiermacher's notes.

# References

Hahn, Barbara. "Der Mythos vom Salon: 'Rahels Dachstube' als historische Fiktion," in *Salons in der Romantik*, Hartwig Schultz ed. (Tübingen: Niemeyer, 1997), pp. 213–34.
"Rahel Varnhagen," in *New History of German Literature*, David E. Wellbery et al. eds. (Cambridge: Harvard University Press, 2004), pp. 551–55.

# 7

# Fichte's Subject and Its Romantic Transformations

Andrew J. Mitchell

One of the allures of late eighteenth- and early nineteenth-century German authorship is its disregard for the genre and disciplinary boundaries between philosophy and literature. Scholarship tends to segregate the figures of the period into two camps, "German Idealists" and "German Romantics," reserving the former appellation for the "philosophers" Fichte, Schelling, and Hegel (all of whom wrote poetry and other works of fiction), and the latter for the "literary figures," Novalis, Schlegel, Hölderlin, and Günderrode, among others (though all of these also wrote their own philosophical works and commentaries). A good place to examine the crossing of such disciplinary boundaries is in the work of Fichte and the critical reception of his thought by Novalis and Schlegel.[1] At the center of this entangled relation is Fichte's notion of a self-positing subject, as articulated in the *Grundlage der gesammten Wissenschaftslehre* (the first full incarnation of the *Wissenschaftslehre* from 1794), and the transformations this subject undergoes in Novalis's *Fichte Studies* (1795–96) and Schlegel's *Lucinde* (1798). In each case, what is at stake is a poiesis of self-creation. My contention is that the Fichtean subject is the poetic subject par excellence; it does not merely lend itself to aesthetic representation, it requires it.

A. J. Mitchell (✉)
Emory University, Atlanta, GA, USA
e-mail: andrew.j.mitchell@emory.edu

# 1 Fichte's Subject and the Space of Positing

The interest in Fichte on the part of both Novalis and Friedrich Schlegel is as a thinker of subjectivity. Fichte's conception of the I as absolute and self-positing is adopted into their work and subjected to their own critical, and ironic, scrutiny. Both seem alert to a certain gap or interval in this subject's self-relation and both exploit this gap in different ways. In both cases what emerges is a concern with the problem of self-creation.

The *Wissenschaftslehre* (1794) opens with Fichte's quest to find a fundamental first principle to use as the basis of his philosophical system: "Our task is to discover the primordial, sheerly unconditional [*schlechthin unbedingten*] first principle of all human knowledge."[2] Fichte is writing in the wake of Kant and under the presumption that philosophy must take the form of a system. Presumed as well is that the Kantian system, for all its achievement, left much to be desired. It could not ground itself on a single fundamental principle while maintaining an irresolvable distinction between the sensible and the supersensible, the phenomenal and the noumenal, sense and intellect. Kant's successors would attempt to perfect and unify his system, maintaining that they held true to the "spirit" of Kant's work, if not strictly to the "letter." Chief among these was Reinhold. Reinhold had already pointed out that there was a lack of unity in Kant's system, that for all its architectonic breadth and detail, it still failed to ground itself on a single principle. Lacking this, it failed as a system. The split between sensibility and intellect remained fatal.

Where the ever epistemically humble Kant gestured at a possible "unknown root" connecting sensibility and intellect, Reinhold rushed in with his own first principle as a solution, that of "the capacity for representation." Properly understood, representation stretched across the sensible/intellectual divide, for sensibility gave rise to intuitions, which Reinhold considered to be "representations," just as the understanding made use of concepts, which Reinhold also considered to be "representations," and reason deployed "ideas," which Reinhold again viewed as "representations." This capacity for representation was held in common between sensibility, understanding, and even reason itself; it thus served Reinhold as the grounding principle for his system.[3]

Fichte's philosophy grew in this rich environment, and he came into his own with his early review of a skeptical attack on Reinhold's system, authored by one Aenesidemus, pseudonym of G. E. Schultz. In the course of Fichte's review, the young Reinholdian Fichte came to see that some of Aenesidemus's points struck home, that Reinhold's system was indeed flawed. But rather than sign on to Aenesidemus's skeptical rejection of the possibility of knowledge, Fichte took another route.

What Fichte realized in the Aenesidemus review was that no system could ever be complete as long as it was based on a principle as hitherto understood. Even assuming Reinhold was correct and that he did, in fact, unify Kant and create a completely unified system, it was still something *objective*, a thought construct that one could take or leave as one wished. That system was a thought-object and this meant it necessarily had something outside of it, a thought-subject, the thinker of the system. So long as the thinker of the system remained outside the system, there was no way that a system could be said to be complete. With this insight gleaned from the Aenesidemus review, Fichte goes on to construct his *Wissenschaftslehre*, incorporating the thinker into the system itself.

Fichte thus begins the *Wissenschaftslehre* in search of an "act" [*Thathandlung*] not a "fact" [*Thatsache*] that will assume the role of first principle.[4] The path to locating this goes through the presumptive first principle of logic, the principle of identity, the fact that A = A. Fichte intends to show that even the most seemingly fundamental of logical facts, A = A, cannot serve as a first principle, since it itself presumes a prior "act." Fichte moves quickly through the analysis: A is A is taken to be simply or sheerly [*schlechthin*] certain, as certain as we can get. It is "simply" certain, not derived from something higher. That we take this for certain shows that we attribute to ourselves the ability to assert, or "posit," something simply in this manner; our positing is not dependent on previously existing premises or grounds. Such propositions, then, have nowhere to come from other than ourselves.

This means that the basis of logic, the fundamental principle that grounds and supports all the subsequent derivations rendered and conclusions drawn, attains its authority through our act of sheer positing alone. Logic depends, in other words, on that act of positing. And it is the I that posits. I simply posit that A = A. Fichte takes this as proof that (an act of) the I underlies logic.

For A to equal A, it must be posited by an I: "If A is posited in the self, it is thereby posited, or, it thereby is."[5] In order to exist, there must be a positing in the I. A = A would not exist were it not for this act of the I. Fichte draws the conclusion that there must be an active self preceding all facts: "Hence it is a ground of explanation of all the facts of empirical consciousness, that prior to all postulation in the self, the self itself is posited."[6] To exist is to be posited in the I, the ground of all empirical facts. But for this I to exist, must not it too be posited? Yes.

The affirmative answer to this question turns on Fichte's famed understanding of self-positing as activity, as *Thathandlung*. Fichte writes:

The self's own positing of itself is thus its own pure activity [*Thätigkeit*]. The self posits itself, and by virtue of this mere self-assertion it exists; and conversely, the self exists and posits its own existence by virtue of merely existing. It is at once the agent and the product of action [*das Handelnde, und das Produkt der Handlung*]; the active, and what the activity brings about [*das Thätige, und das, was durch die Thätigkeit hervorgebracht wird*]; action and deed [*Handlung, und That*] are one and the same, and hence the "I am" expresses an Act [*Thathandlung*], and the only one possible.[7]

*Thathandlung* is Fichte's neologism naming the simultaneity of self-positing and self-posited.[8] It is not immediately evident what this means.

*Prima facie*, this positing would seem like a case of *reflection*, the self in question would simply reflect upon itself. In so doing, the self discovers itself. No one has done more to dismantle this idea than Dieter Henrich in his seminal essay, "Fichte's Original Insight." Henrich argues that the reflection model is inherently flawed, is doubly redundant. First, if it is the self that goes reflecting upon itself, then the self is already at hand and need not reflect to find itself. This is the first redundancy. Second, if the self to be reflected upon first needs to be found, then the reflecting self that searches for it must have a criterion by which to recognize it, in which case, again, the self is already in our possession.[9] The reflection model presupposes the fully formed I that it claims to subsequently discover.

This version of the reflection model has assumed that the reflecting and reflected selves are complete selves. But what if complete selfhood of this sort were the *result* of the reflection, something produced by it. Henrich argues that the reflecting "self" would not be a self in that case. If we modify the model and claim that the I would be the result of the reflection, then the reflecting self would be something different from the I that result from such reflection. But with this, we lose the identity of the two (and Henrich seems to adopt a quite traditional view of identity, and of the copula, in his argument). As Henrich concludes, one "can never achieve the unity of consciousness, namely, the identity 'I = I,' by means of reflection."[10] The problem with the model for Henrich is that in each case I = I represents the I as something objective.[11]

The point is to avoid thinking the self as something that would precede its positing, whether as that which is posited or that which does the positing. Neither self (qua subject, qua object) can precede its positing, because what that self "is" is not anything that can simply "be." The self is an action, a *Thathandlung*. Henrich wants to understand this act as an immediacy:

> When Fichte says that the Self posits itself, he has in mind this immediacy, the fact that the entire Self emerges all at once. [...] Thus we have no basis for objecting that *something* which does the positing must precede the act of positing. The Self *is* the positing, it *is* the act through which it comes to be for itself, through which a Subject-Self becomes aware of itself as Object-Self.[12]

The self would posit itself "all of a sudden," we might say (and Henrich uses the Greek term *eksaiphnês* to indicate this sudden production). Such a view avoids the worries raised by the reflective model, but at some cost.

What is it that Fichte is avowing in his notion of "positing"? To be sure, as Henrich observes, he never defines what he means by this.[13] Nevertheless, a few points seem apparent. That the self posits itself first means that it is not dependent on something else for its existence. Positing is a positing into existence. To self-posit is to enter existence on one's own. The self-posited self is not led into existence or brought into existence or even thrown into existence by anything other than itself. There is a time before the self exists and a time after which it does exist. That is the span of its positing. From this perspective, positing cannot be instantaneous in the way that Henrich wants it to be. Instead, positing would serve to separate the self from itself. As an action, positing cannot be completed all at once. Actions are not instantaneous, they have a beginning, middle, and end. There is an interval endemic to the act of positing. This is evident if we simply consider that "to posit" as used by Fichte is a transitive verb. It takes an object, "something" *gets* posited and then "has been" posited.

The problem only arises if we require the self to be fully finished before it posits or is posited. This seems to be a flaw in Henrich's account. He can only consider the self as a whole. If it is not whole, it is not a self. But this would seem to deny that selves can develop, learn, grow. And this issue of development, indeed infinite development, lies at the heart of Fichte's conception of the self as elaborated in the third part of the *Wissenschaftslehre*. The self has to become what it is. The self that is posited *ab initio* is not the self in all its glory. That self is the result of a development whereby it yearns and longs to be itself and is driven onward to ever more become itself (this in two ways, through self-discipline, on the one hand, and transformation of its environment, on the other).

The positing of the self is never done once and for all. We must be continually posited into position. Henrich's problem is that he assumes there is a self, that a self could be something finished and completed. He is certainly correct in objecting to the reflection model for presupposing the self, but this never leads to him questioning the nature of that self, as it appears within the 1794

*Wissenschaftslehre*.[14] The fundamental problem with reflection is not that it presupposes a self, but that it construes that self as something whole and accomplished. Henrich seems to assume this as well. To be sure, he understands Fichte's self to be an act (*Thathandlung*), but that act is a *fait accompli* for him. For this reason, he cannot think a self in becoming, the self exists all at once for him. It exists immediately and *eksaiphnês*, all of a sudden.

The self must be continually posited. To be posited is to be cut off from something, to be separated from it, otherwise there would be no positing in the first place. To be the product of a positing is to be separated and detached from that act of positing in the production. Thus any posited self is always a finite self, a determinate self. To speak of self-positing does not change this fact. As paradoxical as it sounds, to self-posit is still to separate oneself from oneself and to detach from oneself.

Otherwise put, there is a gap in the self, a ravine it must always traverse to be itself. That gap is what enables self-relation in the first place! The self cannot be thought of as a sphere, as a completed circle or circuit (as something finished), it remains spaced from itself, the circuit must cross a gap: it is more C than circle. This is the posited self; it follows from a blind spot in order ever to be led back to it. In positing the self, there is always a moment of detachment to be crossed before the self recognizes itself as itself.

The separation of the self from itself is simply a result of its finitude, that is, that it has an end, that we exist as delimited. The self is this tumbling (driven) attempt to capture itself and live up to being what it is. With this account of the infinite progressions involved in understanding Fichte's I, we have reached the conception of subjectivity that will exert such a strong effect on Novalis and Schlegel.

## 2  Novalis: The Space of Positing as the Opening to Representation

Novalis's intervention in Fichtean subjectivity displays a keen understanding of the problem of spacing within the self-relation of subjectivity. His *Fichte Studies* is a landmark of romantic aesthetics, if only for the priority accorded the aesthetic. For Novalis locates aesthetic representation at the heart of the subject and in so doing calls into question that subject's avowed self-certainty.

The opening passage of the *Fichte Studies* sets the stage in its discussion of the proposition A = A:

The proposition a is a contains nothing but a positing, differentiating and combining. It is a philosophical parallelism. In order to make *a* more distinct, *A* is divided (analyzed). "Is" is presented as universal content, "a" as determinate form. The essence of identity can only be presented in an *illusory* proposition [*Scheinsatz*]. We abandon the *identical* in order to present it. Either this occurs only illusorily—and we are brought by the imagination to believe it—what *occurs*, already is—naturally through imaginary separation and unification—Or we represent it through its "not-being" [what it is not], through a "not-identical" [what is not identical to it]—a sign—[using] a determined thing for an isomorphic determining thing.[15]

Starting from A = A, Novalis notes that this statement of identity as posited entails a twofold movement of "differentiating and combining." To state the identity of A, we differentiate A from A (we write them twice) in order to then combine them as though the same (we join them with an equals sign). Any simple sense of identity as a matter of the self-same (as a unity) is abandoned in the presentation of it. We cannot present the singular identity of A. To even speak of the "identity" of A is to speak of something that is ultimately "not A." Identity is not A. The "identity" of A involves something that is not A. Identity as presented, that is, A = A, is thus illusory. But we cannot understand identity otherwise.

For us to express identity, a differentiation must take place by means of which A is separated from itself. It rejoins itself a split-second later locked in identity. But that moment of separation is enough to introduce exteriority to A, A is outside of A. This means that identity is either an "illusion" or "we represent it through its 'non-being,' through a 'not-identical'—a sign—[using] a determined [important, determined] thing for an isomorphic determining [important, determining] thing."[16] For A to be A, it must duplicate itself outside itself so that a determination of equivalence or identity can take place. It must put out something that is not itself to stand for itself. In a word, it must represent itself. We represent A by what it is not, this second A; this second A thus stands as a sign for the first A, a representation of it.

This holds not merely of logical identity (A = A), but of personal identity as well (I = I). Novalis expresses the same need for representation in his discussion of consciousness. The argument runs:

> Consciousness is a being outside of being that is within being [*ein Seyn außer dem Seyn im Seyn*].
> But what is that?
> What is outside being must not be a proper being.

> An improper being outside being is an image—So what is outside being must be an image of being within being. Consciousness is consequently an image of being within being.
> A better explanation of the image. /Sign/Theory of signs./Theory of presentation, i.e., of not-being, within being, in order to let being be there for itself in a certain respect.[17]

Novalis does not think consciousness is a kind of being, it is something "outside" of being, other than being. Nevertheless, consciousness is found "within" being. Within being, Novalis thus tells us, an outside of being can be found. Consciousness is a kind of absence that is harbored within presence, a non-being within being, the "nothingness" of existentialism. But if consciousness is outside of being, is other than being, then it is not a "proper" being. Because consciousness is not a being, but appears within being, it is not entirely nothing, either, it does appear. This makes its presence "improper," rather than an absence.

The name for this impropriety that appears within being without being reducible to what it is, Novalis names an image, a representation. The image is not what it is because it always points beyond itself qua representational. It stands for something other than it. To be conscious is thus to bear an image of being within being, to house a representation.

Novalis's notes repeatedly run headfirst into this problem of representation. He searches for what he calls "a better explanation of the image" and this leads him to rethink the notion of presentation itself. Presentation is said to involve a non-being within being. This is undertaken so as to "let being be there." This non-being is necessary for being to be. There would be no being if it did not harbor non-being within it, we might say. Being as a whole, without any non-being, a plenum in the worst sense, would be a suffocating, static whole. Consciousness would be impossible in such conditions. Consciousness trades on non-being, and in so doing, lets there be "being" in a sense no longer identical to that of a plenum.

The self is an improper being. The self can never have itself without first having "represented" itself to itself. This is Novalis's move, right at the moment when the Fichtean self is about to reach itself and thereby successfully reflect upon itself, right there to now insert the demand of representation. Perhaps an image of itself as fulfilled, or Absolute, has guided it all along—an Absolute that is ever only given as just such an image. Novalis interrupts any presumed Fichtean immediacy in the self's relation to itself by the interposing of a representation. The self sees an image of itself, sees itself as represented.

Two things follow from this:

1. The self poetizes. If the self always recognizes itself as a representation, and if the self is always thereby making representations of itself, then the self is poetic. Identity is a creative act.
2. Ineluctable misrecognition. Self-recognition now occurs through the intermediation of a representation. The self must recognize itself in this representation to be itself. This at once entails the possibility of not recognizing oneself, of not finding oneself again, of being at a loss for oneself.

The two are really sides of the same coin. The self that represents itself must recognize itself, but it always can fail to do so. This "always can fail" is not to be understood as a possibility that may or may not befall the attempt at recognition. Failure is constitutive of representation. It is not something that either does or does not occur to representation, instead, as a constitutive possibility, representation is never entirely recognizable. Or rather, we only recognize one thing as one thing, but once we have recognized something we have not yet left the cycle of representation, because we still have this "as." Misrecognition is not a possibility that may or may not befall an otherwise intact or pure notion of representation, misrecognition is inherent to representation, permeates representation, requires that we think of representation as always already missing its target. Complete recognition and complete misrecognition become impossible. Accuracy of representation can no longer be the standard; the creativity of the self is unleashed.

## 3  Schlegel: The Space of Positing and the Impossibility of Representation

Schlegel's novel, *Lucinde* (1798), if no longer deemed "obscene," nonetheless remains subversive.[18] This subversion is not only formal (if a form/content distinction is still allowed here). The disheveled protagonist and ostensible narrator (editor? compiler? composer?) of *Lucinde*, Julius, is the subversion of the stereotypical self-assured, heroic protagonist. This is the subject not only of Goethe's *Wilhelm Meister's Apprenticeship*, the *gebildete*, educated, well-formed subject, but it is likewise the subject of Fichte's *Wissenschaftslehre*. Schlegel's subversion exploits the same gap in the subject's self-relation that Novalis does. Julius is the Fichtean subject gone awry; we can trace all his blundering back to that same gap.

If our focus on Fichte's influence for Novalis was on the first part of the *Wissenschaftslehre*, then with Schlegel we can attend to the third part of the text. Here the abstractions of part one (the articulation of the three fundamental principles) give way to a practical subject, driven to transformative activity in the world. The gap we have diagnosed within the self again plays a central role here, the gap between the self that posits itself and the self that is so posited. The self endeavors to close that gap, to simply be itself alone. But now these attempts at closure take the form of practical acts. In Fichte's account, this is a twofold process of transformation. On the one hand, the self tries to actualize all its potential, on the other, it tries to bring the world into conformity with itself, divesting nature of its otherness. The self's realization of itself becomes a practical endeavor.

This practice has no end. The self can ever only approach complete self-identity, absolute identity remains an unattainable goal that nonetheless orients its striving. The self is thus delivered over to unending striving, infinite seeking. An achievable goal would put an end to the self's quest for identity, and thus to the very self defined by this self-realizing act. Whether achievable or not, the ideal of the Fichtean subject is complete self-possession.

Now there is a sense in which we could say that Goethe's *Wilhelm Meister's Apprenticeship* stages the self-discovery of this Fichtean subject, taking this as its theme. But whereas Fichte sets up self-identity as an infinitely deferred achievement, Goethe presents it as accomplished achievement in his text. Apprenticeship, that is, goal-directed activity culminating in mastery, provides the model of enlightened development here, with our protagonist Wilhelm moving from aesthetics to politics, from representation to self-presentation, from private actor to public decision-maker, from stage manager to figure of destiny. The moment of consummation is Wilhelm's discovery of the scroll of himself, listing all the events in his life and transforming seeming accidental events into necessary and foreseen ones, part of a pre-arranged destiny.[19]

The *Bildung* of this *Bildungsroman* terminates in self-discovery. This is the consummation of the subject's activity and its attainment of itself. The self discovered is now possessed. The self-possessed subject assumes his rightful and mature place. Wilhelm Meister is in command of himself and transparent to himself; he closes the gap.

No one familiar with Julius, the narrator of *Lucinde*, would call him "self-possessed." Indeed, the very subtitle of the book reveals him to be something else, a self-proclaimed "bungler." The subtitle of *Lucinde* is *Bekenntnisse eines Ungeschickten*, translated as "Confessions of a Blunderer." *Bekenntnis* is certainly a "confession," but it is so in the sense of a "profession" or "affirmation." This "confession" is thus not to be mistaken for an apology, for example; it is an avowal. This avowal is made by one defined as *ungeschickt*. Now the German adjective *geschickt* has a sense of something done that is deft, skillful, perhaps even slick. The word carries with it a sense of familiarity with how things are done, it evinces a kind of *phronêsis*, we might say, a practical knowledge of getting about in the world, skillfully and with aplomb. But our protagonist is *ungeschickt*, the opposite of all this, a blunderer, one who is not skillful or tactful in their dealings, one who does not possess a phronetic understanding of the situation, one lacking confidence, deftness, and aplomb.

If we push this a step further, we might find in the *Ungeschickt* an echo of the German *Schicksal*, or "fate." The *Ungeschickt* in this case would be the one who has not been fated, with implications of being ill fated, one who is not among the elect, one for whom all is not guaranteed to work out in advance. A happy fate did not reach our *ungeschickt* subject and was not sent to him. He is perhaps "graceless" in a double sense (inept and unmet by beneficent fate). Etymologically, the fate (*Schicksal*) we are dealing with is understood as something allotted to us, something that befalls us, or, otherwise put, something *sent* to us. Fate, *Schicksal*, is to be thought in terms of the verb "to send," *schicken*.

But if we can press just a little further, this sending shows itself in a new light when thought in terms of the subject. In that case, the "sending," *schicken*, is a "positing," *setzen*. Our *ungeschickt* subject is not merely a blunderer, not merely the one ill fated and without guarantee. Our subject is the one that failed in its self-positing. Our subtitle would then be: *Avowals of One Not Posited* or *Mis-posited*. Julius would thus represent the failed Fichtean subject. He may have posited himself, he must have posited himself, but he does not recognize himself. Julius lacks the assurance of recognizing himself as the self he posited.

The same gap that Novalis sighted in the ego's relation to itself is also spotted by Schlegel. Novalis made the subject's relation to itself a matter of representation; Schlegel trades on the thought that such a representation always entails misrecognition. The subject is inherently an *Ungeschickte*.

Further, in *Lucinde* passivity is lauded and productive activity decried. Its famed celebration of passivity, indeed, of "vegetation," is directed precisely against the activity of the self-actualizing, self-positing, subject. This subject is not rushing out to chase after its own tail or pursue some infinite, unachievable goal. The *appetite* for that is lacking, hence the subject is more plant than animal. Schlegel proclaims: "In a word: the more divine a man or a work of man is, the more it resembles a plant; of all the forms of nature, this form is the most moral and the most beautiful. And so the highest, most perfect mode of life would actually be nothing more than *pure vegetating*."[20]

Vegetative passivity, as Schlegel understands it, does not preclude thinking. He explains, "talking and ordering are only secondary matters in all the arts and sciences: the essence is thinking and imagining, and these are possible only in passivity. To be sure, it's an intentional, arbitrary, and one-sided passivity, but it's still passivity."[21] As such, Schlegel could be said to reject the practical part of the *Wissenschaftslehre*, but still adhere to the theoretical part. Schlegel's notebooks, entitled *Philosophical Apprenticeship*, call into question the structure of the *Wissenschaftslehre*, specifically the ways in which the theoretical and practical parts are grounded. Two notes from the section entitled, "The Spirit of the Fichtean Wissenschaftslehre" (1797–98), read: "The *I ought to be* [Ich soll seyn] must also be capable of analytic demonstration in and for itself, independent of the I = I."[22] The I = I is the foundation of the theoretical section of the *Wissenschaftslehre*; the *Ich soll*, the "I should" or "I ought," is the crux of the practical section, where the I should (ought to) strive toward the realization of its absolute self.

This "ought" is the target of Schlegel's criticism. He accepts Fichte's characterization of the self as self-positing and thus as divided within itself (as I = I). What he cannot accept, however, is Fichte's demand that this division be collapsed in an achievement of absolute identity. Schlegel will not even grant this as an unattainable goal. By Schlegel's reckoning, this practical demand does not follow from the theoretical conception of the I. The practical does not follow from the theoretical, as Fichte would have it, rather, the two are on equal footing: "the one is just as high as the other; there are two fundamental principles, not one."[23] The split self does not need to seek reconciliation with itself. For Schlegel, there is no demand for this. This injunction to activity is rejected in his embrace of passivity.

There is no quest for identity motivating Schlegel's Julius. If anything, the novel reveals him as becoming someone who he never wished to be. The chaotic, erotic, inoperative Julius, ends up a married man, a homeowner, and expectant father. His wife, Lucinde, assumes her corresponding role in this hetero-normative, reproductive union, as mother of the unborn child and keeper of the home, as Julius explains: "But now something else exists which you'll always have to take into consideration, around which your whole world will turn. Now you'll gradually have to adapt yourself to housekeeping [*Ökonomie*]—in an allegorical sense, of course."[24] There can be no doubt that the allegorical here is already corrupted by the literal. But the upstanding family man that Julius would be fails to come about as their child, Guido, is stillborn. Even his betrayal of himself in the embrace of a bourgeois life is blundered. Schlegel's novel illustrates that when the self is dependent on being discovered by itself, then there is always a risk it will not find itself. This risk is so native to the process of self-discovery that there never really is a whole self to find. Even when the self is so discovered, it does not have itself completely; it is never so *geschickt* as to not be an *Ungeschickt*.

## 4 Conclusion

Novalis and Schlegel reveal to us the "dark side" of romantic subjectivity. The Fichtean subject is something of a success story. At the very least, that subject is making every effort toward its goal. Success would mean self-identity, that is, the pole star directing all the subject's endeavors, with respect to both self and world. Fichte diagnoses the condition of subjectivity to be one of diremption and division. He then prescribes endless striving as the means of achieving whatever sense of identity is to be had.

Novalis intervenes to show that the subject never fully possesses itself. That the only way it can have itself is by means of a projection, a representation. The self that posits itself cannot posit itself in an indivisible identity with itself, it must posit itself as divided. This means that it posits itself outside itself, and this means that it represents itself. Such a representation bridges the gap between the self as positing and the self as posited. In so doing, it inscribes representation, and that is to say, poetic creation, into the very nature of the self. Representation at once maintains the gap that separates the self from itself, while also offering a bridge across that gap to allow the circulation of identity.

Schlegel minds this same gap in the subject, but his concern is less with closing it—whether practically, as in Fichte, or representationally, as in Novalis—than with exhibiting the failure and misrecognition inherent in any such divided self. In a word, there is no guarantee that the dirempted self ever finds itself, there is no necessity that it does so. For Schlegel, Fichte's practical demand does not follow from his theoretical conception of the self.

Fichte presented the world with a vision of subjectivity never at one with itself. The early German Romantics exploited this split self, Novalis to show that the subject must always be an artist, Schlegel that it need not be a successful one. Blundering is so ineradicable as to persist even in the midst of success, undermining it, ironicizing it, representing it. Fichte thus bequeaths us a subject for whom aesthetic representation is the condition of identity.

## Notes

1. Notable interpretations of this relationship include Elizabeth Millán, "Fichte and the Development of Early German Romantic Philosophy," in David James and Günter Zöller, eds., *The Cambridge Companion to Fichte* (Cambridge: Cambridge University Press, 2016), 306–325; Ernst Behler, "Friedrich Schlegel's and Novalis' Critique of Fichte" in *German Romantic*

*Literary Theory* (Cambridge: Cambridge University Press, 1993), 184–195; and the first two sections of Dalia Nassar, *The Romantic Absolute: Being and Knowing in Early German Romantic Philosophy, 1795–1804* (Chicago: University of Chicago Press, 2014), 15–156.
2. J. G. Fichte, *Fichtes Werke* I: 91/Fichte, *The Science of Knowledge with the First and Second Introductions*, ed. and trans. Peter Heath and John Lachs (Cambridge: Cambridge University Press, 1982), 93, translation modified.
3. As Reinhold states in 1789, "Every *sensation*, every *thought*, every *intuition*, every *concept*, every *idea* is a representation." Karl Leonhard Reinhold, *Essay on a New Theory of the Human Capacity for Representation*, trans. Tim Mehigan and Barry Empson (Berlin: Walter de Gruyter, 2011), 97. The claim is even stronger in 1791, where he notes of his own philosophy that "In this science alone can it be established through a proof that is universally valid, and will eventually be universally binding, that space and time, the twelve categories and the three forms of ideas, are originally nothing but the properties of mere representations." Karl Leonhard Reinhold, "The Foundation of Philosophical Knowledge," trans. George di Giovanni, in *Between Kant and Hegel: Texts in the Development of Post-Kantian Idealism*, ed. George di Giovanni and H.S. Harris (Albany: State University of New York Press, 1985), 52–103, 68. For more on Reinhold, with particular emphasis on his proto-phenomenology, see the chapter on him in Frederick C. Beiser, *The Fate of Reason: German Philosophy from Kant to Fichte* (Cambridge: Harvard University Press, 1987), 226–265. For more on the romantic influence of Reinhold's conception of representation see Martha B. Helfer, *The Retreat of Representation: The Concept of Darstellung in German Critical Discourse* (Albany: State University of New York Press, 1996), 52–58.
4. Fichte, *Fichtes Werke* 1: 91/*Science of Knowledge*, 93.
5. Fichte, *Fichtes Werke* I: 94/ *Science of Knowledge*, 95.
6. Fichte, *Fichtes Werke* I: 95/ *Science of Knowledge*, 96.
7. Fichte, *Fichtes Werke* I: 96/ *Science of Knowledge*, 97.
8. A year earlier, in the *Aenesidemus* review of 1793, and three years later, in the *New Introductions to the Wissenschaftslehre* of 1797, Fichte will speak of this simultaneity in terms of "intellectual intuition."
9. See Dieter Henrich, "Fichte's Original Insight," trans. David R. Lachterman, in Darrel E. Christensen, Manfred Riedel, et. al., eds., *Contemporary German Philosophy*, Vol. 1 (University Park, PA: Pennsylvania State University Press, 1982), 15–53, 20–21.
10. Henrich, "Original Insight," 21.
11. Henrich, "Original Insight," 21.
12. Henrich, "Original Insight," 25.
13. Henrich, "Original Insight," 25.
14. Too often commentators resort to the 1797 new introductions to explain the 1794 *Wissenschaftslehre*. Henrich's article surveys the whole span of Fichte's

career in pursuing its argument. The self as something whole and complete is rejected by Henrich when considering Fichte's 1801 conception of the *Wissenschaftslehre*, but not prior to that point.
15. Novalis, *Schriften* 2: 104; Novalis, *Fichte Studies*, ed. and trans. Jane Kneller (Cambridge: Cambridge University Press, 2003), 3.
16. Novalis, *Schriften* 2: 104; *Fichte Studies*, 3.
17. Novalis, *Schriften* 2: 106; *Fichte Studies*, 5.
18. For a contemporary revisiting of its obscenity, see Marc Redfield, "*Lucinde's* Obscenity" in *The Politics of Aesthetics: Nationalism, Gender, Romanticism* (Stanford: Stanford University Press, 2003), 125–147.
19. See Goethe, *Wilhelm Meister's Apprenticeship*, ed. and trans. Eric A. Blackall (New York: Suhrkamp, 1989), Book 7, Chapter 9.
20. Schlegel, KFSA 5: 27; Friedrich Schlegel, *"Lucinde" and the Fragments*, ed. and trans. Peter Firchow (Minneapolis: University of Minnesota Press, 1971), 66.
21. Schlegel, KFSA 5: 27; *Lucinde*, 66.
22. Schlegel, KFSA 18: 36.
23. Schlegel, KFSA 18: 36.
24. Schlegel, KFSA 5: 66; *Lucinde*, 112.

# 8

# Friedrich Schiller and the Aestheticization of Ethics

Marina F. Bykova

Friedrich Schiller (1759–1805) is perhaps one of the most celebrated figures in the German literary world. He often referred to himself as a poet-thinker, and this description appears well warranted. A person of wide-ranging interests and knowledge, Schiller was never content to remain bound by any single endeavor, which led his work to traverse a great variety of themes and topics. From his breakout drama *Die Rauber* to his poignant reflection of the *Zeitgeist* in *Der Spaziergang*, it is hard to think of a more versatile and linguistically adept poet and writer of the nineteenth century Germany, perhaps with the exception of Johann Wolfgang von Goethe.

Like Goethe, with whom he had a close personal relationship and almost two decades of productive collaboration, Schiller is usually associated with Weimar Classicism, a German literary and cultural movement that prided itself on its open opposition to purely romantic ideals in literature and other intellectual pursuits and on its attempt to reconcile those ideals with what they found most productive in the Enlightenment, while modeling their own principles on classical antiquity which they sought to emulate. Indeed, the ideals of Weimar Classicism seemed to stand in direct opposition to those advocated by early German Romantics. While classicism emphasized objectivity, analysis, harmony, wholeness, and discipline, Romanticism stressed

M. F. Bykova (✉)
North Carolina State University, Raleigh, NC, USA
e-mail: mfbykova@ncsu.edu

© The Author(s) 2020
E. Millán Brusslan (ed.), *The Palgrave Handbook of German Romantic Philosophy*, Palgrave Handbooks in German Idealism, https://doi.org/10.1007/978-3-030-53567-4_8

subjectivity, synthesis, disharmony, individuality, and spontaneity. At least that was the status quo for which Goethe ardently argued and which he pursued in his own work. Yet Schiller's approach was different. Despite his rather strained relation to early German Romanticism, he was much closer to Romantics than many critics want to accept. In his desire to escape from the excessively didactic trend of the neo-classical school and from the rationalism of the Enlightenment, he did not only adopt a more individualistic, subjective way of writing but also evoked the importance of the emotions and feelings in human nature. Furthermore, Schiller's creative work marks a profound shift in German culture, which brought the question of the power of aesthetic representation to the fore. His legacy encompasses not only the influence and poetic beauty of his own literary creations, but also the studies of Romantic Period aesthetics he pursued. Schiller took this pursuit, famously initiated by Alexander Baumgarten, to heart and made it a central task of his philosophical endeavors. In his quest he followed Kant, the critical reception and transformation of whose work provided the material needed for the realization of his goal. Yet contrary to Kant, he was not interested in establishing aesthetics as a branch of philosophy. He was rather concerned with demonstrating the importance of the aesthetic in human life and the crucial role of aesthetic experience for the development of the individual into a moral being. This approach to aesthetics was very much in accord with the romantic undertaking. Schiller's insistence upon the prime significance of the promptings of aesthetic emotions and sensations and his voiced demand to give these promptings free rein in both everyday life and in the development toward morality served as fertile ground for early German Romanticism and helped to open a path to the centrality of aesthetics that became a hallmark of German Romantic thought. In this sense, an understanding of Schiller's aesthetic quest, which finds its most clear realization in his project of the aestheticization of ethics, is crucial for developing an accurate account of early German Romantic Movement and its intellectual legacy.

\* \* \*

While drama and poetry were certainly Schiller's forte, he also produced works in the fields of history, art criticism, literary studies, and philosophy. Schiller's philosophical publications have long been relegated to a footnote in an otherwise celebrated career, and only recently have scholars begun to give serious consideration to Schiller's contributions to philosophy, most notably to aesthetics, but also to ethics and political theory.[1]

## 8 Friedrich Schiller and the Aestheticization of Ethics

Perhaps Schiller's most important yet puzzling philosophical achievement is an aesthetic turn in ethics that he initiated as a result of his critical reaction to Kant's controversial account of moral agency that gives primacy to duty over inclination. Schiller's response to the troublesome Kantian dichotomy between duty and inclination and Kant's placement of the foundation of *morality* in rationality was his project of the "aestheticization" of ethics that is the main focus of the present chapter.

This project is twofold, and it includes both critical and constructive components, both of which are equally essential to its realization. Schiller's charge against Kant and his moral theory constitutes the critical component, whereas his positive program of introducing aesthetics into ethics represents the genuinely constructive part of the project.

Schiller's productive debate with Kant recently attracted attention from scholars, including those specializing in Kant's ethics, as well as contemporary virtue ethicists.[2] However, in their analysis they focus almost exclusively on Schiller's essay "On Grace and Dignity" (1793), dismissing his *Letters on the Aesthetic Education of Man* (1795) as not adding anything significant to his discourse with Kant and not advancing Schiller's own account of moral motivation any further.

"On Grace and Dignity" is undoubtedly an important work that demonstrates Schiller's sound philosophical understanding of Kant's moral theory and offers a convincing and constructive criticism of the proposition at its very core—that rationality is the supreme principle of morality. Here Schiller argues for an account of moral character according to which the truly virtuous person (who Schiller calls "a beautiful soul" (*schöne Seele*)) is able to exercise ethical duties not by suppressing the sensuous but rather through achievement of a true harmony between the rational and the emotive in man's nature. I would suggest that this account remains incomplete and only provisionally sketched in "On Grace and Dignity." To fully appreciate Schiller's response to Kant and recognize the novelty of the thinker's interpretation of moral motivation, we need to also engage his *Aesthetic Letters*. It is only here that Schiller presents his most rigorous critique of Kant's rational moral psychology, detailing his account of the virtuous (moral) person and bringing to completion his project of the aestheticization of ethics.

My aim in this chapter is to assess Schiller's project by drawing from both of his key philosophical works—"On Grace and Dignity" and the *Aesthetic Letters*. I am interested to see not only what his project entails but also what he attains as a result, both in terms of his disagreement with Kant and of the solution he proposes. In my inquiry into Schiller's contribution to ethics, I am largely motivated by a claim formulated by Frederick Beiser in his groundbreaking monograph, *Schiller as Philosopher*.[3] One dominant theme of the book is the author's contention that what Schiller intended in his writings on ethics is not just to correct Kant's ethics, as many commentators believe, but rather to complete Kant's ethical theory by introducing his conception of the beautiful soul and the associated notion of grace.[4] While I agree with Beiser that Schiller does accept important elements of Kant's ethics that constitute its "rational core," I would argue that, in general, the German Romantic thinker remains unsatisfied with "the spirit and letter" of the rationalist moral psychology advanced by Kant, and this dissatisfaction is evident in his ethical works. Furthermore, Schiller's plan for his own positive program of ethics seems to point to his intention to not just correct or complete Kant's moral theory, but rather to develop a new approach to ethics that would be firmly based in aesthetics. This is the claim I will attempt to justify in this chapter.

I begin my piece by briefly summarizing (in the first part of Sect. 1) the main ideas of Kant's rationalist moral psychology that he puts forward in his *Groundwork of the Metaphysics of Morals* and that Schiller challenges. Later in the same Sect. 1, I turn to "On Grace and Dignity" and analyze Schiller's response to the shortcomings of Kant's ethical theory the German Romantic thinker identifies. Here I argue that despite Schiller's well-grounded assault on Kant's account of moral agency and intended promotion of an aesthetic turn in ethics as a solution to issues he identified in rational morality, in the above essay, he is still not able to fully present his own program of ethics. In need of a plausible explanation for his notion of grace introduced in the essay as a foundation of his conception of beautiful (harmonious) soul, two years later, he engages—now in the *Aesthetic Letters*—in a more specific discussion of what this harmonious state entails and how to achieve this internal harmony. The results of Schiller's search I examine in Sect. 2. I conclude by commenting on the notion of aesthetics that Schiller places at the very foundation of his ethical theory.

## 1 Schiller's Response to Kant in "On Grace and Dignity"

Kant's ethics distinguishes itself through its emphasis on reason and the resulting diminution of the importance of inclination, desire, pleasure, self-love, and satisfaction, as well as any sort of appeal to conscience or moral sense. When founded anywhere besides reason, Kant argues, our moral principles will be merely conditional on the sentiments and inclinations of the individual, whereas it is the very nature of morality that it applies to every man, regardless of his personal inclinations or situation.

For Kant, the very nature of morality is such that its principles are universal laws, binding on all rational creatures by virtue of the nature of reason alone. He tells us that the principles of morality cannot be derived from subjective principles of individual interest ("in favor of some inclination" or any other personal impulses) but must be derived directly from the disinterested, universally binding dictates of reason.[5] Thus, the central concept of morality is duty, which is indifferent to personal inclination. The moral worth of an action does not depend on whether or not the agent achieved (or intended to achieve) pleasure or any other subjective desire, but is rather to be decided according to whether an action proceeds from duty and is done for the sake of duty alone. In Kant's view, only acts done from duty have moral worth, and thus to act morally is to disregard personal interest (inclinations) and act solely for the sake of duty. In this sense, neither the prudent shopkeeper, who treats his customers honestly because he wants his business to prosper, nor the beneficent person, who helps others from philanthropy and his desire to help, displays moral worth, as their motivations are impure. Kant writes:

> To be beneficent where one can is a duty, and besides this there are some souls so sympathetically attuned that … [they] take an inner gratification in spreading joy around them, and can take delight in the contentment of others insofar as it is their own work. But I assert that in such a case the action, however it may conform to duty and however amiable it is, nevertheless has no true moral worth, but is on the same footing as other inclination.[6]

Kant attempts not only to emphasize the irrelevance of inclination to moral worth but also to show that what determines moral character is acting from duty by resisting contrary-to-duty feelings and inclinations. Although Kant labels his position "natural sound understanding,"[7] many of his readers and commentators suggest that, such an account of moral motivation appears very problematic and even conflicts with a commonsense understanding of morality and moral agency. Schiller was one of those who shared this worry and openly challenged Kant in his own writings on aesthetics and ethics.

Schiller spent four long years (1791–1795) carefully studying Kant and his Critical philosophy. During this period the German Romantic thinker produced a number of philosophical essays on topics central to both Kant's aesthetics and ethics. These essays reflect his genuine interest in both disciplines and capture the development of Schiller's own concepts and theories. Among those are his theory of beauty, a more inclusive notion of moral agency, and a new conception of moral motivation, all of which were meant to challenge and eventually resolve problems Schiller detected in Kant's aesthetics and ethics. Some Kant scholars use the similarity of topics in Kant and Schiller, along with the fact that the latter uses the ethical terminology of the former in many of his own predominantly aesthetic works, as firm evidence for Schiller being a true follower of Kant.[8] Profoundly influenced by Kant's philosophy, Schiller, I would argue, never considered himself a disciple of Kant. The latter was for him a main source of inspiration and criticism in both aesthetics and ethics. Indebted to Kant for his thorough account of aesthetic judgment and admittedly borrowing his ideas concerning the sublime and the beautiful, in his own theory of beauty, Schiller went beyond that of his predecessor and developed an aesthetics that essentially advanced Kant's. Attracted to Kant's moral approach to art, Schiller rejected much of the Master's asceticism and moral rigor—for the romantic thinker, involvement of "heart" and "feeling" had always been higher than obedience to universal law. Indeed, Schiller consistently and consciously distanced himself from Kant and his ideas, which is particularly evident in his works on ethics. His essay, "On Grace and Dignity," becomes the first document where he publicly raises his objections to Kant's moral theory and offers his solution to problems left unresolved by Kant.

## 2 Schiller's Project in "On Grace and Dignity"

In his essay "On Grace and Dignity" (1793),[9] Schiller approaches one of the most controversial elements of Kant's conception of moral agency, namely the question of whether it is possible to combine duty and inclination in a moral life. Schiller praises Kant for restoring "healthy reason" to moral philosophy,[10] but he also finds the result of this restoration of reason problematic. His focus is on the role of inclination—the sensuous, emotive side of human nature—in our assessment of moral worth. Criticizing Kant, for whom "inclination is a very ribald companion to moral sentiment, and pleasure a regrettable supplement to moral principles,"[11] Schiller calls moral commands that are unsupported by inclination "ineffective." He points out that "instinct is only set in motion by pleasure and pain," insisting that obedience to reason "must give us cause to take pleasure in it," thus becoming an object of inclination.[12]

It is important to underscore that Schiller sees his task neither in substituting duty by inclination, nor in supplementing one by another. In this case it would be rather a move toward an empiricist model of moral agency and empiricist ethics in general.

## 8 Friedrich Schiller and the Aestheticization of Ethics

It would also be a mistake to interpret Schiller's argument as a simple recognition of the irreconcilable opposition between strict moral commands and admirable but unfulfilled desires. Schiller finds any opposition between the rational and sensuous in moral motivation unsatisfactory. He writes:

> Either the person represses the demands of his sensuous nature to conduct himself in concord with the higher demands of his reasonable nature; or he reverses this relationship, and subordinates the reasonable part of his being to the sensuous part, and thus merely follows the thrust with which the necessity of nature drives him on, just like other phenomena.[13]

Both options, Schiller says, are extreme: the pulling of the soul in opposite directions inevitably leads to moral excess, which, depending on what part of the soul surrenders, manifests itself either as moral severity (by suppressing sensuous nature) or moral laxity (by subjugating the rational). In fact, his chief concern about Kant's ethics is that portraying reason as a constraining force fosters moral severity that causes an unresolvable moral struggle:

> [The man] thrusts everything sensuous from him, and only by this distinction from matter will he attain to the feeling of his rational freedom. But, because sensuousness stubbornly and powerfully resists, a marked force and effort is required of him, without which it were impossible for him to hold off the appetites and silence insistently urging instinct.[14]

Schiller concludes that it is not right that man should sacrifice his natural feelings in order to act morally. It is not that only rational commands have moral significance; man's desires and instincts are equally valuable and effective in moral agency.

Schiller's central argument here is that a full conception of moral life cannot be attained by focusing on duty and reason alone. It is not sufficient to focus merely on what we ought or are obligated to do, as Kant advocated. Only if we recognize the moral value of inclinations and their contribution to moral agency can we reach a satisfactory conception of moral life.[15] Schiller's aim in "On Grace and Dignity" is to formulate a coherent conception of moral (righteous) action that accounts for this positive role of inclination.

His own solution is to establish *harmony* between inclination and duty, which he attempts to accomplish by introducing the notion of grace. Schiller begins his explanation of grace by stating that "all grace is beautiful … but not all that is beautiful is grace."[16] Grace is an objective quality that can be readily distinguished from that which possesses it; thus, the only way an individual can exhibit it is through movement. There are a multiplicity of "beautiful" movements, but grace "can only characterize … moral sentiments."[17] Graceful actions, Schiller claims, when undertaken deliberately, in direct response to our free (rational) volition, appear to be natural and spontaneous, resulting from a harmonious relation between the sensuous and the rational. Schiller explains:

> If, that is, neither reason, ruling over sensuousness, nor sensuousness, ruling over reason, accords with beauty of expression, then shall the sentient condition … where reason and sensuousness, duty and inclination, accord with each other, be the condition under which beauty of play (grace) ensues.[18]

As "sympathetic movements" graceful actions occur "at the behest" of moral sentiment as opposed to pure natural instinct or involuntary actions.[19] Schiller describes such actions as the expression of man's moral character and moral "inner soul." Thus, grace possesses a compelling force that has moral significance, which is established not by a moral imperative, but rather by man's own "moral attitude."

Schiller calls a person who lives in this state of grace a "beautiful soul"; the latter expresses herself through grace. The beautiful soul is able to obey reason "with joy," and not "discard it like a burden." At the same time, she has made moral law her second nature and therefore follows moral law as if it were a sensuous drive. As one who has achieved "mastery of instinct," this person is in "accord with [her]self." For Schiller, the beautiful soul is an ideal of human harmony, which presents the natural "happy contingency" of duty and inclination.[20] This is the harmony between the demand of the senses and the demand of moral law, and this harmony (and the beautiful soul as such) expresses herself through grace. In other words, grace is the key to understanding Schiller's proposal of harmony, for grace is directly related to beauty (beautiful) and eventually to virtue. Grace is a "kind of moveable beauty," and beauty "exercises its appeal" through grace. Schiller warns that grace is not a pure nature, but it charms us because it is spontaneous and seemingly effortless. This is an "imprint of our moral personality,"[21] which appears naturally, and as such it has moral significance without having the form of moral imperative. Yet what delights us when we are in the presence of grace is the harmony of inclination and duty that we are able to achieve in graceful actions. Balance between these two (often conflicting) motivations is the key to achieving grace, and the closer one comes to attaining that balance, the fuller one's moral life becomes.

Schiller, however, acknowledges that circumstances sometimes make that balance impossible and achieving the harmony unmanageable. Yet this, he claims, creates an opportunity for man's "moral greatness" that he himself associates with dignity, which is "the expression of a noble disposition of mind."[22] The person then must defend her dignity by disregarding her sensuous needs and make a moral decision. Like grace, dignity is achieved through finding balance between nature and freedom. However, it is "the physical conditions of (man's) very existence" that confound his efforts to be dignified. Because man is a natural creature, he has bodily needs which ail him from birth and cannot, at any point, deny feeling their effects. Man, however, is more than a beast. Whereas an animal must follow its instincts in every circumstance, man has reason and thus the ability to choose whether to do so. For instance, if the animal is hungry, it cannot choose not to eat, yet a human can purposely starve himself, should he decide to. Similarly, the animal's response to pain is guided purely by its instinct, while humans can resist the force of instinct and act otherwise. Schiller believed that this "mastery of instinct by moral force is *freedom of mind*, and *dignity* is the name of its epiphany."[23]

Although Schiller never states it explicitly, he gives every indication that one acts with dignity in cases of tragedy.[24] This is best exhibited in his example of a person who physically displays dignity. He describes an individual who, for whatever reason, is experiencing painful emotion. While certain aspects of his body reflect his suffering, others do not. His muscles are cramped, but his brow is not burrowed; his chest is swollen, yet his eyes are not tearing. This "composure" in the midst of pain "proves the existence and influence of a force which is independent of suffering," and "becomes the demonstration of intelligence in man and the expression of his moral freedom."[25] It is this force that defines dignity. Man chooses to express dignity, but this choice can only be made when he is put in a position that forces him to subdue virulent and overwhelming emotions. Schiller made it clear that dignity has to do only with the form of emotion, not the content. Dignity is a response, not a stimulus.

Despite the differences in their nature and function, both grace and dignity proceed from freedom. Schiller's primary distinction between the two qualities is that "grace lies in the freedom of willful movements; dignity in mastery over unwillful movements."[26] This seems to present a problem if grace and dignity are supposed to coexist. To say conscious freedom and conscious subjugation can exist simultaneously within the same subject appears to be a contradiction. Yet Schiller believes that the two complement one another, and to show how this was possible he introduces the concepts of love and respect.

Grace produces love, while dignity begets respect. Love is the attraction to an object that occurs when reason is satisfied in sensuousness, which happens when it encounters that which is graceful. Respect comes from the one who acknowledges the tension between inclination and the moral law, and who then comes into contact with a dignified person. Yet no man can claim to be dignified if he lacks grace. Similarly, grace cannot exist without dignity.

Schiller thus insists that only the person in whom grace and dignity are united manifests the complete expression of humanity,[27] which is for him "to be a moral creature."[28] By making grace and dignity a focus of his discussion, Schiller thus reveals the foundation of moral character, providing insight into what it means to be virtuous. For him, virtue is associated with grace and beauty, which introduce an aesthetic dimension into morality. Opposing the reductive conception of moral agency he detects in deontological (duty-driven) ethics, he does not just simply expand the domain of moral motivation to include the sensuous but insists on the harmony of the two motivational forces.[29] He attempts to achieve this harmony by delineating aesthetic experience as the most genuine path toward the true inner self.

However, it seems that in "On Grace and Dignity," Schiller's project of achieving a harmonious state of moral motivation remains largely incomplete. Despite showing that the "beautiful soul" as an ideal of a true harmony between the dictate of the senses and the command of moral law which expresses herself through grace, Schiller does not provide a clear path toward becoming graceful, although the implication appears to be that grace begets grace.

Schiller's explication of grace shows that he believes that physical appearances will ultimately betray intention, and thus that there is no need to constantly concern oneself with one's own or other's underlying motivations.[30]

In "On Grace and Dignity," Schiller openly objects to Kant's conception of moral agency, which underplays the role of inclination in moral action. However, Schiller has not yet departed from Kant's rational moral psychology. This is the path that he pursues in his *Letters on the Aesthetic Education of Man*, where he argues that Kant's moral theory can be put into practice only once it touches the domain of the "heart" and "feeling." Some Kant scholars believe that Schiller's insistence on the necessity of the involvement of "heart" and "feeling" "introduces what is effectively an empiricist model of psychology."[31] I would suggest that the moral psychology that Schiller initiates in his *Aesthetic Letters* is not strictly rational or empirical. The model that emerges here is rooted in the harmony of rationality and sensuality, which is achieved, in his view, only through the incorporation of aesthetics into ethics and its conception of the aesthetic as the core of the ethical.

## 3  *Letters on the Aesthetic Education of Man*

There are several similarities between "On Grace and Dignity" and the *Aesthetic Letters*, which leads some scholars to assign the same goals to these two works. However, if one interprets the *Aesthetic Letters* as expounding upon and providing a foundation for the concepts of grace and harmony associated with the beautiful soul—and thus explaining the aesthetic component of morality—formulated in the earlier essay, Schiller's reasoning becomes much clearer.

Schiller grows confident that if man is to act in a moral way, he must first be internally harmonious.[32] This internal harmony creates a moral creature which can then act as a functioning citizen of a stable society.[33] As Schiller eloquently states,

> Once man is inwardly at one with himself, he will be able to preserve his individuality, however much he may universalize his conduct, and the state will be merely the interpreter of his own finest instinct, a clearer formulation of his own sense of what is right.[34]

Of course, this raises the question as to what is the exact nature of internal moral harmony. This is the question Schiller seeks to answer in his *Aesthetic Letters*.[35] Schiller's primary concern here is the development of man toward the free and truly moral individual. For him, man's surroundings, especially the art produced by a genuinely human culture, is what facilitates the realization of man's moral sensibilities. However, the individual has to come to terms with his own limitations before he can develop an accurate view of reality.

According to Schiller, man's nature is fractured into two opposing "forces" or drives, which he also calls "impulses": the *sense drive* and the *form drive*. The sense drive is linked to man's physical existence, and its focus is on man's finite being and his needs in the present. The form drive proceeds from man's rational nature, and its intent is to find meaning in the world around him by "bring[ing] harmony into the diversity of his manifestations."[36] This drive is responsible for the establishment of universal laws that explain the purpose of man's existence, and it seeks a consistent set of principles that govern the actions taken by man. An individual dominated by this drive may become so ensconced in the realm of thought that he may resist action until he finds a justification for it.

Schiller acknowledges that the different orientation of these two drives could make it appear as if they are destined to eternal opposition, fighting within man and forcing him to decide which he will grant credence. However,

Schiller suggests that when a man experiences both these drives in balance, a new drive can awaken. He calls it "the play impulse" or "the play drive." That is, the drive that ultimately puts man on the path toward true and genuine freedom. Holding the first two drives in harmony, the play drive "frees humans of the domination of each" by reconciling the demand of reason with the interests of the senses.[37]

How does this play drive arise? According to Schiller, this is achieved in the contemplation of that which is *beautiful*. Beauty can be the object of the play drive precisely because it is neither solely a matter of life—which is the object of the sense drive—nor of "shape" or form—which comprises the object of the form drive. Instead, it is an object of both, a combination which Schiller deemed "living shape" or "living form." The true "living form," however, is an ideal, which could never be attained in reality. Yet throughout history man has attempted to produce living form, with varying degrees of success. According to Schiller the culture that had come closest to achieving this ideal was the Greeks.

Greek art not only represented both what man is and what man should be, but it also struck that balance in a way no culture since has managed to replicate. Thus, Schiller concluded that beauty is the eternal pursuit of man and that the path toward that goal is just as essential as the goal itself. Furthermore, he claimed that "it is only through beauty that man makes his way to freedom" and that if man is ever to solve the problems of morality in practice "he will have to approach it through the problem of the aesthetic."[38]

In the *Aesthetic Letters*, Schiller continues attacking Kant's rigorous rational morality that largely suppresses the role of the sensuous in human moral life. Yet, contrary to "On Grace and Dignity," where a critical component of his project of ethics dominates over a constructive one, in *Aesthetic Letters* he comes up with a plausible solution to Kant's challenge by introducing a new—aesthetic—model of ethics.

Here he argues that the reconciliation of man's double nature is achieved by aesthetic production and reception. The goal is to educate the emotions and sensuous impulses of man, in order to bring them into harmony with reason and eventually elevate man to morality. In this way, man must pass through "the aesthetic," moving from the mere physical "state of brute nature," where man is still almost entirely constrained by the sense drive and thus determined by his selfish, infantile emotions, to the rational (moral) state, where the formal drive takes over and man becomes enthralled by the world of thought. Schiller emphasizes the crucial role of "the aesthetic condition" where man "shakes off" the power of the physical, control of which he obtains only in the "moral state." He explains that overcoming the physical and sensuous is possible only through contemplation.

Beauty is that which is to be contemplated. Beautiful objects allow man to discover his ability to contemplate and access his formal drive. Schiller explains that beautiful objects can put man in the state in which he realizes his highest potential. Thus, beauty can finally serve its true purpose and guide man toward complete humanity, for "it is at once a state of our being and an activity we perform."[39]

Those who are familiar with Kant's aesthetics will recognize echoes of his aesthetic ideas in Schiller's own view of aesthetic experience. Indeed, in the *Critique of the Power of Judgment*,[40] Kant offers a well-elaborated conception of aesthetic judgment that assigns a central role to the experience of the beautiful. While Kant denies that art and beauty can give us any knowledge of things at all and that aesthetic judgment is able to educate us in any conventional way,[41] he does recognize that aesthetic experience could be helpful in enhancing our sensory understanding of abstract concepts such as God and love. Such comprehension is possible through the imagination achieved during free play. Furthermore, Kant insists that in the process of synthesizing rationality and sense with nature and freedom, it becomes possible, and even gratifying, for us to grasp certain concepts that cannot be fully understood by purely intellectual means. However, Schiller, who clearly borrows several of Kant's aesthetic ideas, including the notion of our sensuous and rational sides coming together in play during the contemplation of beauty, is unsatisfied with Kant's treatment of beauty and the role he assigns to aesthetic experience.[42] Contrary to Kant, Schiller argues that it is chiefly through aesthetic experience that man gains awareness of higher concepts, both beautiful and moral, thus transforming himself into a harmonious individual able to live a virtuous life.

Attempting to clarify the nature of aesthetic judgment, Schiller relies on Kant's distinction between theoretical and practical reason. While theoretical reason is a faculty that allows one to gain knowledge, practical reason is associated with our ability to act. Similar to moral judgment, aesthetic judgment is for Schiller a product of practical reason, whose primary principle is freedom. In his theory, such properties as proportionality, symmetry, balance, harmony, and so on do not produce beauty. They are rather characteristics of the beautiful. Beauty is not something established by the sensuous perfection of an object. Instead, beauty is the freedom with which an object's sensuous perfection is expressed. As Schiller puts it, "[b]eauty is nothing less than freedom in appearance."[43] What Schiller means by this is that, in the case of beauty, freedom is actually appearing, becoming evident, and manifesting itself. Beauty is the real experience of freedom encountered through perceptions. Thus, building on the Kantian conception of freedom, Schiller constructs his own, "antimetaphysical theory" of aesthetic freedom. Seeking "an objective aesthetic"[44] and rejecting the "perfection-aesthetics" of Baumgarten and Mendelssohn, Schiller reveals the full significance of beauty,[45] which is for him more than just an aesthetic ideal. In his ethics, beauty induces a state of mind, which is truly free, that is, free from emotional, logical, and moral constraints, including external motivations and the externally imposed demands of moral duty.

By acknowledging the existence of not only moral but also aesthetic freedom, he is able to provide a complete account of moral action. He insists that "a free action is a beautiful action" and that "the highest perfection of character in a person is moral beauty brought about by the fact that *duty has become its nature.*"[46] Although Schiller's deduction of beauty in the "Kallias Letters" has some argumentative flaws, his claim that aesthetic judgment belongs to the realm of practical rather than theoretical reason provides the necessary framework for his project to overcome the divide between the moral and aesthetic that he pursues in the *Aesthetic Letters*.[47] In addition, his convincing insistence on the objective character of beauty offers a tenable alternative to Kant's subjectivist account of aesthetic experience.[48]

The significance of aesthetics that Schiller so powerfully demonstrates in the *Aesthetic Letters* is thus defined by its function. It restores "the harmony of man," allowing him fully exercise his own volition. Sensuous man, then, must become "aesthetic" man and learn to appreciate his sensuality in order to be moral. This transformation is not something that happens instantly and by chance, and Schiller suggests that this process continues throughout an entire human life.

A human being who reaches the state of harmony is for Schiller a "beautiful soul." Furthermore, since only such a person is truly free, durable political and moral freedom can only be attained by deliberately fostering such an aesthetic education of man's emotions and inclinations among the population. This is the way of man's cultivation toward humanity, the ideal of *Bildung* central to the neo-humanist tradition of German Romanticism.[49] Yet the exact process of achieving a completed humanity is one that even Schiller admits has no fully discernible pathway. He goes as far as to say that man decides to explore the aesthetic "on the wings of fancy." What is clear, however, is that the one essential component of man's cultivation is *beauty*. Hence, the primary task of education is to subject "to laws of beauty" all spheres of human behavior. Man must encounter and acknowledge beauty if he is to ever have a hope of establishing a lasting society, for, according to Schiller, "it may be his needs that drive man into society, and reason that implants within him the principles of social behavior, but beauty alone can confer upon him a social character."[50]

The *Aesthetic Letters* undoubtedly aid in the interpretation of Schiller's view of a harmonious soul. Whereas "On Grace and Dignity" describes the concept of grace in detail, one of the essays' greatest shortcomings is that it left open the question of how one actually becomes graceful. If the *Aesthetic Letters* are seen as further explicating grace, then the harmonizing of inclination and duty can be seen as the resolution of the conflict between nature and intellect, sensuousness and reason. Further, if beauty is the final product of grace and dignity working concurrently within man's soul, then it becomes clear that man's recognition of what he could become when he views that which is unencumbered by the natural state of conflict is what initiates his journey toward the beautiful soul. The concept of dignity is also easily understood, since grace must sometimes be kept from returning to the sensuousness of which it is at least in part a product. And the notion that the sense drive reconciles with the formal drive, which is analogous to reason itself, at least to some degree helps dispel the concern that to be graceful is also to ignore any consideration of reason and thought.

## 4 Conclusion

Schiller's critical response to Kant involves an important shift in the understanding of the role of aesthetic experience in ethics as well as in the shaping of moral character. While Schiller acknowledges Kant's contributions to both ethics and aesthetics and also borrows some of his predecessor's ideas, he presents a new vision of the relationship between beauty and morality which eventually leads to a unique ethical theory that goes beyond Kant's own. In an attempt to correct the priority Kantian ethics gives to reason and moral duty and its devaluation of the role of human nature's sensuous side, Schiller introduces a significantly new conception of moral agency, which he understands as the harmonious interplay of sense and reason. This harmony, he argues, is possible only through the contemplation of beauty, a powerful aesthetic experience that is central to the transformation of the human being into a virtuous individual. Through this experience, humans do not learn facts and scientific information about the external world but gain an appreciation of beauty that eventually stimulates and fosters their development toward morality, both internally and externally. Furthermore, Schiller argues that aesthetic experience coupled with an active engagement with the beautiful through (aesthetic) education leads to the realization of morality.

This thesis about the relationship between the aesthetic and moral realms is not new and was put forward by Kant and some thinkers before him. Similarly, the idea that aesthetic education may serve as a means for realizing the principles of morality and man's freedom at both individual and social levels is largely in line with corresponding assertions found in Kant's writings, where he discusses a possible pedagogical link between aesthetics and ethics.[51]

However, in his *Aesthetic Letters*, Schiller presents one more argument that often escapes the scholars' attention. Not only does he insist on the ethical significance of aesthetic experience, but he points to the aesthetic experience as the *realm* of the realization of morality and human emancipation. He claims that it is the aesthetic experience and its organization within social and interpersonal relations which allows us to realize morality and establish a free society. In other words, aesthetic experience becomes a main focus here, while both morality and the principle of the free society are formulated in aesthetic terms.

This is a new, radical thesis that clearly goes beyond the relations between aesthetics and ethics suggested by Kant. Schiller changes the very approach to morality. He proposes "aesthetic morality," which is supposed to exist in a free society that abides neither by norms and principles externally forced on individuals nor by ethical, moral maxims determined rationally that present themselves to the individual as a "duty," but rather a society that operates as a system of unmediated aesthetic interrelations among its members.

Schiller's philosophical legacy thus lies not just in stressing the significance of aesthetic experience in development toward ethicality, but rather in proposing morality (what is morally ideal) in aesthetic terms. He argues for an ethics whose very core is a notion of aesthetic experience that becomes a unique practice of freedom and thus an essential component of morality itself. In this sense, the aesthetic experience is not an alternative to ethical experience, but its very foundation, something that allows the cultivation of morality within the social realm.

# Notes

1. See, for example, Frederick Beiser, *Schiller as Philosopher: A Re-Examination* (Oxford: Oxford University Press, 2005); Stephen Houlgate, "Schiller and the Dance of Beauty," *Inquiry*, 51(1), 2008; David Schindler, "An Aesthetics of Freedom: Friedrich Schiller's Breakthrough Beyond Subjectivism," *Yearbook of Irish Philosophical Society* 2008; Anne M. Baxley, "Pleasure, Freedom and Grace: Schiller's 'Completion' of Kant's Ethics," *Inquiry*, 51(1), 2008; Baxley,

"The Aesthetics of Morality: Schiller's Critique of Kantian Rationalism," *Philosophy Compass*, 5(12), 2010.
2. Jeffrey A. Gauthier, "Schiller's Critique of Kant's Moral Psychology: Reconciling Practical Reason and an Ethics of Virtue," *Canadian Journal of Philosophy*, 27(4), 1997; Sabine Roehr, "Freedom and Autonomy in Schiller," *Journal of the History of Ideas*, 64(1), 2003; Katerina Deligiorgi, "Grace as Guide to Morals? Schiller's Aesthetic Turn in Ethics," *History of Philosophy Quarterly*, 23(1), 2006; Deligiorgi, "Schiller's 'Philosophical Letters': Naturalizing Spirit to Moralise Nature," *Philosophical Readings*, 2013(5); Baxley, "Pleasure, Freedom and Grace: Schiller's 'Completion' of Kant's Ethics," *op. cit.*; Baxley, "The Aesthetics of Morality: Schiller's Critique of Kantian Rationalism," *op. cit.*; Zvi Tauber, "Aesthetic Education for Morality: Schiller and Kant," *The Journal of Aesthetic Education*, 40 (3), 2006.
3. Beiser, *Schiller as Philosopher: A Re-Examination*, *op. cit.*
4. Ibid., 81, 178.
5. Immanuel Kant, *Groundwork of the Metaphysics of Morals*, in *Practical Philosophy*, translated and edited by Mary J. Gregor (Cambridge: Cambridge University Press, 1996), Ak 4:394–397.
6. Ibid., *Ak* 4:398.
7. Ibid., *Ak* 4:397.
8. See Daniel Dahlstrom, "The Ethical and Political Legacy of Aesthetics: Friedrich Schiller's 'Letters on the Aesthetic Education of Mankind'," in *Philosophical Legacies: Essays on the Thought of Kant, Hegel, and Their Contemporaries*, edited by Daniel O. Dahlstrom (Washington, DC: The Catholic University of America Press, 2008), 97.
9. "On Grace and Dignity" is the first major published work of Schiller where he decisively criticizes Kant's views of aesthetics and ethics. The essay appeared in July 1793, in the second issue of *New Thalia*.
10. Friedrich Schiller, "On Grace and Dignity," translated by William Wertz. In *Friedrich Schiller: Poet of Freedom*, volume II, edited by Helga Zepp-LaRouche (Washington D.C.: Schiller Institute, 1988), 363.
11. Ibid., 364.
12. Ibid., 363.
13. Ibid., 361.
14. Ibid., 361–362.
15. Deligiorgi, "Grace as Guide to Morals? Schiller's Aesthetic Turn in Ethics," *op. cit.*, 8.
16. Schiller, "On Grace and Dignity," *op. cit.*, 337.
17. Ibid., 340.
18. Ibid., 363.
19. Deligiorgi, "Grace as Guide to Morals? Schiller's Aesthetic Turn in Ethics," *op. cit.*, 13.
20. Beiser, *Schiller as Philosopher: A Re-Examination*, *op. cit.*, 100, 158.

21. Deligiorgi, "Grace as Guide to Morals? Schiller's Aesthetic Turn in Ethics," *op. cit.*, 11.
22. Schiller, "On Grace and Dignity," *op. cit.*, 370.
23. Ibid., 374.
24. Beiser, *Schiller as Philosopher: A Re-Examination*, *op. cit.*, 114.
25. Schiller, "On Grace and Dignity," *op. cit.*, 376.
26. Ibid., 377.
27. Ibid., 380.
28. Ibid., 364.
29. In his direct reply to Schiller's "On Grace and Dignity" in the second edition of *Religion Within the Boundaries of Mere Reason*, Kant praises Schiller's "masterful treatise" and claims that he and Schiller agree on the important principles and need only to clarify their positions to each other to avoid any misconception. However, Kant concedes that he sharply distinguishes between duty and grace as well as grace and dignity, because his overarching aim has been to emphasize the purity of duty, whose main characteristic is "unconditional necessitation, to which gracefulness stands in direct contradiction" (Immanuel Kant, 1998. *Religion within the Boundaries of Mere Reason and Other Writings*, translated and edited by Allen Wood and George de Giovanni (Cambridge: Cambridge University Press, 1998), Ak 6:23n; cf. Ak 6:48n).
30. Deligiorgi, "Grace as Guide to Morals? Schiller's Aesthetic Turn in Ethics," *op. cit.*, 16.
31. Ibid., 17.
32. Schiller's notion of the harmony of one's inner nature is reminiscent of Plato's conception of justice as an inner harmony that the thinker introduces in *Republic* and the discussion of the good life to find in *Philebus*.
33. At the time, political philosophers who adhered to the tradition of Rousseau and Locke were scrambling to make sense of the French Revolution. What was to be the culmination of enlightenment democracy had devolved into a bloody terror, and it was baffling to see every attempt at government fail. This led many, including Schiller, to ask the obvious question: how are men to form a stable, sustainable state? Schiller did not believe that a mere change of circumstances is the ultimate cure for social ills. Instead, he associated human progress with the internal harmony that man must find within himself.
34. Friedrich Schiller, *Letters on the Aesthetic Education of Man*, translated by Elizabeth M. Wilkinson and L. A. Willoughby. In *Essays*, edited by Walter Hinderer, Daniel O. Dahlstrom (New York: Continuum Publishing Company, 1993), 95.
35. Schiller's *Letters on the Aesthetic Education of Man* were originally written in 1793 in a correspondence between Schiller and a Danish Prince Friedrich Christian of Schleswig-Holstein-Augustenborg. The nine original letters burned in 1794 as a result of a fire at the Prince's palace. Almost two years

later, Schiller rewrote the whole set, nearly doubling their length, and published them by installments in *Die Horen*, a journal he founded and edited.
36. Schiller, *Letters on the Aesthetic Education of Man, op. cit.*, 126.
37. Ibid., 127.
38. Ibid., 90.
39. Schiller quoted in Steven Martinson, *Harmonious Tensions: The Writings of Friedrich Schiller* (Newark: University of Delaware Press, 1996), 187. Patrick Murray defines Schiller's goal in almost the same terms, claiming that Schiller saw a "need for a means of powerful moral education which will develop man's capacity for feeling, and reform his sensuous life, rather than directly assail his intellect with moral precepts" (Patrick T. Murray, *The Development of German Aesthetic Theory from Kant to Schiller: A Philosophical Commentary on Schiller's Aesthetic Education of Man (1795)* (Lewiston: Edwin Mellen Press, 1994), 68).
40. See Immanuel Kant, *Critique of the Power of Judgment*, translated by Paul Guyer and Eric Matthews, edited by Paul Guyer (Cambridge: Cambridge University Press, 2000), *Ak* 5:203 ff. (Book 1: Analytic of the Beautiful).
41. According to Kant, knowledge is based on a correspondence between concept and experience. Yet since aesthetic judgment is not associated with any concept, it cannot teach us anything, at least not in the same way as any judgment produced through purely intellectual activity (Kant, *Critique of the Power of Judgement, op. cit., Ak* 5:191, 227–228, 233). For a more detailed discussion of Kant's theory of aesthetic judgment (judgment of taste) see Paul Guyer, *Kant and the Claims of Taste* (Cambridge/New York: Cambridge University Press, 1997).
42. Schiller finds as ungrounded Kant's claim that there could be no objective principle of beauty as well as Kant's insistence that aesthetic experience should be associated with subjective feeling of pleasure, rather than with any property of the object itself. In his view, the subjective-rational theory of beauty developed by Kant, while correctly distinguishing between the logical and the beautiful, "misses fully the concept of beauty" by emphasizing its non-objective character. Schiller, recognizing the need to give reasons for aesthetic judgment, begins relating the latter to objective qualities. In the "Kallias Letters," he proposed a new sensuous-objective theory of beauty, which would largely overcome Kant's own. See Friedrich Schiller, "Kallias or Concerning Beauty: Letters to Gottfried Körner," translated by Stefan Bird-Polan, in *Classic and Romantic German Aesthetics*, edited by J. M. Bernstein (Cambridge: Cambridge University Press, 2003).
43. Ibid., 152.
44. Beiser, *Schiller as Philosopher: A Re-Examination, op. cit.*, 5.
45. Ibid., 60.
46. Schiller, "Kallias or Concerning Beauty: Letters to Gottfried Körner," *op. cit.*, 159.

47. Ibid.
48. Schindler, "An Aesthetics of Freedom: Friedrich Schiller's Breakthrough Beyond Subjectivism," *op. cit.*, 85ff.
49. Frederick Beiser, *The Romantic Imperative: The Concept of Early German Romanticism* (Cambridge, MA: Harvard University Press, 2003), 88–105. See also Marina F. Bykova, "Ludwig Feuerbach and the Humanistic Tradition of Bildung," *Philosophie und Pädagogik der Zukunft. Die Brüder Ludwig und Friedrich Feuerbach im Dialog* (Münster-New York: Waxmann, 2018), 171–172, 184.
50. Schiller, *Letters on the Aesthetic Education of Man*, *op. cit.*, 176.
51. See, for example, Kant, *Critique of the Power of Judgement*, *op. cit.*, *Ak* 5:351–354, cf. ibid., *Ak* 5: 355–356. On linking Schiller's pedagogical concept to this particular argument in *Critique of Judgment*, see David Pugh, *Dialectic of Love: Platonism in Schiller's Aesthetics* (Montreal/Kingston: McGill-Queen's University Press, 1996), 289.

# 9

# Johann Gottfried Herder: Misunderstood Romantic?

Johannes Schmidt

> *Try, like a blind philosopher were to imagine the world!*
> —Herder, "Zum Sinn des Gefühls", in Johann Gottfried Herder, *Werke*, ed. Wolfgang Proß, 3 in 4 vols. (Munich, Vienna: Hanser, 1984–2002), here vol. 2, 244 [in the following as HWP]; all translations are mine unless specifically noted)

During his lifetime Johann Gottfried Herder (1744–1803) resisted categorization, and to this day attempts to compartmentalize him are bound to fail. Yet this did not discourage thinkers from appropriating his broad and wide-reaching thoughts. His name was often ignored, and his ideas were misused to advance personal agendas that had very little in common with his own. Early on Herder's writings were the cause for divergent and conflicting interpretations. And especially during the last decade of his life and then more so in the decades after his death Herder became the source for an increasing polarization in an attempt to proclaim him as either a poet of Weimar Classicism or as a romantic thinker. Additionally due to his opposition to Kantian critical philosophy, he was soon denied the status of a philosopher; whereas his religious-theological writings and activities were separated from his more naturalistic, secular sounding ideas, despite the fact that he thought of them as inseparable. It comes thus as no surprise that Herder has been proclaimed a

J. Schmidt (✉)
Clemson University, Clemson, SC, USA
e-mail: schmidj@clemson.edu

© The Author(s) 2020
E. Millán Brusslan (ed.), *The Palgrave Handbook of German Romantic Philosophy*, Palgrave Handbooks in German Idealism, https://doi.org/10.1007/978-3-030-53567-4_9

representative of German Enlightenment, a strong propagator of German Classicism, as well as "the harbinger" of Romanticism:

> Perceived by his contemporaries as a man of universal interests and talents, an innovator of a new historical thinking, the leading theoretical voice of the Sturm und Drang, and even the harbinger of the emerging Romantic movement in Germany, Herder also had a reputation as one of the most controversial representatives of his time.[1]

The characterization of Herder as the heralder of Romanticism begins with Goethe's reception depicting him in opposite to Johann Christoph Gottsched.[2] In fact, it was Herder's groundbreaking *Treatise On the Origin of Language* (*Abhandlung über den Ursprung der Sprache*, 1772)[3] that influenced a number of authors closely associated with Romanticism: Friedrich Schlegel, Novalis, Hölderlin, and Wilhelm von Humboldt. Language, of course, was one of the major romantic topoi. Yet it is Schelling and not Herder who clads the question of language in romantic-idealistic lingo and locates its origin within a mystical and esoteric space which is empirically inaccessible. Factual data, however, were always of immense importance for Herder.[4]

Herder's thoughts on education and his many proposals to reform general schooling also found numerous admirers among the early German Romantics: certainly Jean Paul, who understood himself as Herder's student, but also Friedrich Schleiermacher, who merged Herder's ideas of humanity, *Bildung*, and religion, and Friedrich Schlegel, who furthered Herder's notion of self-education as divine striving for godlikeness. One can also not deny Herder's influence on Hölderlin, Schelling, and Hegel, as exemplified in *The Oldest Systematic Program of German Idealism* (*Ältesten Systemprogramm des deutschen Idealismus*, 1796/1797).[5] However the connections between Herder and the early German Romantics have not been thoroughly studied. Although Herder's importance for German Romanticism has been mentioned and recognized for specific fields and authors, a general influence on the movement is, in my opinion, highly problematic, as we will see in the following. Herder, as I see it, is too much of an independent and at times arduous thinker that very few could truly be seen as his successors. Herder's ideas were appropriated (often superficially) when favorable and self-serving opportunities arose, whereas his name and his philosophy—often too contentious to be disclosed—were more than often omitted intentionally.[6]

## 1 Between Enlightenment, Classicism, and Romanticism: Herder as an Outsider

Herder is mentioned in one breath with Weimar Classicism, next to no less than Goethe, Wieland, and Schiller.[7] Nevertheless Rüdiger Safranski declares Herder to be the "romantic starting point".[8] Let us consider the opening of Herder's unpublished but crucially influential *Journal of my Voyage in the Year 1769* (*Journal meiner Reise im Jahr 1769*):

> On June 3 I left Riga and on June 5 put to sea—to go I knew not where. Actually a large proportion of the events of our life depends on the vicissitudes of chance. By chance I came to Riga, by chance I assumed my spiritual calling; and so also I got rid of my position, so also I went on my travels. I was not satisfied with myself as a member of society, either in the circle in which I moved or in my self-imposed exclusion from it.[9]

Safranski observes the text's influence on *storm and stress* and Romanticism, popularizing Herder in the following way: "Rocked by the gentle wind of the Baltic, [Herder] gave himself over to the storm of his own thoughts."[10] It is during this voyage that he conceptualizes all of his major ideas. In due course he came to realize that everything is history; not only human experience, but also nature and God's appearance in the world. It is then in Strasbourg between September 1770 and April 1771, while recovering from a painful but failed eye operation, when he met Goethe for the first time, and conversed frequently with a cycle of literary newcomers such as Jakob Michael Reinhold Lenz, Johann Heinrich Jung-Stilling, and Heinrich Leopold Wagner. His influence on these young poets cannot not be underestimated and it is fair to say that because of his influence on *storm and stress* he indirectly also had some influence on German Romanticism. Still it is the young Goethe he impressed the most. With his *Journal*—which Herder most likely shared in his conversations in Strasbourg—Herder awakened in the latter and other poets "the idea of a new German national literature that no longer attempted to imitate foreign paradigms, but rather drew from [their] own sources and traditions"[11].

It is certainly not an overstatement to claim that the Herder of the early 1770s inspired an entire generation of writers to remember their own (German) experiences, emotions, and explorations, to search for their own national ideas of "genius", "nature", and "originality", and to express it by means of their own national language. Rainer Wisbert concludes that, in his colloquies with Goethe, Herder altogether advanced the national culture of Germany (arguably more than any other single thinker).[12] Again Wisbert connects Herder to German Romanticism: "Herder became qua his esteem for mythology and folk tales not only the precursor of the *storm and stress* movement, but also the trailblazer of romanticism."[13] Herder begins in Strasbourg to collect folk songs and convinces others of the importance of this project. It prompted an entire generation of romantics to begin their own collections of folk tales, songs, and sagas. Herder's political thought of the early 1770s was also of importance to his contemporaries. He recognized the political and social function of *Bildung* (education) to unite the ideas of the Enlightenment with the advancement of cultures and nationalities: "Presumably, Herder's political thoughts affected also Wilhelm von Humboldt, Friedrich Schleiermacher, and the other reformers oriented toward the idea of [national and political] *Bildung*." In the *Journal* Herder furthermore develops plans for his philosophy of and need for a universal history, his aesthetical thoughts—to which we will return later—as well as his philosophy of language. Finally, as Wisbert continues, Herder must also be seen as the progenitor of modern geography: Alexander von Humboldt and Carl Ritter sought, just as Herder suggested and demanded already in 1769, to connect a holistic-organic understanding of nature with modern research methods.[14]

However this does not mean we can assume a direct influence on Romanticism as a movement. Hans Adler cautiously comments that Herder was "one of the 'instigators' [*Anreger*] of Romanticism in Germany, who, however, regarded it unfavorably".[15] James Porter notes that the Ossian poems by James Macpherson were made "popular to a reading public in Germany"[16] through Herder's and Goethe's comments, and the poems in turn "continued to shape the course of Romanticism in the arts throughout the eighteenth and nineteenth centuries". Specifically Hölderlin, Klopstock, and Lenz were "deeply affected by Ossian", and the Grimms "felt the power of the poems".[17] And Christina Weiler remarks: "Herder is a predecessor of the Romantics. As a student of Kant he functions as a bridge between Enlightenment philosophy and Romanticism." But she also notes that "Herder differs from the Romantics", observing considerable differences, for example between Herder's and Novalis's use of language: "Novalis understands language as a self-referential system and believes in the power of metaphorical language to romanticize the world."[18] Herder on the other hand saw the development of language as historically inseparable from nature. Weiler thus places Herder closer to Schelling's philosophy of nature.[19] Herder was indeed often skeptical of the ideas brought forth by the movement and distanced himself from individual romantic thinkers. Consequently very few of the early German Romantics spoke favorably of the Herder of the 1780s and 1790s. It was the Herder of *storm and stress* that caught their attention.

In order to illustrate the difficulty of placing Herder within the context of Romanticism further, two additional points must be made. First, when thinking about the Romanticism-Classicism distinction, the latter with roots in Greco-Roman antiquity and the former in medieval poetry and art,[20] we are confronted with serious problems of categorizing Herder's interest in literature, poetry, and the arts. He was as much an admirer of antiquity as of "German" culture, promoting medieval art together with Goethe in *Of German Style and Art* (*Von deutscher Art und Kunst*, 1773). Here Goethe advances the idea that German culture thrived during the middle ages. Goethe's *Architecture* essay, which was edited by Herder, goes as far as equating German with what Goethe and Herder call "Gothic" art; its epitome represented by the Strasbourg cathedral. Yet, at the same time, Herder admired Hebrew poetry, praised ancient Greek and Roman artists, poets and orators, the sculptures of Niobe, Laocoön, Apollo, and Hercules, as well as the renaissance artist Raphael.[21] Then again, he needs to be credited with reigniting an interest in Shakespeare. In fact his essay on Shakespeare appeared alongside his *Ossian* essay and Goethe's Architecture essay in *Of German Style and Art*.[22] The second important point concerns Herder's staunch opposition to medieval, papal Catholicism that he rejected wholeheartedly. In his *Ideas for a Philosophy of History of Mankind* (*Ideen der Geschichte der Philosophie der Menschheit*, 1784–1791) he holds the papacy responsible for some particularly atrocious violence: "With a butchery of Jews began the [crusaders] their holy campaign", writes Herder, "they slew 12,000 [Jews] in some cities along the Rheine, in Hungary [Jews] were slaughtered and drowned like animals."[23] Additionally Christianity nurtured "false enthusiasm" by means of "malicious abuse", and behind "the fullness of Christian zeal hid scurrilous pride, bootlicking haughtiness, shameful lust, stupid foolishness"; the Christians of medieval times "flocked together under bold fraudsters here, and there they adulated the worst souls of tyrannical, opulent rulers as if the latters were to bring the kingdom of God to the world once they built churches for them or deified them with gifts".[24] Then again Herder's idea of *Humanität* is deeply grounded in scripture, in fact Herder sees in the Genesis and in other parts of the Hebrew bible the origins of poetry, culture, and beginning of European civilization.

The reason for the early German Romantics' interest in the early Herder was his shaping of the *storm and stress* movement and in the later Herder for his opposition to Kantian (critical) philosophy (notably after Kant's devastating review of Herder's *Ideas*). His ensuing feud with his former teacher from Königsberg defined him as an un-philosophical thinker. In contrast the admiration he earned came mostly from his contributions to a variety of fields outside of philosophy. Thus not only did Kant's followers question his status as a philosopher, but so did the opponents of Kantian critical philosophy who wanted to see Herder as their ally against cold rationality. Opponents of Kant either criticized Herder for not developing his own systematic critical theory, or rejected the notion of philosophy in principle and thus—sympathizing with Herder's Kant critique—painted him as an un-philosophical writer. At the same time, it is important to note that Herder's firm rejection of Kant's critical theory was not followed by the early German Romantics. More often, the ideas of both thinkers were critically reviewed, broadened, and adopted. Friedrich Schlegel's aesthetics, for example, is indebted to both Herder's historical and cultural differentiation and Kant's skepticism concerning the judgment of artistic beauty.[25] Fichte certainly did not reject Kant's philosophy, but rather implemented Kant's critical thinking consequently, and was able to unite the dichotomies of reason and sensibility, spontaneity and perception, freedom and necessity. But here again, Herder's influence must be acknowledged, for his sensualism, cognition theory, and comments on nature certainly proved fruitful for Fichte. In turn Novalis in his interpretation of Fichte then follows Kant by insisting on two sources of experience (thought and feeling). He is effectively expanding upon transcendental idealism as the only branch of philosophy to explore rationality and its limitations. But like many of his contemporary romantic thinkers, Novalis's ideas are neither Fichtean nor Kantian in nature, they must be seen as emerging in response to and between both thinkers. And here again, I am convinced that further studies are warranted to show how Herder's contributions manifest themselves in Novalis's philosophy as well as in the writings of the other early German Romantics.[26]

Yet this appropriation on both sides is antagonistic to the core of his thinking. It became part of a tendency during the later part of the eighteenth and then most notably so during the nineteenth century to use different movements and schools of art, including literature, to create a cultural hierarchy within and among national arts. For the nineteenth century it may be argued that the cultural distinctions morphed into political-ideological differentiation against other nations, but also within the societal and political order. Maybe not verbatim, but at least conceptually, Herder rejected external evaluations of social groups, political leaders, and national cultures. Furthermore a qualitative-hierarchical distinction of art and literature was for Herder inappropriate, if not even outright misguided. Art for Herder was an expression of the collective potential of a society, a manifestation of its ability to advance humanity at all levels, individually, societal, national, and in the end always for the entirety of the human race.

Finally Herder's place within Classicism or Romanticism largely depends on what specific movement or school of thought is being considered, or with whom Herder is specifically being aligned, be it with the pre-critical Kant and Hamann during his studies in Königsberg and his first appointment in Riga, or with Goethe and Schiller[27] later in Weimar. Wilfried Malsch determines that Herder is closer to the notion of classicism as a historical category than to the epochal definition of a romantic movement or school.[28] Herder was the outsider, even as a member of a classicist group of artists who happened to be in Weimar and who were more or less associated with Goethe and Schiller.[29] Hence Peter Sprengel sees Herder completely isolated from German Classicism, for Herder, together with Friedrich Heinrich Jacobi and Jean Paul, formed an "anti-classicist opposition".[30] Ironically it is an opposition against an understanding and theory of art that was shaped by the members of the Weimar circle with Herder's contributions as an integral part: an appreciation of art that he himself triggered in Strasbourg. Arguably Herder's literary contacts with Goethe and Schiller were much more multifaceted and abundant than his connection with Romanticism.[31] There were certainly admirers of Herder on all fronts, and he may have influenced specific aspects of the writings of individual thinkers. Thus any influence would have to be investigated individually; for each case the relationship will be different and depends always on the chosen context.

A different approach will be undertaken here. By examining Herder's ideas on sculpture the chapter will exemplify their appeal, if not to all of Romanticism, then to some thinkers and artists closely associated with the movement, such as the Schlegels, Jean Paul, and Schelling.[32] Section 4 of this chapter will serve as an example for why German Romantics enthusiastically embraced Herder, and thus incorporated his writings selectively into their own; but also how they, at the same time, deliberately and purposefully disregarded some of his major thoughts and carefully concealed possible influences. First, however, I will provide some background on Herder's anthropology and his notion of *Humanität* (humanity) in order to provide some necessary context which will also shed light on the importance of his ideas for his contemporaries.

## 2   Herder's Concept of *Humanität* and the Human Being as Middle Point

With only the exception of a short period of time[33] Herder was a clergyman and preacher all his life. Still his broad interests render him a generalist in the best sense. His own literary activities (poetry, translations)—while notable—are dwarfed by his other writings; his literary criticism, poetics, and aesthetics expanded the boundaries at the time: anthropology, theology, religious writings and published sermons, epistemology, pedagogical reflections permeated all of his work. But the overarching concept for Herder was his notion of *Humanität* and the human being as the middle being. The title of a central chapter of Herder's *Ideas* reads: "The human being is a middle creature among the animals of the earth".[34] Here Herder summarizes his insights that one and the same anlage—quite in the biological sense—for a common organization is constitutive for all living beings: "Now it is undeniable that for all variousness [*Verschiedenheit*] of Earth's living beings it seems that everywhere a certain uniformity of organization and almost certainly *One main shape* prevails."[35] Yet human beings are indefinitely more refined than animals. Hence the organization of all beings is realized in each individual human being. This makes the human being the middle being, or that being that collected all features of all beings. Herder calls this the "analog of One Organization", or "the great analogy of nature".[36] This allows him to study the human being by studying all of nature and also to understand nature by understanding ourselves. The result of this reciprocal study of human beings and nature accumulate in an all-encompassing concept he calls *Humanität*.[37] *Humanität* "is the purpose of the human-nature [der Menschen-Natur]".[38]

Humanity is of course a principal idea of German classicism. Mankind is to pursue "the full and free self-realization of the individual made possible through the achievements of an enlightened age".[39] At the same time Samson Knoll emphasizes that Herder's concept of *Humanität* differs from the general idea of humanity since it "encompassed the essence of being human in living reality—the human potential latent in all individuals and in all societies".[40] With "*Humanität*" Herder articulates a new concept in order to find a unifying principle capable of grasping all human experiences in all diverse and distinct historical and cultural contexts. At the same time *Humanität* is as inexplicable as human existence, and Herder refuses to define the term systematically and comprehensively. Still his notion of *Humanität* implies a movement from a collective understanding of mankind to a particularized accentuation of human actuality in the world. This individuality—that in its particularity embodies also the plurality of all human beings—extends to a political imperative. It finds its specific expression in Herder's irrevocable call for peace and social justice; "his passionate denunciations of despotism, war, slavery and colonialism".[41] At the core of *Humanität* lies freedom, for without (political) freedom neither the individual nor the society as a whole can fulfill its potential. Ernest Menze and Karl Menges see this as Herder's "groundbreaking efforts toward a synthesis of the concepts of humanity [mankind] and nationality, the universal and the particular".[42]

The universality of Herder's concept of *Humanität* must indeed have been highly attractive to German Romanticism. Herder's *Humanität* applies equally to the entire human race as well as to each individual human being. This is for Herder no dualistic impossibility; he was able to think that which is particular and that which is universal together at the same time. The actuality of all human beings resides in the shape of any human being; thus it is a concept that describes humanity as ultimately self-similar. From a romantic point of view this raises the individual above society. It allows for a cultural relativism that evaluates and judges nations based on their specific geographic, climatic, and situational conditions and not on doctrinaire Eurocentric values.[43] And Adler explains: "To differentiate, for [Herder], was to preserve the occurrence of individuality, variety, diversity."[44] At the same time Herder's notion of *Humanität* rejects a simplified telos that defines human beings' purpose as the fulfillment of history. Instead as a specific end point his concept of *Humanität* suggests a purpose that individually can be reached time and again. This purpose has to be continuously pursued. For Herder the termination of history cannot be the fulfillment of the human race, since it would suggest an unthinkable end of humanity.

Herder's understanding of the complexity of the human being and humanity may be best illustrated with two of his many recurring analogies.[45] In *This Too a Philosophy of History of the Education of the Human Race* (*Auch eine Philosophie der Geschichte zur Bildung der Menschheit*, 1774), the image of flowing water illustrates history's ever-flowing progress and development: "Observe this river [*Strom*] being awash on and on: how it sprung up from a little source, grows, breaks away there, starts (anew) here, ever meanders, and bores further and deeper—remains however always *water*! *river*! drop always only drop, until it plunges into the sea—what if it were the same with the human race?"[46] Herder imagines the human race as an assembly of the countless individuals that all together make up humanity. He augments this analogy with another one: "Or observe that growing *tree*!, that upwards-striving human being!, it must pass through diverse *ages of life*!, all revealingly in *progress*!, a *striving* one for the other in *continuity*!" Herder accepts the idea that human history could be seen in analogy with a single human being's three stages of development: childhood, adulthood, and old age. But between the ages "there are apparent *resting places, revolutions*", and "*changes*", Herder continues. Each age has its own center, its own source of happiness, "[h]owever it is still an eternal striving". Yet the development of a human being progresses in the context of history: "No one is in his age *alone*, one builds on the *proceeding one*, this becomes nothing but the foundation of the *future* [...]." Herder understands this analogy as a universal principle: "Just like the human being appears at the age's diverse stages: just like that time changes everything. The entire human race—indeed the lifeless world itself—every nation, and every family have one law of change [...]."[47] According to Herder, our recollection of our own past—having passed through the different life ages oneself—allows for an understanding of human history. Based on our experience we can feel ourselves into other historical times, places, and situations.

Herder's notion of *Humanität* places the human being at the center of the world. But Herder does not fall back to a Christian, pre-Copernican understanding of the cosmos. In line with the Copernican turn he rejects the belief of the earth's physical center in the universe. For Herder the human being is the intellectual and spiritual middle point. Middle here means "always between" but never central to all things. Herder's anthropology is consequently not anti-Copernican or anthropocentric. It appears rather as a language problem. Herder blends religious imagery with a Newtonian sun-planet cosmology:

> [The human being] is born God's image, middle point of this disposition. As little as proud Saturn has freedom wherever he wants to follow its own straight orbit through all heavens: he ought to be steered by the Sun, and [Saturn] became only that which he is as a consequence of this primitive higher law of the Sun's plan. Likewise is only the human being what he is, as a consequence of higher grace, *ex speciali gratia* [*out of unknown favor*] of the creator, who made him what he is; and thus he has to cling to the creator and his higher positive command. [The human being] has to follow whatever orbit *the* sun requires of him; he can neither learn from himself nor from the snake this orbit which in fact he has to follow *freely*, for *freedom* is middle point of his existence, the grounding of his higher disposition, the Godlikeness that he is able to speak [...].[48]

Herder here uses the analogy of the solar system to illustrate that everything has a center and that the universe just like human experience is based on attraction and repulsion. In terms of the human universe he makes clear that the Sun (God) is the center and that human beings (like planets) cannot deviate from their paths (orbits) around it. To assume a place outside of the universe, or to contemplate the world from the viewpoint of the Sun (God), would not only be impossible but also constitute hubris. Herder unambiguously rejects human's aspiration to be God-like, he objects to an "isolated natural right" for human beings that would otherwise "permit Godlikeness".[49] At the same time Herder situates humans' unique perspective against the insignificance of the individual confronted with a vast universe: the world can only be observed by intelligent beings, thus Herder sees the human being as the only being capable of recognizing the cosmos and its vastness.

Herder's notion of *Humanität* has practical and theoretical consequences, especially for his philosophy of history. The historian as much as the reader of history is required to recognize human action in the past as an emerging image of *Humanität* (either as advancement or regression). In analogy to biological metamorphosis, history is a "becoming of form" ("Gestaltwerdung").[50] Theoretically this means that the writer of history has to construct an all-embracing portrayal of the world created from a multiplicity of forms. Numerous observations of complex historical connections must result in an "observe-all"—the "Allanblick"[51]—to produce "education, specific gestalt, innate existence"[52] for the reader. The external form of the human being (as an image of God) and the inner organization (in analogy to nature) provide the original image or antetype for *Humanität*. Humans as historical beings collect the "finest essence" of all possible human genera ("aller Gattungen").[53] Adler explains further: "Herder adopts an empiricist approach, based on the epistemological axiom that any cognition be derived from experience."[54] Herder rejects philosophical abstractions—since they are only appropriate for philosophers and not the common people (*Volk*)[55]—thus the writing of history is to become literary and artistic production.[56] Herder's notion of *Humanität* morphs from a linguistic into an aesthetic problem, since history or the "Allanblick" must be rendered for the reader as sense-making poetry or fiction of the multiplicity of past, present, and future human experiences. Just like the analogy of the life ages is a poetic depiction of history, any aspect of human experience must be presented in an intelligible story. Story here is to be taken literally; the writing of history transforms itself into story telling.[57] Any cultural expression becomes an artistic representation of history, *Humanität*, and human purpose. And it is especially so in poetry, but also in plastic art, where history as mythology emerges.[58] If art and all other cultural production is the fictionalization of reality then different kinds of reality can be experienced, even those realities that lie outside the direct experience of the individual's surroundings (such as past or future events). Through stories and folk songs, in music (odes) or with sculptures, the artist always creates a representation of human experience, which in turn can then be shared with and felt by other human beings as a sensing of *Humanität*.

## 3 Herder on Sculpture and Poetry

The *Sculpture* essay presents an example how Herder's notion of *Humanität* and his anthropology play out on paper. Yet it will also clarify the thesis of this chapter that Herder has to be seen as an outsider, but that his ideas were, at least partly, attractive to German Romantics. The essay *Sculpture. Some Observation on Shape and Form from Pygmalion's Dream* (*Plastik. Einige Wahrnehmungen über Form und Gestalt aus Pygmalions bildendem Traume*, 1770/1778[59]) is strikingly close to some ideas and motives of Romanticism. Lothar Müller mentions explicitly its influence on August Wilhelm Schlegel's romantic art theory, as it was Herder's essay that helped Schlegel to formulate (in his Jena lectures) that painting too must focus on the single figure of a human being that can be viewed from all sides. As we will see, Herder suggested to a certain degree that a painting could become a sculpture in action when experienced by the imagining observer. Yet Schlegel contests that painting can only survive as a modern art form by distancing itself from sculpture.[60]

Herder's main argument in the *Sculpture* essay concerns in fact the difference between painting and sculpture; a difference that for him is grounded in two ways humans perceive physical objects. Herder identifies sight for the perception of surface, color, and appearance (both "Fläche" and "Gesicht" translate as face, yet the former also means surface), and touch for the sensing of body, form, and depth of an object. The artistic achievements epitomized by statues of antipquity—Herder names Apollo Belvedere, Niobe, the Laocoön group, Hercules, Venus, and the sleeping Hermaphrodite among others—cannot be heightened by contemporary artists; they reached a perfection which cannot be repeated or imitated, Herder insists. Yet what makes the *Sculpture* essay particularly interesting for the early German Romantics is that Herder does not argue from a classicist's position (despite the fact that Winckelmann's influence is conspicuous).[61] Herder is able to productively weigh in on contemporary discussions on art and cognition to formulate his own position.[62] He, unlike Winckelmann, is less interested in the imitation of Greek art, but instead wishes to discuss Greek art in historical terms as a bygone pinnacle of artistic expression. In *Sculpture* he is drawn to ancient art through a contemporary experience. This requires nothing less than a refined art experience and historical understanding of Greek culture from the perspective of an enlightened, educated observer. Thus the essay calls for art education as much as it presents a directive for understanding touch (feelings) and sight as distinct senses. Ultimately Herder approves of all forms of artistic expression not only the visual arts. It is thus not surprising that the *Sculpture* essay originated after the publication of *Fragments on Recent German Literature* (*Fragmente über die neuere deutsche Literatur*, 1766, 1767); about the same time (between 1768 and 1770) Herder began collecting and discussing folk tales and folk songs. As much as classical Greek statues were fitting for the culture of ancient Athens, original German folk songs represent the origins of German culture.

Herder's stay in Strasbourg ended a journey that was supposed to bring him to Italy, to those works of art he is discussing in his essay. Forced to abandon his plans, Herder visited Versailles and the sculpture gallery in Mannheim where he had his first great experience of classical sculpture. Regardless, he suspended his work on the *Sculpture* essay (the manuscript breaks off in section three of a total of eventually five parts), but continued to occupy himself with the topic.[63] Furthermore around 1774 Herder begins with the essay *On the Cognition and Sensation of the Human Soul* (*Vom Erkennen und Empfinden der menschlichen Seele*); and it is clear that as early as 1777 he decides to publish revised versions of the two essays. Herder himself calls the essay *On the Cognition* the twin publication of the *Sculpture* essay.[64] Not only because he worked on both essays during the same period, but because they complement and mirrored each other. The *Sculpture* essay may be seen more as a commentary on art history—with a specific emphasis on the Laocoön group—whereas *On the Cognition* presents a refined version of Herder's theory of perception and cognition. In 1778 he sends both essays to his publisher Hartknoch, only three months apart.

Lastly the *Sculpture* essay is in part based on ideas developed in his "Fourth Critical Forest" which was written between 1768 and 1770 but never published during Herder's lifetime. Even though the 1770 draft of the *Sculpture* essay was not published either, and the 1778 version was published only anonymously, it influenced and animated Goethe, Novalis, August Wilhelm Schlegel, and Wilhelm von Humboldt to develop their own approaches to aesthetic questions. There is no question that the importance of Herder's *Sculpture* essay must be recognized alongside Winckelmann's, *Thoughts on the Imitation of Greek Works in Painting and Sculpture* (*Gedanken über die Nachahmung der griechischen Werke in der Malerei und Bildhauerkunst*, 1755, 1756) and Lessing's *Laocoon* (1766).

The prominence of feeling in Herder's aesthetic epistemology makes some of his thoughts highly attractive for opponents of unconditional rationality.[65] Or, as Rachel Zuckert writes: "It falsifies [...] our mode of existence [...] to understand ourselves solely, [...] or at our most valuable, as 'cold' philosophical, detached, disinterested spectators."[66] Herder associates "cold" philosophizing with seeing and the eye: "Sight is the most artificial, most philosophical of the senses."[67] He follows here the contemporary (Enlightenment) notion of seeing as the sense organ for rational understanding, but reverses the hierarchy of the senses. He declares that the eye sees everything, yet perceives only "a surface" and "diverse visible objects ranged *alongside one another*".[68] Sight does not see the truth, it is picture only, a mere representation: "Sight gives us *dreams*, touch gives us *truth*."[69]

In accordance with his analogy of the life ages, Herder thus considers the sense of touch as the first sense, the predominant and only sense for small children to explore the world:

> Go into a nursery and see how the young child who is constantly gathering experience reaches out, grasping, lifting, weighing, touching, and measuring things with both hand and foot, thereby acquiring securely and confidently the most difficult but also the most primary and necessary concepts, such as body, shape, size, space, and distance.[70]

And in the earlier version of *Sculpture*, which presents a more radical critique of sight, Herder writes: "Ideas by means of touch: [the toddler's] small hands are [to the child] the first organs of the science of the world and the study of nature."[71] The toddler's exploration of the world teaches more "than ten thousand years of mere gawking and verbal explanations".[72] Of course the child will later combine the sense of touch with the other senses, but only after objects have been laboriously grasped by touch do they become familiar. At that point we no longer need to touch the object, we seem to grasp its familiarity immediately at first sight, explains Herder. But "we believe to feel where we only see", because the sight is amended by the recollection of formerly touched objects. Yet this becomes a deception, since quickly "we no longer feel, even where we should not see but [only] feel".[73]

His *Sculpture* essay seems to read as a dismissal of painting. But we have to be careful as Herder rather promotes a theory of perception that takes all the senses into account. In an earlier fragment, entitled "Principles of Philosophy", Herder developed a hierarchical idea of the senses: "I strive to have thoughts: this becomes feeling; thoughts after another: [this becomes] hearing; thoughts next to another: [this becomes] sight [Gesicht]."[74] In *Sculpture* he refines this concept, each sense is applicable to a specific domain. About touch, sight, and hearing he says:

> Things *alongside one another* constitute a *surface*. Things *in succession* in their purest and simplest form constitute *sounds*. Things *in depth* are *bodies* or *forms*. Thus we have distinct senses for surfaces, sounds, and forms; and when it comes to beauty, we have three senses relating to three different *genres of beauty* that must be distinguished from one another just as we distinguish *surfaces, sounds, and bodies*. If there exist forms of art for which the proper domain is to be found in one of these species of beauty, then we know both their internal and external fields of application: on the one hand, *surfaces, sounds, and bodies*; on the other, *sight, hearing, and touch*. These limits or boundaries are imposed by *Nature* herself.[75]

The different forms of art and genres appertain to different forms of representation. But sculpture reached its highest expression in ancient Greek statues portraying mythology. Herder consequently presents a case for contemporary painting, specifically landscape and historical paintings:

> The spacious prospect I see before me, with all its various aspects, what is it other than a picture, a surface? The sky that lowers to the ground and the wood that merges into it, the broad expanse of the field and the water close by, the bank of the river, the motif that dominates the entire picture—these are but an image, a panel, a continuum of things placed alongside one another.[76]

Painting is also superior in depicting action. According to Herder painting presents an appearance and semblance of numerous objects, it is thus better equipped to portray an illusion and vision—the "Allanblick"—of the world:

> [Painting with colors, lights, and shades], the divine instrument of light, the *enchanted world of action*, albeit no matter how varied its interpretation by each new master, remains something *enduring* in painting. [Drawing], as long as it is not made to depend on the fixity of sculpture, borrowing from what is dead, is a magic panel also in *transformation*, a sea of waves, stories and figures, each of which replaces the other.[77]

Rather than recreate Greek sculptures Herder envisions a new approach to art that combines the aesthetic experience of sculpture with that of painting. Just like a statue is not supposed to be touched physically—it is only to be touched in one's imagination—paintings should not only be seen but also touched imaginatively: "Nothing must be merely *observed* and treated as if it were a surface; it must be touched by the gentle fingers of our inner sense and by our harmonious feeling of sympathy, as if it came from the hands of the creator."[78]

The experience of plastic art is thus instructive for both the observer and the painter to allow the depicted scene to come alive. Thus sculpture is still of utmost importance for Herder. The Greek statue presents the human being as the middle point. Here the observer learns imaginary touch. We experience (in our imagination) the body of a Greek statue as being alive, as being beautiful, as truth. And in order to experience the beauty of a work of art it has to become body, this is also true for other forms of art, because "everything has to become body in order to be beautiful for feelings; namely human body. […] A beautiful body is sensual idea of our perfection: it thus reminds the soul of the picture it retained when it created its body",[79] records Herder in his early notes to the *Sculpture* essay. The aesthetic experience of a statue allows us to understand our own soul and feeling. This is analogous to one human being approaching another human being in their desire to understand the emotion of the other. This is ultimately the connection between touch and emotions: "[Through touch] the human soul had more effect, and thought, judged and deduced, missed, and invented more than the greatest man of world wisdom [*der größte Weltweise*] had an effect in a lifetime of abstractions, than the most diligent natural scientist in half a century of experiments!"[80]

In the third part of the *Sculpture* essay Herder describes human activity in analogy to approaching a statue:

> Let us approach a statue as if enveloped in holy darkness, as if we shall discover there for the first time the simplest concept and the meaning of form, the richest, noblest, and most beautiful form of the human body. The greater the simplicity with which we commence this task, the more the mute image will speak to us. [...] The hand and fingers of our inner spirit must bring to life the sacred, energy-laden form that has come from the hands of the creator [*Bildner*] and is pervaded by his breath.[81]

Herder describes the foundation for the individual to understand *Humanität*, to understand one's own purpose. Embracing the human body with imaginary touch and poetic sight constructs the body of the other in one's own soul. This allows one to feel the other, encompass the other, understand the other. By creatively giving body to objects outside our own body, we are able to feel them. Feeling another being's body is to encompass the inner shape of the other. The inner shape in turn is a reflection of its internal physiognomy: it is the shape of the soul. And thus if we grasp the meaning of inner perfection we truly understand beauty and truth.[82] Herder writes:

> Here once again it is of no avail to study letters or the clouds. It is necessary to *exist* and to *feel*: one must be human and blindly register the way in which the soul works *in us* in response to every character, every situation, and every passion—and then touch. This is the clear language of nature itself, perceptible to all peoples, even to those who are blind or deaf.[83]

But Herder emerges not simply as an idealist, which would place him closer to Classicism. He recognizes that in art the deformation of a body, the "ravaged, ugly, or distorted form", and the "contorted figures"[84] can also be sensed—may even be always present—hence ugliness also serves as an object for artistic expression. Herder acknowledges this and relates it to human experience: "*Love* produces the true ideal, the angel; *hate* the devil in us, who rest with us [*der in uns liegt*], and whom we ourselves are often unable to see or find."[85]

Herder additionally discusses pleasure aroused by art, alluding even to sexual sensuality:

> [...] alongside our universal feeling as human beings there is also a specific feeling proper to our sex. Even in our most elevated judgments concerning what it is to be human, this cannot be denied. A man, be he a poet or a ruler, a creator of men or of statues, must always feel as a man, and a woman must always feel as a woman.[86]

Because any aesthetic experience is a sensual experience, it can in fact be a pleasurable experience, as Zuckert contextualizes: "Thus, against the consensus of his time, Herder suggests that touch (or imagined touch) can afford pleasures from the representation of complex order in an object, the artistic skill manifested therein, and (to some degree) mimetic accuracy."[87] Anticipating the criticism that aesthetic experience must not be pleasurable but rather a disinterested and disassociated experience, Herder contrarily suggests that we are interested in the body of a sculpture, because our soul is embodied in a human body, thus aesthetically experiencing a statue reveals something about our own body.[88]

In the *Sculpture* essay Herder contests the notion that aesthetic experience (and this includes any sympathy to other objects, animals, and human beings) must lead to abstract understanding. Even if it is imaginative, all human experience ought to retain a feeling of the other's body. The artistic expression never raises itself above any human experience—as it could be argued for Classicism's perception of art. In fact art is always connected to the human body and vice versa. Art is a reflection of human expression, yet it is the human experience of art that renders art human. This allows for an understanding of another human being, since understanding of, that is to feel oneself into, art becomes the precondition for any understanding of artistic and thus for any human expression. Wolfgang Proß in his commentary on the *Sculpture* essay reflects, "the idea of a soul becomes in the first place only conceivable by means of the appearance of the physical form [of the body]".[89] This may sound like a tautology; we use our awareness of our own body to imaginatively embrace the body of a work of art, which in turn helps us to understand our own body and thus our own soul. Yet this is not truly circular thinking, since during the process of experiencing art we gain a deeper understanding of beauty through art, thus a better understanding of *Humanität*.

Herder in essence redefines the relationship of art and the human form, to the extent that neither is above the other, as it might be true for Classicism where the statue embodies the perfect external appearance of human ideals. Conversely, true human form can only be recognized by another human being through the act of feeling (or sympathetic touch) of one's inner soul: "The more a part of the body signifies what it *should* signify, the more beautiful it is; and only inner *sympathy, that is feeling and transposition of our entire human self* into the figure we touch, is the true teacher and instrument of beauty."[90]

## 4   Herder's Questionable Influence on German Romanticism

Art was for Herder always only a means to educate mankind's capacity for *Humanität*. This is where Herder and Goethe diverge and where the former has to be seen closer to Romanticism. In the last decade of his life, Herder became more and more isolated, not only because of the insurmountable differences with Schiller (and hence also with Goethe), but because of his passionate rejection of Kantian critical philosophy. Very few supporters remained after the publication of his the *Metacritique of the Critique of Pure Reason* (1799), which—together with *On Religion, Doctrines, and Traditions* (*Von Religion, Lehrmeinungen und Gebräuchen*, 1798[91]) and *Kalligone* (1800)—marks his most forceful and polemic response to Kant. Christoph Martin Wieland was one of the few offering a positive review—possibly also in opposition to the Kantian Karl Leonhard Reinhold, his son-in-law—while Friedrich Gottlieb Klopstock limited himself to a supportive letter to Herder.[92] Others who expressed various levels of support included the Duke of Sachsen Weimar, the "German Anacreon" Johann Wilhelm Ludwig Gleim, and the poet and translator Karl Ludwig von Knebel. We also find some support from the early German Romantics. Friedrich Schlegel, for example, mentions Herder favorably together with Goethe in a letter to his brother in 1793.[93] Besides the Schlegels and Wilhelm von Humboldt, it is most of all Jean Paul who emerges as the strongest supporter of Herder with one of the most prominent and arguably most effective defenses of the *Metakritik*. While his reading of Herder is not entirely uncritical or exuberantly enthusiastic, he does not reject Herder's dismissal of Kantian philosophy.

## 9 Johann Gottfried Herder: Misunderstood Romantic?

In 1796, Jean Paul visits Herder in Weimar, and between 1798 and 1800 numerous conversations took place. This must have been important for both; encouraging for the isolated Herder—his friendship with Goethe was more than difficult after Schiller arrived in Weimar—and for Jean Paul because of the reassurance he received from Herder who was not known for habitual praise. However, one cannot help but notice that Jean Paul found in Herder a welcome ally against Kant—and by extension against Schiller, as Wulf Koepke explains: "While Jean Paul, in his definition of Romanticism, polemicizes openly against Schiller, he corrects Herder's perception of modern poetry and the modern era by and large."[94] Jean Paul's criticism draws on Herder, but at the same time, his writings (here specifically the *Introduction to Aesthetics, Vorschule der Ästhetik*, 1804) prove "how much Jean Paul ekes out [erkämpft] his proprietary right against Herder as well".[95] Maybe more importantly Jean Paul also realizes his own uniqueness during this stay in Weimar. It was here where he recognizes the contrast between him and the great German poets of that time, namely Goethe, Wieland, Herder, but also Schiller. Although he criticizes the latter, he nonetheless admires all of them to various degrees. I would add that Jean Paul here also appreciates the difference between him and the previous generation of writers who were more deeply rooted in the Enlightenment and Weimar Classicism. Still there is a deeper connection between Herder and Jean Paul than their mutual opposition to Kant. Both agree that *Humanität* can only be recognized as the individual purpose within the subjective experience of and the individual existence in the world.[96]

It is without question that Herder's wide-spanning works and wide-ranging ideas had much to offer to German Romanticism. However only in a few cases can a direct influence be discerned. These cases are limited to a few, Friedrich and August Wilhelm Schlegel, Wilhelm von Humboldt, and Jean Paul with the possible additions of Schelling, Hölderlin, and arguably Novalis and Brentano.[97] Besides Jean Paul none of these German Romantics emphasized or admitted being strongly influenced by Herder. While Herder's ideas may have been seen as advantageous for their own writings, his name was not seen as the best line of defense, neither against Kantian rationality nor against Weimar Classicism. Herder may be the unique blind philosopher he envisioned in the 1760s, his uniqueness becomes especially prominent in the attempt to establish Herder's influence on German Romanticism. The early German Romantics certainly did not think about the world in Herderian ways.

## Notes

1. Johann Gottfried Herder, *Selected Early Works 1764–1767. Addresses, Essays, and Drafts; Fragment on Recent German Literature*, ed. Ernest A. Menze, Karl Menges (University Park, PA: Pennsylvania State University Press, 1992), 3.
2. Gottsched in turn has been called the harbinger of German Classicism, see P. M. Mitchell's study *Johann Christoph Gottsched (1700–1766): Harbinger of German Classicism* (Columbia, SC: Camden House, 1995).
3. See Franz Vonessen, "Zwei Philosophien der Sprache: Von Hamann und Herder zu Schelling und Jacob Grimm", in: *Romantik* (2000): 105–118 (p. 105).
4. Ibid., 112. Vonessen however simplifies not only Herder's view, but also distorts Schelling's understanding of language in a highly polemic way; favoring a view of German Romanticism as a form of mysticism.
5. See Reiner Wisbert, "Pädagogik", in *Herder Handbuch*, eds. Stefan Greif, Marion Heinz, Heinrich Clairmont (Paderborn: Fink, 2016), 565–622 (p. 599).
6. Goethe's much overlooked *Shakespeare* essay may serve as an example here. Written over a period of several years and published in two parts in 1815 and 1826, respectively, "Shakespeare und kein Ende" must certainly be seen as Goethe's careful discussion not only of Shakespeare's works, but more than anything of Herder's original *Shakespeare* essay (1773). Both essays show the same starting point (the importance of Shakespeare's works for German literature). Goethe repeats a number of Herder's arguments (reading Shakespeare as literature and not drama), and the use of Herder's terms (like "world spirit", "occurrence" [*Begebenheit*], or the "husk and pit (of a fruit)" [*Schlaube und Kern*] analogy). However Goethe not once mentions Herder by name, while the essay's connection to Herder is obvious (see Peter J. Burgard, "Literary History and Historical Truth: Herder—'Shakespeare'—Goethe", in: *Johann Gottfried Herder: Academic Disciplines and the Pursuit of Knowledge*, ed. Wulf Koepke (Columbia: Camden House, 1996), 61–77). More generally, Herder's thoughts on language were frequently repeated throughout the nineteenth century, again often without any specific references to Herder. Kirstin Gjesdal mentions Herder's notion that no two poets use the same language, an idea repeated by Schleiermacher for example (cf. Kirstin Gjesdal, "Human Nature and Human Science. Herder and the Anthropological Turn in Hermeneutics", in: *Herder: Philosophy and Anthropology*, eds. Anik Waldow, Nigel DeSouza (Oxford: Oxford University Press, 2017): 166–184, p. 171n13). Herder scholarship has only just begun to investigate Herder's influence on the generation of philosophers who followed him; for example, Fichte, Hegel, Schleiermacher, Feuerbach, and others. Schelling belongs to those who were well aware of Herder's ideas, but decided not to mention him by name (see

Johannes Schmidt, "Naturphilosophie: Herder and Schelling?", in: *Herder as Challenge*, ed. Sabine Gross (Heidelberg: Synchron, 2010), 83–94.
7. Cf. Klaus Manger, "Herder im Weimarer Viergestirn", in *Herder und seine Wirkung. Herder and His Impact*, ed. Michael Maurer (Heidelberg: Synchron, 2014), 51–60.
8. Rüdiger Safranski, *Romanticism. A German Affair* (Evanston, IL: Northwestern University Press, 2014), 3. Safranski offers a popularizing view of German Romanticism that is at times problematic.
9. Johann Gottfried Herder, *Journal of my Voyage in the Year 1769*, trans., ed. John Francis Harrison (Diss.: Columbia University, 1953), 206.
10. Safranski (2014, 3).
11. Rainer Wisbert, "Wirkung", in: Johann Gottfried Herder, *Werke in zehn Bänden*, eds. Günter Arnold et al., 11 in 10 vols. (Frankfurt a. M.: Deutscher Klassiker Verlag, 1985–2000), here vol. 9/2, 883–889 (p. 885) [in the following as FHA].
12. This view finds its vicious culmination in the modernist Gellnerian (see Ernst Gellner, *Nations and Nationalism* (Ithaca: Cornell University Press, 1983)) understanding of Herder as a romantic nationalist with a direct line to National Socialism of the twentieth century (see for a summary and refutation of this view Dominic Eggel, Andre Liebich, Deborah Mancini-Griffoli, "Was Herder a Nationalist?", in: *The Review of Politics* 69,1 (Winter, 2007): 48–78).
13. Rainer Wisbert, "Wirkung", FHA 9/2, 883–889 (pp. 885–886).
14. Cf. ibid., 887 and 889.
15. Hans Adler, "Einführung. Denker der Mitte: Johann Gottfried Herder, 1744–1803", in *Monatshefte* 95,2: *Johann Gottfried Herder 1744–1803* (Summer, 2003): 161–170 (p. 161).
16. James Porter, "'Bring Me the Head of James Macpherson': The Execution of Ossian and the Wellsprings of Folkloristic Discourse", in: *The Journal of American Folklore* 114,454 (Autumn, 2001): 396–435 (p. 420).
17. Ibid., 396 and 397, respectively.
18. Christina Weiler, *The Romantic Roots of Cognitive Poetics: A Comparative Study of Poetic Metaphor in Herder, Novalis, Wordsworth, Coleridge, and Shelly* (Diss.: Purdue University, 2017), 224, 225.
19. See also Johannes Schmidt, "Naturphilosophie: Herder and Schelling?", in: *Herder as Challenge*, ed. Sabine Gross (Heidelberg: Synchron, 2010), 83–94.
20. See Wilfried Malsch, "Klassizismus, Klassik und Romantik der Goethezeit", in: *Deutsche Literatur zur Zeit der Klassik*, ed. Karl Otto Conrady (Stuttgart: Reclam, 1977), 381–408 (p. 385).
21. Cf. J. G. Herder, *Sculpture. Some Observation on Shape and Form from Pygmalion's Dream*, ed. and trans. by Jason Gaiger (Chicago, London: University of Chicago Press, 2002), 52, 53, and 82 [hereafter HSG]. Herder mentions Michelangelo only once and indifferently (ibid., 91), although

Michelangelo was also a sculptor, whereas Raphael's focus was on painting and architecture. Of the more recent artists, Herder mentions more than any other Hogarth, whom he discusses in ambiguous terms (see ibid., 64).

22. *Ossian* was a collection of Gaelic folk poetry by James Macpherson (1736–1796), a Scottish writer, poet, literary collector, and politician. Macpherson falsely claimed to have translated ancient Gaelic poems he discovered. Even after the poems' true origin was revealed, Herder continued to support the idea of an ancient origin (see generally on Herder's edition of *On German Style and* Art, and specifically on his *Ossian* reception, the commentary in FHA 2, 1106–1111, and 1111–1131).
23. FHA 6, 872.
24. FHA 6, 720.
25. See Hans Eichner, *Friedrich Schlegel* (New York: Twayne, 1970), 35–36.
26. For a discussion on the ambivalent position regarding Kant's critical theory by Fichte, Friedrich Schlegel, and Görres, specifically with respect to some of Kant's political ideas see John Pizer, "The German Response to Kant's Essay on Perpetual Peace: Herder Contra the Romantics", in: *Germanic Review* 82,4 (Fall 2007): 343–367. Here Pizer shows how Herder was both appropriated, however that at the same time Herder surpassed not only the ideas of the early German Romantics, but also argued for a greater level of freedom and a different form of democracy than Kant.
27. Herder's relationship with both, but especially with Schiller, was highly complex, difficult, to say the least, and sometimes outright hostile (see, e.g. Hans Adler, "Autonomie versus Anthropologie: Schiller und Herder", in: *Monatshefte* 97, 3 (Fall 2005): 408–416).
28. Cf. Wilfried Malsch, "Concepts of Romanticism Inside and Outside of German-Speaking Countries", in: *English and German Romanticism: Cross-Currents and Controversies*, ed. James Pipkin (Heidelberg: Winter, 1985), 91–109 (pp. 93–94 and p. 100).
29. It may be more appropriate to align Herder here with someone like Karl Philipp Moritz, whose thinking was also deeply grounded in the German Enlightenment, part of the storm and stress movement, but influenced likewise Weimar Classicisms and early Romanticism. I suspect an interesting connection between Moritz and Herder, specifically in regard to Moritz, "An Attempt to Unify All the Fine Arts and Sciences under the Concept of That Which Is Complete in Itself" (see Elliot Schreiber (intro., trans.), in: *PLMA* 127,1 (2012): 94–100).
30. Peter Sprengel, "Antiklassische Opposition. Herder—Jacobi—Jean Paul", in: *Europäische Romantik* 1 (1982): 249–272 (pp. 267–269).
31. For Herder's closer proximity to German Enlightenment see Michail Rudnizki, "Herder und die Romantik", in: *Herder-Kolloquium 1978: Referate und Diskussionsbeiträge*, ed. Walter Dietze (Weimar: Böhlau, 1980): 386–392, here 387.

32. It should be noted at the same time that Herder is often neglected when the emergence of romantic theory of art is discussed (e.g. Jean-Marie Schaeffer, "The Birth of the Speculative Theory of Art", in: *Southern Humanities Review* 33,4 (1999): 321–360).
33. From 1769 to 1771 during which Herder traveled and accompanied Prince Peter Friedrich Wilhelm of Holstein-Gottorp as private scholar. It was then that he met Gotthold Ephraim Lessing, Johann Joachim Christoph Bode; and later, between September 1770 and April 1771 in Strasbourg, one of the most notably encounters for the German history of ideas took place, when Herder and Johann Wolfgang Goethe engaged in several conversations ranging from Homer and Pindar to Shakespeare and folk poetry (see Hans Dietrich Irmscher, *Johann Gottfried Herder* (Stuttgart: Reclam, 2001), 22).
34. FHA 6, 72; see also Irmscher (2001, 129–131), Greif et al. (2016, 216–218).
35. FHA 6, 73.
36. FHA 6, 76 and 17, respectively.
37. I will continue to use the German term *Humanität* whenever referring specifically to Herder's concept; whereas I use the term "humanity" interchangeable to denote the plurality of all human beings, mankind, the human race, or in Herder's words "die Menschheit"; "der Mensch" I translate as "the (individual) human being", and "die Menschen" as "human beings".
38. FHA 6, 630.
39. Samson Knoll, "Herder's Concept of *Humanität*", in: *Johann Gottfried Herder: Innovator Through the Ages*, ed. Wulf Koepke, Samson Knoll (Bonn: Bouvier, 1982): 9–19 (p. 9).
40. Ibid., 9.
41. Ibid., 18.
42. Ernest Menze, Karl Menges, "Introduction", in: Herder (1992, 1–25, here p. 1).
43. See Sonia Sikka, *Herder on Humanity and Cultural Difference: Enlightened Relativism* (Cambridge: Cambridge University Press, 2011).
44. Hans Adler, "Herder's Concept of *Humanität*", in: *A Companion to the Works of Johann Gottfried Herder*, ed. Hans Adler, Wulf Koepke (Rochester, NY: Camden House, 2009): 93–116 (p. 98).
45. See Hans Dietrich Irmscher, "Der Vergleich im Denken Herders", in: *Johann Gottfried Herder: Academic Disciplines and the Pursuit of Knowledge*, ed. Wulf Koepke (Columbia, SC: Camden House, 1996), 78–97; and Irmscher, "Beobachtungen zur Funktion der Analogie im Denken Herders", in: *Deutsche Vierteljahrsschrift für Literaturwissenschaft und Geistesgeschichte* 55, 1 (1981): 64–97.
46. Johann Gottfried Herder, *This Too a Philosophy of History for the Foundation of Humanity*, in: Herder, *Philosophical Writings*, trans., ed. by Michael Forster (Cambridge: Cambridge University Press, 2002): 272–358 (p. 299), trans. altered (cf. FHA 4, 41).

47. Herder, "Von den Lebensaltern einer Sprache", in: FHA 1, 181.
48. Herder, "Über die dem Menschen angeborene Lüge", in: HWP 2, 729–730.
49. Ibid., 729.
50. See Irmscher (2001, 132).
51. Cf. Hans Adler, *Die Prägnanz des Dunklen. Gnoseologie—Ästhetik—Geschichtsphilosophie bei J. G. Herder* (Hamburg: Meiner, 1990), 170.
52. Herder, *Ideen*, in: FHA 6, 55.
53. See ibid., 64.
54. Adler (2009, 103).
55. See Herder's fragment "[How Philosophy Can Become More Universal and More Useful for the Benefit of the People]" ("[Wie die Philosophie zum Besten des Volkes allgemeiner und nützlicher werden kann]", 1766), in which he instructs his readers to "take note of the meaning of the word philosophy and understand by *Volk* all those who are not such philosophers" (Herder 2002, 7; trans. slightly altered).
56. Adler contrasts philosophical abstractions with holism which he attributes to Herder (see Adler, "Herders Holismus", in: *Herder Today. Contributions from the International Herder Conference, Nov. 5–7, 1987, Stanford, California* (Berlin, New York: de Gruyter, 1990), 31–45, especially, 43–44).
57. See on Herder's understanding of mythos and poetry Karl Menges, "Zeit als Raum: Herders 'Traum' vom Nutzen und Nachteil des Mythos für das Leben", in: Karl Menges (ed.): *Literatur und Geschichte: Festschrift für Wulf Koepke zum 70. Geburtstag* (Amsterdam, Atlanta: Rodopi, 1998: 97–110, especially, 104).
58. Cf. ibid., 102–103.
59. HWP 2, 408–542, and HSG. Herder suppresses the print of the first version, but it is reasonable to think that copies existed and were circulated, and also that Herder has discussed the content with his interlocutors in Strasbourg, cf. Gaiger's "Introduction" (HSG 1–28, pp. 4–5), and Proß's commentary (HWP 2, 984–985).
60. Lothar Müller, "Achsendrehung des Klassizismus. Die antiken Statuen und die Kategorie des "Plastischen" bei Friedrich und August Wilhelm Schlegel", in: *Der Europäer August Wilhelm Schlegel: romantischer Kulturtransfer—romantische Wissenswelten*, eds. York-Gothart Mix, Jochen Strobel (Berlin, New York: de Gruyter, 2010), 57–75, here, 69.
61. Additionally there are no significant "modernistic tendencies" noticeable; see Jürgen Brummack's commentary to the *Sculpture* essay, "Zur Struktur und Gehalt", in: FHA 4, 1006–1011, here 1006–1007.
62. While Herder's *Sculpture* essay is certainly a reaction to Lessing's *Laocoon* essay, it cannot be reduced to this. In fact the essay begins with comments on Diderot and is frequently interrupted by references to Condillac as well as to Winckelmann.

63. For a summary of the genesis of the two versions of *Sculpture* essay and numerous letters on the topic see Brummack, "Entstehung", in: FHA 4, 998–1002.
64. See ibid., especially 1002 and 1080–1081.
65. Herder's sensualism and his high regard and elevation of folk poetry inspired an entire generation of poets in Germany—if only through Goethe—but certainly Karoline von Günderrode, Hölderlin, Novalis, Bettina and Achim von Arnim, and Jacob and Wilhelm Grimm. It would be fruitful to inquiry into Schleiermacher's hermeneutic and how his understanding of religious feelings was influenced by Herder.
66. Rachel Zuckert, "Sculpture and Touch: Herder's Aesthetics of Sculpture", in *The Journal of Aesthetics and Art Criticism* 67, 3 (Summer, 2009): 285–299 (p. 294). On numerous occasions Herder rejects excessive rationality and criticizes the contemporary philosophy of the Enlightenment as "cold"; during the last decades of his life, Kant becomes the characteristic target of his disdain for reason as the only faculty for gaining knowledge (see, e.g. Herder, *Ursprungsschrift*, FHA 1, 786; cf. Herder, "James Beattie", in *Herders Sämmtliche Werke*, ed. Bernhard Suphan, vol. 5 (Berlin: Weidmann, 1891), 460; for Herder's Kant critique cf. Sonia Sikka, "Herder's Critique of Pure Reason", in: *The Review of Metaphysics* 61,1 (Sep., 2007): 31–50, p. 32).
67. HWP 2, 472; HSG 39.
68. Ibid., 35.
69. Ibid., 38.
70. Ibid., 37.
71. HWP 2, 408. Herder's critique of Enlightenment visualism is mostly aimed against the eighteenth century's overvaluation of sight and the reading eye, yet ultimately he sees all human senses as equivalent and not hierarchically ordered in terms of value. Each sense is particularly suited for specific tasks and environments and necessary at different states of human development. His references to the senses are context-dependent: in the *Sculpture* essay Herder emphasizes touch; in his writings on language, hearing and sound predominate; and he employs the help of taste metaphorically when discussing poetry. In contrast to thinkers like Friedrich Schlegel, Herder never fully developed his critical comments on seeing into a full critique of sight. We must understand Herder's thoughts on the matter more as a general theory of cognition, accordingly no specific theory of hearing and sound can be discerned in all of his writings. This is not to say that he did not comment on music or the importance of sound; in fact he was keenly aware of the emerging science of acoustic noise (sound), like Leonhard Euler's "Sciences on musical art" or Joseph Saveur's measurements of sound waves of string and percussion instruments. Building on, but also expanding beyond, the physical phenomenon of sound waves that can be mathematically measured, Herder understands tone or note [*Ton*] as a sound that is only recognized in the ear as

meaningful, or more apt, as beautiful. He evokes this comparison of sound and tone on several occasions (e.g. in the *Fourth Critical Forest*, in: FHA 2: 336–366 (cf. Herder, *Selected Writings on Aesthetics*, trans., ed. Gregory Moore (Princeton, Oxford: Princeton University Press, 2006), 235–256); for a detailed commentary, see Clémence Couturier-Heinrich, "'Der Innigste, der Tiefste der Sinne': Das Gehör in Herders Viertem Kritischen Wäldchen", in: *Herder: From Cognition to Cultural Science/Von der Erkenntnis zur Kulturwissenschaft*, ed. Beate Allert (Heidelberg: Synchron, 2016), 79–94).

72. HSG 37; trans. altered.
73. HWP 2, 410.
74. Herder, "Grundsätze der Philosophie", in: HWP 2, 54.
75. HSG 43.
76. HSG 36.
77. HSG 62, trans. altered.
78. HSG 81, trans. slightly altered.
79. HWP 2, 995.
80. HWP 2, 409.
81. HSG 65–66. Gaiger translates "Bildner" here with Creator in allusion to God, yet, in my opinion "Bildner" here only refers to a sculptor, the creator of a stature. While a religious reading is possible, Herder rejects the idea of a godlike artist.
82. HWP 2, 513.
83. HSG 79.
84. HSG 57 and 59, respectively.
85. HWP 2, 524, my trans., cf. HSG 86.
86. HSG 86.
87. Zuckert (2009, 292).
88. Cf. Zuckert (2009, 293–294).
89. HWP 2, 985.
90. HSG 78, trans. slightly modified.
91. In this fourth collection of the *Christian Writings* (*Christliche Schriften*, 1793–1798), Herder takes on Kant's notion of radical evil, as presented in *Religion within the Boundaries of Pure Reason* (*Die Religion innerhalb der Grenzen der bloßen Vernunft*, 1793). Herder's answer to Kant's philosophy of religion has yet not been thoroughly examined, especially its influence on Schelling and Schleiermacher.
92. See Irmscher's commentary "Wirkung" in FHA 8, 1140–1141; more detailed in Rudolf Haym's *Herder nach seinem Leben und seinen Werken*, vol. 2 (Berlin: Gaertner, 1885), 686–692, here also an overview of the negative responses.
93. See Lothar Pikulik, *Frühromantik. Epoche—Werk—Wirkung* (Munich: Beck, 1992), 16; see also Herder's influence on the formation of the term "romantic", ibid.: 73–79, here 77.

94. Wulf Koepke, "Jean Pauls Romantikkonzept und seinen Auseinandersetzung mit Schiller und Herder", in: *Perspektiven der Romantik*, ed. Reinhard Görisch (Bonn: Bouvier, 1987): 36–49 (p. 36).
95. Ibid., 40.
96. Cf. Götz Müller, "Jean Paul und Herder als Opponenten des transzendentalen Idealismus", in: *Jean Pauls Ästhetik und Naturphilosophie*, ed. Götz Müller (Tübingen: Niemeyer, 1983), 274–284, here 283–284.
97. For Humboldt see "Wirkung" by Rainer Wisbert, in: FHA 9/2, 887 und 889; for Novalis, while questionable, see Brummack, "Wirkung", in: FHA 4, 1012; for Schelling see Greif et al. (2016, 683–685); for Hölderlin see ibid., 649; and for Brentano see ibid., 647.

# 10

## Hermeneutics and Orientation: Retracing the 'Sciences of the Spirit' (*Geisteswissenschaften*) in the Education-Related Writings of Fichte, Schleiermacher and Novalis

John G. Moore

In light of the extensive but altogether indeterminate scholarship that has grown up around the topic of hermeneutics, it is tempting to modify Adorno's famous remark about philosophy and state summarily that hermeneutics lives on because the moment to realize it was missed.[1] Its moment was missed because its original impulse was diverted into a surrogate function it was never intended to fulfill—as an ontological constituent of Dasein's being-in-the-world in Heidegger; as an academic "stand-in and interpreter" for scientific research in Habermas; as an "abnormal" but altogether "edifying" literary agent in support of, what Rorty once called, "normal discourse"; as a psycho-social tool of dialogical understanding in Gadamer and, more recently, as the metaphysical intersection of modernity and Christianity in Lyotard.[2] Indeed, the "unlimited discussion"[3] that hermeneutics was supposed to conduct us toward became, along the way, something more akin to a meta-discussion about the transcendental pre-conditions for having any discussion at all, than a substantive dialogue on the meaning of selected texts in the critical context of, what Humboldt once called, the '*universitas litterarum*.' Ironically, then, it was the sad fate of romantic hermeneutics to be encountered chiefly in the

J. G. Moore (✉)
Lander University, Greenwood, SC, USA
e-mail: jmoore@lander.edu

© The Author(s) 2020
E. Millán Brusslan (ed.), *The Palgrave Handbook of German Romantic Philosophy*, Palgrave Handbooks in German Idealism, https://doi.org/10.1007/978-3-030-53567-4_10

work of authors who failed to treat hermeneutics itself hermeneutically, that is, in terms of its own originating context, and who, instead, thought it was possible to apply Schleiermacher's axiom about knowing an *author* better than he knew himself to knowing a *tradition* better than it knew itself, although, in this case, the tradition in question (viz., the early German Romantics) is made up almost entirely of missed appointments.

In what follows, I would like to suggest one way of re-approaching the subject of romantic hermeneutics by locating it in an historical project that brought together the most extreme antitheses of the era, and was, at one and the same time, both theoretical and concrete, both idealistic and practical, and both romantic and self-critical in its actual genesis, viz. the founding of the University of Berlin.[4] In this way, I hope to show how romantic hermeneutics was initially conceived in a far more delimited and modest way (also, eminently more useful) by its romantic theorizers than its more famous twentieth-century variants (e.g., hermeneutics as it functions in Heidegger and Gadamer),[5] and that, furthermore, much of the reason for its fragmentary character and incompleteness in such romantic authors as Schleiermacher is bound up with its systematic role in delimiting the dialogical space, necessarily open and underdetermined, for what has come to seem a rather fractious and ultimately inefficient enterprise: namely, the college of arts and sciences in the modern research university as the proper place for the progressive and infinite approximation in spoken and written discourse to *something like the truth*.

## 1 The Founding of the University of Berlin: Applied Romanticism? Or Inoperative Idealism?

It is already well documented how influential the University of Berlin was for the development of the modern, research university. Its autonomous stance vis-à-vis the state apparatus; its adoption of the research paradigm as the overarching purpose for every university activity; its orientation toward the pursuit of advanced study and the awarding of advanced degrees (in particular, its designation of the terminal degree in the arts and sciences as the "Ph.D." degree);[6] its division of the professoriate into three distinct levels (roughly corresponding in status and responsibility to our distinction between lecturers, associates and full professors) and its assertion that university governance be a shared responsibility between a faculty-appointed president (i.e., Rector) and a senate made up of full professors, all of these remain a powerful testament to the intrinsic value and judicious exercise of academic freedom; and such commitments—epitomized by Berlin's well known mottoes, '*Lehrfreiheit, Lernfreiheit!*' and '*Universitas Litterarum*'—serve us well even today as a powerful antidote to the corporate model that we increasingly see asserting itself as the successor to the Berlin model.

In fact, the organizational principles for the University of Berlin became the guiding inspiration for the founding of our own Johns Hopkins University, the University of Chicago and the University of California, among many others. Thus, by the end of the nineteenth century, so strong was the gravitational force around its central image that G. Stanley Hall, founder of the American Psychological Association and president of Clark University (itself molded on the Berlin model) could say:

> The German University is today the freest spot on earth.... Never was such burning and curiosity.... Shallow, bad ideas have died and truth has always attained power.... Nowhere has the passion to push on to the frontier of human knowledge been so general. Never have so many men stood so close to nature and history or striven with such reverence to think God's thoughts after Him exactly.[7]

At the time of Hall's remarks in 1891, the philosopher Wilhelm Dilthey, himself the successor to Hegel's chair in philosophy at the University of Berlin, was beginning the first of many attempts to clarify and distinguish the methodologies of the natural from the so-called human sciences by basing the latter on an epistemological instrument he was calling at the time, "descriptive psychology." (Later, he would make clear that "hermeneutics," as previously outlined by Schleiermacher, was a better name for this primary tool of research in the humanities.)[8] Berlin, which was widely venerated during the 1890s for its ground-breaking work in the natural sciences, especially chemistry and physics, but also for its seminal work in the field of cultural history and historiography,[9] was not yet known as the birthplace of the humanities, that is, the *Geisteswissenschaften*, although, due to Dilthey's influence, its name would become, by our time, virtually synonymous with the birth of this other, more contested, legacy as well.[10] But it is this legendary role as the 'mother' of the so-called human sciences that calls for our renewed attention, since it is not clear that the University of Berlin, as it was actually chartered, or as it ultimately developed over time, merits this unique distinction; or that hermeneutics, as it was conceived by Schleiermacher, actually justifies any hard and fast distinction between the arts and sciences. It is toward a clarification of this question, that I would now like to turn, since Schleiermacher championed the role of hermeneutics as a necessary tool in support of not only higher learning (i.e., university research in both the arts and sciences), but also as a necessary ingredient in the dialectical development of cultural *Bildung*. He was also an under-appreciated influence on what became the guiding plan of the University of Berlin, as well as a distinguished member of its inaugural faculty.[11]

## 2   The Hydra-Headed Monster: Schleiermacher and Fichte's Aspirational Proposals for the Founding of the University of Berlin

There has always been something grandiose, but, also, potentially turbulent, associated with the idea of a national university centered in Berlin. This was recognized already by Leibniz, who so detested the dreary and run-of-the-mill lecturers he had encountered that he recommended to Friedrich Wilhelm I that he avoid bringing such scholars to Berlin, and found, instead, a royal society, which might stimulate new and important research without rewarding the tired scholasticism of the university dons by lending them an audience. After Leibniz' death, the King, instead of following Leibniz' advice, appointed three of his court fools as president of the Prussian Academy of the Sciences. But even before the Nazi purges and book burnings of 1933, and well before the professor's revolution of 1848, which, failing to spark a widespread demand outside the university for constitutional reform, Schleiermacher himself noted this misshapen aspect. He wrote in his proposal, "Occasional Thoughts on Universities in the German Sense," regarding the multi-college form the university ought to instantiate:

> It is often remarked that [by basing the university upon] four faculties, namely, the theological, juridical, medical and philosophical, and precisely in the above-stated order, we give the University an extremely grotesque visage. And this is certainly hard to deny.[12]

Attempting, like Kant and Schiller before him, to enlarge (and some would say, ennoble) the task of the higher education so that it might encompass more than merely professional training for what was at that time, three essentially state-licensed occupations (viz., pastoral ministry, legal counsel and medical care), Schleiermacher saw in the synoptic and interdisciplinary discourse of philosophy something like the key to higher education in general, namely, the systematic and self-reflective pursuit of knowledge without regard for immediate applicability or practical worth. But the combined energies of four faculties differing in approach and application as greatly as theology, medicine, philosophy and the law could not have failed to suggest to the great translator of Plato, something like the hydra-headed monster that is summoned by Socrates in Book IX of the *Republic* as a symbol for the human condition when it reveals itself to be the political animal.

In the beginning, one might say, the plan was "grotesque" not because the university would house an unruly and potentially disruptive entity—a multi-headed hydra with the heart of a lion, hellbent on political engagement, and serving the pure scientific interest hardly at all—indeed, none of the blueprints for the university, neither Schelling's, nor Fichte's, nor Schleiermacher's, nor even Humboldt's,[13] suggest anything like Dilthey's methodological distinction between the natural sciences (*Naturwissenschaften*) and the so-called humanities (*Geisteswissenschaften*) as the core disciplines of the Arts and Sciences. (In fact, the term 'Geisteswissenschaften' is nowhere to be found in the early German romantics.)[14] Nor do they anywhere separate and divide the arts and sciences, even where it is a question of disciplinary affiliation (or turf): for Fichte as much as Schleiermacher, "Kunst" and "Wissenschaft" are located under the more general rubric: "die philosophische Fakultät." Rather, the fourfold constitution of the academic faculty seems aesthetically repugnant on Schleiermacher's account because it suggests that the 'pure' arts and science are merely on a par with the professional schools, and that they are being offered a kind of institutional asylum that society at large nowhere else provides them, when, in actual fact, they should lay the intellectual groundwork for any advanced study whatsoever.

Two quotations, the first from Fichte, the second from Schleiermacher, well illuminate this strong conviction shared by both idealists and Romantics alike on this score:

> The spirit of each specific science is a limited [one] and limits [in turn] spirit, which, to be sure, lives within itself, yet is driven [to produce] valuable goods, which neither itself nor another spirited being outside of itself may be able to [completely] understand.… Now, philosophy is that which comprises, scientifically, the whole spiritual activity within which each specific science and any further manifestation of which [finds its ground] … Each one of the specific sciences must be given its 'practice' [Kunst] out of philosophical reflection upon its practice [*Kunstbildung*]. … The spirit of philosophy would be that science, therefore, which understands in itself, first of all, its own practice, so that all

other [scientific] spirits can understand each other through it…. The practitioner in any specific science must be, above all, a practitioner of philosophy, and his specific practice would be a further determination and a unique application of his overall philosophy.[15][my translation]

While Fichte appears to have believed that a strong philosophy department with a fully developed "philosophical catechism" [16] would be the best way to ground the study of the specialized sciences in a common experience—this is why he entitled his contribution to the planning for the university, a "deduced plan" (*eine deduzierter Plan*) in which the university comes to resemble a living "encyclopedia" with philosophical reflection spreading out from the center, illuminating all subsequent activity like a 'sun clear reflection,' the philosophy department itself becomes a vital, forensic space, not unlike the sun at the center of the solar system, in that it provides both the critical space for the revolving disputation of truth claims, but also establishes the respective limits and scope of each scientific sub-field, as though it were granting planetary orbit permissions. [17]

Schleiermacher, on the other hand, echoes the demand in Schlegel's *Athenaeum* for something like 'philosophizing across the curriculum' (or what Schlegel had already designated as "symphilosophy"): "In no other way than this: all university teachers should be rooted in the philosophical faculty."[18] It is important to note here that while Schleiermacher insists that all of the higher faculties become "rooted" in the activity of philosophizing, he stresses that this is especially important for the faculties of theology and law, who would otherwise become unscientific, superficial and trade-oriented:

> This is especially the case for the faculties of law and theology, for study in these disciplines can never be secure from slipping gradually into vocational trades, or becoming spoiled in unscientific superficiality, unless each professor aspires to make a name for himself on the field of pure science, and therefore merit a place as a lecturer.

To emphasize the point that Schleiermacher is here alluding to the *philosophical function* rather than the philosophical faculty, *per se*, Schleiermacher adds the following clarification:

> And, in fact, any professor of law or theology, who doesn't feel in himself the energy or the appetite for [working philosophically], whether it be pure philosophy, or ethics, or the philosophical consideration of history, or philology, deserves to be laughed at and shut out of the university.[19]

It is easy to discern in these, and similar remarks by Novalis (*cf.*, *Fichte-Studien*), why Dilthey thought that his theory of the human sciences was only working up something that was already implicit in the early German Romantics. Even Fichte, who appears to use the term "philosophical faculty" in the most literal sense of all the planners for the University of Berlin, recognized that "philology" is an agreeable substitute for "pure self-reflection" in philosophy, at least in an academic context.[20] Which is to say, reflection on the practice of the sciences must also include reflection on the language and grammatical structures employed by those same sciences in their communications. Philosophy must be supplemented with philology in order to understand how to interpret and reply to the external manifestations of each scientific claim and/or discovery.

But how do we proceed from the pure self-reflection that is characteristic of transcendental philosophy in Fichte's sense of "spirit," properly so called, to anything like the natural sciences or the socio-linguistic sciences we are more accustomed to seeing appraised according to the standards implied in *Geisteswissenschaft* (i.e., scientific scholarship)? It is clear that nothing of empirical value can be simply "deduced" from one's own *a priori* view of the whole, and that the Fichtean "encyclopedia" must be superseded by something that is more world-open and susceptible to critical intervention and dialogue than transcendental reflection appears to be. This is why it is necessary to pause briefly over the Novalis' transformation of Fichtean self-reflection, in order to better discern how it is that Schleiermacher's "philosophical faculty" can seem as much a place of Calliclean disputation and dissent, as it does a symposium (Konversatorien)[21] for Socratic dialogue.

## 3  Novalis and the "Highest Task of Education": The University as an Oasis in "the Deserts of Understanding"[22]

Unlike Schelling, Fichte, Schleiermacher and Humboldt, Novalis does not appear to have set down his thoughts on the possible organization of a university and its core curriculum. A free scholar in every sense of the word, Novalis did not spend the majority of his days (again unlike Schelling, Fichte and Schleiermacher) working within the 'cardboard reality' (Foucault's phrase) of the academy. Nevertheless, Novalis' unique position as a student of Schiller, Fichte and Reinhold, his close relationship with Friedrich Schlegel and the Jena Romantics,[23] plus his altogether novel fusion of philosophy, poetry and criticism open up broad prospects for conceiving anew the nature of the sciences and its relationship, both to the world of nature and to ourselves. Moreover, there does not appear to be anyone who might be said to be capable of endorsing the word 'spirit,' both in its pluralization, and in its coupling with 'science,' in the literal sense of 'Geisteswissenschaften,' as Novalis. (Perhaps, only Walter Benjamin affirmed the obsolescent idioms of magic and alchemical transformation in any sort of self-critical way that is comparable to Novalis.) At any rate, should anyone ever attempt to 'reclaim the sciences of the spirit' for the modern university, and to truly own up to what it might positively imply as a legitimate area of scientific inquiry, such a scholar cannot avoid, it seems to me, having to come to terms with Novalis.

Novalis' recently translated notebooks chronicling his intensive study of Fichte reveal the extent to which Novalis was seeking a way past the terminal moraine of Kant's third *Critique*.[24] Precisely, where Kant had left an unbridgeable divide between the two senses of spirit, that is, between the domain of artistic creativity, on the one hand, and natural teleology (or nature's creativity), on the other (i.e., spirit in its objective manifestation as intelligent design), Novalis appears to follow Fichte in trying to find a way to vault over or across the epistemological divide between natural and artistic creation by resorting to intellectual intuition. In Novalis' hands, however, the simple certainty of A = A becomes double-crossed and repeatedly stressed, such that the budding Romantic is able to say (after parsing the senses of each moment as far as possible, so that each time the number of selves is multiplied): "The absolute I is at once both a united and a divided thing. Insofar as it is divided it must have an empirical consciousness—in short, it must be a mediated I. The divided I must, nevertheless, be united, namely, through the drive to be an I." At which point, Novalis makes the startling conclusion, "We are I." Here, Novalis applies a kind of tropological hermeneutics to Fichte's "A = A," which redoubles to the point of difference the initial claim of identity by applying the figure of identity to itself (something Novalis called 'raising to a higher power'). For example, "We are close to waking when we are dreaming that we are dreaming"[25] (These are akin to enthymemes, it would appear.)

Sometimes, Novalis redoubles an assertion to a self-canceling state, a figure he calls in the *Fichte-Studien*, "neutra" (presumably, for the effect of being self-neutralizing): For instance: "The science of science is a very subaltern science—because it is a very determined one." Another example, also not unrelated to our present task of elucidating Novalis' theory of education and how it might throw light on his plan for a university, had he written one: "The highest task of education is to take control of one's higher self—to be at once the I of its I"[26] (Here the effect of "Potenzierung" is to transform the subject;

however, the science of science, in the example just prior, is hardly transformative.)

In other places, Novalis crosses semantic opposites (or at least terms that come from, ordinarily, quite distinct, even remote, semantic "spheres") in a reciprocal predication[27] that results in a kind of surreal coalescence of the improbable. (In one fragment, Novalis characterizes this hermeneutic strategy as a distinctly "pathological logic," although he does not reveal whether the pathology lies in the objective possibility of such things happening, or whether describing them in such terms, accounts for the pathology). I would call such statements, *transversal predications*; that is, propositions that require the wholesale readjustment of entire sets of already settled statements in order for their sense and reference to become semantically settled.[28] Such propositions are obviously not empirical statements, that is, predicating empirical matter of *a priori* conceptual forms; nor are they aesthetic judgments, since they do not subjectively generalize the particular in terms of an appeal to an underlying *sensus communis*, since most of these statements are, quite clearly, contrary to the norms held by the *sensus communis*, and, thus, run contrary to common sense (i.e., in some sense, they are paradoxical, perhaps even, nonsensical, pseudo-statements). They are not unlike such surrealistic pronouncements as Breton's favorite example of metaphor, "the running is dog."[29]

A few examples, by no means isolated or unique, reveal the range to which Novalis applied this reciprocal cancelation, or rhetorical figure of *chiasmus*:

1. "Idealization of realism and realization of idealism leads to truth. One works for the other—and so indirectly for itself... The proof of realism is idealism—and conversely. ... All proof moves towards the opposite."[30]
2. "We should simply become acquainted with the matter of spirit and the spirit of matter."[31]
3. "The faculty of knowledge is also not knowable as a think in itself"[32]
4. "All change is exchange."[33]
5. "The absence of pleasure is a way to pleasure, as death is a way to life."[34]
6. "If the world is like a precipitate of human nature, then the world of the gods is a sublimate—both occur *uno actu*. No material precipitate without a spiritual sublimate."[35]
7. "In the truest sense doing philosophy is a caress. It bears witness to the deepest love of reflection, to absolute delight in wisdom"[36]
8. "Nature is a magical city turned to stone." [37]
9. "Practical reason is pure imagination."[38]
10. "Physics is nothing but the theory of the imagination."[39]
11. "The poem of the understanding is philosophy."[40]

The last example is more immediately relevant to my earlier claim about working through Fichte's *Wissenschaftslehre* toward something like an encounter with "the sciences of the spirit":

12. "Self equals non-self—the highest principle of all learning and art."[41]

Now, it is interesting to compare this coincidence of self and non-self in fragment #12 with Novalis' last set of remarks in the *Fichte-Studien*: "The human being is as much not-I as I."[42] Clearly, Novalis' strategic use of tropes and 'pathological' predication in the context of a close, hermeneutical reading of Fichte's *Wissenschaftslehre* prompts us to ask whether he is fashioning a destructive hermeneutic, much like Heidegger in *Being and Time*, or whether, these experiments are made in the name of speculative philosophy, and, thus, amount to a kind of *herme-noetics*, rather than hermeneutics, as it has come to be defined by recent theory. Jane Kneller counsels against such an overly 'idealistic' reading of Novalis, writing in her comprehensive translation and critical introduction to Novalis' four hundred-page notebook, the so-called Fichte Studies, that Novalis argues for a position that "marks him out as far more in the spirit of Kantian Enlightenment than those in his idealist cohort."[43] As Kneller reconstructs it, the essential matter is that,

> philosophy may recognize its own absolute when it recognizes that no absolute ground is given. Even in the face of giving up the search for the absolute, or rather, precisely *because* of giving it up, the "drive to philosophize" can never be satisfied, and when we "freely renounce the absolute" there arises in us an "unending free activity" that is "the only possible absolute that can be given us" (#566). Thus, philosophy can only ever provide a negative account of the self. But since this negative characteristic *is* indeed *one* aspect of our nature, it is at least not a falsified account of the human self (which in essence he accuses Fichte of giving).[44]

This is an exceedingly important point to have arrived at, and one that, presumably, marks him out as closer to Schleiermacher in spirit than Fichte, Schelling, Niethammer and other philosophers roaming about on the idealist side of the spectrum. There is something quite like Pyrrhonian skepticism in what Kneller dubs, "this tension laden conception of the self" that doesn't attempt to vault over the phenomenal universe cavorting in a kind of giddy self-certainty. As Kneller points out, it was Manfred Frank, the Schleiermacher scholar and historian of romantic hermeneutics, who first noted in Novalis' affirmation of the *aporia* at the heart of all knowing that his refusal to out-shoot his phenomenological evidence shows that "he affirms only" a non-knowing that knows itself as such.[45] To conclude this brief foray into Novalis' fragments on education and the self of learning, it is useful to formulate where we are at this point with a question: Were such strategies generalized and linked together with Novalis' scattered remarks about the sciences, the nature of inquiry, the semiotic dimension, as well as the pronounced emphasis on gaming and heavily coded information (i.e., riddles) in his fragments and diary reflections, it would prompt us to ask, what form would a university take in Novalis' imaginative crossing of antithetical characters and concepts, were he to "deduce" one, Fichte style, from his own highest premise? "The human being is as much not-I as I." Perhaps, the only thing that would differ is that the names of the faculties would change from physics, chemistry, poetry, and so on, to "magical physics," "magical chemistry," "magical poetry," and so on. Or, perhaps, it would bear a resemblance to a place where even Theology is taken as a progressive science, and all the sciences are housed in the philosophy section of the university: In other words, one quite like Schleiermacher's proposal for the Universal of Berlin.

Now it is exactly here, where the need to account for a meaningful connection between the requirement to be a distinctly unique individual and the simultaneous drive to be, as Novalis puts it, "the I of *its* I" (i.e., the I of the not-self) that the sense begins to dawn that Novalis is using Kant to move beyond Fichte as much as he is using Fichte to move beyond Kant. And it is this last claim that the drive to know the not-self as though it were a self capable of knowing us in turn, which makes Novalis an important figure in the debate about the nature of the humanities. Here the notion of a deliberate perspective-shifting dynamic (via transversal predication, via re-interpretation, via re-figuration and relentless re-examination) can be shown, I believe, to stem, at least, partially, from Kant's aesthetics, especially in those parts, like the four 'moments of a judgment of taste,' where Kant, not unlike Novalis' later uses of chiasmus, crosses up his own concepts (tying normal logic into knots) as he articulates the four moments of a judgment of taste caused by the beautiful manifestation. Rudolf Makkreel notes the many continuities that appear when we line up Kant's writings on aesthetics and his topical essays of the 1790's (when the romantic movement is beginning to make its mark in Weimar and Jena) with the hermeneutic tradition of the late nineteenth century, parallels that he finds explicitly drawn out in the work of Hegel's successor at Berlin, Wilhelm Dilthey. On Makkreel's view, the judgment of taste, which Kant discovers and works out, as a kind of subjective, heuristic way of thinking (testing, tapping, trying things out), connects Kant's early essay, "What is Orientation in Thinking?" with Kant's later essays and work on biblical interpretation, where he distinguishes "doctrinal" from "authentic" forms of "interpretation." As Makkreel puts it, the parallel here has to do with the common experience of feeling disoriented, or lost, in which cases, we rely not on instinctual cues, or prior certainties (which have failed us, hence our sense of feeling lost), so we must appeal to 'worldly' considerations that we have worked out for ourselves by thinking from our standpoint of being aware that we are lost, and need to discover new 'encompassing frameworks' for self-orientation. Makkreel explains it this way:

> The task of reflective orientation is to elicit those conditions that allow us to relate our basic feeling of orientation to some more encompassing frame of reference. In the *Jäsche Logic*, Kant states that one should 'orient oneself in thought or in the speculative use of reason by means of the common understanding. It must be noted however that the orientational framework provided by Kant's 'common understanding,' or by any other encompassing frame of reference such as the *sensus communis* and the inherited medium of commonality, will not give us determinate directions. They only provide markers to help chart our bearings and keep us from straying beyond the bounds of what is communally or historically reasonable as we pursue our own goals or make sense of those of others.... By advocating a reflective orientational approach, we are extending philosophy in the academic sense into what Kant calls "philosophy in the worldly sense.".... It is of interest not just to those skilled in scientific cognition, but to all human beings concerned with the kind of knowledge that enables them to live wisely.[46]

How might such a self-interpretive, orientational use of 'reflective judgment' relate to the modern research university (like Berlin's 'multi-headed Hydra design'), or to the *Geisteswissenschaften*? Or, even to Schleiermacher and Novalis? Let me quote, in conclusion, an important passage from the "Appendix to the Dialectic of Aesthetic Judgment" of the third *Critique*, where Kant pauses over the problem of pedagogy in art. The passage, I believe, is hugely significant for understanding what the early German Romantics, especially Novalis and Schleiermacher, were trying to achieve, although not all in the same way, nor in quite the same 'top-down' way as Kant:

> The propaedeutic for all beautiful art, so far as it is aimed at the highest degree of its perfection, seems to lie not in precepts, but in the culture of the mental powers through those prior forms of knowledge that are called *humaniora*, presumably because humanity means on the one hand the universal feeling of participation and on the other hand the capacity for being able to communicate one's inmost self universally, which properties taken together constitute the

sociability that is appropriate to humankind, by means of which it distinguishes itself from the limitation of animals.[47]

In this passage, it is not difficult to discern the germinal beginnings of a hermeneutic model for approaching the human sciences; indeed, many of the hallmarks of Schleiermacher's later interpretation are already intimated (the emphasis on empathetic identification and sympathy; the universal capacity to engage in conversation, etc.). Moreover, one can well discern how Schleiermacher might have been prompted by such a remark to pursue further the conversational model of dialectic (especially insofar as such a conversation also implies an aesthetic of sociability—which, Schleiermacher made the subject of his first philosophical treatise); also, it is clear that Novalis pursues, with the simmering intensity of a contemplative mystic the way of sympathetic identification with the universe and all that is in it. But just as Schleiermacher's path through the dialectic is not without reference to the aesthetic and rhetorical dimensions of sympathy and audience; so too is Novalis' way through the aesthetics of pan-sympathetic identification not without linguistic disclosure (cf. his repeated use of the coded writing-metaphor, the hieroglyphs, etc.). For Novalis, it would appear, Blanchot's phrase is completely accurate: The external world is "rhetoric become matter" (hence, the magical power of word for Novalis: Only a trope can reverse or alter the effect of another trope).[48] But what phrase is more apt than Blanchot's *Novalisme*, for characterizing a state institution charged with the task of making our senior-most researchers as well as our youngest students feel themselves challenged by the sense of being dislocated, perhaps, even a bit lost?

There is much here that needs further exploration and inquiry. It is hoped that the recently published *Vorlesungen über Hermeneutik* ['Lectures on Hermeneutics'] by Schleiermacher's editors at the Brandenburg Academy of Sciences (which took a little over 200 years to track down the nearly 1000 pages of manuscripts, arrange them by handwriting, and determine page sequencing, lacunae, and so on before finally editing, collating, annotating and indexing), will lead to path-breaking new researches, that will help further distinguish Schleiermacher's quest-for-unity hermeneutics from Dilthey, Nohl and Spranger's humanities-only epistemology. The academic ghettoization of philosophy, comparative religion, classics and foreign literatures, due to that unfortunate misreading of the 'sciences of the spirit' tag is no longer helpful or desirable. With regard to Schleiermacher and Novalis' point-counterpoint relationship—a relationship seemingly only maintained in oblique allusions within one another's letters or texts—perhaps more evidence will surface in the lectures showing deeper affinity than the famous passage in

Christendom or Europe, that some scholars see as an appreciative allusion to Schleiermacher's 'On Religion: Speeches to Its Cultured Despisers,' his anonymously published defense of religious feeling in an Enlightenment world suspicious of rhapsodic, 'enthusiasm' and 'Schwärmerei':

> Where there are no gods, ghosts reign, and the actual period of origin of ghosts in Europe, which also explains their shape almost completely, is the period of transition from the doctrine of the Greek gods to Christianity. So come then you too, all you philanthropists and encyclopedists, into the peace-bringing lodge and receive the fraternal kiss, brush the gray net aside and gaze with young love at the wondrous splendor nature, history, and humanity. I want to conduct you to a brother who will talk with you so that your hearts rejoice and you gird your beloved, expired sensation with a new body, you once again embrace and recognize what you envisioned, and what ponderous, mortal understanding was indeed not able to seize from you. This brother is the new heartbeat of the new age, whoever has felt his presence does not doubt any more that it will come, and he too steps out from the crowd with sweet pride in being a contemporary to join the new band of disciples.[49]

Pauline Kleingeld[50] sees in these lines by Novalis the clearest indication of a cosmopolitan orientation, on Novalis' part, that unites, what appears to be too divergent for unity; if she is correct about that political orientation, then it serves to offset the growing sense that the early German Romantics were nationalists all; the only difference between them being the kind of nationalism they favored:

> It is Novalis's conviction that the "traces of a new world" can be seen in Germany. The Germans (and Novalis must be thinking here of the romantics in particular, especially of Schleiermacher, and of intellectual life in Jena, Weimar, and Berlin in general) have achieved a critical distance from the Enlightenment's one-sided focus on the intellect, to the point where it "shows ... a new universal individuality, a new history, a new humanity, the sweetest embrace of a young surprised church and a loving god, not to mention the intimate conception of a new messiah in its thousand members."[51]

If it is true to see in Novalis' fable-like allusions to a shepherd-like 'brother' who bids us to take up with joy, and enjoy these strongest of affects, the very figure of Schleiermacher (whose name literally means 'veil-maker'), then it also provides a useful clue for how to approach the interpretation of what role hermeneutics was supposed to fill out, within the University of Berlin, if it was not the same as philological exegesis. (Böckhe, Schleiermacher's student who was both a professor and chair of the Philology department left records that indicate no student of philology was to take courses outside the department in 'hermeneutics' but he does not say why in his 'Rules and Guidelines' for students; perhaps, it was just academic protection of turf, like Psychology departments wanting their students to take their own course in statistics rather than the Math department's statistics course. But, it may also be that it gets to deeper issues about societal and cultural interpretation as opposed to textual interpretation and doing 'Quellen-kritik.') Some scholars have written extensively of Schleiermacher's nationalist leanings, and his political sermons, as well as his being suspended from teaching for a short time, due to fears about what he was saying in the classroom; but it may be that hermeneutics was precisely the bulwark he developed from allowing the university and its academic freedom to lose its necessary polarity, or critical gap, between questions and partisan rivalries about the one and the many, self and cosmos, citizen and nation, the authentic and the doctrinal. Such possibilities hold out the hope for a new reading of the University of Berlin, as well as Schleiermacher's involvement with it until his untimely death, as well as Novalis and Schlegel's influence upon his hopes for developing an 'art of understanding.' For instance, the herme-noetics of Novalis' hieroglyphs, and his invocation of something like semiotic consciousness, as well as the need to work out more fully, the place of disagreement and dissent, indeed, of rhetoric as a whole, in Schleiermacher's "general hermeneutics," as well as the relation between philosophy and rhetoric in Schleiermacher's hermeneutics (the endorsement of Callicles is quite striking in this regard). Such work will allow us to better discern what is alive and what is dead in romantic hermeneutics, and whether a post-humanist humanities would also be necessarily post-spiritual, or whether the notion of something like a 'sciences of the spirit' need make any reference to 'man' at all, assuming such is possible, or even desirable.

## 4 A Concluding Reflection About MacIntyre's Challenge in *God, Philosophy, Universities*

In his 2009 study, *God, Philosophy, Universities*, Alasdair MacIntyre eloquently voiced concerns about the modern university's precipitous decline, both in educational quality, and also cultural stature, noting that much of this decline stemmed from the fact that modern reforms made to the university systems in Germany, France, England and the United States, during the early nineteenth century, brought about a research-intensive situation where "the study of theology was marginalized or sometimes abandoned altogether."[52] In such a system, where interfaith dialogue, cross-disciplinary curiosity and the generalist's virtue of bold catholicity are rarely encountered, "the university soon became a place where it is nobody's responsibility to relate what is learned and taught in any one discipline to what is learned and taught in any other"[53]

Noting that many of these nineteenth-century university reformers, like Wilhelm Humboldt, brought about much needed change to the ways in which universities were administered, funded and sustained over time, yet these same changes also made theology "just one more academic discipline,"[54] which itself brought about a parallel divestiture in philosophy, as it "too, became just one more academic discipline, with its own subject matter, its own methods, and its own goals."[55]

While there is much that rings true in MacIntyre's complaint about the over-specialization of modern research, and how the resulting silo-effect of competing, non-overlapping discourse, erects walls of misunderstanding between the teaching and learning that goes on in different disciplines—barriers of nomenclature that make it difficult, if not impossible, for any one scientific specialist to master the idiom of any other discipline, as was seemingly possible in the Renaissance by polymaths such as Leonardo and Descartes; still, there is much that he omits from his Spengler-like narrative of decline. Some of these omissions, such as the acceleration of knowledge capture and the obsolescence of outmoded scientific understanding, are understandable, given that MacIntyre's purpose is not to rehash epistemological arguments about scientific progress; rather, his book speaks to larger, more fundamental issues, which are often overlooked precisely because technological advancement and digital knowledge distribution are ubiquitous parts of our information age, and make it so that the university itself seems obsolescent in the 'do-it-yourself' culture of smart phones, social media and the Internet.

For readers of the German Enlightenment, and the early German Romantics, however, what MacIntyre omits to mention are precisely those very social and political issues that captivated their attempt to unify a divided Germany by effecting a revolution, as Kant once put it, 'from the top down.'[56] These socio-political factors, which led to the reforms in the first place, have very much to do with the hopes and aspirations of the early German Romantics, and especially on the life and work of Friedrich Schleiermacher, who voiced many of these same complaints, and also sought to introduce institutional safeguards that would avoid MacIntyre's 'Spenglerian' (i.e., world-crashing pessimism) conclusion.

## 10 Hermeneutics and Orientation: Retracing the 'Sciences...

In brief, these are what I take to be the ways in which Schleiermacher and Company's plans for the University of Berlin in 1809 attempted to meet, as it were, head-on, the death-by-fragmentation-problems indicated by MacIntyre's suspicions about a university unmoored from philosophical dialogue and theological comprehension:

1. By separating the professional state-licensure programs of medicine, law and pastoral ministry, from the purely academic, research departments, all of which, were known, in aggregate, as the 'philosophy faculty,' Schleiermacher hoped to inspire exactly the kinds of interdisciplinary cross-talk that MacIntyre wants in the modern research university model.
2. By separating theology and philosophy, he effectively isolated the state-fettered theology from the freedom-bound philosophy faculty, but also poised the findings of one with the challenges of the other, guaranteeing a quest for progressive improvements, and a growing quest for comprehension, given the sibling rivalry that he built-in to his structural designs. (Humboldt ultimately drew more from Schleiermacher's design than from Fichte's, Schelling's or Henrik Steffens' counter-proposals.)
3. Schleiermacher's notion of a conversational space positioned at the heart of the university, in the "Occasional Thoughts" treatise, is that *all* of the academic, research, disciplines need to engage in Socratic dialogue, the unfettered quest for comprehension and verification, and that all research claims need to be openly vetted and tested in a challenge-and-response arena (i.e., the 'thesis defense' capstone), which he, presumably, modeled after Plato's *Apology of Socrates*, which the German translator of Plato must have envisioned on analogy with the ancient Athenian agora, by virtue of the fact that he claimed, what would set Berlin apart, would not be its lectures, or its recitations, but rather its collaborative spaces for vigorous, open, discussion. Like Fichte before him, Schleiermacher imagined these disciplinary conversations as mediating between the monologically delivered lectures, led by faculty, and the forensically constructed 'konversatorien,' which shifted the responsibility for leading the discussion to the questioner's side. Schleiermacher's genius for 'unsocial sociability,' led him to innovate a further university practice, which, on the view of some scholars, was Schleiermacher's most lasting contribution, namely, the upper level seminar, created by professor's interested in opening up their workshops to a shared experience of advanced 'work in progress,' and where the equitable norms of round-table discussion helped occasion a surprising turnaround: professors rediscovering their inner learner, and students, their inner teacher.[57]

In such a space, it is hard to see how even MacIntyre's favorite philosophers, Thomas Aquinas and Duns Scotus, wouldn't themselves have enjoyed a place where the traditionally academic 'war of all against all' has been beautifully attenuated as the salon of all with all; and hermeneutics is not a humanities-exclusive study habit, but the name of an aspirational goal for the entire university, the goal of orientational[58] trans-critique.[59]

## Notes

1. "Philosophy, which once seemed obsolete, lives on because the moment to realize it was missed." Cf. *Negative Dialectics*, trans. E. B. Ashton (New York: Continuum, 1995), 3.
2. Karl Reinhold, once professed that the subject he would lecture on at the University of Jena could best be described as "Philosophy without Surnames" (*Philosophie ohne Beinamen*). While it is tempting to apply Reinhold's dictum to the subject of hermeneutics itself, the task is (today, at any rate), no longer possible. Perhaps, only Schleiermacher was ever able to approach the topic without reference to its own effective history. For a sense of hermeneutics as *terra novo*, cf. *Hermeneutics and Criticism*, trans., ed., Andrew Bowie (Cambridge: Cambridge University Press, 1998). For the Reinhold reference, cf. William Wallace's note to Hegel's *Logic* (Oxford: Oxford University Press, 1975), 299.
3. The phrase is Odo Marquard's, although it hearkens back to Schleiermacher's dictum that, although "criticism should come to an end … hermeneutics should not." For Marquard's claim, cf. his stimulating article "To What Question is Hermeneutics the Answer?" in the collection, *Farewell to Matters of Principle* (Oxford: Oxford University Press, 1989), 124. For the Schleiermacher reference, cf. *Hermeneutics and Criticism and Other Writings*, translated and edited by Andrew Bowie (Cambridge: Cambridge University Press, 1998), 4.

   To be sure, Marquard's notion of an unlimited discussion that is distinct from a "discourse" invites comparison with Maurice Blanchot's "infinite conversation," in his influential meditation on the aspirations and legacy effect of the early German romantics: *The Infinite Conversation*, translated by Susan Hanson, Fourth Printing (Minneapolis: University of Minnesota Press, 1993), from the Theory and History of Literature Series, Volume 82; see especially, 242, 315, and 352–359, where Blanchot develops an interpretation of the fragmentary imperative and discusses Schlegel's romantic journal, *The Athenaeum*. For the Marquard reference, see his skeptical meditation on hermeneutics, *Farewell to Matters of Principle*, translated by Robert M. Wallace, with the Assistance of Susan M. Bernstein and James I, Porter (Oxford: Oxford University Press, 1989), 124.

4. The undertaking was clearly also a task that was, needless to say, suspended quite precariously between politics and poetry. Humboldt saw the political implications of the new university more clearly than most when he stated: "Everything depends upon holding to the principle of considering knowledge [*Wissenschaft*] as something not yet found, never completely to be discovered, and searching relentlessly for it as such.... This is because knowledge alone, which comes from and can be planted in the depths of the spirit, also transforms character; and for the state, just as for humanity, facts and discourse matter less than character and behavior." According to Daniel Fallon, in *The German University* (see note 7 below), Humboldt took inspiration in the work of the Swiss education reformer, Pestalozzi, who held that "the taste of modern education was not to nationalize man, but rather to humanize the state" (ibid.).

5. For a different take on this issue, see the article by Vandevelde in this volume on how making hermeneutics a function of Dasein's existential thrownness actually brings it closer to Schleiermacher, not farther away. This is an intriguing suggestion, and resonates with a number of Schleiermacher's well-established commitments, but in overlooking the extent to which Schleiermacher positions hermeneutical understanding as a critical engagement with social forces and action texts, it acts as a kind of bulwark against one-dimensional readings of nationalism, and liberal anarchism, for that matter, as well.

6. For a useful overview of the development and application of the German model of higher education, and its designation of the terminal degree in arts and sciences as the "doctorate in philosophy," see Daniel Fallon, *The German University: A Heroic Ideal in Conflict with the Modern World* (Boulder: Colorado Associated University Press, 1980), especially, 5–53 on the founding of the University of Berlin. (Hereafter cited internally as Fallon.) According to Fallon, the American *Ph.D.* was directly modeled upon the German *Dr. phil*: "The Ph.D. degree itself was a German import. None was awarded before 1861 when Yale awarded doctoral degrees to three students for high attainments in its Department of Philosophy and the Arts. By 1876, when Johns Hopkins opened, the Yale precedent of awarding a 'doctor of philosophy' degree was being followed in 25 American colleges. The 'doctor of philosophy' had been assumed directly from the German *Dr.phil.*, which was the principal academic degree awarded by the German 'philosophische Fakultät' or faculty of arts and sciences" (52).

7. Fallon, 2–3. Fallon also records the following testimony, approximately forty years later by Abraham Flexner, the founder and first director of Princeton's Institute for Advanced Study: "The German university has for almost a century and a half fruitfully engaged in teaching and research. As long as those two tasks combine in fertile union, the German university, whatever its defects of detail, will retain its importance. It has stimulated university devel-

opment in Great Britain; from it has sprung the graduate school of the new world; to it industry and health and every conceivable practical activity are infinitely indebted."

8. See in this regard, Dilthey's qualifying remarks in "The Rise of Hermeneutics" that, although 'descriptive psychology' is still important for approaching the remnants of past historical action, hermeneutics is an "essential component in the foundation of the human studies themselves." See Fredric Jameson's translation of Dilthey's important article, "Die Entstehung der Hermeneutik" in *New Literary History: A Journal of Theory and Interpretation*, 3, no. 2, Winter 1972, 244. For more information about this progressive distillation of hermeneutics out of descriptive psychology, see Rudolf Makkreel's *Dilthey: Philosopher of the Human Studies* (Princeton: Princeton University Press, 1975), 262–272.

9. See Theodore Ziolkowski's deep scan of the central role given to history and the pursuit of narrative truth by the early German Romantics, and how these ideas ultimately became axiomatic in the history/philology side of the Philosophy Seminar in *Clio the Romantic Muse: Historicizing the Faculties in Germany* (Cornell: Cornell University Press, 2003).

10. For a clear and wide-ranging account of Dilthey's role in propagating this reading of the early German romantics, see Frithjof Rodi's *Erkenntnis des Erkannten: Zur Hermeneutik des 19. und 20. Jahrhunderts* (Frankfurt am Main: Suhrkamp Verlag, 1990). Especially useful for the current focus is Rodi's discussion in the second article, "Unverständnis und Wiederverständnis im Umgang mit der Frühromantik," 31–55.

11. Key texts leading up to the founding of the University of Berlin have been gathered together in the indispensable collection, *Die Idee der deutschen Universität*, edited by Ernst Anrich (Bad Homberg: Hermann Gentner, 1959). These include Schelling's *Über den absoluten Begriff der Wissenschaft*, Fichte's *Deduzierter Plan einer in Berlin zu errichtenden höheren Lehranstalt*, Schleiermacher's *Gelegentlichen Gedanken ber Universitten im deutschen Sinn*, plus Heinrich Steffens' *Über die Idee der Universitten*, and Humboldt's unfinished draft, *Über die innere und äußere Organisation der höheren wissenschaflichen Anstalten in Berlin*.

12. Schleiermacher's contribution to the debate about the design of the new university in Berlin was submitted with the title, *Occasional Thoughts on Universities in the German Sense of the Word* [*Gelegentliche Gedanken über Universitäten in Deutschem Sinn*], reprinted in Ernst Anrich's *Die Idee der Deutschen Universität* (Hermann Gentner Verlag: Darmstadt, 1956), 219–308; for Schleiermacher's 'grotesque' characterization, *cf.*, 257. Terrence Tice and Edwina Lawlor have translated it into English with the title, *Occasional Thoughts on Universities in the German Sense* (Lewiston, NY: Edwin Mellen Press, 1996), although this edition appears to have gone out of print.

13. Five key texts shaping the debate around the founding of the University of Berlin have been gathered together in the indispensable collection, *Die Idee der deutschen Universität* (Bad Homberg: Hermann Gentner, 1956). These include Schelling's *Über den absoluten Begriff der Wissenschaft*, Fichte's *Deduzierter Plan einer in Berlin zu errichtenden höheren Lehranstalt*, Schleiermacher's *Gelegentlichen Gedanken Über Universitäten im deutschen Sinn*, plus Heinrich Steffens' *Über die Idee der Universitäten*, and Humboldt's unfinished draft, *Über die innere und äußere Organisation der höheren wissenschaflichen Anstalten in Berlin*.
14. According to Erich Rothacker, the term enters into the German language as a translation of John Stuart Mill's "moral sciences" "[P]erhaps the term *Geisteswissenschaften* first appeared in 1849 in Schiel's translation of Mill's *System of Logic*." Cf. his *Logik und Systematik der Geisteswissenschaften* (Munich: Oldenbourg, 1927/1965), 6. According to Rudolf Makkreel, "Rothacker's claim is incorrect. In 1843, the historian Johann Gustav Droysen had used the term in the preface to the second volume of his *Geschichte des Hellenismus*." Cf. Makkreel's *Dilthey: Philosopher of the Human Studies* (Princeton: Princeton University Press, 1975), 36.
15. For primary texts on the founding of the university in Berlin, I have consulted Ernst Anrich's invaluable anthology, *Die Idee der deutschen Universität* (Darmstadt: Hermann Gentner Verlag, 1956). Although Fichte and Schleiermacher's proposals for the University of Berlin are also found in their own, respective, collected works, Anrich's edition brings together in one handy volume the five different plans submitted by Fichte, Schelling, Schleiermacher, Steffens as well as Humboldt's own, unfinished draft, which permits more readily topical comparisons. All the translations from this volume are my own, as no comparable English version has yet appeared. For the Fichte passage, see, 147–148.
16. Ibid., 150.
17. Ulrich Muhlack's historical reconstruction of the process behind the philosophical proposals solicited by Beyme and Humboldt, provides the clearest and fullest account of this. About Fichte's 'Deduzierter Plan,' Muhlack writes that "[A]llegedly, it appeared out of thin air" and that "although Fichte shared [Minister] Beyme's antipathy against the older universities," Beyme also sensed that Fichte had "indulged his own inclinations by grounding the new model for the university exclusively upon his own idealistic conception of science; that is, by deriving it from the Fichtean philosophy itself. . . . ." See his comprehensive overview, "Die Universitäten im Zeichen von Neuhumanismus und Idealismus: Berlin," in Beiträge zu Problemen deutscher Universitätsgrundungen der frühen Neuzeit, Wolfenbütteler Forschung, Band 4, (Nendeln/Liechtenstein: KTO Press, 1978), 308. My translation.
18. Cf. Schleiermacher's *Gelegentliche Gedanken über Universitäten in deutschen Sinn* (1808), reprinted in Anrich, 261.

19. Ibid., 261–262.
20. "Nächst der Philosophie macht die Philologie, als das allgemeine Kunstmittel aller Verständigung, mit Recht den meisten Anspruch auf Universalität" (Deduzierter Plan, §23, 155).
21. The term is Fichte's and refers to his belief that the traditional philosophical *Vorlesung* should be supplemented with a more informal discussion, led by a philosopher trained in Socratic method. See his *Deduzierter Plan* in Anrich, *op. cit.* § 9, 134. It should be pointed out that, although Schleiermacher disavows, in several places, prior awareness of Fichte's *Plan*, both refer to the *Conversatorien* (spelled by Schleiermacher with an initial 'K').
22. The reference here is to that remarkable page in "Christendom or Europe," in which Novalis appears to draw the figure of Schleiermacher and anticipates, in many ways, Dilthey's case for the historical nature of the *Geisteswissenschaften*. See Stoljar's translation, in *Novalis: Philosophical Writings*, 148, note 26 below.
23. For an excellent explication of Friedrich Schlegel's prodigious and masterful activities as a community organizer for the early German Romantics in Jena, as well as being a prodigious scholar, in his own right, see Elizabeth Millán's, *Friedrich Schlegel and the Emergence of Romantic Philosophy* (Albany: SUNY Press, 2007).
24. See, for example, *Novalis. Notes for a Romantic Encyclopaedia*, ed./trans. David Wood (Albany: SUNY Press, 2007). Also, *Novalis. Fichte Studies*, ed./trans. Jane Kneller (Cambridge: Cambridge University Press, 2003), hereafter, Kneller. I shall also make reference to *Novalis. Philosophical Writings*, ed./trans. Margaret Mahony Stoljar (Albany: SUNY Press, 1997), hereafter, Stoljar.
25. In this section, I have quoted extensively from Margaret Mahony Stoljar's translation and collection: *Novalis: Philosophical Writings* (Albany: SUNY Press, 1997). The meta-dream as 'close to waking' fragment stems from, 25.
26. Ibid., 28.
27. It is tempting to see in this "reciprocal determination" (Novalis' phrase for it in the *Fichte-Studien*; cf. Kneller, 104) something like the rhetorical trope of "chiasmus."
28. "The novel as such contains no definite result—it is not the image or fact of a proposition. It is the visible execution—the realization of an idea. But an idea cannot be comprehended in a proposition. An idea is an infinite series of propositions—an irrational number—it cannot be set (to music)—incommensurable" (Stoljar 70; *NS* II 570).
29. For an exceedingly clear elucidation of Breton's approach to mental insight and the use of grammatical jugglery to achieve such, see Inez Hedges' 1983 article, "Surrealist Metaphor: Frame Theory and Componential Analysis," *Poetics Today*, Vol. 4, No. 2, Metaphor (1983), 275–295.

30. Novalis makes this meta-philosophical remark in No. 32 of "The General Draft"; see Stoljar, *op. cit.*, 131, entitled "Philosophy and Pathological Logic." Referring, quite possibly to Fichte, he continues: "He is a magical idealist, insofar as magical idealists exist. The first person is looking for a wonder movement—a wonder object—a wonder form. Both are logical illnesses." One would want to compare these remarks with their twentieth-century counterparts in the late Wittgenstein.
31. Novalis, *Fichte Studies*, translated and edited by Jane Kneller (Cambridge: Cambridge University Press, 2003), fragment #491, 155.
32. Ibid., entry #523, 159.
33. Ibid., entry #450, 144.
34. Cf., *Logological Fragments*, #92, translated by Stoljar, *op. cit.*, 65.
35. *Cf.*, Novalis, *Philosophical Writings*, *op. cit.*, fragment #95, 41.
36. Ibid., fragment #12, 49.
37. Perhaps, the most reprinted fragment in Novalis' writings, this famous utterance actually is a conclusion to an enthymeme: The entire fragment draws a far wider focus: "Brilliant, noble, divinatory, miracle-working, clever, stupid, etc. plants, animals, stones, elements, etc. Infinite individuality of these beings—their musical sense, and sense of individuality—their character—their inclinations, etc. They are past, historical beings. Nature is a magic city turned to stone." Cf. Novalis, *Philosophical Writings*, Stoljar trans., *op. cit.*, fragment #10, 155.
38. Novalis, *Fichte Studies*, *op. cit.*, #498, 155.
39. Novalis, *Philosophical Writings*, *op. cit.*, #2, 153.
40. Ibid., #24, 54.
41. This concluding example stems from Novalis' "Logological Fragments I," found in Novalis, *Philosophical Writings*, Stoljar trans., *op. cit.*, 59.
42. Cf. Novalis, *Fichte Studies*, *op. cit.*, #561, 166.
43. See Kneller's contextual introduction to her translation of Novalis' *Fichte Studies*, cited below, note 44, vxi.
44. See Kneller's excellent reframing in her Introduction to Novalis' monumental *Fichte Studies*, *op. cit.*, especially xv–xvi.
45. Ibid., xvi.
46. See Makkreel's expansive study in Kantian application, *Orientation and Judgment in Hermeneutics* (Chicago: University of Chicago Press, 2015).
47. Kant, Immanuel. *Critique of the Power of Judgment*, edited by Paul Guyer, and translated by Paul Guyer and Eric Mathews (Cambridge: Cambridge University Press, 2000), Section 60, 229.
48. For Blanchot's phrase, "rhetoric become matter," see his article, "Reflections on Surrealism," in the collection, *Work on Fire* (Stanford: University of

Stanford Press, 1995), p. 89. For the Novalis reference, consider the following, which I gloss, above, as "only a trope can reverse a trope": "Transcendental poetry is a mixture of philosophy and poetry.... From the study of transcendental poetry a tropology can be anticipated – which constitutes the laws of the symbolic construction of the transcendental world." See the "Logological Fragments I," translated by Stoljar, *op. cit.*, 56–57.

49. See Novalis, "Christendom or Europe" in *Philosophical Writings*, *op. cit.*, 148–149.
50. See Pauline Kleingeld, "Romantic Cosmopolitanism: Novalis' *Christianity or Europe*," *Journal of the History of Philosophy*, 46 (2008): 269–284.
51. Ibid., 275.
52. See *God, Philosophy, Universities: A Selective History of the Catholic Philosophical Tradition* (Lanham, MD: Rowman and Littlefield, 2009), 34.
53. Cf. Alasdair MacIntyre's God, philosophy, universities (Lanham, Md.: Rowman & Littlefield Publishers, Inc., 2009), 135.
54. Ibid., 134.
55. Ibid., 135.
56. See Kant's essay, *The Contest of Faculties*, ed. Hans Reiss (Cambridge: Cambridge University Press, 1991), 188: "What sequence can progress be expected to follow? The answer is: not the usual sequence from the bottom upwards, but from the top downwards." This line, from the top down, becomes pervasive in post-Napoleonic Germany of the nineteenth century, and can be found on the tips of many writers' pens, all the way to Bismarck.
57. Schleiermacher, in the *Occasional Thoughts about Universities in the German Sense*, writes the following about the dialogical ethos facilitated by Conversatoria and Seminaria:

> Zwischen ihnen und den Vorlesungen liegen noch die Konversatorien, in welchen die Reaktion des Jünglings zuerst dem Lehrer sichtbar wird; er unterscheidet das minder faßlich Vorgetragene, und gibt es dem Lehrer zur Umarbeitung und Erläuterung zurück; er bringt Zweifel und Einwendungen vor, um sie sich lösen zu lassen. Diese fast wesentliche Form fehlt freilich häufig genug, aber die Lücke muß gewiß sehr fühlbar werden, wo sich nicht etwa eine solche freiere Vereinigung mit in den Seminarien versteckt. Schon bei dieser mehr gegenseitigen Mitteilung erscheinen gewiß nur diejenigen, in welchen der wissenschaftliche Geist sich wirklich regt.

Cf. *Gelegentliche Gedanken*, *op. cit.*, 176. For a fuller discussion of Schleiermacher's innovations regarding the academic seminar and the Konversatorien, see Thomas Karlsohn's wonderfully illuminating article "The Academic Seminar as Emotional Community," *Nordic Journal of Studies in Educational Policy*, 2–3 (2016): DOI: 10.3402/nstep.v2.33724, 1–10.

58. On a recent approach to Kant that views Kant's form of critical inquiry as 'trans-critique,' see Kōjin Karatani's, *Nation and Aesthetics: On Kant and Freud* (Oxford: Oxford University Press, 2017). For the most thorough working out of Kant's hermeneutical dimension, see Makkreel (*op. cit.*).
59. This inquiry owes much to the stimulating work and cross-pollination I have received over the years from Jane Kneller, Karl Ameriks, and Elizabeth Millán Brusslan, whose tireless efforts on behalf of opening up and sustaining scholarly work on the *Frühromantik* tradition is a model of scholarly collegiality. Symposiasts whose questions have stimulated me to take up the problem of thinking through the interpretation of Schleiermacher's aspirations and plans for the University of Berlin, by linking it to broader social and cultural themes of German political unity are Colin McQuillan, whose study on aesthetics and criticism is invaluable for shedding light on Schleiermacher's broader, orientational approach to hermeneutics, and Robert Richards, whose masterful studies of Goethe and Schelling, bring the Romantics still closer to formerly known Idealists, like Schelling, and the 'German Classics,' that is, Schiller and Goethe, revealing a symphilosophical culture that opens up newer, social historical, approaches to philosophers under-promoted in American graduate programs in philosophy. I have read with great profit and admiration the many works of Frederick Beiser on German schools of philosophy, and especially recommend, for these issues, his superb, Oxford study, *The Genesis of Neo-Kantianism, 1796–1880*. For the theological background to Schleiermacher's *On Religion*, his *The Romantic Imperative* is invaluable about the possible links between Spinozism and Lutheran pietism. I await his long-overdue study of Schleiermacher and Steffens, whose many books and writings, each of them, seem to have evaded capture in Beiser's deeply trawling nets.

# Part II

Aesthetics and Romanticism

# 11

## Philosophical Critique and Literary Criticism in German Romanticism

### J. Colin McQuillan

In the "Preface" to the first (A, 1781) edition of the *Critique of Pure Reason* (1781/1787), Immanuel Kant declared his time to be "the genuine age of criticism."[1] Little did he know how much criticism would flourish in the decades that followed the publication of his first *Critique*. Indeed, during the 1790s and the first decades of the 1800s, criticism became a central concern for German thinkers and writers, who extended this concept well beyond Kant's critical philosophy. The early German Romantics were at the center of this development, challenging "the critical age" to become more critical, even self-critical, and to transcend the dogmatism that, in their view, still pervaded philosophical critique and literary criticism.[2]

In the first section of this chapter, I will consider the debates about philosophical critique that took place in Germany in the last decades of the eighteenth century. These debates focused on Kant's critical philosophy as well as post-Kantian philosophies, such as Karl Leonhard Reinhold's *Elementarphilosophie*, and the first works of German idealism, such as Johann Gottlieb Fichte's *Wissenschaftslehre*. It is in the context of these debates that the German Romantics developed a novel conception of philosophical critique. I will argue that the early German Romantics: (1) appropriated from these philosophers the idea that critique is both a philosophical system and a

---

J. C. McQuillan (✉)
Saint Mary's University, San Antonio, TX, USA
e-mail: jmcquillan@stmarytx.edu

subjective standpoint; (2) indicted Kant and his followers for their narrow-mindedness and dogmatism; and (3) rejected the foundationalism of the idealists' search for first principles.

In the second section, I will turn my attention to the German Romantic conception of literary criticism. I will show that the early German Romantics rejected the didactic and nationalistic conceptions of criticism that were common during the Enlightenment, developing their own conception of criticism. Mainly in the works of Friedrich Schlegel, but also in works by Novalis and Schleiermacher, the German Romantics claim that literary criticism plays an essential role in art and culture. By devoting themselves to the individuality and integrity of the work, the German Romantics thought critics could promote and refine artistic sensibilities, encourage historical awareness, and renew philological scholarship.

Finally, in the last section, I will reflect on the relationship between philosophical critique and literary criticism in German Romanticism. Loathe as they were to let distinct disciplines stand in stark opposition to each other, the German Romantics established an important dialogue between philosophy and literature, which helped to bridge the divide between history, philology philosophy, and poetry in the early nineteenth century.

# 1 Philosophical Critique

Although the concept of "critique" was used widely in English, French, and German during the eighteenth century, it assumed a special place in German philosophy with the publication of Kant's *Critique of Pure Reason*.[3]

It has become commonplace for scholars, historians, and teachers to say that Kant's philosophy is "critical" because it rejects dogmatism and skepticism or because it seeks a third way between rationalism and empiricism; yet it is important to note that Kant does not characterize his critique in these terms in the first *Critique*. Instead, he defines his critique as: (1) a court of justice that will distinguish reason's rightful claims from its groundless pretensions; (2) a critique of the faculty of reason that will determine what, and how much, we can know a priori; (3) a transformation of the method of metaphysics, following the model of mathematics and physics; and (4) a propaedeutic to the system of pure reason.[4] The last of these definitions is of particular significance for understanding the early German Romantic conception of philosophical critique, because it inspired post-Kantian philosophers such as Karl Leonhard Reinhold and Johann Gottlieb Fichte to attempt what Kant had not and, perhaps, could not achieve—a move beyond critique, understood as a mere propaedeutic, to a complete system of philosophy.

Despite his reputation as a systematic philosopher, Kant never completed the system of pure reason he promised in the first *Critique*. To construct this system, Kant said he would first have to establish a basic set of a priori principles through a preliminary critique, then derive from these basic principles the rest of the principles of theoretical and practical philosophy, and, finally, present them all in his *Metaphysics of Nature* and *Metaphysics of Morals*. He took himself to have succeeded in cataloging "the entire outline of the science of metaphysics, both in respect to its boundaries and in respect to its entire internal structure" in the first *Critique* by identifying the pure forms of intuition, the pure concepts of the understanding, and the ideas of pure reason—the a priori principles upon which the system of pure reason depends.[5] But instead of deriving the principles that follow from these basic principles, he wrote two more critiques—the *Critique of Practical Reason* (1788) and *Critique of the Power of Judgment* (1790)—and two works on moral philosophy—*Groundwork of the Metaphysics of Morals* (1785) and *Metaphysics of Morals* (1797)—that deviate in important ways from the works he described in the first *Critique*. *Metaphysics of Morals* does not contain all of the principles "which determine action and omission *a priori* and make them necessary" and, in fact, only contain some of the general principles of right and virtue.[6] Kant never completed anything even resembling a *Metaphysics of Nature*—the *Metaphysical Foundations of Natural Science* (1786) is an application of the principles that were to be demonstrated in the *Metaphysics of Nature*, while the "transition project" sketched in the *Opus Postumum* (c. 1796–1801/1936–1938) is meant to provide the link between the *Metaphysical Foundations* and the empirical science of physics.[7] In the end, his failure to extend his system beyond the propaedeutic he presented in the first *Critique* came to be seen by many post-Kantian philosophers, particularly Reinhold and Fichte, as one of Kant's most significant philosophical failures.

Reinhold was an early and important defender of Kant's critical philosophy, but, after being appointed *Professor Extraordinarius* at the University of Jena in 1787, he took it upon himself to go beyond Kant's critique. This aim is stated most explicitly in the first (1790) volume of *Contributions to the Correction of Previous Misunderstandings of the Philosophers* (1790/1794), where Reinhold argues that Kant's critique is a "*propaedeutic to metaphysics* and is so called by its author."[8] By contrast, he says, his own "theory of the faculty of representation" should be called "Elementary Philosophy," because it is "the science of the principles of all philosophy, theoretical and practical, formal and material philosophy, not metaphysics alone."[9] Even more problematic than the partiality of Kant's critique is its failure to identify what Reinhold calls the "ultimate condition" of a system of philosophy—its "first principle." Reinhold argues throughout his Elementary Philosophy that this principle is the Principle of Consciousness, which defines representation as "that which is distinguished in consciousness by the subject from the object and subject, and is referred to both."[10] This means that, in consciousness, the subject distinguishes between itself and the representation of which it is conscious, in addition to distinguishing the representation from the object it represents, while recognizing that any consciousness of a representation must also be related to both the subject and object. Reinhold takes the Principle of Consciousness to define the nature of all representations, whether they are intuitions, concepts, or ideas, and, thus, to explicate what is not only presupposed throughout the critical philosophy, but which also serves as the ultimate condition and first principle for all of the principles of the critical philosophy and, indeed, any possible system of philosophy.[11] Kant's failure to extend his critique from the basic set of a priori principles necessary for metaphysics to the first principle of all philosophy, the Principle of Consciousness, confirmed, for Reinhold, that Kant's *Critique* is merely a propaedeutic and remains incomplete in its grounding as well as in its derivation of the principles of the *Metaphysics of Nature* and the *Metaphysics of Morals*.

Fichte was critical of many aspects of the Elementary Philosophy, but he shared Reinhold's view of the shortcomings of Kant's first *Critique*. In the "Preface" to the first (1794) edition of *Concerning the Concept of the Wissenschaftslehre* (1794/1798), Fichte acknowledges that Kant possessed a "spirit of genius" that "drove philosophical judgment so decisively from the standpoint at which he found it toward its final goal."[12] Yet he follows Reinhold in his insistence that philosophy, as a science, must be grounded in an absolutely certain first principle. "In fact," Fichte argues, "if we consider the innermost character of science, a science could well consist of only one proposition, a proposition which is certain in itself," because it is the certainty of the first principle that grounds and justifies every other principle of scientific knowledge.[13] Fichte agrees with Reinhold that this first principle is not to be found in Kant's critical philosophy, but he also recognizes the utility of beginning his system with a preliminary critique. However, the critique Fichte presents in *Concerning the Concept* differs in important ways from the propaedeutic conception of critique that was embraced by Kant and rejected by Reinhold. Fichte does not think a critique should demonstrate a basic set of a priori principles from which other principles can be derived, because that is the work of philosophy and science itself—the *Wissenschaftslehre*, in Fichte's preferred terminology. Instead, he argues in the "Preface" to the second (1798) edition of *Concerning the Concept* that critique "is related to metaphysics in exactly the same way that metaphysics is related to the ordinary point of view of natural understanding."[14] By this, Fichte means "metaphysics explains the ordinary point of view, and metaphysics is itself explained by critique."[15] In other words, critique is explanatory. It reflects upon, renders intelligible, and justifies the object of its criticism. *Concerning the Concept* is a critique of the *Wissenschaftslehre*, because it explains what the *Wissenschaftslehre* is, why it must be grounded in a first principle, how subsequent principles can be derived from that first principle, and how they give rise to distinctions between theoretical and practical philosophy, as well as other sciences.

In addition to the propaedeutic and explanatory conceptions of critique that we find in Kant, Reinhold, and Fichte, a third conception of critique should also be mentioned. This conception can be found in the third volume of Jakob Sigismund Beck's, *Explanatory Abstract of the Critical Writings of Prof. Kant*, more commonly known by its subtitle, *The Only Possible Standpoint from which the Critical Philosophy must be Judged* (1796). Beck thought Kant's contemporaries had misunderstood the critical philosophy because they had not properly grasped the "spirit" of Kant's critique and did not possess "the right feeling" about "how compelling idealism is."[16] We can infer from these claims in *The Only Possible Standpoint* that Beck thinks understanding the critical philosophy depends, at least in part, on one's subjective disposition—the cognitive and affective state in which one reads and thinks about philosophy. A similar view can be found in a number of works by Fichte. In the first (1794) "Introduction" to the *Foundation of the Entire Wissenschaftslehre* (1794–1795), for example, Fichte distinguishes the starting points of idealism and dogmatism—the subject and object—and shows how they lead to two mutually incompatible systems of philosophy. Fichte argues that the "the ultimate basis of the difference between idealists and dogmatists is thus the difference of their interests," suggesting that realists embrace dogmatism because they want to preserve the independence and external reality of what appears, while idealists embrace critical philosophy, because it affirms the independence and self-sufficiency of the I.[17] This makes critique the name for the standpoint of those who begin their systems with the freedom of the I and embrace idealism. Unfortunately, Fichte struggled with those who shared this standpoint as well as with those who did not. Subsequent versions of his introduction ("For Readers Who Already Have a System") and later presentations of the *Wissenschaftslehre* (*A Crystal Clear Report to the General Public Concerning the Actual Essence of the Newest Philosophy: An Attempt to Force the Reader to Understand*) indicate that his readers were more resistant to the

*Wissenschaftslehre* than they ought to have been, if they were interested in freedom.

Schelling's early writings contain perhaps the most sustained and systematic reflections on philosophical critique among the German Romantics. In *On the I as Principle of Philosophy* (1795), Schelling follows Fichte in characterizing dogmatism and critique as antithetical philosophical systems. That Schelling thinks these systems derive from the different standpoints of their adherents is clear from his account of the origin of the principle upon which critique is based—the I. He explains that critique derives from "those philosophers who really wanted the I, and not the not-I as the principle of philosophy, but they did not want to abandon the concept of fact," so "they had to choose the I … as the principle of all philosophy."[18] Again, it is the subjective desires and interests of the adherents of the critical philosophy—their standpoint—that leads them to privilege one principle over another and to affirm one system rather than its opposite. Similar arguments are also to be found in Schelling's *Philosophical Letters on Dogmatism and Criticism* (1795), which was published the same year. After rejecting claims that Kant's critique should be understood as a moral proof for the existence of God or as an account of our "cognitive faculty," Schelling argues that the "genuine essence" of critique concerns something very different and more profound.[19] Indeed, he says, "the *Critique* is destined to deduce from the essence of reason the very possibility of two exactly opposed systems; it is destined to establish a system of criticism (conceived as complete) or, more precisely, a system of idealism as well as in exact opposition to it, a system or dogmatism or realism."[20] The standpoint of critique is not, therefore, a particular, subjective disposition that might be distinguished from other dispositions. On the contrary, it is the standpoint of the Absolute—the point from which all philosophical systems emerge, even mutually opposed systems like dogmatism and criticism, realism, and idealism.

There are also a number of comments on philosophical critique in the works of Novalis, though they are scattered and, as a result, more difficult to interpret. Still, they are noteworthy, because they show that not all of the German Romantics regarded critique as a standpoint associated with idealism and opposed to dogmatism. In his *Notes for a Romantic Encyclopedia* (1798–1799), Novalis says "it was Kant's plan to supply a universal—an encyclopedic critique—yet he was not able to carry this out, and with respect to its individual elements, he was not so fortunate in his execution."[21] This passage echoes Reinhold's objection to Kant's critique—that critique, as a propaedeutic, must be partial and incomplete—and goes on to raise a similar objection against Fichte's *Wissenschaftslehre*. According to Novalis, Fichte is "the reviser of the Kantian critique—the 2nd Kant—the higher organ, insofar as Kant is the lower organ .... He sets the reader down at the point where Kant takes them up. His *Wissenschaftslehre* is therefore the philosophy of the critique—its introduction—its purer part. It contains the principles of the critique. Yet, to my mind, it is still greatly lacking in this ideal. It only encompasses one part of the philosophy of the critique—and is just as incomplete as the critique itself."[22] Together, these remarks show that Novalis understood the preparatory nature of Kantian critique—critique as a propaedeutic—as well as the goals of Kant's critical philosophy—the construction of a system of pure reason—and Reinhold's criticism of Kant's failure to complete that system. The extension of Reinhold's criticism of Kant to Fichte also helps us understand the ambitions of Novalis' encyclopedia. Indeed, when we examine his notes, we see that Novalis complains, under the heading "encyclopedistics," about the one-sidedness of philosophical systems and the arbitrariness of the principles philosophers have used to construct them. In response to those who have "selected several of the criteria without criticism, and consequently obtained a confused system," Novalis insists "a critique of philosophical criteria is of utmost importance for philosophy—just as a critique of natural historical criteria is for natural history."[23] This claim is reminiscent of Fichte's explanatory conception of critique, though the criteria Novalis has in mind for his "encyclopedistics" are very different from those Fichte articulates in *Concerning the Concept of the Wissenschaftslehre*, which Novalis regarded as "rather *dogmatic*."[24] Instead of searching for a single, first principle, Novalis sought to produce a classification of the various "scientific operations" that would render their "order and sequence" comprehensible. The result is undoubtedly complicated, but undeniably pluralistic.

Finally, there are several fragments about philosophical critique in the works of Friedrich Schlegel. In the *Athenaeum Fragments* (1798), he writes that "since nowadays philosophy criticizes everything that comes in front of its nose, a criticism of philosophy would be nothing more than justifiable retaliation."[25] This fragment seems to complement the first fragment in the *Athenaeum*, which suggests that "nothing is more rarely the subject of philosophy than philosophy itself."[26] In effect, Schlegel is accusing philosophy of being eager to criticize others, but unwilling to subject itself to the degree of self-critical scrutiny. Other fragments extend this criticism to Kant and his followers. In one of these fragments, Schlegel writes that "those people who have made a profession of explaining Kant to us were either of the sort that lacked the capacity to gain an understanding for themselves of the subjects about which Kant has written; or else such people as only had the slight misfortune of understanding no one except themselves; or such as expressed themselves even more confusedly than he did."[27] These fragments refer to the subjective standpoint from which Kant and his followers construct their systems, implying that Kant's standpoint is ahistorical and philosophically dogmatic, leaving his followers ignorant and confused. This leads Schlegel to conclude that "the philosophy of the Kantians is probably termed critical *per antiphrasin*; or else it is an *epithet ornans*."[28] In other words, philosophical critique is either contradictory or meaningless, because it is not self-critical and, as a result, does not even consider the issues that are most important for philosophy to address.[29] There are, however, other fragments that address different conceptions of critique. In one of these fragments, Schlegel calls Fichte "a Kant raised to the second power," because the *Wissenschaftslehre* is "simultaneously philosophy and philosophy of philosophy."[30] This is clearly a reference to Fichte's explanatory conception of critique, which is not simply concerned with the subject matter of science or philosophy, but also with the form of their exposition. It is by examining the form of the *Wissenschaftslehre* that Schlegel thinks we can grasp the unity of Fichte's and Kant's philosophy, though he also takes his distance from Fichtean critique, noting, at the end of the fragment, that "one can never be too critical."[31]

## 2 Literary Criticism

Art and literary criticism played an even larger and more important role in European culture during the eighteenth century than they did during the period of Kant's critical philosophy. In the eighteenth century, criticism became a staple of periodicals such as *The Tatler* (1709–1711) and *The Spectator* (1711–1715) in Britain, as well as their German versions, for example, Gottsched's *Die vernünftige Tadlerinnen* (1725–1725) and *Der Biedermann* (1727–1729). The readership of these periodicals differed in important ways from the small circle of academic specialists for whom criticism was, in the previous century, primarily concerned with philological questions about ancient literature. Periodicals were read by large and diverse audiences who may or may not have had formal academic training in classics. They were also read in public spaces, like tea, coffee, and chocolate shops, where debates about social and political issues mixed with discussions of modern art and literature.[32] In German-speaking lands, during the second half of the eighteenth century, these discussions were often informed by journals such as the *Allgemeine deutsche Bibliothek* (1765–1806), which sought to review every new book published in Germany, as well as anything else of scientific and literary merit. Friedrich Nicolai, the editor of the *AdB*, expresses sentiments typical of the German Enlightenment when he enumerates the virtues of criticism, saying "precise and sound criticism is the only means of achieving and determining good taste" and also when he says "it is certain that the most exact criticism is indispensable to us, if we expect works by German geniuses to be worthy of the respect of posterity."[33] Not for nothing did Kant call this time "the genuine age of criticism."[34]

It is in relation to Enlightenment conceptions of literary criticism, like Nicolai's, that we should understand the German Romantic conception of literary criticism. The German Romantics recognized and affirmed the prominent place criticism occupied during the Enlightenment, as well as its role in the development of modern literature. They rejected the image of the critic as the persecutor of literary genius that is often attributed to them. Yet they were also wary of the kind of criticism being published in periodicals like the *AdB*. Nicolai's pedagogical interest in shaping the tastes of his readers was problematic for the German Romantics, as evidenced by a fragment from Schlegel: "The function of criticism, people say, is to educate one's readers! Whoever wants to be educated, let him educate himself. This is rude: But it can't be helped."[35] This fragment challenges the authority of the critic to determine what readers should know and value. Schlegel also seems to affirm a more individualist or, perhaps, more personalistic view of education as *Bildung* than we find in Nicolai's enlightened didacticism—his attempt to educate the judgment and taste of German readers. Instead of gaining the respect of future generations by conforming to universal and timeless standards of "good taste," Schlegel suggests that education is a process of personal development, growth, and discovery that distinguishes one individual from another. Schlegel's conception of a "universal progressive poetry," which would unite philosophy and rhetoric, verse and prose, genius and criticism, art and nature, is also sharply at odds with the nationalistic tendencies of Enlightenment criticism.[36] While Gottsched and Nicolai hoped to promote the development of literature in the German language, within the German territories, for the German people, the German Romantics did not limit their efforts to any one language, place, or group of people. They championed works by Dante, Boccaccio, Cervantes, Shakespeare, Calderon, and Goethe as representatives of romantic poetry, regardless of their linguistic or national origins, articulating, in the process, a cosmopolitan view of literature and culture that crossed national boundaries.[37]

Yet we cannot understand German Romantic literary criticism simply by contrasting it with seventeenth-century philology or German Enlightenment criticism. Literary criticism was an object of both theoretical reflection and practical engagement for the German Romantics. Take, for example, Friedrich Schlegel's review (1798) of Goethe's *Wilhelm Meister* (1796). Schlegel regards Goethe's novel, along with the French Revolution and

Fichte's *Wissenschaftslehre*, as "the greatest tendencies of the age."[38] He even suggests that whoever was able to interpret the work "would have expressed what is now happening in literature" and could retire from "literary criticism" forever.[39] However, in his review of *Wilhelm Meister*, Schlegel does not simply praise Goethe's genius or list the perfections of his work; he also reflects on the nature of criticism. According to Schlegel, "the view of Hamlet to be found scattered partly here [in the third and fourth books] is not so much criticism as high poetry."[40] This claim implies that there is an important distinction to be drawn between poetry and criticism. Poetry is said to be something that comes about "when a poet in full possession of his powers contemplates a work of art and represents it in his own," which suggests that it is the result of an artist contemplating art itself, instead of diligently working on the creation of a particular poem.[41] This makes art, or, perhaps, the work, into an idea or an ideal—something to which poetry and poems aspire.[42] In a series of fragments written in response to Schlegel's review, Novalis puts the point as follows: "every work of art has an ideal *a priori*—It has a necessity of itself to exist."[43] Novalis goes on to claim that it is only through this "ideal *a priori*" that "true criticism" is possible.[44] Schlegel would, I think, agree. In his review, he argues that criticism "does not act as a mere inscription, and merely say what the thing is, and where it stands and should stand in the world."[45] On the contrary, Schlegel thinks the critic aims at "developing and elaborating an insight which is fundamentally single and indivisible" in a way that is fundamentally different from the artist or poet. The difference is presented in an ambiguous way when Schlegel says "the poet and artist … will want to represent the representation anew, and form once more what has already been formed," while the critic "will add to the work, restore it, shape it afresh."[46] These two functions could be taken to be equivalent, since it remains unclear how "representing the representation anew" differs from "restoring" the work and "shaping it afresh." Yet it seems that Schlegel takes "restoring" and "refreshing" to refer to the poem rather than to the idea of the work, so that, for the critic, the poem itself serves as an ideal. That is why he says the critic "will only divide the whole into articulated parts and masses, not break it down into its original constituents, which in respect of the work are dead things, because their elements are no longer of the same nature as the whole; however, in respect of the universe they are certainly living, and could be articulated parts or masses there. The ordinary critic relates the object of his art to these, and so he is inevitably bound to destroy his living unity, sometimes breaking it down into its elements, sometimes regarding it as an atom itself within a greater mass."[47] The analytical restraint that Schlegel advocates in this passage is justified by the integrity of the object of criticism, its organic unity, and wholeness, which defines its individuality and its character. Representing the individuality and character of the poem is the work of the critic who, like the artist, devotes themselves to an ideal that is higher than their own art. A practical example of this devotion can be found in the review in which Schlegel's reflections are situated. At each step, as he describes the "quiet unfolding of an aspiring spirit" in Goethe's novel, Schlegel attends to the charm, beauty, depth, and grandeur of its four parts, considered in themselves and in relation to the whole to which they belong.[48]

The value of criticism that attends to the uniqueness and integrity of the work is explained in Schlegel's *Lessing's Thoughts and Opinions* (1804). The "General Introduction" to the work is subtitled "Concerning the Essence of Critique" and provides an overview of "the concept of criticism"—a concept that, according to Schlegel, provides a summary of all of Lessing's intellectual activities, including his writings about classical antiquity, grammar, literature, and dramaturgy.[49] Schlegel begins with a short history of criticism, tracing the origins of the concept to the ancient Greeks, who "invented and established it, and, at the same time, took it almost to its highest point of development and perfection."[50] Schlegel associates Greek criticism with the work of selecting and ordering the works that best represent their poetic tradition, as well as the philological and editorial work of correcting the multiple forms in which classical works were preserved and transmitted. He praises the method the Greeks employed, noting that they "did not consider to be excellent, fully formed, and worthy of eternal imitation that which was free of mistakes," because a work that is "free of mistakes" often lacks the "force of excess" that marks it as "the first, the highest, or the ultimate in its genre, even when it gives offense to a limited sensibility."[51] Schlegel thinks the Greeks were uniquely sensitive to the quality of such works, because their "artistic sensibility" had not been corrupted by the invention of the printing press and the expansion of the book market—forces that led to the corruption and confusion of modern taste.[52] The Greeks read and reread their classical writings, refining their artistic sensibilities, the maturity of their critical judgment, and their culture as a whole. This did not take place in Rome; the Roman conception of criticism was imported from Greece, and was, as a foreign tradition, appreciated only by a small group of scholars.[53] Nor did it take place in modern Europe, despite the richness of modern languages and literature. Schlegel argues that "the Provençal ballads, the Old French creations, and the masterful works of old German poetry have been lost," because, "unlike in Greece, no age of criticism followed the great age of poets, such that, although the power to bring forth new beauty may no longer have been present, at least the old beauty could have been handed down to later ages."[54] This leads Schlegel to conclude that "no literature can exist for long without criticism and no language is secure from corruption that does not maintain the monuments of its poetry and nourish their spirit."[55] Because criticism is "the common pillar on which the entire edifice of knowledge and of language rests," he ends his introduction, not only by praising Lessing, to whose thoughts and opinions the work is devoted, but also by presenting a sort of manifesto for German criticism. He rejects the attempts by German philosophers to transform criticism into aesthetics, which strives "merely to explain artistic sensibility, rather than universally practicing, applying, and constructing it further."[56] It is likely that he had in mind philosophers like Gottsched, who sought to ground his poetics in rationalist philosophy; Baumgarten, who tried to formally define beauty and enumerate its perfections; and Kant, who claimed to have discovered the a priori principles of judgments of taste. More fruitful than the systems of these philosophers, Schlegel argues, is Lessing's attempt "to differentiate strictly between the various genres of art—indeed, to determine the concept of each with scientific precision," because the latter has important practical applications.[57] Indeed, Schlegel maintains that it is the "exemplary striving" of artists and critics toward what is essential to art, "which actually lays the basis for an improved notion of criticism that is to restore to us the former, lost one." He even insists that it leads, sooner or later, "to a historical construction of the whole of art and poetics" that is "the primary and most essential condition for a criticism that is really able to fulfill its high calling," because it situates works and genres in the language, culture, and context from which they arise.[58] Finally, Schlegel argues that criticism requires a renewal of philology, understood as "that interest which can be aroused for anything that can in any way be said to be of literary interest, even that which is of interest to a true *literator* or librarian merely because it once was of interest."[59] Lessing stands as a model of this renewed philology, because he extends his philological inquiries beyond Greek and Latin into modern German, English, French, Italian, and Spanish literature; unites scholarship with an artistic sensibility and historical understanding; and presents his work in a way that remained "popular and universally applicable."[60] Schlegel's conception of romantic literary criticism, as it is articulated in his fragments and in his review of *Wilhelm Meister*, follows this model precisely.

Schleiermacher probably did more than any of the German Romantics to advance Schlegel's conception of criticism as renewed philology. Although he does not often mention Schlegel by name, we can see how closely the concepts of criticism and philology were related to Schleiermacher, and how closely they were related to his hermeneutics. This is apparent, not only in his translations of Plato (1804–1828), but also, more theoretically, in the lectures on hermeneutics and criticism that he delivered in Berlin (c. 1819). It has often been noted that, in his translations of Plato, Schleiermacher promotes a "foreignizing" approach to translation—one that challenges the reader to understand the author, instead of making the author more comprehensible to the reader.⁶¹ This is already evident from the "General Introduction" in the first (1804) volume of his translation. Schleiermacher refuses to speculate about the biography of the author of the dialogues or his philosophical views, because "a worthy reader of Plato can entertain the notion of wishing to strike out a light upon the sentiments of the philosopher," can learn these things "from the works themselves," and has no need to rely on "multifariously told and deformed trifles."⁶² Schleiermacher also refuses to provide a contextualizing survey of Greek philosophy and science, since such a survey would either repeat conventional wisdom or speculate about matters that remain uncertain, making it more difficult for readers to adopt "the right point of view" for appreciating Plato's dialogues. Schleiermacher would prefer readers to read the dialogues for themselves, acquaint themselves with Plato as a "philosophical artist," and attend to the unique character of his works, though this task is complicated by the Greek philosopher's "utter deviation from the ordinary forms of philosophical communication."⁶³ Schleiermacher's response is to challenge modern criticism to account, not only for the philosophical doctrines present in Plato's dialogues but also for their literary form, and the interconnections between the matter and form of philosophy.⁶⁴ Going further, Schleiermacher challenges critics to reconstruct "the natural order" of the Platonic dialogues—the way in which "the exposition of philosophy" proceeds "from the very first excitement of the original and leading ideas" in one dialogue to the "original and leading ideas" of another dialogue, and establishes "a natural sequence and a necessary relation in these dialogues to one another."⁶⁵ By reconstructing the history of the dialogues, understood as the sequence of insights that led their author from one work to the next, Schleiermacher thinks we will be in a better position to appreciate Plato's literary artistry, as well as his philosophy. He does not shy away from philological technicalities in his approach to history; on the contrary, he encourages critics to try to establish the authenticity of the dialogues and to study Plato's use of language, along with the range of subjects he discusses in the dialogues and the form of the dialogue. And he discusses the technical requirements of these tasks in the lectures on hermeneutics and criticism that he delivered in Berlin, at a time when he was still in the process of publishing his Plato translations. In the "General Introduction" to his lectures, Schleiermacher characterizes hermeneutics and criticism as philological disciplines that presuppose one another. Hermeneutics is defined as "the art of understanding particularly the written discourse of another person correctly," while criticism is "the art of judging correctly and establishing the authenticity of texts and parts of texts from adequate evidence and data."[66] Hermeneutics presupposes criticism, because "explication can only be sure of its establishing the meaning if the authenticity of the text or part of the text can be presupposed."[67] Yet criticism also presupposes hermeneutics, insofar as we engage in criticism in order to correctly understand an author, and this process of understanding continues even after criticism has been successfully concluded—if it is even possible for criticism to be complete.[68] The ongoing investigation of the critic serves hermeneutics by attending to the details of grammar and texts and by constantly comparing "single products with their idea."[69] Schleiermacher explains this claim later in the lectures, where he claims that "for every human work there is a primal image," in comparison to which "the particular must be judged as appearance."[70] This seems to rely on a conception of the work as what Novalis called an "ideal *a priori*," which the critic uses to judge, not only the charm, beauty, depth, and grandeur of a work—the values with which Schlegel was concerned in his review of *Wilhelm Meister*—but also the kind of philological minutiae that might only be of interest to "a true *literator* or librarian"—the final requirement for a renewed philology, according to Schlegel's account of "the essence of critique." Schleiermacher also insists that criticism is historical and that its scope is "wider than the classical"—indeed, he says it is even broader than "the literary domain as a whole"—making the relationship between Schleiermacher's criticism and Schlegel's renewed philology quite clear.

## 3    Critical Romanticism

So far, I have presented philosophical critique and literary criticism in German Romanticism as if they were separate. In the section on philosophical critique, I identified the ways in which the German Romantics took up three different conceptions of critique that rose to prominence in German philosophy in the wake of Kant's first *Critique*—critique as a propaedeutic to a philosophical system, critique as reflective explanation, and critique as a subjective standpoint. In the section on literary criticism, I showed that the German Romantics understood criticism through its devotion to the ideal of the work and its unique character; that they thought it was essential to knowledge, language, and culture; and saw it as distinct from aesthetics, though closely related to history and philology. However, it is important to note that German Romantic conceptions of philosophical critique and literary criticism were actually closely intertwined, despite the appearance of separateness that the organization of this chapter might create.

The connections between philosophical critique and literary criticism in German Romanticism can be partially explained by the close personal relationships among the Romantics during their time in Jena—often referred to as the period of "Jena Romanticism" (1798–1804). During this time, Novalis, Schlegel, and Schleiermacher were deeply engaged in discussions of Kant's critical philosophy, Reinhold's Elementary Philosophy, and Fichte's *Wissenschaftslehre*, which were shaped by the lectures Reinhold, Fichte, and Schelling had delivered at the university. At the same time, the German Romantics were engaged in their own literary pursuits, many of which were collective undertakings. Take, for example, the literary journal *Athenaeum*, published between 1798 and 1800, which I have quoted many times throughout this chapter. Edited by Friedrich and August Wilhelm Schlegel, *Athenaeum* contains fragments written by Novalis, both Schlegels, and Schleiermacher, as well as Dorothea Schlegel, Caroline Schlegel (later Caroline Schelling), and several others. It also mixes fragments on philosophy, literature, history, politics, and many other subjects, suggesting that it would be a mistake to draw sharp distinctions between philosophical critique and literary criticism—they are one and the same *Kritik* and appear together in the same work, which is both literary and philosophical at the same time.

If we go beyond biography and history to examine the content of their writings, the close relation between German Romantic conceptions of philosophical critique and literary criticism becomes apparent in a number of passages that seem to be primarily about philosophical critique. For example, Schlegel calls Kant a "half critic," because "a critique of philosophizing reason cannot succeed without a history of philosophy" and Kant's thought is "not at all historical enough even though it is filled with historical relations and he attempts to construct various systems."[71] This suggests that Kant's philosophical critique remains uncritical because it is insufficiently historical—an essential component of his conception of literary criticism. Schlegel also emphasizes the importance of history for philosophical critique at the end of the introduction to *Lessing's Thoughts and Opinions* (1804). There Schlegel even says that "critique" should be understood as "a middle term between history and philosophy, one that shall join both, and in which both are to be united to form a new, third term."[72] The work of this new conception of critique is also described in terms that are reminiscent of Schlegel's account of literary criticism. He says that "a history of philosophy such as the one that is at stake here can have as its object of investigation a single system, a single philosopher alone." In order to comprehend this system, Schlegel says critique must be able to "reconstruct its course and its structure" in a way that allows us to appreciate its distinctive character of "a work, an intellect." Thus, "characterizing," which was associated with literary criticism, also becomes "the inner essence" and "highest task" of philosophical critique.[73]

Nor should we neglect the philosophical dimension of German Romantic conceptions of literary criticism. By conceiving of the work of art as an idea or ideal, the German Romantics committed themselves to a metaphysics that is, or could be, even more idealistic than Kant's or Hegel's idealism. Some commentators have called early German Romanticism "the greatest revival of Platonism since the renaissance" because it conceived of the work of art as a transcendent reality that could only be grasped by aesthetic intuition.[74] Whether the German Romantics explicitly affirmed such an idealistic metaphysics, or whether they embraced it ironically, remains a matter of debate. The early German Romantics may have seen works of art as instantiations of ideal forms, but the historical and philological dimensions of their conception of literary criticism complicate any straightforwardly idealistic interpretation of their philosophy of art—art is bound, not only to its ideal a priori but also to times, places, and peoples. Finally, we should not underestimate the metaphysical implications of their conception of literary criticism as "characterization." The German Romantics did not dismiss attempts to identify and classify literary natures and kinds—genres—but their sensitivity to the complex ways in which genres mix in modern literature, to the individuality of works of art, and to the peculiarity of the fragment all indicate that they adhered to a distinctively particularistic metaphysics, even if they did not present this view in the form of a treatise or defend it with philosophical arguments. If, for the early German Romantics, the task of the critic is to attend to the particular character of the work, in all its complexity and individuality, then criticism is as philosophical as it is literary.

## Notes

1. Immanuel Kant, *Critique of Pure Reason*, trans. Paul Guyer and Allen W. Wood (Cambridge: Cambridge University Press, 1998), Axi. The English words "critique" and "criticism" are used throughout this chapter to render the German word *Kritik*—sometimes spelled *Critic* or *Critik* in the eighteenth and early nineteenth century. I have used "critique" to translate *Kritik* when it is used in philosophical contexts and "criticism" to translate the same term when it refers to art and literary criticism. Differentially translating the same German term creates the appearance of a difference, which helps to

clarify the different functions *Kritik* served in different contexts. However, it may not reflect a fundamental conceptual distinction between philosophical and literary *Kritik*, least of all for the early German Romantics.

2. Jochen Schulte-Sasse, *Theory as Practice: A Critical Anthology of Early German Romantic Writings (Schlegel, On Incomprehensibility)* (Minneapolis: University of Minnesota Press, 1997), 261. For the purposes of this chapter, "early German Romanticism" (*Frühromantik*) refers to the movement associated with Novalis, Schelling, August and Friedrich Schlegel, and Friedrich Schleiermacher, in Jena and Berlin, between 1794 and 1808.

3. See, for example, the entry on *kritik* by Claus von Bormann, Giorgio Tonelli, and Helmut Holzhey in Joachim Ritter, et al., *Historisches Wörterbuch der Philosophie, Bd. 4* (Basel: Schwabe Verlag, 1976), 1250–1282.

4. Kant, *Critique of Pure Reason*, Axii, Bxxii, A10/B24-A13/B26. See also J. Colin McQuillan, *Immanuel Kant: The Very Idea of a Critique of Pure Reason* (Evanston: Northwestern University Press, 2016), 63–88.

5. Kant, *Critique of Pure Reason*, Bxxii.

6. Kant, *Critique of Pure Reason*, A841/B869. See also Immanuel Kant, *Practical Philosophy (Metaphysics of Morals)*, trans. Mary Gregor (Cambridge: Cambridge University Press, 1996), 365.

7. Immanuel Kant, *Theoretical Philosophy After 1781 (Metaphysical Foundations of Natural Science)*, ed. Henry Allison and Peter Heath (New York: Cambridge University Press, 2002), 184–185; Immanuel Kant, *Correspondence (Kant to Christian Gottfried Schütz, September 13, 1785 & Kant to Christian Garve, September 21, 1798)*, ed. and trans. Arnulf Zweig (New York: Cambridge University Press, 1999), 229, 551.

8. Reinhold, Karl Leonhard Reinhold, *Beiträge zur Berichtigung bisheriger Mißverständnisse der Philosophen, Bd. 1*, ed. Faustino Fabbianelli (Hamburg: Felix Meiner Verlag, 2004), 193. A similar argument is found in *The Foundation of Philosophical Knowledge* (1791), where Reinhold notes that Kant's critique "fails to ground the whole of philosophical knowledge; on the contrary, it *only* grounded ONE PART of it." "In short," he continues, "the only part of philosophical knowledge that Kant grounds is that philosophical science called *metaphysics*," which is understood as "the *science of objects proper*, that is to say, of objects that are distinguished in consciousness from all mere representations or the properties of representations." See George Di Giovanni and H.S. Harris, *Between Kant and Hegel: Texts in the Development of Post-Kantian Idealism (Reinhold, The Foundations of Philosophical Knowledge)* (*Revised Edition*, Indianapolis: Hackett Publishing, 2000), 63–64.

9. Reinhold, *Beiträge zur Berichtigung bisheriger Mißverständnisse der Philosophen (Bd. 1)*, 193.

10. Di Giovanni and Harris, *Between Kant and Hegel (Reinhold, The Foundations of Philosophical Knowledge)*, 72.

11. Reinhold first argues that the concept of representation is presupposed by but undefined in Kant's Critical philosophy, as well as being the ultimate condition and first principle of all philosophy in Karl Leonhard Reinhold, *Essay on a New Theory of the Human Capacity for Representation*, trans. Tim Mehigan and Barry Empson (Berlin: Walter de Gruyter, 2016), 25–26.
12. Johann Gottlieb Fichte, *Early Philosophical Writings (Concerning the Concept of the Wissenschaftslehre)*, ed. and trans. Daniel Breazeale (Ithaca: Cornell University Press, 1988), 96.
13. Fichte, *Early Philosophical Writings (Concerning the Concept of the Wissenschaftslehre)*, 104.
14. Fichte, *Early Philosophical Writings (Concerning the Concept of the Wissenschaftslehre)*, 97.
15. Fichte, *Early Philosophical Writings (Concerning the Concept of the Wissenschaftslehre)*, 97.
16. Di Giovanni and Harris, *Between Kant and Hegel (Beck, The Standpoint from which Critical Philosophy is to be Judged)*, 206–207.
17. Johann Gottlieb Fichte, *The Science of Knowledge*, trans. Peter Heath and John Lachs (Cambridge: Cambridge University Press, 1982), 15–28.
18. Friedrich Wilhelm Joseph Schelling, *The Unconditional in Human Knowledge: Early Essays by F.W.J. Schelling (On the I as Principle of Philosophy)*, trans. Fritz Marti (Lewisburg: Bucknell University Press, 1980), 80. Schelling suggests that the adherents of the critical philosophy—Kant and Reinhold—initially privileged "the empirically conditioned I" over the "absolute I," at least until they discovered that "the perfect system of philosophical science proceeds from the absolute I ... as the one unconditionable" that "conditions the whole chain of knowledge, circumscribes the sphere of all that is thinkable and, as the absolute all-comprehending reality, rules the whole system of our knowledge." See Schelling, *The Unconditional in Human Knowledge (On the I as Principle of Philosophy)*, 80–81.
19. Schelling, *The Unconditional in Human Knowledge (Philosophical Letters on Dogmatism and Criticism)*, 161.
20. Schelling, *The Unconditional in Human Knowledge (Philosophical Letters on Dogmatism and Criticism)*, 169.
21. Novalis, *Notes for a Romantic Encyclopedia*, ed. and trans. David W. Wood (Albany: SUNY Press, 2007), 77. On this passage, see Dalia Nassar, *The Romantic Absolute: Being and Knowing in Early German Romantic Philosophy* (Chicago: The University of Chicago Press, 2014), 72.
22. Novalis, *Notes for a Romantic Encylopedia*, 77. It is noteworthy that Schlegel not only calls Fichte a second Kant, but also refers to him as "a Kant raised to the second power." See Peter Firchow, *Friedrich Schlegel's Lucinde and the Fragments (Athenaeum Fragments)* (Minneapolis: University of Minnesota Press, 1971), 202.
23. Novalis, *Notes for a Romantic Encyclopedia*, 76.

24. Novalis, *Notes for a Romantic Encyclopedia*, 9.
25. Firchow, *Friedrich Schlegel's Lucinde and the Fragments (Athenaeum Fragments)*, 168.
26. Firchow, *Friedrich Schlegel's Lucinde and the Fragments (Athenaeum Fragments)*, 161.
27. Firchow, *Friedrich Schlegel's Lucinde and the Fragments (Athenaeum Fragments)*, 166.
28. Firchow, *Friedrich Schlegel's Lucinde and the Fragments (Athenaeum Fragments)*, 167.
29. Firchow, *Friedrich Schlegel's Lucinde and the Fragments (Athenaeum Fragments)*, 167.
30. Firchow, *Friedrich Schlegel's Lucinde and the Fragments (Athenaeum Fragments)*, 202. Similar point in Novalis, *Notes for a Romantic Encyclopedia*, 463–464.
31. Firchow, *Friedrich Schlegel's Lucinde and the Fragments (Athenaeum Fragments)*, 202.
32. On the importance of tea, coffee, and chocolate shops as sites for public discourse in early modern Europe, see Habermas, *The Structural Transformation of the Public Sphere*, trans. Thomas Burger (Cambridge: MIT Press, 1989), 32–33.
33. Friedrich Nicolai, *Kritik ist überall, zumal in Deutschland, nötig: Satiren und Schriften zur Literatur (Briefe über die itzigen Zustand der schönen Wissenschaften, 17. Brief)*, ed. Wolfgang Albrecht (Leipzig: Gustav Kiepenheuer, 1987), 197, 201.
34. Kant, *Critique of Pure Reason*, Axi.
35. Firchow, *Friedrich Schlegel's Lucinde and the Fragments (Critical Fragments)*, 153.
36. Firchow, *Friedrich Schlegel's Lucinde and the Fragments (Athenaeum Fragments)*, 175.
37. On the cosmopolitanism of early German Romanticism, see Kleingeld, "Six Varieties of Cosmopolitanism in Late Eighteenth Century Germany," 521–524.
38. Firchow, *Friedrich Schlegel's Lucinde and the Fragments (Athenaeum Fragments)*, 190.
39. Firchow, *Friedrich Schlegel's Lucinde and the Fragments (Athenaeum Fragments)*, 158.
40. J.M. Bernstein, *Classic and Romantic German Aesthetics (Schlegel, On Goethe's Meister)* (Cambridge: Cambridge University Press, 2003), 281.
41. Bernstein, *Classic and Romantic German Aesthetics (Schlegel, On Goethe's Meister)*, 281.
42. This aspect of the early German Romantic theory of art is emphasized in Walter Benjamin, *Selected Writings, Vol. 1: 1913–1926 (The Concept of Criticism in German Romanticism)*, ed. Marcus Bullock and Michael W. Jennings (Cambridge: Harvard University Press, 1996), 153–156.

43. Novalis, *Philosophical Writings (On Goethe)*, ed. and trans. Margaret Mahony Stoljar (Albany: SUNY Press, 1997), 117.
44. Novalis, *Philosophical Writings (On Goethe)*, 117.
45. Bernstein, *Classic and Romantic German Aesthetics (Schlegel, On Goethe's Meister)*, 281.
46. Bernstein, *Classic and Romantic German Aesthetics (Schlegel, On Goethe's Meister)*, 281.
47. Bernstein, *Classic and Romantic German Aesthetics (Schlegel, On Goethe's Meister)*, 281.
48. Bernstein, *Classic and Romantic German Aesthetics (Schlegel, On Goethe's Meister)*, 269, 285.
49. Schulte-Sasse, *Theory as Practice (Schlegel, Concerning the Essence of Critique)*, 268.
50. Schulte-Sasse, *Theory as Practice (Schlegel, Concerning the Essence of Critique)*, 268.
51. Schulte-Sasse, *Theory as Practice (Schlegel, Concerning the Essence of Critique)*, 269.
52. Schulte-Sasse, *Theory as Practice (Schlegel, Concerning the Essence of Critique)*, 269–270.
53. Schulte-Sasse, *Theory as Practice (Schlegel, Concerning the Essence of Critique)*, 270.
54. Schulte-Sasse, *Theory as Practice (Schlegel, Concerning the Essence of Critique)*, 271.
55. Schulte-Sasse, *Theory as Practice (Schlegel, Concerning the Essence of Critique)*, 271.
56. Schulte-Sasse, *Theory as Practice (Schlegel, Concerning the Essence of Critique)*, 273. On Schlegel's critique of aesthetics, see also Lacoue-Labarth and Nancy, *The Literary Absolute*, 103–104.
57. Schulte-Sasse, *Theory as Practice (Schlegel, Concerning the Essence of Critique)*, 273.
58. Schulte-Sasse, *Theory as Practice (Schlegel, Concerning the Essence of Critique)*, 274.
59. Schulte-Sasse, *Theory as Practice (Schlegel, Concerning the Essence of Critique)*, 274–275.
60. Schulte-Sasse, *Theory as Practice (Schlegel, Concerning the Essence of Critique)*, 275.
61. For an account Schleiermacher's practice as a translator, see Susan Bernofsky, "Schleiermacher's Translation Theory and Varieties of Foreignization." *The Translator* 3, no. 2 (1997), 175–192.
62. Friedrich Schleiermacher, *Introductions to the Dialogues of Plato (General Introduction)*, trans. William Dobson (London: John William Parker, 1836), 1–2.

63. Schleiermacher, *Introductions to the Dialogues of Plato (General Introduction)*, 4–5.
64. Schleiermacher, *Introductions to the Dialogues of Plato (General Introduction)*, 14.
65. Schleiermacher, *Introductions to the Dialogues of Plato (General Introduction)*, 18–19.
66. Friedrich Schleiermacher, *Hermeneutics and Criticism*, ed. and trans. Andrew Bowie (Cambridge: Cambridge University Press, 1998), 3.
67. Schleiermacher, *Hermeneutics and Criticism*, 3–4.
68. A.W. Schlegel refers to the work of art as "an immeasurable field, an infinite domain in the most authentic sense," so it follows that the work of the critic would be also an "infinite task" that could only ever approximate completeness. See Benjamin, *Selected Writings, Vol. 1: 1913–1926 (The Concept of Criticism in German Romanticism)*, 174. See also Frank, *Philosophical Foundations of Early German Romanticism*, 23–37.
69. Schleiermacher, *Hermeneutics and Criticism*, 158.
70. Schleiermacher, *Hermeneutics and Criticism*, 161.
71. Quoted by Elizabeth Millán in her introduction to Manfred Frank, *The Philosophical Foundations of Early German Romanticism*, trans. Elizabeth Millán-Zaibert (Albany: SUNY Press, 2004), 13–14. See also Elizabeth Millán-Zaibert, *Friedrich Schlegel and the Emergence of Romantic Philosophy* (Albany: SUNY Press, 2007), 117–132.
72. Schulte-Sasse, *Theory as Practice (Schlegel, Concerning the Essence of Critique)*, 276.
73. Schulte-Sasse, *Theory as Practice (Schlegel, Concerning the Essence of Critique)*, 276–277.
74. Frederick Beiser, *The Romantic Imperative: The Concept of Early German Romanticism* (Cambridge: Harvard University Press, 2003), 59.

# 12

## Romantic Irony

Karolin Mirzakhan

Several characteristics distinguish the early German Romantic Movement (1794–1808) from its predecessors. These features include a critique of first principles or anti-foundationalism, a distrust of closed all-encompassing systems, and an emphasis on the limitations of philosophy. Philosophy, the early German Romantics contend, must be united with other disciplines, most notably poetry. Philosophizing is an activity without end; it is the infinite yearning for the Absolute.[1] Novalis beautifully captures the difficulty of the yearning that characterizes the romantic relationship to the Absolute in his first *Pollen* fragment when he writes, "We *seek* the absolute everywhere and only ever *find* things."[2] Translated more literally, this fragment reads: "everywhere we seek the "unthinged" [*das Unbedingte*] and find only things [*nur Dinge*]." In spite of this challenge, philosophizing, from a romantic perspective, is concerned with an infinite striving for the Absolute, that is, a striving for the whole or that which is unconditioned.

Romantic irony performs the infinite striving for the Absolute in a dynamic and non-linear way. My claim is that the phrase, "romantic irony," which describes the method for enacting this striving, is itself an ironic iteration. In order to understand how the simpliciter "romantic irony" is itself an instance of irony, I will break it into its two component parts before reuniting them. First, I will address irony; I will argue that Friedrich Schlegel, one of the

---

K. Mirzakhan (✉)
Kennesaw State University, Kennesaw, GA, USA
e-mail: kmirzakh@kennesaw.edu

foremost thinkers of the early German Romantic Movement, transforms the traditional meaning of irony from a means of dissimulation to the presentation of paradox as such. Then, I will turn to the ideal of romantic poetry in order to provide an account of how the qualifier "romantic" alters the meaning of the phrase. Finally, I focus my attention on Schlegel's contemporary and friend Novalis (Friedrich von Hardenberg) who employs "romantic irony" as the method of his *Romantic Encyclopedia*. I will argue that, for both thinkers, "romantic irony" is the continuous, playful joining of opposites that performs the absoluteness for which it is striving.

## 1 Schlegel's Transformation of Irony

Friedrich Schlegel's philosophical writings during the early German Romantic Period are comprised primarily of the fragments he published in the *Athenaeum* journal. The journal was co-founded with his brother August Wilhelm and included Novalis and Schleiermacher as contributors. Although the *Athenaeum* was only published from 1798–1800, it was a major vehicle for the views of the early German Romantics. Schlegel also composed a short essay in response to critics who accused those fragments of being incomprehensible (aptly titled "On Incomprehensibility"). There, he suggests that it is the irony of the fragments that led to their being misunderstood; however, he does not attempt to unpack the meaning of the fragments for his critics, a gesture that would remove their irony and violate his project by destroying the very force that enacts romantic striving. Rather, Schlegel argues for the value of incomprehensibility, claiming that not everything ought to be scrutinized by the understanding, which comprehends by breaking apart what it seeks to know.

Schlegel provides one of his clearest definitions of irony in Critical Fragment 48 where he defines it as the "form of paradox."[3] Irony, on Schlegel's definition, joins two contradictory claims in one short statement, thereby forcing the reader to consider both simultaneously. Describing a cultivated work, in *Athenaeum* fragment 297, Schlegel writes that "[a] work is cultivated when it is everywhere sharply delimited, but within those limits limitless and inexhaustible; when it is completely faithful to itself, entirely homogenous, and nonetheless exalted above itself."[4] Here, Schlegel's ironic description of the work of art forces his reader to consider it as both limited and self-contained *and* as limitless and reaching beyond itself. Irony holds these two claims in tension with one another, without conflating the two or reducing one to the other. It is through tarrying with two irreconcilable claims held in tension by the irony of the fragments that Schlegel's reader is brought nearer to the Absolute, which must 'emcompass' both.[5] Irony functions to simultaneously posit contradictory claims, and in so doing, to always leave room for another meaning of a given claim. Irony allows for the expression of absoluteness in its shifting between two opposing poles, in the case of the artwork between its description as both bounded and limitless. As the "*form* of paradox," irony allows for both meanings to be held simultaneously; irony creates the space that facilitates their co-existence.[6]

This oscillating movement produced by irony can be best understood through the model of a conversation, i.e., as that dynamic to and fro movement between the dialogue partners, in which each posits claims, counterclaims, and so on. The conversation is not only a helpful metaphor for understanding the structure of the ironic fragments, but also romantic striving itself. Romantic striving, like a conversation, does not begin with a first principle nor does it have a definitive end point. The movement of the conversation is prompted not only by the statements made by each of its participants, but also by the spaces in-between, that is, the moments of incomprehensibility that produce the possibility for further inquiry into the matter at hand. Romantic striving is a communal effort achieved through the relationship between the author and reader, between philosophical interlocutors, as well as through an inner dialogue with ourselves; Schlegel uses the term "symphilosophy" to refer to these relationships, which he considers to be "sacred."[7]

The role of irony in Schlegel's fragments, which I have sketched above, is a departure from irony's traditional meaning. In order to demonstrate how Schlegel's definition of irony is a transformation of its meaning, I will now draw on the interpretations of Ernst Behler and Paul de Man. Both thinkers recognize Friedrich Schlegel as an important thinker of irony who was central in broadening its scope. Behler draws attention to Schlegel's invocation of Socrates as marking a shift in irony's meaning, whereas De Man emphasizes the radical nature of this shift, which he claims scholars have attempted to downplay.

In *Irony and the Discourse of Modernity*, Ernst Behler proposes that there was a decisive extension of irony from a figure of speech to a basic critical term at the end of the eighteenth century.[8] This turning point occurs with Friedrich Schlegel's proclamation in Critical Fragment 42 that "Philosophy is the true homeland of irony, which one would like to define as logical beauty."[9] Schlegel defines irony ironically, in this fragment, by joining two opposing terms: logic and beauty. Behler points out that the "true homeland of irony" is a clear reference to Socratic irony as the "first manifestation of the ironic mood in the West."[10]

Before Schlegel's transformation of the term, irony was defined as a "figure of speech by which one wants to convey the opposite of what one says."[11] This traditional meaning of irony operates through an agreement between the speaker and listener and an "absolute notion of truth."[12] As a figure of speech, irony allows the speaker to convey the opposite of what she actually means; however, the listener understands the real intention of the speaker, which is communicated through intonation, emphasis, or gesture.[13]

Schlegel ushers in the new meaning of irony through Socrates, the father of philosophy in the West, when he writes in Critical Fragment 108:

> Socratic irony is the only involuntary and yet completely deliberate dissimulation. It is equally impossible to feign it or divulge it. To a person who hasn't got it, it will remain a riddle even after it is openly confessed. It is meant to deceive no one except those who consider it a deception and who either take pleasure in the delightful roguery of making fools of the whole world or else become angry when they get an inkling they themselves might be included. In this type of irony, everything should be playful and serious, guilelessly open and deeply hidden. It originates in the union of *savoir vivre* and scientific spirit, in the conjunction of a perfectly instinctive and perfectly conscious philosophy. It contains and arouses a feeling of indissoluble antagonism between the absolute and the relative, between the impossibility and the necessity of complete communication.[14]

Prior to Schlegel's transformation of the term (in the above description of Socratic irony), the Greek *eiron* was conceived of as a master dissimulator who deceived his listener for personal gain; this image of the *eiron* was that of the liars and charlatans of Aristophanic comedies.[15] In Aristotle's *Nicomachean Ethics*, the *eiron* is still connected to dissimulation, but, now it is the noble self-deprecation of the interlocutor who understates what he knows; irony, on this account, is a deficiency with regard to the virtue of truth-telling.[16] Through Schlegel's transformation of irony, the ironist is no longer the master dissimulator who simply pretends in order to gain something. Irony, in Schlegel's work, is no longer a mere figure of speech, which allows the speaker to communicate the opposite of what she says. Irony is no longer merely saying one thing and meaning another, but the form of paradox as such.

With Schlegel's characterization of Socrates in Critical fragment 108, irony's meaning is altered and, as the form of paradox, it is simultaneously deliberate and involuntary, both serious and playful. Because it expresses both claims at once, without meaning only one or the other, direct communication is no longer possible. Irony is not based on a complete agreement between listener and speaker, in which the listener understands (through, e.g. the speaker's tone) that she means the opposite of what she says. Insofar as the speaker now means both contradictory claims at once, the listener may only take one of the meanings to be true, and therefore only partially understand the speaker; in this case, the ironic communication would fail.

In "The Concept of Irony," Paul de Man argues that the radical nature of this shift in the meaning of irony by Schlegel has been diffused by scholars who have attempted to reduce it to a mere rhetorical device. De Man's analysis relies on Schlegel's unpublished fragment from *Zur Philosophie* (1797) where Schlegel defines irony as "permanent parabasis."[17] De Man explains that a parabasis is the interruption of a discourse or of a narrative line by a shift in the rhetorical register.[18] By stating that irony is not merely a parabasis, but rather a "permanent parabasis," Schlegel, on de Man's reading, is not claiming that parabasis occurs at one point in a narrative, but rather at all points. As permanent parabasis, irony would not only disrupt all narratives but also all theories of the narrative. Irony is the trope (or, the turning away from a literal meaning toward a figurative one) that interrupts and thereby disrupts any attempt to construct a system of meaning.

If de Man is right and irony disrupts any attempt at creating a narrative, then what follows is that the romantic narrative of an infinite and progressive striving toward the Absolute is also radically disrupted by irony (the very technique that Schlegel uses to achieve this striving). While de Man's reading is provocative, by emphasizing irony's role in destabilizing and interrupting all narratives, his reading strips Schlegel's philosophical project of its Romanticism. Moreover, the fragment that de Man cites can also be read as an instance of irony as the form of paradox, that is, Schlegel is forcing his reader to consider an interruption that is permanent. As I claimed in the introduction, Romanticism is marked by an earnest and unending striving for the Absolute, and irony is a means for achieving this striving. If de Man is right, then irony, the method for enacting the striving toward the Absolute, actually undercuts the efforts of the romantic philosopher. Instead, I argue, irony must be joined with the ideal of romantic poetry.

## 2 Joining Opposites: Romantic Irony

Whereas irony is the form of paradox, which disrupts system making, Romanticism is characterized by a yearning for the Absolute and the progressive movement toward it. The ideal of Romanticism is romantic poetry, which Schlegel defines in *Athenaeum* fragment 116 as

> a progressive, universal poetry. Its aim isn't merely to reunite all the separate species of poetry and put poetry in touch with philosophy and rhetoric. It tries to and should mix and fuse poetry and prose, inspiration and criticism, the poetry of art and the poetry of nature; and make poetry lively and sociable, and life and society poetical; poeticize wit and fill and saturate the forms of art with every kind of good, solid matter for instruction, and animate them with the pulsations of humor.[19]

Romantic poetry is not merely an aggregate of the different species of poetry or the static unity of philosophy and poetry, but it is the aesthetic ideal that names the animated and playful joining, separating, and connecting that strives toward the Absolute. Wit is the tool used by the philosopher, much as a chemist uses chemicals for her mixing and experimenting.[20]

Irony as the "form of paradox" is a force that is able to bring together and hold two or more contradictory claims without diluting or conflating either of them. Because of this capacity, irony is both the motor for the activity of creative joining that characterizes romantic poetry as well as the force that limits that striving. Irony's operation is ironic; it both impels our striving and places a restraint on our pretensions to know the whole.

Schlegel alludes to this dual function of irony in *Athenaeum* fragment 53 when he describes the mind's need for systematicity: "It is equally fatal for the mind to have a system and to have none. It will simply have to decide to combine the two."[21] Systems are necessary for striving, for without any structure it would be impossible to know anything; however, irony reveals that humans cannot completely capture what which they seek to know. A mind capable of both having and not having a system is an agile mind, and agility is strengthened with exposure to ironic texts. Paradoxically, by encouraging our striving (for comprehensive systems) and limiting our striving (by showing us that these systems fail to be complete), irony brings us closer to that which we seek to know but can never reach through the structures of human knowing. As a check on human knowing, irony humbles us. As a linguistic device, irony demonstrates that words often outwit those who try to use them; it shows us that words have affinities with one another (and thus a kind of autonomy) and that, through their secret relationships and doubled meanings, words can evade our desire to control them. Words, Schlegel instructs the readers who misunderstood his fragments, "often understand themselves better than those who use them."[22]

By posing multiple meanings simultaneously, irony instructs us about our failures to know, and, at the same time, through the presence of an absence (the inability of a system to be complete) the reader approximates the Absolute. In order for the ironic form to propel an oscillating movement, there must be space that allows for that movement to happen; the space is strictly speaking no-thing; it is neither of the propositions, but it allows for their relationship. This space, which is not present, facilitates the dynamic movement of the fragment between the two poles of meaning.

Taken together, the disruptive quality of irony combined with the progressive and universal quality of romantic striving transforms into "romantic irony": a continuous, playful joining of opposites that performs the striving for the Absolute which is the essence of romantic philosophy. I now turn to Novalis' *Encyclopedia* in order to argue that it is a text of romantic irony and to more fully flesh out what is meant by the term "romantic irony."

## 3  Novalis' *Encyclopedia* and Romantic Irony

The *Romantic Encyclopedia* (*Das Allgemeine Brouillion*) was composed by Novalis between September 1798 and March 1799 and contains over 1100 entries.[23] The entry titles range from Philosophy, Medicine, Physiology, Psychology, Politics, Religion, and Physics to Musical Physics, Magic, and Encyclopedistics. The entries on Encyclopedistics focus on the method of creating the encyclopedia, a supreme task of writing, which Novalis refers to as a Bible. In this context, Novalis is not using the term "Bible" in an overtly religious sense, but rather, he uses this term to refer to the science of all sciences or the book of all books. Novalis is primarily known as a lyric-poet, but he also trained in mineralogy, and both influence his method; the encyclopedia is a poetic-scientific work. For example, in entry 473, entitled "Encyclopedistics," Novalis outlines the classification of minerals in terms of the relationships to each other and in terms of their constituents, and thus uses mineralogy as a classification system for philosophy, psychology, and other disciplines: "Geognosy = the theory of relations between minerals. Oryctognosy is the theory of the relations between the (*external*) characteristics of minerals … Chemical mineralogy is concerned with the constituents of minerals—their separations—*their transitions*."[24] In this entry and others on Encyclopedistics, or the method of the encyclopedia, Novalis proposes a union of philosophy and mineralogy, which takes the relationships in the mineral kingdom as its organizational structure. All sciences could be classified under "the grand science and art of the mineral kingdom."[25] Novalis does not merely bring together poetry, mineralogy, and philosophy in his fragments. He aims to unite music with algebra and physics, mathematics with physiology, medicine with philosophy, and physics with grammar (just to name a few examples). For example, in entry 274 entitled "Psychology," Novalis brings medicine to bear upon thinking in order to claim that too much abstract thinking leads to bodily weakness, and conversely that too much reflection leads to bodily strength.[26] This formula is repeated throughout: in other places, he connects the emotion of joy with sensing and nutrition, whereas sadness is associated with secretion and thinking.[27]

What might such a project have in common with romantic irony? It appears that Novalis' Bible project aims at a closed system or encyclopedic knowledge, and that it is at odds with the direction of the romantic circle, which emphasizes philosophy as an infinite activity. But, I wish to argue that Novalis' project is romantic in several ways. First, it is romantic in its incompleteness. This is not simply because Novalis was unable to finish it; rather, its fragmentary style allows for its continual modification; it remains open-ended and capable of metamorphosis.[28] Like Schlegel's ironic definition of the work of art as both self-contained and reaching beyond itself, the *Encyclopedia* is simultaneously a self-contained body of knowledge and always opens to alteration. Second, because it is a poetic-scientific work, the *Encyclopedia* accomplishes the romantic ideal of uniting philosophy with poetry; it poetizes the world and makes science poetical. Poetry, in turn, becomes scientific. A third sense in which the text is romantic is in its method. Novalis uses the term "romanticize" to describe the elevation of the mundane. In these oft-cited lines from 1798, Novalis wrote:

> The world must be romanticized. This yields again its original meaning. Romanticization is nothing other than qualitative potentization. In this operation the lower self becomes identified with a better self. Just as we ourselves are a potential series of this kind. This operation is still entirely unknown. By giving the common a higher meaning, the everyday, a mysterious semblance, the known, the dignity of the unknown, the finite, the appearance of the infinite, I *romanticize* it—For what is higher, unknown, mystical, infinite, one uses the inverse operation—in this manner it becomes logarithmicized—It receives a common expression. Romantic Philosophy. *Lingua romana*. Reciprocal raising and lowering.[29]

Novalis intertwines romantic philosophy with mathematics in this definition; however, as David Wood clarifies, "the results of this process are not dry mathematical combinations, but artistic and philosophic *elevations*."[30] Novalis also describes this process of elevating the world, especially in Goethe's novels, as the production of a never-ending romance. A novel is an example of a text that functions analogously to Novalis' Bible. Both join seemingly disconnected ideas; they elevate the mundane by including it in a narrative and, at the same time, give an ordinary expression to the mysterious. It is the task of the author to risk these combinations; romanticization emerges through the labor of writing.

The fourth sense in which Novalis' project is romantic is due to his recognition of the possibility of the failure of the fragments and the necessary role of error in striving for the whole. Novalis writes in *Pollen* fragment 104, "[the] art of writing books has not yet been invented. But it is on the point of being invented. Fragments of this kind are literary seed-houses. True, there may be many a barren grain among them. But meanwhile if only a few germinate ..."[31] In this fragment, published in the *Athenaeum* journal, Novalis admits that many of the fragments will not germinate even as he holds out hope that *some* of the fragments will develop. He expresses this potential for maturation in multiple references in the *Encyclopedia* to his own fragmentary work as laying out a method or planting the seed of the Bible, the science of sciences. For example, he writes in entry 526 (and later crosses it out, indicating it was likely a note to himself): "*Critique of my undertaking*—Theory—and countertheory ... If my undertaking becomes too large to execute—then I will only present my method of working—and examples from the *most general part*, and fragments from the specialized parts."[32] Even if Novalis' project cannot be completed, and indeed, he did not finish it, the fragments would lay out the seed of the project as its method.

Novalis' approach borrows from mathematics in recognizing the necessity of error in our striving for truth. In entry 566, Novalis claims that a problem must be solved (in math and philosophy) from many different angles; error is a part of the path to truth and not merely an obstacle. Novalis makes this latter claim explicit in entry 601 when he says that "error is the necessary instrument of truth."[33] Moreover, striving can only truly be called striving when one does not so easily come to their goal; that is, if there is no error in striving, then that means there really was no striving at all. Every science, for Novalis, has a God that is also its goal, and this goal-God is what forever encourages and frustrates its striving.[34] If we achieve our goal without error, then that means we already knew the results before we began, and there was no true activity of philosophizing.

Novalis' project, by seeking a seed for the science of all sciences, or the Bible, does not aim to find a first principle or a foundation. Rather, this seed is the rhythm of the work. Novalis describes the seed as the elemental in entry 555, "If I have really completed a genuine part (element) of my book then the highest peak has been scaled."[35] He returns to the theme of the seed in entry 557: "My book shall be a scientific Bible ... a real, and ideal model—and the **seed** of all books."[36] The Bible is the science of all sciences; however, in these passages, Novalis is not claiming that this scientific Bible includes all other sciences as parts of itself, but rather that it is their seed. This "seed" of all books is what in other places Novalis calls the "rhythm" of all writing, or its musicality; by expressing that musicality, his text is the "seed" of all other books. Rhythm is a foundation that is not an absolute foundation. The rhythm of the *Encyclopedia* is the continual coupling of the various disciplines in each of the entries in order to provide a complete understanding of the world. From a romantic perspective, it is only through the uniting of philosophy and poetry, poetry and science, medicine and psychology, that an understanding of the whole can be achieved. Novalis' aim in the *Encyclopedia* is to find that which unites all the different sciences, and that is the seed or the rhythm of the work. Novalis' *Encyclopedia* does not aim to be Absolute in its completeness, an impossible task, but rather, it repeats a formula of romantic irony (of the playful and continuous joining of opposites) throughout its entries.

As a text imbued throughout with romantic irony, Novalis' *Encyclopedia* is both complete and completely open-ended and infinite. The fragments are repeated instances of romantic irony as the joining of disciplines in creative combinations that force the reader to think concepts together in novel ways. The text's irony allows for the chemical process of bonding to occur and also ensures its continuation: there is always room for another combination to arise. This emptiness of the ironic fragment—its openness to a new meaning—is precisely what allows it to perform absoluteness in each fragment. As simultaneously self-contained and reaching beyond itself, each fragment contains the formula for the Absolute, which allows that which is and that which is not to dwell together. Each fragment contains the combinations of two disconnected, or at least apparently disconnected ideas, and because the fragments are multiple, there is an openness to the creation of more combinations, to the steady addition of links in this fragmentary chain. The fragments contain two, often opposite claims, and also contain (which is to say they never fully contain) the space that allows for the continued emergence of new meanings. Not all of the fragments will be successful in communicating the Absolute to their reader; many in this experiment will fail. Because the fragments are ironic, and no longer based on a complete agreement of language between reader and writer, they may be misunderstood by their reader. Or, they may fail in their facticity, since some of the claims represented in them are no longer recognized by the scientific community. However, by their association with one another, these hundreds of fragments produce an overall effect; they produce the rhythm that is the seed of the Bible.

## 4   Conclusion

If philosophical thinking, in its attempt to know the unconditioned, necessarily applies conditions to it, then philosophy must be united with poetry, particularly with poetry's capacity for irony. For it is irony that can at once limit and set free from limits. Philosophy and science must become poetical. Irony is the *form* of paradox because it is what allows the paradox to hold without conflating or reducing it. The ironic fragments contain the simultaneous positing of two contradictory claims and the emptiness that makes possible their co-existence. But to say the fragments 'contain' emptiness is to also say they allow for the presence of non-presence, of that which, strictly speaking, cannot be contained. By allowing that which is (the stated propositions), and that which is not (the non-presence that facilitates their relationship), the ironic fragments perform absoluteness in a way that does not attempt to dominate or reify the empty space that cannot be grasped. Irony can never be wholly intentional because it only marks that which it does not say; irony points us to the limits of human knowing and to what must be "left in the dark" in order for those structures to function; it holds an empty space for that which has yet to be said, or which cannot be said.[37] In pointing us to the limits of what we can know, irony brings us nearer to (not further from) the Absolute. But this nearness, I have tried to argue, is not linear or spatial.

Irony joined with romantic striving transforms into "romantic irony," a term that names the continuous, playful joining of opposites that performs the act of the striving for the Absolute. The creativity of combinations found in Novalis' *Encyclopedia* illustrates the romantic imperative to join the disciplines in order to understand the whole. This on-going process relies on the ingenuity of the philosopher-poet-scientist (or the scientist-poet-philosopher), but it is not arbitrary. It is both impelled by and limited by irony. Irony is never a mere demonstration of the sovereignty of the author-artist. The sovereignty of the artist is undermined by words that, as Schlegel says, have a "secret brotherhood" among themselves.[38] Irony humbles the one who tries to use words to express herself.

The success or failure of the ironic fragments depends upon their readers who may not understand the author's use of irony, and therefore are prone to misunderstand their author. Schlegel's fragments were indeed charged with being incomprehensible by readers and critics. The ironic fragments have an implicit dialogical structure. The fragments rely on their reader who may misunderstand them, but they also train the reader through repeated encounters with them; after all, the fragments are always multiple. The ironic fragments will often frustrate the reader whose aim is to comprehend them. They are, to borrow a phrase from Ricarda Huch, "hard-shelled nuts." She explains that "[without] the reader's energetic intellectual engagement they are totally incomprehensible."[39]

Because the ironic fragments are not easily digestible, they train the reader's mind to be agile. It is by way of this agility that the reader realizes the Absolute. As an illustration of the agility, think of the image in which both a duck and a rabbit can be seen. This image made famous by Ludwig Wittgenstein in his *Philosophical Investigations* is of either a duck or a rabbit, depending on how the image is viewed. The duck and the rabbit of this image can be likened to the two sides of a contradiction that irony simultaneously presents to its reader. Through repeated encounters with ironic texts, the reader gains an agility of mind and is able to move quickly between opposing positions, as one could move more and more quickly between seeing a duck, then a rabbit, and back and forth. An agile mind can move quickly between multiple images or propositions; the more agile the mind, the smaller the gap is between seeing one image or the other.

In the fragments of both Schlegel and Novalis, romantic irony is the method by which they perform a continual coupling of disconnected, or at least apparently disconnected, propositions, which tirelessly and sincerely strive toward the Absolute. The fragments are romantic insofar as they are continually and earnestly endeavoring to reach the Absolute; they are ironic insofar as their form is paradox. Each fragment is a burst of wit, which joins together opposites. The fragments are never singular, but always multiple; this playful combining in the earnest seeking of the Absolute happens again and again. In each of Novalis' *Encyclopedia* entries, a variety of disciplines speak to each other; however, the aim is not to create a completed system, but rather to repeatedly perform the form of absoluteness—through the joining of opposites, a dynamic whole is created, which is not only composed of presence, but also that space of non-presence necessary for the joining to occur and for ensuring its continuation.

# Notes

1. References to Schlegel's fragments are cited according to their number and abbreviated as follows: AF = Athenaeum Fragments, CF = Critical [Lyceum] Fragments, I = Ideas. References in the original German are from Friedrich Schlegel, *Kritische Friedrich-Schlegel-Ausgabe*, ed. Ernst Behler, Jean Jacques Anstett, and Hans Eichner (München: F. Schöningh, 1958) [=KFSA]. Translations are from Friedrich Schlegel, *Friedrich Schlegel's Lucinde and the Fragments*, trans. and ed. Peter Firchow (Minneapolis, MN: University of Minnesota Press, 1971). Citation to Novalis is to *Schriften*, ed. P. Kluckhorn and R. Samuel (Stuttgart: Kohlhammer, 1960 ff.) [=NS], by volume number, followed by encyclopedia entry number. Parallel citation to: *Philosophical Writings*, trans. & ed. M. M. Stoljar (Albany: SUNY Press, 1997) [=PW], or to Novalis, *Notes for a Romantic Encyclopedia: Das Allgemeine Brouillon*, ed. and trans. David W Wood (Albany: State University of New York Press, 2007) [=AB].
2. Novalis, *Philosophical Writings*, trans. Margaret Mahoney Stoljar (Albany: State University of New York Press, 1997), 23. NS 2, 412.
3. "Ironie ist die Form die Paradoxen. Paradox ist alles, was zugleich gut und groß ist." KFSA 2, 153, CF 48.
4. Friedrich Schlegel, *Friedrich Schlegel's Lucinde and the Fragments*, trans. Peter Firchow (Minneapolis: University of Minnesota Press, 1971), 204. KFSA 2, 215, AF 297.
5. Although, I use terms like "nearer," "closer," or "encompass" throughout, my claim is that the way in which irony brings its reader in contact with the Absolute, as part of the romantic project of striving for the Absolute, is neither linear nor totalizing. The language describing the way irony operates will undoubtedly fail to capture the work that irony does.
6. KFSA 2, 153, CF 48. Emphasis mine.
7. Schlegel, *Lucinde and the Fragments*, 156–157. KFSA 2, 161, CF 112. In Critical fragment 112, Schlegel describes this relationship with his reader as the "sacred relationship of symphilosophy"; unlike the analytical writer who approaches her reader as she is and accordingly sets out to make the proper impression upon that reader, the synthetic writer approaches her reader as "alive and critical."
8. Ernst Behler, *Irony and the Discourse of Modernity* (Seattle and London: University of Washington Press, 1990), 73.
9. Critical Fragment 42, Quoted in Behler, *Irony and the Discourse of Modernity*, 73.
10. Behler, *Irony and the Discourse of Modernity*, 73–74.
11. "French Encyclopedia of 1765," quoted in Behler, *Irony and the Discourse of Modernity*, 76.

12. Behler, *Irony and the Discourse of Modernity*, 82.
13. Ibid., 76.
14. Schlegel, *Lucinde and the Fragments*, 155–156. KFSA 2, 160, CF 108.
15. For more on this view of the Greek *eiron* see Eric Miller, "Masks of Negation: Greek Eironeia and Schlegel's Ironie," *ERR European Romantic Review* 8, no. 4 (1997).
16. Behler, *Irony and the Discourse of Modernity*, 77.
17. "Die Ironie ist eine permanente Parekbase." Paul de Man, *Aesthetic Ideology*, 179. KFSA 18, 85. De Man translates "permanente Parekbase" as "permanent parabasis" rather than "permanent parekbasis." Etymologically, both terms have very similar meanings. "Parabasis" denotes a stepping to the side and "parekbasis" denotes a stepping *out* to the side. Parabasis was the term that marked the moments when the chorus directly addressed the audience in Old Attic Comedy, whereas parekbasis tended to be used by writers on rhetoric to note a digression in a text. In the sections where I am providing de Man's reading of Schlegel's fragment, I will retain the term as he translates it in his lectures. Because parabasis is the term that de Man actually uses, I will not alter the translation when I discuss his interpretation. Furthermore, since the meanings are so similar, I do not think this translation issue alters Paul de Man's reading of Schlegel. "Greek Word Study Tool," accessed March 25, 2016.
18. Paul de Man, *Aesthetic Ideology*, ed. Andrzej Warminski (Minneapolis: University of Minnesota Press, 1996), 178.
19. Schlegel, *Lucinde and the Fragments*, 175–176. KFSA 2, 182–183, AF 116.
20. For more on the chemical model in Schlegel's fragments see Michel Chaouli, *The Laboratory of Poetry: Chemistry and Poetics in the Work of Friedrich Schlegel* (Baltimore: Johns Hopkins University Press, 2002).
21. Schlegel, *Lucinde and the Fragments*, 167. "Es ist gleich tödlich für den Geist, ein System zu haben, und keins zu haben. Er wird sich also wohl entschließen müssen, beides zu verbinden." KFSA 2, 173, AF 53.
22. Friedrich Schlegel, "On Incomprehensibility (1800)," in *Classic and Romantic German Aesthetics*, ed. J. M Bernstein (Cambridge: Cambridge University Press, 2003), 298. KFSA 2, p. 364.
23. The title and the number of entries were added later by editors. The work was not meant to be published in its current form. However, Novalis did critique the project and went through marking out personal notes and adding titles of entries.
24. Novalis, *Notes for a Romantic Encyclopedia: Das Allgemeine Brouillon*, ed. and trans. David W Wood (Albany: State University of New York Press, 2007), 80–81. NS 3, #473.
25. Ibid.
26. Ibid., 41. NS 3, #274.

27. For example, in entry 190 entitled "Psychology," Novalis describes sadness and joy in terms of secretion and nutrition, respectively. "Sadness is a symptom—a mood of secretion—joy, a symptom of enjoyment—of nutrition./ The arteries carry out the process of nutrition, and the veins, the process of secretion./" Ibid., p. 29. In entry 273 (also entitled "Psychology"), he aligns thinking with secretion and sensing with devouring, that is, nutrition.

"Is thinking also secreting? Then perhaps sensing is devouring. Self-reflection is perhaps a life process—both a process of devouring and secretion. Both thinking and sensing." Ibid., 40.
28. Ibid., xxix.
29. HKA 2, p. 545, quoted in *Notes for a Romantic Encyclopedia*, David W. Wood, xvi.
30. Ibid., xvi.
31. Novalis, *Miscellaneous Remarks*, Fragment 104, in *Classic and Romantic Aesthetics*, ed. Bernstein, 213.
32. Novalis, *Notes for a Romantic Encyclopedia*, 93. NS 3, #526.
33. Ibid., 106. NS 3, #601.
34. Ibid., 46. NS 3, #314.
35. Ibid., 98. NS 3, #555.
36. Ibid., 98–99. NS 3, #557.
37. Friedrich Schlegel, "On Incomprehensibility (1800)," 305. KFSA 2, 370.
38. Ibid., 298. KFSA 2, 364.
39. Huch, Ricarda, *Die Romantik: Blütezeit, Ausbreitung und Verfall.* (Tübingen: Wunderlich, 1951), quoted in Dennis McCort, "Jena Romanticism and Zen," *Discourse* 27, no. 1 (2005), 104.

# 13

# The Role of the Fragment in German Romantic Philosophy and Nietzsche

Guy Elgat

This chapter concerns itself with one central literary form embraced (especially) by the early German Romantics: the fragment. In addition to the fragment, the early German Romantics also adopted many other literary genres such as the critical literary review, the dialogue, the poem, and the novel, but exhibited an intriguing preference for the fragmentary form. The texts that highlight this in great detail are: Friedrich Schlegel's early *Critical Fragments* (1797, also known as the *Lyceum Fragments*); Novalis' *Miscellaneous Observations* (most of which were published in 1798 as *Grains of Pollen* in the journal *Athenaeum*); Novalis' *Logological Fragments* (from his notebooks dating from 1797 to 1798); the *Athenaeum Fragments* (1798, published in the journal *Athenaeum*), written mostly by Friedrich Schlegel with the participation of his brother August Wilhelm, Novalis, and Schleiermacher[1]; and Friedrich Schlegel's later *Ideas* (1800, in the journal *Athenaeum*). As my focus shall be on romantic aesthetics, the main issue I will explore in the following is the nature of the fragmentary literary-philosophical form and the relation between this form and the substantive views of aesthetics held by the early German Romantics.

First, a short, general account of the fragmentary and aphoristic form in its relation to philosophy will be given. Here I will argue that while there is no

G. Elgat (✉)
School of the Art Institute of Chicago, Chicago, IL, USA
e-mail: guyelgat2011@u.northwestern.edu

© The Author(s) 2020
E. Millán Brusslan (ed.), *The Palgrave Handbook of German Romantic Philosophy*, Palgrave Handbooks in German Idealism, https://doi.org/10.1007/978-3-030-53567-4_13

important philosophical chasm separating the fragment from the aphorism, and while a precise definition of either is not forthcoming,[2] it is nevertheless possible to supply a general characterization of the philosophical fragment or aphorism. Then, on the basis of an analysis of some of the early German Romantics' views on art, the chapter will turn to ask in what way, given these philosophical commitments, the fragmentary or aphoristic form is an especially suitable stylistic choice. Specifically, I will argue that the fragment or aphorism is seen by the early German Romantics as a suitable medium for a form of aesthetic perspectivism of the Absolute. Finally, on the basis of an identification of Friedrich Nietzsche as a romantic (despite the latter's protestations), a comparative analysis of Nietzsche's use of the aphoristic and fragmentary form will be given. I will argue that while Novalis did not unconditionally subscribe to this literary form and while Schlegel did not fully exploit its potential, it is with Nietzsche that the fragmentary form is more fully realized.

## 1    The Aphorism and the Fragment

The first order of business is to provide some characterization of the fragmentary form, which, needless to say, was not invented by the romantics but has a long and reputable pedigree that can be arguably extended as far back as to the writings of Hippocrates and Democritus. In effect, even though the early German Romantics refer to their collection of short pieces of writings as fragments, some of those short paragraphs could also adequately be described as aphorisms (Schlegel and his circle were highly influenced here by the aphoristic writings of Chamfort, namely, his *Maximes et Pensées*).[3] And indeed, the line separating the aphorism from the fragment is terribly thin and practically philosophically negligible, so that I believe it is ultimately unfruitful to insist on some essential and profound difference between the two. I will, therefore, for the most part, deal with these two forms in the same breath and will use the terms almost interchangeably.

But even if we acknowledge the closeness of kin of the aphorism and the fragment, the problem of how to define the aphoristic or fragmentary form remains.[4] Unfortunately, as Gary Saul Morson in his recent book on the short literary form writes: "there is no agreed upon definition" of these terms[5], to such an extent that "[I]f one struggles to arrive at the true meaning of these terms, one will surely be lost in an endless labyrinth".[6] Morson therefore turns to "classify the works themselves and then, merely for the sake of consistent usage, apply a term to each class, with the understanding that a different term could have been chosen".⁷ He uses the term "aphorism" to refer to the entire family of the various brief literary forms, and classifies the various short genres "according to their worldviews, the distinct sense of human experience that each conveys".⁸ Thus, for example, the "apothegm" for Morson pictures the world "as fundamentally mysterious",⁹ the "maxim" "unmask[s] vanity, self-deception, and egoism disguised as virtue",¹⁰ and the "thought" "offers a private meditation, still incomplete and tentative, as it first occurred to the author".¹¹

A different, perhaps more traditional way to define the aphorism and distinguish it from other related terms is offered by R.J. Hollingdale:

> In its pure and perfect form the aphorism is distinguished by four qualities occurring together: it is brief, it is isolated, it is witty, and it is "philosophical". This last quality marks it off from the epigram, which is essentially no more than a witty observation; the third, which it shares with the epigram, marks it off from the proverb or maxim: its point, though intended seriously, is supposed to strike the reader, not with the blunt obviousness of a palpable truth ... but rather in the way the point of a good joke should strike him ... In this pure form the aphorism disdains all giving of reasons and presents only a conclusion, so that it is often plainly intended to provoke instant contradiction in the sense that the payoff line of a joke is intended to provoke instant laughter.¹²

This might be true of what Hollingdale defines as the aphorism in its "pure" form, but many of Pascal's and Nietzsche's writings, for example, while conforming to some of the traits Hollingdale mentions, fail to attain the purity that is found to a much greater extent in a paradigmatic case such as that of La Rochefoucauld and, for example, rather than "brief", can at times be quite lengthy.¹³ Conversely, some of the early German Romantics' *Athenaeum Fragments* could be seen as closer to the aphorism in its pure form,¹⁴ and we would not want to comb through these collections and exclude from our discussion of the romantic "fragment" those texts that appear too aphoristic to us and yet appeared to the early German Romantics themselves as worthy of being included in their "Fragments".

Hollingdale, of course, admits that the aphorism can expand "into a miniature essay"¹⁵—at which point we can say, if we are so inclined, that the aphorism becomes a *fragment* (or a "fragmentary reflection"),¹⁶ though, we can assume, no sharp boundaries in terms of length, or any other determinant, can be drawn between the two.¹⁷

Hollingdale, however, insists that even in the case of the expanded aphorism the feeling of a punchline is one of the aphorism's "defining characteristics".[18] This quality of the aphorism is related to its power to shock and unsettle.[19] Many *Athenaeum* fragments are characterized by such a quality (I return specifically to the topic of wit below); for example, "The historian is a prophet facing backwards".[20] But clearly many aphorisms—whether long or short—are neither witty nor take the form of a joke (e.g. "Whoever doesn't pursue philosophy for its own sake, but uses it as a means to an end, is a sophist").[21] In general, though, we can say on the basis of empirical examination of the various texts that the longer the aphorism is and the more it becomes a "fragment", the more its pun-like or surprising nature tends to dissolve.

Further—to return to Hollingdale's characterization—arguments and justification, while perhaps absent from the "pure" form, are far from being completely absent from many aphoristic or fragmentary writings—a feature which brings such forms closer to philosophy in its more traditional discursive format. Indeed, it is what Hollingdale calls the "philosophical" nature of the aphorism which is of central importance here. Hollingdale does not explain what exactly he has in mind here, but it seems to mean, first, that an aphorism or fragment is philosophical if it can be seen to operate within a recognizable philosophical context: either as instituting one or responding to already extant philosophers or philosophical issues. This is clearly the case with the romantics, whose philosophical orbit belongs within post-Kantian and post-Fichtean philosophy, where the seeds of absolute idealism were sown.[22] Second, an aphorism or fragment is philosophical, we might say, when it aims to present us with a general, "deep", truth about humanity or the world. Further, as philosophical, aphorisms and fragments formulate general thoughts: they are, as Cioran—himself an aphoristic philosopher—puts it, "instantaneous generalizations"[23]: they are not merely a recording of an author's private and subjective thoughts as in a diary, but make a general, objective, claim.

Though we can maintain that the aphorism is philosophical in its aspiration to convey some deep truth, the question remains whether the aphorism or fragment is ever true in the same way as commonplace true statements of facts (e.g. "the cat is on the mat"). Joseph Stern, in his discussion of the aphorism in his book on Lichtenberg, denies this and asserts that the aphorism "aspires to another, less stable kind of truth …: the truth of a suggestion or illumination".[24] Nevertheless, he agrees that after the initial blinding experience of the aphorism, it can become a "stable and lucid insight" or merely revealed to be a "chimera".[25] The "illumination" referred to here will be of central importance when we turn to consider the romantics' view of aesthetics.

Let us now turn to the second trait on Hollingdale's list: the aphorism and fragment are isolated from other aphorisms and fragments; this is their discontinuous form.[26] This of course does not mean that consecutive aphorisms or fragments cannot be found to deal with the same topic or question. Thus, in La Rochefoucauld, one can find, for example, a series of successive reflections on love,[27] though he clearly expresses his wariness of organizing his thoughts in this manner for fear of "boring the reader".[28] Similarly, many of Novalis' texts laud the revelatory and creative power of the imagination. The fragment's isolated nature lies rather in its being typically discursively cut off from those that precede or follow it: the fragment ends and a new one begins which, even if it addresses the same topic, approaches it afresh, as if from scratch, without drawing any explicit conceptual or justificatory links to the content of the other fragments. In this way, the "truth and validity" of the aphorism or fragment "is to be weighed individually".[29] This means, of course, that one can understand it without drawing on the ideas of the surrounding aphorisms—it is "self-contained".[30] Schlegel expressed a similar view when he wrote—and I will return to this aphorism below—that "a fragment … has to be … complete in itself like a porcupine".[31] And this in turn implies that typically one can dip into a book of aphorisms or fragments at any point without suffering any deficit in understanding the author's thoughts: one can read the aphorisms in whatever order one wishes.[32]

But we have to be careful here: the fact that in some cases one can peruse through an author's fragments in no particular order does not necessarily mean that the author's ideas cannot be stitched together to form a coherent and well-ordered set of ideas or worldview or were not put forward as an expression of such a worldview. We will come back to this question below—the question whether fragmented form necessarily implies fragmented *thought*. But already at this stage, we can remark that arguably one way to differentiate the fragment from the aphorism is to focus on "the way it is meant to be received: the aphorism need not be read as part of a whole" while the fragment is to be seen as forming a part of a system.[33] But though I agree that with the early German Romantics' (especially Schlegel) fragments were meant to be part of a system of sorts,[34] the author's intention cannot supply us with a criterion for distinguishing the fragment from the aphorism, for the way a text is meant to be received is not something that can be read off the text itself or its stylistic form but requires extensive background knowledge regarding the intentions and metaphilosophy of the text's author. Second, as we will see, even Nietzsche's *aphorisms* were not meant to be taken in isolation.

We can now better understand Morson's reluctance at providing a definition of the aphorism and its closely related short literary forms. This perhaps should not surprise us, given that, as Nietzsche says in aphoristic style, "only that which has no history is definable",[35] and given the complex and rich history of the aphoristic literary form and the manner in which it crisscrosses and grows out of the history of the other related literary forms such as the epigram or the proverb.[36] Nevertheless, we have managed to provide a general profile of the *philosophical* aphorism or fragment: it is relatively short, offers a general truth or responds to a recognized set of philosophical questions, and is isolated or discontinuous.

## 2   Art and Romanticism

It is a widely accepted view[37] that early Jena Romanticism's philosophy could be read as a reaction to a perceived loss of meaning brought about in the wake of the rise of Enlightenment philosophy. More specifically, Romanticism is seen as a reaction to Kant's influential views as put forward in his *Critiques* which not only curbed the philosophical aspirations of philosophical reason to grasp absolute reality and put an end to all dogmatic theology and metaphysics, but also precipitated a fragmentation in the sphere of the phenomena that are accessible to human experience and knowledge. Thus, the traditional Platonic triad of the True, the Good, and the Beautiful was split asunder under the force of the Kantian argument and made each the provenance of separate mental faculties: the world of empirical knowledge is split off from the realm of freedom and morality, and both are to be distinguished from the field of aesthetic experience and the pleasure of the beautiful.[38] These separate fields are now seen as discontinuous in a way which does not allow for them to be glued back together: there are no bridging principles that would allow one to move from the one to the other. They now constitute what Lyotard has called a "differend".[39]

It might be thought that in light of this philosophical background the romantics' adoption of the literary form of the fragment is almost self-explanatory: the romantic response to the fragmentation of the world, according to this view, is to accept it and employ a means of expression most suitable to it. If, according to the romantics, the world is split off into shards that do not amount to "puzzle pieces",[40] then the only way to engage it philosophically is to offer short reflections that are characterized, as we saw above, precisely by one of the central features of the aphorism and the fragment, namely, by discontinuity. As Joseph Stern puts it:

> The romantic stress on individual experience, the atomization of thought and feelings, the absence of commonly accepted religious beliefs, metaphysical presuppositions and moral standards, and the disintegration of modern culture—all these represent a mode of thought and feeling explored in many books and

essays in the wake of Friedrich Schlegel, Leopardi, Baudelaire, Schopenhauer and Nietzsche. The parallel between this modern consciousness and the aphorism is striking. In both cases fragments are endowed with values once resident in the whole.[41]

But while there is some truth to this view, this cannot be the whole story, for while the early German Romantics were indeed impressed and distressed by this fragmentation, "the key word in the Romantic ideology is incontestably Unity".[42] Thus, on Frederick Beiser's interpretation, according to which the romantics can be viewed as fledgling Absolute Idealists, instead of acquiescing in the disappearance of unity, the romantics sought to reconstitute it by developing a metaphysics of the Absolute.[43] According to this metaphysics, which seems to flout all Kantian restrictions on what can be considered legitimate claims to knowledge, all of reality's different aspects are but expressions of one underlying substance or Being, which is conceived as a dynamic, developing organism, where the whole is dependent on the parts, and the parts depend on each other, as well as on the whole.

What is the role of art in this worldview? Though there are some significant differences between their views, Friedrich Schlegel and Novalis, at the early stages of their thinking, put forward an essentially similar view of the role of art. According to this view, works of art, and especially poetry, have the power to break through the limitations of the understanding imposed upon it by the Kantian critique. While according to Kant, the understanding, with the help of its pure concepts, the categories, can only provide cognitive access to phenomena and amount to empirical knowledge, for the early German Romantics, works of art, at their best, can pierce through the order of phenomena and enable us to catch a glimpse of the thing-in-itself, the Absolute. While, according to Schlegel, the understanding can only explain phenomena, an image or an allegory can *present* us with the Absolute[44]—it serves us with a kind of direct intuition of that which goes beyond the realm of everyday experience. In this way, it compensates for the limitations of the understanding. More—in this way, it compensates for the inadequacies of discursive *philosophy* itself, that is, for its demonstrated inability to grasp existence as a whole or the very ground of being. Hence, art's importance with respect to philosophical thinking and the reason why both Schlegel and Novalis[45] tended to attribute greater significance to poetry than to philosophy (though it should be borne in mind that poetry with the romantics is broadened and "comes to include within its extension verse, novels, and even some theoretical writing").[46] Thus, Novalis claims that "poetry is as it were the key to philosophy, its purpose and meaning"[47] and adds that the poet is the "voice of the universe" and "always remains true" while the philosopher "changes within the eternally enduring".[48] And, as Manfred Frank puts it, for Novalis, "only the inexplicable meaningfulness of the work of art can positively show what I cannot definitely dissolve in knowledge" ("Nur die unausdeutbare Sinnfülle des Kunstwerks kann positiv zeigen was sich nicht definitiv in Wissen auflösen lässt").[49] Similarly, Schlegel held that poetry can reach the heights of philosophy when it is permeated by a "mood that surveys everything and rises infinitely above all limitations".[50] And in his *Gespräch über die Poesie*, he claims in a Spinozistic spirit that every finite is pervaded by the infinite, which is the task of poetry to reveal.[51]

It is important to note, though, that the recourse to art does not immediately imply any form of irrationalism on the early German Romantics' part, as has often been assumed. Rather, successful works of art induce aesthetic experiences that enable the subject to intuit the heart of being, in a manner akin to the quasi-visual experience that for Plato is involved in our coming to grasp the Forms or Ideas directly. In Novalis, we can see this as part of an attempt to develop a "notion of reason that … takes into account the experience of art, literature, and religious and affective sentiments of various kinds".[52]

But how can the fragment or aphorism enable us precisely to *overcome* the fragmentation of reality, and what does the fragmentary form have to do with the early German Romantic's conception of the importance of poetry or art in general? I will now turn to address these issues.

## 3    The Significance of the Fragment

Though many of their works are fragmentary, neither Schlegel nor Novalis has left us any worked-out account for this choice of medium. In some cases, of course, the many notes these thinkers have left behind are precisely that—(merely) notes, and as such, were never meant for publication but are to be regarded as sketches of ideas that were either dropped or were later integrated or made use of in texts written in the non-fragmentary style. This however leaves out of consideration those most important fragmentary texts that *were* either published or composed for the purpose of publication.

So—we need to ask again—why the fragment? Let us start with a consideration of Schlegel's views. Though a fledgling absolute idealist,[53] Schlegel did not adhere without reservation to the idea of a philosophical *system*, where an entire set of philosophical claims about the world can be deduced from a number of basic and self-evident assumptions so as to generate a final and conclusive philosophy of the whole. Schlegel's skepticism and mistrust of any First Philosophy[54] prevented him from developing any such comprehensive view of being. Nevertheless, this did not mean for him a complete abandonment of the attempt to develop a philosophy that is systematic but in a more relaxed sense—a philosophy, that is, which is not, on the one hand, based on first principles and, on the other hand, does not assume to ever attain the whole. Indeed, for Schlegel, being systematic in some sense is indispensable: "It's equally fatal for the mind to have a system and to have none. It will simply have to decide to combine the two".[55] The alternative Schlegel conceived of was to posit the idea of a system as a regulative ideal,[56] as something to *strive* for, in a manner which continuously posits new ideas, draws connections between them, and moves beyond them toward what can be hoped for is a more complete and more coherent conception of the whole—a conception, it is important to emphasize, that will never actually be complete. The activity of philosophy is thus open-ended. This is in line with the romantic conception of poetry, famously presented in *Athenaeum Fragments* 116[57] as "progressive, universal poetry", as that which "reunite[s] all the separate species of poetry and put[s] poetry in touch with philosophy", as that which "alone can become … a mirror of the whole circumambient world" and yet is "capable of the highest and most variegated refinement", while, at the same time, *essentially* "in the state of becoming". Thus, a mirroring of the whole, in a progressively refined and comprehensively uniting view, which in its very essence is incompletable.[58] But how is the fragment related to the romantic conception of poetry? And isn't the fragment precisely anti-systematic, even in this more relaxed sense?

Let us take these questions in order. It is first important to note that Schlegel adds in that same fragment that "Romantic poetry is in the arts what wit is in philosophy",[59] and this provides us with an angle from which to think about the aphorism and the fragment: the wittiness of the short philosophical form is supposed to enable it to perform for philosophical thought what poetry succeeds in doing in the arts. To see how, it is helpful, second, to distinguish in Schlegel (and possibly also in Novalis) two axes of thought: the "intensive" dimension of thought which approximates the Absolute, and the "extensive" dimension which involves "accumulative means" of further reflection in ever more fragmentary formulations.[60] Now, correlating to these two dimensions, one can find in the early German Romantics two so-to-speak vectors of "wit" in virtue of which the romantics' fragments and aphorisms can proceed along these two dimensions of thinking. Thus, with respect to the intensive dimension, "wit" is the "lightning bolt of the imagination" and is akin in its revelations to those of "mysticism"[61]: an intuitive going-beyond which penetrates the depth of things. Here wit "perceives immediately and through inspiration"[62] and its "expressions aren't long and wide enough" for those whose "sensitivity is only a darkly imagined mathematics".[63] This accords with Schlegel's early skepticism of definition, analysis, and proof in philosophy and his championing of the capacity to posit or propose an idea directly without the retinue of reasons and other adulterations.[64] And, as we saw above, one central characteristic of the aphorism or the fragment is its avoidance of the more traditional philosophical manner of providing arguments and detailed articulation of justifications.

But wit, for Schlegel, also refers to the "capacity to discover similarities and to form ideas"[65]: this corresponds to the extensive dimension of thought, where surprising connections are made that can potentially traverse the Kantian fragmentations. Thus, wit has the power to bring about a "disintegration of spiritual substances which, before being suddenly separated [by Kantian critique] must have been thoroughly mixed".[66] Thus, we can appreciate how the fragment, thanks to its wittiness, can play in philosophy an analogous role to that played by poetry in the romantic's conception of it: on the one hand, in moments of immediate insight it can provide intuition into that which goes beyond the Kantian limitations on philosophy, and on the other, it helps overcome the fragmentation of reality and bring about (or restore) its unity by forming imaginative links between phenomena.[67]

Second, with respect to the anti-systematic aspect of philosophy, as Millán claims, "The literary form that Schlegel favored to reflect that open-ended nature of philosophy was the fragment".[68] But how can this tentative and open-ended nature of fragmentary philosophy amount to some kind of system? As Firchow explains, there was no objection to systematicity in the *Athenaeum Fragments*: the fragments refer to one another[69] and thus can stand as a "substitute"[70] for a system that, unlike the traditional one, need not exclude contradiction or even self-contradiction: "[the fragments] can and do bring the entire noisy federation of literary and philosophical quarrels under one roof".[71] The fragment, in its wittiness, possesses the "capacity to create correspondences suggesting an essential unity of totally diverse phenomena, and thus of the whole world".[72] Importantly, the piecing together of the fragments does not presuppose a conception of the fragment as a "residue of a broken ensemble",[73] as if this whole once existed in some fashion and was at some point smashed into pieces that can now be reattached together, as if in a puzzle, so as to reconstruct the whole. As we saw, the early German Romantics precisely rejected this "puzzle picture" conception of knowledge.

Furthermore, the progressiveness of romantic poetry, the striving toward the whole in ever-renewed attempts without any presumption for a final synthesis, is a trait that can be seen to be shared by the fragmentary or aphoristic text in its extensive dimension: despite its disjointed nature, the fragment can be seen as persistently trying to form links between diverse phenomena,[74] forming a net of insights—"a chain or garland of fragments"[75]—that continuously expands yet always fails to capture its "prey" in a final and complete synthesis. In this way we can see how the fragment and Schlegel's conception of irony complement each other: while the fragment in its wit enjoys a "fragmentary geniality" or "selective flashing" in which a unity can momentarily be seen,[76] irony opens us up to the infinity of the Absolute and thus to the never-ending task of trying to comprehend it: it is the "clear consciousness of eternal agility, of an infinitely teeming chaos".[77]

A problem with this reading of the role of the fragment arises with respect to one of the very few explicit reflections on the nature of the fragment that the romantics offer—the well-known *Athenaeum Fragment* 206: "A fragment, like a miniature work of art, must be entirely isolated from the surrounding world and be complete in itself like a porcupine". On the one hand, the fragment is here compared to a work of art and is thus credited with the same power ascribed to art in general: to provide access, however limited, to the whole or the Absolute. On the other hand, the idea, articulated above, that fragments can be chained together to form a more complete conception of the Absolute is here seemingly explicitly rejected: fragments are to be seen as "entirely isolated" from the world and thus presumably from other fragments as well. Moreover, as the image of the porcupine suggests, the fragment is positively resistant to the attempt to integrate it into a whole larger than itself.

Millán addresses fragment 206 by relating it to Schlegel's comments on Goethe's *Wilhelm Meister* where Schlegel praises the work's composition and claims that "it would not be wrong to regard the first part, irrespective of its relationship to the whole, as a novel in itself".[78] She then argues that while "Schlegel is not speaking directly of fragments in this description of the organization of Goethe's novel … his emphasis on the fact that individual parts can also be seen as wholes in themselves helps shed light on what he means [in fragment 206] … Fragments are parts of a whole; parts that have independent value or meaning but that nonetheless should be read in connection with the whole of which they are a part" (Ibid.). But this is again to insist on the idea that fragments should be related to other fragments, which fragment 206 seems to explicitly deny.

A possible yet, I think, unsatisfying way out of this inconvenience is to invoke Firchow's idea that the system to be composed of fragments need not exclude contradiction: we thus should not be troubled by the realization that we have discovered a fragment that contradicts the very philosophy behind the choice of the fragment as a philosophical tool. A variant on this approach which is perhaps more successful is to notice that in a peculiar sense the fragment at issue contradicts *itself*: on the one hand, it aims to say something about fragments in general, but on the other hand, it asserts that all fragments must be absolutely disconnected from everything else, so, being a fragment, it should be read as having no bearing at all on all other fragments and on the idea that they can connect to form a progressive system. Thus, this fragment—ironically—cancels itself out.

## 4   Nietzsche and the Aphorism—A Comparison

In this final section, I wish to compare Nietzsche's use of the aphorism with that of the early German Romantics. Now, while Nietzsche, perhaps influenced by Goethe, considered Romanticism a sickness,[79] the case could nevertheless be made that in a number of important respects Nietzsche could be considered a romantic. Thus, like the early German Romantics, he rejected the idea that the rationalistic or scientific approach can provide answers to all questions[80] or that it could even provide us with the best answers.[81] In the same spirit, Nietzsche was not of the view that all answers must necessarily cohere with each other and appreciated the "marvelous uncertainty and rich ambiguity of existence".[82] Further, similarly to the romantics he held in a Kantian vein that we have no "organ for knowledge", meaning that we have no cognitive faculty that provides immediate access to the thing-in-itself.[83] Moreover, Nietzsche's ethics, in general, could be seen as closely tracing the main contours of the romantic "ideal of excellence",[84] articulated by Friedrich Schlegel, Novalis, Schleiermacher, and Hölderlin. It is explained by Frederick Beiser as consisting of "three basic components: (1) *totality*, that a person should develop *all* his or her characteristic human powers; (2) *unity*, that these powers be formed into a whole or unity; and (3) *individuality*, that this whole or unity should be individual or unique, characteristic of the person alone".[85] Thus, Nietzsche was always critical of the idea that one should fight against one's passions or extirpate one's instincts and desires.[86] Rather than attempt to annihilate or repress the desires, one should try to refine or sublimate them so as to harness their power. But—to turn to unity—the passions should not be spiritualized in a disorderly fashion, as separate and isolated psychological powers; instincts in anarchy spell danger and imminent corruption.[87] Rather, order should govern the structure of the soul, where a hierarchy of forces is constructed to form a unified "social structure of drives and affects".[88] As for individuality, Nietzsche champions the idea that one should become "new, unique and incomparable"[89] by giving laws to oneself, thus creating oneself. Finally, and obviously, Nietzsche adopted the aphoristic/fragmentary style of

## 13 The Role of the Fragment in German Romantic Philosophy...

writing and has arguably become the philosopher most identified with this genre of writing. This is not of course to deny the differences in view between Nietzsche and the early German Romantics (e.g. Nietzsche, importantly, did not share the organic view of Being), but it does balance the impression one might get in light of Nietzsche's predominantly negative evaluation of early German Romanticism.

How does Nietzsche compare to the romantics with respect to the aphorism/fragment? One possible suggestion, made by Palmowski, is that Schlegel and Nietzsche "both mixed philosophy with poetry ... They both wrote philosophy in the form of poetic aphorism, the form which, because of its fragmentary nature, invites contradiction".[90] And contradiction, according to Palmowski, as well as the mixing of genres, is a mark of the irony which both philosophers practiced in their writings. While there is something to this assessment, it is important to emphasize that the meaning of "irony" invoked here draws on Richard Rorty's conception of irony and includes, among other features, an anti-metaphysical stance which refuses to make substantive claims about the nature of reality. Nevertheless, as a budding absolute idealist, Schlegel cannot be too easily described as an ironist in this sense.

Another suggestion[91] is to conceive of the irony that Schlegel and Nietzsche practice in their fragmentary writings along Socratic lines. Here philosophy is conceived not as substantive, that is, not as a discipline that puts forward systematic metaphysical theses about the nature of man and world, but as a kind of practice, specifically, as a way of incessantly interrogating and questioning our taken-for-granted beliefs, exposing them for their lack of rational grounds and thus opening the way for a reassessment of our commitment to them. By doing so, it also *engages the reader* and incentivizes him or her to reflect critically on their own opinions. The ironical fragment thus makes a claim, simultaneously questions it, and pushes the reader beyond it toward further reflections. The fragment is thus a most suitable literary vessel for the communication of this Socratic irony, for, "every text is only a fragment which the reader must complete".[92] The following fragment from Schlegel's *Ideas* expresses a similar idea:

> The mind understands something only insofar as it absorbs it like a seed into itself, nurtures it and lets it grow into blossom and fruit. Therefore scatter holy seed into the soil of the spirit.[93]

In "Nietzsche and the Art of the Aphorism", Jill Marsden offers a similar view: the aphorism consists in the "provocation to think".[94] It does so through its surprising and precise use of language,[95] which has the effect of breaking commonsensical thoughts and preconceptions in the attentive reader, engaging their sensibility and their body, thus rousing him or her out of their passivity and spurs them to actively think in a new way.[96] This view about the philosophical significance of the aphorism/fragment is plausible enough, but it seems that all innovative and ground-breaking philosophy achieves these effects. Further, conceiving of Nietzsche and Schlegel as ironists in the Rortyan or Socratic sense is in tension with their systematic aspirations. In order to elaborate on this last point, the question of the systematicity of Nietzsche's philosophy must first be addressed.[97]

Here we have, on the one hand, scholars who seek systematicity (in the weaker sense) in Nietzsche, either by focusing on one of Nietzsche's central ideas (perspectivism, will to power) or by putting at the center of their analysis a specific "problem or crisis" which Nietzsche's philosophy systematically responds to.[98]

On the other hand, there are those who refuse to attribute any system in whatever sense to Nietzsche. This point is seemingly supported by Nietzsche's own words when he writes: "I distrust all systematizers and avoid them. The will to a system is a lack of integrity".[99] But the point Nietzsche makes here can be read differently: presenting one's thoughts *as a* system lacks honesty about the personal nature of those thoughts and how one arrived at them. The will to a system thus betrays lack of integrity about the activity of philosophizing and its autobiographical nature.[100] Crucially, Nietzsche arguably would nevertheless insist that a philosophy, even an aphoristic one, could express a person's *specific* physio-psychological profile, a single "taste", and could thus amount, not to a system in the strong sense (complete and comprehensive view based on unshakeable foundations) but to a more or less coherent world view. As he puts a similar idea elsewhere in interrogative form: "Do you think that this work must be fragmentary because I give it to you (and have to give it to you) in fragments [*Stücken*]?"[101]—where the expected response of the reader should obviously be "No". So Cioran was arguably wrong when he wrote that Nietzsche's aphorisms are the sum of his attitudes and that it is therefore a mistake to look for something like a system in Nietzsche.[102] The "therefore" here is where the fallacy lies: different moods could still be expressive of a single person and could have coherence to the extent that the person herself has a more or less coherent personality and is not merely a heap of valuations and opinions. As Nietzsche puts it: "For assuming that one is a person, one necessarily also has the philosophy that belongs to that person".[103] It thus seems that much like Schlegel, Nietzsche could be read as offering a systematic philosophical view (in a weaker sense) composed mostly of aphorisms and fragments.

## 13 The Role of the Fragment in German Romantic Philosophy...

An interesting point of comparison in this respect has to do with Nietzsche's perspectivism. While I cannot go into a detailed discussion of the topic,[104] in general it can be held that for Nietzsche there is no God's view of reality—a single comprehensive and final picture—but only various differing and often contradictory perspectives taken by different agents whose view of reality is shaped by their sense-apparatus, their psychology, their values and beliefs, and their conceptual scheme. In order, then, to approach a somewhat comprehensive view of reality, it is incumbent upon the thinker to multiply his or her perspectives and to consider things from various different sides in an attempt to fuse these views together or reach some form of balance between them. This is Nietzsche's concept of intellectual justice, where things are given their due cognitively.[105]

Now the idea—for which the fragment is so well suited—that the thinker should examine things from different sides, is remarkably celebrated in AF 121 where Schlegel writes that:

> [T]o transport oneself arbitrarily now into this, now into that sphere, as if into another world … with one's whole soul; to freely relinquish first one and then another part of one's being, and confine oneself entirely to a third; to seek and find now in this, now in that individual the be-all and end-all of existence, and intentionally forget everyone else: of this only a mind is capable that contains within itself simultaneously a plurality of minds and a whole system of persons … [and] has grown to fullness and maturity.

And here too we find the idea of holding those partial points of view together in one mind, an idea that is reminiscent of the romantics' idea of "symphilosophy": the art of "amalgamating individuals", of creating "communal works" by "several complementary minds".[106]

But despite these similarities, Nietzsche's usage of the aphorism/fragment differs from both Schlegel's and Novalis'. I will now outline these differences with respect to three points of comparison. First, a striking difference arises when one examines the *substance* of Nietzsche's and Novalis' and Schlegel's (early) texts. While, as I argued, the fragmentary form in early German Romanticism could be seen as a potential means of philosophizing beyond the bounds of Kantianism, in effect, many of Schlegel's and Novalis' fragmentary writings are *programmatic* in content, that is, they announce and elaborate on what should or could be done and accomplished in art, criticism, philosophy, learning, religion, and so on,[107] without actually setting out to achieve it. Further, a kind of Kantian architectonic and a penchant for definition and classification pervades a large number of them.[108] The result is that in many cases rather than actually philosophizing about Being, morality, or knowledge, what we have are preparatory remarks which merely seem to lay the ground for a future romantic philosophy (compare here with Novalis' grand project for an encyclopedia, which was never consummated).[109] They are more of a manifesto than an actual execution: an explosion of philosophical enthusiasm that, alas, at least at this early stage, is never fully developed.

Second, although, like the romantics, Nietzsche too rejects the traditional idea of philosophy as a system which is derived logically from solid foundations and can provide final and ultimate answers to philosophy's central questions, he adhered more fully to the fragment as a medium for experimental philosophizing. To philosophize in the experimental mood is to formulate ideas, not on the basis of any prior conviction that these make up the final truth and not on the basis of any metaphysical scheme that one takes to be necessary in guiding one's thinking. Accordingly, one does not derive them from what one takes to be certain axioms. Rather, one acts in the spirit of trial and error: one expresses an idea that strikes one as true or worth pondering, and examines—or lets the reader examine—its ramifications, consequences, or connections with other similarly tentatively expressed thoughts.

As can be readily seen, the aphoristic and fragmentary form is especially amenable to this form of philosophizing: aphorisms or fragments are not presented as following logically from various basic and certain assumptions, and the relatively relaxed logical connections that obtain between them allows one to dispose of some while retaining others. In contrast, the more traditional philosophical form allows for much less leeway in this regard: once one rejects one of the central argumentative building blocks of the theory or system (e.g. Spinoza's definitions, axioms, or propositions), the whole structure threatens to collapse.

This conception of the fragment or the aphorism as a provisional experiment and thought has a history that precedes both Nietzsche and the romantics at issue here. Thus, Francis Bacon was one of the first to draw a connection between the aphorism and the experiment-based inductive method: "For [Bacon], the aphorism is the genre in which this induction can most effectively be practiced because, as a brief and self-contained assertion, it proceeds directly from experience and observation, rather than being systematically derived from already established truths".[110]

Famously, Nietzsche occasionally expresses sympathies for the experimental mode of philosophizing: "I favor any *skepsis* to which I may reply: 'Let us try it!', but I no longer wish to hear anything of all those things and questions which do not permit any experiment".[111] Given that the experimental aphorism is the proper way to philosophize, it is no surprise that he calls the philosophers of the future "attempters" or "experimenters".[112] Not perceiving a sharp break between one's life and one's philosophy, Nietzsche even often advocates seeing life itself as an experiment.[113]

How does this experimental stance compare to that of the early German Romantics? I will consider the case of Novalis and argue there is reason to doubt his full allegiance to philosophy in the experimental mode. It has been held that, like Schlegel, Novalis abandoned the idea of an all-encompassing and final system and attempted "to think systematically but without allowing thought to stagnate in a final set of truths or dogma. Philosophy ought to be open-ended".[114] This might give the impression that Novalis shares Schlegel's view regarding the philosophical value of the fragment.[115] However, when we turn to look at Novalis' own views regarding the value of the fragment, a different picture emerges. Thus, in *Miscellaneous Observations* 104, Novalis claims that the fragments he has composed are "literary seedlings" of which some "may indeed be sterile" while others may yet grow, presumably into non-fragmentary conceptions and formulations. Similarly, at the end of another set of fragments, Novalis writes the following:

> As one progresses so much becomes dispensable … so that I should not have wished to work on a single point before the exposition of the great, *all-transforming idea*.[116] That which is imperfect appears most tolerably as a fragment—and thus this form of communication is to be recommended above that which is not yet finished—and yet has single noteworthy opinions to offer.[117]

These remarks strongly suggest that for Novalis the fragment form is not a new means of expression conformable to a new metaphilosophy, but is rather a *faute de mieux*—the "most tolerable" form of expression in the absence of a more suitable one. Rather than being part of a non-systematic system in constant need of revision, fragments are merely provisional expressions of one's views, to be ultimately abandoned and transcended by a more complete and perhaps systematic philosophical vision—the "great, *all-transforming idea*". This means that for Novalis the use of the fragment was itself experimental, and that consequently, insofar as fragments are conducive to an experimental mode of philosophizing, there is reason to believe that Novalis, despite appearances, was not fully committed to the idea of philosophy as *continuously* experimental. Thus, despite Novalis' penchant for and training in the sciences,[118] it seems that while he indeed formulated his views in the fragmentary and thus seemingly experimental mode, he did not genuinely adhere to the notion of fragmentary and fallibilistic inquiry but took his fragments to be ultimately overcome by a final and systematic philosophical view.

Finally, and perhaps most important in terms of drawing a distinction between Nietzsche and the early German Romantics, Nietzsche dispenses with the idea of the Absolute. In Nietzsche, there is no transcendent Being or Thing-in-itself, and mystical insight, of the kind that the intensive dimension of thought purports to provide, is seen as shallow, despite its profound appearance.[119] Even the will to power is just a perspective, just another hypothetical interpretation.[120] In other words, Nietzsche goes further than Schlegel for whom irony and poetic philosophy remain guided by the Absolute, where, even if that Absolute remains unattainable, it serves a guiding principle. From this point of view, Schlegel's early philosophy constitutes a fork in the road of the history of German philosophy: one can either retain the Absolute and drop perspectival and fragmentary irony (and go with Hegel) or one can retain perspectivism and drop the Absolute (and go with Nietzsche). While in Schlegel, we have a search for knowledge that is marked with a kind of *Sehnsucht* for the Absolute—in Nietzsche there is just nomadism, for God is dead. Whether this absence of the intensive dimension of the fragment in Nietzsche is to be considered as a loss or as a gain, depends partially on one's metaphysical sensibilities: distaste for the Absolute can incline one to regard the loss of this dimension as liberation of the fragmentary form from any metaphysical anchorage that hinders its perspectival and experimental roaming; a liberation that can be seen as releasing the fragment to come to its own.

## 5    Concluding Remarks

I have argued that fragment or aphoristic form employed by the romantics is a means of expression that, much like art, can enable the thinker to overcome Kantian fragmentation and strictures on cognition and can thus indicate as well as circumnavigate the Absolute. In this respect, the choice of the fragment as a medium can be seen as motivated by romantic considerations as to the nature and power of art. I have also argued that despite many similarities, Nietzsche's fragmentary and aphoristic writings provide us with an arguably fuller realization of the idea of the philosophical fragment: an interconnected and experimental set of insights that is on the move, open-ended and perspectival, substantive and fully committed to the fragmentary medium *sans* metaphysical additives.

## Notes

1. Lacoue-Labarthe and Nancy argue that the *Athenaeum Fragments* were all composed by a collective subject, but according to Firchow, the authors of each fragment can be reliably identified (Firchow, 15–16), even if they all participated in the same endeavor and shared the same spirit. See Philippe Lacoue-Labarthe Jean-Luc Nancy, *The Literary Absolute: The Theory of Literature in German Romanticism*, trans., Philip Barnard and Cheryl Lester (Albany: State University of New York Press, 1988), 45 (hereafter *The Literary Absolute*) and Peter Firchow "Introduction", in *Friedrich Schlegel's Lucinde and the Fragments*, trans. with an introduction by Peter Firchow (Minneapolis: University of Minnesota Press, 1971), 15–16 (hereafter Firchow).
2. With the possible exception of the "pure" aphorism—see below.
3. See Firchow, 15.
4. The discussion that follows draws on my "Aphorisms and Fragments", forthcoming in the *Palgrave Macmillan Handbook of Philosophy and Literature*.
5. Gary S. Morson, *The Long and the Short of It: From Aphorism to Novel* (Stanford: Stanford University Press, 2004), 4.
6. Ibid.
7. Ibid.
8. Ibid., 5.
9. Ibid., 6.
10. Ibid., 7.
11. Ibid., 8.
12. George C. Lichtenberg, *The Waste Books*, trans. with an introduction by R.J. Hollingdale (New York: New York Review Books, 1990), x–xi.
13. Thus, Nietzsche refers to his *Human, All too Human*, which consists of sections of various lengths, as a "collection of aphorisms" (*On the Genealogy of Morals*, in *On the Genealogy of Morals and Ecce Homo*, ed. W. Kaufmann/ trans., R.J. Hollingdale (New York: Vintage, 1967), Preface, section 2). Cited henceforth as GM followed by essay and section number.
14. For example, *Athenaeum Fragments*, Nr. 63, in Schlegel, Friedrich, *Friedrich Schlegel's Lucinde and the Fragments*, translated with an introduction by Peter Firchow, Minneapolis, Minnesota: University of Minnesota Press, 1971. References to *Athenaeum Fragments* will be given as AF followed by the fragment's number; references to the *Critical Fragments* will be given as CF followed by the fragment's number; references to *Ideas* will be given as I followed by the fragment number. Both the *Critical Fragments* and the *Ideas* are to be found in Schlegel 1971.
15. Hollingdale, Introduction to *The Waste Books* (*op. cit.*), x–xi.

16. See Joseph P. Stern, *Lichtenberg: A Doctrine of Scattered Occasions—Reconstructed from his Aphorisms and Reflections* (Bloomington: Indiana University Press, 1959), 216, and Will G. Moore Will, *La Rochefoucauld: His Mind and Art* (Oxford: Oxford Clarendon Press, 1969), 84.
17. One can insist that a necessary, though not a sufficient condition, for being an aphorism, in contrast to the fragment, is being exactly one sentence long. But, again, this will go against how the terms are used both by Nietzsche (who refers to longer sections as "aphorisms") and the early German Romantics (who include such pure aphorisms in their collection of fragments), and would not yield any clear philosophical payoff.
18. Hollingdale, Introduction to *The Waste Books* (*op. cit.*), xii.
19. Moore, *La Rochefoucauld: His Mind and Art* (*op. cit.*), 5.
20. AF 80.
21. AF 96.
22. See Frederick C. Beiser, *German Idealism: The Struggle against Subjectivism, 1781–1801* (Cambridge, MA: Harvard University Press, 2002).
23. Emil M. Cioran, *Oeuvres* (Paris: Quarto Gallimard, 1995), 1736.
24. Stern, *Lichtenberg: A Doctrine of Scattered Occasions—Reconstructed from his Aphorisms and Reflections* (*op. cit.*), 217.
25. Ibid.
26. Cioran: "Aphorisms … [belong] to discontinuous thought" (Cioran, 1995, 1736).
27. La Rochefoucauld, *Collected Maxims and Other Reflections*, E.H. Blackmore, A.M. Blackmore, F. Giguère (trans. and introduction), Oxford: Oxford University press, 2007, v: 68–v: 78.
28. In La Rochefoucauld, "The Publisher to the Reader", 3.
29. Introduction to La Rochefoucauld, xxviii.
30. Stern, *Lichtenberg: A Doctrine of Scattered Occasions—Reconstructed from his Aphorisms and Reflections* (*op. cit.*), 194.
31. AF 206.
32. There are, of course, exceptions: Nietzsche's *On the Genealogy of Morals*, for example, though composed of what can be called extended, aphorisms (Nietzsche himself seems—though there is some uncertainty here—to refer to the sections comprising the *Genealogy* "aphorisms", see GM Preface, 8), follows a certain logical, if complex, order. The various aphorisms of Wittgenstein's *Tractatus* lack justification too, in the sense that Wittgenstein does not offer arguments in their favor, though arguably the work as a whole could be read as one long *reduction* argument (see Ludwig Wittgenstein, *Tractatus Logico-Philosophicus* (New York: Dover Publications, 1990), and Alfred Nordmann, *Wittgenstein's Tractatus: An Introduction* (Cambridge: Cambridge University Press, 2005), for this interpretation). Further, though they could perhaps be read in a different order in which they were published, Wittgenstein marked the relative importance of the aphorisms by assigning

numbers to them. As he puts it: "The decimal figures as numbers of the separate propositions indicate the logical importance of the propositions, the emphasis laid upon them in my exposition. The propositions *n*.1, *n*.2, *n*.3. etc., are comments on proposition No. *n* ..." (Wittgenstein, footnote to first proposition).

33. Elizabeth Millán-Zaibert, *Friedrich Schlegel and the Emergence of Romantic Philosophy* (Albany: SUNY Press, 2007), 225, fn.91.
34. Indeed, this is arguably why Schlegel preferred the term "fragment" over "aphorism", namely, because it connotes the author's view that one can aim at the whole precisely by joining *fragments* together.
35. GM II 13.
36. See Moore, *La Rochefoucauld: His Mind and Art, op. cit.*, 80–83 for the case of La Rochefoucauld's maxim and for a general discussion of the form, Ben Grant, *The Aphorism and Other Short Forms* (London: Routledge, 2016), 6–37.
37. See, for example, Rüdiger Safranski, *Romanticism: A German Affair*, trans., Robert E. Goodwin (Evanston: Northwestern University Press, 2015); Jean-Marie Schaeffer, *Art of the Modern Age: Philosophy of Art from Kant to Heidegger*, trans., Steven Rendall (Princeton: Princeton University Press, 2000); Frederick C. Beiser, *German Idealism: The Struggle against Subjectivism, 1781–1801* (Cambridge, MA: Harvard University Press, 2002).
38. Which is not to deny that Kant did try in the *Critique of Judgment* to put back together that which was shattered by drawing connections and identifying intersections between the three spheres. Romantic philosophers were by and large unconvinced by these attempts (see Beiser, Ibid., 369–70).
39. See Jean-François Lyotard, *The Differend: Phrases in Dispute*, trans., Georges Van Den Abbeele (Minneapolis: University of Minnesota Press, 1989).
40. Isaiah Berlin, *The Roots of Romanticism*, Second Edition (Princeton: Princeton University Press, 2013), 26–27.
41. Stern, *Lichtenberg: A Doctrine of Scattered Occasions—Reconstructed from his Aphorisms and Reflections* (*op. cit.*), 221.
42. Jean-Marie Schaeffer, *Art of the Modern Age: Philosophy of Art from Kant to Heidegger*, trans., Steven Rendall (Princeton: Princeton University Press, 2000), 68.
43. To be clear, Beiser claims that more than a reaction to the Kantian fragmented world, the romantic advancement of absolute idealism should be seen as a rejection of some of the perceived failures of Fichte's view (Beiser, *German Idealism: The Struggle against Subjectivism, 1781–1801* (*op. cit.*), 359–361). Later, however, Beiser adds that the Spinozism of this absolute idealism attracted its adherents because it offered a way to overcome dualisms also found in the Kantian system (Ibid. 363). For a push-back against Beiser's claim with respect to the early German Romantics' relation to Fichte,

see Ayon Maharaj, *The Dialectics of Aesthetic Agency: Revaluating German Aesthetics from Kant to Adorno* (London: Bloomsbury, 2013).
44. Beiser, Ibid., 461 and compare with Novalis speaking of the "Darstellung des Undarstellbaren" in Manfred Frank, *The Philosophical Foundations of Early German Romanticism*, trans., Elizabeth Millán-Zaibert. (Albany: SUNY Press, 2004), 164.
45. See Schaeffer, *Art of the Modern Age* (*op. cit.*).
46. See Fred Rush, *Irony and Idealism: Rereading Schlegel, Hegel, and Kierkegaard* (Oxford: Oxford University Press, 2016), 60. In addition, Schlegel and Novalis by no means regarded philosophy as dispensable. Thus, Novalis held that "without philosophy a poet is incomplete. Without philosophy a thinker—or a judge—is incomplete" (*Logological Fragments* I Nr. 24 in *Philosophical Writings*, ed./trans., Margaret Mahony Stoljar (Albany: SUNY Press, 1997)). The *Logological Fragments* will henceforth be cited as LF followed by a Roman numeral and section number. The *Miscellaneous Observations*, also to be found in *Philosophical Writings*, will be henceforth cited as MO followed by a section number.
47. LF 25.
48. Fragment Nr. 49, in *Last Fragments*, in Novalis, *Philosophical Writings*. Henceforth these fragments will be cited as LF followed by section number.
49. Manfred Frank, *Unendliche Annäherung: Die Anfänge der philosophischen Frühromantik* (Frankfurt am Main: Suhrkamp Verlag, 1997), 255.
50. CF 42, cf. I 13.
51. See Beiser, *German Idealism: The Struggle against Subjectivism, 1781–1801* (*op. cit.*), 450, and compare with Novalis' definition of Romanticism as making the finite infinite and the infinite finite in LF I 66.
52. Kristin Gjesdal, "Georg Friedrich Philipp von Hardenberg [Novalis]", *The Stanford Encyclopedia of Philosophy* (Fall 2014 Edition), ed., Edward N. Zalta, URL = <https://plato.stanford.edu/archives/fall2014/entries/novalis/>.
53. See Beiser *German Idealism: The Struggle against Subjectivism, 1781–1801* (*op. cit.*).
54. Ibid. and Millán-Zaibert *Friedrich Schlegel and the Emergence of Romantic Philosophy* (*op.cit.*)
55. AF 53.
56. Beiser, *German Idealism: The Struggle against Subjectivism, 1781–1801* (*op. cit.*), 446–447.
57. See also Novalis MO 45.
58. Lacoue-Labarthe and Nancy understand the *Athenaeum Fragments* as being in the process of individuation, which corresponds, in their view, to fragment 116 which, as we saw, defines Romantic poetry as "forever be becoming and never be perfected". But if this process of individuation involves a sharpening of the content and meaning of each fragment, then, in good

coherentist fashion, it seems that this "individuation" can be achieved precisely only through the linking together of the various fragments in the striving toward a system. See Lacoue-Labarthe and Nancy, *The Literary Absolute* (*op. cit.*).
59. AF 116.
60. Rush, *Irony and Idealism: Rereading Schlegel, Hegel, and Kierkegaard* (*op. cit.*), 46–47.
61. I 26.
62. Firchow, Introduction to Schlegel, 30.
63. AF 120.
64. AF 82. See also Beiser *German Idealism: The Struggle against Subjectivism, 1781–1801* (*op. cit.*), 436.
65. Firchow, 30.
66. CF 34.
67. Rush discounts the importance of wittiness and consigns this property to the aphorism only, which he distinguishes from the fragment "proper" (Rush, *Irony and Idealism: Rereading Schlegel, Hegel, and Kierkegaard* (*op. cit.*), 81). But as I argue, wit is actually crucial for the philosophical function of the fragment, even if, admittedly, not so many of the early German Romantics' fragments are witty in the colloquial sense.
68. See Millán-Zaibert, *Friedrich Schlegel and the Emergence of Romantic Philosophy* (*op. cit.*), 47.
69. Firchow, 16.
70. Ibid., 18.
71. Ibid., see also Rush, *Irony and Idealism: Rereading Schlegel, Hegel, and Kierkegaard* (*op. cit.*), 86–89.
72. Andrew Bowie, *Aesthetics and Subjectivity: from Kant to Nietzsche* (Manchester: Manchester University Press, 1990), 53.
73. Lacoue-Labarthe and Nancy, *The Literary Absolute*, 42.
74. Cf. AF 37.
75. AF 77.
76. See Frank, *The Philosophical Foundations of Early German Romanticism* (*op. cit.*), 216, quoted in Speight, Allen, "Friedrich Schlegel", *The Stanford Encyclopedia of Philosophy* (Winter 2016 Edition), Edward N. Zalta (ed.), URL = <https://plato.stanford.edu/archives/win2016/entries/schlegel/>.
77. I 69.
78. Quoted in Millán-Zaibert, *Friedrich Schlegel and the Emergence of Romantic Philosophy* (*op. cit.*), 158.
79. *The Gay Science* 370, *Assorted Opinions and Maxims* Preface 2. In the following works by Friedrich Nietzsche will be cited with the corresponding abbreviation followed by section number: *Beyond Good and Evil*, trans., W. Kaufmann (New York: Vintage, 1966). [BGE]; *The Birth of Tragedy* in *The Birth of Tragedy* and *The Case of Wagner*, trans., W. Kaufmann (New

York: Vintage, 1967). [BT]; The *Will to Power*, trans., W. Kaufmann and R.J. Hollingdale (New York: Vintage, 1968). [WP]; *The Gay Science*, trans., W. Kaufmann (New York: Vintage, 1974). [GS]; *Human, All Too Human*, trans. M. Faber (London: Penguin Books, 1984). [HH]; *Assorted Opinions and Maxims The Wanderer and His Shadow*, in *Human, All Too Human*, trans., R. J. Hollingdale (Cambridge: Cambridge University Press, 1966). [AOM] and [WS]; *Kritische Studienausgabe*, compiled under the general editorship of G. Colli and M. Montinari, Berlin and (New York: Walter de Gruyter, 1999). [KSA]; *Twilight of the Idols*, in eds., A. Ridley and J. Norman and trans., J. Norman, *The Anti-Christ, Ecce Homo, Twilight of the Idols: And Other Writings* (Cambridge: Cambridge University Press, 2005). [TI].
80. For example, in *The Birth of Tragedy*.
81. GS 373.
82. GS 2, see also 373.
83. GS 354.
84. Beiser *Hegel* (New York: Routledge 2005), 39.
85. Ibid. 39.
86. TI, Morality, 1.
87. TI, Socrates, 9.
88. BGE 12.
89. GS 335.
90. Michal Palmowski, "Antimetaphysical Philosophy and Ironic Discourse. Nietzsche and Schlegel", in *Friedrich Schlegel und Friedrich Nietzsche: Transzendentalpoesie oder Dichtkunst mit Begriffen*, ed. Klaus Vieweg (Paderborn: Ferdinand Schöningh, 2009), 71–79, 74.
91. See Kathleen M. Wheeler, "Socratic Irony and the Fragment Form in Friedrich Schlegel", in *Friedrich Schlegel und Friedrich Nietzsche: Transzendentalpoesie oder Dichtkunst mit Begriffen*, ed., Klaus Vieweg (Paderborn: Ferdinand Schöningh, 2009), 81–93.
92. Wheeler, Ibid., 84.
93. Ideas 5. Wheeler references this fragment to support her argument but ascribes it erroneously to Novalis (Wheeler, Ibid., 84).
94. Jill Marsden, "Nietzsche and the Art of the Aphorism", in *A Companion to Nietzsche*, ed., Ansell K. Pearson (Oxford: Blackwell Publishing, 2006), 25.
95. Ibid., 28.
96. Ibid.
97. The following discussion of systematicity in Nietzsche draws on my "Aphorisms and Fragments", forthcoming in the *Palgrave Macmillan Handbook of Philosophy and Literature*.
98. See Bernard Reginster, *The Affirmation of Life: Nietzsche on the Overcoming of Nihilism* (Cambridge, MA: Harvard University Press, 2006), 4–5.
99. TI, Maxims and Arrows, 26.
100. BGE 6.

101. AOM 128.
102. Emil M. Cioran, *The Temptation to Exist*, trans., H. Richard (Chicago: Quadrangle, 1970), 151.
103. GS Preface 2.
104. For an overview of possible interpretations of Nietzsche's perspectivism see Ken Gemes, "Life's Perspectives", in *The Oxford Handbook of Nietzsche*, eds., J. Richardson and K. Gemes (Oxford: Oxford University Press, 2013), 553–75.
105. See, for example, GS 333. For a development of this view see Guy Elgat, *Nietzsche's Psychology of* Ressentiment: *Revenge and Justice in* "On the Genealogy of Morals" (New York: Routledge, 2017).
106. AF 125. See also Maharaj on Schlegel's conception of irony: "Irony, for Schlegel, denotes the capacity to move *laterally* among opposing perspectives: instead of settling into a single perspective and thereby reverting to foundationalism, the ironist is able to test and inhabit multiple perspectives at will" (Maharaj, *The Dialectic of Aesthetic Agency* (*op. cit.*), 97).
107. For example, I 22, AF 3 76 92 117 167 434.
108. For example, AF 91 106 121, 439, 440, 443.
109. Thus, the burgeoning idealism that is only in its nascent stages in the early German Romantics only gets realized in the philosophies of Schelling and Hegel.
110. Ben Grant, *The Aphorism and Other Short Forms* (London: Routledge, 2016), 15.
111. GS 51, see also GS 110.
112. For example, BGE 42. The German word Nietzsche uses is *Versucher*, which is ambiguous between "attempters" and "seducers" or "tempters".
113. GS 319, 324. But see, on the other hand, Nietzsche's wariness that an extreme adoption of the experimental mode where everyone becomes an "actor" is potentially harmful for the growth and sustenance of the future (GS 356).
114. See Gjesdal, *op. cit.*
115. Admittedly, Gjesdal later goes on to add that the "affiliation with empirical science is another point at which Novalis' understanding of the fragment differs from that of Friedrich Schlegel. Whereas Schlegel establishes a close link between philosophy and poetry—at times he even dismantles the distinction between them—Novalis is convinced that if human reason seeks everywhere for the unconditioned (*das Unbedingte*) but finds nothing but things (*Dinge*) (MO 1), then we better study these things closely and try to make sense of them". But Novalis' stronger interest in and appreciation for the natural sciences does not in itself imply any different understanding of the nature or philosophical role of the fragment.
116. Stoljar, in a footnote to this fragment, speculates that the idea Novalis refers to here is his "theory of magical idealism" (in Novalis' *Philosophical Writings*,

fn. 14,175). See Beiser, *German Idealism: The Struggle against Subjectivism, 1781–1801* (*op. cit.*), 407–434 for a discussion of magical idealism.
117. LF II 55. See also Novalis' remarks in LF II 20, where fragments are presented as a sort of caricature of the real world and as such are "more interesting" and "more picturesque" but also "more untrue—more unphilosophical—more immoral". This again strongly suggests that Novalis was not full-heartedly committed to the fragment.
118. Novalis, *The Birth of Novalis: Friedrich von Hardenberg's Journal of 1797, with Selected Letters and Documents*, ed./trans. with an introduction by Bruce Donehower (Albany: SUNY Press; Reprint edition, 2015), 119.
119. GS 126. *Pace* Rush, who holds that in Nietzsche too there is a constant striving to multiply perspectives so as to possess "more ways … to take the world and adumbrate the absolute" (Rush, *Irony and Idealism: Rereading Schlegel, Hegel, and Kierkegaard* (*op. cit.*), 72, fn. 102).
120. BGE 22.

# 14

# Early German Romanticism and Literature: Goethe, Schlegel, Novalis and the New Philosophical Importance of the Novel

## Allen Speight

Early German Romanticism is characterized in no small part by the distinctively *literary* revolution it launched. Heralded most famously, of course, by Friedrich Schlegel's inclusion of Goethe's novel *Wilhelm Meister* in a list of "tendencies" of the age that included the political and philosophical events of the French Revolution and the publication of Fichte's *Wissenschaftslehre*, the literary revolution of the early German Romantics raised important new questions about the mode of philosophical writing.[1] Among other things, the romantics can be credited with the origination or new appropriation of a number of different literary forms, including the fragment and the novel, as well as in general the reconsideration of the relationship between philosophy and literature and the larger new role the early German Romantics accorded to the task of "poetry."

Among the most celebrated romantic projects in literature was the novel—a genre taken to have a particular intimacy with Romanticism itself, *Roman* being the German word usually translated as "novel," but construed by the early German Romantics in a way that transcended the narrower conception of it as a genre designation. Coming to terms with the profusion of new novelistic works and romantic theories of the novel is by no means an easy task. The *philosophical* consideration of the nature and new importance of the novel

---

A. Speight (✉)
Boston University, Boston, MA, USA
e-mail: casp8@bu.edu

© The Author(s) 2020
E. Millán Brusslan (ed.), *The Palgrave Handbook of German Romantic Philosophy*, Palgrave Handbooks in German Idealism, https://doi.org/10.1007/978-3-030-53567-4_14

among the early German Romantics have been discussed in a number of different ways by a variety of scholars, but two of them—Ernst Behler and Walter Benjamin—are particularly useful for framing the exploration that will follow.

Behler claimed a distinction between "idealist" and "romantic" attempts to come to terms philosophically with the new status of the novel. In the idealist tradition (which originates in Schelling and Hegel and can be traced to its wider influence in figures like Lukács), Behler claimed that the novel was understood primarily as a form having kinship with ancient epic—in particular, that epic and novel were "different manifestations of *one and the same type of narration*," a comparison employed not always to the interpretive advantage of the novel. In the romantic tradition, by contrast, Behler claimed that the novel was "a modern art form *sui generis*," revealing its break from ancient forms not only in the distinctively ironic voice which novelistic narration can employ but also in the wide range of materials (narrative, song, discourse) that can now be included in its wider purview.[2] ("In vain do we hope for a Homer," Friedrich Schlegel said, even suggesting that if one wanted an ancient form to compare with the novel, one should focus on tragedy rather than on epic as the most relevant point of comparison).[3] Benjamin's influential essay, "The Concept of Criticism in German Romanticism," illuminated the importance of the novel by emphasizing the romantics' conception of the notion of prose as the "idea of poetry." "The conception of the idea of poetry as that of prose determines the whole Romantic philosophy of art," Benjamin claimed, arguing that since the romantic conception on his understanding saw the unity of poetry "as a whole, as one single work" constituting a poem in prose, the novel therefore afforded "the highest poetic form."[4]

While both Behler and Benjamin offer crucial perspectives on the philosophical importance of the novel that have shaped much subsequent commentary, there are a number of elements in their claims that need further exploration. Although Behler's remark captures an important difference in the idealist and romantic receptions of the novel, the philosophical consideration in these two traditions is actually more diverse than is represented, and a re-exploration of the interpretive approaches in the context of the romantic novel is worthwhile. On the one hand, more can be said for the idealist perspective, and on the other hand, there is significant divergence within the romantic approach across a range of issues, including those of what makes a novel (*Roman*) a "romantic" work of art in the sense of the new age and the relation between novels as works of art and ("ordinary") life. And while Benjamin's view of the new importance of the novel as a *prose* form is historically important for the understanding of German Romanticism, it neglects some of the valences of "prose" and "prosaicness" relevant for understanding the novelistic productions of the period.[5]

In this chapter, I want to focus on the question of the philosophical and literary potential within the romantic novel, and I will do so first by looking at the particular novel which Schlegel made clear had unique importance for the romantics: Goethe's *Wilhelm Meister's Apprenticeship*. Goethe's novel was not only the literary point of reference in Schlegel's assessment of the "tendencies of the age," but in addition the very work, as Benjamin pointed out, which Schlegel used to articulate the notion of romantic criticism and the standards appropriate to it, as well as a source of inspiration for novelistic efforts on his own part and that of Novalis.

As Benjamin points out, Schlegel "answered fully to his ideal of criticism only in his review of *Wilhelm Meister*."[6] So crucial in fact is getting a perspective on *Wilhelm Meister* for Benjamin that he argues in the "Concept of Criticism" essay for a relation between the particular influence of *Wilhelm Meister* in the context of the early German Romantics and the necessity of understanding the romantic conception of poetry as prose. Being clear about the latter claim is requisite, he argues, because "[o]nly from this viewpoint can the theory of the novel be understood in its profoundest intention and be extricated from the empirical relation to *Wilhelm Meister*."[7] It's not clear what would count for Benjamin as an "extrication" from the "empirical relation" to Goethe's novel (or even what, apart from anxiety of influence issues, might especially motivate the need for such liberation), but his further remarks about the development of the romantic novel make clear the larger stakes of thinking through the early German Romantics' relation to *Wilhelm Meister*. As Benjamin explains in the section that follows this claim, there are two important romantic concerns bound up with the novel that can be confused in this context—its formal ability to *include varied material* (narration, songs, conversation) and its general *prose* style—that need to be disentangled. It's Novalis, he claims in the essay, who more thoroughly takes up the issue of prosaicness:

> It is probably in allusion to the unifying function of prose that Novalis says: 'Shouldn't the novel comprehend all genres of style in a sequence differentially bound by a common spirit?' Friedrich Schlegel grasped the prosaic element less purely than Novalis, though he intended it no less deeply. Thus, in his exemplary novel *Lucinde*, he sometimes cultivates the multiplicity of forms (whose unification is his task) perhaps more than he does the purely prosaic (which fulfills this task). He wanted to insert many poems in the second part of the novel. But both of these tendencies, the multiplicity of forms and the prosaic, have in common

an opposition to limited form and an aspiration to the transcendental. Except that in some places in Friedrich Schlegel's prose, this is less demonstrated than postulated. Even in Schlegel's theory of the novel, the notion of prose, although it undoubtedly conditions its characteristic spirit, fails to stand clearly at its center.[8]

In what follows, this chapter will explore the kind of model *Wilhelm Meister* is (or isn't) for Friedrich Schlegel and Novalis. In the first section, it will explore the novelistic project that Goethe carried out. In the second section, it will examine the responses of Frierich Schlegel and Novalis as romantic readers of Goethe's novel. The third section of the chapter will explore the inspiration both positively and negatively that Schlegel and Novalis took from *Wilhelm Meister* in their own novelistic projects in *Lucinde* and *Heinrich von Ofterdingen*. In *Lucinde*, Schlegel explored the issue that Benjamin framed in terms of "multiplicity" by seeking out the space for contestation of different types of novel within it. But as Benjamin's comments about multiplicity and prose suggest, the question of novelistic differentiation—even in the romantic period—cannot be framed simply in terms of the genre's inclusiveness. Schlegel himself comes to categorize *Wilhelm Meister* as both "modern" and "poetic" but not as "romantic" (saving the latter term for *Don Quixote*). Novalis' novelistic exploration takes up the question of romantic form in a more deliberate distancing from Goethe's work: although he had gone so far as to call *Wilhelm Meister* the "absolute novel," he later insisted that it was not only not romantic—a point that Schlegel had made—but not even poetic. Novalis' use of "prosaic" has a different valence from the positive ones that Benjamin discerns in the "Criticism" essay (*Wilhelm Meister* is "in certain ways thoroughly prosaic—and modern—the Romantic in it is thereby destroyed," Novalis claimed, going so far as to call it "a *Candide* directed against poetry") and his novel *Heinrich* offers one of the clearest windows onto the different approach he took to a construal of the potential of the novelistic form.[9]

Looking at the sort of model each of these three works (*Wilhelm Meister*, *Lucinde* and *Heinrich von Ofterdingen*) represents will offer an exploration of three different philosophical perspectives on the nature and potential of the novel. With Goethe, the novel offers an exploration of the connection of events within a space of ironic play; with Schlegel, a notion of the novel as the place in which the interpretive struggle over different modes of expression may range; and with Novalis, a sense of what he calls *Übergangsjahre*—the development, at once internal and external, which poetry in its extension may offer for a connection between infinite and finite. In the end, I return to the question Behler has raised of competing idealist and romantic conceptions of the relation among these novelistic styles and to Benjamin's broader concern with what Romanticism's critical theory of the novel accomplished, but with an eye to the philosophical afterlife of the romantic novel in the nineteenth and twentieth centuries—an afterlife that in many ways has led philosophical exploration of art and literature to go well beyond the romantic conceptions of the novel.

(A word, briefly, about the method before taking up the novels in question: in a Schlegelian vein, this discussion will begin *in media res*, with a focus on the concrete works of literature in question and on what follows in the philosophical attempts the early German Romantics and idealists make in trying to come to terms with them aesthetically. In focusing on these three novelistic models which, despite the divergences in their style and purpose, bear such a close relation to one another (*Wilhelm Meister's Apprenticeship*, *Lucinde* and *Heinrich von Ofterdingen*), there is much within both the theory and praxis of the romantic novel that will be left aside. The range of novelistic production within German Romanticism is striking, and a more complete account of the constellations that gave rise to the romantic novel would involve a careful consideration of the philosophical and literary resonances of works such as Ludwig Tieck's *Franz Sternbalds Wanderungen* or Clemens von Brentano's *Godwi*. What the close examination of these three works together can offer, however, is a concrete sense of commonalities and divergences within the romantic project of the novel.)

## 1  Goethe's Novelistic Project in *Wilhelm Meister's Apprenticeship*

What made Goethe's *Wilhelm Meister's Apprenticeship* such a revolutionary force within the romantic circle, such that it was singled out by Friedrich Schlegel both as exemplary of the "tendencies of the age" and as the sort of work that attracted his most explicit attention to the emerging problems of contemporary criticism? If we look at the outset simply at stylistic concerns, it is worth noticing, as Behler points out, that *Wilhelm Meister* diverged radically from the novels of the eighteenth century—in its manner of composition, "unprecedented compactness" and its "absolutely organized coherence."[10] All of these stylistic factors, as we will see, play a role in the reception of the work by Schlegel and Novalis, but to grasp the sheer force of the novel and the attention which it garnered requires a look at Goethe's own production as a key to what made this novel the singular work that it is. Initially begun as a much more conventional novel similar to other earlier eighteenth-century works, *Wilhelm Meister's Apprenticeship* involved not just a reappropriation on Goethe's part of earlier writing but a significantly altered mode of approach to composing a novel. Instead of the project that Goethe had been working on in the 1770s but had abandoned—what he called *Wilhelm Meister's Theatrical Mission*, which shaped both the character we find in *Wilhelm Meister's Apprenticeship* and Goethe's interest in the stage—what emerged from his pen in the mid-1790s was a novel that employed a different mode of narration/irony and approach to the central question of literature and its relation to life. While the Wilhelm of the earlier work and his theatrical passion had been described from the narrator's perspective, Goethe now saw fit to have the character himself narrate his own early fascination with the stage—a move which allowed some ironic distance, since the most ardent of his early narrations involves his girlfriend falling asleep during the stories he told: Wilhelm is now a character whom Goethe invites the reader to see from more than one perspective (his own later temporal view as a narrator and that of those around him).[11] This shift to the distance of a narrator's stance and the irony implicit in it comes particularly to the fore in romantic criticism: as Schlegel's review puts it, Goethe never mentions his hero "except with some irony and seeming to smile down from the heights of his intellect upon his work."[12]

Interestingly, the point at which Goethe's early engagement with Wilhelm as a character broke off becomes a moment of a very different sort in the new novel when Goethe takes it up again in the 1790s. The moment involves Wilhelm's attempt to play Hamlet in a performance of Shakespeare's play, and the new stance that Goethe takes toward that critical scene is revelatory of the different sort of novel that *Wilhelm Meister's Apprenticeship* has become: now the Hamlet performance will represent not just a culmination in Wilhelm's acting career but a real turning point in his own life. In the *Apprenticeship*, Wilhelm's playing Hamlet is preceded by a larger conversation he has with figures that have been only mysterious up to this point but who are revealed as the novel progresses as part of a larger "society" (still no less mysterious) which has been pulling strings behind the scenes. One of the strings they play is to put a real ghost on the stage in front of Wilhelm during the crucial scene of Hamlet's encounter with his father at the beginning of the play, such that Wilhelm's reactions of fright are just those which he himself is actually experiencing in that moment and not the ("theatrical") gestures a professional actor would be trained to employ to convey such fright to an audience. Wilhelm's performance (it turns out in fact to be Wilhelm's only attempt at acting in the novel) is successful, in other words, not because of his *artistic* abilities but precisely because he is not playing a role at all at the climactic moment. And the scene represents an important transition in terms of the novel's development insofar as Wilhelm gives up his artistic ambitions and starts to develop a different relationship to a number of the central characters.

Beyond the play with narrational voice and ironic perspective in the novel, Goethe also includes within it a wide range of characters from diverse backgrounds, as well as a variety of thematic material and distinct modes of writing. In particular, the songs of Mignon, who becomes an important character within romantic readings of the novel, are directly included, as are the seemingly independent "Confessions" of a figure Goethe (as well as Schiller, Schlegel and Hegel) called the "beautiful soul."[13] And Goethe's evident larger concerns with the relation of literature and life—as framed not only by the famously sententious remarks in the *Lehrbrief* Wilhelm receives toward the novel's end (*Die Kunst ist lang, das Leben kurz*), but also by Goethe's own lifelong work of revision and expansion of his treatment of the figures and themes of the novel—are among the elements that have wider romantic resonance.[14]

## 2    Romantic Readings of *Wilhelm Meister*

Both Schlegel and Novalis offer early praise of the artistic achievement of Goethe's novel. "*Wilhelm Meister* is entirely a product of art, a work of the intellect," Novalis says in fragments from 1798, and suggests a comparison with ancient poetry: "Goethe may not be a match for the ancients in rigor, but he excels them in content – though that is not to his credit. His Wilhelm Meister approaches them pretty closely. It is the Absolute Novel, without qualification [*schlechtweg, ohne Beiwort*]—and that is a great deal in our time."[15]

Schlegel makes clear that the book is "absolutely new and unique": "[o]ur usual expectations of unity and coherence are disappointed by this novel as often as they are fulfilled" and gestures away from reading it in terms of conventional novelistic expectations ("as it is usually taken on the social level: as a novel in which the persons and incidents are the ultimate end and aim").[16] In the context of this new artistic form, Novalis is drawn to the novel's ability to link significance and contingency: "One notes a remarkable quality of Goethe's in his connecting small, insignificant incidents [*Vorfälle*] with important events. He appears to have no other intention than employing imagination in a poetical way with a mysterious play [*Spiel*]. Ordinary life is full of similar fortuitous connections [*Zufälle*]. They comprise a play [*Spiel*], which, like all play, goes on its way with surprise and disappointment."[17] In Schlegel's view, "[b]oth the larger and the smaller masses reveal the innate impulse of this work, so organized and organizing down to its finest details to form a whole. No break is accidental or insignificant..."[18] Schlegel emphasizes the progressive ability of the narrative to incorporate newness ("novelty") while appropriating events that have already happened, a narrative structure in terms of ever-expanding points of departure within the novel itself: "every book opens with a new scene and a new world ... every book contains the germ of the next, and with vital energy absorbs into its own being what the previous book has yielded" (as Behler puts it in summarizing Schlegel's views: "newness is never entirely new or disruptive and familiarity is never completely familiar or merely old").[19]

Besides emphasizing these narrative connections, Schlegel reads *Wilhelm Meister's Apprenticeship* as producing a series of stages of consideration of art in progression, from the earliest, most instinctual level of play-acting (Wilhelm was drawn as a child to puppetry) to increasingly higher perspectives, above all "the art of all arts, the art of living"[20] in an articulation of "stage after stage of every natural history and educational theory in living progression"[21]:

> For example, in this period of his apprenticeship, Wilhelm is concerned with the first, most elementary beginnings of the art of living. Hence this is where the simplest ideas about art are also presented, the most basic facts and the crudest efforts—in short, the rudiments of poetry: the puppet plays, the early childhood years of poetic instinct common to all people of sensibility ... Then there are the observations about how the learner should practice his art and make his judgments, and about the impressions made by the miners and by the tight-rope walkers; there are the poetic passages on the Golden Age of early poetry, and on the acrobat's art, and there is the improvised comedy during the excursion on the river.[22]

This presentation of stages of artistic engagement with the world "might suggest that the novel is as much an historical philosophy of art as a true work of art," but "that is not so: it is all poetry—high, pure poetry": "This marvelous prose is prose, and yet it is poetry."[23]

The result is not a conventional novel in which "persons and incidents are the ultimate end and aim," but a work that demands to be judged (against conventional expectations) instead "on its own terms"; in fact, says Schlegel in a remarkable claim, "it turns out to be one of those books which carries its own judgment within it, and spares the critic ... Indeed, not only does it judge itself; it also describes itself."[24]

## 3   Romantic Novelistic Responses: Schlegel's "Contest" of Novels and Novalis' Turn Against Goethe's "*Candide*"

Despite the public praise of *Wilhelm Meister's Apprenticeship* in his review, Schlegel in his notebooks had drawn back from offering his *highest* praise to *Wilhelm Meister* in the context of the romantic assessment of the prospects of novelistic writing. Goethe's novel, as he classified it, was "modern" and "poetic"—but *not*, however, "romantic"—the latter term he reserved instead for Cervantes' *Don Quixote*[25] (given the connections Schlegel drew between the *Roman* and the world of knights and gallantry). A little later on, after he'd encountered it, Tieck's *Sternbald* was to receive Schlegel's accolades for being a "romantic" novel.[26] While Schlegel's critical assessment in the review had been immanently focused on *Wilhelm Meister* as a work offering its own standard, the wider stakes for the romantic novel in his view required seeing the relation of *various* novels in light of one another. His own novelistic practice underscores this in the sort of contest of novels that arises within his own novel *Lucinde*.[27] The playful contest among novels in the "Allegory of Impudence" section of *Lucinde* raises a number of questions about romantic critical practice in the process, in particular the question of the relation of an individual work—with the standard Schlegel held appropriate to it—to the larger world of criticism (the larger romantic "work" of innumerable authorial efforts that becomes decisive for Benjamin's assessment of the *Kunstkritik* of Romanticism).

Novalis' critical distance-taking from *Wilhelm Meister* in light of his own literary practice was much more intense. As mentioned above, Novalis' first engagement with Goethe's novel was, like Schlegel's, characterized by a positive sense of the task of interpreting its importance. While there has been some dispute about when and why Novalis' assessment of *Wilhelm Meister* began to change, it is clear that Novalis came to see Goethe's novel as less romantic and poetic than he had before.[28] Novalis' critical comments in this later period (starting in 1799) are unstinting: *Wilhelm Meister* was "an embarrassing and silly book" (*Es ist im Grunde ein fatales und albernes Buch*) which was "*unpoetic in the highest degree*" (*undichterisch im höchsten Grade*), "in certain ways *thoroughly prosaic*—and modern" such that the romantic was destroyed (*gewissermassen durchaus prosaisch—und modern. Das Romantische geht darin zu Grunde*).[29] In the end, said Novalis, it was a "*Candide* directed against poetry," a "*satire on poetry and religion*," one so stringent that "whoever took this work truly to heart would never read another novel."[30]

Given Benjamin's stress on Novalis as what he takes to be the more thorough of the two romantics in working out the notion of prose as the "idea of poetry," it is worth asking how we should construe the clearly more negative valence of Novalis' characterization of Goethe's novel as "thoroughly prosaic" and "unpoetic"—one that has little resonance with Benjamin's notion of prosaic "sobriety" and more to do with the seemingly conventional notion of prose as the more "vulgar" or "common" medium closer to everyday speech. (The latter, by the way, is a view of prose that is not only its resonance in seemingly conventional discussions of literary form but is also employed to more interesting theoretical purposes by a range of critics from Hegel to Bakhtin).[31] One resource we can look at is Novalis' own sketch of a theory of prose and poetry, which he articulated in a letter to Friedrich Schlegel's brother, A. W. Schlegel:

> If poetry wishes to extend itself, it can do so only by limiting itself, by contracting itself, by abandoning its caloric matter and congealing. *It will acquire a prosaic look* [*Schein*], its constituent parts will no longer stand in the same close community—or, therefore, under such strict rhythmic laws—and it will become more capable of portraying that which is limited. *But it remains poetry* and hence faithful to the essential laws of its nature; it becomes, so to speak, an organic being, whose whole structure *betrays its origin from the flux, its originally elastic nature, its unlimitedness, its omnipotence*. Only the mixture of its elements is without rule; the order of these, their relation the whole, is still the same. Every charm extends outward on all sides. Here, too, only the parts move around the one, eternally resting whole … The simpler, more uniform, and calmer the movements of the sentences are here, the more harmonious their mixtures in the whole and the looser the connection, the more transparent and colorless the expression—*so much the more perfect is this indolent poetry in its seeming dependence on objects, and its contrast to all ornate prose*. Here poetry seems to slacken off from the rigor of its requirements, to become more complacent, more tractable. But it will soon become evident to one who makes trial of poetry under these conditions how difficult it is to realize it fully in this form. Such *extended poetry* is precisely the highest problem of the poetic artist—a problem that can be solved only by approximation and that is actually part of the higher poetry …. Here is still an immeasurable field, an infinite domain in the most authentic sense. One could call this higher poetry the poetry of the infinite.[32]

The context of this extended discussion of poetry and prose offered by Novalis is in opposition to A. W. Schlegel's essay on Goethe's *Hermann und Dorothea*, which argued that prose should be viewed as an earlier and less "ornamented" form of literature which later becomes poetry. In contrast to this view, Novalis clearly holds that the novel should be understood as an "extension" of poetry, rather than the reverse, as A. W. Schlegel had claimed. Against Benjamin's reading of this passage (he quotes the entirety of it in the "Criticism" essay), it should be emphasized that in this context Novalis does not seem to be arguing that poetry is (ultimately or always) more comprehensively taken up in the "idea" of prose, but rather that one could conceive of a novel in the form of prose that in some ways should be considered as an *extension* of poetry, one that has the *Schein* of prose but that reveals its elasticity just in taking that form.[33] One could conceive of a novel that was "higher poetry," in other words, but one could also conceive of prose that has no poetry behind it—and Novalis apparently had begun to think that *Wilhelm Meister* was such a novel. When poetry, on the other hand, is conceived to be somehow *underneath* its prosaic utterances, one can conceive of what Novalis calls "indolent" poetry—note, seemingly, in its "dependence on objects," a point to which we will return—in contrast to the "ornate" prose that A. W. Schlegel sees as the connection between prose and poetry. (A similar view seems to be at issue in the fragment that Behler cites, where Novalis takes issue with the literalness of conventional construals of the poetry/prose distinction: "It would be an appropriate question whether the lyric poem is properly a *poem*, plus-poetry, or rather prose, minus-poetry? Just as people have taken the novel for prose, they have taken the lyric poem for poetry—both unjustly. The highest, most characteristic prose is the lyric poem."[34])

In order to understand the importance of Novalis' way of understanding the poetry/prose relationship—and why he can no longer construe Goethe's novel as "poetic" in the deepest sense—we must look at his own novelistic practice, especially the decisive description of his intention to write a novel that, while having *Wilhelm Meister* and the structure of the *Bildungsroman* in mind, clearly will be a different sort of project. Novalis' intentions can be seen in his letter to Caroline Schlegel of Feb. 27, 1799, which is worth quoting in detail. In the letter, Novalis speaks about turning his "whole life" to a novel which "alone would comprise an entire library":

> perhaps it ought to contain the apprenticeship [*Lehrjahre*] of a *nation*. The word *apprenticeship* is false: it expresses a particular destination [*ein bestimmtes Wohin*]. In my view it should mean nothing besides *years of transition* [*ÜbergangsJahre*] from the infinite to the finite [*vom Unendlichen zum Endlichen*]. I hope thereby at the same time to satisfy my historical and philosophical yearning [*Sehnsucht*].[35]

Many questions have been raised about how best to understand Novalis' intentions in this letter. Some of these questions are biographical (while it is not certain, e.g., he is speaking about *Heinrich von Ofterdingen*, that seems most likely),[36] but philosophically what is most of interest is what Novalis might mean by "years of transition." For one thing, there is the complication that Novalis both eschews a *telos* (there should be "no particular destination") but at the same time, he insists that the novel he has in mind should effect some form of "transition," and in particular a transition from the infinite to the finite. Many readers have been puzzled by the directionality of that transition, assuming that Novalis must have meant to write about a transition *from finite* to *infinite* (Behler, in a clear rejection of the *lectio difficilior* here, simply translates the sentence this way, while indicating Novalis' actual words must be a mistake).[37]

Alice Kuzniar has suggested a reading according to which transition just means non-teleologically "pure change,"[38] but this would not appear to help us come to terms with the sense of the *zu* in the phrase "from the infinite to the finite" (this is a problem even if one takes Behler's reading of "finite to infinite"; in any case, Kuzniar thinks that Novalis does not even have in mind "even" a Kantian sense of regulative ideal when he talks about the infinite).[39] A more affirmative reading of the passage has been given by Johannes Mahr, whose reading of the poet as coming to his vocation nonetheless sounds, as Kuzniar argues, like it might transgress the first part of Novalis' claim—that it is precisely the telos or *wohin* implicit in the notion of *Lehrjahre* that he wants to avoid.[40]

If we take Novalis' intention of writing an *Übergangsjahre* rather than *Lehrjahre* as reflective of his goals in *Heinrich*, we can see how Novalis might have understood his novel as a "poetic" attempt to capture something that had been prosaically denied in the ultimate shape of *Wilhelm Meister*. A careful comparison will suggest, in fact, not a sort of poetry/prose binary, but rather an interesting case of romantic appropriation (or, in Novalis' term, "inversion"). The key lies in seeing that one important sense of "transition" that Novalis may have taken from Goethe is one that comes not merely from the *Wilhelm Meister* but from the scientific works, as well—in this case, specifically from a reading of Goethe's *Metamorphoses of Plants*. Novalis knew Goethe's scientific work well—in fact, in the 1798 fragments where he praises *Wilhelm Meister's Apprenticeship*, he begins his discussion about Goethe's cultural influence by noting the range of his scientific achievements ("His observations on light and on the metamorphoses of plants and insects both confirm and demonstrate most convincingly that the perfect style for instruction is also part of the artist's range").[41] In the *Metamorphoses*, Goethe insists that in considering nature one must not proceed from parts to whole but rather the reverse, given a subject that is "alive and active": "if we want to arrive at some living intuition of nature, we must keep ourselves as flexible and plastic [*beweglich und bildsam*] as nature herself, and in accordance with the example she offers us [*nach dem Beispiele mit dem sie uns vorgeht*]" (LA I, 9, 7).

The particular importance of the *Metamorphoses of Plants* lies in Goethe's insistence that, in order to understand an organic phenomenon like plant development, one must be able both to gain "complete knowledge of the phenomena themselves, and then to make them our own by reflection upon them ... When we are able to survey an object in every detail [*in all seinen Teilen*], grasp it correctly and produce it again in our mind [*im Geiste wieder hervorbringen können*], we can say that we intuit it in a real and higher sense [*im eigentlichen und höhern Sinne*]" (*NA* II, 11, 165). In the case of plants, this means looking not at the plant as a static object but seeing how its various parts will develop from seed to fruit: as Eckart Förster has put it, what matters "are the transitions, the *Übergänge*, not so much the formed parts or products, and these transitions I experience only in the observation of my own formative (*nachbildend*) thinking."[42]

If this connection to Goethe's own notion of *Übergang* is right, we might notice that one of Novalis' particular developments in *Heinrich von Ofterdingen* is again of a kind of *series* of shapes that bears comparison with Goethe's and with Schlegel's interpretation of the successive "stages" presented in *Wilhelm Meister*, but that they have been articulated in a different way. Novalis' novel offers not a Goethean portrayal of moments in the development of a character who is losing a sense of artistic mission but rather a series of scenes that move from an underlying dream (the "blue flower" in both Heinrich's and his father's dreams) to the vocation of the poet in search of that dream. The connections as well as the contrasts between the two novels seem clear: Schlegel had noticed in his review of Goethe that *Wilhelm Meister*'s story began in a sort of "dream-world" and then moved toward an engagement with social reality for its central character; for Novalis, the origin of Heinrich's poetic vocation in the dream of the blue flower is crucial to the beginning of a story in which Heinrich undergoes a set of encounters (with the knights, the miner, Klingsohr) that afford an experience that is at once "knowing self as world and world as self."

This reading suggests that Novalis has "inverted" Goethe's project in *Heinrich von Ofterdingen*: composed with inspiration from Goethe's larger scheme of connections and stages, but then turned in such a way that these structural elements offer not an ironic "*Candide* against poetry" but rather into an invitation toward the poetic vocation of connecting infinite and finite. For Novalis, this project involves what he called in the letter to Dorothea Schlegel above an expression of his historical and philosophical "yearning," a remark that can be usefully thought about not only in connection with his claim that *Wilhelm Meister* was a satire directed at poetry *and* religion but also in connection with Benjamin's claim that the "core" [*Zentrum*] of early Romanticism "is religion and history."[43] Benjamin's larger project about the notion of *Kunstkritik* that can be drawn from the "sobriety" of prose as it takes up these "messianic" concerns cannot be fully addressed in the space remaining, but in the final section, I will try briefly to talk about the broader scope of critical approaches to novelistic literature in the post-romantic world.

## 4 Romanticism, Idealism and the Novel: Conclusions and Questions

We've looked at three novels which had a central bearing on the emergence of Romanticism and the aesthetic understanding of the literary form that the romantic novel was in the process of becoming. Goethe's *Wilhelm Meister's Apprenticeship*, as we've seen, had revolutionary import for the re-imagination of the task of the novel by the young German Romantics and prompted consideration of new critical standards that opened up the project of the distinctively romantic novel in the generation of Schlegel and Novalis. Friedrich Schlegel's *Lucinde* and Novalis' *Heinrich von Ofterdingen* each offered a different view of the stages of art and life that Schlegel's review had suggested can be seen as outlined by *Wilhelm Meister*: in the case of *Lucinde*, with an aim of engaging with the multiplicity of possible content that can be appropriated by the novel; and in the case of *Heinrich von Ofterdingen*, in order to make use of a Goethean scheme by turning a *Candide* against poetry against itself, as it were.

What is the relation of these novelistic models to one another? What does a consideration of them suggest for the questions about the relation between idealist and romantic traditions of interpretation of the novel that Behler raised and about the questions concerning the relation among poetry, prose and criticism in Benjamin? In this final section, I will briefly take up these wider interpretive questions.

From what we have seen in an exploration of these three novels, one line of "romantic" interpretation might be construed to run this way in the focus on the relation between art and life that has been suggested in each case. The plot of Goethe's *Wilhelm Meister's Apprenticeship* turns, as we have seen, on a scene in which the central character moves from attempting to *play* Hamlet in a theatrical context to a broader concern with art's relation to the larger play of life—a fact within the narrative itself which Goethe's life-long project of revision of the *Wilhelm Meister* theme (virtually co-extensive with his life-long absorption in the *Faust* theme) poses at the level of the artist. Schlegel in his review of Goethe's novel stressed that the various stages of engagement with the arts and various professions in the novel lead ultimately to a consideration of the "art of all arts" as the "art of living" (a formulation which in its context offers an interesting anticipation of Nietzsche's formulation of "science in the perspective of art and art in the perspective of life" in the "Attempt at Self-Criticism" written for the revised edition of the *Birth of Tragedy*). And Novalis wants to turn his "whole life" to the novel that *Heinrich* is. On Lacoue-Labarthe and Nancy's reading of the two authorial modes of engaging Romanticism's fragmentary literature, this is the sort of infinite task that means the poet giving his life.[44] For Goethe and Schlegel, especially, this engagement with life is not of course absorption in the bourgeois realm but one that requires a constant sense of irony, something which is presumably the great worry of the Hegelian idealist about the romantics.

But Hegel's position (in the end unlike that associated with, say, the Shklovskyan process of "defamiliarization") is not that poetry removes or distorts prosaic life in the lower sense of that term, but that it actually draws a kind of intense life into itself (art's overall purpose, after all, in Hegel's view, is to "awaken and vivify [*beleben*] our slumbering feelings, inclinations and passions").[45] Seen from this perspective, it might be worth considering what the idealist line of interpretation of the novel offers that goes beyond the focus that Behler (admittedly correctly) finds in the idealist construal of the novel as deriving from ancient epic.

Following this line of interpretation, one might make a case in this context for, say, Lukács' (still "idealist") attempt to find an epic "largeness" missing in post-romantic literature except Dostoevsky and to some extent Tolstoy. A fair treatment of this would require putting aside Lukács' own typology of "idealist" and "romantic" novels, which he himself came to criticize, and which pick up rather different valences of the two terms than we have mostly been using here.[46] And one might look also at Hegel's broader "unofficial" engagement with the romantic literary tradition, visible less in the Berlin lectures on art than in his earlier encounter in the *Phenomenology of Spirit* with a typology of modes of conscience found within the romantic *Zeitgeist*, where Hegel directly takes up Schlegel's notion of a "contest," writing in the process what might be considered a counter-novel of his own, while treating Novalis' mode as a quiet wasting-away. For Hegel, these figures are central to a world in which the claims of highest individuality and conscience are directly linked to the larger religious atmosphere that both Schlegel and Novalis were interested in, with the importance of art lying precisely in a claim that absolute spirit entered the picture just here.[47] The treatment accorded Schlegel and Novalis in Hegel's assessment here (with Goethe as the larger background) tallies reasonably neatly with Schlegel's own typological distinction between "exoteric" and "esoteric" novels (the former, like *Wilhelm Meister's Apprenticeship*, representing the ideal of the beautiful in everyday life, and the latter, like *Heinrich von Ofterdingen*, offering a "transition from novel to mythology").[48]

It is of course a very good question how helpful any typology, romantic or idealist, can be for giving a sense of the novel of the post-romantic future—for either philosophical engagement with the novelistic products of the nineteenth and twentieth centuries that follow or for our own.[49] What is clear from examining Goethe's, Schlegel's and Novalis' novels together, however, is how important the different modes of their romantic re-imagining of the novel remain.

## Notes

1. "The French Revolution, Fichte's philosophy and Goethe's *Meister* are the greatest tendencies of the age" (KFSA 2, *Athenäum Fragment* Nr.216). While Schlegel takes these three "tendencies" as characteristic of the mid-1790s, there is a wider literary explosion in the last two decades of the eighteenth century that, as Dieter Henrich has pointed out, follows in the wake of Kant's *Critique of Pure Reason*.
2. Ernst Behler, *German Romantic Literary Theory* (Cambridge: Cambridge University Press), pp. 165–66. (Italics in the first Behler quotation are mine.)
3. Schlegel, *KFSA* 1334; *KFSA* 2, 335.
4. Walter Benjamin, "The Concept of Criticism in German Romanticism," in Marcus Bullock and Michael W. Jennings, eds., *Walter Benjamin: Selected Writings: Volume I, 1913–1926* ed. (Cambridge: Harvard University Press, 1996), 174.
5. It is, of course, important not to conflate these two terms: as Marcus Bullock points out, "The concept of prose cannot, in Schlegel, be identified with the prosaic" ("The Coming of the Messiah or the Stoic Burning: Aspects of the Negated Text in Walter Benjamin and Friedrich Schlegel," Germanic Review 60(1) (1985): 2–15, reprinted in Walter Benjamin: Critical Evaluations in Cultural Theory, ed. Peter Osborne, vol. II: Modernity (Routledge, 2005), 29–55, at 38). The larger importance of the relation between prose and "prosaic" for an assessment of the Benjaminian notion of criticism as the 'exhibition' of the 'prosaic core of every work' would require another essay.
6. Benjamin, "The Concept of Criticism in German Romanticism," op. cit., 118.

7. Ibid., 174.
8. Ibid., 174–75.
9. Novalis Schriften. Die Werke Friedrich von Hardenbergs, edd. Richard Samuel, Hans-Joachim Mähl and Gerhard Schulz (Stuttgart: Kohlhammer, 1960–2006), III.646.
10. Behler, *German Romantic Literary Theory*, 165.
11. For a discussion of the development of Goethe's *Wilhelm Meister* theme between these years, see the essay by Sarah Eldridge in *Goethe's "Wilhelm Meister's Apprenticeship" and Philosophy* (Oxford: Oxford University Press, 2020).
12. Friedrich Schlegel, "On Goethe's *Meister*," translated in *German Aesthetic and Literary Criticism: the Romantic Ironists and Goethe*, ed. Kathleen Wheeler (Cambridge: Cambridge University Press, 1984), 64.
13. For more on the figure of the beautiful soul, see my *Hegel, Literature and the Problem of Agency* (Cambridge: Cambridge University Press, 2001), 94–121.
14. The reception of Goethe's wider treatment of the *Wilhelm Meister* theme, in his later *Wilhelm Meister's Journeyman Years* is beyond the scope of this chapter, but it raises a range of additional themes that move the discussion of the philosophical and literary context of the era from the mid-1790s to the 1820s (where such concerns as industrialization and emigration are now to the fore).
15. Novalis, "On Goethe," in *Classic and Romantic German Aesthetics*, edited by J. M. Bernstein (Cambridge: Cambridge University Press, 2002), 228, 229.
16. Schlegel, "On Goethe's *Meister*," 64, 65.
17. "Eine merckwürdige Eigenheit Göthes bemerckt man in seinen Verknüpfungen kleiner, unbedeutender Vorfälle mit wichtigen Begebenheiten. Er scheint keine andre Absicht dabey zu hegen, als die Einbildungskraft, auf eine poëtische Weise, mit einem mysteriösen Spiel, zu beschäftigen. Auch hier ist der sonderbare Mann der Natur auf die Spur gekommen und hat ihr einen artigen Kunstgriff abgemerckt. Das gewöhnliche Leben ist voll ähnlicher Zufälle. Sie machen ein Spiel aus, das, wie alles Spiel, auf Überraschung und Täuschung hinausläuft." (NS II, 424 [text here using N's own spelling in the Handschrift he labeled "Vermischte Bemerkungen"]).
18. Schlegel, "On Goethe's *Meister*," 63.
19. Schlegel, "On Goethe's *Meister*," 66.
20. Schlegel, "On Goethe's *Meister*," 71.
21. Schlegel, "On Goethe's *Meister*," 63.
22. Schlegel, "On Goethe's *Meister*," 64–5.
23. Schlegel, "On Goethe's *Meister*," 64.
24. Schlegel, "On Goethe's *Meister*," 64, 65.
25. KFSA 16,133; 16,176.
26. KFSA 16, 206.
27. See the discussion of Schlegel's notion of a "contest" of novels (and Hegel's response to it) in Speight, *Hegel, Literature and the Problem of Agency*, 100–12.

28. To what extent Novalis' shift of view about *Wilhelm Meister* had to do with Schlegel's influence—also becoming more negative at this point—is a good question. The binary opposition of some readers who want to see *Heinrich* either as a *riposte* or counter-narrative to Goethe or a (seemingly imitative) *model* seems not to do justice to the self-conscious practice of romantic appropriation or to the literary richness of both works. (For an example of the binariness in the literature, see Robert T. Ittner, "Novalis' Attitude toward *Wilhelm Meister* with Reference to the Conception of His *Heinrich von Ofterdingen*," *The Journal of English and Germanic Philology* Vol. 37, No. 4 (Oct., 1938): 542–554).
29. *NS* III, 536.
30. Novalis, NS, *Urteile über Wihelm Meisters Lehrjahre*, 679.
31. See my "Hegel on Poetry, Prose and the Origin of the Arts," in Marina Bykova and Kenneth Westphal, eds. *Palgrave Hegel Handbook* (New York: Palgrave/McMillan, 2020).
32. Novalis, Letter to A. W. Schlegel, January 12, 1798 (*NO* 4.245); translation in Benjamin, "The Concept of Criticism," *op. cit.*, 174.
33. More would need to be said than space allows here about Benjamin's own interpretive practice, in particular the concern critics have expressed with his use of quotations in the *Criticism* essay: see, among others Winfried Menninghaus, "Walter Benjamin's Exposition of the Romantic Theory of Reflection" and Rodolphe Gasché, "The Sober Absolute: On Benjamin and the Early Romantics," both in Beatrice Hanssen and Andrew Benjamin, eds., *Walter Benjamin and Romanticism* (New York/London: Continuum, 2002).
34. *NO* 3.536, cited in Behler, *German Romantic Literary Theory*, 209.
35. "… ich habe Lust mein ganzes Leben an Einen Roman zu wenden—der allein eine ganze Bibliothek ausmachen—vielleicht Lehrjahre einer *Nation* enthalten soll. Das Wort *Lehrjahre* is falsch—es drückt ein bestimmtes *Wohin* aus. Bey mir soll es aber nichts, als—*ÜbergangsJahre* vom Unendlichen zum Endlichen bedeuten. Ich hoffe damit zugleich meine historische und philosophische Sehnsucht zu befriedigen …" (NO IV. 281):
36. Ittner, "Novalis' Attitude toward *Wilhelm Meister* with Reference to the Conception of His *Heinrich von Ofterdingen,*" *op. cit.*
37. Behler, *German Romantic Literary Theory, op. cit.*, 214.
38. Alice A. Kuzniar, *Delayed Endings: Nonclosure in Novalis and Hölderlin* (Athens and London: University of Georgia Press, 1987), 87.
39. Ibid., 81.
40. Johannes Mahr, *Übergang zum Endlichen: der Weg des Dichters in Novalis' "Heinrich von Ofterdingen"* (Munich: Fink, 1970).
41. Novalis, "On Goethe," in Bernstein, *op. cit.*, 227.
42. Eckart Förster, "Goethe and the 'Auge des Geistes,' Deutsche Vierteljahrsschrift für Literaturwissenschaft und Geistesgeschichte, 75 (2001): 87–101, at 93.

43. Walter Benjamin, Letter to Gerhard Scholem, June 1917, *The Correspondence of Walter Benjamin*, ed. Gerschom Scholem and Theodor W. Adorno, trans. M. R. and E. M. Jacobson (Chicago: University of Chicago Press, 1994), 88; Benjamin, *Briefe*, ed. Gerschom Scholem and Theodor W. Adorno (Frankfurt am Main; Suhrkamp, 1966), I.138.
44. Lacoue-Labarthe and Nancy suggest two paths toward the Absolute emerging from literary Romanticism's concern with the fragment. See *The Literary Absolute: The Theory of Literature in German Romanticism* (Albany: State University of New York Press, 1988): Novalis' path, which they represent as "simultaneous combination and dissolution," a dissolution that "includes the sacrifice in all its ambiguity, of the poet" and Schlegel's "energy" (the "infinitely flexible … universal power through which the whole man shapes himself"), 56.
45. Hegel, MM 13:70, VKunst I:46.
46. Lukács, *Theory of the Novel*. Lukács' "idealist" novel is *Don Quixote* (the cynosure of the romantic novel, according to Schlegel) and his "romantic" one is *Sentimental Education*, with *Wilhelm Meister's Apprenticeship* as a medial form.
47. For a comparison of Hegel's and Schlegel's contemporaneous concerns with the relation between religion and art, see my "Art, Imagination and the Interpretation of the Age," in *The Imagination in German Idealism and Romanticism*, eds. Gerad Gentry and Konstantin Pollok (Cambridge: Cambridge University Press, 2019).
48. I am glossing a larger issue of the relation between Goethe and the romantics which is posed in the afterword of the "Concept of Criticism" essay, where Benjamin suggests a neat dichotomy between the romantics and Goethe: where the romantics are interested in form and the idea and are engaged in a far-reaching project of art's criticizability, Goethe's artistic stance can be categorized, he thinks, instead by its appeal to matter, the ideal and non-criticizability. The romantics aimed thus in the end for a notion of infinity in totality, while Goethe aimed at unity in plurality. A charitable reading of the Hegelian project with respect to both figures—Goethe whom he admired and the romantics whom he took to define the artistic and literary workspace within which his own philosophical project was born (for so one can read the final sections of the "Spirit" chapter of the Phenomenology of Spirit)—might be to suggest an attempt at bringing both projects together into a philosophical synthesis. With an eye to the ancient Greek inheritance that Goethe and Schiller took so seriously, Hegel's philosophy of art preserves the notion of an ideal (the embodiment of the Idea in a sensible form), but his own articulation of that ideal presents itself as arising within a genealogy where the idea of art and poetry has arrived in a fashion that makes Winckelmann and Schlegel the key figures that they are within Benjamin's essay.
49. This is a version of the question that Lacoue-Labarthe and Nancy pose: "From the moment that the novel, in the romantic sense, is always more than the

novel, what happens to the novel itself, in the restricted sense?" (*The Literary Absolute, op. cit.*, 98). Their concern is with the novel's "depreciation" or "dissolution in its chemical form": "the novel cannot or will not become the 'romantic genre' until it becomes equal to the subject-work" (*The Literary Absolute, op. cit.*, 99).

# 15

# The Cinematic Afterlife of German Romanticism

Laurie Johnson

## 1   Introduction: Romanticism and Film, Romanticism on Film[1]

When students in my undergraduate German courses watch Éric Rohmer's *The Marquise of O* (*Die Marquise von O*, 1976), they often remark on how slow-paced and quiet the film is. Indeed, Rohmer's film, like Heinrich von Kleist's novella of 1808, sets an utterly implausible story in a highly realistic setting. Rohmer tells Kleist's tale—of a woman who is apparently unaware she had sex, and who places an advertisement in the newspaper seeking the father of her unborn child—without a soundtrack and with dialogue that is often measured and characterized by long pauses. This style is at odds with the extreme emotions and melodrama at the story's heart. Rohmer's ability to capture this contrast is perhaps what makes his film one of the better-known cinematic treatments of German Romantic literature.

Rohmer (born Jean-Marie Maurice Schérer), a French director known for his contributions to French New Wave cinema, made an intriguing choice when he recreated one of the most famous texts of German Romanticism.[2] In a sense, Rohmer's *Marquise of O* represents how some aspects of German Romanticism are seen from outside Germany. In other countries, Germany

L. Johnson (✉)
University of Illinois, Urbana-Champaign, Champaign, IL, USA
e-mail: lruthjoh@illinois.edu

itself is associated strongly with a certain kind of Romanticism; and, "Romanticism" has come to signify certain traits in art, literature, film, and philosophy that are associated with Germany. Outside Germany and German Studies, German Romanticism often is associated with, at best, apolitical aestheticism, and, at worst, a proto-fascist focus on folk culture and politics. From the early nineteenth century on, prominent German intellectuals, including Kleist, responded to the philosophy and politics of the Enlightenment with reactionary fears of outsiders and of change, and an emphasis on whatever was considered to be purely "German." Some argue that these regressive views emerged later in the nineteenth century as part of a quintessentially Germanic aesthetic in Richard Wagner's idea of the "total work of art," which in turn influenced Adolf Hitler's totalitarian politics.

Set in the northern Italian town of "M—," a settlement besieged by Russian invaders, *The Marquise of O* is characteristic of Kleist's tendency to displace action from Germany to elsewhere. The displacements of territory are mirrored in the confusion and disorientation of the characters, whose sense of being trapped in inescapable identities and places is still strong. Even when elsewhere, Kleist seems to indicate, we are burdened by the same problems, the same tragedies. In other words, by moving his stories' events to Italy, Switzerland, or South America, Kleist does not reveal *differences* between cultures or histories so much as he exposes how *similarly* crime, violence, and injustice unfold wherever one is.

Kleist's novella, and arguably his Romanticism more generally, can be read as marked by paranoia and cynicism about others—including foreigners, or those not part of the majority group. This Romanticism conveys an extreme emotional expressivism that is highly kinetic, yet does not really go anywhere: Kleist's work is full of characters who are fighting the same battles, over and over. This is also how Rohmer's film interprets Kleist, if not all of German Romanticism. For instance, by the end of the film, as in the novella, the heroine can no longer deny the identity of her child's father, and therefore her own knowledge of his crime (and her possible complicity in it). But for Kleist, knowing the difference between good and evil does not change the fact that an enemy eventually will conquer us, most likely literally from within. At the end of the film and novella, the Italian Marquise agrees to marry the Russian Count, who fought for the force that invaded her hometown, and the novella and film end with the proclamation that a "whole series of young Russians" followed the birth of their first child. The Marquise's womb is now occupied territory. But it is an invasion she clearly welcomes and desires. Rohmer's carefully paced, quiet film simultaneously distances the audience from and exposes the audience to the extreme focus on emotional life, accompanied by a reactionary politics that characterizes Kleist's novella as well as a common view of German Romanticism.

In a sense, Rohmer's film translates Kleist's novella into the language of moving images—the language of cinema. One could argue that *The Marquise of O*, with its move from a relatively widely "framed" opening battle scene to a series of "close-ups" of the Marquise's psychological battle, already had pre-cinematic qualities. But the 1976 film helps us recognize those qualities. In 1923, Walter Benjamin used the term "afterlife" to indicate a certain kind of relation between present and past. In "The Task of the Translator" (*Die Aufgabe des Übersetzers*), Benjamin proposes that translation defers, as well as reshapes, an "original" text.[3] He also suggests that translation preserves something *non*-translatable: some element (or elements) of the text's original language that is (or are) unique. That is, the present translated work preserves, or brings into the present, the knowledge that we cannot know the past text completely. One implication of this way of thinking is that neither the original text nor the translation is really aimed at an audience.[4] Rather, original and translation interact with one another, and the translation interacts with its own *inability* to fully reproduce the original.

In the novella and the film, the Marquise does not recognize the father of her child, in any event not consciously, and this introduces at least some small doubt about him into the mind of the reader or viewer as well. The Marquise insists that she "does not want to know" that her savior is also a rapist. On the page and on screen, the rape itself is elided (in the text, by a hyphen, and in the film, by a blackout and change of scene). The plot revolves around the past while refusing to fully reveal it: the text re-imagines, or "translates," battles between nations, between men and women, and between one's own conscious and unconscious mind, and the film re-imagines, or "translates," those battles into moving images. But instead of fighting those battles over and over—in other words, instead of merely repeating them—the novella and the film express a persistent desire to know the past while acknowledging that it can only be known partially, via a deferral into the present, or via translation.

Appropriating Benjamin's term, we can understand Rohmer's film as a kind of translation of, and thus also as part of the afterlife of, aspects of German Romanticism. German Romanticism does not mean any one thing, in film or in any other type of cultural product. In what follows, I argue that what I am calling a "romantic" cinema develops and re-interprets several of the most progressive and skeptical features of German Romanticism. These features include an exploration of the limits of Enlightenment thinking about nature, individual consciousness, and community, and the conviction that while we can never fully grasp the past or the others who inhabit our present, we must make urgent efforts to do so. Tensions that the romantics emphasized, between reason and instinct and between control and contingency, find expression in these films' portrayals of radical "otherness": sublime environments, or people who engage in life-endangering feats. Perhaps paradoxically, the pace of these films is often slow and the sound subdued, features that evoke past-ness in a non-nostalgic manner. In other words, by keeping the focus on the emotions and choices of figures who are exploring extreme experience, and (generally) not amplifying those emotions and choices via expressive soundtracks and quick cuts, these films evoke realism in the service of a specific set of romantic ideals.

Without directly "translating" the original texts or events that they re-represent, the films I am considering convey key elements of German Romantic philosophy and aesthetics. This re-representation in turn establishes a "tradition" of German Romanticism from a contemporary position. Joseph Leo Koerner's work on Caspar David Friedrich's aesthetic vision complements Walter Benjamin's theory of translation here, as Koerner argues that the way Friedrich's paintings make sense of the past actually is oriented toward the future. Koerner borrows Sigmund Freud's notion of *Nachträglichkeit*, translating it as "afterwardsness." In Friedrich's paintings, "afterwardsness" expresses itself in scenes that look like "something *viewed*."[5] They are scenes full of realistic detail (we recognize cliffs, thickets, and waterfalls as such), but they are, Koerner says, "not familiarized" due to the artist's positioning of the implied spectator (and sometimes of a spectator within the painting itself, often with his back to us). Friedrich combines realistic detail with a lack of directly referential context: for example, although we know the chalk cliffs are on Rügen, it is difficult to reproduce this view precisely in reality, in part because Friedrich worked with pieces of sketches of different locales when he composed the final painting. This combination of reality and imagination is partly what compels us to do the work of making sense of the scene; or, in Koerner's phrasing, to see "all the order (in Friedrich's spaces as) the order of (our) gaze."[6] But Friedrich's use of light and perspective to confound distinctions between night and day, between imagined (and thus man-made) objects and nature, and between proximity and distance, makes us uncertain as to whether the order of our gaze corresponds reliably to the whole of what is represented.

The films I consider here occasionally echo Friedrich's aesthetics quite clearly (Werner Herzog, for instance, has acknowledged that at least some scenes in his films are reminiscent of Friedrich's paintings[7]). But more often, they re-represent the temporal aesthetics of "afterwardsness" that the German Romantics crystallized in their philosophical and literary works. This temporality, which combines retrogression (the present making sense of the past) with progression (a sense that the past is sending us—its future—an enigmatic message) is intimately intertwined with early German Romantic identity philosophy, and specifically with the notion of apperception. Apperception, a self-consciousness that Johann Gottlieb Fichte likened to a dynamic "activity in which an eye is inserted," requires a sort of constant re-representation of oneself in space and time.[8] The films that I contend are part of a modern romantic cinema "translate" a Friedrichean aesthetic in that their protagonists function as inserted "eyes" in the films: among other things, the characters often look at what we are intended to see and thus invite us to identify with them as fellow spectators. In a move parallel to romantic thinking about the interplay of images in consciousness and self-consciousness, Friedrich's, and these filmmakers', figures both draw attention to the power of our subjectivity and to its limits. Like the early German Romantics, these directors shape this awareness of the gap between our own formidable sense-making apparatus and another source of sense that is fundamentally independent of us. In *The Marquise of O*, this "other" source of sense may be the Marquise's own unconscious mind, or the interaction between her "inner" (but not conscious) knowledge and the inner knowledge of others. In the mountain films to which I turn my focus, the "other," and ultimately never completely knowable, source of meaning is nature—a nature portrayed as indifferent and yet imbued with suggestive significance.

In the remainder of this essay, I argue that some contemporary films re-envision not just aspects of romantic philosophy, but overlooked aspects of German Romanticism as a whole. These films *animate*, for instance, romantic understandings of relations between reason and passion, civilization and wild nature, and knowledge and belief. Among other things, romantic philosophy, and in particular early German Romantic philosophy, presents evocative imaginings of alternative political and aesthetic ideals. I examine the ways in which some of these ideals are expressed and made animate in films directed by Werner Herzog and Joseph Vilsmaier.

I begin by tracing a few additional characteristics of early German Romanticism that contribute to a modern form of spectatorship which, in Herzog's and Vilsmaier's films, is translated into and onto specific landscapes. These landscapes, in turn, are translated into psycho-topographies of the men who climb them. Like the German Romantics, Herzog and Vilsmaier grapple with the task of making meaning in a post-metaphysical world, and in so doing turn to the power of the aesthetic, and in particular to the promise of the aesthetic for granting access to an inner universe, or to a psychological landscape. But this aesthetic and psychological turn does not necessarily entail a flight from engagement with the world. On the contrary, Romanticism is, in Richard Eldridge's phrase, "a set of commitments" *to* the world. Eldridge identifies "imagination, nature-place, [and] prophetic ordinary language" as the core elements of that set of commitments that undergird Romanticism's poetic and philosophical practices.[9] These commitments persist from the days of the early German Romantic and Idealist thinkers in the 1790s throughout the long nineteenth century, from writing by Novalis, Friedrich Schlegel, and Schelling to work by Nietzsche, Freud, and Kafka, in spite of the differences among those authors and texts.[10] Romantic commitments to imagination, nature-place, and to "prophetic ordinary" language can only be expressed incompletely, in fragments (philosophical, literary, or scientific) produced in the spirit of ironic approximation of an ultimately unreachable absolute goal: the goal of unifying knowledge and belief, past and future, reason and emotion.

The aesthetic and epistemological mode in which the romantic self and signs often take shape is one of melancholy sensibility. This romantic sensibility, or mode of aesthetic expression of knowledge, is not anti-realist. In other words, the romantics who shaped and participated in the discourse I am describing here definitely were preoccupied with portraying the world, and with attaining knowledge about it. But romantic melancholy takes into account the notion, often considered axiomatic in Western philosophy, that our knowledge of reality is fundamentally limited by our perceptive abilities, including our vision. This simultaneously liberating and confidence-shattering insight provokes a melancholy response.[11]

To paraphrase Ian Baucom, who locates a "melancholy counterdiscourse of modernity" in the long nineteenth century, this realistic *and* romantic expressive mode explicitly draws attention to spectatorship. The melancholy romantic spectator views history as "composed … of imaginary *scenes* strictly consistent with fact … (the) key unit (of this melancholic approach) is neither the type nor the average but the sentimental, romantic, or melancholy case, scene, or fact."[12] The melancholy romantic expresses neither nostalgic yearning for a return to the past nor the desire to protect and preserve the authenticity of his or her object of study. Instead, he or she is aware that the illusions we create and observe, about ourselves and the world, are very real: imagination is where we live. Romantic melancholy, the mode in which the self and its signs are expressed, is thus an experimental and creative rather than an inertial mode.[13] Participants in this post-Enlightenment, modern, melancholy discourse, which winds through not only philosophy and literature but also psychology and economics in the long nineteenth century, are in a sense all working on a "theory of what it means to be a historical spectator."[14] The modern melancholy spectator observes the world at a distance, and yet feels involved and moved to act: often by creating aesthetic responses to his or her own sense of transience and yet also meaningfulness.

Although Baucom's work concentrates on ways in which both enlightened *and* romantic texts focus on spectating—with the Enlightenment generally valorizing a "disinterested" model of viewing history, and the German Romantics admitting to investment (and expressing this with a generally melancholy effect)—his proposition that there is a "late eighteenth and early nineteenth-century romantic counterknowledge of the modern" is useful for framing and contextualizing a melancholy and ironic romantic aesthetics, whether in literature or in film. Melancholy is not politically unproblematic: its distanced insistence on an observational perspective can make it essentially complicit in modernity's crimes (such as the foci of Baucom's study, which include the slave trade and colonial regimes). But for the romantics around 1800 and their intellectual descendants, melancholy had and has a truly critical potential.

Werner Herzog's and Joseph Vilsmaier's films borrow heavily from and reactivate the romantic discourse I have outlined above, in ways that resemble an often melancholy self-conscious extension into the world more strongly than they do a retreat into a one's own imagination or a personal world of images. Both films that I focus on here feature mountain climber Reinhold Messner (born 1944). One is a documentary, one a feature film, but Vilsmaier's feature, *Nanga Parbat* (2010), tells the historical tale of Reinhold and his younger brother Günther's traumatic climb of Nanga Parbat in 1970, the climb during which Günther died. Reinhold discusses his brother's death in Herzog's *The Dark Glow of the Mountains* (1984), in a sequence that makes clear that all of Reinhold's later climbs, including the one highlighted in *Dark Glow*, are in part an extended series of deferrals of the meanings of that 1970 climb. The films contribute to a contemporary Romanticism that retells, translates, and projects an early romantic spatio-temporal aesthetic into the present and future.

## 2   The Onscreen Sublime: The Dark Glow of the Mountains (1984)

*The Dark Glow of the Mountains* (*Gasherbrum—Der leuchtende Berg*, 1984) treats Messner's climb, in the summer of 1984, of Gasherbrum I and II, part of the Karakoram mountain range, which stretches along the borders of

China, India, and Pakistan and includes the largest number of mountains of a height of 8000 meters or higher in the world. Together with Hans Kammerlander, Messner crossed the peaks of both Gasherbrum I and II in one trek, without returning to base camp. In a long aerial shot of the Gasherbrum I face near the beginning of their two-peak journey, Messner and Kammerlander are tiny black specks whose movement across a vast expanse of snow is barely detectable.

The long shots and wide pans of the mountainscape, here and elsewhere in the film, contrast starkly with close-up shots in very tight spaces, such as Messner's tent. While the sequences in the tent invite viewers to watch Messner "re-watching" his own traumatic past, and use the enclosed space of the tent to create an almost suffocating psychological close-up, the mountain sequences venture into re-representing the romantic sublime: the experience of something so overwhelmingly vast as to be incognizable, and thus only partially comprehensible to the viewer or to the self-reflective climber. In addition to the fundamental "moves" of romantic aesthetics and philosophy elaborated earlier, *The Dark Glow of the Mountains* comes close to expressing the simultaneous terror and exhilaration of the romantic sublime. In so doing, Herzog re-invokes specific romantic thinkers' preoccupation with mountains and mountain climbing, as well as with the potential of mountains to express (or translate, "afterwards") psychological realities, including the terror and guilt involved in our responsibility to others.

Writing primarily about the function of the sublime in English Romanticism, David Simpson says that the

> romantics' interest in the grand and threatening objects of nature went along with their general obsession with categories of otherness. Even when their poems and writings image the subsumption or displacement of this otherness, as they sometimes do, the terms of the dialectic are at least still there to be recovered and thought through. Wordsworth's misunderstanding someone always reminds us that there is someone there.[15]

A shared experience of the sublime—a shared experience of spectatorship in which we are overwhelmed, awed, and possibly frightened—can be a way to bring us into closer proximity to others, but the dilemma remains that the sublime, like its less challenging aesthetic alter ego, the beautiful, may also promise a kind of transcendence that implies an escape from feelings of responsibility or guilt. If we are overwhelmed, we cannot be expected to be responsible.

Mountains, perhaps the objects in nature most readily associated with the sublime, indeed often seem to offer a way to escape the pressing demands of conventional life, including political and ethical demands. Peter Arnds writes:

> Mountains in nineteenth-century literature provide the possibility of an escape from the nation-state as the location in which the individual's poetry of the heart, as Hegel once called it, has to be given up for the prose of circumstances. Especially for the hero of Romantic literature the journey into the mountains becomes a way of rekindling the poetry of his heart.[16]

For Ludwig Tieck, for instance, physically challenging experiences in nature, and above all walking in mountains, far from the constraints of social life, were the best route to aesthetic ecstasy, at least when he was a young man. In *On the Sublime* (*Über das Erhabene*, likely 1792), an essay that remains a fragment, Tieck writes that a trip to the Harz mountains in that same year, when he was 19, was an "ecstatic" experience.[17]

Tieck's description of experiencing strenuous and dangerous nature as ecstatic anticipates the attitude of Christoph Ransmayr's protagonist Josef Mazzini in *The Terrors of Ice and Darkness*, who defends his desire for dangerous travel in a diary he kept on his arctic expedition. Mazzini's diary contains the following critical observation:

> Once we have closed up shop for the day, surely it is always the same embarrassed desire to break away that makes us dream of marches through jungles, caravans, or glistening floes of ice. We send our deputies where we cannot go ourselves—reporters who will tell us what it was like.[18]

But Mazzini, like Tieck—and like Messner, Ransmayr, and Herzog—does not send a deputy. Instead of yearning for adventure, instead of bemoaning the fact that, as he continues: "Nothing moves us anymore. Nor does anyone truly inform us. No one moves us, they entertain us," these authors and artists embark and encounter the sublime themselves. And, to a certain extent, they make it their mission to take us with them. Instead of acting as our deputies or reporters—or, as Herzog might say, as our accountants—these explorers use art to convey the ecstasy and awe of the experience of the sublime, desiring to move us rather than to entertain us.

Ransmayr, in literature, and Herzog, in film, give us scenes in which our gaze falls into neither of the traps the sublime might create: our reading, or viewing, of their scenes is neither voyeuristic nor fetishistic.[19] That is, we neither attempt to subsume the other (or: the sublimity of the landscape) into ourselves via the possessive gaze, nor is the sublime vista a substitute or supplement for ethical engagement with the world. That world needs our engagement, even if that engagement comes in the observational mode often espoused by both Herzog and Ransmayr, both of whom regularly avoid taking explicit political stances. For neo-romantics like Herzog and Ransmayr, the language of politics by and large is not the poetry of the heart. As Herzog writes in a related vein in a proposal for an unrealized film with the working title *The Aztec Project*, "perspective is not a mere technicality of where the camera is positioned. The question is: where are we, the spectators, with our hearts."[20]

Alan Singer argues that Herzog has his own "particular version of the sublime," one that reflects romantic irony while wielding the camera in ways that update and extend the theories of the sublime produced by the philosophical tradition. Singer explains that in

> Herzog's most enigmatic images ... his mise-en-scène presents the spectacle of a sumptuously particularized reality that, by its very exorbitance, seems to elude conceptualization and so to deny knowledge of its origins—the only knowledge that might anchor our faith in a world of appearances. The meaning of Herzog's images ... gives the inference of a whole that is more than the multiplicity of its parts.[21]

This denial, or at least only partial revelation, of knowledge of an image's origins serves not only to create scenes in which space and time are defamiliarized, as they are in the romantic tradition of painting. The inference of a more complete knowledge "out there" that cannot be fully comprehended is also precisely what creates the desire for more knowledge, and the desire to keep looking at surfaces in the hope that more sense will appear. Like the romantics', Herzog's images are still anchored in a world we recognize. But these images displace conventional certainties about that world, and make us wish to keep nearing a different kind of truth, via aesthetic form. Singer adds that the desire for that different knowledge, the desire to "fill in" the concealed, secret knowledge of an image's origins, is most effectively elicited by the sublime.

But Singer cautions that we should not take the sublime in Herzog's films at its face (or, rather, surface) value. While, as Singer writes, "it is indeed tempting to see Herzog as the mystic seer of sublime intuitions," the filmmaker's use of the categories of the sublime—and, I would add, of the beautiful as well—is instead the "operative illusion of Herzog's filmic sleight of hand." Instead of using the sublime to check out of reality, and of history,

Singer argues, Herzog wields it as a trick to get us to think about how we unavoidably do live in history: his filming of nature as sublime in particular ultimately offers a "critical perspective on the habits of human history" and acknowledges "the difficulties of inhabiting human time."[22] In addition to prompting us to ask "where are we, the spectators, with our hearts," Herzog's visions of human figures in overwhelming nature, whether in the Amazon, the Himalayas, on Guadeloupe, or under the sea, are also visions of human relations. Sublime settings are the places where relations between self and other are thrown into sharpest relief, in part because Herzog films these settings as psycho-topographies, always making connections between the minds and hearts of his subjects and the extreme circumstances to which they have willingly exposed themselves.

In an interview in 2002, Herzog reflects: "Life in the oceans must be sheer hell. A vast, merciless hell of permanent and immediate danger. So much of a hell that during evolution some species—including man—crawled, fled onto some small continents of solid land, where the lessons of darkness continue."[23] This statement attributes a clear, if depressing, history to human development, and ties humans inextricably to nature's history as well. Mountain climbers, one could argue, also have sought out a "vast, merciless hell of permanent and immediate danger." The lessons they do, or do not, learn have fascinated Herzog for decades. While the Alpine freestyle climbing technique espoused by Messner, one of Herzog's most famous climbing subjects, is a topic hotly debated in the mountaineering world, as ever, the technicalities of the activity are not what primarily interest the director. In *Dark Glow*, Herzog says: "We weren't so much interested in making a film about mountain climbing *per se*, or about climbing techniques. What we wanted to know was 'what goes on inside mountain climbers'? … Aren't these mountains and peaks like something deep down inside us all?" Herzog's interviews with Messner in the film imply that the answers to such questions are clearest when climber and filmmaker are at the mercy of the sublime.

In the aforementioned highly claustrophobic tent sequence in *Dark Glow*, Herzog, also in the tent, asks Reinhold Messner questions about the death of his brother Günther on Nanga Parbat. During the interview, Messner explains that he has the feeling that not his brother, but rather he himself died on the expedition, when he lost consciousness on the mountain. He then woke up and, after searching fruitlessly for Günther, walked down the rest of the mountain and began his life again.[24] Messner is composed until he describes telling his mother, "face to face" ("von Angesicht zu Angesicht"), that her son is dead. At this point he begins to cry, and says that she understood him completely. This scene, in which Messner acknowledges involvement with, although not responsibility for, his brother's fate conveys the possibility of a unification of surface and depth, or of appearance and essence. The idea that only the "face," or surface, permits any access to essential meaning is part of pre-romantic and romantic thinking about "appearing sense," or how meaning only unfolds with and through manifest expressions.[25]

The echo of Paul's first letter to the Corinthians in Messner's phrase "from face to face" ("von Angesicht zu Angesicht") implies that only when he saw his mother did he see the complete truth of the situation, in that moment, he both recognized another (his mother) and was himself fully recognized by her.[26] But the very fact of his brother's death in the past, on Messner's very first Himalayan climb, coupled with the fact that Messner continued to go on extremely dangerous and extremely similar climbing expeditions for many years thereafter—even insisting in 1978 on re-enacting, now successfully, the climb along the Diamir Face of Nanga Parbat, the route where Günther died in 1970—could be read as an exaggerated expression of an awareness that on some level we only have access to the other's appearance, surface, or face.[27] His obduracy arguably represents an avowal of the distance between the self and the other, one whereby no one can take responsibility for another.

The psychiatrist R.D. Laing reframes a post-Kantian, romantic view of subject-object relations in psychoanalytic terms:

> The analytic theory of object-relations is based on the finding that the recognition of our own separate existence, and the separate existence of the other person, is gained only slowly and often painfully. [...] Anxiety remains an ultimate risk even in mature object-relations, since there is no escape from the tragic paradox that whereas our relatedness to others is part of us, the real other person is not.[28]

The connection to Romanticism is thus not only in the romantic fascination with mountains such as one finds in E.T.A Hoffmann's tale "The Mines of Falun" ("Die Bergwerke zu Falun," 1819) or in Ludwig Tieck's "The Runenberg" ("Der Runenberg," 1804). The mountains and their hidden peaks, in this case, are the site of deep recesses and hidden secrets that Herzog has continued to explore (with the help of an added third dimension) in, for instance, *Cave of Forgotten Dreams* (2010). Here, however, I am concerned with the fact that German Romantic philosophy presupposes a relationship of correspondence rather than collapse between self and other; it avows that the other cannot be collapsed or incorporated into the self. This relationship, akin to those associated with twentieth-century psychoanalysis, acknowledges difference and thus has a melancholy or anxious aspect—our very proximity to the other makes us aware of the unbridgeable gap between us. Thus, the ability to see another "face to face" is also a reminder of transience and of loss.[29]

In this way Romanticism offers insight into mourning, and Messner's return to the mountain—his reenactment of the past—engages Freud's romantically inflected discourse on introjection, one that inherits from, for example, Friedrich Schlegel, who insists that similarity and sympathy with the other are real, yet also acknowledges that we can never become one with that other.[30] There is always a danger of becoming trapped in a world of inner images—as if, Schlegel warns, in an "endless row of mirrors."[31] But the anxiety that this realization can precipitate emerges in a context of what Schlegel called love—precisely that to which the aforementioned verses in Corinthians are devoted. Here, again, is the relevant passage in Friedrich Schlegel's fragments:

> Inasmuch as we can very well call *love* that *perception and apprehension* of the object, this marriage of the *perceiving I* and the perceived spirit (of the other), then we can posit *without love no meaning; meaning, understanding depends on love*.
> (Und sofern wir dies *Wahrnehmen und Ergreifen* des Ichs des Gegenstandes, diese Vermählung des *wahrnehmenden Ichs* und des wahrgenommenen Geistes sehr gut *Liebe* nennen, können wir den Satz aufstellen, *ohne Liebe kein Sinn, der Sinn, das Verstehen beruht auf der Liebe*.)[32]

Love is only possible if the beloved both is, and is not, me. But this classically romantic view of the relation between self and other is revealed in Herzog's film, as it is in the work of members of early German Romantic philosophers (including Schlegel, Tieck, and Hölderlin), is far from straightforward. The assertion that the relation between love and understanding is axiomatic does not exclude the existence of guilt and responsibility nor does it provide any guidance for navigating those elements of intersubjective relations—something about which the romantics in general are quite silent. Despite Messner's denials of responsibility for Günther's death, for instance, even Herzog's sympathetic direction permits us to see that doubt about Messner's responsibility remains, in the world at large and within Messner's mind. His breakdown in the tent at least leaves room for the possibility that he feels culpable.

The fundamental relationship and responsibility to another are measured in *Dark Glow*, in the context of psychic and natural extremes. In the voiceover narration for the film, Herzog states that he is not really interested in making a movie about mountain climbing, but rather (as mentioned above): "What we wanted to know was 'what goes on inside mountain climbers'? ... Aren't these mountains and peaks like something deep down inside us all?" Messner asserts "I've never asked myself why I [climb] … I wouldn't know the answer," which echoes the desire to travel until there is nothing "behind" him. Both statements reject the search for answers within the self, or within the past. Yet Messner simultaneously discusses his motivations for mountain climbing in considerable detail, describing the activity as an addiction, as a kind of illness; after a few months without climbing, he needs to climb again. In a monologue filmed at base camp beneath the Gasherbrum peaks, Messner says "I think mountain climbing is a sign of degeneration in mankind [...] [people who have to work for a living in the mountains] are *afraid* of mountains," but those who climb them for sport are addicts, artists, creators—and, echoing elements of Nietzsche's thesis from *The Birth of Tragedy*, Messner remarks, "creative activity is a sign of degeneration." It is no coincidence that "degeneration" is a term with biological as well as philosophical provenance in the nineteenth century. Whether knowingly or not, Messner here reaches back to a concept popular among romantics concerned about the consequences of the Industrial Revolution and preoccupied with proto-evolutionary thinking in the biological sciences. It was not an enormous leap from Fichte's philosophy of an epigenetic, self-generating self-consciousness to the concern that this self-consciousness could also devolve as the boundaries between man and machine and between man and animal seemed to dissolve.[33]

In the film, the "degenerative" activity of climbing is measured in part by affinity for and distance from others: in other words, by relation. Messner and Herzog's dreams of ambulating through a life lived purely in the present are also dreams of utter self-reliance. After Günther's death, Messner became an even stronger advocate for Alpine freestyle climbing, in which belay ropes are rarely used and each climber is responsible for himself alone, not for his partner. In a scene with Hans Kammerlander looking on, Messner says, "Each of us, without really saying it, assumes the responsibility for himself. There's no other way. Not until I know that's clear do I have the peace of mind and self-assurance to ask someone else to join me." In the film, Messner's extreme self-reliance seems related to a need, after his brother's death, to abdicate responsibility for his partner. Or, perhaps mountain climbing and the self-reliance it demands provide a sort of absolution—an acknowledgment that each of us, without really saying it, always is responsible ultimately only for ourselves, not needing anything behind us. In any event, Messner's discussion of his brother's death here is relatively elliptical. Only his description of his encounter with his mother, when he told her about Günther's death, is detailed.

## 3   Ineffable Experience: *Nanga Parbat* (2010)

*Nanga Parbat* gives us some of the details, and therefore at least the feeling of getting some of the "answers," that Reinhold Messner and Werner Herzog withhold from viewers of *The Dark Glow of the Mountains*. This fictionalized rendering of the tragic climb in 1970 (Reinhold Messner was a consultant on the film) integrates Günther Messner as a character, and depicts the brothers' childhood relationship as not only emotionally close, but as focused on their common obsession with climbing. The childhood scenes, however, depicted in flashback, already make clear that Reinhold (Florian Stetter) is considerably more daring and risk-taking than Günther (Andreas Tobias), and that Günther's wish to follow his charismatic older brother repeatedly outweighs his inherent caution.

Early in the film, while climbing a rock face in the Dolomites in 1968, Günther Messner accuses his brother of dangerous climbing tactics. Reinhold climbs the final feet of the rock face without belays or bolts, consistent with his insistence on Alpine freestyle climbing without additional supportive equipment. Günther foreshadowingly says: "At some point you will kill yourself. And me too" ("Irgendwann bringst du dich um. Und mich mit"). Reinhold points out that the only option in those final feet of the climb was to keep going, saying: "Turning back is the same as not going at all" ("Zurück ist nicht 'gangen"). Günther remonstrates with him, but eventually agrees to next try something no one has done before: the freestyle climb of Nanga Parbat.

The sequences depicting the Messner brothers' childhood imply that it is possible to understand their decisions psychologically—that is, if we understand their past (their childhood home is positioned in front of an Alpine rockface) and their relationship, we can understand why they undertook arguably irresponsible climbs. But the film's flashback technique also serves to reinforce the brothers' bond as one so strong and essentially ineffable that it transcends death. In other words, the scenes of the brothers' past affirm Reinhold's declaration in the future that he never betrayed his brother, and that he did not act irresponsibly (either on the mountain or in his retelling of the events leading to Günther's death). Narrating the tragedy in a style reminiscent of Ludwig Tieck's aforementioned description of mountaineering in *On the Sublime*, Messner says of himself and Günther:

> We climbed as if on a distant star, according to our own rules. We were brothers, friends, partners, a conspirative rope team. The Alpine scene was small. You only got recognition for taking the most difficult routes. It wasn't about the peak. It was about dangers, abysses, risk. About taking new routes with as little

technology as possible. And it was about happiness. About the moment before the last big step. About the second, in which nothing seemed impossible anymore.

(Wir kletterten wie auf einem fernen Stern, nach unseren eigenen Regeln. Wir waren Brüder, Freunde, Partner, eine verschworene Seilschaft. Die alpine Szene war klein. Anerkennung fand nur, wer die schwersten Routen g'gangen ist. Dabei ging es nicht um den Gipfel. Es ging um Gefahren, Abgründe, Risiko. Darum, neue Routen zu gehen mit so wenig Technik wie möglich. Und es ging ums Glück. Um den Moment vorm letzten großen Schritt. Um die Sekunde, wo Dir nichts mehr unmöglich scheint.)

This tone continues throughout the film, as Messner proudly proclaims his—and Günther's—affinity with risk and danger, instead of acknowledging that they should have been more careful or not gone at all. Although in later years Reinhold Messner asserted that Alpine freestyle climbing is better because it protects the environment, in 1970—and in Vilsmaier's film—he defends the style because it is the most risky.

The real dangers of climbing would seem to contradict the aesthetic experience of the sublime, which is essentially one of spectatorship. Karl Philipp Moritz, whose aesthetic theory was highly influential for the German Romantics, stresses the vicarious thrill of viewing. When we perceive another's peril, but are not imperiled ourselves, says Moritz, this "shakes and elevates" our souls. In a passage that sounds like a description of an epic battle on film, Moritz says: "When thousands fall to the sword on one day, that is something *great*. And the *great* is what we want; our souls desire expansion, our imagination wants to encompass a *lot*" (Wenn Tausende an einem Tage vor dem Schwertstreich fallen, das ist doch etwas *Großes*. Und das *Große* wollen wir ja; unsre Seele will ja erweitert sein, unsre Einbildungskraft will *viel* umspannen).[34] But it is not only the film's viewer who is in that spectator position, but the film's version of Messner, for key segments of the picture. By staging early scenes in the post-accident period, the film emphasizes Messner's delayed narration of the events on Nanga Parbat, and his posterior projection determines our view of the anterior situation—of what Joseph Leo Koerner calls a "future-oriented … enigmatic message" from the past.[35] In this film, the tragedy on Nanga Parbat "shakes and elevates" our souls rather than making us question the Messner brothers' freestyle approach.

*Nanga Parbat* does allude to the conflict in the mountaineering world between aficionados of Alpine freestyle climbing and those who climb expedition-style (so-called siege mountaineering). Near the beginning of the film, physician and climb organizer Karl Maria Herrligkoffer (Karl Markovics) calls Nanga Parbat the "Germans' mountain of destiny" (the "Schicksalsberg der Deutschen").³⁶ Herrligkoffer organized the Sigi Löw Memorial Expedition on Nanga Parbat in 1970—the climb during which Günther Messner died. Herrligkoffer is unflatteringly portrayed as wanting to "conquer" ("besiegen") Nanga Parbat. When he and Herrligkoffer meet for the first time, Messner counters: "We don't have to conquer it (the mountain) right away. It's enough for me to climb it" ("Wir müssen ihn nicht gleich besiegen. Mir reicht, ihn zu besteigen"). And, Herrligkoffer cravenly attempts to get Reinhold, who is already semi-famous, to raise more money for the trip when finances falter, in Pakistan. Herrligkoffer insists to wealthy potential financiers: "I have always counted the Austrians as Germans" ("Ich habe die Österreicher immer zu den Deutschen gezählt"); this occurs after Reinhold has reminded the prospective donors that Hermann Buhl, an Austrian rather than a German, first climbed Nanga Parbat in 1953.

Earlier in the film, but later in the history of events, while giving a lecture about the (now-past) expedition and standing in front of a projected image of snowy Nanga Parbat, Herrligkoffer asserts that it is not his duty to discern "how much guilt Reinhold Messner has burdened himself with" ("wie viel Schuld Reinhold Messner auf sich geladen hat"). But clearly Herrligkoffer has reached his own conclusions, saying: "He must carry this burden. To the end of his days" ("Diese Bürde muss er tragen. Bis ans Ende seiner Tage"). A watching crowd of journalists then surges toward Messner, demanding to know whether he feels guilty.

In a sequence that portrays the Messner brothers as children, the boys scale a churchyard wall instead of ascending nearby steps. When the pastor confronts them, Reinhold asserts: "The wall was guilty. It was in the way" ("Die Mauer war schuld. Sie stand im Weg"). The pastor reinforces that the brothers themselves should feel guilty, asking them to imagine their parents' pain if they were killed while climbing. In the tent in *The Dark Glow of the Mountains*, Reinhold indeed breaks down when remembering telling his mother about Günther's death. In Vilsmaier's film, when the brothers are leaving for the expedition to Nanga Parbat, the Messners' mother (Lena Stolze) whispers to Reinhold: "You bring Günther back to me safe. Promise me?" ("Du bringst mir den Günther heil zurück. Versprichst du's mir?"). Reinhold promises, simultaneously implicitly affirming both that he is the better climber, and also that he is indeed his brother's protector.

As children, the Messner brothers attend church and hear the pastor rhetorically ask: "Am I my brother's keeper?" ("Bin ich der Hüter meines Bruders?") He then answers in the affirmative. In *Dark Glow*, Reinhold avoids the story of Cain and Abel, but refers to another Biblical passage, Paul's first letter to the Corinthians, and its evocation of only achieving complete knowledge when one is completely known oneself, "from face to face." Unlike the adversaries Cain and Abel, the Messner brothers are comrades, adventurers who ascend the surface, or "face" of the mountain instead of plumbing the depths of the psyche and its concomitant questions of responsibility. Despite their differences as filmmakers, Vilsmaier might agree with Herzog's assertion, in the 1970s, that talking about psychology is "too much 'talk show'" ("zu sehr Talk-Show").[37]

And yet *Nanga Parbat*, like *Dark Glow*, is rich with allusions to psychology, but exhibits a seeming disdain for taking apart the psyche's pedestrian components. The mountain is just as much a psycho-topography for Vilsmaier as for Herzog, but it is a map with no clear routes—it is inscrutable, ineffable. In both films, nature, including the mountain, is indifferent to human feelings and fates. But in *Nanga Parbat*, this indifference tends in the direction of an exculpation of Reinhold Messner, while *Dark Glow* transfers the mountain's inscrutability right back onto Messner's own behavior and the question of responsibility. In both films, however, Messner is "his brother's keeper" in that he keeps Günther's memory, and "afterwardsness," alive—but he does this primarily by continuing to climb, rather than by taking a hard look at how his climbing practices could have played a role in the tragedy. In *Nanga Parbat*, Herrligkoffer tells Messner that it is necessary to keep climbing, and to climb Nanga Parbat specifically, because that actually honors those who died there, and in a sense continues their lives. In this instance, Herrligkoffer refers to the death of his own half-brother, Willy Merkl, on Nanga Parbat in 1934, but only briefly and allusively. And yet that death clearly is the impetus for many, if not most, of Herrligkoffer's future expeditions.

Herzog and Vilsmaier could perhaps be accused of using aesthetic tactics to avoid probing questions of guilt and responsibility. Or, put another way, the romantic aesthetic strategies in these films preserve ineffability and secrecy, in that they privilege images over language, and thus seem to reveal surfaces rather than depths. All participate in the kind of "re-enchantment" of nature that preoccupied the early German Romantics; all wish to counter the notion, as Alison Stone puts it, that nature ever can be "wholly intelligible to reason."[38]

Romanticism is a multivalent movement, with various afterlives, and Vilsmaier's cinematic Romanticism certainly differs from Herzog's in important respects. But like Herzog, Vilsmaier is Bavarian (both were born in Munich; Vilsmaier in 1939 and Herzog in 1942). Both were children during the Third Reich, and have made films that assert a German cultural identity via regionalism. Herzog has asserted that all of the landscapes, in all of his films, are Bavarian—like Kleist, he displaces Germany to other locations, creating generalizations of an idea of a place rather than depicting specific national or provincial spaces.³⁹ Vilsmaier has released a cinematic ode to his home region: *Bavaria. Traumreise durch Bayern* (2012). About this film, Vilsmaier has said: "I want to express how beautiful our state is, and that people here are doing well" ("Ich möchte zum Ausdruck bringen, wie wunderschön unser Land ist, und dass es den Menschen hier gut geht").⁴⁰ However, unlike Herzog, Vilsmaier does not evoke a sense of Bavaria in far-flung locations. Instead, he actually shows Bavaria itself, albeit mostly from the air (with a Cineflex camera), and therefore not in the way that most people "really" see it. *Bavaria* arguably is Herzogian in this respect, as in many films, *The White Diamond*, *Little Dieter Needs to Fly*, and *Wings of Hope* to name just a few, Herzog is preoccupied with air travel and/or with filming from the air. Still, *Bavaria* is arguably closer to *verité* filmmaking than anything Herzog has done.

And, the style and tone of *Bavaria*, like that of *Nanga Parbat*, is marked by a lack of irony. In a sense, Vilsmaier's films echo aspects of German Romanticism (including the re-enchantment of nature, self-consciousness and a simultaneous awareness that the psyche can never be completely known, and a sense of always progressing) without incorporating romantic irony. The music used in *Nanga Parbat* could be considered an example of this lack of irony. Vilsmaier introduces the sections of the film that take place in Pakistan and the Himalayas with what is subtitled as "Far-Eastern music" ("fernöstliche Musik"), patently signifying that the Messners have entered the land of the Oriental "other." Herzog's use of the music of Popol Vuh in *Dark Glow*, by contrast, is otherworldly rather than ethnically "other."

But both *Dark Glow* and *Nanga Parbat* represent what Ian Baucom calls the "deathly afterlife of past historical situations."⁴¹ What makes us empathetic, as viewers, is not the sufferer's anguish but our ability to imagine what happened to him. In *The Theory of Moral Sentiment* (1759), Adam Smith says: "Sympathy, therefore, does not arise so much from the view of the passion [e.g., the suffering of another], as that from the situation that excites it … When we put ourselves in his case, [then] that passion arises in our breast from the imagination."⁴² This attitude is related arguably to Friedrich Schlegel's aforementioned understanding of love as a form of sympathy: an attentive, perceptive apprehension of and concentration on the other.

Herzog's and Vilsmaier's films are allusive rather than indicative, but both do invite us to identify with their protagonists at a distance: as "something *viewed*." Herzog never really invites us to take Reinhold Messner's side, but he does give Messner the chance to speak and be heard, and to demonstrate his passion for (and addiction to) climbing. And Vilsmaier's flashback techniques do remind us that Günther Messner's death is being re-told and re-represented here, by himself and by Reinhold, and that we are thus receiving the past's enigmatic messages only through the present's filmic technologies.

## 4 Conclusion

Intriguingly, Reinhold Messner came up with the idea for Werner Herzog's film *Scream of Stone* (*Cerro Torre: Schrei aus Stein*, 1991), in which a climbing accident is portrayed in considerable detail. Although in this very graphic scene (from the original treatment for the film) a storm is enveloping the hapless climbing team, nevertheless their view, and therefore also our view, of a lengthy and horrible accident is mercilessly unobstructed. As the scene begins, two climbers are trapped on a cliff face, a leader and a belayer, roped together in a system meant to ensure their safety, but which instead leads to doom.

> We see a smooth-scrubbed, partly ice-enclosed, vertically looming wall of granite … In this inferno we suddenly discover—we do not believe our eyes—an apparitional figure: a climber hangs on the wall. The wind tugs at him and threatens to rip him from the rock ledge, which is not even as broad as a hand, on which he braces himself with a toehold. He convulsively clasps a tightly stretched rope. Our gaze follows the rope upwards, and in the dense mist we recognize a second climber, who is trying to master an overhang. Suddenly a shrill scream breaks through the howling wind: the second climber has fallen and dangles helplessly above the abyss. … Both men try to communicate, screaming, but in the roar of the storm only snatches of sentences can be heard. The man on the ledge has, in his fall, tightened the safeguarding rope across his breast and this squeezes the breath out of him. He squirms in snake-like movements. Then the climbing hook that must hold the fallen man's entire weight begins to wobble, the cliff crumbles, the hook breaks out of the granite, and the fallen man falls another five meters into the deep, and hits the cliff wall hard. In his second fall the rope has been ripped over the larynx of the belayer, and threatens to strangle him. … The man on the cliff is choking as he tries in vain to wrestle out of the rope's stranglehold. In his terror he is able to draw a knife. … The rope tumbles over the cliff's edge; it is almost completely shredded. We see the face of the fallen, contorted with terror, his wide-open eyes, we see him fall.
> 
> [Wir sehen eine glattgescheuerte, stellenweise eisgepanzerte, senkrecht aufragende Granitwand … In diesem Inferno entdecken wir mit einem Mal—wir trauen unseren Augen nicht—eine schemenhafte Gestalt: Ein Kletterer hängt in der Wand. Der Wind zerrt an ihm und droht ihn von der nicht einmal handbreiten Felsleiste wegzureissen, auf der er sich mit den Fußspitzen abstützt. Krampfhaft umklammert er ein straff gespanntes Seil. Unser Blick folgt dem

Seil nach oben, und in den dichten Nebelschwaden erkennen wir einen zweiten Kletterer, der gerade einen Überhang zu bewältigen versucht. Plötzlich durchdringt ein gellender Schrei das Heulen des Windes: Der zweite Kletterer ist abgestürzt und baumelt hilflos über dem Abgrund. ... Die beiden Männer versuchen sich schreiend zu verständigen, doch im Tosen des Sturms sind nur Wortfetzen zu verstehen. Dem Mann auf der Felsleiste hat sich das sichernde Seil durch den Sturz stramm um die Brust gespannt und drückt ihm die Luft ab. Er windet sich in Schlangenbewegungen. Da beginnt der Umlaufhaken, der das ganze Gewicht des Gestürzten halten muß, zu wackeln, der Fels bröckelt, der Haken bricht aus dem Stein heraus, und der Abgestürzte fällt weitere fünf Meter in die Tiefe, schlägt hart gegen den Fels. Durch den zweiten Sturz wurde das Seil über den Kehlkopf des Sichernden gerissen und droht ihn zu strangulieren. ... Der Mann am Fels röchelt, vergeblich versucht er, sich dem Würgegriff des Seils zu entwinden. In seiner Todesangst gelingt es ihm gerade noch, ein Messer zu ziehen ... Das Seil scheuert weiter über die Felskante, es ist fast schon völlig aufgefasert. Wir sehen das angstverzerrte Gesicht des Gestürzten, seine weit aufgerissenen Augen, wir sehen ihn fallen.][43]

The spectators' perspective here is a sublime one, and their simultaneous safe distance from and horrible proximity to the accident is emphasized by the phrases "Our gaze follows ..." and "we see." These phrases function here as cinematographic instructions as well, as they also remind the filmmakers of what viewers will see while watching the film. But these phrases also reveal what is romantic about this simultaneously highly realistic scene. Viewers of the film will watch the viewing climbers watching the accident, small against the vast mountain and in the mighty storm; the narrating, watching climbers are frightened and frightening re-embodiments of Caspar David Friedrich's rear-view figures. The watching climbers do not trust their eyes, and yet they have no choice but to do so—they must "insert" their eyes into this activity.[44] But this activity cannot save the doomed climbers, any more than those climbers' efforts to communicate with one another verbally can. It seems likely that Reinhold Messner intended for the belaying practice to bear much of the blame for the accident. The message of the scene seems to be that when climbing partners, via the belaying system, are responsible for one another instead of for themselves alone, they actually are being highly irresponsible. Messner's stance here could be understood as a romantic warning against overextending ourselves *into* others' worlds and thus interfering with their ability to climb (or: achieve, walk, think) for themselves. True sympathy and respect (or, for Schlegel, love) arises from apprehending—or, viewing—the other as different from oneself, and thus respecting the other's autonomy.

The production documents for *The Dark Glow of the Mountains* include excerpts from Edward Whymper's volume *Scrambles Amongst the Alps in 1860–'69*.[45] Whymper describes a deadly fall on the Matterhorn in 1865 that seems to have served as the direct inspiration for the accident in *Scream of Stone*, given its inclusion in the production materials. The accident scenes in *Scrambles*, which are accompanied by graphic pencil illustrations, are so similar to those in the film treatment for *Scream of Stone* that the influence of the nineteenth-century accounts, and images, on the twentieth-century film is undeniable. But it is impossible to consider the accident in *Scream of Stone* without also thinking of the death of Günther Messner, especially given that Reinhold Messner influenced the story and making of the film. The inclusion of *Scrambles Amongst the Alps* in the production materials for *Stone* and the strong resemblance between the illustrations in the nineteenth-century book and the events in the film seems to constitute a fundamental instance of deferral, a way to order experience and memory during the "afterwardsness" of trauma. The accident in *Scrambles* substitutes for Günther Messner's accident, a century before his accident happened—demonstrating, perhaps, that such accidents happen again and again, and that no one is to blame, and that, as Messner says, whenever we talk about yesterday, we describe the future.

The production materials for and the production history of *Dark Glow of the Mountains*, as well as the content of the film itself, thus are permeated with and surrounded by simultaneously graphic and elliptical descriptions of death, and by the awareness of the ever-looming possibility of a violent death in nature in which one is ultimately alone, even when with a partner or team. What is "degenerative," perhaps, is not only the need and willingness to risk everything in dangerous adventures in sublime surroundings, but also the need to acknowledge an intense similarity with, yet difference from, the loved one. In other words, relation itself has a degenerative component parallel to that found in creative activity and in the creative drive. And these two things, activity and relation, seem ineluctably linked in Herzog's and Vilsmaier's films and in Messner's writing: the relation between self and other is truest, most authentic, in the moment in which one both does and does not depend on that other for one's life, in dangerous activity performed in the midst of a stunning and stunningly indifferent nature.

*The Dark Glow of the Mountains* and *Nanga Parbat* use images of nature to "re-enchant" not only nature but also their post-Enlightenment subjects. Alison Stone explains that for Friedrich Schlegel, "to perceive nature as partly mysterious is equally … to see its behaviour as partly magical, deriving from sources that are occult to us. An 'enchanting' view of nature, on which the character and behaviour of natural phenomena can never be entirely grasped or predicted, also implies ... the appropriateness of care for these phenomena."[46] In these films, mountains, and their histories—including the histories of all who died there—remain fundamentally ineffable and sublime, partly magical and never entirely graspable or predictable.

For the early German Romantics, images explicitly communicate our knowledge of *not* knowing, in part because our position is ever-changing, and in part because the images we view are in motion as well. This focus on not knowing implicitly guides our vision toward the future rather than encouraging nostalgia for the murky past. At the same time, romantic thinking about the image always involves turning back to ourselves, to an awareness of ourselves as spectators.

In the film *Encounters at the End of the World* (2007), Herzog speaks with a mechanic named Libor Zicha, who lives on the McMurdo science station on Antarctica. Zicha, we are informed, is from "behind the Iron Curtain." He begins to speak to Herzog about the "drama" of his escape from somewhere in the East bloc (the exact location is never stated), but he has difficulty. Off-camera Herzog intones, "You do not have to talk about it." Zicha thanks him and then shows Herzog, and us, the complete contents of a backpack (which he opens for the camera) that he keeps loaded at all times with survival and travel supplies. Zicha's implicitly traumatic past, the "it" about which he need not talk, is both his own individual past and an "it" that here stands for other traumatic events of the mid-twentieth century as well. The location of the interview with Herzog in Antarctica displaces the memories of those catastrophes, but cannot erase them. Antarctica is a representation of a lacuna, a blank spot—or, here, a literally white spot. Like remote and dangerous Nanga Parbat, Antarctica seems to be a place where everything and nothing happens. Here Herzog's film participates in a longer discourse about the relationship between seeing, speaking, and knowing, opposing psychoanalysis's contention that to speak is to know. And in *Nanga Parbat*, the character of Reinhold Messner evokes a similar stance when he takes the stage at Herrligkoffer's lecture ostensibly to explain himself, but expresses dramatic sentiments about climbing "as if on a distant star." In *Dark Glow*, the real Reinhold Messner describes his brother's death as his own resurrection, in highly image-driven terms. Herzog indeed privileges the visual and the visible, as ways to knowing, over language. And yet his films also rely on storytelling, on a form of "talking about it," that underlies the images on screen.

In Éric Rohmer's film of Heinrich von Kleist's *The Marquise of O*, the characters also rely on psychology's insights while simultaneously denying them (in particular, when the Marquise insists that she "does not want to know" what *we* know she must on some level already know). While the German

Romantics were preoccupied with origins, the denial that we can ever know the complete truth about either beginnings or endings is highly characteristic of the entire Romantic Movement, even through all of its different iterations. Instead, the representation of the past becomes, in the words of Friedrich Schelling, a new myth, a "truth of its own kind" (a "Wahrheit eigener Art").[47] Rather than promising to reveal the facts about what really happened, these films provide immersion in the truths of the present aesthetic construction.

Herzog and Vilsmaier arguably exemplify *auteur* cinema, which in some ways is easier to categorize in stereotypically romantic terms: the director functions as a strong central author or authority—and in Herzog's case, this is often even more apparent due to his frequent voiceover narration. And, the protagonists of the films explored here are extremely independent adventurers who seem to "author" their own lives. But the afterlife of German Romanticism in these films and others by these directors is less easy to categorize. The melancholy sensibility, self-conscious attention to spectatorship, and the sense of deferred meaning, or of "afterwardsness" that permeates the films coalesces in films that are, in a sense, "screen memories" of aspects of German Romantic philosophy.

## Notes

1. Some of the material in this essay is based on material in: Laurie Ruth Johnson, *Forgotten Dreams: Revisiting Romanticism in the Cinema of Werner Herzog* (Rochester: Camden House, 2016).
2. It is perhaps less surprising that New German Cinema director Hans-Jürgen Syberberg would film Kleist's work. Syberberg's political views have been criticized as reactionary, and, in addition to Kleist, he has chosen Richard Wagner's work as a focus. In 1989, Syberberg directed *The Marquise of O: From the North to the South* (*Die Marquise von O. Vom Süden in den Norden verlegt*, 1989), in which the star of Rohmer's film from 1976, Edith Clever, declaimed Kleist's entire novella. See https://mubi.com/films/the-marquise-of-o-from-the-north-to-the-south.
3. Walter Benjamin, "The Task of the Translator," in *Selected Writings, Volume I: 1913–1926*, eds. Marcus Bullock and Michael W. Jennings (Cambridge: Belknap Press/Harvard University Press, 1996), 253–263.
4. Walter Benjamin, *Gesammelte Schriften*, eds. Rolf Tiedemann and Hermann Schweppenhäuser (Frankfurt am Main: Suhrkamp, 1991) vol. 4.1:9.
5. Joseph Leo Koerner, *Caspar David Friedrich and the Subject of Landscape* (London: Reaktion Books, 2009), 12.
6. Koerner, *Caspar David Friedrich and the Subject of Landscape*, 12.

7. In the screenplay for *Nosferatu*, for instance, Herzog notes that in one scene, the character Lucy Harker "stands there, like the *Monk by the Sea*, and looks into the distance" ("Da steht Lucy, wie der Mönch am Meer, und schaut in die Weite"). Werner Herzog Collection, Deutsche Kinemathek, Berlin.
8. Johann Gottlieb Fichte, *System der Sittenlehre*, *Sämmtliche Werke* 4 (Berlin: Veit, 1845–1846): 32–33.
9. Eldridge, *The Persistence of Romanticism* 2.
10. In the 1990s, work done by the philosopher Dieter Henrich and others transformed our understanding of how the early German Romantics of the 1790s helped shape these four philosophical-aesthetic criteria (=anti-dogmatism, progressivism, community, irony), among other elements of the subject philosophy that was emerging at that time. Prior to the 1990s, the contribution of Early Romanticism largely was considered to consist of a set of more or less discrete responses to the critical philosophy of Immanuel Kant and the idealism of Johann Gottlieb Fichte. Henrich and his colleagues argued that the German Romantics' new concepts of subjectivity and the aesthetic theory emerged within collaborative groups, or constellations. "Constellation research" shows that concepts we now associate with Romanticism did not develop in a philosophical vacuum, but rather that in Romanticism, from the movement's earliest days in Jena and Tübingen, philosophy, literature, science, and visual culture formed a larger aesthetic and intellectual force field. For instance, Karl Leonard Reinhold, Friedrich Heinrich Jacobi, Friedrich Hölderlin, Novalis, Schelling, and Friedrich Schlegel intervened significantly in the development of critical and absolute idealism in the 1790s. Novalis, Schelling, and Schlegel in particular shared expertise in the natural sciences evident in their philosophical output. Their work intersected with other "constellation" members' focus on aesthetic theory and literature; the larger group included Caroline Schlegel-Schelling, Dorothea Veit-Schlegel, August Wilhelm Schlegel, and Ludwig Tieck.
11. Although Herzog's melancholy differs from Freud's understanding of melancholy in significant ways, Freud, like Herzog, inherits what I am calling the alternate discourse of Romanticism on precisely this issue. I rely on two texts about melancholy that bookend the long nineteenth century: Freud's essay "Mourning and Melancholia" (1917) as well as Adam Smith's *The Theory of Moral Sentiments* (1759). My understanding of Smith is aided greatly by Ian Baucom's provocative reading in *Specters of the Atlantic: Finance Capital, Slavery, and the Philosophy of History* (Durham: Duke University Press, 2005).
12. Ian Baucom, *Specters of the Atlantic*, 222; emphasis mine. Baucom identifies a "late eighteenth and early nineteenth-century Romantic counterknowledge of the modern" whose melancholy expressions emphasize "imaginative sympathy" and the "evident" (242–243). This knowledge serves as a critical counterpoint, for Baucom, to a speculative modern realism (focused on "imaginary value" and "evidence") that instrumentalizes its objects of study—and is com-

plicit in literally instrumentalizing bodies (of slaves, colonized peoples, and others). The "figure of the spectator" around 1800 is the site at which these two discourses join: the spectator has both a "'disinterested,' speculative, Enlightenment guise and [a] haunted, witness-bearing, melancholy incarnation." This modern spectator represents for Baucom "an internally fissured, doubly self-conscious, simultaneously and antagonistically speculative and melancholy Atlantic modernity" (243).

13. Baucom describes modern melancholy as "less a condition than a determination, less something we suffer than something we choose, less a way of being wounded by the world than a way of entering into it," *Specters of the Atlantic*, 259.
14. Baucom, *Specters of the Atlantic*, 257.
15. David Simpson, "Commentary: Updating the Sublime," in *Studies in Romanticism* 26.2 (1987): 258–259.
16. Peter Arnds, "From Eros to Thanatos: Hiking and Spelunking in Ludwig Tieck's *Der Runenberg*," *Heights of Reflection: Mountains in the German Imagination from the Middle Ages to the Twenty-First Century*, eds. Sean Ireton and Caroline Schaumann (Rochester: Camden House, 2012), 177. Arnds cites Hegel in *Vorlesungen über die Ästhetik III* (Frankfurt am Main: Suhrkamp, 1970), 393.
17. Ludwig Tieck, *Über das Erhabene, Schriften 1789–1794*, ed. Achim Hölter (Frankfurt am Main: Deutscher Klassiker Verlag, 1991): 1137–1170. Patrick Bridgwater notes that both Tieck and his direct inspiration on the topic of the sublime, Carl Grosse, were responding to Friedrich Schiller's notion of the "sublime villain" (erhabener Bösewicht) in the play *Die Räuber* of 1781. See *The German Gothic Novel in Anglo-German Perspective* (Amsterdam: Rodopi, 2013), 225.
18. Christoph Ransmayr, *The Terrors of Ice and Darkness* (New York: Grove Press, 1991), 12.
19. Laura Mulvey provides now-standard definitions of these types of gazes in "Visual Pleasure and Narrative Cinema," *Screen* 16.3 (1975): 6–18.
20. Werner Herzog, *The Aztec Project*, undated guideline for a draft of a screenplay, 2, Werner Herzog Collection, Deutsche Kinemathek, Berlin. Abbreviated henceforth as DK.
21. Alan Singer, "Comprehending Appearances: Werner Herzog's Ironic Sublime," *The Films of Werner Herzog: Between Mirage and History* (New York: Methuen & Co., Ltd., 1986), 183.
22. Singer, "Comprehending Appearances," 185.
23. Paul Cronin, ed., *Herzog on Herzog* (London: Faber and Faber Limited, 2002), 301.
24. This "scene" from Reinhold Messner's narration is retold particularly faithfully in Ransmayr's *Der Fliegende Berg*.

25. This relationship between meaning and manifestation is explicated, for instance, in Karl Philipp Moritz's aesthetic theory, and in particular in his thinking about aesthetic autonomy. For Moritz, the artwork's surface can provide direct experience of meaning; artworks whose signs refer "only to themselves" ("nur auf sich selber zeigen"), substance has *become* surface, and vice versa. In art of his own time, Moritz says, "appearance and reality … have become the same" ("Die Erscheinung ist mit der Wirklichkeit … eins geworden"). See Moritz, *Über die bildende Nachahmung des Schönen*, in *Beiträge zur Ästhetik*, eds. Hans Joachim Schrimpf and Hans Adler (Mainz: Dieterichsche Verlagsbuchhandlung, 1989) 78.
26. The standard German translation of the passage is "von Angesicht zu Angesicht," the same words used by Messner. See 1 Corinthians 13: 11, 12.
27. Messner was a romantic where his mountaineering was concerned. In his 1971 manifesto against the over-use of climbing equipment, "The Murder of the Impossible," he compares himself to the medieval German hero Siegfried and asks: "Who has polluted the pure spring of mountaineering?" *Mountain* 15 (1971), accessed at http://upwardtrail.multiply.com/journal/item/1/The_Murder_of_the_Impossible.
28. R.D. Laing, "An Examination of Tillich's Theory of Anxiety and Neurosis," *British Journal of Medical Psychology* 30.2 (1957): 90.
29. Schlegel's theory of love is the most detailed exposition of romantic alterity and intersubjectivity. See *Kritische-Friedrich-Schlegel-Ausgabe*, ed. Ernst Behler (Munich: Schöningh, 1964) 12: 350–351, 435. Abbreviated henceforth as KFSA, with volume and page number.
30. KFSA 12: 435.
31. KFSA 12: 351.
32. Schlegel, KFSA 12: 350–351.
33. Helmut Müller-Sievers discusses Fichte's view of self-consciousness, and of philosophy itself, as "self-generating" in *Self-Generation: Biology, Philosophy, and Literature Around 1800* (Stanford: Stanford University Press, 1997): 65–89. David Farrell Krell explicates the interest of Novalis, Hegel, Friedrich Schlegel, and Schelling in developments in biology around 1800 in detail in *Contagion: Sexuality, Disease, and Death in German Idealism and Romanticism* (Bloomington: Indiana University Press, 1998).
34. Karl Philipp Moritz, *Werke*, ed. Horst Günther (Frankfurt am Main: Insel, 1981) 3: 301.
35. Koerner, *Caspar David Friedrich and the Subject of Landscape*, 294.
36. This nickname itself refers to a film: *Berg des Schicksals*, of 1924 (dir. Arnold Fanck), about an Alpine climbing accident. Herrligkoffer's claim that the mountain of destiny is *German* is proved controversial, later in the film, when Messner, Herrligkoffer and prospective financiers meet in Pakistan prior to the 1970 expedition. Messner informs *Burda* and guests that Hermann Buhl, an Austrian, not Germans, climbed Nanga Parbat in 1953. Herrligkoffer was

the controversial organizer of numerous expeditions in the Himalayas; like Messner, he had lost a relative on Nanga Parbat (Herrligkoffer's half-brother Willy Merkl died on the mountain in 1934). Herrligkoffer subsequently organized the expedition on which Günther Messner died in 1970, the "Sigi-Löw-Gedächtnisexpedition." Herrligkoffer was successful in financing expeditions, which made it possible for more climbers to take part. Vilsmaier's film (which Herrligkoffer's son criticized strongly for its unflattering portrayal of his father) de-emphasizes Herrligkoffer's role in the Messner brothers' ascent of Nanga Parbat, and depicts Herrligkoffer as invested in blaming Reinhold for Günther's death, rather than any organizational aspects of the 1970 climb.

37. *I Am My Films: A Portrait of Werner Herzog (Was ich bin sind meine Filme. Ein Porträt von Werner Herzog*, dir. Christian Weisenborn and Erwin Keusch, Part I, 1976–1978).
38. Alison Stone, "Friedrich Schlegel, Romanticism, and the Re-enchantment of Nature," *Inquiry* 48.1 (February 2005): 3–25, here 5.
39. Paul Cronin, ed., *Herzog on Herzog* (New York: Faber and Faber, 2002), 23.
40. *Süddeutsche Zeitung*, July 31, 2012.
41. Baucom, *Specters of the Atlantic*, 258–259.
42. Adam Smith, *The Theory of Moral Sentiments*, cited here in Baucom, *Specters of the Atlantic*, 259.
43. "Schrei aus Stein. Nach einer Idee von Reinhold Messner," treatment for *Schrei aus Stein*, Werner Herzog Collection, DK. Translation mine.
44. As cited in the introduction, Johann Gottlieb Fichte refers to self-consciousness as a form of seeing; it is an "activity in which an eye is inserted." In *System der Sittenlehre, Sämmtliche Werke* 4 (Berlin: Veit, 1845–1846): 32–33.
45. Edward Whymper, *Scrambles Amongst the Alps in 1860–'69* (London: J. Murray, 1871). The excerpts from Whymper's work cited here are housed together with the production documents for *The Dark Glow of the Mountains* at the Deutsche Kinemathek in Berlin.
46. Stone, "Friedrich Schlegel, Romanticism, and the Re-enchantment of Nature," 4.
47. Friedrich Schelling, *Ausgewählte Schriften*, ed. Manfred Frank (Frankfurt am Main: Suhrkamp, 1985) 6: 657.

# Part III

Romanticism and the Sciences

# 16

## Romantic Biology: Carl Gustav Carus at the Edge of the Modern

Robert J. Richards

The early German Romantic Movement of the late eighteenth and early nineteenth centuries transformed the aesthetic literature of the period. The Ur-texts of the movement, especially those by Johann Wolfgang von Goethe, generated immediate enthusiasm and imitation. Not only did Goethe's *Leiden des jungen Werthers* (Sorrows of a young Werther, 1774) cause young men throughout Europe to be tempted by the hero's resolution of his hopeless love affair, the Emperor Napoleon, in his march across the Germanies, commanded Goethe's presence to discuss the novel that he had read six times—he had some suggestions for the author.[1] The poet Friedrich von Hardenberg, writing under the name Novalis, introduced a new kind of sensibility into the poetry of the period and provided an icon of the poet as doomed lover. When Coleridge returned from Germany, after visiting there with Wordsworth, he took up the philosophy of Kant and Schelling, sometimes verbatim, in his contributions to *Biographia Literaria* (1817), a founding text of English Romanticism.[2] That a literary-philosophical movement should have an impact within the confines of its own provenance raised little protest among the critics. But the Movement's influence on science seems to have breached boundaries that were slowly being erected during the middle of the nineteenth century.

R. J. Richards (✉)
University of Chicago, Chicago, IL, USA
e-mail: r-richards@uchicago.edu

Goethe, of course, had credentials as a naturalist. His work in botany and in the area of his newly defined science of morphology was admired from the beginning. By contrast, his studies of optics, developed in strong opposition to Newton's theories, were thought to have foundered on the shoals of his poetry.[3] Schelling kept up with the latest literature in the medical areas of anatomy and physiology but cast that knowledge into the framework of idealism, which caused even friendly critics to dismiss his proposals. Those scientists who yet took up the challenge of Schelling's philosophy, such as Lorenz Oken and Carl Gustav Carus, have been cast together as introducing the higher absurdities into the discipline of biology. In his monumental history, *The Growth of Biological Thought*, Ernst Mayr, one of the forgers of the modern synthesis of evolutionary biology and genetics, dismissed romantic biology with the swat of a sentence: "Oken, Schelling and Carus [were] authors whose fantasies the experts could only ridicule and whose silly constructions the modern reader can only read with embarrassment."[4]

Had Mayr not waded through the backwash of German Romanticism in the early twentieth century, when he became a biologist of disenchanted positivism, he might have given more effort to cut through the lush language of the romantics to recover the empirical bones of their body of doctrines. I would like to offer Carus as a test case, a case that challenges Mayr's assessment in two ways: first, a straightforward analysis of Carus's accomplishment reveals, I believe, a meticulous anatomist and a biologist of enormous depth; second, a historical analysis of the consequence of Carus's proposals will indicate how his ideas have slipped into the main stream of biology in the nineteenth century and have become foundational for Darwin's theory of evolution. Carus provides a particularly instructive test case, since he acknowledged as his mentors, Goethe, Schelling, and Oken. The latter two were the very individuals disdained by Mayr. Moreover, Carus made vivid in his accomplishments the romantic mandate of Friedrich Schlegel: "All art should become science and all science art; poetry and philosophy should be made one."[5] Carus's talent in anatomy, his sharp methodological acumen, brought him right up to the edge of the modern and his ideas became foundational in the modern project of evolutionary thought. But he remained on the other side of that boundary. Why?

# 1 Carus's Education Under the Cloud of Napoleonic War

Carl Gustav Carus was born in Leipzig on January 3, 1789, to August Gottlob Carus (1763–1842) and Christiane Elisabeth Carus (née Jäger, 1763–1816). His father ran a successful wool-dyeing business, and his mother's side of the family boasted of several physicians, philosophers, and naturalists. As a boy at the Thomasschule, he was provided instruction in Greek, Latin, and little else—no mathematics or physical science. He did show a talent for drawing and received lessons in sketching and painting. When Carus enrolled at Leipzig University (1804), his father hoped he would concentrate on chemistry since that would be useful in the wool-dyeing business. But chemistry, for which he had some inclination as a young boy, became tedious and dull when the teenager encountered it at the university. He did show more curiosity about physics, but the course was taught by "an old barely alive man [*ein alter fast abgelebter Mann*]." His own reading propelled an interest in anatomy, which caused a new trajectory: Carus, at age 16 (1806), decided to enter medical school.[6]

Carus's time studying medicine occurred during the early battles (spring through early fall of 1806) of Napoleon's conquest of the Germanies. The Emperor's Grande Armée occupied the Thuringian cities of Leipzig, Dresden, Jena, and Weimar. After the Third Corps of the Grande Armée marched into Berlin, the Prussian and Saxon forces signed an uneasy truce with the French, and a troubled peace quickly settled on the German lands. Carus threw himself into his medical studies, especially into "the secrets of the human structure, and generally that of animals, all of which pulled me along with strong cords."[7] Carus pursued anatomy under the tutelage of Johann Christian Rosenmüller (1771–1820) and two young professors, Karl Friedrich Burdach (1776–1847) and Johann Christian Heinroth (1773–1843), both of whom Carus greatly admired. Yet, he felt his knowledge of the human and animal bodies was fragmented and somewhat incoherent. He longed for the kind of unifying principles that would render his study a real science, a *Wissenschaft*. He said he found the desire realized in the *Naturphilosophie* of Friedrich Joseph Schelling (1775–1854) and the developmental principles of Lorenz Oken (1779–1851):

> No longer would I represent nature and the animal world as an accidental, infinitely varying, unintelligible mass, something that always left me with an awful feeling; rather, I had discovered the conceptual key to this variability. I needed no longer only to love the body of creation; I now recognized its soul and that renewed my spirit.[8]

Schelling's hypothesis of the *Weltseele*, the world-soul, implied that all of nature was bound together as a living balance of forces.[9] Oken, whom Carus regarded as one of the "new priests of nature," introduced a distinctive principle of life, "the principle of development [*Princip der Entwickelung*]."[10] Comparative study of human development revealed to Oken that from the earliest embryonic formations up through those of the young child, the individual passed through morphological stages parallel to the development of lower species, from the simplest infusoria up through invertebrates to mammals. When Oken spoke about species development, however, he was not referring to a real evolution of species, say in the sense of Lamarck or Erasmus Darwin, but of ideal relationships in a hierarchy of morphological forms. This developmental idea, though, would later be reformulated as the principle that ontogeny recapitulated phylogeny and would become associated chiefly with the evolutionist Ernst Haeckel (1834–1919).[11] For Carus, the principle of development would become central to his later demonstration of the vertebral theory of the skull, formulated initially by Goethe, and to the construction of archetype theory, which became the channel by which Carus's ideas would flow into the larger stream of evolutionary thought. More generally, however, the principle of development implied, at least for Carus, that one had to understand both nature and human consciousness in historical terms. Carus's own mental development proved to him the power of the recapitulation hypothesis: he continually traced back conceptions of his mature self to the notions of his younger self.

While engaged with the medical curriculum, Carus still found time to pursue his life as an artist. For about a year, he attended drawing classes at the Leipzig Art Academy, where his teachers, Johann Friedrich Tischbein (1750–1812) and Veit Hanns Schnorr (1764–1841), thought he showed real ability.[12] A few years later, in 1816, that talent was formally recognized in an exhibition at the Art Academy in Dresden, where four of his paintings were displayed.

Carus began clinical training in 1809 at the Leipzig Maternity Clinic under the expert eye of Johann Gottfried Jörg (1779–1856), an innovative obstetrician. The young student—he was just 20 years old—thought treating the "tender sex" quite congenial to his temperament. The experience allowed him to appreciate in the female "more profoundly all of her distinctive features."[13] He would later become director of the maternity department at the Dresden Institute for Medicine and Surgery. In his many travels, especially to Italy, his artist's eye would continue to appreciate the distinctive features of the female form.

In the *annus mirabilis* of 1811, Carus received a liberal arts master's and a PhD; he also habilitated with a dissertation on the general doctrine of life. At the end of this year of unremitting effort, he was awarded a medical degree. These scholastic accomplishments brought him an appointment as assistant to Professor Jörg in the new Triersches Maternity Hospital in Leipzig. And during this headlong dash over one academic hurdle after another, Carus married a distant relative, Christiane Caroline Carus (1784–1858). The wedding, in 1811, the same year Carus received his several degrees, was likely precipitated by the birth of their daughter, Sophie Charlotte (1810–1838), who anticipated her parents' wedding by six months. They became a devoted couple, eventually producing 12 children, 7 of whom made it out of infancy.

## 2 Teaching and Research at Leipzig

Carus's habilitation allowed him to lecture in comparative anatomy at Leipzig, which he began in 1812. While working in the maternity hospital and in the clinic for the poor, he became convinced that his real vocation lay not in medical practice but in research.[14] So while lecturing on comparative anatomy, he worked to complete a research monograph, his *Versuch einer Darstellung des Nervensystems und insbesondere des Gehirns nach ihrer Bedeutung, Entwicklung und Vollendung im thierischen Organismus* (Essay on a representation of the nervous system, particularly the brain, in light of its significance, development, and mature state in the animal organism, 1814). That work would set the norm for his subsequent publications and would quickly establish his reputation.

Carus's study of the nervous system required many hours at the bench dissecting the fetal and adult brains of a variety of animals—fish, amphibians, birds, mammals, and humans—and many hours drawing the illustrations and overseeing the production of the copperplates used in the printing of the images. The goal of this empirical work was to lay out the developmental sequences in the formation of the brain within the different classes of vertebrates and to compare these sequences of structure across classes, with the ultimate aim of formulating "the idea of the archetype [*Urtypus*] of the central organ of sensibility," that is, a model of structures common to all the vertebrates.[15] But in this early monograph, Carus never quite achieved the goal of an archetype of brain structure—or skeletal structure—that united representations across the different classes of animals, though he continued the pursuit until he finally did, arguably, meet with success in the magnificent work of 1828, his *Von den Ur-Theilen des Knochen-und Schalengerüstes* (On the primitive parts of the bones and skeletal framework).[16] The notion of an archetype is mentioned in these early years as a goal, one which he pursued with ever greater avidity as he learned more about Goethe's morphological views and those of Goethe's rival, Lorenz Oken.

Carus introduced the empirical work described in his *Versuch einer Darstellung* by a set of philosophical considerations of a type that would be in constant development throughout his life. He worried about the metaphysical context of the mind-body relationship. From empirical appearances alone, he could not decide between the two poles of possibility—idealism and realism. His pragmatic recourse initially was simply to work out the regular relationships governing the appearances and express those relationships as natural laws—in Kant's terms, to turn a *Naturlehre* (doctrine of nature) into a *Naturwissenschaft* (natural science).[17]

In his comparative study, Carus eventually drew a deeper metaphysical conclusion, one expressive of his ideal of unity. He argued that the nervous system and the soul formed, not two independent entities but rather a single substance having two aspects: "in the nervous system we detect the spatial representation of the soul and, simultaneously, in the soul, the temporal appearance of the life of the nervous system."[18] Though the different faculties of the soul had their locations in the nervous system, those faculties were dynamically related to one another such that in perception and thought, for example, the various faculties operated sympathetically together and their corresponding brain areas were connected through networks of nerves. This conception of the interaction of various facultative brain-sites formed the basis for Carus's long-time objection to Gall's phrenology, which located particular mental activities in specific brain locations, with no concern for the interaction of those areas.

The details of Carus's comparative study confirmed the general outlines of Oken's hypothesis of recapitulation. The hypothesis held that the relationships governing the vast number of different animal species revealed a progressive developmental history of the animal organism, from the simplest infusoria to the higher animals and ultimately to human beings, and that a comparable sequence could be found in the development of the human fetus, which "repeated the different developmental stages of the animal world."[19] Carus, though, insisted that the stages of human fetal development demonstrated only general morphological similarities to the developmental history of lower animals. This parallel would nonetheless allow, say, the physician to recognize that an unfortunate infant whose brain had only achieved structures characteristic of a given species of lower animal would likely have a comparably diminished psychic ability.[20] Carus had these relationships of developmental deficiency sadly confirmed by the pathologies he attended in his Maternity Institute. He would later escalate these developmental conclusions into a study of skulls, which would provide an index of different mental traits within the human races and between the races. The metric, however, would not be a quantitative measure but an aesthetic one.[21]

## 3 A Physician During the Battle of Nations

In the midst of an auspicious start to a productive career, Napoleon intervened in Carus's life, as well in the lives of countless others.[22] In June 1812, the Emperor's Grande Armée of half a million men crossed the Russian border and marched toward Moscow. When they finally entered Moscow in early September, after following the despoiled trail left by the retreating Russian forces, they found an abandoned and burning city. In early November, unable to conduct a decisive battle with the Russians, Napoleon began pulling his forces back south. The retreating French army was besieged along the way by raiding parties of Cossacks, devastating hunger, and the onset of the Russian winter. Of the over 650,000 troops that had advanced into Russia, only about 25,000 made it safely back. Napoleon quickly returned to Paris to raise a second *Grande Armée* lest the German lands slip from his grasp. In March 1813, the Prussians formed a coalition with Great Britain, Sweden, and Russia to defend against the second coming of Napoleon. At the beginning of May, the opposing forces clashed initially outside of Leipzig, the onset of what came to be known as "the Battle of Nations." Of the 160,000 men engaged in the ferocious struggle, some 30,000 fell dead, or were wounded. Carus organized a group of young physicians to care for the injured and sick and in June took command of a French military hospital, a former dairy barn reconstructed with makeshift wards in the stalls and an area for surgery. His experience in tending to the dying brought him a sobering recognition:

> I understood for the first time … how little a human life seemed to count in the ledger books of the world. A rich country was drained of the blood of its young men. Thousands of families must send off what had been cultivated for long years with love and care and full of hope—so that they would be tossed aside without a thought. … Whole generations were cut down by the merciless angel of destruction and there was no one there who seemed to have noticed … Certainly, it is not possible to have attained the elevated concept of the wonderful structure of man and of the value of the character of the human spirit and not feel a deep shudder when one—it cannot be expressed otherwise—becomes aware of the contempt had for humanity in its masses.[23]

In late August, a French battalion shocked the allies outside of Dresden with a decisive defeat of the latter's much larger force. Though suffering heavy losses, the allies began winning smaller battles against scattered French contingents occupying different parts of the central Germanies. At Leipzig, on October 16, an opening salvo ignited the largest battle Europe would experience before the First World War. The slaughter turned against the French. During the night of the 18th, Napoleon began a retreat from the city. He fled back to Paris and within a year was forced into exile on the island of Elba. In his wake, hundreds of thousands of corpses washed up on the island of the dead. The Battle of Leipzig alone contributed flotsam of about 100,000 men dead or wounded on both sides. Carus himself almost died from typhus, which spread rapidly through the remaining wounded and those attending them.

## 4 Move to Dresden: Anatomy and Gynecology

Given the vast destruction of the Napoleonic campaigns, the rapid return to semi-normal life is quite surprising. By the new year of 1814, Carus felt strong enough to begin work again on his manuscript describing the science of the brain and nervous system, and to find a few moments to take his sketch pads into the Rosenthal, the woods around Leipzig. In mid-summer, he was called to a professorship in obstetrics at Dresden in the newly reorganized Academy for Surgery and Medicine; the offer included the directorship of the Maternity Institute, a very modest salary, but free housing.[24] What he did not appreciate at the time was the kind of rebuilding necessary after the destruction of Dresden; initially, his maternity clinic would be conducted in an armory left over from the war. Yet, recognizing the opportunity, he quickly accepted the offer.

On December 1, 1814, the Carus family welcomed its youngest member and thereby brought the brood of children to three, and simultaneously the father began his duties as director of the maternity clinic, physician in the maternity wards, and lecturer on gynecology to medical students. The crush of work was eased, as he explained to his friend Johann Gottlob Regis (1791–1854), by the natural environment of Dresden, which allowed him to accomplish some of his best artistic work.[25]

He described to his friend the kind of scene that stimulated both his painterly eye and his scientific mind. As he came home one evening from a walk at dusk, he gazed on the Elba river, flecked with small white islands of ice and hidden at either end by a gray, lingering mist and flowing under a distant bridge:

> I was completely engaged in watching how out of the fog the ice flow came closer, with its own rushing monotone sound, and finally disappeared behind the dark band of the bridge. For me it was as if I had observed the current of time and had seen uncountable numbers of species come out their dark source, be swept along, and disappear. I thought about this a lot.[26]

It was after such evening walks, when he returned home, that he began keeping notes of the impressions made on him by the various scenes in and around the city. These notes would become sources for his *Neun Briefe über Landsaftsmalerei* (Nine letters on landscape painting, discussed below).[27]

As his lecturing on gynecology continued apace in spring of 1815, he conceived of writing two student handbooks, one on comparative anatomy and the other on gynecology. The former would rely on his Leipzig lectures, with the aim of representing the differences in animal structure from the perspective of a "higher unity." The latter would be constructed out of his then-current lecture course to medical students and would have the purpose of leading students "into the mysterious nature of women, both in health and in sickness."[28] In remarkably short order, he brought both plans to fruition with his two-volume *Lehrbuch der vergleichenden Zootomie* (Handbook of comparative animal structures) in 1818 and his two-volume *Lehrbuch der Gynäkologie* (Handbook of gynecology) in 1820.[29]

Though treatises touching on female anatomy, physiology, pregnancy, and diseases date from the ancient period, Carus's *Lehrbuch der Gynäkologie* was the first systematic study of what would become a medical specialty, uniting both obstetrics and the particular functions and diseases of women's reproductive organs, both under the rubric of his newly coined term "gynecology [Gynäkologie]." His treatise gained its authority not only from his anatomical prowess but from his clinical work in the delivery ward of his institute, where, from the beginning of his directorship until the publication of his *Lehrbuch*, some 1293 pregnant women were treated, many with very complicated conditions—for instance, various kinds of breach births, closed cervixes, malformed neonates, and conjoined twins.[30]

In his *Lehrbuch der Zootomie*, the other student manual produced at this time, Carus (Fig. 16.1) distinguished the vegetative sphere of animal life from the sphere of animal life per se. The former domain comprised respiration, nutrition, secretion, and reproduction, all functions that animals shared with plants. Animals and plants also shared a comparable compositional element:

**Fig. 16.1** Carl Gustav Carus (1789–1869), at about age 35; portrait (1824) by Carl Rössler

plants exhibited cells, from which their larger structures were formed; and animals exhibited "globules [*Kügelchen*] swimming in a slimy fluid," serving the same basic function as cells in plants. (The assumption of "globules" instead of cells was undoubtedly an artifact of the low resolving power of Carus's microscope.[31]) Carus divided the animal sphere proper into the sensory system, the motor system, and the general nervous system. Instead of beginning with the simplest animals and describing each of their systems and then moving to the next highest creature, he consider it less confusing to provide a coherent description of each division of the vegetative and then the animal systems in their respective progressive development through the series of animals up to man. This allowed him more easily to follow Oken's principle that in a given system the higher stages would incorporate the lower.[32] So, for instance, he compared the brain of fish to that of man: "the brain of fish appears little more than a series of pairs of ganglia on the upper side of the medullary stem; it strikes one that these brain masses—since each is *behind* the other, not one *under* the other—are as far from the spherical structure of the well-formed human brain, as they are near in their structure to the brain of the very early human embryo."[33] Neither the *Zootomie* nor *Gynäkologie* engaged in the kind of philosophical considerations characteristic of his earlier work in comparative anatomy. Undoubtedly, his students were grateful.

## 5  Friendship with Caspar David Friedrich and Johann Wolfgang von Goethe

Sometime in 1816, Carus met Caspar David Friedrich (1774–1840). Friedrich's reputation as a landscape painter—and as a troubled individual—was already well-recognized. As their friendship solidified, the two would often go on long rambles into the surrounding countryside with sketch pads, chalks, and pencils. Carus thought his friend had a profound impact on his own practice and on his painterly sensibilities, especially in matters of imaginative expression. Friedrich offered Carus many suggestions on how to achieve certain effects in his paintings, especially in representing light. The impact of Friedrich's tutelage is easily detected from a comparison of their works (e.g., see Fig. 16.2). Carus thought his friend's practical suggestions and nomic expressions could be made more clear and could become the basis for a "future science of art."[34] He pursued this possibility in a series of essays, began just after meeting Friedrich, that were later published under the title *Neun Briefe*

**Fig. 16.2**  (a) Caspar David Friedrich, *Mondaufgang am Meer* (1822). (b) Carl Gustav Carus, *Blick auf Dresden bei Sonnenuntergang* (1822)

**Fig. 16.2** (continued)

*über Landschaftsmalerei, geschrieben in den Jahren 1815–1824* (Nine letters on landscape painting, written during the years 1815–1824).[35]

Carus had two aims in the composition of his essays: to elevate landscape painting in the estimation of painters and the public and to show that significant landscape painting must depend on scientific knowledge of the natural environment. In this latter effort, Carus depended on insights from Goethe and Alexander von Humboldt. Carus, like Goethe, predicated of the artistic genius the "freely creative productive and reproductive power" that imitated "the eternally creative power of the cosmos."[36] And like Goethe, Carus maintained that art and science were interdependent ways of coming to terms with nature: science required an artistic sense of ordering of ideas and words, and art required scientific awareness. Both modes expressed the kind of divine, creative power that genius is able to recruit, the same power by which nature produces her creatures.

Carus contended, in letter three of the *Neun Briefe*, that the principal task of landscape painting was "to represent a certain mood [*Stimmung*] of psychic life [*Gemüthlebens*] through the replication of a corresponding mood in the life of nature [*Naturlebens*], the first producing *meaning*, the second *truth*."[37] In short, the landscape painter seeks to represent in a *true* depiction of a natural scene the mood (the aesthetic *meaning*) induced in his or her soul by the scene, with the intention of reproducing that mood in the soul of the viewer. Carus thus defined the "objective correlative" long before T.S. Eliot identified the principle in 1919.[38]

The life of nature, in Carus's account, displays a kind of general physiognomy in which the various plants and animals, climate and geography, form a morphological whole, which the landscape painter attempts to capture. Alexander von Humboldt, in his *Ansichten der Natur* (*Views of Nature*, 1808), described a similar physiognomy of various regions, the complex morphology of a locale:

> What the painter describes as Swiss nature or Italian sky is based on the vague feeling of these local, natural characters [*Naturcharacters*]—the blue of the sky, the lighting, the haze gathering in the distance, the forms of animals, the succulent grasses, the sheen on the leaves, the outline of the mountain; all these elements determine the total impression of a region.[39]

Carus went further than Humboldt, however. Like Goethe, he argued that the landscape painter had to comprehend not only the laws governing relationships of external forms—climate, mountains, lakes, plants, and animals—the artist had to be aware of the inner structure of these elements and their development over time. Moreover, the artist had also to understand "the laws of vision, the different refractions and reflections of light, and the source of colors."[40] In short, to depict the morphology of a scene, the artist, like a scientist, had to understand the anatomy and physiology of the dynamic systems of nature, as well as how her features might strike the observer.

Carus would later, in 1821, send Goethe a few of the early letters on landscape painting. By that time, however, he had already made contact by sending the master a copy of his *Lehrbuch der Zootomie*. After spending a few hours with the book, Goethe immediately wrote back that "I already see, on every page and in every plate, my hopes realized. What others proposed, knowledgeably, but scattered in thousands of essays and articles, you have synthesized and in your own way have newly brought to completion."[41] In return, Goethe sent Carus his own gift, the first number (1817) of his series *Zur Morphologie* (1817–1824). And so was initiated a correspondence and frequent exchange of books and articles, as well as gifts of some of Carus's paintings and illustrations, that lasted till Goethe's death in 1832 (Fig. 16.3).

Carus had been planning a trip to Italy for some time, with an ultimate destination of Genoa. He hoped to visit several art galleries and collections of paintings along the way. At Genoa, he believed he might explore the riches of sea-life to be found around that port-city. The beginning of his journey in July 1821 gave him opportunity to stop in Weimar and meet Goethe for the first time.

**Fig. 16.3** Johann Wolfgang von Goethe (1749–1832). (Portrait [1828] by Joseph Karl Stieler)

He arrived on July 21 at 11:00 o'clock that morning at Goethe's house *am Frauenplan*. As he recalled, he sat nervously waiting in the parlor of the large house, surrounded by classical statuary lining the walls. "Finally, a lively step through the adjoining room announced the esteemed man himself. He was outfitted in a simple blue frockcoat, boots, and displaying short, lightly powdered hair and the well-known, deeply lined face from smoking. With a strong bearing, he stepped up to me and led me to the sofa. His seventy-two years have made little impression on him." Carus began describing to the older man the new research he was conducting on the vertebrate skeleton, which would confirm for Goethe "his earlier supposition that the head consisted of six vertebrae." When Carus sketched for him the structures constituting the skull of a fish, "he interrupted me with an approving exclamation and joyful nods of the head: 'Yes, yes, the matter is in good hands.'"[42]

## 6 Carus's Demonstration of Goethe's Vertebral Theory of the Skull

Goethe's vertebral theory of the skull arose, paradoxically, out of his study of plants. In his *Versuch die Metamorphose der Pflanzen zu erklären* (*Essay to explain the metamorphosis of plants*, 1790), Goethe had argued, based on careful observations of plant development, that one feature of a plant could be transformed into another, the stem-leaves into the calix, the calix into the petals, and petals into the stamens and pistil, and so on. He assumed that an underlying structure, which he called the *ideal leaf*, could be transformed, through forces of contraction and expansion, into all the parts of the plant. He extended this developmental conception to animals. As Goethe told the story, during a trip to Venice in 1790, he and his amanuensis Paul Götze were walking along the Lido, near a Jewish cemetery, when Götze suddenly tossed him a broken sheep's skull. Goethe later recalled that when he had examined the skull it struck him that the plates forming the skull "had arisen from transformed vertebrae," much as the plant consisted of transformations of the ideal leaf.[43] The play with the sheep's skull would be used by Goethe as evidence in his priority dispute with Lorenz Oken about who first formulated the theory that the vertebrate skull consisted of transformed vertebrae.[44] Now Carus was ready to enter the discussion, not to take sides, but to provide graphic evidence for the theory.

A few months after Carus returned from Italy, he sent Goethe two prints from the copperplates of the book on the vertebrate skeleton that he was still working on. Goethe had hoped that Carus would expeditiously finish his work on the volume. The research and writing took a much longer time than Carus had estimated. Seven years later, on March 21, 1828, Carus sent Goethe a copy of his great, folio-sized *Von den Ur-Theilen des Knochen-und Schalengerüstes* (*On the primitive parts of the bones and the skeletal framework*).[45]

In the *Ur-Theilen*, Carus credited Goethe with bringing to clarity what had been a vague presentiment of many previous naturalists, namely, "the idea of a metamorphosis of the bony structure [of the vertebrate skull], that is, awareness that the different particular structures are more or less modifications of one and the same original formation [*Ur-Gestaltung*]."[46] Carus affirmed that Goethe had initially expressed this principle of the archetype in his essay on comparative osteology (1796) and then applied it to his earlier discovery of the vertebral composition of the skull.

Carus had to perform a diverting *pas de deux* with each of his two partners, Goethe and Oken. He accepted Goethe's assertion that he had made the discovery during his trip to Italy in 1790 and that he only revealed it to the public in his *Zur Morphologie* in 1819, 30 years later. So, Goethe had the clear priority. But Carus allowed that Oken made the first public announcement of the theory in his pamphlet *Über die Bedeutung des Schälknochen* in 1807.[47] Despite this Solomonic resolution, Oken was not happy. In responding to a presentation copy of Carus's *Ur-theilen*, Oken protested:

> I don't know why you are so ready to ascribe the discovery of the vertebra [theory of the skull] to him [Goethe]. If this idea were so brilliant, why had he kept quiet while some have ridiculed and laughed at my tract 'Meaning of the Skull'? After this doctrine suddenly gained approval with you, Meckel, Bojans, and others and after I had thoroughly developed the idea, he lusts after this doctrine. Thus, ten years after the appearance of my tract he finds the idea acceptable and finds it acceptable to act as if this idea were his.[48]

After the publication of Oken's pamphlet, many French and German anatomists did begin to recognize the general principle of the archetype and its specific application in understanding the development of the vertebrate skeleton. But what was missing in the previous discussions was a systematic approach to the theory and, even more importantly, an empirical justification. Carus designed his volume to provide the observational evidence for the theory.[49]

Every organic individual, Carus declared in the *Ur-Theilen*, forms a unity governing its parts, and each individual, in its turn, can be regarded as a part of its type. All individuals form the ideal whole: the whole of the realm of plants is the Ur-plant; the whole of the realm of animals is the Ur-animal. The main feature of plant life is generation [*Zeugung*]: the generation of the individual through assimilation and growth and the generation of the species [*Gattung*] through reproduction of similar individuals.[50] Animals exhibit through their nervous systems an inner unity, which allows awareness [*Wahrnehmung*] of the relationship of their parts and through sensibility a relationship to an external world. In the case of the most perfect animal—man—self-determination further requires reason and freedom. Carus thus understood human beings as a continuation and perfection—"the most perfect inner unity"—of the animal state,[51] and with that observation, perhaps also an invitation to the theory of evolution.

Carus's division of the animal realm followed conventional distinctions but designated them by unconventional names: the sphere of egg-like animals (protozoa and radiolarians), the sphere of corporal animals (having two divisions—mollusca and articulata), the sphere of cephalic animals (having four divisions—fish, amphibians, birds, mammals), and, as a separate sphere, human beings. Carus regarded the external structures of individual members of these various animal spheres as developed out of a common Ur-part, comparable to the ideal leaf in plants as Goethe conceived it. He named this common part the "vertebra [*Wirbel*]," though recognizing that only the cephalic animals exhibited proper vertebrae. The term functioned symbolically to refer to that fundamental body part that was transformed into the several structures of an organism; the term semantically distilled Carus's doctrine of the archetype much in the way that the "leaf" captured Goethe's comparable doctrine. The most powerful support for this conception was the empirical demonstration of the vertebral theory of the vertebrate skull. Carus's doctrine of the archetype and the vertebral theory of the skull have survived in Richard Owen's conception of homology and in Charles Darwin's argument for the unity of type; both naturalists cite Carus, though without really giving him his due.

Carus examined the skulls and skeletons of several classes of animals: jawless fish, teleost fish, sharks, tortoises, snakes, several birds (eagle, chicken), mammals (dogs), and humans (Fig. 16.4). In considering the skulls of each class of animal, he focused on the three boney plates forming the braincase and the three major plates forming the face. He showed in sequential illustrations how these six plates gradually changed as they passed from the jawless fish, where the distinction between the anterior spinal column and the skull hardly existed, through intermediate skulls, to the plates forming the braincase and face of the most advanced creature, man.[52] He also furnished an illustration of "the simplest schema," or archetype, of the skeleton of a cephalic animal, which consisted of a vertebral column and rib-like processes off the vertebrae (see Fig. 16.4, top). In scanning Carus's illustrations, a reader might well imagine the gradual transformational processes by which anterior vertebrae became incrementally restructured in passing through the series of lower skulls up to that of the human. The idea that all members of the vertebrate phylum realized a basic plan became known as archetype theory and served to help convince Darwin of the transmutation of species. But were these transformations as illustrated by Carus only ideal, or did he have in mind historical transformations of the kind Lamarck, Erasmus Darwin, or Charles Darwin proposed? This issue put Carus right at the edge of the modern age. I will explore the question in the next section of this chapter.

Carus sent Goethe a copy of his book, and the great man responded in wonder that the young doctor "had brought forth into the light of day from

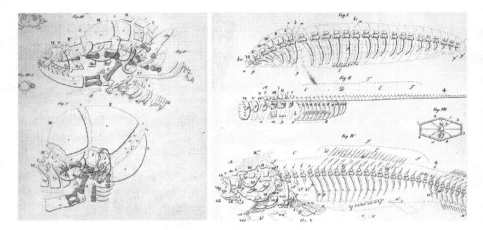

Fig. 16.4 (a and b) The lower plate illustrates a human skull (lower image) and skull of a dog, with six skull bones marked in Roman numerals; the upper plate illustrates a teleost fish, a Jawless fish (fig. 2), a vertebra (fig. 3), and the "simplest schema" (fig. 1), or the archetype, all with the six anterior skull bones identified. Other plates trace the six skull bones in many other animals. From Carus's Von den Ur-Theilen des Knochen- und Schalengerütes (1828)

the simplest form an infinite manifold of forms in their connections." It was, the poet thought, "a great and unbelievable accomplishment."[53] A few days after receiving Goethe's letter, one came from Alexander von Humboldt: "Five days ago, I obtained, through the kindness of councilor Schulze, your wonderful book on the structure of the bones, and for five days I have been continuously busy with it. It has been a long time since anything has moved me as much as has your magnificent view of nature."[54]

## 7 Carus and Evolutionary Theory

Carus's developmental analyses in his several books and especially in his *Von den Ur-Theilen* balance precariously on the edge of modern evolutionary theory. But did he jump over into that theory? He considered the question of transformational development ten years later in his *System der Physiologie*. By 1838, the Lamarckian hypothesis had become well known and was essentially endorsed by several German naturalists, such as Gottfried Treviranus (1776–1837) and Friedrich Tiedemann (1781–1861). Carus, however, expressed reservations: "strictly speaking, we know nothing of the origin of mankind."[55] He recognized that the geological work of such naturalists as

Georges Cuvier (1869–1832), Alexandre Brongniart (1770–1747), and William Buckland (1784–1856) indicated a period of earth's history when only plants covered the earth and a subsequent period when no-longer-existing animals—such as giant lizards, megatheriums, and mastodons—populated the land. Only in the last period of earth's history did human beings appear, likely in the highlands of Asia, and thereafter they spread over the earth. Still, "a mysterious darkness envelops the earliest evolution of humanity [*Entwickelung der Menschheit*]."[56] Despite the darkness, Carus urged that the real evolution of humankind was mental and cultural, and that the most important ability was speech, which unfolded into ideas and then into science and art. The best evidence of this kind of gradual mental evolution was provided by the varieties of mankind. Just as the individual went through periods of development, from infancy through adolescence to adulthood, so the various groups of humans displayed a comparable evolution, from the fetal stage of the Papuans to the adult stage of the Europeans. The Europeans demonstrated the greatest variability of talents, with certain individuals (e.g., Kant, Goethe) showing the immense potential of humanity.[57] In his later years, even after the publication of Darwin's *Origin of Species*, the darkness surrounding the origins of human beings did not lift for Carus.

## 8  The Transformation of Carus's Ideas in Owen and Darwin

Travel over long distances in the early nineteenth century was arduous. Even within the confines of Europe, one had to plan in advance to arrange coaches and ships (to use waterways as more efficient ways of travel). Carus yet undertook several major journeys within a 25-year span. In July and August 1821, after visiting Goethe in Weimar, he travelled on to Switzerland and down through the northern part of Italy to Genoa, where he collected sea-animals for his research. In August to October 1835, he journeyed through the Rhineland to Paris, where he met Alexander von Humboldt and Fredric Cuvier, among other illustrious naturalists. After he became personal physician to the kings of Saxony,[58] he travelled on two extensive tours as part of the royal retinue to Switzerland and Italy (April to August 1828) and to England and Scotland (May to August 1844). During these excursions, he tried to view major art collections and significant churches in Paris and London, and in the Italian cities of Florence, Rome, and Naples, while also visiting scientific institutions and meeting prominent naturalists. In London, he met three times with Richard Owen, twice in the Hunterian Museum, which Owen directed, and once seated next to him at a dinner in honor of the King of Saxony.[59] As a result of these meetings, Owen also came to know Carus's *Von den Ur-Theilein* quite well. His copy is still held in his *Nachlass* at the Kensington Natural History Museum, along with his notes on the book. Carus's argument and illustrations were appropriated by Owen in two books that developed the idea of homology, his *On the Archetype* (1848) and *On the Nature of Limbs* (1849).[60]

In his *On the Archetype and the Homologies of the Vertebrate Skeleton*, Owen maintained that the researcher had to pierce through the variability of organisms to their underlying nature so that the "same" bones in different vertebrate species might be called by the same names. This effort required that comparisons be made across different vertebrate species. Thus, he proposed, in the *Nature of Limbs*, that the bones in the claw of the mole, the pectoral fin of the dugong, and the wing of the bat displayed homologously similar bones, though they were only analogously similar to the structures in the "arm" of the crab.[61] Owen thus introduced the concept of homology riding on the back of Carus's theory of the archetype. In both of Owen's books, not only were the same comparative methods employed as in Carus's *Von den Ur-Theilein*, but virtually the same illustrations were taken over by Owen from Carus's volume. The evidence is the illustration of the archetype itself, as represented by both Carus and Owen (see Fig. 16.5).

Darwin thought the discipline of morphology "the most interesting department of natural history, and may be said to be its very soul."[62] That feature of morphology he had particularly in mind was archetypal relationships, as specified in Owen's concept of homology: "What can be more curious," he asked, "than that the hand of a man, formed for grasping, that of a mole for digging, the leg of the horse, the paddle of the porpoise, and the wing of the bat, should all be constructed on the same pattern, and should include the same bones, in the same relative positions?" This curious relationship became clear, he maintained, if "we suppose that the ancient progenitor, the archetype as it may be called, of all mammals, had its limbs constructed on the existing general pattern."[63] Darwin, thus, maintained that the morphological relationships were explained realistically if we suppose that the archetype was not merely an ideal plan, as Owen and Carus originally believed, but that it was the ancestor of the vertebrate phylum, that even human beings were transformations of the archetypal ancestor.

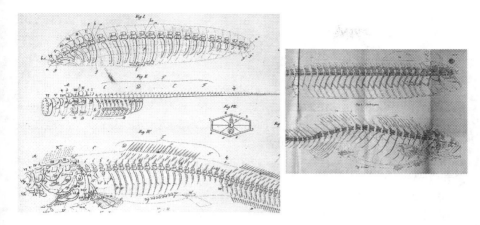

**Fig. 16.5** On the left, Carus's image of the archetype and two fish, from his *Von den Ur-Theilen und den Knochen-und Schalengerüstes* (1828); on the right, Owen's image of the archetype (top) and a fish, from his *On the Archetype and the Homologies of the Vertebrate Skeleton* (1848)

## 9 Conclusion: Romanticism and Evolutionary Theory

Carus was quite aware of Darwin's proposal, as well as the similar earlier views of Erasmus Darwin and Lamarck. His theory of the archetype crossed the border into the modern age via an appropriation by Richard Owen. Moreover, his thesis of recapitulation—that the embryo goes through the same morphological stages as the phylum—became a pillar of Darwin's (and Haeckel's) evolutionary theory. Carus was poised on the very edge of the modern, but what held him to the other side of that border? His own developmental conceptions would have made it easy to have crossed into that area he regarded as mysterious—the origins of mankind. He was, despite the reservations of historians and scientists like Ernst Mayr, a consummately skilled anatomist, who perceived the deep connections of the human form to that of animals. I think the answer lies in the area that makes him such a compelling thinker and scientist: his romantic perspective.

Consider the marks of romantic biology:

1. The metaphysical assumption of most romantic naturalists was monism; matter and spirit [*Geist*] were one, though the spiritual side was usually stressed. They thus accepted the fundamental tenet of Spinoza: *Deus sive Natura*, which meant that nature herself was creative. This was Goethe's view and that of Carus. Later Ernst Haeckel would make it fundamental

to his own philosophical conception of nature, and, of course, that is the general message of natural selection.
2. Nature is the repository of values, aesthetic, and moral. Both Goethe and Carus assumed this to be the case. And this belief allowed Darwin to formulate his theory of the evolution of morality.
3. The fundamental principle of romantic biology is organicism, not mechanism. The animal body is not a machine, but organic. Though many historians have represented Darwin as having introduced mechanism into nature, a deeper penetration into his accomplishment would reject that judgment.[64]
4. As organic, creatures are thus to be teleologically explained; that is, they exhibit parts whose existence must be understood as caused by the whole structure and its environment. Another feature of Darwin's accomplishment is his teleology, often denied by scholars. But let those scholars reckon with Darwin's notebook remark that "man is the one great object, for which the world was brought into present state."[65]
5. Certain other biological principles are often invoked—for example, archetype theory, embryological recapitulation, and hierarchy of species. These are all elements in the repertoire of romantic biologists such as Goethe, Oken, and Carus, as well as Darwin.
6. The romantic biologist maintains that the fundamental character of the organism can be conveyed not only analytically (in the cognitive domain) but also aesthetically, that is, through drawing, painting, sculpture, poetry, and so on. Both science and art are thus concerned with uncovering the same kinds of fundamental principles governing organisms. This mark of romantic biology caused Carus, I believe, to hesitate about human evolution.

Carus's fundamental objection to Darwinian notions about the evolution of human beings seems to have been largely aesthetic.[66] In the 1840s, Carus had not foreclosed the possibility of human evolution. He did wish to insist that the basic feature of human development was mental; he argued that human civilization, the evolution of the arts and sciences, was a gradual process dependent on speech and social organization.[67] This much does not obviously preclude the theory that human beings descended from lower animals; indeed, the incremental development of human civilization has been embraced by many evolutionary thinkers. But Carus was an artist, and it was an artistic—and naturalistic—principle that stayed his hand. In considering the entire morphology of the gorilla, the best model for an antecedent of the human line, Carus stood back in revulsion.

As president of the German Academy of Sciences, Carus delivered an address in 1863 entitled "Further Remarks on the Gorilla and in Opposition to Darwin's Hypothesis."[68] In the address, Carus initially sided with Owen about the osteological differences between human beings and the gorilla, despite the opposition of Thomas Henry Huxley. So, from the anatomical point of view, the relationship was not likely. But the crucial distinction that set the gorilla in a completely different class was aesthetic. In his *Nine Letters on Landscape Painting*, Carus had argued in the mode of Humboldt that the elements of a scene formed a morphological whole and exhibited a distinctive aesthetic value. Likewise, when one considered the morphological whole composition of the heads of man and ape, the differences became aesthetically obvious. In the case of gorilla, the morphological complex had a negative value:

> Partly by the general smallness and imperfect development of the brain, ... partly by the entire formation of the head, which clearly astonishes one by the small crushed ears, by the gawking, narrow eyes, by the depressed flatness of the small dome, yes also by the raw, animal mouth without a chin.[69]

In the case of cretins or microcephalic individuals, even with those pitiable distortions, the lineaments of the true human being could still be discerned, Carus maintained.[70] Even by comparison to these malformed humans, the Gorilla is "gruesomely stained [*Hässlichkeit färbt*]."[71] Carus expressed the judgment of great artists from the Greek period even to the present day; the human frame is a wonder of perfection—as so judged by human beings. The beauty of humankind simply precluded any animal origin.

## Notes

1. See Goethe account of the encounter with the Emperor, in his conversations with Eckermann: Johann Peter Eckermann, *Gespräche mit Goethe in den Letzten Jahren seines Lebens*, 3rd ed. (Berlin: Aufbau-Verlag, 1987), pp. 299–301 (April 7, 1829).
2. Richard Holmes, *Coleridge: Early Visions* (New York: Penguin Books, 1990), 232n.
3. That was the evaluation of Hermann von Helmholtz. See his "Ueber Goethes wissenschaftliche Arbeiten," in *Populäre wissenschaftliche Vorträge*, vol. 1 (Braunschweig: Friedrich Vieweg und Sohn, 1865). Helmholtz would later change his mind about Goethe optical studies.
4. Ernst Mayr, *The Growth of Biological Thought* (Cambridge, MA: Harvard University Press, 1982), 130.

5. Friedrich Schlegel, *Kritische Fragmente, 115*, in *Friedrich Schlegel: Studien Ausgabe*, ed. Ernst Behler and Hans Eichner (Paderborn: Ferdinand Schöningh, 1988), I: 249.
6. Carl Gustav Carus, *Lebenserinnerungen und Denkwürdigkeiten*, 4 vols. (Leipzig: Brockhaus, 1865–1866). I: 52.
7. Carl Gustav Carus, *Mnemosyne: Blätter aus Gedenk=und Tagebüchern* (Pforzheim: Flammer und Hoffmann, 1848), 414.
8. Carus, *Lebenserinnerungen*, I: 72.
9. In the Third Critique, Kant had supposed, for heuristic purposes, that organic structures had to be considered the result of intelligence, of mind, which explained the goal-directed activities of creatures. Schelling rejected Kant's restriction of teleology to a merely regulative status; he rather made it constitutive of the activities of organisms. Schelling's survey of contemporary naturalists—Alexander von Humboldt (1769–1859), Johann Friedrich Blumenbach, Carl Friedrich Kielmeyer (765–1844), and Johann Christian Reil (1759–1813)—confirmed the necessity of applying teleological concepts to organisms in order to understand and explain their activities. Humboldt and Kielmeyer in particular applied the concept of teleology to relations among organisms, showing the more far-reaching organic character of nature generally. Shelling deployed the ancient concept of a world-soul to express this higher unity. See Robert J. Richards, *The Romantic Conception of Life: Science and Philosophy in the Age of Goethe* (Chicago: University of Chicago Press, 2002), 137–45.
10. Carus, *Lebenserinnerungen*, I: 71.
11. For a discussion of Oken's developmental morphology, see Robert J. Richards *The Meaning of Evolution: The Morphological Construction and Ideological Reconstruction of Darwin's Theory* (Chicago: University of Chicago Press, 1992), 39–42.
12. Carus, *Lebenserinnerungen*, I: 76–78.
13. Carus, *Mnemosyne*, 440.
14. Ibid., 440.
15. Carl Gustav Carus, *Versuch einer Darstellung des Nevensystems und insbesondre des Gehirns nach ihrer Bedeutung, Entwickelung und Vollendung im thierischen Organismus* (Leipzig: Breitkopf und Härtel, 1814), 4.
16. Carl Gustav Carus, *Von den Ur-Theilen des Knochen- und Schalengerüstes* (Leipzig: Gerhard Fleischer, 1828).
17. Carus, *Versuch einer Darstellung*, 1–22.
18. Ibid., p. 299. Carus's metaphysical commitments varied throughout his life. In his autobiography (*Lebenserinnerungen*, II: 181), he expressed the relationship between the sensible and supernatural worlds somewhat differently: "The relationship of a sensible world to a supersensible (*übersinnlichen*) world had struck me once so clearly as never before: one cannot, by means of kind of sublimation, absorb the sensible into the supersensible, rather they must

remain two wholly different worlds, which move eternally in themselves and through one another; and one must have the courage to live in both simultaneously, or dispense with both."
19. Ibid., 2.
20. Ibid., 311–12.
21. See Robert J. Richards, "The Beautiful Skulls of Schiller and the Georgian Girl: The Quantitative and Aesthetic Scaling of the Races, 1770–1850," in *Johann Friedrich Blumenbach: Race and Natural History, 1750–1850*, eds. Nicolaas Rupke and Gerhard Lauer (Routledge, 2018), 142–76.
22. I have consulted several sources for the history of the Napoleonic Wars, especially Georges Lefebvre, *Napoleon*, trans. Henry Stockhold, 2 vols. (New York: Columbia University Press, 1969), II: 309–52.
23. Ibid., 122.
24. Ibid., 143. The Academy was reestablished by the Russian governor of the region, Prince Nikolai Repnin Wolonski (1778–1845). The regency was agreed to by the coalition since the Saxons had been allied with the French after the Battle of Jena in 1806. The Prince also reorganized the Dresden Academy of Fine Arts.
25. Carus to Regis (November 20–26, 1814), MS Briefe 3, 1; Dresden University Archive, transcribed by Marianne. Prause.
26. Carus to Regis (November 20–26, 1814), MS Briefe 3, 2.
27. Carl Gustav Carus, *Neun Briefe über Landsaftsmalerie, geschrieben in den Jahren 1815–1824* (Leipzig: Gerhard Fleischer, 1831).
28. Carus, *Lebenserinnerung*, I: 159.
29. Carl Gustav Carus, *Lehrbuch der Zootomiel, mit stäter Hinsicht auf Physiologie aus gearbeitet, und durch zwanzig Kupertafeln erlätert* (Leipzig: Gerhard Fleischer, 1818); and *Lehrbuch der Gynäkologie, oder systematische Darstellung der Lehren von Erkenntniß und Behandlung eigenthümlicher gesunder und krankhafter Zustände*, 2 vols. (Leipzig: Gerhard Fleischer, 1820).
30. To be more precise, from 1814 to 1821, Carus's Institute in Dresden admitted 1293 pregnant women, 86 suffering a breached condition, with 1285 children born, of which 102 were born dead and 89 died shortly after birth of various complications. They lost only 25 women in childbirth. Carus's tabulations from his Institute confirmed the unequal sex-ratio first noted by the English physician-mathematician John Arbuthnott in 1710: namely, that male births regularly exceed female births by a small margin. Between 1815 and 1821, 13% more males were born than females in Carus's Institute. See Carl Gustav Carus's report on his Institute in his *Zur Lehre von Schwangerschaft und Geburt physiologische, psthologische und therapeutische Abhandlungen*, 2 vols. (Leipzig, Gerhard Fleischer, 1822–1824), 1: 132–34.
31. Carl Gustav Carus, *Lehrbuch der Zootomie*, 2 vols. (Leipzig: Gerhard Fleischer dem Jüngern, 1818), I: 13–14. Plant cells are much larger and more rigid than animal cells. The resolving power of Carus's microscope was simply not strong enough to detect the same cellular formation exhibited in animals as

found in plants—hence globules. Cell-doctrine, formulated by Matthias Schleiden (1804–1881) and Theodor Schwann (1810–1882), was still two decades in the future.
32. Ibid., 22: "We find it as a well confirmed law that the higher formation takes up the lower in itself, and instead of being formed from a new, never before existing type, it repeats in a more perfect form the already achieved lower stage."
33. Ibid., 236.
34. Carus, *Lebenserinnerung*, I: 208.
35. Carl Gustav Carus, *Neun Briefe über Landsafismalerei, geschrieben in den Jahren 1815–1824* (Leipzig: Gerhard Fleischer, 1831).
36. Carus, *Neun Briefe über Landschaftsmalerei*, 17.
37. Ibid., 41.
38. T.S. Eliot defined "objective correlative" in his essay "Hamlet and Its Problems" (1919), in *The Sacred Wood: Essays on Poetry and Criticism* (New York: Alfred A. Knopf, 1921), p. 92: "The only way of expressing emotion in the form of art is by finding an 'objective correlative'; in other words, a set of objects, a situation, a chain of events which shall be the formula of that particular emotion; such that when the external facts, which must terminate in sensory experience, are given, the emotion is immediately evoked."
39. Alexander von Humboldt, *Ansichten der Natur*, 2 vols. (Tübingen: Cotta'schen Buchhandlung, 1808), 1: 173–74.
40. Ibid., p. 143. In her forthcoming book, *The Romantic Roots of Alexander von Humboldt's Presentation of Nature*, Elizabeth Millán Brusslan discusses the complementary relationship of Humboldt and Carus on the issue of *Naturgemälde* (Nature painting).
41. Goethe to Carus (March 23, 1818), in Stefan Grosche, *"Zarten Seelen ist gar viel gegönnt," Naturwissenschaft und Kunst im Briefwechsel zwischen C. G. Carus und Goethe* (Göttigen: Wallstein Verlag, 2001), 11.
42. Carus, *Lebenserinnerungen*, 2:9–11.
43. Goethe had made some kind of discovery in 1790 relevant to morphology, at least he so claimed to friends at the time, but he did not specify what that discovery was. Only in his later collection, *Zur Morphologie* (1817–1824), did he claim that the play with the sheep skull led to his vertebral theory. The quotation comes from his essay "Bedeutende Fördernis durch ein einziggs geistreiches Wort," *Zur Morphologie*, 2.1 (1823), in Goethe, *Sämtliche Werke*, 12:308. Goethe first publicly mentioned his conviction that the vertebrate skull was composed of six transformed vertebrae in the conclusion to his essay "Dem Menschen wie den Tieren ist ein Zwischenknochen der obern Kinnlade zuzuschreiben," *Zur Morphologie*, 1.2 (1820), in Goethe, *Sämtliche Werke*, 12:190.
44. Most scholars believe that Goethe had the priority and that Oken got wind of his theory, which inspired a like view. I think there is a strong evidence that the usual assumption is incorrect. I believe both Goethe and Oken came

independently to the idea and that Goethe's own construction was retrospective. I have discussed this in *Romantic Conception of Life*, 497–502.
45. Carl Gustav Carus, *Von den Ur-Theilen des Knochen- und Schalengerüstes* (Leipzig: Gerhard Fleischer, 1828).
46. Ibid., vii.
47. Lorenz Oken, *Über die Bedeutung des Schälknochen: Ein Programm beim Antritt der Professur an der Gesammt-Universität zu Jena* (Jena: Göpferdt, 1807).
48. Oken to Carus (December 28, 1828), as quoted by Rudolph Zaunik, in "Oken, Carus, Goethe: Zur Geschichte des Gedankens der Wirbel-Metamorphose," in Karl Sudhoff (ed.), *Historische Studien und Skizzen zu Natur und Heilwissenschaft* (Berlin: Julius Springer, 1930), 118–129.
49. I have put Carus's justification of the vertebral theory of the skull in the context of early evolutionary views in "The Foundations of Archetype Theory in Evolutionary Biology: Kant, Goethe, and Carus," *Republic of Letters* Volume 6, Issue 1 (March 2018); on-line at: https://arcade.stanford.edu/rofl_issue/volume-6-issue-1.
50. Carus, *Von der Ur-Theilen*, 7.
51. Ibid., 8.
52. Forming the human braincase, there is a frontal plate, a parietal plate, and an occipital plate. In the infant skull, the frontal plate consists of two plates (left and right) joined at the metopic suture; the parietal plate also consists of two plates joined at the sagittal suture. During childhood and early adolescence, these sutures fuse.
53. Goethe to Carus (June 8, 1828), in Grosche, *Zarten Seelen*, 51–52.
54. Alexander von Humboldt to Carus (June 15, 1828), quoted in Carus, *Lebenserinnerungen*, 2: 289.
55. Carl Gustav Carus, System der Physiologie, 3 vols. (Leipzig: Gerhard Fleischer, 1838–1840), I: 131.
56. Ibid., 138.
57. Ibid., 138 and 142.
58. Carus gave up his university posts in late 1827 to become personal physician to the Saxon kings Anton I (1755–1836) and Friedrich August II (1797–1854).
59. See Carl Gustav Carus, *The King of Saxony's Journey through England and Scotland in the Year 1844*, trans. S.C. Davison (London: Chapman and Hall, 1846), pp. 59–60 (June 2, 1844), 93–4 (June 9, 1844). Nicolaas Rupke mentions the dinner seating in his *Richard Owen, Biology without Darwin*, revised ed. (Chicago, University of Chicago Press, 2009), 60.
60. Nicolaas Rupke has argued, quite convincingly, that Owen used Carus's illustration in the *Von den Ur-Theilen* while failing to acknowledge the dependency. See *Rupke's Richard Owen*, 123–25.
61. Richard Owen, *On the Nature of Limbs* (London: John Van Voorst, 1849), 5–8.
62. Charles Darwin, *On the Origin of Species* (London: Murray, 1859), 434.
63. Ibid., 435.

64. The role of organicism versus mechanism in Darwin's theory is the subject of the book that I have co-authored with Michael Ruse, *Debating Darwin* (Chicago: University of Chicago Press, 2016).
65. Charles Darwin, *Charles Darwin's Notebooks, 1836–1844*, eds. Paul Barett et al. (Ithaca, NY: Cornell University Press, 1987), E Notebook MS 49, 409.
66. This is the convincing argument of Jutta Müller-Tamm, in her *Kunst als Gipfel der Wissenschaft* (Berlin: de Gruyter, 1995), 130–31.
67. Carus, *System der Physiologie*, I: 138
68. Carl Gustav Carus, "Weiteres über den Gorilla und gegen die Hypothese Darwin's," *Leopoldina, amtliches Organ der Kaiserliche Leopoldino-Carolinischen Deutschen Akademie der Naturforscher* 4 (October 1863), 58–61.
69. Ibid., 60.
70. Carus had intimate experience with malformed infants in his gynecological practice.
71. Ibid.

# 17

## Goethe's Philosophy of Nature

Tim Mehigan and Peter Banki

According to a popular view Goethe was an "Augenmensch",[1] literally, an "eye person", a mind touched in notable ways by the power of visual images. This descriptor, to which a passage from Faust has added further weight,[2] is useful in that it highlights a prominent aspect of Goethe's sensibility—his response to physical beauty and the strong emotions it arouses, a feature of his early love poetry, and his intellectual interest in the origin and nature of physical light and what can be drawn from knowledge of its effects, such as we find in pithy observations throughout his major works,[3] or, more programmatically, in the *Colour Theory*, Goethe's quarrelsome disquisition leveled against Newton. We can even go further and see in Goethe's profound, celebratory awareness of the attributes and suggestiveness of the manifestations of physical life an anticipation of the modernity he helped engender, the tendency of the modern to concretize and sensualize images in a visual regime that would speak of the cognitive achievement of canonical vision. The "eye person" Goethe, from this angle, seems thoroughly our ancestor, a visionary who helped loosen the constrictions of medieval Europe, which cleaved perhaps more to the aural sense and, at best, inner sight, and who, in figures such as

T. Mehigan (✉)
University of Queensland, St Lucia, QLD, Australia
e-mail: t.mehigan@uq.edu.au

P. Banki
Western Sydney University, Penrith, NSW, Australia
e-mail: p.banki@uws.edu.au

© The Author(s) 2020
E. Millán Brusslan (ed.), *The Palgrave Handbook of German Romantic Philosophy*, Palgrave Handbooks in German Idealism, https://doi.org/10.1007/978-3-030-53567-4_17

the enigmatic Faust, helped us grow comfortable with the forms and contradictions of modern materialism. It seems quite natural to us, then, that we should organize our understanding of Germany's greatest poet to conform to this sense of his modernity and to find in him a picture of the emerging commitments of our own age. In this vein, T.J. Reed observes in his primer on Goethe:

> The first half of Goethe's life coincided with the later Enlightenment. Though he is not usually thought of as part of it, its principles are present in his work as an unspoken foundation: empiricism, attachment to the sensuous world, intellectual independence and secularism, confidence in man's nature and particularly in his own, a forthright clarity of thought.[4]

If we take these statements at face value, however, we are apt to be led astray. For if we hold too strongly to the *Augenmensch*, we fail to grasp the ways in which Goethe does not wholly stand on the foundation of the visual, just as we also fail to grasp Goethe's uniqueness as a thinker and as a mind which cannot be comfortably assimilated into its own era, much less into ours. While the first half of Goethe's life indeed coincided with the later Enlightenment, as Reed observes, Goethe saw no profit in the enthronement of vision-led reason, nor in the various attempts of his age to construct intellectual positions derived from it. And while Goethe's precipitous decision to decamp to Italy in 1786 was, first and foremost, a response to the cloistered life that had surrounded him for much of his first decade in Weimar, it is also the case that an arresting public discussion in German intellectual circles around the merits of progressive "enlightenment", which had been initiated in a Berlin journal barely two years before, had patently failed to arrest *him*. And so it was that Goethe, the putative "eye person", completely missed the moment when the merits of a new impetus in thought, which had no small stake in visual disclosure of the real, were the topic of intense public discussion in the German lands. Goethe may well have been informed about the recruitment to the Chair of Philosophy at the nearby University of Jena of the Kantian philosopher Karl Leonhard Reinhold in 1788, one of the effects of this discussion if we consider Kant's influential role in the public debate about "Enlightenment". After all, Goethe's fellow-writer and friend Christoph Martin Wieland, who also lived in Weimar, was Reinhold's father-in-law. But it seems unlikely that Goethe, sojourning in Rome, would have been consulted about Reinhold's "call" to Jena, though his advice as Privy Councillor to Carl August, the local Duke of Saxe-Weimar, was later to be considered essential when it came to future appointments at Jena after his return from Italy. Instead of sharing in an exciting intellectual ferment in Germany in the late 1780s, then, Goethe indulged a late release into sexual love in the eternal city, about whose personal significance for the poet the sensually rich and evocative *Roman Elegies* give report.

Our inquiry into the nature of Goethe's philosophical leanings—to the extent that any cogent philosophical position can be ascribed to him—must take account of these circumstances. If Goethe was a philosopher, his was a type of philosophy that took no interest in established intellectual positions, did not swim, nor seek to swim, in the tide of current thinking, no matter how fast and strongly that tide ran, and whose commitments were forged in dialogue with the voice within—the second self of Faust, say, for whom the academic pursuit of knowledge has lost all meaning and who accordingly conscripts Mephistopheles in the service of a project that aims to penetrate further than any academically licensed project of knowledge is entitled to go. Kant might have commended to his age the virtues of *sapere aude* in his Enlightenment essay of 1784. Goethe's counter-position was premised on the insight that neither rational knowing per se nor the type of sensible limits Kant set out for the conduct of public reason had anything significant to contribute to an intelligence that sought a fundamentally different comportment toward knowledge, an intelligence, moreover, which was committed to comprehending, in the words of Faust, what it is that "makes the world, in its innermost being, hold together".[5]

If Enlightenment in the hands of its proponents in the *Berlinische Monatsschrift* of the 1780s was a philosophy that found no reason to break with the appearances, discerning, as Kant was soon to propose in the *Critique of Judgment* (1790), in the thought-figure of the sublime an outer limit of the appearances, Goethe defended a series of positions in his writings that effectively made the case in support of a contrary position. From his breakthrough work, *The Sorrows of Young Werther* (1774), through to *Elective Affinities* (1809), a product of his maturity and one of his greatest intellectual achievements, Goethe's thinking forever chafed at the kind of limits Kant's philosophy prescribed. Goethe's thought thus does not aim to locate a point of modest reach consistent with the conditions attending human cognition, but was constantly tutored by the prior need to find and follow a deeper and more insistent demand—the demand of the ethical. It is in this priority that Goethe's independence as a thinker lies. Instead of the separation between moral and natural orders on which Enlightenment philosophies were overtly or covertly premised, Goethe turned toward the order of nature to understand what it held within—the quintessence of the ethical relation. For this reason, Goethe was apt to appear out of step with his time, a throwback to an earlier, more intuitive way of thinking and feeling, an impression the "classicism" of his middle period only appeared to deepen. Despite these impressions, however, Goethe's thinking was not anachronistic, but rather an expression of a cosmically extended nature, an interpenetration of the divine with nature even deeper than that of Spinoza—something his secularizing age had rarely witnessed in this intensity and whose existence it had been increasingly unwilling to ratify.

## 1   Goethe's Metaphysics

We gain little, then, when we seek to locate Goethe's intellectual bearings in the context of late Enlightenment thought, as if the poet's interest in the sensuous image betrayed, as a matter of course, a wider sympathy for a philosophical movement arguably derived from that same interest. But it would not be right, either, to say that Goethe was exclusively led by the processes of his own thought, say, in the manner of Heinrich von Kleist, an idiosyncratic poetic voice whose genius Goethe respected (he staged a Kleist play in Weimar in 1808), but whose unruly spirit he ultimately found repellent. Goethe was certainly alive to the value of cogent philosophies and viewpoints and frequently made reference to them. His *Maxims and Reflections*,[6] a work made up of well over a thousand rich observations, are full of insightful comment about ancient and modern thinkers and the profit to be gained from them. Goethe was undoubtedly a devoted student of the thought of the past—the interest in Greek and Roman antiquity in his middle years would not have been possible without this attribute. Yet the conundrum the often philosophically astute maxims present is the same conundrum his poetic writings present: everywhere there is the thinker, the wise and patient investigator, the thought-experimenter who drives forward toward knowledge, but nowhere, it seems, is there the philosopher outright, the author of a clearly articulated program of ideas, the purveyor of cashable knowledge. Albert Schweitzer, noting this conundrum about Goethe, devoted a series of appreciative essays to the question of a mind that appears to lack a coherent philosophy and yet is still worthy of attention as a thinker in his own right.[7]

Goethe outstrips our attempts to locate his philosophy precisely because he *abjures the philosophical*. To restrict the reckoning to the leading thinkers of his era, Goethe finds neither in the rationalism of Cartesian thought, the empiricism of Locke and Hume, the idealism of Berkeley or Schelling, nor in any combination of these, a basis for his own thinking. The scientists were nearer to Goethe than these philosophers, but even then, as already mentioned, he found grounds to oppose them. In Newton's empiricism, as exemplified by the contrivance of the prism to observe the spectrum of light,

Goethe did not find a convincing picture of the experiential world, nor a binding view about how human beings should understand light as a structuring principle of being. Among other scientific pioneers of the day, Bacon's anti-Aristotelian program of the *Great Instauration* was also not disposed to please him[8] (as it did, say, Kant), precisely because, in its concern to strip away the anticipations of the inquirer, it remained at a remove from the real nature of the object. Goethe's intellectual outlook demanded understanding of the inner quality of living forms as well as what could be known of their physical manifestations. His outlook fell between the two aspects of empiricism and rationalism according to which, in his own time, objects were considered to present themselves to human perception. Goethe is certainly attentive to the complexity of the scientific viewpoint when, in *Elective Affinities*, he considers, but finally rejects, the single magisterial view of the object. Yet the tragic events of this novel imply that there is nothing of final value in the scientific project, even if the imperfections governing its viewpoint might be overcome. For the constitutive view of the object, for this reason, Goethe does not substitute a more modest "regulatory" approach, an awareness of the bounds within which human perception incrementally builds knowledge of objects and on which modern science erects its hypothetico-deductive experimental procedure. It is thus not merely the case that Goethe's science is differently premised (as the quarrel with Newton reveals). It is also that Goethe's inquiry is exercised on different questions, those, for example, which do not aim to neutralize the distortions of the human viewpoint, but which precisely require them. To this extent, it appears legitimate to conscript Gadamer's sense of the value of these distortions, the value of the prejudices which drive human awareness, when it comes to the task of assessing what human knowing is able—and perhaps required—to accomplish in the world.[9] In line with this insight, Goethe appears not as a scientist in the modern sense nor as an Enlightenment thinker in his own day for whom, as Gadamer points out, prejudices were anathema and had to be combatted.

Goethe, then, is not a modern scientist in part because he fails to obey the first rule of empirical science as laid down by Bacon—"obey in order to command".[10] Yet, on the other hand, he is not a philosopher either because he also fails to exercise a high level of deference toward formal concepts. From this angle, it is the agile, symbolic quality of Goethe's thinking that, on one side, interrupts thought's apparent schematism and its reliance on a fixed time-space continuum, and, on the other, melds thought with feeling, opening thinking up to what, in the midst of the experience of life, concepts cannot properly reveal about the true inner workings of the self in its relation to matter. We get further with an assessment of Goethe's intellectuality when we see in its most characteristic forms the structuring role that intuition plays—whose significance, in turn, allows us to speak of Goethe's thought, in its primary preoccupations, as metaphysical rather than propositional. Metaphysical thought in this meaning would be "pre-critical" in Kant's sense, which is to say, thought that fails to distinguish between noumenon and phenomenon, between direct cognition that produces the content of its own intuitions and indirect cognition that only receives the content of its intuitions, but has no direct access to the thing-in-itself.

Nevertheless, Goethe's thought is apt to appear nearer to the spirit of Kant and his followers than to other philosophers. It is certainly the case that Goethe spent time absorbing the thought systems of Kant and his followers, especially Fichte, Schelling and Hegel. This effort alone has given some commentators reason for assuming compatibility, say, between Goethe's and Hegel's metaphysics,[11] since both types of thought appear to extend into the theological. Yet Goethe's relation to Kantian and post-Kantian thought is less than it might appear, as can be gleaned from the following passage in the drama *Faust*:

> Geschrieben steht: 'Im Anfang war das *Wort*!'
> Hier stock ich schon! Wer hilft mir weiter fort?
> Ich kann das Wort so hoch unmöglich schätzen,
> Ich muß es anders übersetzen,
> Wenn ich vom Geiste recht erleuchtet bin.
> Geschrieben steht: Im Anfang war der *Sinn*.
> Bedenke wohl die erste Zeile,
> Daß deine Feder sich nicht übereile!
> Ist es der Sinn, der alles wirkt und schafft?
> Es sollte stehn: Im Anfang war die *Kraft*!
> Doch auch indem ich dieses niederschreibe,
> Schon warnt mich was, daß ich dabei nicht bleibe.
> Mir hilft der Geist! auf einmal seh ich Rat
> Und schreibe getrost: Im Anfang war die *Tat*! (*Faust* I, v. 1224–37).[12]

These words, of course, are Faust's, not Goethe's. Even so, they mark out a set of steps, a logical progression, that can be reasonably considered to approximate the intellectual background for Goethe's own thought. According to this progression, the word—standing for language, writing, the nominalist viewpoint as such—does not, perhaps cannot, constitute the ground of metaphysical understanding. The reverence for the word as the sacred vessel through which the divine spirit is conveyed is accordingly rejected. Faust's thinking, and, perhaps, Goethe's as well, severs the bond between the word and the spirit, which not only means that it traverses a different route from that of Hegel, where the word and the spirit are pointedly kept together (e.g., in the figure of Jesus), but also that it is already secular in point of principle. From this angle, language may certainly be one of the by-roads traversed by metaphysical understanding, but it will not constitute the highway leading to it—a condition that holds, worryingly, perhaps, for the poet, for poetry no less than it does for the spiritual view.

If the word does not encapsulate the metaphysical, neither, as Faust contends, does *Sinn*—"consciousness" or "mind". Faust at this point appears to oppose the import of Enlightenment theories of mind that saw in the cognitivist interest the main way to access the significance of human experience. The net that Faust casts out here catches a great variety of representationalist positions in both the rationalist and empiricist traditions from the mid-seventeenth to the late eighteenth centuries. Faust, and arguably Goethe with him, includes Descartes and Leibniz in this catch no less than Locke and Hume. As we have seen, there may be grounds for excepting Kant's middle road between these two dominant traditions from inclusion in this list of expendables, but doubtless not that of Kantian thinkers like Reinhold, for whom representation, notably in his *New Theory of the Human Capacity for Representation* (1789), is the main support for a foundationalist argument about consciousness and its achievements. In this passage, therefore, we witness the moment of final dismissal of the position, widely promoted in Kant's day (and erroneously ascribed to him), according to which comprehension of the features of the conscious mind could constitute the royal road to understanding human beings and their core moral commitments.

Once nominalism and consciousness are dispensed with, Faust moves to consider the question of *Kraft*, which might be translated as "force" or "impulse" and stands for the energy inherent in the life instinct itself. In the *Sturm und Drang* ("Storm and Stress") phase of his early period, Goethe doubtless considered this kind of energetic power a significant driver of human experience. This "force" of the self, moreover, held a sexual potency within it that seemed to explain why love was such a powerful element within human beings. In the memorable early poem "Heidenröslein" ("Little Rose of the Field"), for example, the youth feels the urge to pluck the rose, though the price for doing so will be a painful prick that will "eternally" remind him of the injury he does to the rose. And yet still he plucks her. In a poem of a later period, "Gefunden" ("A Find"), Goethe finds a different way to appreciate a flower's beauty and a different recognition of her virtues. In both cases the power of human affect looks consistent, but it is subject to a process of change that still appears entirely natural. Even in the register of the ballad, which

Goethe turns to under the influence of his early mentor Herder, the power of the emotions remains ever-present. In "Erlkönig" ("Earl King"), for example, a father is driven to embark upon a fruitless ride through the night to save his son. His own fear of loss of the child mixes with the deathly premonitions of his son to the point where the two perspectives become one. Yet as much as the passions animate and direct the subjects in whom they stir, Faust, in the passage under consideration, means to give them short shrift. A philosophical project, one might conclude from this move, cannot be built on a theory of the emotions any more than it can be put in the service of a "folk soul", as commended to Goethe by Herder in a way that decisively influenced the movement of *Sturm und Drang*.

Rejecting the attachment to elemental force reminiscent of *Sturm und Drang* and typical of the flavor of later German Romanticism, Faust finally settles on *Tat*, the ground of the deed, of action per se. By Goethe's middle period when these lines were penned, this reference to action was apt to look like a version of Fichte's theory of the ego, which equally thought of the *Tathandlung* ("fact-act") as pivotal for a theory of inner and outer life, on the assumption that there was ultimately no meaningful distinction between these two aspects. It cannot, indeed, be discounted that Fichte's notion of the deed is an important source for Goethe's portrait of Faust's material interests, since in crucial respects the play is an exploration of precisely what is seen to result from the enshrinement of the principle of action, or of a type of acting facing, with awareness, toward a philosophy of the deed as the first law of the cosmos. It is noteworthy, then, that in both parts of *Faust* the actions themselves often do not go well and do not appear to advance the cause of the soul's salvation, the moral issue associated with Faust's wager with the devil. We may further wonder, in view of the parallel with Fichte, whether "intellectual intuition"—with its almost magical suspension of the limitations of material life akin to the Faustian wager with Mephistopheles—will prove to be the means by which to close the gap between the sanctum of "self" and an outer world of "not-self" from which it seems terminally separated. Will the knowledge that purports to bridge this gap—that induces the human being who achieves it to utter the words "Verweile doch! Du bist so schön!" (*Faust I*, v. 1770: "Stay a while! You are so lovely!")—be at the same time the kind of knowledge that effects a proper ethical progression, an unambiguous movement of the inner self toward something admitting of the prospect of moral redemption? And would such a knowledge, were it obtainable, also move the human being to a new, more "modern", position where ethics is no longer a species of religious reflection, as it was in the cloistered Middle Ages that Faust means to leave behind, but rather a science, a form deducible from the practice of living capable of orienting human beings in the increasingly complex social spaces they are destined to move through in life?

## 2   The Philosophical Relevance of Goethe's Friendship with Schiller

There can be no doubt that these are the type of questions Goethe's imaginative works aim to respond to from the outset. And yet it is also the case that they become especially pointed in the period that coincides with Goethe's friendship with the dramatist, essayist and historian Friedrich Schiller, that is, the period from 1794 extending through Schiller's early death in 1805 to the end of the first decade of the nineteenth century. This period is often considered to mark a summit in Goethe's development, a movement from the nature-pantheism of "storm and stress", through the increasingly contemplative,[13] but still notably self-absorbed,[14] courtly dramas of *Egmont* and *Torquato Tasso* of the early to middle period, to the more measured and outward focused novel *Wilhelm Meister's Apprenticeship* (1795–96), and the two towering achievements *Faust* I (completed in 1806) and *Elective Affinities* (1809)[15] of Goethe's maturity. It is accordingly important to weigh up Schiller's influence on Goethe in this period in any assessment of Goethe's overall outlook as a thinker.

The question of Schiller's influence on Goethe is far from straightforward. On the one hand, when the surface detail is assessed, such influence seems self-evident: Goethe's visits to Jena, where Schiller held a teaching post in history at the University of Jena, were frequent during the mid-1790s and almost always involved lengthy exchanges between the two. Moreover, the deeper acquaintance with Schiller began at a time of Schiller's own immersion in the philosophy of Kant. Goethe's *Wilhelm Meister* project, which expounds something like a philosophy of *Bildung* (formation), as we discuss further below, thus had a counterpart by the 1790s in the form of Schiller's many lengthy disquisitions on the cross-over between art and philosophy—disquisitions that arose as a result of Schiller's reading of Kant's *Critique of Judgment*. The most important of these reflections, Schiller's *Letters on the Aesthetic Education of Man*, was published in Schiller's new journal *Die Horen* in 1795.

The first issue of this journal containing the first third of the *Aesthetic Letters* was a joint undertaking with Goethe and Fichte. Goethe's contribution to the journal was solicited—and freely offered—in an atmosphere of dismay at the progress of the French Revolution, which did not result, as Schiller had hoped, in an increase of freedom and the development of a form of republican democracy in France, but rather led to the dramatic excesses of the Reign of Terror, a weakening of the cause of republican government amid an orgy of increasingly indiscriminate violence. Goethe and Schiller's friendship developed around the need to find an adequate response to this disastrous social development in France, and the resources to do so for both were to be drawn from literature and philosophy. Heine's later assessment about the role played by philosophy in Germany at this time thus also applies to the two architects of Weimar Classicism. For Heine, Germany was spared a social revolution on the streets, but in the emergence of German philosophy at this time, it had incubated a revolution with possibly more far-reaching consequences.[16] Heine, of course, was referring to Kant's Copernican Revolution in thought first and foremost. But among other signs of this revolution were Schiller's Kantian writings, which expressly linked Kant's critical project to a political theory of republicanism based on the centrality of art and aesthetic education. While Goethe was no Kantian in the vein of Schiller, the *Conversations of German Emigrés*, Goethe's contribution to the first issue of *Die Horen*, for its part, saw in an idea of dignified conversation a force directed toward the preservation of social mores and thus a principle of societal conservation. At the heart of the literary friendship between Goethe and Schiller, indeed, lay a shared commitment to the notion that art could nurture as well as reform, preserve yet also innovate in ways that would make the delicate fabric of society ripped through by the French Revolution ultimately more durable.

The classicism for which this friendship is remembered was therefore a classicism of a particular sort. On the one hand, Goethe and Schiller saw the threshold moment of forward historical movement represented by the French Revolution as the continuation of a familiar debate—the quarrel between the ancients and the moderns. This understanding on its own revived the question of cultural traditions and what significance to attach to it at a moment of paradigmatic change. On the other hand, Goethe and Schiller were not minded to settle this question unambiguously in favor of the ancients. The term "classicism", indeed, would be a misnomer if it suggested that Goethe and Schiller rejected the progressive impulse at the heart of the modern or somehow believed that antiquity had provided the cultural standard for all later ages. The appeal of the term "classical" is that it suggests a normative function for art at a time when philosophy, as Heine also saw, was possibly even more unsettling than social revolution. Under Schiller's pen, especially in the politically powerful *Aesthetic Letters*, this normative aspect is linked to the conservative function of art. Schiller states openly in these *Letters* that only the disposition of art can truly bridge the gap between nature and culture and, by implication, heal the social rift that revolution had exposed. The question now is: how far did Goethe really share this kind of normative sentiment, however much it chimed with his own view of the importance of art and literature? As we discuss in the following section, an examination of Goethe's morphological thought helps us formulate a response to this question.

## 3   Goethe's Morphological Thought and *Bildung*

In the opening remarks of his treatise *On Morphology* (1807–17), Goethe observes:

> German has the word *Gestalt* for the complex of beings, for an effecting essence. Through this expression [however] there is an abstraction from what moves, on the assumption that a complex being is something held together, closed off and fixed in its character. But if we look at all these *Gestalten*, especially the organic ones, we discover that nothing in them in permanent, nothing is at rest or closed off—everything is in a flux of continual movement. Thus our language has the word *Bildung* which refers both to the end product [*dem Hervorgebrachten*] as well as to the process of production [*dem Hervorgebrachtwerdenden*]. If we want to develop a morphology, then, we must not speak of *Gestalt*.[17]

For Goethe, then, Being is fundamentally dynamic in nature. This does not just mean that the objects of the world are subject to perpetual flux. Goethe goes further—and even beyond the Spinozistic associations to which he was initially attracted in his *Sturm und Drang* phase—in establishing that the phenomena are subject to open-ended processes of emergence according to which putatively stable entities, when observed, have already entered new metamorphosis, a new process of becoming. The word Goethe finds for this dynamic conception of mutually interpenetrating being is "*Bildung*", a word which, like "*Gestalt*", has many different associations specific to the German language. *Bildung* highlights both the dynamic and energetic processes at play in any work of formation, as well as the end product of these processes—the realized form, the formation itself. When we cast around for parallels with later thinking, Goethe's emergentism looks like an early version of thermodynamic theory and the principle of conservation postulated in its first law.[18] As Tantillo observes, the reckoning here need not be confined to Goethe's writings on morphology, for even in *Faust*, Helmholtz could see a principle of conservation of energy at work. Tantillo, for her own part, postulates a dynamic principle of "compensation" in Goethe's thinking, by which "nothing can be added … without something being taken away".[19] Doubtless, there is something of value in such views, though it needs to be underscored that Goethe's primary interest seems to pertain to open rather than closed systems, and accordingly to forms of activity that are not systemically delimitable and in which states of equilibrium only apply in local ways. The takeaway in terms of *Bildung*, therefore, is that the fields of activity across which Goethe's dynamic energy flows are not closed off, but uphold potentially limitless relations with all other entities including with time itself (which lacks the a priori significance it has for Kant). Drawing out a further consequence of this view, Goethe notes that these shifting sands of flux and perpetual change hold as much for the viewpoint of the scientific observer as for the observable phenomena themselves:

> When something has acquired a form it metamorphoses immediately into a new one. If we wish to arrive at some living perception of nature we ourselves must remain as quick and flexible [*so beweglich und bildsam*] as nature and follow the example that it gives.[20]

The philosophical ramifications of this view of nature are significant. First, there can be no in-principle distinction between living and non-living beings. The interest in questions of normativity—the cultural focus mentioned above—must diminish in consequence. This position immediately distinguishes Goethe's thinking from that of his contemporaries, especially Kant and Blumenbach,[21] and indeed also from the entire German Enlightenment tradition, which, as we have seen, proceeds on the basis of a fundamental distinction between natural and moral orders, and, in so doing, potentially also provides for the subordination of the natural world to the human (moral) world (and its alleged purposes). When we read passages from Kant's *Critique of Judgement* (1790) that are consistent with Blumenbach's viewpoint,[22] we therefore must also note how far they lie from Goethe's dynamic view of the cosmos. In section 81, for example, Kant argues it would be contrary to reason "that life should have sprung from the nature of the lifeless, that matter should have been able to dispose itself into the form of a self-maintaining purposiveness". He goes on to state: "The mechanism of nature alone does not enable us to think the possibility of an organized being, but (at least according to the constitution of our cognitive faculty) it must be originally subordinated to a cause working designedly".[23] Goethe's morphological project finds itself fundamentally opposed to these views.

Secondly, in its full compass, the concept of *Bildung* carries within itself an in-built dynamic of self-transformation. This aspect helps explain why, in later applications to educational theory, *Bildung* has come to mean not just "formation", the forming of individuals through the education process, but also "self-formation", the reflexive dynamic of formation within that individual itself. The sort of becoming *Bildung* signifies, for this reason, is at once teleological and non-teleological, purposive and non-purposive. This conception of *Bildung*, understood as an evolving transformation which crosses all borders, was taken up by the Jena Romantics, notably by Friedrich Schlegel in *Athenaeum Fragment 116* (1798), who famously defined romantic poetry as "progressive universal poetry":

> Its destiny is not merely to reunite all of the different genres and to put poetry in touch with philosophy and rhetoric. Romantic poetry wants to and should combine and fuse poetry and prose, genius and criticism, art poetry and nature poetry. It should make poetry lively and sociable, and make life and society poetic …. The romantic form of poetry is still in the process of becoming. Indeed, that is its true essence, that it is always in the process of becoming and can never be completed …. Romantic poetry alone is infinite, just as it alone is free and recognizes as its first law that the poetic will submits itself to no other law.[24]

The literary application of Goethe's morphological thought can be found in *Wilhelm Meister's Apprenticeship*. The importance given to the conditions under which phenomena appear, the inclination to see a harmonious transition between organic nature and human development, and finally the conception of a developmental process as both limited and unending are organizing principles in this work even more than they are compelling ideas. The protagonist of this novel, the eponymous Wilhelm Meister, begins his "journey of formation" in the conviction that he must give up the safety and security of home in order to access those "manifold experiences" that Wilhelm von Humboldt, a close friend and correspondent of Goethe over nearly four decades, believed to be an essential ingredient in the emergence of the fully integrated human being.[25] This intellectual exchange with Humboldt, indeed, is clearly of high importance for the novel, though it must also be noted that Goethe, unlike Humboldt, was reluctant to assign any final purpose to human striving as such. As his literary and auto-biographical works attest, Goethe's emphasis lay rather with the individual's process of self-development and discovery. In *From My Life: Poetry and Truth* (1811–33), Goethe accordingly observed:

> A human being may seek his higher destiny [*Bestimmung*] on earth or in heaven, in the present or in the future, yet within he remains exposed to an eternal fluctuation, to effects from without which always disturb him, until he once and for all makes a decision to declare that what is right is what is in accordance with him.[26]

The prominence of the theme of formation in *Wilhelm Meister's Apprenticeship* was to lead later observers to canonize the novel as the exemplary *Bildungsroman* (novel of formation) of its age.[27] Dilthey, in the later nineteenth century, even considered the *Bildungsroman* to have borrowed its key commitments from the Enlightenment, downplaying or ignoring the German Romantic aspects later accruing to the term. In the *Bildungsroman*, Dilthey argued, could be witnessed

> [a] regular development [...] in the life of the individual: each of the stages has its own intrinsic value and is at the same time the basis for a higher stage. The dissonances and conflicts of life appear as the necessary points of passage through which the individual must pass on his way to maturity.[28]

But this emphasis on regularity is misleading and, in relation to the *Wilhelm Meister* project, tugs Goethe too severely toward a rationalism he never endorses. In fact, from the outset, the novel stages a conflict between two worlds or realms, between, on the one hand, art and *Bildung*—the realm of the emerging romantic disposition—and, on the other, economic functionalism and social conformity, a set of values that better approximate the goals of Enlightenment even if it might not be coextensive with them.

Wilhelm, the focalizing figure of the narrative, begins his journey of formation by leaving behind the inherited world of his upbringing in order to pursue a calling in the theater. In so doing, he gains release from the pressures of bourgeois society, whose values are represented in the narrative by his childhood friend Werner. Through his passion for the theater and love for a woman, Wilhelm claims for himself the right to *Bildung*, which is to say, to life experiences and possibilities of learning which are open-ended and consciously eschew the utilitarian. In the construction of these circumstances, Goethe stages a version of his own ambivalence toward conventional society that had driven him from Weimar years before. And yet, as becomes clear in the narrative, claiming such a right provides no effective counter to the economic imperative on which the conditions of life otherwise depend. Perhaps for this reason, Wilhelm's journey is repeatedly subject to error and disappointment. Following the loss of Mariane, his first love, Wilhelm abandons his artistic ambitions and falls back on the commercial world familiar to him from his upbringing. This decision, in turn, brings to light the central dilemma examined in the story: how is the "quiet dutiful industry" required for success in such a world to be reconciled with the individual's need for personal happiness, which would appear to depend exclusively on personal inclination and freedom from external constraint? To speak the language of Kant, how is a principle of autonomy that the sovereign will requires to give itself its law to be reconciled with de facto heteronomy, with the need to balance diverse interests including the establishment of an economic foundation for life in bourgeois society? It is all the more remarkable at this point in the novel that Wilhelm does not obviously founder on a frustrated or broken principle of autonomy but, on the contrary, makes some sort of success of his new life:

> To the astonishment of Werner and to the great delight of his father, no one was more industrious than Wilhelm in the counting house, on the exchange, in the office or the warehouse. He dealt with correspondence and bills and everything else assigned to him with the greatest efficiency. Not indeed with that joyful eagerness which is its own reward when one executes in an orderly fashion what one is born to do, but with a certain quiet dutiful industry, based on solid foundations and sustained by conviction, self-rewarding on the whole. But sometimes he was unable to suppress a sigh even when his best qualities were being engaged.[29]

It would not be unreasonable to read this passage as a challenge to Kant's moral philosophy. Kant erected his ethics on the confidence that a universally binding moral law—one that would lay down a maxim of action that holds "categorically" for any rational being and therefore in all like circumstances—can be deduced from rational precepts to meet the demands of ethical life. By contrast, striving to be happy cannot in Kant's outlook give rise to a moral maxim of this sort because happiness is determined in accordance with the empirical needs of individual subjects. Desire, as Kant sees it, should play no role in ethical determinations, as he notes in the *Critique of Practical Reason*:

> To be happy is necessarily the wish of every finite rational being, and this, therefore, is inevitably a determining principle of its faculty of desire …. But precisely because this material principle of determination can only be empirically known by the subject, it is impossible to regard this problem as a law; for a law being objective must contain the very same principle of determination of the will in all cases and for all rational beings.[30]

Duty—the compulsion to follow the categorical imperative—and personal inclination thus remain incompatible with each other. And so when Wilhelm Meister temporarily abandons his artistic inclinations and cultivates the "certain quiet dutiful industry", it is arguably this Kantian notion that the novel means to contradict. Later in the eighth book of the novel, Kant's moral philosophy again appears in Goethe's crosshairs when Wilhelm, with one eye on his son's future, proclaims:

> All moralizing is unnecessarily strict! [...] Nature turns us, in her own pleasant way, into what we should be. Strange indeed are those demands of middle-class society that confuse and mislead us, finally demanding more from us than nature itself.[31]

As this passage attests, Wilhelm's capacity for moral action arises from the dictates of his own inner nature. It is this same nature that renders Kantian duty inoperative. The novel contests a dualistic understanding of human being where spirit and nature find themselves split off from, and at odds with, each other. The countervailing position Goethe argues for aims at achieving a unification of feeling with virtue. *Wilhelm Meister's Apprenticeship* thus conceives of a morality that does not mistrust the naturalness of humanity, but can ratify it as a social force. Rather than opposing human nature and moral action, the natural order becomes the very basis of the moral order because the human striving for happiness—against Kant's express thoughts concerning the matter—comes about itself as an ethical demand. Thus, in a manner consistent with the approach taken by Goethe in his scientific writings, *Wilhelm Meister's Apprenticeship* aims at finding legitimation in nature for a social commitment. The novel explores how the autonomy of the individual and the needs of rational society can be brought into dialogue if not alignment.

In the seventh of his *Letters on the Aesthetic Education of Man*, Friedrich Schiller characterizes the cause of the individual's unhappy consciousness as attributable to the growing specialization and compartmentalization of work in modern society. In such a society, an integrated life is only possible in a mechanical way. With Schiller's influence in mind, it is all the more instructive that the vision of life and work in the wider society in *Wilhelm Meister's Apprenticeship* is endorsed at a level that rises above that of the characters:

> It is beyond belief what a cultivated man can achieve for himself and others, if, without trying to lord it over others, he has the temperament to be the guardian of many, helping them to find the right occasion to do what they would all like to do, and guiding them toward the goals they have clearly in mind without

knowing how to reach them. Let us then join together in a common purpose—that is not mere enthusiasm, but an idea which can quite well be put into practice, and is indeed often implemented, though not always consciously.[32]

## 4  Goethe and Platonism

In *Wilhelm Meister's Apprenticeship*, then, Goethe settles accounts with the issue of natural and moral orders. For Goethe, the discrepancy between these realms is only apparent. Beyond these realms, as Goethe's morphology contends, lies an infinitely vaster lived connectivity of the human with the non-human, the human and the non-human with the cosmos. The question now arises of whether the dynamic "formation" philosophy the novel appears to defend shares any of the features of the neo-Platonism to which the early German Romantics were drawn.

In the *Maxims and Reflections*, Plato, though sparingly referenced, is cited as a touchstone for the right approach to thinking:

> In order to rescue oneself from the unbounded multiplicity, dismemberment and complication of the modern theory of nature one must put this question before oneself: how would Plato, with thorough simplicity, have responded to nature as she may appear to us in her great variety? (Maxim 662)

In these remarks, it is less reverence for Platonism as a philosophy that can be heard than interest in a manner of conceiving the world that arises from the virtues of simplicity. Such simplicity is commended because it acts as a foil against the "limitless multiplicity, dismemberment and complication" attending modern views of nature. Of course, Goethe is no enemy of modern complexity—such complexity is soberly recalled in other maxims where, for example, the difficulty, as well as the necessity, of distinguishing between cause and effect is highlighted (Maxim 594), a comment which appears to highlight Goethe's understanding of the value of scientific experimentalism, or where the expansion of knowledge brings as a natural consequence of its hypothetical procedures wider problems to light (Maxim 557). The modern, in this way, is indeed "multiplicity, dismemberment and complication"—one of many possible systemizations cashed out on the basis of the epistemology on which it relies (cf. Maxim 568).

When this is borne in mind, Goethe's interest in antiquity appears less in the content of its thought than with its method. This interest in method, admittedly, could be translated into the Platonic view that the forms or essences are always other than the "real" effects and therefore ultimately more binding than they are. On the other hand, the ancient focus on objects has the benefit of cutting away from the modern question of normativity, which presents itself in the gap between subjects and objects as the problem, as Goethe puts it in Maxim 564, that no average can represent the difference between a rule and the exception to it. Whereas, for Schiller, the interest in generality overrides all other interests, Goethe's metaphysics is motivated above all by the desire to give full weight to exceptional individual experience:

> Of the absolute in a theoretical sense I dare not speak; but I am permitted to maintain that whoever recognizes it in the appearance and always keeps it in view stands to make a great profit by it. (Maxim 571)

To talk generally—to theorize—about the Absolute is to indulge in a form of theology. But to find in the manner of appearing (*in der Erscheinung*) the higher quality of an essence, something like the Absolute, yet not provably that Absolute, is to acknowledge the truth of something perhaps merely intuited, yet also beyond doubting. For all the language of the visual evident in this remark, it is notable that Goethe does not ratify any cognitive claim for this type of knowledge. He speaks cautiously about the profit to be had from it, and he observes a Kantian protocol about the objects that present themselves to pure reason. Elsewhere in the *Maxims and Reflections*, Goethe cites Kant's finding, approvingly, that appearances cannot meaningfully be separated from the observer—the appearance, as he puts it, is "devoured" by the individuality of the observer and the ways in which observers are inextricably tied (*verwickelt*) to that which they observe.[33] But the consequence he draws from this limitation is not to remain mindful of limits nor to be guided by a rule-bound understanding toward a regularity whose terms must first be properly worked out. Rather, even in his mature writing, Goethe's interest lies with outlining the excessive power of affect, the overwhelming, and for the human being, ultimately defining, quality of inner nature itself.

## 5  Concluding Remarks

In "Selige Sehnsucht" ("Blessed Longing"), composed in 1814, Goethe comes close to laying out a catechism—a private religion—in full knowledge of the fact that it will be popularly misunderstood, even derided. On the one hand, the poem is steeped in the German Romanticism from which Goethe can scarcely be properly separated. Its subject matter repeats the early German Romantic interest in excess since it celebrates the instinct of the moth (Goethe calls it a "butterfly" in the poem) to seek the flame that will extinguish its life. For Enlightenment philosophy, knowledge of the behavior of the moth is a piece of useful knowledge, perhaps advantageous for biological control or for some other purpose. But Goethe professes no interest in such knowledge. Instead, the moth's nature and human nature are located on a continuum; the human appears tied to a wider dispensation that must be fully appreciated if the full import of human being is to be understood. This is the reason the "you" of the poem, the moth the poet addresses at the start, metamorphoses into the human "you" the poem ultimately means to reach by the end of the poem:

> Und so lang du das nicht hast,
> Dieses: Stirb und werde!
> Bist du nur ein trüber Gast
> Auf der dunklen Erde.[34]
>
> And as long as you lack this,
> This: Die and become!
> You will be but a gloomy soul
> On the dark earth.

The moth reaches no fulfillment in obedience to instinct, its inner life force. Faust, as we have seen, rejects this "force" as it does not advance any controlling interest of the human being, no material profit for the self. But in this poem, Faust's materialism is itself overcome, and it is overcome precisely on the grounds that there is some sensed connection between the immanent and the transcendent sphere, the conditioned and the unconditioned. The light that draws the moth is both a flame and a greater Enlightenment, grasped and yet not graspable, known and not knowable. Yet if the *Flammentod* (death by fire) is to be read as symbol, its instructions for use remain materially indecipherable. Nature for Goethe is no book to be finally comprehended, however much it is a book to be read and closely observed. The suggestive power in the personal religion the poem outlines arises out of its ethical outlook—its desire to augment human understanding with a set of principles that can only be sensed, but not rendered formally or materially available.

Yet what kind of ethics can this be? Like Kant, Goethe accepts a form of ethical alignment between the conditioned and the unconditioned. Unlike Kant, Goethe thinks nothing categorical can be derived from it. For Kant's interest in the ways in which common sense is organized and regularized, Goethe substitutes a reverence for the emotional surplus to which the category of the sublime draws attention (and whose effects the Kantian sublime aims to subdue). In this sense, Goethe's ethics, taking its cues from nature, breaks with those of Kant, which are finally exercised in—and only mean to take stock of—the realm of culture. Goethe's relevance for our own age lies precisely in this move back to a greater, cosmically extended power in relation to which nature attains its true significance. Goethe's gift as a metaphysical thinker is to make this naturalizing move appear plausible.

As Schweitzer observes, the problem for every philosophy of nature is how to move from nature to ethics. Whereas the Stoics "affirm, without being able to prove ..., that life in harmony with nature has in itself a moral character", others, like Spinoza, "found their ethics ... upon considerations which at bottom are alien to their natural philosophy and which they attach to it afterwards".[35] Goethe's ethics is simpler than these accounts, and today we might also say, more ecological. The ethical factor for Goethe is given in the very idea of nature; only reverence for nature can properly evince it. Goethe was out of step with his age because the great thought systems of his own time—those of Kant, Fichte, Schelling and Hegel—assumed a dualism between nature and culture that Goethe could never share. This put ethics on one side of a dualism, where, to transport it the other side, it had to be deduced, artfully configured or simply asserted. Schiller's philosophy subdued this dualism under the influence of aesthetic ideals, but since this philosophy came from Kant, the dualism was incipient and could not be silenced. So even the project of Weimar Classicism proved to be a passing moment in the career of the writer. Goethe is most true to himself when we witness in works such as *On Morphology* and poems such as "Selige Sehnsucht" something greater than this dualism and something undefeated by it: the power and transcendent quality of inner nature. Only when viewed from the outside, perhaps, does this idea of nature resemble a metaphysics. On the inside it is, or at least means to be, an ethics, an immanent creative power whose attunement to the demands of physical life and whose profundity for human beings living that life Goethe perpetually sought to make evident through the means of writing.

# Notes

1. See David Wellbery, "Augenmensch: Zur Bedeutung des Sehens im Werk Goethes": *Deutsche Vierteljahrsschrift für Literaturwissenschaft und Geistesgeschichte* 75/1 (Sonderheft) (March 2001): 176.

2. "Zum Sehen geboren, /Zum Schauen bestellt" ("Born to see, /made for beholding"): *Faust* II: v. 11, 289–90. All translations unless otherwise indicated are by Mehigan and Banki.
3. For example, in *Faust* II, v. 4727: "Am farbigen Abglanz haben wir das Leben" ("Our lives are conducted in the reflected splendour of color").
4. T.J. Reed, *Goethe* (Oxford: Oxford University Press, 1997), 6.
5. All translations unless otherwise indicated are by Mehigan and Banki. Johann Wolfgang Goethe, *Werke: Hamburger Ausgabe in 14 Bänden*, ed. Erich Trunz (Munich: Deutscher Taschenbuchverlag, 1994), Vol. 3: *Faust* I: v. 382–3. Hereafter, *Werke*.
6. Goethe, *Werke* (Ibid.), Vol. 12, 365–547.
7. Albert Schweitzer, *Goethe: Five Studies*, trans., Charles Joy (Boston: Beacon Press, 1961).
8. Bacon's program is mentioned, with restraint, in Maxim 506 (Goethe, *Werke* [*op. cit.*], Vol. 12, 434).
9. See Hans-Georg Gadamer, 1989. *Truth and Method*, trans., Joel Weinsheimer and Donald G. Marshall (London and New York: Continuum, 1989), 273–5.
10. Henri Bergson, *The Creative Mind: An Introduction to Metaphysics*, trans. Mabelle L. Andison (New York: Carol Publishing, 1992), 126.
11. See, for example, Leif Weatherby, *Transplanting the Metaphysical Organ: German Romanticism between Leibniz and Marx* (New York: Fordham University Press, 2016).
12. This is Luke's translation (Johann Wolfgang Goethe, *Goethe: Selected Verse*, ed. David Luke (London: Penguin, 1964), 185): "'In the beginning was the *Word*.' Here I am stuck already! Who will help me on? To set so high a value on 'word' is impossible: I must translate it in some other way, if the spirit is giving me real enlightenment. It is written: 'In the beginning was *Mind*.' Consider the first line well, let your pen not move on too fast! Is it by *Mind* that all things are done and made? It should read: 'In the beginning was *Energy*.' And yet, at the very moment of writing it down, something warns me not to leave it at that. The spirit moves me! I suddenly see the answer, and boldly write: 'In the beginning was the *Deed*.'"
13. The preparation for this reflexive turn in Goethe's writing may well be the *Römische Elegien*, which Nicholas Boyle aptly describes as poems which are "as much … about thinking as they poems about sensual experience" (Nicholas Boyle, *Goethe: The Poet and the Age* [Oxford: Oxford University Press, 1991], 633).
14. For Tantillo, indeed, Werther's self-absorption even leads to his self-destruction (Astrida Orle Tantillo, *Goethe's Modernisms* [New York: Continuum, 2010]), 101.
15. What then postdates this period is consolidation at the summit of this development and the finalizing of projects: the first version of *Wilhelm Meisters*

*Wanderjahre* in 1821 and its extension in 1829, and the completion of *Faust II* in 1831, a year before his death.

16. Heinrich Heine, *Zur Geschichte der Religion und Philosophie in Deutschland*, ed. Jürgen Ferner (Stuttgart: Reclam, 1997).
17. Goethe *Werke* (*op. cit.*), 55; Goethe, *Schriften zur Morphologie*, ed. Michael Holzinger (Berlin: Berliner Ausgabe, 2016), 6–7. Hereafter, *Morphologie*.
18. Cf. Rudolf Clausius, "Über die bewegende Kraft der Wärme und die Gesetze, welche sich daraus für die Wärmelehre selbst ableiten lassen." *Annalen der Physik* 79 (1850): 368–397, 500–524.
19. Tantillo, *Goethe's Modernisms* (*op. cit.*), 5.
20. Goethe, *Werke*, 56; Goethe, *Morphologie* (*op. cit.*), 7.
21. Blumenbach, one of the founders of physical anthropology, had posited the notion of a *Bildungstrieb* or formative drive (*nisus formativus*). He had argued that it is a mark of living beings to possess such a drive and that their structure, function and powers can only be fully understood in line with this drive.
22. This is richly evident in the question of originating causes, in which Blumenbach professes a high interest but from which Goethe turns completely away. As we will outline in relation to the *Maxims and Reflections*, Goethe considers that the only proper starting point for philosophy—in accordance with the view of the ancients, particularly Aristotle—is the direct experience of natural objects. Thus, instead of grounding his scientific project in the search for causes, Goethe assigns priority to *the context in which phenomena may be observed*. In *On Morphology* Goethe therefore notes, "We will not be looking for causes, but rather for the conditions under which these phenomena appear" (Goethe, *The Essential Goethe*, ed. Matthew Bell [Princeton: Princeton University Press, 2016]).
23. Immanuel Kant, The *Critique of Judgment*, trans. J.H. Bernard (2nd ed. revised). (London: Macmillan, 1914), 345–346. A version of this argument was recently put forward by Dalia Nassar in a lecture to the Annual Conference of the Society for German Idealism and Romanticism (2018), December 6–7, 2018, Department of Germanic Studies and Department of Philosophy, University of Sydney.
24. Friedrich Schlegel, *KFSA* 2, 182. Our translation.
25. Wilhelm von Humboldt, "Ideen zu einem Versuch, die Gränzen der Wirksamkeit des Staates zu bestimmen." in *Werke in fünf Bänden, Band 1* (Darmstadt: Wissenschaftliche Buchgesellschaft, 1969), 64.
26. Goethe, *Aus meinem Leben. Dichtung und Wahrheit*, ed. Peter Sprengel, Münchner Ausgabe, Vol. 16 (München: Hanser, 1985), 496 f.
27. The concept of the *Bildungsroman* was first introduced by Karl Morgenstern 25 years after the publication of the novel (Tobias Boes, "Modernist Studies and the Bildungsroman: A Historical Survey of Critical Trends", *Literature Compass* 3/2 (2006): 230–243), but it was not made canonical until Wilhelm Dilthey employed it in his biography of Friedrich Schleiermacher (1870).

28. Wilhelm Dilthey, *Das Erlebnis und die Dichtung. Lessing, Goethe, Novalis, Hölderlin* (Leipzig: Teubner, 1922), 394.
29. Goethe, *The Essential Goethe* (*op. cit.*), 936.
30. Kant, *The Critique of Practical Reason*, ed./trans., Mary Gregor (Cambridge: Cambridge University Press, 1997), 23.
31. Goethe, *The Essential Goethe* (*op. cit.*), 1621–1622.
32. Goethe, Ibid., 1792.
33. Maxim 512, p. 435.
34. Goethe, *Werke* (*op. cit.*), Vol. 2, 18; v. 17–20.
35. Schweitzer, *Goethe: Five Studies* (*op. cit.*), 113.

# 18

## Romantic Acts of Generation

Jocelyn Holland

This chapter focuses on an aspect of German Romantic thought that can best be described—at the risk of redundancy—as the generation of generation. The tidy formulation refers to a phenomenon that occurred in the early years of Romanticism, which witnessed a proliferation of terms that have to do with processes of generation (including making, constructing, *poiesis*, producing and reproducing, creating and procreating, along with many others). The phrase "generation of generation" also shares an affinity with the recursive structures and reflexive gestures endemic to early romantic writing, where one finds numerous examples of texts that call into question the circumstances of their own existence and processes of making. In order to manage what at first glance seems to be a chaotic assemblage of notes, aphorisms, fragments, and novelistic writing about generation and its network of closely related topics, this chapter will focus on the work of two prominent thinkers who were also great friends: Friedrich Schlegel and Friedrich von Hardenberg, who is better known by his pen name, Novalis. In their writing, Schlegel and Novalis draw upon sources that played an important role in the discussion of generation at the end of the eighteenth century. These sources include the speculative physics of Johann Wilhelm Ritter and Friedrich Schelling, Immanuel Kant's discussion of the organism in his *Critique of the Power of Judgment* (1790), Johann Gottlieb Fichte's philosophy of the self-positing subject, the

J. Holland (✉)
California Institute of Technology, Pasadena, CA, USA
e-mail: jholland@caltech.edu

© The Author(s) 2020
E. Millán Brusslan (ed.), *The Palgrave Handbook of German Romantic Philosophy*, Palgrave Handbooks in German Idealism, https://doi.org/10.1007/978-3-030-53567-4_18

reproductive theories of Johann Friedrich Blumenbach and Carl Friedrich von Kielmeyer, Antoine Lavoisier's writings on chemistry, and the mystical writings of Jacob Böhme, to name just a few. The focus on Schlegel and Novalis will accordingly be counterbalanced by references to a rich interdisciplinary environment. A primary goal of the chapter is therefore to provide curious readers with an overview of the vast discursive reach that characterizes German Romantic thinking about generation, one which extends from the organic realm (which at that time included animals, plants, and minerals), to the intellectual (including the production of thoughts and the work of art), and even the technological. A second, narrower goal is to think more precisely about the topography of a discursive landscape whose primary characteristic—the essence of generation—is change. What implications does a state of constant change have for creative subjects, their products, and the very instruments of production?

In keeping with the mutable nature of its subject matter, this chapter offers no hard and fast definition of generation, but rather uses it provisionally as a neutral term that refers equally to processes of technological and poetic making as well as modes of organic growth and development. The first section begins, in true romantic spirit, with the self; it explores generation in terms of self-production. The second section then addresses generation as a problem of genre, where acts of generating and production are inherent to the romantic understanding of the literary text to an astonishing degree: it is no stretch of the imagination to say that romantic texts have the capacity to write themselves and to be written by their readers. The third section takes a step back to consider how romantic generation also draws from elements of the natural sciences and the contemporary philosophical school, *Naturphilosphie*.[1] This chapter concludes with a reflection on the romantic tool, instrument, and organ concepts, also as a heuristic means of organizing the potentially unmanageable scope of romantic thinking about generation. By the end of this chapter, once readers have become better acquainted with the complex terrain of romantic generation, at least one feature of this landscape should have become more clear: for all that early German Romanticism emerges within an intense reflection on the subject, the centrality of this perspective does not define the writing of Schlegel and Novalis as a whole. Instead, as this chapter will argue by shifting its attention away from the self, it is possible to observe that one consequence of the early romantic "generation of generation" and its multiple creative modes is to decentralize the romantic subject by outsourcing, as it were, its creative function to other focal points.

## 1  Generating the Self

If it sounds odd to the uninitiated reader to describe the period of early German Romanticism as a time of extensive philosophical reflection on the act of self-generation, it might help to keep in mind that for those involved, such activity was understood to be a real and authentic form of (intellectual) labor. To judge from their notes, thinking about the self and its activities—which includes thinking about processes of thinking itself—was a common occurrence for Novalis and Schlegel. In part, their focus on the self constitutes a response to a late-eighteenth-century development in philosophy, often associated with Johann Gottlieb Fichte, which attempted to account for the emergence of an "I" (*Ich*) and its manifold relations to the world. Schlegel and Novalis responded to Fichte's philosophy on their own terms and tried to make something of it, and these acts of making are embedded within the language of generation.

The second volume of the critical edition of Novalis' writings contains many of these initial responses, which have been collected in the "Fichte Studies" (a title chosen by the volume's editors that has been the subject of some dispute).[2] Through his reading of Fichte, Novalis encounters the idea of an absolute I that contains within itself a division between the "I" and the "not-I." In the "Fichte Studies," Novalis refers to an initial intellectual act of self-positing or *Urhandlung* that, as Jane Kneller describes in the introduction to the English translation, replaces the "immediate act of self-positing" described by Fichte with a "mediated act of representation."[3] The act of self-reflection therefore has an aesthetic dimension for Novalis because it produces an illusion whose status *as* illusion can only be revealed through further reflection.[4] The work of the thinking, reflecting individual is therefore at the same time creative and concerned with the act of creation. With a slight difference of emphasis, Novalis is able to say that the I is both "act and product."[5] This aspect of Novalis' philosophical thinking—including his criticism and revision of Fichte's basic philosophical principles—has been treated in great detail by Manfred Frank.[6]

Responding to and adapting the Fichtean notion of a powerful self-generating I, Novalis is able to envision a conceptual landscape—the "paradise of ideas" explored in Gerhard Neumann's eponymous work[7]—whose unique features do not completely obscure the intellectual terrain that precedes it:

In every system—individual group of thoughts—which may either be an aggregate or a product etc.—One *idea*, one observation, or several such, have *especially flourished* and stifled the others—or have remained over. We must now gather them together in the system of spiritual Nature—granting each its own specific soil—climate—its particular cultivation—its specific *neighborhood*—in order to form a *paradise of ideas*—this is the true system./Paradise is the ideal of the *earth*.[8]

To produce with one's own intellectual products and map out a grander paradise of ideas that is at the same time a renewal of paradise lost: that is an intellectual ideal for Novalis, the work of his time and of philosophers yet to come. The idea is rooted in an intellectual tradition that extends well beyond the most obvious references to Fichte and the Bible. To highlight just one example, one can turn to the chapters Neumann devotes to Lichtenberg, whose own commitment to the I as product comes to light in the laconic aphorism: "Man as nature-product; as product of his race (of society); the product of himself, the educated, knowledgeable man."[9]

The motoric of self-production that emerges within philosophy takes on different guises in romantic thought as it is re-constructed and re-narrated from diverse vantage points. Some of these guises recall the fact that in the German tradition, and particularly around 1800, philosophy is a science. Indeed, it is the "science of sciences," as Fichte writes in *Ueber den Begriff der Wissenschaftslehre oder der sogenannten Philosophie* [Concerning the concept of the doctrine of science or the so-called philosophy].[10] For his part, Novalis seems to enjoy speculating about whether the same patterns of self-generation described in the primal actions of an emerging "I" can be applied to nascent scientific discourses. One of the most important in this regard is chemistry, whose status was contested by another philosopher of great importance to Schlegel and Novalis: Immanuel Kant. In *The Metaphysical Foundations of Natural Science* (1786), Kant writes that "chemistry can be nothing more than a systematic art or experimental doctrine, but never a proper science, because its principles are merely empirical, and allow of no *a priori* presentation in intuition."[11] Novalis is less concerned with the legitimacy of chemistry as a science than with the usefulness of chemical language to advance his understanding of the subject:

219. Previously an absolutely simple thesis was sought—now [we seek] an absolute synthesis/for chemists the former is simple, the latter is composite, matter. /Thesis is the residue of that which acts—the simple basis. Absolute synthesis—absolute thesis—the former is the imagination as such—the latter is the

imagination itself in *opposition* to its product—or in relation to the product. The subject is thus only an idea—it is only that which is set in opposition to the representation or intuition, absolutely nothing more. But the subject must necessarily lack causality—just because it [the subject] is only a residue. To what extent will the subject, that is, the product, be able to relate to itself? Basically, never. How can one speak of freedom? Or how can causality be ascribed to the subject at all?[12]

The note, which is quite critical in tone about the status of the subject, frames the subject in chemical terms such that the philosophical product exists in analogy to the chemical "residue." The note's impetus arises from the awareness of particular affinities: between the empirical and the theoretical, and between the logic governing a particular science and the structures produced by "the" science of philosophy. Such claims call to mind the work of Friedrich Schelling, another philosopher whose most significant initial publications appeared in tandem with early German romanticism, in the years around 1800. Schelling grounds his early thinking in the idea of a deep affinity between the structures of nature and the structures of the mind.[13] For him, these philosophical ideas will eventually be refigured within a philosophy of art. In the case of Schlegel and Novalis, whose philosophical thinking takes up more overtly aesthetic concerns at an earlier historical moment, one can see how romantic figurations of self-production concretize in the figure of the artist and a more general aesthetic concern with the production of signs, as Manfred Frank, Herbert Uerlings, and others have noted.[14] In a note discussed by both Frank and Uerlings, Novalis refers not to the traditional figure of the artist (*Künstler*) but to a neutrally gendered "one who represents" or "signifies" (*das Bezeichnende*). The note could be read as a story of Fichtean intellectual production:

> The first signifier [*Bezeichnende*] without noticing it will have painted its own picture in the mirror of reflection, not forgetting to paint the feature, that the picture is painted in the arrangement that it [the first signifier, JH] itself paints[.][15]

In the description of an "it" who stands before the "mirror of reflection" and paints its own image, Frank sees a reference to the beginning of the "Fichte Studies" (where the consciousness is equated to an "image" [*Bild*] of being, within being).[16] Uerlings develops this idea even further: for him, the quintessence of early romantic theories of representation is the act of making aware its illusory, constructed status (*Schein-Charakter*). Uerlings also describes how the peculiar pattern of an oscillatory positing and removal that keeps any firm notion of "truth" in representation at bay forms the basic structure of romantic irony. Or, as Uerlings phrases it, "in terms of subject theory it leads to a *rhetorical* definition of the ego: 'The ego must posit itself as representing' … The ideal of such representation is the 'free representation,' which has, to a great extent, released itself from mimetic representation."[17] If there is one thing to be learned from the above examples, it is that romantic reflections on the self, as abstract as they might seem at first glance, emerge *ab ovo* as it were, within a discourse shaped by philosophical, scientific, and aesthetic concerns. The next section will explore the latter of these in greater detail.

## 2   Generation as *Poiesis* and Literary Genre

The early German romantics, when fantasizing and philosophizing about radical gestures of self-creation, such as the unsettling image of the artist who creates himself through the reflection of his own act of self-portraiture, as described above,[18] also sought to develop other organs of experimentation. They found them in poetic genre. The degree to which the Schlegel and Novalis reconceptualize both traditional and new genres cannot be overstated: whereas earlier, more rule-bound centuries created rigid taxonomies of poetic form (and therefore tended to write in accordance with particular genre restrictions), the writers of German Romanticism appropriate genre in order to test out their philosophical ideas. For that reason (among others), established genre forms become almost unrecognizable. The "fable," for example, which has traditionally been conceived as a short prose piece with a moral message, often delivered by animal characters, is referred to in Novalis' notes as the "expression of an entire thought" and "in itself a complete production of the *higher faculty of language*."[19] Through the emphasis on "expression" and "production," genre becomes understood in terms of function: to define a romantic genre is therefore to explain what it does. Such a functional, productive understanding of genre reaches the peak of complexity in a particular genre: the novel. This section takes as a case study Friedrich Schlegel's novel *Lucinde* (1799) to illustrate the different ways in which, even among romantic genres, the novel is special; it embodies the romantic arch-tendency to "generate generation."

Readers of *Lucinde* who are new to German romanticism will likely find it a challenge. *Lucinde* is a love story—where the title character does not get to speak for herself. Its chapters are a mishmash of various poetic genres. Narrative tone and mood shift abruptly, without clear psychological motivations. All the characteristics which might, at first glance, be attributed to literary idiosyncrasies (or, if one is feeling less charitable, to an immaturity of style) take on different meaning when focused through the prism of romantic philosophy. From that perspective, *Lucinde* emerges as an intellectual exercise in the theoretical mediation between procreation and auto-production, as well as between organic generation and techniques of literary *poiesis*. How can that be the case? One way in which Schlegel brings these different modes of generation together is through the deliberate use of *creatio ex nihilo*, a figure whose path his philosophical notes have already traced from theology to philosophy (especially Fichte's), literature (especially Sterne's), and beyond.[20] Schlegel conceives of creation from nothing in terms of an "absolute leap," a figure with connotations that range from embryology (as in the *punctum saliens* that, in William Harvey's work, marks the emergence of organic life) to Fichte's act of self-positing. The creation from nothing, as an "absolute leap," has the ability to bridge the physical and the metaphysical gap, but Schlegel puts the creative subject in place of the divine instance, something that he refers to as an "ethically ethical" proposition to be equated with absolute individuality.[21]

*Lucinde* begins with such an absolute leap.[22] Its first chapter is framed within a context of "doing nothing" when a daydream is disturbed—a daydream that is a lustful fantasy of procreation. Schlegel's novel therefore posits both natural and poetic orders as "emerging from nothing" and links them to the idea of a creative subject who needs only the contingency of interruption (a kind of poetically contrived "chaos," to borrow another word from the romantic lexicon) to get going.[23] To underscore the fact that the poetic gesture that grounds Schlegel's novel has a broader currency in romantic-era thought, one could turn to two other contemporary texts where the creation from nothing resides at the juncture of ethical and aesthetic discourses. One is the *Das älteste Systemprogramm des deutschen Idealismus* [The oldest systematic program of German Idealism] of 1796–1797, a text fragment of disputed authorship (alternately attributed to the G.W.F. Hegel, Friedrich Hölderlin, and Friedrich Schelling). The other is Schlegel's *Rede über die Mythologie* [Speech on mythology], which forms one part of his important poetological text, *Das Gespräch über die Poesie* [Conversation about poesy] from 1800.

The *Systemprogramm* fragment raises the question, what kind of self or world should be created in the case of "the only true and conceivable *creation from nothing*" which would be the creation of the self as an "absolutely free being."[24] It asks where society will find its transcendent legitimation in an age where reason has divested it of its traditional recourse to God. The answer lies in poesy, as the highest art. According to the *Systemprogramm*, poesy will assume the synthesizing function that mythology previously had. This poesy will be a new mythology: literature not just for individuals but for society as a whole. The second text, one that also invokes the creation from nothing in tandem with a call for a new mythology, is Schlegel's *Rede über die Mythologie*. Spoken by the character Ludoviko, it too posits the creation from nothing as an aesthetic and ethical project. Ludoviko claims that modern poesy lacks a collective center. For the modern poet, every creative act exists only for the individual and is a creation from nothing. There are echoes of the *Systemprogramm* here, but the emphasis is on the emergence of the social from within a poetological discussion. Every act of subjective creativity exists not just for the individual, but for all. For both Schlegel and Novalis, creation from nothing is creation of and for society. This idea is most succinctly illustrated in Novalis' claim that we are "personified, all-powerful points," a note that depicts this very transition from the individual to the political unit of the family: "[o]nly insofar as man conducts a happy marriage with himself—and makes up a beautiful family, is he at all capable of marriage and family."[25] When he writes about marriage, he says that this institution is to politics "what the lever is for the theory of mechanics" and that "[t]he state is comprised not of individual people, but rather of pairs and societies."[26] For Novalis, then, the basic unit of the functioning state is not simply the personified point, or the individual as hypomochlion, but a lever whose two arms connect the disparate conditions of woman and man.

We can see that for the romantic novel, "generation" is a complex matter indeed, given that ontological and literary modes of generation emerge from an overdetermined "creation from nothing" and develop within a poetics of calculated disorder. I have argued elsewhere that, in the case of *Lucinde*, Schlegel provides us a way of combining these different elements by offering a model of interpretation grounded in epideictic oratory, where the qualities of a person, thing, and place are put on display by the speaker (*rhetor*) for the audience (*theoros*).[27] Epideictic oratory is traditionally self-reflexive and concerned with its own artifice; for Schlegel, who refers to these and other rhetorical terms in his philosophical notebooks, *epideixis* is a calculus of language, a constantly self-surpassing limit whose figure is synonymous with the creation of literature itself. Julius' epideictic speech exposes both himself and Lucinde. From the establishment and chance disruption of an imagined procreative coupling, there emerges both chaotic order and a turn to autoproduction. Of equal importance is the fact that epideixis is an emphatically positive (because creative) amplification with no corresponding negative impulse. In the framework of a creation from nothing, it seems to posit Being without destruction (in contrast to, for example, the movement of romantic irony, which oscillates between creation and destruction). Epideixis has a significant role to play in the collection of terms related to generation in romantic thought, because it formalizes the creation and revelation of Being within literature.

## 3  Generation in Broader Contexts

Thus far, the array of terms associated with the concept of generation in German Romanticism has been managed by limiting the focus of the discussion quite narrowly to particular aspects of romantic "self-production" and the production of the literary text. The challenge of articulating any unified perspective of romantic "generation," or of producing an adequate metalanguage with which to sort and organize the profusion of related terms, will quickly become apparent once more when the scope of the inquiry is broadened beyond generations of the self and the poetic text to include the organic theories that were of such great interest to the German Romantics. The distinction between *Zeugung* (procreation) and *Fortpflanzung* (propagation) presents one particularly interesting case. One most often encounters *Zeugung* in the context of animal generation. It is, according to one early nineteenth-century dictionary, "the activity wherein one brings forth one's own."[28] Despite its essentially heteronormative status (given that *Zeugung* was usually conceived of in terms of a coupling of male and female members of a species), romantic thinkers are just as interested in its logic of self-similarity, whereby like produces like.[29] Such an emphasis feeds naturally into the autopoietic fantasies of romantic literature, where *Zeugung* emerges as the production of a new individual in terms of its kinship with the parent. *Fortpflanzung*, for its part, though initially linked to the context of plant reproduction (as the name suggests: *Pflanze* = plant), was also adapted into broader contexts. Romantic thinkers use it as a model to describe the propagation of other things as well, including the various categories of procreating individuals (such as the propagation of a genus or a species[30]). It could also, from a theological perspective, refer to the transmission and inheritance of original sin. *Zeugung* produces an individual that is somehow indebted to its parent or creator (but whose ontological status in romanticism is fluid: it can be a human, but also an idea, or a work of art). The emphasis of *Fortpflanzung*, through the incorporation of singular acts of *Zeugung*, reproduces part-whole relationships on a larger scale by maintaining a collective that includes the individual.

We can see a wide range of examples of this phenomenon. Friedrich Schelling, the nature-philosopher whose early intellectual interests so often align with those of early German Romanticism, understands *Zeugung* to be directly accessible through the physical medium of the organism or the materiality of objects in the world, whereas *Fortpflanzung* is indirectly accessible through a different kind of "medium," one that only becomes visible (i.e., is granted a form) through the appearance and disappearance of physical bodies. In Goethe's case as well, if we accept him as someone whose intellectual interests are at least nominally compatible with those of German Romanticism,[31] the connection between *Zeugung* and *Fortpflanzung* can express a relationship between part and whole. This is particularly true in Goethe's writings on plant generation and morphology: in terms of time, where *Zeugung* is one empirical stage of development in the *Fortpflanzung* of the organism; in terms of a conceptual distinction that permits *Fortpflanzung* to be greater than or equal to individual acts of *Zeugung*; and in terms of the relation between a medium and its elements, where the spiritual or virtual dimension of *Fortpflanzung* is only revealed through empirical observation.

In the work of Johann Wilhelm Ritter, a physicist with close ties to Novalis, we see how these terms, and in particular *Fortpflanzung*, find purchase in the inorganic realm. Bettine Menke has shown how *Fortpflanzung* takes on new meaning in Ritter's work, where, in the context of acoustical experiments, it becomes pure operation and motion, and the subject is merely the medium of inscription. In other words, Ritter's writing on acoustics encourages us to imagine an unusual decoupling of these two concepts—a pure *Fortpflanzung* without *Zeugung*—where the organism in question is only medium and duration. The degree to which Ritter was willing to entertain this possibility is evident in the following passage taken from the appendix to the fragment project:

> In the *tone*, generally, where discontinuity in time *nonetheless* produces continuity, would be the first place to ask whether *different qualities which border one another merely in time* … could perhaps not also produce *processes* and processes of a *particular* kind among each other?—Already something similar lies in every *Fortpflanzung* of something, since namely here a time still really passes, until the process, etc., of *a* in *b*, of *b* in *c*, etc., has arrived.[32]

The difference in the temporality between, on the one hand, Ritter's metaphor of acoustical *Fortpflanzung* and, on the other, Goethe's discussion of *Fortpflanzung* and *Zeugung* in his writings on metamorphosis is striking. For Goethe, *Zeugung* is characterized by simultaneity, it is the event of a moment, whereas the *Fortpflanzung* of the species was characterized by a constant sequentiality and duration. In Ritter's acoustical speculations, however, his fantasy of a real *Fortpflanzung* is actualized. The propagation of sound can overcome temporal lapses because tones generate their own unique processes—"discontinuity … produces continuity."[33] As elements, the tones allow for a form to be propagated, which endures in time. In other words, the essence of *Zeugung*, as the production of one's own (invoked earlier in the phrase *seines Gleichen*, and here, *eigner Art*) has been reworked into the language of propagation. Though grounded in acoustical phenomena, the tendency of this passage is to take the acoustical model of *Fortpflanzung* and generalize it: if one can observe this process in a series of tones, then, as Ritter asks, why not in every act of *Fortpflanzung*?

The above examples have been included in order to supplement an overview of generation in romantic thought with close-up snapshots that give readers a sense of the language and thought processes unique to the intellectual epoch. We have observed that romantic thinkers have a particular agility when moving between the parts and the whole, whether in the context of the thinking, reflecting subject, within a landscape of interconnected scientific discourses or when taking advantage of the idiosyncratic meanings and usages offered by the particular terms of generation, as we saw in the case of *Zeugung* and *Fortpflanzung*. With the advantage of perspective, it is possible to say that there are two tendencies at play that might seem, at first glance, to be at odds with one another. These tendencies, linked to notions of part-whole relations that are readily adaptable to new contexts, are for figures of the period to think either holistically in terms of a large-scale process of generation of a particular "system" (be it the self, the novel, the plant, etc.) or of smaller moments or events within that system. A final example, which uses the concept of the mathematical series as a way of narrativizing procreative models, will help to illustrate the co-existence of the two tendencies:

> 81. Physics. Should every *embrace* be at once an embrace of the entire *couple*—as One nature, with One art (One spirit), and the child the unified product of the twofold embrace? Should plants perhaps be the products of the feminine nature and a masculine spirit—and animals the products of a *masculine* nature and the *feminine spirit*? And plants, say, the young girls—animals, the *young boys* of nature?
> Or are the stones the products of the root generation—plants—of generation$^2$—animals—generation$^3$—and the human being $^n$—of generation$^\infty$ or—?[34]

Novalis begins with a procreative pairing that sees in every human embrace the coupling of nature and art—the children of such a union are physical and transcendental products. The second sentence remains within an anthropocentric model of generation which then expands to include other realms: he detaches the word pair masculine/feminine from the human and integrates it within two distinct scenarios to account for the creation of plants and animals as well. He thereby generates an entire organic economy through a set of arithmetical equations whose components are chiastically inverted such that "feminine nature + masculine spirit = plants [girls]" and "masculine nature + feminine spirit = animals [boys]." In each case, nature, rather than mind (or "spirit"—Novalis uses the word *Geist*), determines the gender of the offspring. Up until this point, the note follows an arithmetical pattern, indexed by the synthesis of pairs and the structuring of the equations through additions and multiplications. The last sentence departs from the pairings to offer an alternate model of generation that integrates plants, animals, and humans into an exponential series. Novalis' designation of stones as the "root generation" reflects both their proximity to the earth and their value within the exponential series—*Wurzel* also refers to the square root ($\sqrt{}$) or mathematical radical sign. The series then skips to plants, whose generation is raised to the power of two, followed by the generation of animals to the power of three. These first members of the series exist in approximate proportion to one another: the ratio of 3 to 2 is approximately the same as that of 2 to $\sqrt{2}$. Yet, it is impossible to determine the latter ratio with precision. This is so because of a fact already discovered by mathematicians of antiquity, namely that $\sqrt{2}$ is an irrational number which cannot be precisely measured (hence "irrational" in the literal sense of without "ratio"). For that reason, the position of the stone generation in the series is subject to an infinite process of adjustment: its distance to the plant generation is immeasurable. The last term in the series, "humankind," forms a pendant to the stone generation: it too articulates an immeasurable gap through generation raised to a potentially infinite degree.

It bears keeping in mind, when re-constructing the conceptual environment of romantic thinking about generation, that from a historical perspective, the perception of what constitutes organic life was much different than ours. Novalis' positioning of stones within a "root generation" that exists in relationship to other, more developed, forms of life already gives a sense of this, and Ritter's fragments contain similar remarks.[35] At the same time, the romantic fascination with mining, the mineral realm, and the study of earth, informed as it was by the conviction that rocks and minerals were considered living and growing products, can scarcely be overestimated. Theodore Ziolkowski has documented this phenomenon extensively in a chapter on mining in *German Romanticism and Its Institutions*. He connects a historical fact—that Germany was the most important source of precious metals in

Europe through the end of the eighteenth century[36]—with the belief founding the "rational basis for alchemy" that "minerals and metals grow and, in the process, become increasingly refined" and that, as a result, "all the baser metals tend toward silver and gold."[37] A similar line of argument can be found in Irene Bark's *Steine in Potenz*:

> Thus the attempt to found the material causes of the living through chemical-physical means implied, at the same time, the claim of a reciprocal convergence of mathematical-mechanical and organological points of view with the goal, beyond that of closing the 'divide' between the realms of the anorganic and the organic, of also achieving a bridge between established modes of explanation of purely material phenomena ('physics') and the attempt of a scientific grounding of processes in the realm of consciousness ('theory of reason').[38]

It is astonishing how many romantic-era writers were educated in mining. Their numbers include Goethe, Novalis, Clemens Brentano, Joseph von Eichendorff, Henrich Steffens, Theodor Körner, Alexander von Humboldt, Franz von Baader, and Gotthilf Heinrich Schubert.[39] There is an equally enormous amount of writing on the subject, but as a point of departure, one could consult, for example, Steffens' *Beyträge zur innern Naturgeschichte der Erde* [Contributions to the internal natural history of the earth] from 1801, which described the earth as a site for the transformation of inanimate to animate objects; or Schubert, who wrote that "the whole kingdom of metals … seems to have arisen at the boundaries of the two worlds, from the decline and deterioration of the anorganic, and to bear within itself the seeds of the new organic age."[40] The most canonical literary texts in this area were penned by Novalis, Ludwig Tieck, and E.T.A. Hoffmann. In Novalis' novel, *Heinrich von Ofterdingen*, the protagonist asks, "Is it possible that beneath our feet a world of its own is stirring in a great life? That unheard-of births are taking place in the depths of the earth, distended by the inner fire of the dark womb to gigantic and immense shapes?"[41]

## 4 Technological Production

The study of mining is closely connected with the topic of tool-use. Novalis' notes attest to the fact that he encountered tools and technical instruments in the course of his studies at the Freiberg Mining Academy (1798–1799) and during his subsequent appointment as saline assessor in Weißenfels. Whether his professional work inspired a more theoretical interest in the concept of the tool or whether such interests emerged via other directions, such as his philosophical reflections on human agency, the fact remains that there is a pervasive theoretical interest in the concept of the tool in his notes and fragments. This fact still seems somewhat at odds with German romanticism's preoccupation with organic modes of generation, and their corresponding figures kind of self-generation or autopoiesis. To focus exclusively on organic generation nonetheless risks overlooking an equally pervasive interest in making that is more technological in its orientation. The tool concept is not just important for various romantic statements about craftsmanship, however. It is deeply embedded into processes of organic generation to the point where any rigorous attempt to distinguish between organic generation and technological production occurs at the expense of missing the point altogether: the word used for tool, *Werkzeug*, is itself a medium of reflection about the intersections of organic and mechanical processes of generation.

First, a brief terminological clarification is useful. *Werkzeug* is a peculiar word in German. It can refer to an instrument or tool, like a hammer, but it can also be a sensory organ or a philosophical organon. In Novalis' lexicon, the *Werkzeug* is shaped by Kant's writing on the organ in the *Critique of Judgement* from 1790. As organ, the *Werkzeug* has what Kant calls a "natural purpose." It is organized and self-organizing: each part is there both through and for every other part and the whole; each part is both *Zweck* (purpose) and *Mittel* (means). As natural purposes, organs appear to have a teleology, but, as Kant argues, such purpose cannot be interpreted by human faculties. Novalis' reception of Kant's perspective on the *Werkzeug* is evident through a heightened interest in reciprocal relationships, leading to a more complex model of production. Novalis then develops his new organically inflected model of the *Werkzeug* further to include other types of productivity (such as the relationship between artist, instrument, and artwork) as well as auto-production. In a statement that is as programmatic as it is ambivalent, Novalis claims that man is a *Selbstwerkzeug*: an instrument (or tool? or organ? of the self). He also takes advantage of this term's fundamental ambivalence to explore new territory through the creative use of analogies. The generative capacity of the *Werkzeug* lies in the fact that it is a vehicle of mediation between the human and the world. This same feature poses significant conceptual challenges, however, such as the problem of self-implication. If the *Werkzeug*, as tool or instrument, is so deeply embedded in processes of making, how are we supposed to distinguish its particular functioning from human agency? In German romanticism, this question takes on a particular urgency. Given that the *Werkzeug* mediates between various modes of making, production, and even organic generation, to what degree can one connect its poietic function with that fiction-building that, in Novalis' theory of language, overcomes the differentiation between subject and object? The examples provided below will give a sense of how the early German romantics thought about the question of the instrument's mediation between subject and object, both in contexts of artisan craftsmanship and in other contexts greatly abstracted from all material origins.

The young Heinrich von Ofterdingen, for example, learns the skills and pleasures of manual craftsmanship before those of poetry. It is also a well-known fact that the *nom de plume*, Novalis, ostensibly chosen from a repertoire of ancestral names, deserves to be included within the discourse on tools circulating throughout his oeuvre: *Novale* refers to newly plowed land. Without departing entirely from more "pragmatic" concepts of tool-use, Novalis also pursues numerous theoretical reflections about the nature of tools and their manifold relations to tool-users and the products they create. Consider, for example, this statement about the *Werkzeug*:

> Every *Werkzeug* is vehicle of a foreign utterance—efficacy. It modifies and is modified. The execution is a product of the individual composition of the *Werkzeug* and of the *Gestion*. Both can be variable—thus too the product becomes variable. Yet the case could arise, that they are as poles variable—and then the product is *constant* and the same.[42]

This fragment is important for Novalis' thinking on the *Werkzeug* because it implicates the elements of agent, instrument, and product within a process whereby each is constantly being modified by the other, perhaps an allusion to the organic register associated with the *Werkzeug* as organ. Although the focus of the fragment is on function, it also gestures to the rhetorical tradition: as a vehicle of transferal, a medium between agent and product, the *Werkzeug* performs the work of a metaphor. What is more, through his emphasis that agent and tool constantly inform one another, Novalis foregrounds the fact that the tool does not just act like a metaphor, it *is* one in the sense that it condenses mechanical and organic discourses, thus performing new couplings—new acts of generation—before our very eyes. Novalis' programmatic statements on the *Werkzeug* continue in the second paragraph, where the emphasis is on the relation between instrument and product. The degree to which his thinking oscillates between the abstract and the concrete is noteworthy. Having made the general statement that "Die *Gestalt* (Natur) des Werckzeugs ist gleichsam *das eine Element* des Produkts" [The *shape* (nature) of the tool is as it were *the one element* of the product], he shifts his attention to material constraints, while retaining the more general term, "element":

> I cannot be effective with a *Werkzeug* in any other way except the one which determines its natural relations. Thus I can only push, scrape and cut or crush with a chisel, insofar as it is sharp *iron*, or use it electrically, as metal for a galvanic excitator. In the two latter cases it no longer works as a chisel. I feel myself therefore through every specific *Werkzeug* limited to a certain kind of efficacy.[43]

As much as the *Werkzeug* is "modified" and is the "expression" of eternal agency, it too has the power to shape the "forces and thoughts of the artist" as well as to impact the material to which it is applied. These observations can be connected directly back to the question posed at the beginning of this chapter: what particular features define the romantic topography when it comes to the discourse of generation? The *Werkzeug* provides us with an important clue: in the hands of Novalis and Schlegel, it signals a de-centralization of romantic agency. It is not the self per se, not the "I," but rather an instrument whose autonomy waxes and wanes as it inscribes this new terrain. In retrospect, and framed in somewhat different terms, we are reminded of the balance between procreation and propagation, a shift away from pure iterations of the self.

I would like to conclude this section with reference to two further connections in early romantic thinking about the *Werkzeug* in processes of generation. The first is to late eighteenth-century physiological theory, and the second requires a return to romantic concepts of the novel and general reflections on language; these are spheres where the *Werkzeug*, through cognitive processes, can produce a language which has its own materiality. When manipulating language, the *Werkzeug* performs multiple simultaneous functions, just as in the fragment cited previously which summoned a reciprocal relationship between agent and product. On the one hand, the *Werkzeug* externalizes thoughts into near-tangible apparitions; on the other hand, it works in the opposite direction, moving from the acoustics of language to a supersensory poesy, which results in a hieroglyphic "total instrument" (*Gesamtwerkzeug*[44]), what Novalis will call "language to the power of two."[45] The reciprocity between the sensory and the supersensory, internal and external, tangible and intangible can be thought of within the framework of late eighteenth-century physiology. Novalis was familiar with a theoretical model discussing the relations of organic forces to one another thanks to Carl Friedrich Kielmeyer's 1793 essay, "Ueber die Verhältniße der organischen Kräfte unter einander in der Reihe der verschiedenen Organisationen, die

Geseze und Folgen dieser Verhältniße" [*On the relations of the organic forces to one another in the series of the various organizations, the laws and consequences of these relations*]. In this essay, Kielmeyer posits five forces in living organisms and develops a theory of compensation, where a noticeable decrease in one force was balanced by the increase of another. For example, sensibility (the capability of having impressions, such as on the nerves, produces ideas) and irritability (the capability of the muscles or other organs to move when stimulated) decrease as the force of physical reproduction increases. This idea was taken up as a way of describing the balance between physical and intellectual faculties and to claim man's specificity as the creature with the greatest sensitivity: whose lessened physical reproduction, when compared to other species, was compensated by the production of ideas. The heightened productivity of the virtual *Werkzeug* is based on the same economy, which leads to a heightened generation of intellectual activity.

Novalis also explores the potential of the *Werkzeug* for poetic creation in his novels and his aphoristic writing. Between the two genres, however, it is the novel that addresses the *Werkzeug* more directly as a problem for poetics and literary creativity. *Heinrich von Ofterdingen* and his second novel, *Die Lehrlinge zu Sais* [The Apprentices of Sais], each connect the concept of the *Werkzeug* directly to a particular literary genre. *The Apprentices of Sais* grants the fairy-tale the function of an epistemological tool by inserting one in the center of its philosophical discussions. *Heinrich von Ofterdingen* experiments with different literary forms, including references to the novel and the fairy-tale, but identifies the fable as the "total *Werkzeug*" that organizes Heinrich's world; this expression, already mentioned at the beginning of this chapter, receives a different emphasis in the context of Novalis' instrumental thinking. In the novel, he invokes the genre of the fable as *Werkzeug* in the sense of an *organon*, a construct which permits him to expand his knowledge and awareness beyond the present world: "thus, in the theory of the fable, life is reproduced for a higher world in the poetic expressions that have emerged in the most wonderful way."[46] There is a connection to be made between, on the one side, Heinrich's certainty that the fable, as poetic organon, completely informs his world and, on the other side, the fairy-tale told by the character Klingsohr, which allegorizes a metamorphosis from the individual to the total *Werkzeug*— from tool to poesy.

## 5   Concluding Remarks

The two goals for this chapter have been to provide a sense of the expansive and varied landscape associated with the notion of generation in German Romanticism and to consider the consequences of a discursive landscape predicated on modalities of change that encompass organic growth as well as technological production. As far as the first is concerned, the reader should now have a better sense of the discursive reach of romantic thinking about processes of generation, broadly understood. What about the second goal? What particular landscape features have emerged from our composite view of romantic writing on generation? Or, to add another, arguably romantic, level of redundancy to an already circular line of questioning: what does the generation of generation generate?

One feature to emerge is that of a decentralized, disunified self. Whereas early German Romanticism is often, and not incorrectly, characterized in terms of recursive, self-implicating gestures that seem to concentrate the self within the self, there are other tendencies that do just the opposite. We see this most clearly when the emphasis is placed on their concept of the tool, but distinctions made between different modes of generation (such as between *Zeugung* and *Fortpflanzung*) also suggest a more "outwardly" moving self. This argument connects to a line of thought articulated in Leif Weatherby's recent book, *The Metaphysical Organ*. Consider, for example, the definition he gives of the romantic organ. Weatherby argues that "rather than producing a representation of a world, a Nature, or a history, the early German Romantics' focus on organs was meant to recast any possible sense of 'world,' 'nature,' or 'being,'" and that "by naming the parts of any of these wholes 'organs,' the Romantics did not wish to replace one picture of the world with another—they meant to undermine the merely pictorial or representational sense of the world."[47] For this reason, he continues, "organs delimit and open the space between the possible and the actual—as Aristotle had shown—and thus change the metaphysical question about the primacy of thought or being from one having to do with representation (thought 'pictures' being; an ultimately represented world produces the thought that does the representing) to one centered on function and reproduction."[48] Evidence arguing in favor of a shift of emphasis from a language of representation toward one of function and reproduction has already been provided by some of the cases discussed above, and further examples can be found in my own research on structures of procreation in German Romanticism.[49] Collectively, these perspectives do not argue that we give up on some notion of the "self" altogether, but rather that we reconsider it through a language of production that connects its physical and metaphysical aspects. We are left with an alternative to a conventional, centralized model: one that allows for all manner of creative extensions, projections, and dislocations, all under the auspices of generation.

## Notes

1. One concise formulation of the state of *Naturphilosophie* before Friedrich Schelling's arrival on the scene can be found in J.S. Beck's *Grundriß der critischen Philosophie* [Outline of the critical philosophy] from 1796. Beck identifies two strands of *Naturphilosophie*: the dynamic and the mechanical. Whereas the first relies upon "the difference of the connection of the original forces of expansion and attraction," that is, the model that forms the basis for Kant's description of matter, for the second, "the varying figure of the absolutely hard *first particles* (atoms) is … the principle, from which the specific variation of matter is derived." In the work of Schelling and others such as Carl Eschenmayer, we see not a rejection of these two models, but rather an attempt, through a project Schelling refers to as a "speculative physics," to understand object-oriented theories of nature as existing within the same continuum as theories of the ego (a goal which was, in essence, more compatible with the Kantian understanding of a nature philosophy based on forces of expansion and contraction).
2. Manfred Frank. *Foundations of Early German Romanticism*.
3. Kneller, "Introduction," xv.
4. Ibid.
5. Novalis, *Schriften*, II.294.
6. Frank's *Philosophische Grundlagen der Frühromantik* was initially published in the journal *Athenäum*, eds. Günter Oesterle, Jochen Hörisch and Ernst Behler, vol. 4 (1994), 37–130. Translated into English as *The Philosophical Foundations of Early German Romanticism*, trans. Elizabeth Millán-Zaibert (Albany: SUNY Press, 2004). The translated lectures had not been published before they appeared in the Suhrkamp 1997 *Unendliche Annaeherung. Die Anfaenge der philosophischen Fruehromantik*. Frank has discussed this matter in both places.
7. Gerhard Neumann, *Ideenparadiese. Untersuchungen zur Aphoristik von Lichtenberg, Novalis, Friedrich Schlegel und Goethe* (München: Fink, 1976).
8. Novalis, *Notes for a Romantic Encyclopedia*, trans. and ed. David W. Wood (Albany: SUNY, 2007), 165, n. 927. The German text is located in Novalis, Schriften, 3446–7, 929.

9. "Der Mensch als Natur-Produkt; als Produkt seines Geschlechtes (der Gesellschaft); das Produkt seiner selbst, der gebildete, gesittete, wissende Mensch." Quoted in Neumann, *Ideenparadiese*, 91.
10. Fichte, *Ueber den Begriff der Wissenschaftslehre oder der sogenannten Philosophie*. 2nd edition (Jena and Leipzig: Christian Ernst Gabler, 1798), 12. In this passage as well, one finds a metaphor of arable land similar to the one contemplated for the growth of a paradise of ideas.
11. Kant, *Metaphysical Foundations of Natural Science* in *Theoretical Philosophy after 1781*. Edited by Henry Allison and Peter Heath. Translated by Gary Hatfield, Michael Friedman, Allison and Heath. Cambridge University Press (2002), 186.
12. Novalis, "Fichte Studies," 66–7. For the German, see Novalis, *Schriften*, 2.168.
13. See, for example, Marie-Luise Heuser's essay, "Dynamisierung des Raumes und Geometrisierung der Kräfte" in 'Fessellos durch die Systeme.' *Frühromantisches Naturdenken im Umfeld von Arnim, Ritter und Schelling* and also Leif Weatherby's discussion of Schelling in his *Transplanting the Metaphysical Organ: German Romanticism between Leibniz and Marx* (New York: Fordham UP, 2016).
14. Herbert Uerlings, "*Darstellen*. Zu einem Problemzusammenhang bei Novalis."
15. Novalis, *Fichte Studies*, 10. For the German, see *Schriften*, vol. 2. Ed. Richard Samuel, with Hans-Joachim Mähl and Gerhard Schulz. Stuttart, etc. (W. Kohlhammer, 1981), 110.
16. See Frank [x], quoted in Uerlings 376.
17. Uerlings, Herbert. "Darstellen. Zu einem Problemzusammenhang bei Novalis," in *Romantische Wissenspoetik. Die Künste und die Wissenschaften um 1800*. Ed. Gabriele Brandstetter and Gerhard Neumann. Würzburg: Königshausen & Neumann, 2004, 373–392, 380.
18. For further reading on the concept of art and figure of the artist in German romanticism, see Brad Prager's *Aesthetic Vision and German Romanticism. Writing Images* (Rochester: Camden House, 2007).
19. Novalis, *Schriften* 2.588.264.
20. Schlegel, *Kritische Ausgabe*, 18.iii.15.
21. See Schlegel *Kritische Ausgabe* 16.v.216 and *Kritische Ausgabe* 16.xii.30.
22. For further reading on Schlegel's *Lucinde* from other theoretical perspectives, see Eleanor Ter Horst, "The Classical Aesthetics of Schlegel's *Lucinde*," *Goethe Yearbook* 23 (2016), 123–140 and Mark Bauer, "Der verborgene Mittelpunkt: Issues of Death and Awareness in Friedrich Schlegel's 'Lucinde,'" *Monatshefte* 92.2 (2000), 139–163.
23. On the topic of chaos, see Bianca Theisen and Kelly Barry, "$\chi^\alpha$ Absolute Chaos: The Early Romantic Poetics of Complex Form," *Studies in Romanticism* 42.3 (Fall, 2003), 301–321.
24. "Oldest System Programm" in Joseph Tanke and Collin McQuillan, eds., *The Bloomsbury Anthology of Aesthetics* (New York: Bloomsbury, 2012), 300.

25. "Nur insofern der Mensch also mit sich selbst eine glückliche Ehe führt—und eine schöne Familie ausmacht, ist er überhaupt Ehe und Familienfähig. Act der Selbstumarmung" (Novalis, *Schriften* 2, 541.74).
26. "Die Ehe ist für die Politik, was der Hebel für die Maschinenlehre. Der Staat besteht nicht aus einzelnen Menschen, sondern aus Paaren und Gesellschaften. Die Stände der Ehe sind die Stände des Staats—Frau und Mann. Die Frau ist der sog[enannte] *ungebildete* Theil" (Novalis, *Schriften* 3, 470.1106).
27. "Lucinde: the Novel from 'Nothing' as Epideictic Literature" in *Germanisch-romanische Monatsschrift* 54.2 (2004), 163–176.
28. "Zeugung": "von dem Verbo zeugen, generare, am häufigsten im thätigen Verstande, die Handlung, da man seines Gleichen hervor bringet." See Johann Adelung, *Grammatisch-kritisches Wörterbuch der hochdeutschen Mundart*, vol. 4 (Vienna: B. Bauer, 1811), col. 1701.
29. This is thought of as the "breeding criterion" in late eighteenth-century physiology.
30. See Novalis, *Schriften*, 3.433.849: "Die Definition ist die Constructionsformel d[er] Begr[iffe] etc. Aller Erzeugung—*Generation*—Erzeugung d[es] Geschlechts—geht eine Specification—der Specification eine Individuation voraus."
31. I do not consider Goethe a (German) "Romantic" per se, but the distinctions between his philosophical approach to nature and that of Schlegel and Novalis are beyond the purview of this chapter. For a more detailed analysis, see Dietrich von Engelhardt's essay "Natur und Geist, Evolution und Geschichte: Goethe in seiner Beziehung zur romantischen Naturforschung und metaphysischen Naturphilosophie" in *Goethe und die Verzeitlichung der Natur*, ed. Peter Matussek (Munich: C. H. Beck, 1998).
32. Ritter, appendix to the fragments, 497.
33. Ibid.
34. Novalis, *Notes for a Romantic Encyclopaedia*, 13. For the German, see Novalis, *Schriften*, 3.255.81.
35. See, for example, the opening of Fragment 64: "Everything, which is, preserves itself organically. Every stone emerges anew in every moment, produces itself on into the infinite."
36. Ziolkowski, *German Romanticism*, 25. Please give full bibliographic information.
37. Ziolkowski, *German Romanticism*, 30.
38. Irene Bark, *Steine in Potenzen. Konstruktive Rezeption der Minerologie bei Novalis* (New York: de Gruyter, 1991), 291.
39. Ziolkowski, *German Romanticism*, 20.
40. Gotthilf Schubert, *Nachtseite der Naturwissenschaften*, quoted in Ziolkowski, *German Romanticism*, 31.
41. Novalis, *Heinrich von Ofterdingen*, quoted in Ziolkowski, *German Romanticism*, 31. Tieck's novella, "Der Runenberg" (1804) and Hoffmann's

novella, "Die Bergwerke zu Falun" (1819) are required reading for those interested in further reading.
42. Novalis, *Schriften*, 2:552.120. My translation.
43. Ibid. 2:553.120. My translation.
44. Novalis, *Schriften*, 1.331.
45. Novalis, *Schriften*, 2:588.264.
46. Ibid. 1.333.
47. Leif Weatherby, *Transplanting the Metaphysical Organ: German Romanticism between Leibniz and Marx* (New York: Fordham UP, 2017).
48. Ibid. Weatherby also writes, "the project of Romantic metaphysics become 'technological,' that is, it becomes a matter of constructing working systems that can produce and reproduce (rather than merely represent) in what appear to be multiple orders of things"; and, in a more summary statement, "the organ of philosophy must be operationalized, it must be recognized as a *Produzieren*. All that remains is to find the proper cognitive medium for the realization of that recursive immediacy, or of the conscious intuition of the self" (Weatherby, *Metaphysical Organ*, 201).
49. In my book, *German Romanticism and Science: the Procreative Poetics of Goethe, Novalis, and Ritter* (Routledge 2009), I show in greater detail how the procreative tendencies in Novalis' philosophical and scientific aphorisms: where philosophical, chemical, or galvanic narratives of production were articulated as gendered couplings, proto-narratives that a few common tendencies: while draw freely from diverse theories of organic generation, they place as much emphasis on the process as on the product of procreation.

# 19

# Arts of Unconditioning: On Romantic Science and Poetry

## Gabriel Trop

This chapter examines the operations of romantic poetry and science inasmuch as they form part of a common project undertaken from two distinctive strategic sites and discursive logics. Both of these sites—poetry and science—can be regarded as forms of signification that organize and disorganize themselves in the light of a conception of the Absolute as something that is without condition and limitation: the Absolute as *unconditioned* (*das Unbedingte*) and hence as the source of a power of *unconditioning*.

The force of unconditioning that inheres in romantic semiosis unleashes a subterranean energy and seeks to make present the drone or hum of a persistent chaos capable of reconfiguring our imaginative tendencies and our ethical and political investments (Novalis' *Europe or Christianity*, which I will discuss in the course of this chapter, provides a concrete example of the politics of unconditioning). This account of the imbricated operations of romantic poetry and science—as arts of unconditioning—distances itself from the following understandings of the romantic project: poetry and art as ineffable (and hence as primarily non-discursive and non-scientific); art as something that mystically restores contact with an Absolute that evades our capacity to represent it or grasp it; the Absolute as a "regulative idea" that, although we can never grasp it, can nevertheless orient our behavior; the unification of humanity and nature through art as a messianic fulfillment; or the

G. Trop (✉)
University of North Carolina, Chapel Hill, NC, USA
e-mail: gtrop@email.unc.edu

establishment of a restorative and utopian ideal (the return of a "golden age") through the reconciliation of art and nature.

In order to understand romantic poetry and science as arts of unconditioning, one must begin with conditions. Conditions are figures of stabilization: they designate what must be the case in order for an expected operation to function properly (e.g. the production of truth, the binding of a contract, the norms, both implicit and explicit, governing personal, social, legal, or political life). Regarding romantic poetry and science as arts of unconditioning uncovers a counterforce to all transcendentalizing gestures by attending to whatever is external to conditions. This chapter will thus first examine romantic poetry from the perspective of an oscillation between processes of stabilization and destabilization that depends upon the production of alterity: knowledge in contact with that which cannot be integrated into the production of knowledge. This chapter will then turn to an investigation of the isomorphic dynamics of poetry and science, above all as they manifest themselves in the romantic concept of poetry (*Poesie*) and in the discourse of Schellingian nature-philosophy. Before briefly considering different conceptions of the imbrication of poetry and science (Johann Wilhelm Ritter's *Fragments from the Papers of a Young Physicist*, Goethe's morphology), this chapter will show how the material and semiotic forces of "unconditioning" culminate in the romantic notion of a new mythology. The "new mythology" draws upon that which extends beyond the human (e.g. force and matter) and attempts to translate these dynamics into human practices, thereby releasing a power of reconfiguration into the order of the sensible. However, the poetry of this period does not merely celebrate the emancipatory potential of the new mythology, but also foregrounds its limitations, as will be demonstrated in the work of Karoline von Günderrode.

## 1   Distant Philosophy

An evocative remark in Novalis' *Notes for a Romantic Encyclopedia* imagines a type of philosophy as a call in the distance.[1] What would it mean to practice *distant philosophy*? Distant philosophy as envisioned by Novalis contains an implicit imperative: bring the presence of the everyday world into contact with the contours of an obscure horizon that intimates a different organization of beings. This injection of alterity into the present comprises one of the most significant operations of romanticization: "distant mountains, distant human beings, distant events etc. all become romantic."[2] Philosophy, when directed toward the distance, activates a sense of possibility and disorients as much as it orients: it conjures the "poesy of night and dusk."[3]

The function of poetry (*Poesie*) in Novalis' conception of distant philosophy directs itself against epistemological security, or more broadly, against any discursive operation that seeks to neutralize the mystery of the unknown.[4] Poetry thereby differentiates itself from discourses that posit the production of knowledge as a telos. It is perhaps for this reason that German Romantic philosophy has, over the course of its long and varied reception history, often been associated with a form of aesthetic mysticism, one that values an intuition of something ineffable or inexpressible over whatever can be discovered through empirical investigation or articulated in discourse.

According to this view of the romantic project, the truth of science and the truth of art may implicate one another, but they must ultimately remain forever distinct: even if the energies of magnetism, electricity, chemistry, and other scientific discourses move through romantic textuality, even if romantic scientific writings speak with the language of poetry, science and art essentially diverge in their particular way of making beings speak, in the way each domain generates ontological insight. Science would depend upon and produce the articulation of truth within discursive orders, whereas art would bring into focus a non-cognitive or pre-cognitive—and hence non-discursive—domain that could only be accessed through intuition and would thus signal a void within all acts of discourse.[5] Art—or *poetry*, when understood as a mode of attunement to the world rather than as a linguistic form, literary genre, or something that is merely encoded as information—would then represent a privileged point of entry into what many early German Romantics sought to achieve, namely, participation in an absolute realm that would infuse a disenchanted, mechanistic world with the breath of the sacred. In this view, the holistic intertwining of art, truth, politics, and religion would constitute the signature of the event of Romanticism. It is for this reason that a thinker like Alain Badiou characterizes the later Heidegger's prioritization of the truth of the work of art as a quintessentially romantic project.[6]

This understanding of Romanticism is in many ways limited. Some of the dominant modes of romantic thought attribute a disclosive function to empirical investigation, scientific experimentation, the observation of the phenomenal world, and the production of knowledge in and through genres and disciplines that can be constellated and recombined with one another. If there is something like an event of German Romantic thought, its most significant operations will not be found in the separation of various regimes of truth or in a distinction between domains of practice, each with its own internal coherence and consistency, but rather in an attraction to discursive contamination, impurity, troubled boundaries, and boundary troubles. Let us return briefly to Badiou, as his understanding of philosophy can provide us with a clear contrast to the investments of romantic thought. Whereas Badiou understands philosophy not as a discourse that generates truths but one that "seizes" truths that have been generated—through "truth procedures" that take place in love, politics, science, and art, for example, which constitute the "conditions" of philosophy—romantic thought posits the boundaries of discursive and imaginative zones only to relate them, suspend them, mix them, displace them, and reposition them. Faced with the void of an event, Badiou's philosophy stabilizes and delimits conditions; part of the romantic imperative consists in the following injunction: *uncondition* the conditions.

There is a certain strand of romantic thought that can therefore be grasped as a living practice opposed to what Badiou will call the "purity" of the idea. Badiou writes, "But what is purity? It consists, I would argue, in the composition of an Idea that as such is not retained in any bond. This is an idea that captures being's indifference to every relation, that captures its separated scintillation, its multiplicity without Whole. This is the idea's coldness … its disjunction."[7] Pervasive patterns in romantic thought tend toward a diametrically opposed notion of the order and disorder of beings: even when Being is conceptualized as a zone inaccessible to reflection that excludes differentiation (as happens in Novalis' *Fichte Studies*), one may discern a higher-order form of Being that consists in perpetual oscillation between opposing polarities (e.g. Being as *movements* between reflection and feeling rather than as a non-differentiated unity accessible *only* to feeling)[8]; the field organizing beings is experimental in that any discrete element can be joined with any other to generate a novel discursive reconfiguration[9]; if there is a notion of the Whole that runs through Romanticism, this holism is not merely integrative and restorative but equally disruptive and even sometimes traumatic[10]; and the central movements of Being are paradoxical, consisting in operations that are both disjunctive and conjunctive, solidifying and fluidifying, attractive and repulsive.

## 2 Force and Unconditioning

These patterns of romantic thought can best be understood as an attempt to think beyond the power of one of the most pervasive stabilizing discursive figures, namely, that of the condition (*Bedingung*). Kant's Critical Idealism is a philosophy of conditions: our "interests of reason"—*what can I know, what should I do, what may I hope*—must first be approached by elucidating the

## 19  Arts of Unconditioning: On Romantic Science and Poetry

*conditions of possibility* (*Bedingungen der Möglichkeit*) of knowledge, morality, and happiness.[11] Kant's notion of reason, however, has paradoxical characteristics inasmuch as it is simultaneously stabilizing and destabilizing; reason itself is the condition of possibility of morality, but there is also a drive structure inherent to reason that pushes human beings into making judgments and assertions about that which they can have no possible experience. Hence, the necessity of a *critique* of reason, where critique signals the demarcation of a boundary line and an injunction to avoid transgression, does not go beyond the realm of possible experience toward something outside of all conditions, unless it is merely in a regulative sense, and thus only as an idea that *orients* thought.

In contrast to the ideas, imperatives and lines of demarcation characteristic of Kant's critical project, romantic thought does not remain confined to conditions of possibility, but more significantly, seeks the possibility of the unconditioned. In the first aphorism of Novalis' *Pollen*, we read, "We *seek* the Absolute [*das Unbedingte*, the unconditioned] everywhere and only ever *find* things."[12] It is easy to read this aphorism as a compressed narrative of frustrated desire: we yearn for an Absolute that forever withdraws from our capacity to hold it, grasp it, and cognize it.[13] This reading projects an *adversative Romanticism* into the structure of the aphorism: we desire the Absolute, *but* we find only things. However, alongside this reading—which, in Kantian fashion, seems to posit the Absolute as something *beyond* things, something that merely orients us in a regulative sense—we intimate another possibility: a *conjunctive Romanticism*. Here we attend to the power of the conjunction that binds the two statements in the fragment: we seek the Absolute *and* we only find things. Such, after all, is what the aphorism says. Finding things in the world is commensurate with seeking the Absolute. Or one may express the insight as follows: seeking the Absolute is a specific way of always finding only things.

The romantic project does not consist merely in a manner of finding things in any way whatsoever, but in a way that is inflected by that which is without condition, thereby introducing a fundamental difference into the orders that seem to govern quotidian reality. This "unconditioned" that feeds into practices and reconfigures them is functionally equivalent with *poetry* (*Poesie*) or with *romanticization*.[14] Poetry, in this sense, is an operation rather than a genre; it occupies the functional position of a different sort of imperative, namely, not to become frozen in stabilizing forms of thought and feeling. Seen from this light, the unconditioned or Absolute is not the holistic dream of a totalizing mythology aiming to unite all of humankind and usher in a new golden age, but becomes a drive toward the production of difference, catapulting individuals out of their most entrenched investments and positions. Whereas the Fichtean Absolute *posits* (*setzt*, stakes out a position), fundamental operations of the romantic Absolute *uncondition* (unsettle the positions).[15]

To be sure, this "unconditioning" cannot be thought without its opposite, namely, the necessity of the opposing movements of conditioning: a counterforce without which the unconditioned could never come to light. In his study of romantic ballistics or a general romantic mechanics and dynamics that encompasses Leibnizian calculus, parabolas, hyperbolas, circles, rotating figures, and curves, Daniel Lancereau writes of a "series of technologies" that draw romantic authors, on the one hand, to a process of infinitization that would occasion a dissolution of forms and, on the other hand, to a form of restraint that allows them to *generate* forms; the central romantic tension consists in the fact that the romantic is simultaneously "the friend of the infinite *and* the friend of forms."[16]

Such a tension infiltrates romantic practices of signification. The most fundamental romantic patterns of representation operate within a cosmos of forces and polarities that cut across discursive fields, moving not only through magnetism, chemistry, medicine, and so forth, but also through poetry and philosophy, indeed interpenetrating *every field*.[17] The forces that manifest themselves through polarities are never fixed, but exhibit an oscillating dynamic structure that feeds into an entire way of life, a *poetry* of existence: through such oscillations, one seeks out whatever does not fit within a consistent field of practices, patterns of intelligibility, or in any specific position or condition whatsoever, and then one relentlessly pursues this darkness in order that it might flow back into practices and recondition them. Such is the meaning of Novalis' paradigmatic articulation of *distant philosophy*.

Philosophy itself, then, is less a meta-discourse that governs all the others than itself a medium of the Absolute of force: a thematization of the unconditioned as the production of a dynamic oscillation. Here one must attend to the *form* of philosophy rather than its content. For example, the content of Friedrich Schlegel's philosophy is resolutely anti-foundationalist: "an absolute understanding is not at all possible in our opinion."[18] The movements of philosophy do not cease once the philosopher has determined that the Absolute cannot be cognized; on the contrary, the absence of an absolute "understanding" sets discursive and reflective processes into motion. The energy of romantic philosophy—what movements it incites in mind and matter—travels through sensuous forms invested with a power of reconfiguration. The *form* of Schlegel's discourse thus has a revelatory function that organizes itself along the pulsations of a higher-order Absolute of force, a movement modeled on the structure of the magnet; it suggests an Absolute not of perfect identity that would culminate in some ultimate ground, but an Absolute that continually moves among relations.[19]

Such an Absolute would move throughout philosophical discourse as well. Thus, when Friedrich Schlegel claims that "truth is relative,"[20] it is not merely a statement about the impossibility of ever grounding truth foundationally, but rather, he expresses the insight that truth organizes itself *in relations* that are continually reconfiguring themselves. Schlegel's idealism thereby embraces the structure of a magnet, "where truth is the indifference of two opposed errors."[21] Even here can be seen, at the heart of a romantic idealism, a latent nature-philosophy (*Naturphilosophie*) or absolute physics. Truth is functionally equivalent to that point in a magnet, the "point of indifference" in the language of the Dutch physicist Anton Brugmans, at which contrary forces (in this case, contrary "errors") cancel one another but nevertheless remain present as structuring polarities.[22] Truth becomes a higher-order movement *through errors*, and the relativity of truth involves the way in which these "relations" both exist as differences and cancel one another out when one moves from one polar opposition to the next. It is not enough to say that philosophy is magnetic; rather, the same invisible forces that constitute both the magnet's conditions of possibility *and* its real materiality can be found in the concrete movements of philosophy, of thought, and of discourse. Romantic experiments with literary form—for example, the "fragment"—are thus not primarily mimetic; they do not mirror a static ontological order, nor do they suggest an "unattainability" of truth to which we shall never accede, as much as they attempt to continually generate new relations that themselves *are* the movements of the Absolute.

Schlegel's ultimate formulation of a "philosophy of philosophy" is not a simple ironic infinite self-reflection or mise-en-abîme, but the folding of philosophical discourse itself into a self-perpetuating oscillation between opposing forces. Like Schlegel, Novalis, in his fragment on distant philosophy, grasps the practice of philosophy as a medium of prosaic "indifference" rather than as poetically charged (positive or negative). As a neutralizing discourse of knowledge, philosophy is surrounded on both sides by the polarized energetics of poetic mystery: "on both sides, or around it, there lies + and minus poesy."[23] The first poetic mystery (negative poetry) results from a deficit of knowledge, and the second poetic mystery (positive poetry) results from a *passing through* knowledge. Novalis does not dismiss the zone of indifference of prosaic philosophy; rather, it is a zone that is structurally necessary for the force of the poetic imagination to remain operative. However, it is a zone that one must pass through, a zone in which "knowledge is a means of once again acquiring *ignorance.*"²⁴ Once philosophy becomes a call in the distance, its "consonants," or its structuring and conceptual operations, are transfigured and rendered open, made *vocalic*, "for every call in the distance becomes a vowel."²⁵

The traces of an Absolute of *dynamic forces* that moves throughout sensuous reality, throughout the mind and its signifying practices—rather than an Absolute as a plenitude of Being that remains forever beyond our grasp and beyond signification—saturate Novalis' philosophical reflections. The full import of the doctrine of "magical idealism," for example, cannot be adequately grasped without this dynamic, as "magical idealism" must be offset by a "magical realism":

> [There is] a Magical Idealist, just as there are Magical Realists. The former seeks a wondrous movement—a wondrous subject—the latter a wondrous object—a wondrous figure. Both are logical afflictions—types of delusions—within which, nonetheless, the ideal manifests or reflects itself in a twofold manner—holy—isolated beings—who wonderfully refract the higher light—Genuine prophets.²⁶

The magical idealist seeks to make everything appear as a manifestation of his or her own subjectivity; the magical realist, however, makes everything, including his or her own subjectivity, the manifestation of an externalized, objective form. Although Novalis calls both of these personality types "logical illnesses," these illnesses—as thinking outside the norms of health—nevertheless have a revelatory capacity, namely, as a *refraction* of the ideal into multiple forms. Both poles—magical idealism and magical realism—are critical to the movements of romantic art, and an oscillation between both prevents the totalization of one over the other. While much has been made of Novalis' magical idealism, it cannot be understood without an opposing force: attentiveness to the magical realist zones of Romanticism asks us to linger in an open conceptual space, that of the real, with its own particular refraction of the ideal. Novalis' form of Romanticism is therefore a very specific sort of realism: the cultivation of a sensitivity to an exteriority to the space of the mind. In turn, the power of the exterior becomes a source of a peculiar form of perturbation, one whose power relativizes and limits the human, and at the same time, by gesturing toward a domain over which we hold no empire, affirms the cosmos as a limitless and expansive horizon of possibilities.

One may see the imbrication of science and poetry in the polar movements of force and the presence of an exteriority that infuses these movements with a disruptive power. In what follows, I intend to illustrate and explicate this particularly significant node of romantic discourse and imagination—the node occupied by romantic science and poetry—through the pervasive presence of operations of *conditioning, unconditioning*, and *reconditioning*.

In this task, my method will follow closely that of the early German Romantics' own understanding of the task of criticism. The romantic notion of criticism harbors a poetic potential, guided by the thought that reality can be *poetized* by contact with something outside of explanatory frameworks and that whatever poetry is, it is irreducible to the production of knowledge; poetry thereby "unconditions" the historical conditions of possibility of its own intelligibility. Furthermore, within this constellation, the romantic organization of knowledge abjures master discourses. Philosophy therefore cannot function as a framework that explains *why* the sciences, the arts, and the whole world must be romanticized, but rather, is itself also part of the world that must be romanticized. No discourse can claim a privileged status, but rather, discourses become lenses that can be put on and taken off at will depending on the specific strategic interest, and the romantic language of criticism moves through the orders and disorders of the sensible world in order to intensify these interests. Approaching the knot of poetry and science in this manner would constitute an *intervention* rather than a description and would harness a force of perturbation; a romantically inflected criticism would not merely seek to capture the "truth" about a state of affairs, but would actively unsettle the ossification of thought.

To be sure, just as light passes through a prism and transforms its direction and appearance, so too can romantic poetic, scientific, and philosophical practices be refracted through a discursive lens: economics, mathematics, physics, organology, chemistry, sexual differentiation, heredity, medicine, with as many points of entry as there are fields of knowledge.[27] For the romantic critic, however, scientific discourses do not simply produce truth; they have the effect of associative resonance chambers, semiotic models, and even corresponding moods that reverberate in the imagination. Going beyond a mere *description* of the historical conditions of emergence of knowledge, the romantic critic would see his or her own act as something that would facilitate the unconditioning and reconditioning of the real. And here—to anticipate one of my conclusions—is to be found a distinctive form of romantic politics, a politics utterly distinct from ideologies that derive their power from organicist models of community whereby a people is constituted through processes of identification. Such political operations can be found instead in the localizable semiotic and imaginative operations that saturate both scientific and poetic textual forms: movements of attraction and repulsion, binding and dissolving, condensing and dispersing, differentiation and the suspension of differentiation.

## 3   Scientific Poiesis

In the so-called Earliest Program for a System of German Idealism (1796)—a document written in Hegel's handwriting but composed in the Tübinger *Stift* and thus likely to have been influenced, if not co-authored, by Schelling and Hölderlin—we read about a desire "to restore wings to our plodding physics, which is weighed down by laborious experiments."[28] The text's celebration of a "mythology of *reason*"[29] suggests that the problem with physics lies not in its epistemological character, but rather in its form of representation, namely, in the experiment, its tempo, and the affect that surrounds it. Hampered by casuistry, resistant to narrativization (*mythos*), "plodding" physics becomes overwhelmed by a force of gravity or inertia, ironically falling victim to one of its own privileged objects of study (gravitational force). Only poetry can deliver the upward swing that would release physics from its imaginative sterility. The "Earliest Program" thus has revolutionary ambitions in excess of its professed political desire to eliminate the machinery of the state and pave the way for a life without conditions free to create itself. The text mobilizes an energetic counterforce in the art of poetry (*Dichtkunst*) in order to refashion the entire field of nature and its scientific representations: it aims to reconcile *physis* with *mythos*.

Goethe as well, in "The Experiment as Mediator between Object and Subject" (1792), understood the scientific experiment as an inversion of art; the scientist, through countless variations and iterations, aims to exhaust the possibilities of the object of study, without imaginative remainder: "The scientist has precisely the inverted duty of an author who would like to entertain."[30] The genre of the experiment, however, which seems to aim at the *exhaustion of the phenomenon*, would acquire precisely the opposite valence in romantic scientific practice as it unfolded over the following years: the aesthetic thrust of scientific experimentation in the romantic period would become a generative matrix, a staging of the *inexhaustibility* of the variant forms of the sensible world, and a simultaneous modal concatenation of necessity, reality, *and* contingency.

Physics itself, the shape and effects of its discourse, no longer becomes subject to the downward pull of gravity, but discovers an expansive aesthetic counterforce within its own horizon. The scientist Johann Wilhelm Ritter, in his lecture *Physics as Art*, describes physics as the "greatest of all the arts"[31]; the experiment becomes the medium of an aesthetic practice, or in the words of Jocelyn Holland, a *procreative poetics*.[32] Ritter, who notoriously used his own body as a medium of scientific experimentation,[33] understood the aesthetics of science as an infinitely variable practice of the self: "What is a *knowledge* which is not capable of *practice*, and what is this *practice* forthwith *itself?*— And if what *knowledge* creates is *infinite*, then according to this knowledge the *ability* to practice it, wherefore only it exists, must be *equally infinite*."[34] The "highest art" was one that could make *everything* into an art, a *techne*. Ritter makes the discourse of science (*Wissenschaft*) into a process of creation, what knowledge *creates* (*was Wissen schaft* [sic]).[35] The existence of the discourse, the only reason why it is "there" (*wofür es einzig da ist*), becomes folded into the potentiality of a capacity to be developed (*Können*).[36]

So too does Goethe's morphology necessitate an imaginative or aesthetic *askesis*, a training and production of perception and a way of looking at the world.[37] Morphology attempts to cognitively grasp and imaginatively represent invariant patterns of emergence in developmental processes, thereby bringing a hidden internal order out of its latency within the flow of sensuous becoming.[38] Although morphology challenges the capacities of a subject to condense successive images extending over time (e.g. of the stages of a plant developing) into one mental representation, thereby initiating an internal contractive movement (from the multiple to the one), the morphological gaze equally expands outward (from the one to the multiple) to encompass all appearances. For all that morphology is concerned with the emergence of boundaries and individuated forms, as a discourse and as an ontology of transformation, it knows no bounds; there is no beginning or end to morphological processes, only patterns in circumscribed observational fields. Morphology becomes expansive and all-encompassing, folding all things, including the observing subjects, into its material, spiritual, and formal dynamics; subjects themselves become living morphological experiments.[39]

Although Goethe and Ritter both understand a certain aesthetic practice or *askesis* as commensurate with scientific observation and representation, and both share a conception of nature as an infinite process, there are distinctive differences in their regimes of exercise. Ritter equates life with combustion, re-describing "life-science" as "fire-science" (*Lebenswissenschaft* as *Feuerwissenschaft*).[40] The reclamation of physics as an art shows how this transformative fire moves through the history of science itself, as each discovery conditions (and unconditions) the next. The revelatory capacity of the magnet and the "electrical fire" produced through polarity ultimately pushes Ritter to the epiphany of unity through the combustibility of matter: "everything was able to burst into flames and to burn."[41] Seeking the unconditioned or the Absolute within sensuous reality through scientific experimentation and discourse culminates in an art of infinite energy transference that can travel from any element to any other element that it touches (since the Voltaic pile works through sheer contact). Combustion becomes a poetic and scientific medium. In his *Fragments from the Papers of a Young Physicist*, one may perceive this energy of contiguity as the physicist moves from vegetation to the placement of altars in temples to the equation of light with God to reflections on the work of art as that which makes present something that is absent.[42]

In contrast, Goethe is attracted to the ontological integrity of the condition, the unfolding of discrete stages of existence, the necessary boundedness of the individual. Goethe writes in one of his maxims: "Researching into nature we are pantheists, writing poetry we are polytheists, morally we are monotheists."[43] Different domains of practice produce a different organization of the sacred: science is organized around a concept of the whole of existence as it concerns the totality of the real; poetry is organized around the multiple, and often, as in Goethe's notion of the daemonic, incommensurable orders, possible and impossible worlds; and ethics is organized around the one, the universality of the moral law. Suturing all of this together is the life of the "we" that can move from domain to domain, thus suggesting a second-order polytheism as an alternation between the various regimes of practice. However, it is in the polytheism of the work of art that Goethe explores the unconditioned as a way of Being: in Werther, in Faust, in Eduard and in Ottilie of *Elective Affinities*. The ontological integrity of the bounded individual, of any condition of becoming that posits a norm as part of the order of the given, is for Goethe a sensuous *attraction* rather than an a priori structure; any manifestation of order can be distorted, suspended, dissolved, or overwhelmed by a force of perturbation. Indeed, Goethe gave the name of "the daemonic" to precisely this upsurge of contingency and internal inconsistency that persists in practices oriented toward the disclosure of the cosmos as a well-ordered whole.[44]

One of the most conspicuous features of the discourse of the Absolute or the unconditioned circulating around this time is the great variety of the logics, mythologies, semiotic models, modes of organization, ethical and political consequences, and forms of access that accompany the thought of the whole; axiomatically and somewhat paradoxically one may claim, looking from afar (or practicing "distant philosophy") at the works of Hölderlin, Hegel, Novalis, Schlegel, Schelling, Goethe, Baader, and many others, *there is not one Whole.* In many articulations of the supposedly totalizing operations proliferating in romantic thought, there is nevertheless a recurrent pattern: unity and totality often coexist with dissolution, disarticulation, internal inconsistency, and paradoxicality.

Romantic holism, or the attempt among romantic authors to philosophically or poetically approach the ontological totality of the field of beings, often produces and intensifies such internal tensions rather than alleviating them. In Schelling's *First Outline of a System of the Philosophy of Nature* (1799), which raises the question "to what extent *unconditionedness* might be ascribed to Nature,"[45] nature appears as a paradoxical, inconsistent system, one in which each "condition" of ontological unfolding is undone by another condition that appears to undermine the claim of the first to constitute an ultimate ground of appearances.[46] On the one hand, there is nature as infinite productivity, infinite activity that rushes onward, bringing about the elimination of all differentiation; on the other hand, there are impediments, forces within nature working *against* nature, that inhibit this elimination of differentiation. These impediments internal to nature through which productivity becomes product give rise to the condition of *organic life*, which is nothing other than a result of a system of nature internally divided, turned against itself, "the work of opposed tendencies."[47] Life, or the concretization of nature in an organic product, is therefore both the manifestation of an internal order as well as a misfiring internal to this order.

Romantic holism does not so much repair these tensions as hold them fixed in a disjunctive synthesis. In Schelling's *On the Relation of the Real and Ideal in Nature*, which accompanied Schelling's second edition of *On the World Soul*, "totality" and "unity" are represented as contradictory velocities and operations, corresponding respectively to the movements of light and gravity: totality expands outward, disperses to encompass everything, whereas unity contracts and gathers all things together.[48] Appearances as a whole result from a higher-order copula emergent from these two conflicting tendencies.

Schelling, unlike other romantic thinkers, is invested in an agonism of the whole of nature: the unconditioned as *oppositional* forces. Novalis, in contrast to Schelling, writes, "Science does not begin with an antinomy—binomy—but with an infinitinomy."[49] The "infinite" in this instance *unconditions* the very structure of a polarity and opens onto a thinking of the proliferation of laws as the infinite multiplication of sheer difference rather than oppositionality.

## 4 Romantic Mythology and Speculative Physics

Drawing on the potentially differential, agonistic, paradoxical, and relational dynamics of romantic holism outlined above, the intercourse between poetry and science could be re-described in this period as contributing to the conditioning and unconditioning of the entirety of existence. The terms of such a project culminated in speculative engagement with the grammar of a "new mythology." At stake in the new mythology is the provisional exploration of semiotic operations that weave the scientific and material manifestations of a nature-philosophical Absolute *beyond* the human—for example, in the chaos of matter and the agonism of impersonal forces—into the folds of the destiny of the human.[50]

Already in Karl Philipp Moritz's *Doctrine of the Gods* (*Götterlehre*)—which is a central text of aesthetic theory essential for an understanding of German Romantic thought, and not a compendium of myths—one may find the idea of mythology not as a poetic invention of human beings, nor as an allegorical signifying system that says one thing but means another, nor as a didactic system meant to impart a moral lesson, but rather as an aesthetically autonomous, self-referential system of signs, a "language of fantasy" taken in the most literal sense of the term.[51] Mythology is structured like a language: a language that is immediately sensuous, concretized in images, consisting of a web of relations, labile, and capable of an infinite number of pragmatic realizations. Moritz will call mythology a web rather than a system—*Gewebe*—since striking on one strand can call forth resonant effects that will reverberate throughout the whole. Moritz's text itself can be read as yet another realization of this mythological matrix: it constructs the generative grammar of its own textual system, which it then uses to construct yet another narrative, a *mythos*. *The Doctrine of the Gods* itself, as the mythologization of its own mythology, has an arc with trajectories, deviations, and interweaving episodes, beginning with chaos and the emergence of the beautiful through darkness, conflict, violence, and ending with an erotic reconciliation and redemption through the marriage of Amor and Psyche.

The "new mythology" of the early German Romantics does not simply spiritualize the materiality of the real, but materializes the ideal (or more significantly, concretizes the "indifference" between the real and the ideal in the case of Schelling), drawing on the dynamics of matter as they come to light in physics in order to inject alterity into practices of life. It is important to grasp that the new mythology of the romantics does not utilize the natural sciences as a mimetic source for concrete poetic images—it is precisely not a matter of personifying electrical charges, for example—but rather, it coheres with speculative physics inasmuch as it draws upon an unconditioning power. Ludoviko, in Friedrich Schlegel's *Speech about Mythology* (part of the *Dialogue on Poetry*), says, "Just try once to contemplate the old mythology, filled with Spinoza and with those views that modern physics must arouse in any reflecting person, and see how everything appears to you in a new light and life."[52] It is not the *unifying* function of Spinoza and his concept of substance that lays the ground for a new mythology, not its capacity to function as source, but rather, the *perturbation* that this doctrine produces in acts of reflection. Spinoza reconfigures the world, upends the system of relations in which we act, and makes the atmosphere refract a light that intimates a different organization of beings. Thus poetry, inasmuch as it has a mythological function, is at the same time a grammar that *conditions* the world of appearances and that *unconditions* it at by leading it back to an unruly chaotic horizon of possibilities: there is a conditioned poetry of form and an unconditioned poetry "formless and unconscious" that moves *through* forms and consciousness.[53] These two types of poetry intermingle with one another in the romantic practices of signification.

The romantic dream of a new mythology is thus not a simple humanism, replete with gods to mirror our forms and our desires, but the becoming-sensuous of a grammar of all appearances as an expansion of the possible. In Schelling's 1802–3 lectures on the philosophy of art, he writes, "In recent times, one has often heard the thought, that it would be possible to take from physics—inasmuch as it is speculative physics—the material for a new mythology."[54] Speculative physics, in contrast to empirical physics, does not produce empirically verifiable truths, which are conditioned, but regards the emergence of such empirical truths in the light of unconditioning: it attributes to physics an ontologically disclosive function (revealing how beings are organized and disorganized) rather than an epistemological function (discovering experimentally falsifiable "truths" about the cosmos). Mythology would channel that which is disclosed in speculative physics into practices of existence.

Mythological signification, as Schelling construes it in his earlier writings (which differs in important ways from his treatment of this theme in his later writings), merits closer examination as a practice within which the codes of science and poetry meet, intertwine, and are imbued with a power of personal, social, and political disruption. Underlying the new mythology is an ontology of immanence coupled with forces, localized textures, and physical-semiotic operations: movement, resistance, attraction, binding, permeability, and passage through zones of indifferentiation that make possible state changes or changes of identity. Schelling hints at the concretization of such an ontology when he writes, "It is not we who want to give the idealist culture its gods through physics. We rather await its gods, gods for which we are already holding the symbols ready perhaps even before they have developed in the culture itself independently from physics."[55] The poet-physicist-philosopher has a *preparatory* agency; she or he cannot simply create a collective mythology, since mythology exhibits a self-organizing, emergent logic over which the individual has only limited control. The philosopher-physicist-poet can, however, draw upon the generative dynamics of speculative physics from whose movements mythological signification might one day be realized.

Such a speculative dynamic organization, if it were one day to be mythologized, would be *polytheistic* (or, were it to embrace monotheism, would construe monotheism through the lens of an infinite generative process commensurate with multiplicity, as one can find in Schelling's later works). It would not be organized around a monotheistic God for whom the world of particulars is simply a period of transition into a transcendent world or eschatology (i.e. Christianity and its "allegorical" tendencies to subordinate the finite to the infinite), but rather, it would manifest itself through the "indifference" of the finite and the infinite, saturating and interpenetrating the finite with the infinite. The continual production of the infinite *in* the very way finite beings organize themselves would be polytheistic since finite beings are irreducibly multiple and capable of an infinite variety of combination and recombination.

This complete saturation of the infinite *in* the finite is precisely what Schelling understands by the symbol, and is generally distinguished from allegory, which reads the finite only inasmuch as it means something infinite that points beyond its own finite form.[56] However, for Schelling, allegory and symbol are not oppositional since the allegorical tendency of Christianity is itself symbolic inasmuch as it is also part of the emergence of the Absolute as process. More importantly, instead of the dichotomy allegory-symbol, there is a triad: allegory-symbol-mythology, a triad in which each term differs from the others but is not opposed to one another. If the symbol "indifferentiates" the particular and the universal, the mythological consists in a specific form of symbolization. Mythology describes a second-order symbolic operation, a re-particularization of the symbol that would describe how the symbol enters into the intelligibility of shared practices.[57] Mythology is therefore symbolic in a particular way: inasmuch as it can be comprehended historically, bringing symbolic operations into patterns of intelligibility such that they would potentially be capable of structuring collective practices—even if, as in the modern age, there is no such totalizing collective practice that might apply to all individuals.

Moreover, the type of binding form that might be poetically constructed through the symbols of speculative physics would not be identitarian or predicated on some stable, unchanging essence. Unity could only be produced through that which is unconditioned, and therefore any form of unity would remain constantly open to being poetically reconfigured; individuals would be bound only inasmuch as they would be conditioned by something unbound.

The central task of the new mythology consists not merely in binding humans to a transcendental ideality, but just as significantly, to a dynamic *materiality* inasmuch as a mythology based on speculative physics would draw operations inherent in the immanence of matter out of their latency. This new mythology, reduced to its basic operative structure, can be defined as the translation of material force into the force of aesthetic signification. In contrast to Moritz, for whom the autonomy of a mythological signifying system belongs to the structure of the human mind as *fantasy*, romantic mythology brings into the fold of human practices the dynamics of Being as such, all matter, the real and the ideal, including the unruly domain of the inorganic.

## 5    Arts of Unconditioning

Through the lens of Schelling's philosophy of art, one may regard the romantic practice of mythology as aesthetic-existential translations of material-physical dynamics. The unconditioning power of romantic mythology does not merely make its presence felt in physical dynamics that surface explicitly as the content of a representation—for example, in the presence of magnetic forces in Klingsohr's fairy tale in Novalis' *Heinrich von Ofterdingen*—but also, and perhaps less evidently, in the intricacy of poetic form, in the oscillating movements through which language organizes and disorganizes itself. It is precisely through the movements of art that the unconditioning power of the Absolute can reconfigure the sensible world and generate unexpected social and political bodies.

Novalis' essay *Europe or Christianity* can be regarded as mythological in precisely this sense. On the surface, the document seems to provide a blueprint for an ideologically regressive romantic politics: the dream of a Europe that is united in a Christian identity. However, the seeming holism of this document conceals a latent dynamic that produces nothing less than the unconditioning of Christianity as an identity, which is to say, a perturbation of the conditions under which it might count to be Christian. Novalis writes:

> Christianity has three forms. One is the creative element of religion, the joy in all religion. Another is mediation in general, the belief in the capacity of everything earthly to be the wine and bread of eternal life. Yet a third is the belief in Christ, his mother and the saints. Choose whichever you like. Choose all three. It is indifferent.[58]

The triad constructed here—which mirrors and at the same time distorts the trinitarian logic of Christianity—does not define Christianity as much as include as one of its possibilities the evacuation of Christianity of any sort of substantial definition. Instead of a definition or a singular condition of Christianity, there is an oscillation between conditions and the emergence of a potentially combinatory logic that indifferentiates forms of Christianity (*choose whichever you like, choose all three, it is the same thing*). Christianity thereby becomes subject to the mythology of speculative physics through this dynamic of oscillation, indifferentiation, and multiplication; thus romanticized, Christianity modeled on Novalis' notion of science could potentially become an *infinitinomy*. In only one of these forms—*the belief in Christ, his mother, and the saints*—would Christianity properly be called "Christian" (although, it must be noted, this substantialized ideology of Christianity is nevertheless maintained *as* a possibility by Novalis). Novalis nevertheless makes Christianity as substantial ideology into a historically contingent form, as the other two forms of Christianity—joy in all religions and the purely formal operation of symbolic mediation—need never make any reference to Christ, Mary, or the saints.

The mythological unconditioning of Christianity can simultaneously be applied to the idea of Europe: if Europe is defined by Christianity, and Christianity is nothing other than an oscillating field of possibility between imaginative operations, the "unity" of Europe could potentially consist in nothing other than an aggregate of romanticized subjects. Novalis' romantic mythologization of Christianity contains as one of its possible configurations a radically deterritorialized conception of Europe; the door has been opened to a form of Christianity without Christ and a Europe without any distinct European identity, without borders or limits, incapable of being localized on a map.[59]

One of the most significant procedures of the new mythology—touched upon by Novalis here—takes its point of departure from stabilizing or binding conceptual operations or conditions (e.g. space, time, identity, morality, community, politics, and knowledge), some of which are transcendental in nature (e.g. as "conditions" of possible experience). It then views these conditions from the perspective of that which is without condition and postulates how reality must be sensuously transfigured when these conditions are refracted through the light of the power of unconditioning. As Schelling suggests, the symbolic value of speculative physics plays a central role in the romantic mythological arts of unconditioning. One may trace here a metamorphosis in the semantics of the Absolute that expands its mythological capacity, rendering it capable of entering into practices and reconfiguring the real. Already Newton had postulated a notion of absolute space as homogeneous and immobile, a form of space external to all relationality through which motion could be thought to be *true* (as opposed to just motion relative to other bodies); Kant, in his *Metaphysical Foundations of Natural Science*, reinterprets Newtonian absolute space as an "idea of reason," one whereby a common center of gravity could be posited for all appearances but never grasped, since such a conception of space would necessitate moving to ever-expanded frames of reference, eventually encompassing the entire cosmos; and Schelling, in his *Ideas for a Philosophy of Nature*, asks not how matter *fills* an absolute space, but rather, how the Absolute produces itself *as* matter, which in turn is nothing other than the agonistic play of opposing forces of attraction and repulsion.

By means of the simultaneously transcendental and ontological forces of attraction and repulsion (transcendental because they are the condition of possibility of matter, ontological because they *are* matter), Schelling's *Naturphilosophie* becomes a medium of mythologization. Artists of this period—including those operating far beyond the horizon of Jena Romanticism—explore in poetic artifacts the unconditioning potential of an Absolute of forces: whether in the Eternal Feminine of Goethe's *Faust* that "attracts us onward" (*zieht uns hinan*),[60] in Schlegel's and Novalis' oscillation through the production of differentiation, or in the *nature-philosophical* Absolute that comes to light even in the works of Hölderlin, structured around the functional tension between the earth and the aether, where earth implies a gravitational force that creates differentiation and stability (thus signaling the sensuous limitations of the real) and the aether implies a plenitude of space with no intrinsic differentiation (thus signaling pure possibility).[61] In Hölderlin's poem "To the Aether," the aether stands in for precisely such a notion of absolute space as an expanded horizon of existential possibility or space distributed in such a way as to make room for all beings: "Room enough for all. The path is indicated to no being" (*Raums genug ist für alle. Der Pfad ist keinem bezeichnet*).[62] And if the poet, after confronting the risk of losing himself in the infinite of absolute space, eventually reconciles himself to the "flowers of the earth" (*Blumen der Erde*), it is only because a space radically free from *position* and *condition* becomes capable of being integrated into the conditioned practices of the sensible world. Far from being postulated as the "other" of material reality, the unconditioned aether descends from the heights and infiltrates all beings, endowing them with an expansion of possibility. It is from such contact that the potentially abyssal and violent chaos of revolutionary politics—or the loss of order in a suspension of differences and laws—becomes capable of generating new differences, new laws. It is in this sense that one may speak of Hölderlin's mythology—which is also a nature-philosophical mythology or a mythology that blends historical gods (Christ, Dionysus, and other demigods) and the gods of speculative physics (attraction and repulsion, gravity and light, earth and aether)—as a revolutionary art of unconditioning.

## 6  Critique of the Unconditioned

If the basic operation of the new mythology consists in the translation of material force into the force of aesthetic signification, the act of reading demands moving through the dynamics that organize themselves in sensuous matter. While this new mythology embraces practices of unconditioning in order to recondition the real—giving rise to new conditions that may previously have seemed impossible, improbable, or might simply have been unforeseen and unforeseeable—poetry itself becomes an experimental crucible, a testing ground for the power of the new gods and the possible emergent reconfigurations of subjects, social orders, and political forms.

Among the poets who experiment with the mythological symbolization of speculative physics as an art of unconditioning, Karoline von Günderrode deserves special mention.[63] However, in her work, one may also find a *critique* of this mythologization in the sense of a determination of its limits: what happens when the unconditioning power of romantic mythology fails to generate an expansion of imaginative and existential possibility? Whereas the absolute space of Hölderlin's aether *descends* to infiltrate the entire field of beings, in the following poem by Karoline von Günderrode, the creature *ascends* toward an intuition of cosmic order only to eventually be subject to the more powerful force of a downward pull:

> The Aeronaut
> In the unsteady ship I sailed
> In the bluish ocean,
> Flowing around the blazing stars,
> Greeted the heavenly powers.
> Absorbed in their observation,
> Drank the eternal aether,
> Divested myself fully of earthly garb,
> Recognized on high the writings of the stars
> And in their circling and turning,
> Saw depicted the holy rhythm,
> Forcefully dragging every sound

To harmony's undulant urge.
But O! it pulls me down,
Mist veils my gaze,
And once more I see the limits of the earth,
Clouds drive me back.
Alas! The law of gravity
It claims its right,
No man of earthly race
May elude its pull.

[Der Luftschiffer

Gefahren bin ich in schwankendem Kahne
Auf dem blaulichen Oceane,
Der die leuchtenden Sterne umfließt,
Habe die himmlischen Mächte begrüßt.
War, in ihrer Betrachtung versunken,
Habe den ewigen Aether getrunken,
Habe dem Irdischen ganz mich entwandt,
Droben die Schriften der Sterne erkannt
Und in ihrem Kreisen und Drehen
Bildlich den heiligen Rhythmus gesehen,
Der gewaltig auch jeglichen Klang
Reißt zu des Wohllauts wogendem Drang.
Aber ach! es ziehet mich hernieder,
Nebel überschleiert meinen Blick,
Und der Erde Grenzen seh' ich wieder,
Wolken treiben mich zurück.
Wehe! Das Gesetz der Schwere
Es behauptet nur sein Recht,
Keiner darf sich ihm entziehen
Von dem irdischen Geschlecht.[64]]

The figure of the aeronaut had previously appeared in Jean Paul's *Giannozzo the Aeronaut's Seabook*. In this work, part of the *Comic Appendix* to the novel *Titan*, the aeronaut is an ironist: one who ascends and descends, one who travels horizontally and vertically, one who thus does and does not belong to the terrestrial world, and one who ultimately meets his fate through an encounter with contingency, *a storm* in the clouds above him, which brings him crashing down to earth.

In contrast, Günderrode's poem appears particularly apt as an intervention in the new mythological poetics of force: it too is structured around force (the circular movement of the stars that draws beings on high) and counterforce (the law of gravity), rising and falling, a Neoplatonic desire to contemplate divine order by "divesting oneself of earthly garb" that is immediately countered by a downward movement toward the earth, toward conditions, and toward boundedness (the limits of the earth, *der Erde Grenzen*). The descent of the poet is occasioned not by a contingent event (or the advent of contingency, as in the sudden burst of storm clouds) but by the sheer unconditioned force of gravity that acts upon all beings.

For Günderrode, it seems there can be no mythological continuum between a Neoplatonically inflected transcendence and the physics of force; the poem brings to light a break, a caesura (*But O!*) that divides the harmony of *divine powers* (*Mächte*) from the perturbation of natural force (*Kraft*).[65] The cosmic order disclosed in the upward trajectory in first half of the poem is thus overwhelmed by the material operation of force or gravity (*Schwerkraft*) in the second half of the poem. And along with this entrance into the world of force comes the fall of the subject.

And we the readers fall with the subject. We can feel the pull of gravity in the very act of reading as our eyes are pulled from left to right and from top to bottom. And although the expansive upward thrust seems to constitute the majority of the poem—twelve lines of an ascent to eight lines of a descent—a closer look reveals that, in this poem, one is always falling. The first twelve lines are, after all, in the past tense; the last eight lines are in the present. We can thus temporally and spatially pinpoint the position from which the poet speaks: for it is precisely at the point of the mythological caesura, the *Aber ach!*, that we enter explicitly into the present, and this present moment is one of descent (*it pulls me down*). The first twelve lines of ascent must thus be folded into the last eight lines of descent, as each line proclaims: I *saw* the holy cosmic rhythm but *now* I am falling. The entire poem is thus governed by the law of gravity, by a fall into differentiation. Moreover, the law of gravity produces a stochastic effect in the poetic structure of the poem: the harmony of the initial rhymes (*aabbcc*) becomes crossed, producing alternating rhymes after the caesura (*hihi*), only to include a dyad that does not rhyme at all in the final four lines (*Schwere* and *entziehen* do not rhyme at all, yielding the rhyme scheme *jklk*). Gravity *scrambles* the order of harmony, which nevertheless continues to shine, albeit through a distortion field.

This examination of the intersection of romantic science and poetry has, up until now, been attentive to an exteriority and productive of an impurity, a perturbation in the structure of the given: the index of an external force that unconditions whatever happens to present itself *as* a condition. Here, however, the unconditioning power itself seems to become a condition impeding the fulfillment of desire, the desire *for* the unbound.

How does this new mythology appear when refracted through the lens of Günderrode's poem? The chaotic materiality of the poem becomes concretized in our sensuous encounter with the text as a dynamic that inheres in our very practices of reading. We as readers are falling together with the poet as our eye moves down the page, and indeed the very phenomenology of reading is linked to the stochastic chaotic descent; we see, then, that the new mythology is irreducible to a utopian mythology of redemption, a way of being that could uncondition the law and culminate in an ultimate fulfillment of desire; indeed, the very unconditioning power can itself be used to restrict possibility. The desire for the loosening of identity itself—for example, of a gender, of a hierarchical social order, of a political form, and of a mode of subjectification—thus might find itself thwarted by the pull of an unconditional force. Already the first syllables of the poem in its opening phrase—"Driven have I," *gefahren bin ich*—contain the index of the danger, or in German, *Gefahr*, that permeates the new mythology of force.

But we can go further. And the relentless force of the romantic poem is precisely this: to go further, to chart the narrow path toward the exterior, something alien and unknown that transfigures the order of the sensible— transfiguring in the sense not of imbuing the immanent with a transcendent force, but of making an immanent order *pass over* into a new or unexpected figure. After all, for the first twelve lines of the poem, even if in the mode of something past, the poet suspends the pull of the fall—precisely when the fall is taking place—in order to poetically reproduce a celestial and oceanic rhythm, to make this rhythm visible at the precise moment when it no longer corresponds to the conditions of reality. In the attempt to contravene the omnipresent Absolute of force, Günderrode, in the end, uncovers yet another move in the art of unconditioning: the discovery of the counterforce of the imagination at the very moment of catastrophe.

## Notes

1. Novalis, *Notes for a Romantic Encyclopaedia: Das allgemeine Brouillon*, trans. and ed. David W. Wood (Albany: State University of New York Press, 2007), 51.
2. Ibid., 51–2.
3. Ibid., 52.
4. The concept of romantic poetry (*Poesie*) extends far beyond the literary domain and exerts its formative power over the shape of a life, social bodies, forms of political practice, and so on. For this reason, one might be tempted

to differentiate between *poesy* as a romantic operation and *poetry* as a literary genre; however, while the romantic notion of *Poesie* exceeds the literary genre of poetry, it nevertheless draws an imaginative power from this genre that would be lost were one to insist too strongly on a strict differentiation between *poesy* (as broad romantic concept) and *poetry* (as narrow generic form).

5. For such tendencies in romantic thought, see, for example, Manfred Frank, *Einführung in die frühromantische Ästhetik* (Frankfurt a.M.: Suhrkamp, 1989), 233.
6. See Alain Badiou, *Handbook of Inaesthetics*, trans. Alberto Toscano (Stanford: Stanford University Press, 2005), 6.
7. Alain Badiou, *Conditions*, trans. Steven Corcoran (New York: Continuum, 2008), 59.
8. Novalis writes, "Should there be a still higher sphere, it would be the sphere between being and not-being.—The oscillating between the two." Novalis, *Fichte Studies*, trans. and ed. Jane Kneller (Cambridge: Cambridge University Press, 2003), 6.
9. See Joseph Vogl, *Kalkül und Leidenschaft: Poetik des ökonomischen Menschen* (Zürich: diaphanes, 2008), 260.
10. Schelling, in his *First Outline*, draws attention to nature as an agonistic, paradoxical, inconsistent system that seeks to return differentiated life to a state of universal indifference: "The same forces which have for a time maintained life finally destroy it too." F.W.J. Schelling: *First Outline of a System of the Philosophy of Nature*, trans. Keith R. Peterson (Albany: State University of New York Press, 2004), 68. The "whole" of nature is thus a generative-destructive, paradoxical system that unfolds through internal tensions, oppositions, and inconsistencies.
11. See Immanuel Kant, *Critique of Pure Reason*, trans. and eds. Paul Guyer and Allen W. Wood (Cambridge: Cambridge University Press, 1998), 677.
12. Novalis, *Philosophical Writings*, trans. and ed. Margaret Mahoney Stoljar (Albany: State University of New York Press, 1997), 23.
13. See, for example, Manfred Frank, *"Unendliche Annäherung". Die Anfänge der philosophischen Frühromantik* (Frankfurt am Main: Suhrkamp, 1997), 28.
14. I follow Frederick Beiser here, who argues for an expanded understanding of *romantic poesy*; see Frederick Beiser, *The Romantic Imperative: The Concept of Early German Romanticism* (Cambridge, Mass.: Harvard University Press, 2003), 6–22. For the specificity of how the aesthetic flows into practices of life, an idea important to many romantics, I use the term *mythology*.
15. For one of the most compelling accounts of the romantic philosophy of nature as a philosophy of the "unconditioned," see Iain Hamilton Grant, *Philosophies of Nature after Schelling* (New York: Continuum, 2006).
16. Daniel B. Lancereau, "Leibniz, Novalis, Gödel: Balistique du romantisme allemand," in *Arts et sciences du romantisme allemande*, Daniel Lancereau and

Andre Stanguennec (Rennes: Presses Universitaires de Rennes, 2018), 239–272.
17. The labile nature of polarity leads Antje Pfannkuchen and Leif Weatherby to call it an "absolute metaphor" that cuts across discursive fields, both science and poetry; see Antje Pfannkuchen and Leif Weatherby, "Writing Polarities: Romanticism and the Dynamic Unity of Poetry and Science," *The Germanic Review* 92:4 (2017): 336.
18. Friedrich Schlegel, *Transcendentalphilosophie* (Hamburg: Meiner, 1991), 102.
19. For the notion of a "relational" Absolute, see Dalia Nassar, *The Romantic Absolute: Being and Knowing in Early German Romantic Philosophy, 1705–1804* (Chicago: University of Chicago Press, 2014).
20. Schlegel, *Transcendentalphilosophie*, 92
21. Ibid., 93.
22. For the significance of magnetism and indifference for romantic science and Johann Wilhelm Ritter in particular, see Jocelyn Holland, "Die Zeit der Indifferenz. Johann Wilhelm Ritter und die Weiblichkeit," in *Narration und Geschlecht. Texte–Medien–Episteme*, ed. Sigrid Nieberle and Elisabeth Strowick (Köln: Böhlau, 2006), 335–47.
23. Novalis, *Notes for a Romantic Encyclopaedia*, 51.
24. Ibid.
25. Ibid.
26. Novalis, *Notes for a Romantic Encyclopaedia*, 116.
27. The studies that adopt such "refractive" strategies are too numerous to mention exhaustively, although any of the following could function as points of departure: Michel Chaouli, *The Laboratory of Poetry: Chemistry and Poetics in the Work of Friedrich Schlegel* (Baltimore: Johns Hopkins UP, 2002); Stefani Engelstein, *Anxious Anatomy: The Conception of the Human Form in Literary and Naturalist Discourse* (Albany: State University of New York Press, 2008); Daniel Lancereau, "La poétique de la terre chez Novalis," *Cahiers du Géopoétique* 3 (1992), 59–76; Christine Lehleiter, *Romanticism, Origins, and the History of Heredity* (Lewisburg, PA: Bucknell University Press, 2014); Howard Pollack-Milgate, "Gott ist bald $1 \cdot \infty$—bald $1/\infty$—bald $0$: The Mathematical Infinite and the Absolute in Novalis," *Seminar* 51:1 (2015), 50–70; John H. Smith, "Kant, Calculus, Consciousness: The Mathematical Infinite in Us." *Goethe Yearbook* 23 (2016), 95–121; Benjamin Specht, *Physik als Kunst*, 2010; Joseph Vogl, *Kalkül und Leidenschaft*, 2008; Leif Weatherby, *Transplanting the Metaphysical Organ: German Romanticism between Leibniz and Marx* (New York: Fordham University Press, 2016).
28. G.W.F. Hegel et al., "Earliest Program for a System of German Idealism," in *Theory as Practice: A Critical Anthology of Early German Romantic Writings*, trans. and ed. Jochen Schulte-Sasse et al. (Minneapolis: University of Minnesota Press, 1997), 72–73; 72.
29. Ibid., 73.

30. Johann Wolfgang Goethe, "Der Versuch als Vermittler von Objekt und Subjekt," in *Sämtliche Werke*, eds. Wolf von Engelhardt and Manfred Wenzel, vol. 1, no. 25 (Frankfurt a.M.: Suhrkamp, 1989), 33.
31. Johann Wilhelm Ritter, *Physics as Art*, in *Key Texts of Johann Wilhelm Ritter (1776–1810) on the Science and Art of Nature*, trans. and ed. Jocelyn Holland (Leiden: Brill, 2010), 523–583; 581.
32. See Jocelyn Holland, *German Romanticism and Science: The Procreative Poetics of Goethe, Novalis, and Ritter* (New York: Routledge, 2009).
33. See Joan Steigerwald, "The Subject as Instrument: Galvanic Experiments, Organic Apparatus and Problems of Calibration" in *The Uses of Humans in Experiment: Perspectives from the 17th to the twentieth Century*, eds. Erika Dyck and Larry Stewart (Leiden: Brill 2016), 80–110.
34. Johann Wilhelm Ritter, *Physics as Art*, 581.
35. Ibid., 580.
36. Ibid.
37. See Joan Steigerwald, "Goethe's Morphology: *Urphänomene* and Aesthetic Appraisal," *Journal of the History of Biology* 35 (2002): 291–328.
38. For a more thorough analysis of the relation between Goethean morphology and German Idealism, see Eckart Förster, "Die Bedeutung von §§76, 77 der *Kritik der Urteilskraft* für die Entwicklung der nachkantischen Philosophie [Teil 1]." *Zeitschrift für philosophische Forschung* 56 (2002): 185–6.
39. As Eva Geulen writes, "Goethe's series is a medium of hesitation in the service of going further"; see Eva Geulen, *Aus dem Leben der Form. Goethes Morphologie und die Nager* (Berlin: August, 2016), 116.
40. Johann Wilhelm Ritter, *Physics as Art*, 551.
41. Ibid., 553.
42. Johann Wilhelm Ritter, *Fragments from the Estate of a Young Physicist*, in *Key Texts of Johann Wilhelm Ritter (1776–1810) on the Science and Art of Nature*, trans. and ed. Jocelyn Holland (Leiden: Brill, 2010), 3–507; 451.
43. Johann Wolfgang Goethe, *Maxims and Reflections*, trans. Elisabeth Stopp, ed. Peter Hutchinson (London: Penguin, 1998), 109.
44. For a more detailed analysis of the concept of the daemonic, see Angus Nicholls, *Goethe's Concept of the Daemonic: After the Ancients* (New York: Camden House, 2006).
45. F.W.J. Schelling, *First Outline of a System of a Philosophy of Nature*, trans. Keith R. Peterson (Albany: State University of New York Press, 2004), 13.
46. For a description of Schelling's philosophy of unconditioning as the continual hypothesization of "antecedents," see Iain Hamilton Grant, "The Hypothesis of Nature's Logic in Schelling's *Naturphilosophie*," in *The Palgrave Handbook of German Idealism*, ed. Matthew C. Altman (New York: Palgrave Macmillan, 2014), 478–98.
47. Schelling, *First Outline*, 17.

48. See F.W.J. Schelling, "Treatise on the Relationship of the Real and the Ideal in Nature," trans. Dale Snow, *International Philosophical Quarterly* 55.2, issue 218 (2018): 239–249; 246.
49. Novalis, *Notes for a Romantic Encyclopaedia*, 153.
50. I have recently examined this poeticization of the nature-philosophical Absolute in the works of Schelling and Nerval in "Mythological Indifference in Schelling and Nerval," *The Wordsworth Circle* 50.1 (2019): 108–126.
51. Karl Philipp Moritz, *Götterlehre*, ed. Horst Günther (Frankfurt am Main: Insel, 1999), 9.
52. Friedrich Schlegel, *Dialogue on Poesy*, in *Theory as Practice: A Critical Anthology of Early German Romantic Writings*, trans. and ed. Jochen Schulte-Sasse et al. (Minneapolis: University of Minnesota Press, 1997), 180–193; 187.
53. Ibid., 180.
54. F.W.J. Schelling, *The Philosophy of Art*, trans. and ed. Douglas W. Stott (Minneapolis, University of Minnesota Press, 1989), 74.
55. Ibid., 76.
56. For a detailed analysis of the context of romantic theories of the symbol and of Schelling's contribution in particular, see Daniel Whistler, *Schelling's Theory of Symbolic Language: Forming the System of Identity* (Oxford: Oxford University Press, 2013).
57. As Whistler writes, myths "exhibit the indifference of meaning and being, but through an excess of the real." Ibid., 154.
58. Novalis, "Christianity or Europe: A Fragment," in *The Early Political Writings of the German Romantics*, ed. Frederick Beiser (Cambridge: Cambridge University Press, 1996), 59–80; 78.
59. I touch briefly on this point in "Fléchissement transcendantal et procédé hyperbolique: les mouvements de l'absolu chez Novalis et Hölderlin," in *Arts et sciences du romantisme allemande*, eds. Daniel Lancereau and Andre Stanguennec (Rennes: Presses Universitaires de Rennes, 2018): 153–180.
60. Johann Wolfgang von Goethe, *Faust*, in *Sämtliche Werke: Briefe, Tagebücher und Gespräche*, vol. 1.7/1, ed. Albrecht Schöne (Frankfurt am Main: Deutscher Klassiker, 1994), 464.
61. See Jürgen Link, "Aether und Erde. Naturgeschichtliche Voraussetzungen von Hölderlins Geo-logie," *Hölderlin-Jahrbuch* 35 (2006–2007), 120–151.
62. Hölderlin, *Sämtliche Werke*, 177.
63. For an attempt to view Günderrode's work as a contribution to the romantic "new mythology," see Helga Dormann, *Die Kunst des inneren Sinns. Mythisieren der inneren und äußeren Natur im Werke Karoline von Günderrodes* (Würzburg: Königshausen & Neumann, 2004). It is worth nothing that Günderrode was drawn to Schelling's *Naturphilosophie*, although this attraction does not entail that she uncritically accepted his ideas. See also Anna Ezekiel's contribution in this volume, "Women, Women Writers, and Early German Romanticism." Ezekiel's discussion of Günderrode's "Idea of the Earth"—as indicative of a

combinatory logic of aggregation that draws upon attraction to generate new entities—provides a vivid example of how she uses a nature-philosophical mythology of forces to uncondition gender and erotic identities, for example.

64. Karoline von Günderrode, *Sämtliche Werke und ausgewählte Studien*, vol. 1, ed. Walter Morgenthaler (Basel: Stroemfeld, 2006), 390.
65. It must nevertheless be noted that the aeronaut's ascent is not merely Neoplatonic and that the poem cannot be divided along the difference between antiquity and modernity; the intuition of cosmic order is not dependent on the vision of the mind itself, but requires the body and more significantly, the technological apparatus that transports the body into the heavens.

# 20

## Romantic Conceptions of Life

### Leif Weatherby

Romantic poetry is not only "progressive" and "universal," according to Friedrich Schlegel. It is also

> capable of the highest and most all-sided formation [*Bildung*]; not only from the inside outward, but also from the outside in; by organizing all parts to resemble each one which is meant to be a whole in its products—by this procedure the view onto a limitlessly growing classicity is opened to it.[1]

Poetry is like an organism, we might say. It is plastic in response to its internal drives, adaptable to its environment, and built up of units that resemble the whole in organization. Rather than crystallizing into classical form, it gains a *view* onto that form even as it grows. The comparison of poem and animal is at least as old as Aristotle, but Schlegel suggests that romantic poetry "sees" and has a view onto "limitlessly growing classicism." It is not only a formal comparison then, but one that combines form and life as a mode of representing. Schlegel continues:

---

This chapter relies on a wealth of scholarship in various areas related to romantic literature, science, and philosophy. I have tried to cite liberally and specifically from this scholarship, without claiming to engage it fully, as this would have been impossible, to support the suggestion I make here. I hope the reader will profit as much from the sources in the footnotes here as I have.

---

L. Weatherby (✉)
New York University, New York, NY, USA
e-mail: leif.weatherby@nyu.edu

> Only [romantic poetry] can become, like the epic, a mirror of the whole surrounding world, an image of our epoch. And yet it too, more than any other writing, hovers in the middle between the represented and the representing [*zwischen dem Dargestellten und dem Darstellenden*], free from all real and ideal interest on the wings of poetic reflection, continuously potentiating this reflection and multiplying itself like in an endless series of mirrors.[2]

The plasticity of the romantic text allows it to fulfill its historical mission by resolutely remaining between what it depicts and its mode of depiction.[3] To know by romantic lights is to be an adaptable, reflexive form that signals something both about the world and about its own mode of signaling. Irony, reflexivity, and recursion—all are built into the romantic text by this simple affordance of attention to the blurry boundary between the depicted and the means of depiction. The ability to hover between these—perhaps even to be unsure what is object and what is expression—is distinctive of the romantic concept of life, which is the basis for romantic poetry. Schlegel compares the form of poetry not only to that of the organism but also to the ability to know, to depict, and to distinguish, in the very structure of the organism. Poetry is not an imitation of the structure of the organism. Rather, it *is* and is about that structure. To signal is to give signs of life.[4]

The question concerning a specifically romantic conception of life hovers between poetry and science, individual and society, constraint and autonomy. "Life," it is generally agreed, is not the model or the metaphor by which the romantics understood textual production or metaphysics. Yet "life," in the crucial penultimate moment before its ratification as the autonomous subject of a science called "biology," was crucial not only to the sources the early German Romantics relied on but also to their own scientific endeavors, philosophies, and indeed even poetry. The question is not whether life mattered but how and what sort of life. The scholarship is currently in a sort of lag mode, in which the problematic "life" plays the role of keeping the time out of joint. A wealth of recent scholarship has deepened and expanded our sense of what "life" meant around 1800, while literary interpretation retains a theoretical opposition to any "organicism," holding it to imply an untenable metaphysical closure or collapse of signifier and signified. The goal of this chapter is to describe this conjuncture and to suggest that the difficulty, and the way forward, lies in the conception of *life* as *semiosis*. I argue that life was defined between the proliferation of forces after Albrecht von Haller's physiology took root—including various attempts to define a "life-force" around 1795—and the reflexive attempt to grasp life as a mode of knowing, most clearly developed in German Idealism. The romantic contribution emerged just when these two pressures on the concept of life converged on the phenomenon of local electricity, giving rise to a doctrine of signs embedded in life (and matter) as such. Romanticism and *Naturphilosophie* bound semiotics and life deeply together in a configuration that would have lasting effects not only in literature but also in what became the theory of technology and media.

## 1  Historiographical Lag

Historians of science have spent the last generation in turns refining, rejecting, and extending Michel Foucault's claim that until 1800, "life itself did not exist. All that existed were living beings, which were viewed through a grid of knowledge constituted by *natural history*."[5] The term "biology," as is well known, first appeared several times around 1800.[6] But the *science* came into institutional and professional existence only slowly over the course of the nineteenth century, as Lynn Nyhart has shown.[7] The question of *life*, then, gained conceptual autonomy before it achieved disciplinary security. Foucault describes this process as participating in the emergence of a notion of the human as what he calls the "empirico-transcendental doublet,"[8] in which a region of Being is marked out as having its own, independent rules, yet within the confines of those rules makes itself available to empirical inquiry and determination. Foucault's reading runs close to, and draws from, Immanuel Kant's notion of a transcendental idealism that is also an empirical realism, achieved by means of a critique that, in Foucault, avoids reducing the phenomenon at hand to some other entity (e.g., the reduction of organism to physical substrate) but also rejects promising a final and complete knowledge of that object.[9] Life cleaved off from Being, becoming an independent subject of empirical inquiry just because it also had proprietary rules that transcend empirical manifestation. These rules, in turn, were the topic of fierce and ideological debate throughout the German Enlightenment, and there was indeed an intensification and sense of forward movement in the natural-philosophical circles in Germany in the final decade of the nineteenth century. Life was autonomous, holistic, and spontaneous. And yet its newfound autonomy immediately gave it blurry borders with apparently opposed categories such as passivity, immateriality, and constraint.

It is in this historiographical no-man's-land that both anti-organicist and organicist approaches to German Romanticism have thrived.[10] The centrality of the conception of life to early German Romanticism in particular has been debated since Rudolf Haym gained historical purchase on the movement in his magisterial work, *The Romantic School* (1870).[11] But since Walter

Benjamin's 1919 dissertation at the latest, a line of philosophical-literary inquiry has sidelined or explicitly rejected "life" as the defining category of early German Romanticism in particular. The tradition that has emerged from Benjamin's redefinition of the "concept of art" in German Romanticism has produced the most influential readings of romantic notions of writing, text, genre, and medium.[12] Maurice Blanchot's short article, "The Athenaeum," is a central source for Philippe Lacoue-Labarthe's and Jean-Luc Nancy's watershed book, *The Literary Absolute*.[13] Building on Blanchot's notion that the fragmentary project in Jena was literature announcing that it was "taking power," in a sense both "revolutionary" and yet separate—*ab-solutus*—from any other organizational instance, Lacoue-Labarthe and Nancy argue that the literature becomes "the genre of generation."[14] (For more on this notion of generation, see Jocelyn Holland's chapter in this volume.) And yet, as they repeatedly emphasize, this literature both closes in on itself in apparent "organic" totality and presents the "immediate projection of what it nevertheless incompletes."[15] Philosophy operates by use of an *organon* (tool), the authors tell us, with the goal of an *efficacy* that literature exempts itself from in becoming absolute. These formulations are meant to capture the double gesture in all signification for the German Romantics, of appearance or image and significance or the directing of attention. We can already see here that the text is made of *signs*, and the argument that these signs are not merely meant to cohere into a beauty imitative of life has been largely persuasive in recent decades. Perhaps even more explicitly anti-organic is the standard-setting reading of Paul de Man in his essay, "The Rhetoric of Temporality," which proposes that the mode of European Romantic literature—de Man's central example is Rousseau's borrowings from Jean de Meun's *Roman de la Rose*—is *allegory* allied with *irony*. These modes discover an "authentic temporality" that brooks no teleological coherence: "they are ... linked in their common demystification of an organic world postulated in a symbolic mode of analogical correspondences or in a mimetic mode or representation in which fiction and reality could coincide."[16] Unlike the at least implicitly organic "symbol," allegory operates in an infinite iteration of signifiers, laterally one to the other, resignifying by metonymy, not in imitation of a world but in continuation of a self-conscious or reflexive use of signs. In this tradition, the romantic notion of art, text, writing, and sign is generally taken to be *valid* in some enduring way. De Man states that the "dialectical play" between the modes of allegory and irony "make up what is called literary history."[17] The autonomy of literature expressed in the romantic Absolute is a light shone upon literature itself.

Romanticism is less a historical moment in literature than its emergence *as literature*—and as semiotics in general. Severed from any model other than its own, literature cannot be based on "life."

We are now in a better position to understand the lag in the interpretation of German Romanticism. When Frederick Beiser advances the thesis that early German Romanticism is in possession of a convincing philosophical program that is continuous with German Idealism and maintains an "organic conception of the absolute"[18] or "in metaphysics ... developed an organic concept of nature to compete with the mechanical paradigm of the Enlightenment,"[19] then some miscommunication has occurred. I am less interested in whether he is "right" or "wrong" than in the misfit between the large-scale research programs described here. They all circle around the conception of life—even if by rejection—and point collectively to its persistence and opacity in the romantic program. I want to address this lag by proposing that early German Romanticism associated life with signs and sign-making. But the romantic conception was based on the *expression of force*, standing as it did between the Idealist and the natural-philosophical understandings of that characteristically eighteenth-century preoccupation. Life was the *energy of writing*, in a sense that Schlegel and Novalis first expressed. In this respect, it was not fundamentally other to some "dead" matter. This point is, I suspect, what has given rise to the notion of "organicism" as a model of Being. Rather than modeling one region of Being on another, however, the early German Romantics took matter and life to be locked in permanently expressive and dynamic passage from condition of possibility to concrete state—a passage from actuality to possibility and back again that leaves material marks in its expressive wake. Those marks are potential signs, signs that stand on the threshold between force and consciousness. The intimacy of life and semiosis, under proper focus, might require the philosophers to pay more attention to the problems of signification and mediation that so preoccupied the early German Romantics while requiring the literary critics to afford German Romanticism historical and theoretical closure, efficacy, concreteness, instead of only deferral, delay, theoretical bad infinity. The combination of these two must be located in the relation of force and meaning around 1800.

## 2  Force and Meaning

Life around 1800 was the interface between two concepts: force and mind.[20] Newton had thrown down the gauntlet for any serious science. He had famously quipped that he did not "feign hypotheses," meaning he refused to speculate about the metaphysics of the forces at work in nature. To be sure, there were such forces—the one most associated with Newton is gravity—but we could know only their phenomenal effects. From those effects we could construct mathematical formulas to depict the laws of nature, but no more than these rules could be known. Newton's tripartite method spread quickly throughout Europe.[21] In the incipient life sciences, it created productive chaos since the notion of quantifying the laws of organisms seemed far off, if not impossible. Embryology, physiology, and eventually what came to be known as biology took shape in the struggle with Newton's model. None of these areas of inquiry remained innocent of philosophical speculation, and by 1800, they stood proximate to two rapidly developing movements: German Idealism and German Romanticism, with their focus on mind, judgment, and signs. It was the negotiation between force and norm that gave rise to the romantic conception of life.

The twin inheritors of Newton's program, it could be argued, were Albrecht von Haller and Immanuel Kant. Haller—often cast as the last true polymath in the early modern tradition—gave modern physiology its initial shape. Caught for decades in debate about how embryos formed, Haller changed his mind twice. Haller initially embraced the position known as "performation," in which the embryo exists sub-microscopically in full form. This doctrine allowed Newtonians to avoid the proliferation of (potentially ungodly) forces. He then changed his mind, embracing "epigenesis," meaning generation "out of" or "on top of," indicating the belief that some force internal to the egg or sperm guided the formation of the embryo—only to reconvert to preformationist orthodoxy later. He also carried on a public debate with Caspar Friedrich Wolff, who theorized that epigenesis was drive by an "essential force" or *vis essentialis* that gathered and formed the parts and capacities of the embryo.[22] By the 1750s, Haller had partly moved on to other questions of force. Having experimented on the muscular tissue of some hundreds of dogs, he distinguished two capacities of organic tissue: irritability, in which the tissue contracts or shortens when incited, and sensibility, in which it gives rise to a representation (*Vorstellung*).[23] This is at least the most celebrated, if not the first, experimental result that called Cartesian anthropology, based as it is on a strict separation between extended and thinking things, into question in the eighteenth century. A second gauntlet had been thrown down, raising the question of how force and mind could interact. This question recurs throughout and deeply informs the work of Immanuel Kant.

One essay from Kant's early cluster of publications already asks if the concept of "negative magnitude" can be introduced coherently into philosophy.[24] Kant introduces the example of a ship moving down a river with a contrary wind in its sails. Mathematically, there is no question that we should interpret forces with plus and minus signs, yet Kant hesitates to give ontological force to the contradictory motions. This dilemma takes on various forms in his thinking, but in its most general guise, it is what led to the formulation of the critical philosophy, which attempts to preserve the Newtonian picture of force by making the laws of physics almost entirely synthetic a priori judgments with their legitimacy based on the laws of our thought, not on a posited nature outside us.[25] The separation—and subsequent synthesis in judgment—of force and concept allows Kant to depict his critical philosophy as an "epigenesis of pure reason," suggesting that mind is spontaneous, self-forming, and free of divine imprint—like the organism.[26] But just because it is free, the mind is limited and cannot determinately judge precisely those things that do not conform to Newton's mathematical method: organisms. The famous formulation of the *Critique of Judgment* is that there can be "no Newton for a blade of grass."[27] To know the organism determinately would be to know the principle that guides its purpose-like (*zweckmässig*) behavior, requiring an intuitive intellect denied to humans. The organism acts as though each part was permeated by the whole, and vice versa, in a kind of circular causality.[28] Intellect encounters something like itself in its conception of life, but it is too shallow—its tools are "unfit," to use Kant's phrase[29]—to plumb either its own depths or that of the living. It may *observe* living and perhaps understand how it functions in the mechanical order, but it will never be able to reduce life to mechanism, which is to say, to its own Newtonian understanding.

The same year that Kant published the *Critique of Pure Reason*, Johann Blumenbach published a short treatise called *On the Formative Drive* [*Über den Bildungstrieb*], generally viewed as the final statement in the epigenesis controversy. Blumenbach had observed that the regrowth of the starfish's arm does not produce the same, but instead a smaller arm. He reasoned that a divine will would have infinite matter at its disposal and would not commit such an "error." Reproduction, nutrition, and indeed formation itself must rest upon this "drive," which gathers fluids and mixes them into a form not given in the materials but emerging from the drive's action upon and in them. Haller had died in 1777, and no comparable figure could defend preformation. The debate came to an end.[30] Blumenbach had invoked Newton's method for his conclusion:

> I hope that for most readers the reminder will be quite superfluous that the word "formative drive" [*Bildungstrieb*], just as much as the words "attraction," "gravity," etc. should serve no more and no less a purpose than to designate that their constant effects can be recognized in experience, but that their cause just

as much as the cause of those other named and universally recognized forces of nature, is for us a *qualitas occulta*. What Ovid says goes for all these forces: *caussa latet, vis est notissima*.[31]

Kant, though impressed, remained unconvinced by Blumenbach's claims. He called Blumenbach's doctrine "virtual preformationism," accusing his colleague of "the explanation of one unknown by another unknown."[32] Kant left principled explanation, as we have seen, beyond the limits of our knowledge. Life reflects to the understanding a mode it does not determinately possess. The question of the ontological status of life for us—and for the scientist—has been a bitter bone of contention in scientific-historical accounts of this conjuncture.[33] However, one views this question with respect to the eventual emergence of biology, there can be no question that the conceptual conflict between force and mind was central to the concept of life when German Romanticism came into full swing in the final decade of the eighteenth century.

In 1791, a new force entered the scene: "galvanism," the electrical current named after the Italian scientist Luigi Galvani, who had claimed to see it traverse a frog's leg. His countryman Alessandro Volta claimed that while the leg could conduct electricity, the electrical effect itself was based on polarized metals, demonstrating that zinc and copper could reduplicate the effect with no animal tissue when immersed in sulfuric acid. Stacking zinc and copper, he created what was known as the "Voltaic pile," the predecessor to the modern battery. But Galvani's discovery—which would eventually lead to electrophysiology in the 1840s, as Karl Rothschuh has documented—could not be laid to rest so easily, and both Alexander von Humboldt and Johann Wilhelm Ritter would demonstrate properly animal electricity over the course of the 1790s.[34] Both were connected to the emergent German Romantic Movement (more on Ritter below), and electricity gave the movement's most scientifically-minded philosopher a path toward the mind-force interface.

Friedrich Schelling made the force/mind distinction a focus of his version of transcendental idealism. Penning no fewer than three separate treatises between 1797 and 1799 on what was increasingly known as *Naturphilosophie*, Schelling responded to Kant's epistemic modesty with an increasing focus on electrical phenomena, consciousness, and its aesthetic artifacts. We will return to Schelling below, but it is worth noting here that his stated genealogy of the notion of the organic went by way of Johann Gottfried Herder and Carl Friedrich Kielmeyer, whose lecture of 1793, "On the Relations of Organic

Forces," had sent a wave of inspiration through the German publics sphere, adding to Haller's irritability (muscle-contraction) and sensibility (perception) the forces of reproduction (in Blumenbach's term, *Bildungstrieb*), secretion, and propulsion. In the systems of Herder and Kielmeyer, Schelling summarized, a set of compensatory laws arranged the forces of nature. What Schelling called "comparative physiology" showed how inorganic force balanced itself against organic, and how the latter was internally balanced as a combination of reproductive force, irritability, and sensibility, alongside a smattering of other organic forces. Note that irritability and electricity are on the same row in the diagram below. Sensibility involved a balance of electricity, and only this balance could provide an analytical focus for the project of showing nature's buildup to mind.[35] This interface, and not the question of force itself, was the romantic inheritance from the philosophical and experimental notions of life in the eighteenth century.

Less than a year after this work, Schelling published his *System des transcendentalen Idealismus*. The two projects, *Naturphilosophie* and *Transcendentalphilosophie*, ran parallel through the 1790s. Even when Schelling decided to join them into a single presentation in the so-called identity philosophy of 1801, the twin goals remained: to display nature's ability to culminate in mind and to self-objectify mind into nature.[36] Forces must balance to create intellect; intellect must allow the objective to emerge from itself.[37]

Mind will recognize its highest calling in nature and realize that calling only in art. But this operation can only occur through the analysis of forces. Schelling lays them out as follows:

| Organic | General[38] | Anorganic Nature | |
|---|---|---|---|
| | Formative Drive | Light | Chemical Process |
| Irritability | Electricity | Electrical Process | |
| Sensibility | Cause of magnetism? | Magnetism?[39] | |

Each of the columns depicts a sort of region of nature defined by the force named first in the column. The three following items constitute the overall area through their interactions. In the case of the "organic," a formative or reproductive drive stands in opposition to irritability. Only their balance results in sensibility or the capacity to have representations. For Schelling, *Bildung* is clearly positive: it involves the combinative creation of a new being. Irritability is negative, because it is passive—it records shocks absorbed into the animal's body. Sensibility combines these two, synthesizing the two electrical poles of the organ's capacity. What should be impossible is really the foundation of the order (the organic order, for our purposes), and it is also what allows that order to interact with another one. The general and inorganic forces must combine to allow for the creation of life; life must balance itself into (electrical) neutrality to create knowledge, which in turn is *about* the other spheres of nature. This means, for this case, that the isolated and dumb forces of reproduction and muscle-contraction, when they are combined by their simultaneity in an organ (in this case, the brain), make possible a reference to another order: the inorganic, and even the "general" forces. In other words, it is the indifference of the organ to its positive and negative charges, or the combination of passivity and activity, that constitutes the beginnings of cognition as it emerges from animal life. Nature allows mind to emerge.

In the fifth section of the *System*, Schelling gives a beautiful rereading of Kant's notion of organic nature. Schelling argues that we see the unification of knowledge in the objective world in living nature, but *not as ourselves*. In other words, we see *what* the system wants to deliver—the *I* objectified—but not *as the I*. This means that the knowledge that nature gives us, and which we know underlies our ability to represent and think at all, is known to us only externally. In a sense, this section passes judgment on the schema above—or better, points to its intentional limitation. The *System* goes on to argue that it is in art that we find the highest calling of transcendental philosophy, the subject realized as object. The neutrality of forces leads to a cognition that cannot complete itself in gazing back onto the nature that produced it: it must *leave traces* of itself in that nature.[40] Those traces are the subject realized as object, forces realized as semiosis. The recursion in Schlegel's romantic poetry is retained, but we can now see that it does not except itself from the world of forces, remaining aloof. "Life" is what occurs on this continuum between force and sign.

## 3   Galvanic Signs, or Being Outside of Being Within Being

Ritter would put the matter this way: "In galvanism the earth comes to reflection about itself."[41] The project Ritter penned as the *Fragments from the Estate of a Young Physicist* maintains that a variety of forces culminate in a semiotic cosmology. Schelling is, Ritter tells us, "an actual philosophical electrician or electrical philosopher,"[42] though this is not enough on its own. Physics will yield a cosmic sign, written as "⊗." This sign is a combination of process and element, positive and negative—it is what Ritter's friend Novalis (who appears in the *Fragments* as "N") might call a "hieroglyph" or an "Aeolian harp" which is played by the wind. Ritter engages extensively with Ernst Chladni's famous "sound figures" while fashioning his physical semiotics, and readers from Siegfried Zielinski to Bettine Menke have shown how sound and medium are intimately connected around 1800.[43] Ritter's sign must not only document but also produce physical synthesis. Jocelyn Holland has shown that this sign is not merely a documentation for Ritter, but a "construction."[44] If animal electricity leads to consciousness—even perhaps to "world-reflection," which runs close to what Schelling had dubbed the "world soul"—it cannot avoid semiotic mediation. Ritter has gone down in scientific history, among other things, for self-experimentation, attaching positive and negative electrodes of galvanic circuits to his sense organs and recording the taste, smell, and provoked visual patterns. Perhaps these experiments, too, show us the constructive element of physiological semiotics. Nature can only have patterns if we make them into signs, and signs must be material through and through. Ritter translates Schelling's interface into a life constituted of signs. Life is no mere region of force, but the constructed, semiotic unity of matter, pattern, and spontaneity.

Novalis would agree that "spirit galvanizes the soul by means of the crude senses. Its self-activity is *galvanism*—self-contact *en trois*."[45] The triad of spirit, soul, and senses matches Ritter's physics: to galvanize is to write something in memory or in matter. To galvanize is also to give physical incitement or *Reiz*—which leaves a trace, giving material force to the signal. Nothing is only recorded, for Novalis, but instead is constructed *as* recording. Signs can only be *of life* even if they are also properties of physical systems. Borrowing from John Brown's medical system, in which incitements affect a mechanical scale of strength and weakness that determines the state of health of the body, Novalis realizes the romantic insistence on life as semiosis most forcefully.[46] Paraphrasing Fichte, he writes that "the I must posit itself as representing [*darstellend*]," drawing on a "force for representation."[47] We can only awaken this self-positing activity by "giving to it incitatory matter [*reitzenden Stoff*]." Once awakened, the representative force externalizes the

> inner state, internal changes—the inner object comes to appearance. /The external object alternates through and in the I with the concept and there is produced the intuition. The inner object alternates through and in the I with a *body*

> *appropriate to it* and there arises the sign. There the object is the body—here the object is spirit. Common consciousness confuses the result, the intuition and the sign, with the body, because it does not know how to think abstractly [*abstrahieren*]—it is not *self-active*, but instead only necessarily *passive*. Only *half*, not *whole*.[48]

Sign and intuition are both physical imprints, neither complete on its own, each demanding the whole circuit of Ritter's physics in order to complete themselves. Representation is itself a force that consciousness as self-activity can only realize by fashioning signs that can signal their own physical limitations.[49] The interface of force and meaning is a physical one—spontaneous yet reflexive, recursive yet real. Novalis' doctrine of signs connects this complex operation not only to self-consciousness but also to life.

The sign, Novalis writes, is a "Not-being" [*Nichtseyn*] that allows the presentation of something that is. Consciousness cannot do without such signs and in fact, as we have already seen, is structurally dependent on semiosis. This is because knowing is the setting of relations, Novalis tells us, and as such it is "a being outside of being in being" [*ein Seyn außer dem Seyn im Seyn*], meaning an "image" of Being that is not in Being.[50] This image is, in turn, the sign, which "allows being to be *there in a certain way* for itself."[51] Mere Being is nothing, containing no relation at all. The I is nothing *but* the setting of a relation by means of a "Not-being" or image—the sign—which can leave Being as it is only by shifting it into relation with the I. To *be between* Being and not-Being, to hover between them—as Schlegel said of romantic poetry's ability to hover between the represented and the means of representation—is the "concept of life."[52] Life is whatever pattern exists between relation and non-relation, Being and the I. That pattern is the concrete cognition of the I and its expression all at once. It requires electrical impulse, *Reiz*, and the constructive recording of that impulse. It is a "composite of synthesis, thesis and antithesis but none of the three."[53] It is the "character" that accrues to this process, the balance of force and construction, impression and spontaneity. This is why Novalis can ascribe to the I a "hieroglyphistic force."[54] To be self-conscious is to be alive as a sign-generating and sign-receiving Being. Life is not a region of Being, but also not a simulacrum of consciousness. Life is the mediation of Being, the pattern it takes as a series of signs.

## 4 Sensibility and Extension, or *Naturphilosophie's* Life Science

The movement that grew from Schelling's writings on nature—*Naturphilosophie*[55]—is dogged by the underestimation of the role of the sign in the romantic conception of life. When we encounter Joseph Görres' claim, for example, that the brain is the "central sun of the microcosm,"[56] which he shifts from William Harvey's designation of the heart as the same (*cor animalium … Microcosmi Sol*), the problem is patent. Either this is a nominal connection of signs, or it is an ontological assertion. If the sun and the brain are related in Being, revealing a logical similarity expressed by the order of things, then we land in the pre-modern episteme Foucault defined as relying on *resemblance*.[57] Either the brain is the central sun of a microcosm heuristically or else the comparison must be based on a deeper logic, the search for the principle of which had long gone missing, somewhere between Copernicus and Kant. *Naturphilosophie* always seems to slip behind some philosophical, scientific, or rhetorical consensus, whether historically or historiographically. But perhaps this is because we see *Naturphilosophie* as a part of a history of an incipient science. Its focus on physiology, as in Görres' statement, with life and organics as ontological horizon, presents an inverted image of the same physiological focus, but with a newly mathematical physics as its horizon, in positivism.[58] Seen retrospectively from the worldview canonized by Hermann von Helmholtz, *Naturphilosophie* must be seen as a strangely systematic series of analogies with no ontological value. But if we think of *Naturphilosphie* as continuous with the Romanticism that gave rise to it, with its focus on life as semiosis, we can locate a different and perhaps surprising legacy for *Naturphilosphie*: the "philosophy of technology," a phrase first used by the early media theorist and student of Hegel and *Naturphilosophie*, Ernst Kapp.

Lorenz Oken's influential 1809 *Lehrbuch der Naturphilosophie*—dedicated to Schelling and fellow *Naturphilosoph* Henrich Steffens—describes the sciences as narrating the "generation [*Zeugung*] of the world" as the "eternal transformation of God into the world."[59] The Spinozan overtone here dovetails with the ambition to write a cosmology that culminates in the emergence of the organic and the rational. The ambition stems from Herder's *Ideas*, which Schelling had also cited. Force becomes organ, and from the organic arises consciousness. *Naturphilosophie* would be a science that did not exclude life in its romantic sense. The genre of cosmology-with-anthropology took on different forms—many traceable to Herder's influence—and remained popular throughout the nineteenth and arguably into the twenty-first century.[60] Its tendency to embrace teleology, both rational and Eurocentrist, did not prevent Young Hegelians and others from participating, perhaps because it retained a compelling programmatic question inherited from German Romanticism about the relation of life and signs.

The year before his textbook appeared, Oken published a pamphlet called *On the Universe as a Continuation of the Sensory System* [*Über das Universum als Fortsetzung des Sinnensystems*]. This small treatise retains the continuity of life, electrical signal, and sign that is so crucial to Romanticism. Oken writes that

> sense is immediate consensus of the nervous system with the world ... sensation and movement are absolutely unified in the nervous system.[61]

Like Novalis, Oken is concerned with what is passed in both directions through the nerves. The world, he suggests, must maintain a "consensus" of organs in order to allow feeling and motion to be identical. If they were not—at least for our cognition—then no coherence could be ascribed to our knowledge. The question is not how organs work, but what sort of Being they suggest. This leads Oken to define the cosmos as a series of functions—we might almost say sign-functions. Extending Görres' heart/sun metaphor, Oken writes,

> The universe is only *one* animal, whose sensorium commune or self-consciousness is the human, the animals its brain, the plants its senses, and the trunk is everything that remains, what you call "inorganic." There is nowhere an interruption; just as essentially as the sense-organ is one with the brain, is just the distributed brain, so is the sense-object just as essentially one with the sense-organ, and is simply the sense organ further spread out into the universe. The brain extends itself through the sense-nerve, which extends itself into its organ, this extends itself into its object, and this extends itself into the endlessness of the universe.[62]

Again, it is hard not to ask if this is merely an analogy. Does Oken really mean that the universe is structured like an animal? From the standpoint of an emergent discipline called "biology," this does not appear to be literal discourse. But if we read Oken against the background of German Romanticism, we can see that he is most interested in the connective tissue between world and representation or between different regions of that connection. *Naturphilosophie* in Oken's sense would be about the world as inclusive of, and constituted by, life as knowing, life as representation, life as sign. He goes on to define "natural functions" as the only way to overcome the apparently fatal dualism between "external" and "internal." This is the only way to avoid a *"salto mortale"* that leaves world and subject in permanent disjunction. Rather than something "separate from the body" influencing the body, "it is simply two organs of the body working together."[63] The very word *Fortsetzung* in the title speaks to the ambition to unite science with its own medium, language, and signs. Its readiest translation is "extension," but it can also be construed as "continuation." Nerves, representations, and signs are all functions constituting the life that writes science, that knows the world.

This sliding scale of functions providing the joints of the universe in his treatise concatenates ontology and semiotics. It is this combination that creates a through-line to media theory. For the *Naturphilosophen* did not disappear with the rise of positivism, and equally importantly, many of them did not die until the middle of the nineteenth century. Schelling lived until 1853; Carl Gustav Carus, author of the twin nature-philosophical works *Physis* and *Pysche,* until 1869. It was Carus' articulation of a theory of the unconscious as the "key to all conscious life"[64] that allowed Kapp to turn the material screw in his own philosophy of technology. Technology, for Kapp, was the "unconscious projection of organs" on the part of the human. Kapp took inspiration from a backwoodsman he had met in his post-1848 exile in Texas, who had spoken of a "philosophy of the axe." Noting that the American axe mocked the sinews of the arm, Kapp speculated that technology was a series of such projections: the railroad for the circulatory system, the telegraph wires for the nervous system, and so on. But this projection was not intentional: in a dialectical twist, Kapp argued that humans unconsciously projected these technological forms, only afterward to discover their resemblance to themselves. In fact, he went so far as to argue that physiology as a discipline could only exist in the light of these technologies.[65] He had, in a sense, turned Oken's theory on its head. The connective tissue of the universe was in an unconscious labor that precipitated in machines. The world of signs and language was, for Kapp, a kind of reflexive or internal projection, the beginning of the any distinction between the natural and the artificial. Organ projection—of which I have only provided a thumbnail sketch here—inherited the material semiotics of German Romanticism by way of Hegel and *Naturphilosophie*. If it shifted the paradigm from "life" to "technology," that can only reinforce our sense of the power of the romantic conception of life. So far from modeling Being or anything else on some pre-established organicism, the German Romantics deeply entangled the semantics of life with the problem of material semiosis. To shift the register to technology is only to ask how we may live with communicative machines.

Romanticism has been recruited to virtually every theory that flourished in the late twentieth century on a continuum from deconstruction to systems theory.[66] Given that Foucault's theory of biopolitics puts the emergence of the statistical administration of life in the eighteenth century, we should not be surprised to find German Romanticism also recruited to the theory of life as population.[67] What underlies these attempts, as I have attempted to show in this chapter, is the distinctive view of life as semiosis. The German Romantic Movement came into Being just as electricity came to be recognized as sign-generative. The electric telegraph was still decades away, although the automaton already firmly existed, both in reality and in imagination. Jessica Riskin has recently argued that these automata testify to a conception of "living matter" and that they "simulate life" rather than merely mocking up one or the other function.[68] But life, and even matter, was not just a type of Being for the German Romantics: it was continuous with self-consciousness as a semiotic process. Attempts to make Romanticism fit into histories of a post-hoc scientific worldview, like attempts to recruit the romantics to one or another theory, tend to require simplification that levels the highly complex theory of life that we find in German Romanticism. To be sure, that theory was crafted in deep dialogue with science and anticipated questions of material artificiality of semiotic processes. Its historical reach is, after all, connected to its conception of life. But that conception can be neither the infinite deferral of signs nor the description of some region of Being dubbed "organic." It has to be both, even if that identity resists definition.

## Notes

1. Friedrich Schlegel, Kritische Friedrich-Schlegel-Ausgabe. Ed. Ernst Behler, Jean Jacques Anstett, and Hans Eichner (Munich: Schöningh, 1958–). Cited as KFSA 2, 181. Translations mine unless otherwise noted. I have translated the extremely difficult syntax of this passage with a view to analytical clarity, not to the reproduction of style.
2. KFSA 2, 181–82.
3. In *Die Lesbarkeit der Welt*, Hans Blumenberg captures this semiotic plasticity this way: "Romanticism didn't only erase the boundaries between literary genres, or boundaries in general in favor of the impression or the symbolization or even only of the illusion of infinity—it also dissolved the difference between signification and signified [*von Bedeutung und Bedeutetem*] in favor of a kind of universal plasticity that allows anything to stand in for anything else" (Frankfurt a.M.: Suhrkamp, 1981: 236–37).

4. This sets the German context off from British Romanticism, which famously maintained a notion of "organic form," taking inspiration from Kant's *Critique of Judgment* and Coleridge's interactions with the Jena Romantics. It lies beyond the bounds of this chapter to connect its argument to the excellent work ongoing in this parallel field, such as Robert Mitchell's *Experimental life: Vitalism in Romantic Science and Literature* (Baltimore, Johns Hopkins, 2013), Denise Gigante's, *Life: Organic Form and Romanticism* (New Haven: Yale University Press, 2009), Sarah Guyer's, *Reading with John Clare: Biopoetics, Sovereignty, Romanticism* (New York: Fordham, 2015), and Amanda Jo Goldstein's, *Sweet Science: Romantic Materialism and the New Logics of Life* (Chicago: University of Chicago, 2017). Goldstein's work also highlights the crucial role of material semiotics, inherited from Lucretius, in the romantic imaginary and in Goethe's work.
5. Michel Foucault, *The Order of Things: An Archaeology of the Human Sciences* (New York: Routledge, 1970/2005), 139.
6. But see the attempted revision by Peter McLaughlin, "Naming Biology," *Journal of the History of Biology*, 35 (1) (2002): 1–4.
7. Lynn Nyhart, *Biology Takes Form: Animal Morphology and the German Universities, 1800–1900* (Chicago: University of Chicago, 1995).
8. Foucault, *Order of Things*, 347–51. For the connection to Kant, see also Foucault's complementary thesis, *Introduction to Kant's Anthropology from a Pragmatic Point of View* (Los Angeles: Semiotext(e), 2008).
9. Ibid., 349.
10. A group of recent attempts to cast Romanticism as "mechanical" are of note here, including Jocelyn Holland's forthcoming study, *The Lever as Instrument of Reason*, as well as her earlier study, *German Romanticism and Science: The Procreative Poetics of Goethe, Novalis and Ritter* (New York: Routledge, 2009). I have also argued against the primacy of "organicism" in my *Transplanting the Metaphysical Organ: German Romanticism between Leibniz and Marx* (New York: Fordham, 2016). For French Romanticism, see John Tresch, *The Romantic Machine: Utopian Science and Technology after Napoleon* (Chicago: University of Chicago Press, 2012). This chapter attempts to clear ground for these forward-looking works by treating the lost interface between life and sign in early German Romanticism. Goldstein's *Sweet Science* also pursues this line of thought. Perhaps the most pro-organicist account is that of Kristian Köchy, *Ganzheit und Wissenschaft: Das historische Fallbeispiel der romantischen Naturforschung* (Würzburg: Königshausen und Neumann, 1997).
11. Rudolf Haym, *Die romantische Schule: ein Beitrag zur Geschichte des deutschen Geistes* (Gaertner: Berlin, 1870).
12. Walter Benjamin, *Werke und Nachlaß. Kritische Gesamtausgabe. Band 3: Der Begriff der Kunstkritik in der deutschen Romantik*, ed. Uwe Steiner (Frankfurt/Main: Suhrkamp, 2008).

13. Maurice Blanchot, "The Athenaeum," trans. Deborah Esch and Ian Balfour, *Studies in Romanticism* 22: 2 (1983): 163–72; Philippe Lacoue-Labarthe and Jean-Luc Nancy, *The Literary Absolute: The Theory of Literature in* German Romanticism (Albany: SUNY Press, 1988). Other studies that broadly follow this line include Winfried Menninghaus, *Unendliche Verdopplung: Die frühromantische Grundlegung der Kunsttheorie im Begriff absoluter Selbstreflexion* (Frankfurt a.M.: Suhrkamp, 1987), and Werner Hamacher, "Position Exposed: Friedrich Schlegel's Transposition of Fichte's Absolute Proposition," in *Premises: Essays on Philosophy and Literature from Kant to Celan* (Stanford: Stanford University Press, 1999): 222–61.
14. Lacoue-Labarthe and Nancy, *Literary Absolute*, 49.
15. Lacoue-Labarthe and Nancy, *Literary Absolute*, 43.
16. Paul de Man, "The Rhetoric of Temporality," in Paul de Man, *Blindness and Insight: Essays in the Rhetoric of Contemporary Criticism* (Minneapolis: University of Minnesota), 187–228, here 222.
17. Ibid., 226. Nancy and Lacoue-Labarthe also seem to think of German Romanticism as *correct*; Blanchot places the romantics in his own avant-garde canon; in 1919, something like this seems to be true about Benjamin, too. I will return to this issue at the end of this chapter.
18. Frederick Beiser, *German Idealism: The Struggle against Subjectivism, 1781–1801* (Cambridge: Harvard, 2002), 357.
19. Frederick Beiser, *The Romantic Imperative: The Concept of Early German Romanticism* (Cambridge: Harvard, 2003), 2.
20. Here I agree with Thomas Khurana, "Force and Form: An Essay on the Dialectics of the Living," *Constellations* 18:1 (2011): 21–34. See also his monographic treatment of the "Lebensphilosophie" of German Idealism, *Das Leben der Freiheit: Form und Wirklichkeit der Autonomie* (Frankfurt a.M.: Suhrkamp, 2017).
21. See Simone de Angelis, *Von Newton zu Haller. Studien zum Naturbegriff zwischen Empirismus und deduktiver Methode in der Schweizer Frühaufklärung* (Max Niemeyer, Tübingen, 2003), and also John Zammito, *The Gestation of German Biology: Philosophy and Physiology from Stahl to Schelling* (Chicago: University of Chicago, 2018), esp. 13–37 and 37–71.
22. See the definitive account in Shirley A. Roe, *Matter, Life, and Generation: Eighteenth-Century Embryology and the Haller-Wolff Debate* (Cambridge: Cambridge UP, 2003).
23. See Hubert Steinke, *Irritating Experiments: Haller's Concept and the European Controversy on Irritability and Sensibility, 1750–90* (New York: Rodopi, 2005).
24. Immanuel Kant, "Versuch den Begriff der negativen Größen in die Weltweisheit einzuführen," in Immanuel Kant, *Kant's gesammelte Schriften* (Berlin: Reimer, 1900–.), vol. II, *Vorkritische Schriften II, 1757–1777*: 165–205.

25. See Eric Watkins, *Kant and the Sciences* (New York: Oxford, 2001), and Michael Friedman, *Kant and the Exact Sciences* (Cambridge: Harvard University Press, 1992).
26. See Béatrice Longuenesse, *Kant and the Capacity to Judge: Sensibility and Discursivity in the Transcendental Analytic of the Critique of Pure Reason*, trans. Charles T. Wolfe (Princeton: Princeton, 1998); Catharine Malabou. *Before Tomorrow: Epigenesis and Rationality*, trans. Carolyn Shread (Cambridge: Polity, 2016).
27. See Immanuel Kant, *Kant's gesammelte Schriften* (Berlin: Reimer, 1900–.), vol. V, 400.
28. The relevant passages are §§64–65 of the *Critique of Judgment*. The standard account—among a flood of recent scholarship on Kant's biology—is perhaps still Reinhard Löw, *Philosophie des Lebendigen: Der Begriff des Organischen bei Kant, sein Grund und seine Aktualität* (Frankfurt a.M.: Suhrkamp, 1980), and more recently Jennifer Mensch, *Kant's Organicism: Epigenesis and the Development of Critical Thought* (Chicago: University of Chicago Press, 2013).
29. Kant, CPR B334/A278.
30. See Helmut Müller-Sievers, *Self-Generation: Biology, Philosophy, and Literature around 1800* (Stanford, CA: Stanford University Press, 1997); compare John Zammito, *Kant, Herder, and the Birth of Anthropology* (Chicago: University of Chicago Press, 2002).
31. Johann Friedrich Blumenbach, *Über den Bildungstrieb* (Göttingen: Dieterich 1791), pp. 32–34; emphasis in original. See also James Larson, "Vital Forces: Regulative Principles or Constitutive Agents? A Strategy in German Physiology, 1786–1802," *Isis* 70: 2 (1979).
32. Kant, AA V 422–24.
33. Timothy Lenoir's *The Strategy of Life: Teleology and Mechanics in Nineteenth-Century German* Biology (Chicago: University of Chicago Press 1989) revitalized interest in *Naturphilosophie* by marking a clearly Kantian research paradigm that led circuitously to Darwin, using life as a regulative notion by which to explore the mechanisms in use in organisms. This approach was countered by Robert Richards' important study, *The Romantic Conception of Life*, which argued that the explicit ontological commitment to a robust notion of part and whole, spontaneity and activity, was continuous from Jena and its literary program through to Schelling, Goethe, and again Darwin. Richards confirmed but reversed the charge from Peter-Hanns Reil, as articulated in *Vitalizing Nature in the Enlightenment* (Berkeley: University of California Press, 2005), that Romanticism rejected Kant's notion of a regulative balance between life and dead matter. For Reil, this rejection meant that romantic *Naturphilosophie* was a metaphysical departure from the royal road to empirical biology, the path battened down by Enlightenment natural philosophers. For Richards, it is the opposite: to make life *real* was the way to render it historical, to give it dynamic form and eventually (in Goethe) a

notion of species-transformation. John Zammito's recent, *The Gestation of German Biology* achieves a new synthesis by tracing the emergence of a science of life from the vitalist-mechanist debates between Herman de Boerhaave and Georg Ernst Stahl in Halle through to the Göttingen paradigm (also Lenoir's point of departure) in the successive generations of Albrecht von Haller and Johann Blumenbach. *Gestation* shifts the focus onto the question of the expression of force, a lead I follow here. Joan Steigerwald's, *Experimenting at the Boundaries of Life*, due out later this year, promises to make another crucial intervention in the field. The sum of this literature has placed German Romanticism firmly between Newton, whose dual programs of experimentalism and mathematical formalism with respect to natural laws put great pressure on any aspirations to life science, and Darwin, who represents a final—or for Richards a not-so-final-after-all—break with the holistic and teleological understanding of life that is thought to have flourished in the breach created by Newton.

34. Johann Wilhelm Ritter, *Johann Wilhelm Ritter: Key Texts on the Science and Art of Nature*, trans. and ed. Jocelyn Holland (Amsterdam: Brill, 2010), x; see also K. E. Rothschuh, "Von der Idee bis zum Nachweis der tierischen Elektrizität," *Sudhoffs Archiv für Geschichte der Medizin und der Naturwissenschaften* 44: 1 (1960): 25–44, and K. E. Rothschuh, "Alexander von Humboldt und die Physiologie seiner Zeit," *Sudhoffs Archiv für Geschichte der Medizin und der Naturwissenschaften* 43: 2 (1959): 97–113.

35. Friedrich Schelling, *First Outline of a System of the Philosophy of Nature*, trans. Keith R. Peterson (Albany: State University of New York, 2004), 141. On the various forces at work in Schelling's *Naturphilosphie*, the best resource remains Francesco Moiso, "Magnetismus, Elektrizit.t, Galvanismus," in Friedrich Schelling, *Historisch-kritische Ausgabe*, ed., Jörg Jantzen, Thomas Buchheim, Jochem Hennigfeld, Wilhelm G. Jacobs, and Siegbert Peetz (Stuttgart: Frommann-Holzboog, 1976). Cited as Schelling, HKA 5/9, 165–375. See also Benjamin Specht, *Physik als Kunst: Die Poetisierung der Elektrizität um 1800* (Berlin: de Gruyter, 2010).

36. *HKA* I: 9, *System des transscendentalen Idealismus*, 30–32. For alternate accounts emphasizing the independence of Schelling's *Naturphilosophie*, see Iain H. Grant, *Philosophies of Nature after Schelling* (New York: Continuum, 2006), and Dalia Nassar, "From a Philosophy of Self to a Philosophy of Nature: Goethe and the Development of Schelling's Naturphilosophie," *Archiv für Geschichte der Philosophie* 92, 3 (2010): 304–21.

37. "*das Objective aus ihm entstehen zu lassen*," (To allow the objective to develop out of it) Schelling, *System* 32.

38. The universal unifying force is, of course, the *Weltseele* in the 1797 writing of that name.

39. Schelling, *First Outline*, 9.

40. I have argued elsewhere that these artifacts can be construed as not only aesthetic but *artificial*, and that Schelling here anticipates crucial elements of the philosophy of technology, more on which below. See Weatherby, *Transplanting*, 171–206.
41. Ritter, *Key Texts*, 296.
42. Ritter, *Key Texts*, 435.
43. Bettine Menke, "Töne—Hören" in *Poetologien des Wissens um 1800*, ed. Joseph Vogl (Munich: Wilhelm Fink, 1999): 69–96; see also Siegfried Zielinski, "In Praise of What Is Not Systemic About the Arts: For a *cultura experimentalis*," in Siegfried Zielinksi, *[… After the Media]: News from the Slow-Fading Twentieth Century*, trans. Gloria Custance (Minneapolis: Univocal, 2013): 125–173. Bernhard Siegert has also suggested that a sort of physical self-writing by means of electrical phenomenon in the eighteenth century was crucial to the emergence of the digital more than a century later, subjecting Georg Lichtenberg's figures that appear on insulating materials to analysis. See Bernhard Siegert, *Passage des Digitalen: Zeichenpraktiken der neuzeitlichen Wissenschaften, 1500–1900* (Brinkmann & Bose: Berlin, 2003): 255–75. On acoustics and emergent patterning in aesthetics and the sciences and embryology, see also Janina Wellman, *The Form of Becoming: Embryology and the Epistemology of Rhythm, 1760–1830*, trans. Kate Sturge (New York: Zone Books, 2017).
44. Jocelyn Holland, "The Silence of Ritter's Symbol ⊗," *Germanic Review* 92: 4 (2017): 340–54. See also Specht, *Physik als Kunst, Op. cit.,* 199–216.
45. Novalis, *Novalis Schriften: Die Werke Friedrich von Hardenbergs*, ed. Paul Kluckhohn and Richard H. Samuel (Stuttgart: Kohlhammer, 1960–2006). Cited as: NS II, 545: 192
46. See Nelly Tsouyopoulos, *Asklepios und die Philosophen: Paradigmawechsel in der Medizin im 19. Jahrhundert*, ed. Claudia Wiesemann, Barbara Bröker, and Sabine Rogge (Stuttgart–Bad Cannstatt: frommann-holzboog, 2008), and Nelly Tsouyopoulos, "The Influence of John Brown's Ideas in Germany," *Medical History*, Supplement no. 8 (1988): 63–74; see also John Neubauer, *Bifocal Vision: Novalis' Philosophy of Nature and Disease* (Chapel Hill: University of North Carolina Press, 1971).
47. NS II 633: 282.
48. NS II 637: 283–84.
49. It would require a separate chapter just to summarize the brilliant work on Novalis' semiotics. Cited here are only those works which I have often consulted and which have influenced the presentation given here. Azade Seyhan, *Representation and Its Discontents: The Critical Legacy of German Romanticism* (Berkeley: University of California Press, 1992); Martha Helfer, *The Retreat of Representation: The Concept of Darstellung in German Critical Discourse* (Albany: SUNY Press, 1996); William Arctander O'Brien, *Novalis: Signs of Revolution* (Durham: Duke University Press, 1995); Herbert Uerlings,

"Darstellen. Zu einem Problemzusammenhang bei Novalis," in *Romantische Wissenspoetik: Die Künste und die Wissenschaften um 1800*, ed. Gabriele Brandtstetter and Gerhard Neumann (Würzburg: Königshausen und Neumann, 2004), 373–93; Winfried Menninghaus, "Die frühromantische Theorie von Zeichen und Metapher," *German Quarterly* 61: 1 (1989): 48–58.

50. NS II 2:106.
51. Ibid.
52. NS II 3: 106.
53. NS II 3: 107.
54. NS II 6: 107.
55. Dietrich von Engelhardt distinguished three kinds of *Naturphilosophie*, as Timothy Lenoir recounts in his "Göttingen School." *Studies in the History of Biology* 5 (1981): 11–205: a Kantian type focused on mechanical-teleological balancing acts; a Schellingian type; and a Hegelian type. The latter two both suffer from the discursive problem I lay out, and both to some extent can be read more profitably with an eye to semiosis and their legacy in the philosophy of technology and media theory.
56. Joseph Görres, *Exposition der Physiologie: Organologie* (Koblenz: Lassaulx, 1805), 161.
57. Foucault, *Order of Things*, 19 ff.
58. Johann Müller forms the most important institutional link between *Naturphilosophie* and positivism, as Laura Otis has shown in *Müller's Lab: The Story of Jakob Henle, Theodor Schwann, Emil du Bois-Reymond, Hermann von Helmholtz, Rudolf Virchow, Robert Remak, Ernst Haeckl, and Their Brilliant, Tortured Adviser*(Oxford: Oxford University Press, 2007); on the philosophical link between the two movements, see Thomas Kuhn, *The Essential Tension: Selected Studies in Scientific Tradition and Change* (Chicago: University of Chicago Press, 1977): 66–105.
59. Lorenz Oken, *Lehrbuch der Naturphilosophie* (Frommann: Jena, 1809), vii.
60. Nasser Zakariya, *A Final Story: Science, Myth, and Beginnings* (Chicago: University of Chicago, 2017).
61. Lorenz Oken, *Über das Universum als Fortsetzung des Sinnensystems* (Frommann: Jena, 1808), 11.
62. Ibid., 10.
63. Ibid., 15.
64. Carl Gustav Carus, *Psyche. Zur Entwicklungsgeschichte der Seele* (Flammer and Hoffmann: Pforzheim, 1846), 1.
65. See Ernst Kapp, *Elements of a Philosophy of Technology: On the Evolutionary History of Culture*, trans. Lauren K. Wolfe (Minneapolis: University of Minnesota, 2018). For a fuller analysis of Kapp's work, see my introduction, co-authored with Jeffrey Kirkwood, to this volume.
66. See note 14 above. See also Niklas Luhmann, "A Redescription of 'Romantic Art,'" *MLN* 111: 3 (1996), 506–22; Joseph Vogl, *Kalkül und Leidenschaft:*

*Poetik des ökonomischen Menschen* (Diaphanes: Berlin, 2004); Theisen "χα Absolute Chaos: The Early Romantic Poetics of Complex Form," *Studies in Romanticism* 42: 3 (2003): 301–21; and Edgar Landgraf, "Comprehending Romantic Incomprehensibility. A Systems-Theoretical Perspective on Early German Romanticism," *MLN* 121: 3 (2006): 592–616.

67. See Sarah Guyer, *Reading with John Clare*, and my "Police Psychology: E.T.A. Hoffmann's Technological Narrative," *Romantic Circles: Praxis*, "New Work on German Romanticism," 2016, visited March 25, 2019.

68. Jessica Riskin, "The Defecating Duck, or, the Ambiguous Origins of Artificial Life," *Critical Inquiry*, 29: 4 (2003): 599–633.

# Part IV

## Legacy

# 21

## Women, Women Writers, and Early German Romanticism

Anna Ezekiel

Early German Romanticism is sometimes claimed to present a radical challenge to the gender norms of the late eighteenth and early nineteenth centuries.[1] However, critics argue that the romantic concern with the efforts of an active "male" subject to rediscover its lost wholeness and create an aesthetic self through interactions with a "feminine" nature, often through the intercession of women, has reinforced a dichotomous view of gender, along with its damaging stereotypes.[2] In particular, women are often presented in early German Romanticism as connected to nature and able to mediate the divine, already experiencing the unity with nature and the absolute that the alienated male subject must retrieve.[3] Overt statements that associate women with passivity, motherhood, non-discursive reasoning, and "otherness" add to the moments in which early German Romanticism risks reinscribing, rather than undermining, the long-standing association of women and the feminine with nature and their exclusion from reason and subjecthood. Even Schlegel's famous call for a "gentle masculinity" and an "independent femininity," which would mitigate the characteristics bestowed on men and women by nature, arguably presupposes the dichotomies that he aims to subvert. The same can be said of Novalis' depictions of gender fluidity, in which male protagonists become "feminized," and thereby productive, through taking on the features of the female characters with which they interact. The early German Romantic ideal of a unified humanity that

A. Ezekiel (✉)
Hong Kong, Hong Kong SAR

merges masculine and feminine characteristics and re-integrates the alienated subject and object, together with the modes of knowledge of discourse and intuition, arguably does not reject gender stereotypes, but can only function as part of a paradigm in which these gendered characteristics are seen as fundamental.

Nonetheless, this chapter argues that a critique of gender norms is present in early German Romanticism, although it appears inconsistently and competes with a more conservative model. The first two sections of the chapter respectively describe the thought of Friedrich Schlegel and Novalis on women and gender and present feminist criticisms of this model, without attempting to defend early German Romanticism from this critique. A third section explains the integral place of gender in early German Romantic thought, showing why problems with the early German Romantic model of gender create more thoroughgoing difficulties for the romantic project in general. Section 4 provides a partial defense of early German Romanticism against the criticisms raised in Sects. 2 and 3, arguing that early German Romantics such as Schlegel and Novalis were well aware of the difficulties and pitfalls of attempting to move beyond the perspective of the subject, and, in particular, of the implication of this subject in a masculinist discourse. However, I argue that, despite this self-awareness, the emancipatory potential of some early German Romantic ideas about women cannot be realized within the romantic project of self-poiesis as it is conceptualized by Friedrich Schlegel, Novalis, and other male romantics, that is, within a world characterized in dichotomous terms that are heavily gendered.

The last two sections of the chapter focus on the work of two female writers associated with early German Romanticism, arguing that these writers provide a more consistent critique of gender norms and that their writings show promise for creating a model of self and world that escapes these problematic stereotypes. Dorothea Veit-Schlegel's novel *Florentin* highlights problems with the romantic model of self-poiesis, while Karoline von Günderrode challenges the dualistic view of nature that forms the starting point for early German Romanticism, and with it its dichotomous view of gender. In rejecting a model that presents the subject as constituting itself through interactions with its complementary opposite, these writers also create alternative conceptualizations of the tension between fragmentation and wholeness, and the quest for identity and unity, that is central to the early German Romantic project.

## 1 The Early German Romantic Account of Gender and Its Emancipatory Aspirations

It has sometimes been claimed that early German Romanticism presents a radical and emancipatory view of women, gender, and gender relations, particularly in the early work of Friedrich Schlegel. Hans Eichner, for example, states that "Schlegel's *Lucinde* is a passionate protest against the inequality of the sexes and the condemnation of sexuality."[4] In particular, Schlegel's essays "On Diotima" (1795) and "On Philosophy: To Dorothea" (1799) and his novel *Lucinde* (1799) question conceptions of the nature and role of women that prevailed at the time and attempt to undermine a rigid division of characteristics according to gender. The same effort to undermine fixed gender categories is found in the work of Novalis and other writers associated with early German Romanticism such as Schleiermacher, Eichendorff, E.T.A. Hoffmann, Kleist, and Johann Wilhelm Ritter.[5]

Schlegel wrote against a background of debate about whether women were capable of pursuing an intellectual education and whether they ought to even if capable, and in which the natural suitability of women to domesticity and motherhood was widely asserted.[6] The early Schlegel argued that women could and should be encouraged to develop intellectually, and that they should especially study philosophy. He devoted "On Diotima" to demonstrating that women in certain periods and states of ancient Greece were educated, aesthetically creative, and participated in public life, to no detriment of health or morals, and claimed, in "On Philosophy," that "philosophy is indispensable to women[.]"[7] Schlegel recognized, furthermore, the social constraints affecting women's development, arguing that women's expected roles as wives and mothers placed burdens on them that prevented their full flourishing:

> Not the vocation of women but their *nature* and *position* are domestic. And I hold it for a more useful than pleasant truth that even the best marriage, motherhood itself, and the family can so easily entrap and pull them down with needs, with economy and the world, that they are no longer mindful of their divine origin and likeness.[8]
>
> The lifestyle of women has the propensity to limit them ever more and more and to bury their spirit[.][9]

Closely associated with these claims was a theory of gender that Schlegel linked to his philosophy. To Schlegel, full humanity would comprise an integrated whole of masculine and feminine characteristics, whereas the strict separation of these characteristics into different individuals resulted in incomplete human beings: "In fact masculinity and femininity, as they are usually taken and practiced, are the most dangerous hindrances to humanity, which, according to an old legend, is at home in the middle and can only be a harmonious whole, which suffers no segregation."[10]

Accordingly, the realization of full humanity would require a mitigation of the extremes of gender characteristics:

> Only gentle masculinity, only independent femininity is the right, the true, and beautiful. If it is so, then one must in no way further exaggerate the character of gender, which is only an inborn, natural profession, but rather seek to mitigate it through strong counterweights, so that individuality may find a potentially unlimited space, in order to move freely in the whole region of humanity[.][11]

Thus, men should attempt to become more complete human beings by mellowing their masculine characteristics and taking on characteristics of femininity, while women should develop more masculine traits. Schlegel concludes from this that women should pursue philosophy, developing their intellectual faculties to counteract their "poetic" and "religious" nature. Men, conversely, have a "philosophical" nature and should pursue poesy.[12]

As this last point indicates, while Schlegel claims men and women should each combine masculine and feminine characteristics, he *does* maintain that there are essential differences between men and women. In the above quote, he claims that gender is an "inborn, natural profession," even if it can be "mitigated" by "strong counterweights." Elsewhere, he states that "Every *man* has genius; harmony is the essence of woman"[13] and that woman's "innermost essence is poesy."[14] At various points, Schlegel explicitly connects women by nature to poesy, religion, moral goodness, intuition, beauty, harmony, love, passivity, and sympathy, and men to philosophy, independence, energy, rationality, activity, genius, and the sublime.[15] These align with associations between these categories and characteristics of masculinity and femininity that were propounded by Schlegel's contemporaries.[16]

Schlegel thus claims that men and women do have stereotypically gender-coded essential characteristics, but that, in pursuit of perfected humanity, efforts at self-development should aim to mitigate, rather than exaggerate, these differences: "the sex-difference is only an externality of human existence and in the end indeed nothing more than a good establishment of nature, that one indeed cannot arbitrarily destroy or reverse, but certainly may subordinate to reason, and form according to its higher laws." The result will not be unfeminine women or unmasculine men; the development of the opposing characteristics will round out, rather than obscure, those that each gender naturally possesses. In the case of women, "the concern of suffering damage to moral innocence and especially femininity through this gain of spiritual development [...] seems to me to be as ungrounded as it is unmasculine! For where once femininity is present, there is no moment in which it does not remind its owner of its existence[.]"[17]

Schlegel's ideal end-point for this exchange of characteristics would be an androgynous being that combined male and female characteristics.[18] However, this end-point is only a regulative ideal. On Schlegel's model, the characteristics of sex and gender that are bestowed upon human beings by nature can be shaped, enhanced, minimized, and exchanged, but in the end women will remain feminine and men will remain masculine. The realizable objective that Schlegel hopes can emerge is a reduction in the extremes of masculinity and femininity that, he believes, limit individual human beings. This is to occur through a continual back-and-forth exchange of characteristics between the two poles of a masculine and a feminine being. As Lisa Roetzel notes, "In the play of *Wechsel* [alternation, or exchange], [...] each side takes on the qualities of the other without losing its own fundamental characteristics."[19]

In *Lucinde*, Schlegel presents his theory of gender in the romantic form of the novel. In one passage, the protagonist, Julius, describes to Lucinde the significance of playfully reversing the roles expected of male and female lovers:

> One [of the shapes and situations of happiness] above all is wittiest and most beautiful: when we exchange roles and in childish high spirits compete to see who can mimic the other more convincingly, whether you are better at imitating the protective intensity of the man, or I the appealing devotion of the woman. [...] I see here a wonderful, deeply meaningful allegory of the development of man and woman to full and complete humanity.[20]

For the early German Romantics, the practical outcomes of this exchange for the development of individual human beings include a coherent, meaningful life and the development of creative genius. Both Schlegel and Novalis present the adoption of feminine characteristics by men as essential to the emergence of a higher level of human existence, represented by the artist. In *Lucinde*, an "Apprenticeship for Manhood" describes Julius' development through interactions with various women, especially Lucinde, into an artist and complete human being. This development culminates in Julius' relationship with Lucinde, who he describes as uniting all the characteristics of women—"at once the most delicate lover, the most wonderful companion, and the most perfect friend"[21]—and representing the unity of nature: "you know of no separations; your being is one and indivisible."[22] Julius experiences that unity himself and recognizes himself in the other through the mirror of Lucinde: "In you [my most cherished and secret intention] has come to fruition and I'm not afraid to admire and love myself in this mirror. Only here do I see myself complete and harmonious, or rather, see all of humanity in me and in you."[23] Once Julius is in a relationship with Lucinde, his life acquires cohesion and meaning and he finally enjoys success as an artist: "Just as his artistic ability developed and he was able to achieve with ease what he had been unable to accomplish with all his powers of exertion and hard work before, so too his life now came to be a work of art for him[.]"[24]

A similar movement drives Novalis' novel, *Henry of Ofterdingen*, in which Henry becomes a poet through the mediation of women, particularly his fiancée Mathilde. As in the work of Schlegel, Novalis' writings present gender as, to some extent, fluid and allowing an exchange of gendered characteristics between men and women, or at least from women to men. Like Schlegel, Novalis claims that gender characteristics are not absolutely tied to physical sex but can also be developed in the opposite sex, stating, for example, that "man is to an extent also woman, as woman is man."[25] *Henry of Ofterdingen* involves numerous examples of men taking on stereotypically feminine characteristics and absorbing women into themselves. Most literally, in a story told by Mathilde's father Klingsohr, the ashes of a dead mother are consumed by the surviving characters, who seem transfigured by this act.[26] Several scholars mention the feminization of Henry himself, especially in frequent references to his lips and mouth,[27] which are presented as open, receptive, and productive, suggesting, as Alice Kuzniar notes, "a conflation of parturition and conception metaphors."[28] Kuzniar points out the connection in the novel between voices—especially women's voices—and the lips or mouth, which are used to speak and, in several cases, to transfer the ability to sing and write poetry from women to Henry or other male characters.[29] In particular, it is Mathilde's opening of Henry's lips with her kiss and whispering into his mouth that allows Henry to "give birth to poetry," as Kuzniar puts it.[30] As Kuzniar concludes, "Novalis aligns motherhood with poetic creativity, with the result that the male hero must ultimately become feminized in order to write."[31]

As in Schlegel's writings, in Novalis' work women function as mirrors to male protagonists, revealing the protagonists as ultimately one with nature and the universe, and mediating unification with that oneness—a return to their original, absolute self. For example, in "Hymns to the Night," the narrator's dead beloved appears in a vision and connects him to eternity.[32] In *Henry of Ofterdingen*, too, the ultimate unity that is mediated by women to men is unity with the Absolute. Henry says of Mathilde, "Does a distinct, undivided being not belong to her contemplation and worship?"[33] and, to her: "You are the saint who brings my wishes to God, through whom he reveals himself to me[.]"[34] In *Henry of Ofterdingen*, as in "Hymns," this unity is ultimately achieved through death. In the unfinished second volume, it is after Mathilde's death that Henry finds his voice and becomes a poet, prompted by hearing Mathilde's voice echoing from a rock. In the published part of the novel, this event is prefigured in Henry's observation of Mathilde, shortly before dreaming of her death, that "She will dissolve me into music. She will become my inmost soul, the guardian of my holy fire."[35] In "Hymns," the narrator's dead beloved plays this role of mediator of the infinite. The idea that death will enable the final unification of an alienated (male) subject with nature (represented by a female figure) is also suggested by Schlegel. For example, in *Lucinde* Julius imagines Lucinde's death and the subsequent continuation of his own life: "The years slowly passed by and one event tiresomely succeeded another; one task and then another achieved its end [...]. They were only holy symbols for me, all of them referring to the only beloved one, who was the mediator between my dismembered self and indivisible eternal humanity."[36] This echoes Henry's reflection, following the manifestation of the dead Mathilde's voice, that "Voice and language became living again within him and everything seemed to him more known and prophetic than before, so that death appeared to him a higher revelation of life[.]"[37]

The ability of women, associated with nature, to mediate unity, selfhood, and completion to men is thus an important theme in early German Romanticism. Although this chapter does not explore the work of other male romantic writers, others have argued that Schleiermacher, Eichendorff, E.T.A. Hoffmann, and Johann Wilhelm Ritter also present gender categories as fluid and women as having a high moral or religious value that they can mediate to men.[38]

Another important aspect of the position of women in early German Romanticism is the status granted to sexuality. Schlegel maintained that the ideal relationship between lovers would be both sexually fulfilling and spiritually significant. As Sara Friedrichsmeyer puts it, in *Lucinde* "sexual love, the prototypical combination of dichotomous entities, was vested with the metaphysical force to symbolize all such unions within the universe and could consequently be proffered as a saving religion."[39] In associating sexual intercourse between a man and a woman with spiritual development, Schlegel aimed both to undermine the conventional separation of sexuality and sensuality from spirituality and to challenge the concomitant idealization of women as either asexual spiritual beings or lovers—hence Julius' belief, in *Lucinde*, that "he possessed united in one person all those things which before he had loved separately and disjointedly: the beautiful newness of the senses, the ravishing passion, the modest activity, the docility, and the noble character."[40] Lucinde is both friend and lover, both earthly wife and spiritual mediator.[41] By presenting women—and relationships of men with women—as ideally both spiritual and sexual, Schlegel contributes to rescuing sexuality from the social opprobrium with which female sexuality in particular has often been regarded, presenting it as a fulfilling and even spiritually important part of human development.

Although the early German Romantic understanding of gender does not challenge the existence of stereotypical gendered characteristics, it arguably weakens gender dichotomies by maintaining that extreme manifestations of masculinity and femininity are undesirable. Instead, the development of masculine characteristics in women and feminine characteristics in men is both possible and desirable. This, along with its positive view of sexuality, underlies claims that the early German Romantic view of women was radical for its time and had the potential to emancipate women.

## 2   Criticisms of the Early German Romantic Model of Gender

A number of commentators point out that, although early German Romantics such as Schlegel intended to undermine gender dichotomies by advocating an exchange of gendered attributes between male and female partners, in fact this model reinforces the gendered constructions it claims to mitigate, since it must presuppose them in order to function.[42] This reliance on gender stereotypes emerges in frequent references to the characteristics of men and women by Schlegel and Novalis which, as noted above, follow the same categories as stereotypical conceptions of gender. In "On Philosophy" and *Lucinde*, Schlegel refers to women's "nature,"[43] and Novalis, too, speculates about the "nature" of women and, occasionally, men, retaining a traditional assignation of gendered characteristics (e.g., women "live in the true state of nature"[44] and "Reason is in man, feeling in woman"[45]). The undermining of the male-female dichotomy that Schlegel and Novalis imagined is thus not as profound as might be expected based on their advocacy of exchanging masculine and feminine characteristics. This exchange is premised on an original possession of gendered characteristics by men and women, which can be mitigated, but never obliterated.

Furthermore, the romantics portray the development of an individual toward complete humanity in terms of an asymmetrical appropriation of supposedly feminine characteristics by a male subject.[46] One commentator describes *Lucinde* as "an egocentric account of how Lucinde, and to a lesser extent one or two of the earlier women whom Julius meets, contributed to his sexual, emotional, and intellectual *Bildung*[.]"[47] As we have seen, the same movement occurs in Novalis' *Henry of Ofterdingen* and "Hymns." As Friedrichsmeyer notes, in Novalis' depictions love "is primarily an exploitative union and one which benefits the male protagonist[.]"[48]

In addition to its heteronormativity, this relationship does not benefit the female partner in the same way it benefits the male. As many writers argue,[49] women in early German Romanticism are instrumentalized, idealized, and excluded from the kind of moral and creative development experienced by men. This asymmetry is not accidental, but is based on early German Romantic conceptions of gender and gender relations. As we saw above, Novalis and Schlegel present women as intrinsically connected to nature, spirituality, and love. This idealization ostensibly confers high status on women, as it presents them as unalienated from nature and the divine and as naturally grasping moral and religious truths. However, it also depicts women as less active and intellectual than men, repeating the stereotypical association of masculinity with activity, consciousness, and reason and of women with passivity, intuition, feeling, and mysticism.[50]

This model excludes women from the moral and spiritual development that is at the heart of the early German Romantic conception of the subject. The idealization of women as inherently connected with the unity of nature and with love posits that women are by nature suited to mediating unity to men, and that they themselves do not need this kind of development toward oneness.[51] For example, we saw above how *Lucinde* describes Julius' development, through a series of relationships with women, especially Lucinde, into a successful artist and complete human being. By contrast, Lucinde, who was also an artist when Julius met her, does not experience a similar development; in fact, the culmination of her humanity achieved through her relationship with Julius is her pregnancy. That Schlegel equates Lucinde's fulfillment in motherhood with Julius' as an artist is further suggested by the fact that when he learns Lucinde is pregnant, Julius claims she should receive a poet's laurel.[52] Elsewhere, Schlegel claims that "love is for women what genius is for men"[53] and Novalis asks: "Should an inspiration in a woman not be able to express itself through a pregnancy?"[54]

In *Henry of Ofterdingen* it is through the mediation of women that the protagonist matures into a poet, while these women not only do not develop, but seem to lose their status as artists through their contact with him. Henry learns music from Zulima, who is not heard from again, and Mathilde teaches him guitar but then, rather than becoming a poet alongside him, dies. Similarly, the beloved in Novalis' "Hymns" is dead, and in Schlegel's *Lucinde* two women who are instrumental to Julius' development, Lisette and Lucinde, suffer real and imaginary deaths, respectively.

Both women's deaths are associated with their pregnancies, and Elena Pnevmonidou notes that Novalis and Schlegel connect pregnancy with female death and male creativity.[55] In *Lucinde*, Lisette is associated with an early, failed effort by Julius to become an artist; when she becomes pregnant he leaves her and she kills herself. By contrast, Julius greets Lucinde's pregnancy with joy—he is now a successful artist and views her pregnancy as her corresponding manifestation of their union; however, he still dreams of her death. In Klingsohr's tale in *Henry of Ofterdingen*, the consumption of the mother's ashes allows the capacity for creativity to pass from the dead mother to the remaining characters, and in Novalis' "Hymns," the dead beloved provides a route for the male narrator to sink into the "father's womb."[56]

Several writers argue that this association of pregnancy, women's deaths, and men's creativity reflects the romantic male poet's need "to appropriate woman's child-bearing capabilities[.]"[57] While women manifest the union of male and female in heterosexual love through the birth of a child, the male genius needs to manifest this generative creativity in another way. The artist's search for creative self-expression thus becomes a search for male procreativity. Corresponding to this elevation of the male genius as bearer of the fruits of heterosexual union is the exclusion of women from creativity and their marginalization from pregnancy itself. The generative power of women is appropriated by men for their creative endeavors, after which women themselves become superfluous.[58]

The achievement of lost wholeness that the early German Romantics depict as the goal of the male subject, epitomized by the male artist, is not a goal they envision for women. In fact, in one fragment Novalis explicitly asks: "Is woman the goal of the man, and is woman without a goal?"[59] As intrinsically whole and connected to nature, woman is already at her goal. Consequently, there is no future for her in the early German Romantic model; female characters often die, their feminine characteristics absorbed by the male subject who combines "feminine" access to nature, the divine, love, inspiration, and creativity with their own active form-giving in painting, music, and song.[60]

In addition to the above problems, scholars have pointed out the failure of early German Romanticism to advocate concrete social and political changes to accompany the supposed conceptual emancipation of women. Richard

Littlejohns notes that "Schlegel never deals directly in *Lucinde* with the economic or legal position of women in marriage or their status in society[.]"[61] Barbara Becker-Cantarino agrees, arguing that Schlegel was interested in "'femininity' as completion and station towards his own self-development to 'masculinity' as poet, but not the social position of actual women."[62]

More than failing to undermine traditional roles for women, early German Romanticism may promote and even exacerbate them. Julius and Lucinde's relationship reflects traditional gender roles, with Lucinde as mother and companion while Julius fulfills his vocation as an artist,[63] and, as we saw above, both Schlegel and Novalis describe motherhood and love of a man as the desired state for women. In fact, the situation for women within the paradigm of love as presented by Schlegel and Novalis may be worse than in traditional marriages. According to this paradigm, women should provide their husbands with sexual satisfaction, romantic fulfillment, and spiritual enlightenment in addition to their existing duties as mothers and household managers.[64]

The focus of writers like Schlegel and Novalis on sexuality as a natural and even spiritually important aspect of human life is sometimes seen as transgressive and liberating—a protest against bourgeois social mores and late eighteenth-/early nineteenth-century prudishness. But, as Becker-Cantarino notes, it is men and men's pleasure that are liberated, not women or women's pleasure.[65] Women, on early German Romantic accounts, remain intrinsically connected to nature and to motherhood, to passivity, objectification, and appropriation, and early German Romanticism describes their role in sexual intercourse in terms that reflect this. This emerges in what has been described as "Romanticism's most transgressive philosophical moment":[66] Novalis claims that "Rape is the strongest pleasure."

Unfortunately, this is not merely an isolated[67] or chance remark by Novalis, but is drawn from ideas about women's connection to nature, the body, and maternity that are widespread in early German Romantic writings. Like other writers of the time, including Schlegel,[68] Novalis uses an analogy with plants to link women essentially with motherhood, passivity, and receptivity, while likening men to animals, as actively consuming and fertilizing.[69] He states, for example, that: "The life of plants is, compared to the life of animals—an unceasing conceiving and giving birth—and the latter, compared to the former—an unceasing eating and fertilizing."[70] And, more explicitly: "*Conception* is the feminine enjoyment—consuming the masculine."[71] This is problematic in the first place because it links women's nature essentially to the role of motherhood—a view shared by Schlegel, even in relatively early pieces such as *Lucinde*, as we saw above. In "On Philosophy," for example, Schlegel claims that "the female organization is wholly directed toward the one beautiful purpose of maternity."[72] Novalis, meanwhile, notes "[w]omen's similarity to plants. [...] (Flowers are vessels.)"[73] But the connection of women essentially to the combination of passivity and conception, and perhaps even more problematically the connection of men to both activity and consumption, has worse consequences. Novalis draws the implication from this that women's sexual enjoyment is linked to the passive role he grants them in conception, and consists in the pleasure of being overcome. Men's sexual enjoyment, meanwhile, is linked to the pleasure of overcoming resistance: "She wants—but her sensations resist and can only be suspended for a moment by means of a foreign power. / He senses—but he does not want—and his will can only be suspended for a few moments by a foreign yielding."[74] The conclusion of a line of reasoning that links women to receptive plants, and women's pleasure and purpose to conception, which is presented as passive—the same line of reasoning that links men to activity and animals, and men's pleasure to fertilizing and devouring—is: "The more lively the thing to be devoured resists, the livelier the flame of the moment of pleasure will be. [...] Rape is the strongest pleasure."[75]

## 3  The Role of Gender in Early German Romantic Philosophy

While the above criticisms should raise concerns about the conceptualizations of women and gender relations in early German Romanticism, there is a larger problem insofar as these conceptualizations are implicated in central aspects of early German Romantic Philosophy. These include fundamental dichotomies that Novalis and Schlegel saw as characterizing the world—activity and passivity, form and material, spiritual and physical—with their long, gendered history, and the human vocation, as they saw it, of reconciling these differences by integrating the world of the object into the mind of the subject and the subject's creative imposition of form on the object. This gendered background also informs the early German Romantic conception of the genius and its theories of language and representation.

The fundamental movement of early German Romanticism is from an original unity of the divine, spirit, or universe, through a fragmented and alienated state of individuation—the world as we experience it—to a future reconciliation of these alienated individuals with the divine.[76] The human vocation, and goal of early German Romanticism, is to work toward this reconciliation of alienated entities.⁷⁷ For the early German Romantics, heterosexual love is an instance of, analogy for, and initiation into this reconciliation of dualities.

Underlying the ability of heterosexual love to play this role is the fact that early German Romanticism conceived the dualities characterizing the fragmented universe of earthly life in gendered terms. On this model, the original division of the universe into subject and object underlies other divisions, including those between the individual entities that make up the world and between the characteristics that accrue to the subject—mind, cognition, consciousness, reason, form—and those that accrue to the object—nature, body, feeling, intuition, imagination, material.⁷⁸ These attributes have, of course, often been ascribed, respectively, to men and women, including on the early German Romantic theory of gender. As a result, for the romantics heterosexual love can instantiate and begin to realize the union of the male-coded world of the subject, or mind, and the female-coded world of the object, or body, nature, and original unifying ground. For example, Novalis depicts sexual love as prefiguring the dissolution of the individual male self in a feminine nature:

> Whose heart does not [...] skip delightedly, when the deepest life of nature in its whole fullness comes to mind! when then that powerful feeling, for which speech has no other name than love and lust, expands in him, like a powerful, all-dissolving mist, and he sinks quivering with sweet fear in the dark, alluring womb of nature[.]⁷⁹

One might argue that the problem with this model is relatively superficial: the gendering of the divisions it depends on, rather than the divisions themselves. In other words, one might conceive of a world divided dualistically along the same lines without the baggage of traditional gender stereotypes. However, even if we can rid ourselves of the time-worn associations of masculinity with the active, observing subject, the mind, reason, and form, and of femininity with the passive, observed object, the body, emotions, and material, early German Romanticism does not do so, but adopts the gendering of these divisions as a central metaphor.

This metaphor plays a formative role in important areas of early German Romantic Philosophy, including the quest of the individual subject for wholeness and the associated concept of genius. We saw above how early German Romanticism presents the reunification of the world and the alienated individual as achieved through the appropriation by the (male) subject of aspects of the (feminine) object. This is illustrated in the stories of Julius and Henry, and in the romantic theory of the genius, which Julius and Henry exemplify. The epitome of the human being who re-integrates the lost elements of the self is the poet, artist, or genius—the individual who, like Julius and Henry, absorbs the alienated aspects of the world and is consequently able to create art, in the process raising, poeticizing, or romanticizing[80] the world. Thus, according to Novalis, the poet "represents in the truest sense *subject object—mind and world*[.]"[81]

Although the concept of the genius is ostensibly gender-neutral, the gendered dualities that underlie it imply that it can accrue to men only—and Novalis and Schlegel draw this implication. As we saw above, early German Romanticism depicts women as already unified with nature and connected to the divine. Consequently, there is no mechanism for women to follow the human vocation of overcoming alienation, or to become geniuses. Women may require intellectual development to overcome their nature as inherently natural, intuitive, and poetic—hence Schlegel's claim that philosophy is indispensable to women. However, as we saw, Schlegel and Novalis do not depict women's interactions with men as leading to women becoming artists (or even philosophers). Rather than integrating masculine characteristics and achieving genius in a mirror image of the process by which men become geniuses, women's roles are presented as mediating artistic ability to men and becoming mothers. In fact, Schlegel explicitly describes women as possessing "love" and "harmony" where men have "genius."[82]

Gender also plays a role in the early German Romantics' attempt to retrieve what they saw as the neglected other of the enlightenment, and in the ideas about language that emerge from this attempt. One of the complaints of early German Romanticism, indeed a driving force of the movement, was the overvaluation of characteristics belonging to the mind in enlightenment science and society, and the corresponding denigration and exclusion from our sense of identity of the other side of the equation, including the body, the emotions, nature, and things considered feminine.[83] The solution, according to Romanticism, is the revalorization of the latter aspects and their retrieval for our sense of self.[84] It is for this reason that early German Romanticism is sometimes called a "feminine philosophy":[85] as a counterweight to the enlightenment emphasis on "masculine" reason and discourse, Romanticism places a high value on "feminine" intuition and forms of communication, and attempts to create ways of speaking, writing, and thinking that incorporate these.

In keeping with this view, early German Romantic theories of language attempt to retrieve aspects of experience that are outside discourse—the gaps, unspoken things, intimations, and failures of thought and language. This project underlies Novalis' claims about the impossibility of literal communication[86] and his statement that "The sense for poetry [....] represents the unrepresentable."[87] Schlegel's claims about irony and incomprehensibility also reflect this effort to use language to represent what is beyond language.[88]

The early German Romantics explicitly viewed these things as "feminine."[89] They also applied these characteristics to real women, expecting these to be the ways that women understood the world and communicated. Thus, Novalis claims: "Man must transform his sensations into concepts, woman her concepts into sensations."[90] Schlegel frames "On Philosophy" as an attempt to put "masculine" writing and argumentation in dialogue with "feminine" conversation, embodied by his partner, Dorothea Veit-Schlegel. He claims to be writing the essay partly "to tease such a decided despiser of all writing and letters" and adds: "A conversation would perhaps be preferable to you."[91] The unrepresentable and mysterious "feminine" aspects of the universe, as well as the unwritten perspectives of women, are presented in male writing and indicated by references to their absence, for example in Schlegel's deferrals in "On Philosophy" to the opinions of the "you" of Veit-Schlegel.

Notably, these elements are retrieved by language on the same basis as the alienated other of nature is appropriated by the individual subject in its quest for wholeness. The incomprehensible "feminine" is expressed by men, whether in language—using allegory, irony, fragments, and reference to an unspeaking "you" to point beyond what is said—or in the perfected humanity of the poet-genius and his artistic creations, through his appropriation of female characteristics to articulate what is given in nature and express it in a "higher" form.

Early German Romantic ideas about women are thus interwoven with their basic picture of the world, idea of the human vocation, concept of human genius, and theories about language. Romanticism maintains the traditional association of women with the mysterious, unspoken, unconscious, undifferentiated, with nature, feelings, and intuition. It increases the importance of this association by making it the task of the subject to integrate these elements with itself, and by making that task the vocation of humankind and the means by which the purpose of the universe—its self-differentiation in order to know itself—is realized.

## 4 Complexities in the Early German Romantic Approach to Gender

To be fair, the deliberately self-critical and polyvalent nature of early German Romantic discourse complicates the above picture. Novalis and Schlegel were aware of many of the problems just noted and gave some of them a central position in their work. In particular, they were very conscious of the impossibility of fully integrating the world of the object in the representations of the subject, and the need to address other perspectives, including those of women, alongside the perspective of the male subject. Some commentators argue that Romanticism describes "competing discourses on gender[,]" using female voices and perspectives to critique the dominant, male-centered model.[92] Indeed, on one view, a central purpose of early German Romanticism is to perform a self-critique of masculine culture.[93]

From the outset, the early German Romantics presented the goal of the individual's reunification with aspects of the world it experiences as outside itself as a regulative ideal rather than something that could actually be realized. It is largely for this reason that death held such significance for early German Romanticism, as the site of complete unification of the individual with its greater self.[94] While alive, the individual can never completely overcome its individual perspective; the subject can never fully absorb or represent the object; and, correspondingly, the efforts of the poet or genius to communicate about what is beyond language and thought are always only guideposts and approximations. Similarly, Schlegel's idea of a *Wechsel*, or exchange, of characteristics between men and women envisions a mitigation, rather than obliteration, of the differences between the poles of masculinity and femininity, as we saw above. All these situations are based on the same principle of separate dualities that, while the differences between them can never be totally overcome, are nonetheless capable of interaction, communication, and exchange.

This idea of a dynamic exchange between opposites was an important feature of early German Romanticism, differentiating their approach in particular from that of Fichte. Novalis and Schlegel were dissatisfied with Fichte's focus on the subject as the place in which the object would be recreated through philosophy. Instead of deciding between basing their philosophy on the world of the object (what Fichte called "dogmatism") or the world of the subject ("idealism"),[95] they imagined a foundation for philosophy in mutual exchange: a *Wechselerweis* or *Wechselgrundsatz*—a principle of reciprocity.[96] Thus they explicitly opposed the idea, apparently illustrated in their accounts of male *Bildung* and the genius, that the subject should appropriate the world of the object and represent it; instead, they imagined the two realms participating in a friendly exchange.[97]

In keeping with this model, the early German Romantics aimed to engage women as the other that is imperfectly represented by male discourse, and as representing the other of the rest of the world. For early German Romanticism, women and nature are not passive objects of the creative activity of the male subject, but participate in the poeticization of the world, joining in dialogue with the subject—especially the genius—and speaking through his words and images.⁹⁸ Consequently, women were called on to engage with the writings of male romantics—within certain limits, of course, as their input was supposed to contribute the neglected "feminine" perspective, which should be connected to nature, the divine, and the beautiful, and grasped through emotion and intuition rather than structured reasoned argument.⁹⁹

Of course, this model presupposes gender stereotypes, especially the association of women with intuition and the world of the object (nature) and their inability to articulate ideas in systematic form. Furthermore, the outcome of this interaction is always represented by the male subject in language, art, and thought. In other words, the realm of the object, including women, does not so much speak as it is spoken for.

Even granting this, however, there is a strong argument that early German Romanticism deliberately critiques its own narrative of male appropriation of an ideal female sphere. Alongside the dominant heterosexual model of the subject's development, romantic texts often incorporate a homoerotic or homosocial subtext which suggests an alternative model and, as Martha B. Helfer puts it, "subtly debunks the feminine ideal."¹⁰⁰ Helfer argues that early German Romanticism often uses female muses as foils for men who are the "real source of poetic inspiration[.]"¹⁰¹ She analyzes a number of texts that ostensibly present women as the source of unity, poetic inspiration, and male development, but subordinate them to a male character. For example, in *Henry of Ofterdingen*, Mathilde supposedly mediates unity and artistic development to Henry, but is repeatedly presented as a "projection" of her father Klingsohr.¹⁰² She teaches guitar to Henry, but emphasizes that she learned it from her father; Henry first notices and is attracted not to Mathilde but to Klingsohr; and Mathilde seems to be "the spirit of her father in the loveliest disguise."¹⁰³ Helfer also points out the importance of male narration in *Henry of Ofterdingen* and the paucity of female narratives. Klingsohr, Henry's father, a male stranger, merchants, and a miner all tell stories that inspire Henry, prefigure events in his life, and promote his development as a poet. By contrast, women in the novel rarely speak and, when they do, do so "through male narration, omitted storytelling, insipid conversation, as the projections of male desire, or through death."¹⁰⁴ Thus, claims Helfer, in *Henry of Ofterdingen* "male discourse—language written, spoken or sung by men—[…] is the inspiration, source, and ground of Romantic poesy[,]" and the novel "works to expose the traditional female poetic ground—woman and her voices—as constructed within and controlled by a male representational system."¹⁰⁵

According to Helfer, Novalis' re-gendering of the "originary poetic ground" as male—and corresponding feminization of the poet Henry—is deliberate, and aims to draw attention to what Helfer describes as Romanticism's "constructedness of gender and subjectivity within its own patriarchal representational system."[106] In other words, Novalis recognizes his status as a man writing from a man's perspective and, consistently with early German Romantic ideas about communication, rather than attempting to complete the picture by adding the pieces he knows are missing, he instead highlights this inadequacy. As Helfer puts it:

> Novalis as male author writes woman's originary poetic voice *as mediated by man, as ultimately unnecessary to man.* In accordance with Romantic theory the text calls attention to its own casting of woman as the source of true poesy ironically and self-critically, and presents a counter-paradigm in which the male poet produces the male subject as text, i.e., as a discursive construct.[107]

Helfer traces this self-critique back to the early German Romantic's engagement with Fichte, arguing that Romanticism's dominant goal of reunifying the individual self with its world undermines itself through a competing paradigm of the self-construction of the subject in language. In other words, the subject attempts to go beyond itself and integrate with itself aspects of the object-world that lie outside it, but can always only construct itself within its own system of representation. Thus, according to Helfer, "the self-positing of the male subject must occur within a 'male' representational system," or "male discourse[.]"[108]

Gender stereotypes are foundational to early German Romantic metaphysics, account of the human vocation, and ideas about language and representation, but Schlegel and Novalis were aware of their perspective as male authors writing within a discourse controlled by men. They foregrounded the one-sidedness of their account, especially its inability to fully represent the "other," and questioned their own paradigm of male self-poiesis though the appropriation of feminine characteristics. When interpreting early German Romantic claims about women, it is therefore necessary to recognize simultaneously their efforts to provide increased value to women and the feminine, their reliance on gender stereotypes, and their own—not always successful—attempts to acknowledge and address this failing.

## 5   Early German Romantic Women

In addition to Schlegel, Novalis, and the other male romantics mentioned above, a number of women were associated with early German Romanticism, including several published authors. These include Dorothea Veit-Schlegel

## 21 Women, Women Writers, and Early German Romanticism

and Karoline von Günderrode (discussed below), Bettina von Arnim, Henriette Herz, Sophie Mereau, Caroline Schlegel-Schelling, and Rahel Varnhagen. Given the involvement of women in the production of romantic literature and thought, as well as early German Romanticism's statements about the importance of women's contributions to philosophical dialogue, and simply in the interests of comprehensiveness and accuracy, it is essential to consider what women romantics had to say about gender.

Although there is a body of scholarship on women associated with early German Romanticism, these women are often depicted as muses and assistants for male philosophers and facilitators of interactions between male intellectuals rather than as contributors to early German Romantic Philosophy in their own right.[109] It is also sometimes claimed that while male early German Romantics wrote and theorized about Romanticism, the women of this movement embodied this theory in their lives. For example, Roetzel states that "for Schlegel-Schelling and Veit-Schlegel, Romantic critique meant *living* as Romantics[,]"[110] and Helfer suggests that "one might read Günderrode's suicide as the highest expression of Romantic theory."[111] Although this position may seem strange, especially since many of these women were published authors, it reflects early German Romantic ideas about gender. On this model, women have no goal of their own except to help men achieve creative development; women enjoy conversation, not writing, and can have intuitive access to truths that are beyond men, but it is men who write down these ideas and give them systematic form. In keeping with this view, Veit-Schlegel in particular worked hard in support of her husband's work. She edited and critiqued his writings, copied out his manuscripts, and published reviews, translations, and her novel *Florentin* under Schlegel's name.

The idea that women lived Romanticism while men wrote it has pernicious effects, undermining the significance of women's writing, which is construed as secondary to their roles as wives, mothers, muses, helpers, and spiritual mediators, while the latter acquire increased significance as the only authentic sites for women to engage with Romanticism. Nonetheless, women did write on topics related to early German Romantic philosophy. Whether we understand these contributions as representing the "feminine" perspective that early German Romanticism recognized was missing from its work—as some scholars view Veit-Schlegel's writings[112]—or as critiquing or standing beside the work of male writers, these women provided significant commentary on and interpretations of ideas that are better known in the work of their male colleagues.

The last two sections of this chapter explore the writings of Veit-Schlegel and Günderrode, which critique and provide alternatives to the ideas of male romantics. Veit-Schlegel's novel *Florentin* situates the early German Romantic model of the self-poiesis of the artist subject in a real world that does not fit neatly into the developmental trajectories suggested by Schlegel and Novalis. Meanwhile, Günderrode creates a non-heteronormative vision of unifying love that avoids the dualisms and gender stereotypes that pervade the work of Novalis and Schlegel.

## 6  Veit-Schlegel's (anti-)Bildungsroman

Dorothea Veit-Schlegel is counted among the women of early German Romanticism almost automatically because of her marriage to Friedrich Schlegel and her contributions to his work, as well as because of her status as supposedly embodying the romantic ideal of the feminine philosopher.[113] However, there are other reasons to consider Veit-Schlegel an author of Romanticism. In particular, her novel *Florentin* provides a perspective on early German Romantic ideas of self-poiesis, the artist, gender, and social roles that is grounded in recognition of social realities, especially those affecting women.

*Florentin* is sometimes considered a counterpart to *Lucinde*, perhaps constituting Schlegel's promised sequel from the "feminine" perspective.[114] However, although the novel resembles a *Bildungsroman*, *Florentin* focuses not on the self-creation of an ideal woman, but on failures in the romantic ideal of self-poiesis. As such, it critiques the early German Romantic model of the development of the artist-subject, and has been described as an "anti-*Bildungsroman*."[115]

The novel centers on the arrival of a young man, Florentin, in a noble country household shortly before the wedding of the daughter of the house, Juliane, to Eduard. The name Juliane connects the heroine to Julius, the hero of Schlegel's *Lucinde*, suggesting that *Florentin* will describe Juliane's development in relation to Florentin, analogously to Julius' development in relation to Lucinde in Schlegel's novel. However, that is not what happens in Veit-Schlegel's story. If that were the case, we would see Juliane maturing to a more balanced womanhood and, possibly, motherhood, as she adopts masculine characteristics mediated by male characters, especially Florentin. But instead, the book focuses on Florentin's search for identity, while Juliane's only effort to transgress gender boundaries (discussed below) results in failure and her relieved return home, where she marries Eduard. The novel ends with Florentin's disappearance.

In *Florentin*, it is not Juliane, but Florentin, whose story most resembles Julius'. Like Julius, Florentin is an artist, and attempts to create an identity for himself largely through interactions with others. However, in Florentin's case, these others more obviously include men, notably in his passionate relationships to Manfredi, Eduard, and the Doctor. Helfer argues that *Florentin*'s homoeroticism subverts the masculinist discourse of Schlegel's *Lucinde*[116]—a more overt critique of the construction of the romantic subject in male discourse than that given by Schlegel or Novalis. Meanwhile, Florentin's relationships with women end in disappointment: his "mother" casts him out; his "sister" stays in a convent rather than escaping with him; his wife has an abortion and leaves him; Juliane marries Eduard. In this way, Veit-Schlegel undermines the early German Romantic ideal of heterosexual romantic love as the culmination of the artist's successful effort at self-poiesis. Instead, she emphasizes the importance of circumstance and social context for relationships, especially marriage.[117] In direct reference to Schlegel's description of Lucinde, Florentin complains: "What use is it that I found everything my wishes could grasp united in *one*? She is the loving bride of [Eduard]!"[118]

As others have noted, Florentin's disastrous relationships with women depict failed attempts of the romantic subject to idealize and appropriate women for his own self-construction—an effort that stumbles against the unwillingness or incapacity of real women to embody these ideals.[119] Veit-Schlegel makes this point vividly in an episode that parallels Julius' relationship with Lisette in *Lucinde*. Florentin's wife is an artist's model, who he paints as different ideals of womanhood. When she becomes pregnant, Florentin (unlike Julius) is delighted, believing he has found his true vocation as a father, and anticipates enjoying his own lost childhood through his child.[120] While Florentin is happily fixated on the prospect of fatherhood, his wife feels increasingly constrained by her role as mother-to-be, and eventually has an abortion. Florentin is so angry that he throws a knife at her, nearly killing her,[121] and flees, leaving his dreams of fatherhood and life as a successful artist behind him.

As Pnevmonidou states, this episode is "an explicit de-mythologizing of Friedrich Schlegel's *Lucinde*."[122] Romantic stories of masculine development such as *Lucinde* and *Henry of Ofterdingen* depend on idealized images of women, which suppress the ways real women do not meet these ideals or resist figuration as mediators of male fulfillment. Florentin's wife's desire not to bear children frustrates Florentin's use of her to enable his paternity and his artistic development.[123] In addition, in contrast to Schlegel's *Lucinde*, early German Romanticism's claims about women, and prevailing opinion at the time, which present women as naturally fulfilled by motherhood, Veit-Schlegel depicts Florentin, and decidedly not his wife, as anticipating fulfillment in parenthood.

The above episode also indicates the significance of Florentin's lost childhood: Florentin's search for identity is at the same time the quest for a homeland, a family, and his origins. This appears congruent with the early German Romantic notion of an alienated subject seeking unity with its original greater self. However, Florentin's search differs from those of Schlegel's Julius and Novalis' Henry in a number of ways, including its disassociation of femininity from the unity and sense of belonging that the subject seeks. While some writers claim that Florentin's true quest is the quest for his mother,[124] this is only part of the story—Florentin is seeking his lost childhood and therefore not only his mother but also a father. He frames his journey to Juliane's father as: "I have always been an orphan and a stranger on earth, and so I will call that country fatherland where I first hear myself called father[,]"[125] and the book includes many other references to fathers as well as mothers.[126] Nonetheless, Florentin's ultimate encounter—or near-encounter—with his childhood occurs when he meets Juliane's aunt Clementina, who may be the woman Florentin grew up believing was his mother. Florentin finds Clementina's features familiar and, watching her, hears music he remembers from his childhood; meanwhile, Clementina is so struck by seeing him that she faints.[127] However, Florentin never notices this possible connection and leaves without realizing he may have found his "mother," and at the same time his home and the means to learn his true identity.

As several commentators note, Florentin's obsessive self-focus and self-image as an alienated individual seeking a homeland result in his frequently missing points of connection with others, and at the same time failing to create a stable identity for himself and find a place he belongs.[128] In one episode, Florentin describes himself as "the poor, the lonely, cast out, the child of chance[,]" to which Eduard replies "why would you think yourself always alone? In our midst, alone?"[129] Florentin's interactions with others, especially women, are shaped by delusion and an aestheticization of his experiences that do not address individuals in their concrete, complex reality.[130] He paints his wife in costumes; he describes Juliane's mother Eleanore as like "an image of the beneficent Ceres"; he first encounters Clementina in the form of a portrait, which also includes a portrait of Juliane as a child.[131] Veit-Schlegel thus presents the romantic subject's attempts to create an identity by aestheticizing relationships with others as foundering in narcissism and self-delusion.[132]

Florentin's efforts to create an identity and find a home, like the stories of Julius in *Lucinde* and Henry in *Henry of Ofterdingen*, depict a male subject attempting to develop artistic genius and achieve unity with the lost original sphere of nature and the divine. However, whereas in *Lucinde* and *Henry of Ofterdingen* the protagonists' efforts show a progression, culminating in their successful emergence as artists, the incidents comprising Florentin's history do not bring Florentin closer to his longed-for "fatherland" or to successfully constituting himself as an individual, let alone an artist. From one episode to another, Florentin remains steeped in self-delusion, isolation, and failures to recognize the others around him. The novel begins with Florentin lost in a forest: "Sunk in enjoyment of the magnificence that surrounded him and in fantasies that swept him now forwards, now backwards, he had lost the right path[.]"[133] The last line of the novel, "Florentin was nowhere to be found[,]"[134] simultaneously shows Florentin leaving his potential home with Juliane and Eduard's family and indicates the failure of his construction of identity.

While Florentin's story critiques the romantic ideal of male self-poiesis as unstable, delusional, and foundering in narcissism, Juliane's trajectory undermines the idea of a self-creative *Bildung* for women[135] and critiques the idea of gender fluidity as it applies to women. Juliane is destined to marry Eduard from the outset. Her only attempt to step outside social norms occurs when she dresses as a boy to go out with Eduard and Florentin. This episode ends in disaster as Eduard abandons self-restraint and attempts to embrace Juliane, which frightens her, and the three are forced to shelter from a storm in the house of a miller and his wife. There, Juliane faces the embarrassing and unpleasant fact that the miller's wife does not recognize her as a noblewoman. She insists on revealing her identity and returns gratefully to her home, with its usual social constraints.[136]

In this episode, Veit-Schlegel does not present gender fluidity as liberating or otherwise desirable for women, but as stripping away the protections of social conventions. As Elisabeth Krimmer notes, "Cross-dressing in *Florentin* does not reclaim male privilege for women but induces a dissolution of established gender roles that leaves the disguised woman unprotected and helpless. [Veit-]Schlegel seems to suggest that traditional gender roles, though restrictive, also function as safeguards against male license[.]"[137] This episode is paralleled by Florentin's attempt to help his "sister" escape her confinement to a convent, which ends in failure as she refuses to leave, accepting the role defined for her, although she was originally sent to the convent against her will.[138] Florentin, by contrast, escapes. Veit-Schlegel reminds her readers of the social realities and dangers that constrain women's ability to choose their vocation.

Nonetheless, Veit-Schlegel does sketch ways that women's roles can be extended, while remaining broadly consistent with social expectations. Juliane's mother Eleonore broke with tradition by accompanying her husband to war, but did so out of love and in order to care for him.[139] Clementina composes music, adopting a role typically reserved for men, but her compositions lie exclusively within the feminine-coded spiritual or religious realm.[140] Eleonore's traditionally feminine role as household manager extends to the affairs of the village.[141] Liesl Allingham argues that Veit-Schlegel depicts these extensions of women's roles in order to create possibilities for female *Bildung* within the traditionally feminine private sphere "us[ing] the very constructions designed to limit women's participation in the public sphere, such as loyalty to one's husband and maternal instincts."[142]

Veit-Schlegel's novel highlights problems in early German Romanticism's focus on the aesthetic self-creation of the subject, which not only occludes the experiences of the women—and men—around him, but also results in a perpetually lost and disconnected subject and the failure of the romantic project of reconciliation. On Veit-Schlegel's reading, the problem with overemphasizing the perspective of the male subject is not primarily the reinforcing of gender stereotypes, but the failure of this project to provide a path for recuperating the lost world of the object in a way that is not delusional. Veit-Schlegel's critique in *Florentin* not only identifies the problematic narcissistic appropriation of others in the early German Romantic model of self-poiesis, but also demands that social roles and constraints are acknowledged in considering an individual's identity and relationships, including romantic relationships.

## 7 Karoline von Günderrode, Gender, and the Idea of the Earth

Unlike Veit-Schlegel, Günderrode was not a member of the Jena circle that included Schlegel and Novalis, although she studied their writings along with those of Fichte, Schelling, and others. Her work incorporates features of early German Romanticism, including ideas of the universe as progressing toward unification through a succession of raised or more adequate forms, death as the site of final unity with other individuals and the natural world, and love as unifying force. However, a non-dualistic metaphysics underlies Günderrode's approach, which means gender stereotypes cannot play the central role they do in the work of Schlegel and Novalis. Despite this, Günderrode, like Veit-Schlegel, is keenly attentive to issues of gender, especially regarding social roles for women and their impact on women's identity and ability to act. This combination of factors makes Günderrode's writings an alternative to early German Romantic models that reinforce traditional conceptions of gender.

Like Novalis and Schlegel, Günderrode presents love as a unifying force, emphasizing the capacity of love to unite individuals in death. For example, in "The Malabarian Widows," she writes that "Death will become sweet celebration of love, / The separated elements unified" and that "the previously sundered flames of love / Are struck ardently together into one."[143] In "The Bonds of Love" she depicts a connection between the living narrator and a dead "beloved," writing that "This bond is called love."[144] And "The Kiss in the Dream" describes a longing for a lover's kiss that can only be satisfied in death. However, unlike Novalis and Schlegel, Günderrode does not present this unifying love as necessarily heterosexual. Many pieces, including "The Malabarian Widows," "Timur," "Mora," and "Don Juan," depict romantic love between a man and a woman, while others, including "The Bonds of Love" and "The Kiss in the Dream," do not mention the sex of the narrator and can therefore be interpreted heteronormatively. But other pieces, especially the ballad "Piedro," are homoerotic, leading some writers to claim that Günderrode presents homosexual love as paradigmatic of union.[145] In fact, however, Günderrode's account of the unifying force of attraction between individuals privileges neither heterosexual nor homosexual love—nor romantic love at all.

This is evident in Günderrode's philosophical dialogue "The Manes," which describes the connection a "student" feels with a long-dead king. The student's teacher explains that there exist hidden connections between things that are similar, that is, that "harmonize" with each other, and that such a connection exists between characteristics of the student and characteristics of the dead king. These allow the king to affect the student and, in a sense, to live on in him: "As surely as all harmonious things are connected, whether they are visible or invisible, just as surely we, too, are connected with the *part* of the spirit world that harmonizes with us"; "he lives on in you only insofar as you have a sense for him, insofar as your system makes you capable of receiving him inwardly, insofar as you have something homogeneous with him. What is foreign in you enters into no connection with him[.]"[146]

The "separate elements" that are unified in death in "The Malabarian Widows" are not, therefore, the two separate individuals of husband and wife. Rather, they are the many elemental forces that constitute the husband and wife, like all other human beings and other entities, some of which harmonize with each other and which, once released from their earthly constraints in two separate bodies, can join together. Günderrode explains this idea more fully elsewhere. In her unpublished essay "Idea of the Earth" she presents the world and every entity within it, including human beings, as created from "elements" that, over time, group together, then separate and recombine to form new entities, as individual creatures live and die, while "the life-principle in the elements is immortal; it requires only contact and connection again like before and the new life blossoms."[147]

Günderrode states explicitly that the recombination of elements occurs through "attraction" and "laws of affinity."[148] What we experience as love—whether romantic, between friends, or in a perhaps less intense form as a draw or pull toward others, living or dead—is an expression of inner harmony between elements of our own individuality and elements of theirs. After death, the attraction between these harmonious elements brings them together to create new entities. We saw above how, in Schlegel and Novalis' dualistic universe, heterosexual love was paradigmatic of the unification of polar opposites through mutual exchange. Günderrode's model of love also functions as a paradigm of unification within her universe, which is characterized, not by dual polarities, but by a large set of elements. Consequently, on Günderrode's model gender is irrelevant to love, the emergence of unity, and, therefore, the human vocation.

As we saw, on Novalis' and Schlegel's account, the task of human being, especially the poet or genius, is to reshape what is given in nature in higher forms—the "cultivation of the earth," as Novalis puts it.[149] "Idea of the Earth" suggests a course of action that corresponds to this task. For Günderrode, the succession of forms in which the universe manifests itself can constitute a more or less perfect whole, ideally progressing toward complete unification: "each mortal gives back to the earth a raised, more developed elemental life, which it cultivates further in ascending forms, and the organism, by assimilating ever more developed elements, must thereby become ever more perfect and universal."[150] Human beings can help or hinder progress toward this point, as their actions serve to either increase harmony (virtuous actions) or decrease it (unvirtuous actions).[151] In this way, the rest of the world is (potentially) reclaimed for the individual self by the merging of elements with others that are, increasingly, like its own. Unlike the model of reunification presented by Novalis and Schlegel, in which the fragmented parts of the universe are reconciled through the appropriation of one pole (the object) by the other (the subject), Günderrode's account entails a non-hierarchical joining of elements through self-improvement and mutual attraction.

Although gender is irrelevant to Günderrode's metaphysics, she does see gender as important for how identities are constituted and how people live their lives. Many of her writings explore the implications of gender for agency, subjecthood, and self-determination, in particular addressing the different ways that men and women are viewed and treated and the possibilities for action and self-image that these open or close. For example, in "Hildgund," the heroine must decide whether to marry Attila in order to forestall his invasion of her homeland—but first she must establish her right to act on her own behalf in the face of her fiancé Walther's machismo.[152] In "Mora," the title character wears her male lover's armor in order to protect him and assert her decision not to marry his rival, who wants to kill Mora's lover to claim her. And, as Allingham has argued, in "Darthula" Günderrode's refocusing of the action of Ossian's piece onto Darthula herself involves a nuanced consideration of the ways male and female heroism is constructed.[153]

Some writers suggest that Günderrode understood gender according to conventional categories,[154] and she did occasionally make statements that presuppose stereotypical ideas about gender. For example, in a letter to a friend she exclaims: "Why was I not a man! I have no sense for feminine virtues, for feminine happiness. [...] It is an unfortunate but incurable discrepancy in my soul; and it will and must remain so, for I am a woman, and have desires like a man, without manly strength."[155] However, whereas for Schlegel and Novalis gendered characteristics are essentially related to men and women, and can only be partially mitigated through exchange between the sexes, nothing in Günderrode's work entails a necessary connection between men and masculine characteristics or women and feminine characteristics, even as a starting point. To be clear, Günderrode does not indicate decisively either that gendered characteristics are to some degree essential or that they are entirely socially determined. Her depictions of women show that she imagined women possessing characteristics and adopting roles that are traditionally considered masculine. For example, Hildgund makes decisions coolly and rationally (while the male characters around her are too weak or emotional to act effectively), and Hildgund, Darthula, Mora, and many other female characters are brave and willing to kill to protect their loved ones and for the sake of honor and their country. However, Günderrode does not specify whether this reflects a lack of essential gender characteristics or an ideal of "independent femininity" such as that advocated by Schlegel, in which an originally "feminine" nature adopts "masculine" characteristics to temper its one-sidedness.

Whichever is the case, Günderrode's treatment of her heroines highlights the significance of how women are viewed and treated by others for their ability to act outside the roles determined for them, to control their own destinies, and even to constitute themselves as active subjects. Thus, like Veit-Schlegel's *Florentin*, Günderrode's work highlights the need to consider the social conditions under which the self develops its identity, vocation, and relationships.

## 8   Conclusion

Scholarship has barely begun to address women's contributions to early German Romantic thought, but already it is clear that neglected authors such as Veit-Schlegel and Günderrode provide sharp criticism of the dominant, male-authored paradigm of early German Romanticism, and suggest routes to solving some of the issues identified by critics. In particular, these two authors highlight the importance of social conditions for the quest of the individual to create an identity and achieve reconciliation with alienated aspects of itself. Veit-Schlegel's unmasking of the narcissism and self-delusion that underlie this quest and lead to its eventual failure, and Günderrode's situating of women's actions in the context of their interpellation by others, along with her monistic metaphysics, indicate directions that could be followed in addressing the problematic aspects of early German Romanticism that are noted by critics.

The integral place of gendered concepts in the work of Schlegel and Novalis means that their reliance on gender stereotypes has wide implications, affecting their ideas about language and representation, genius, the self and its vocation, and metaphysics. Attention to the work of women writers associated with early German Romanticism contributes both to recognizing these failings and finding new ways to address them. The question remains whether changes to our understanding of early German Romanticism that address contributions by Veit-Schlegel or Günderrode would result in a metaphysics and an account of human identity and the human vocation that are still recognizably romantic. Nonetheless, given the problems with the dominant model of early German Romanticism that have been described in this chapter, it may be time to rethink our understanding of early German Romanticism, which until now has been based almost exclusively on the writings of men.

## Notes

1. For example, Hans Eichner, "*Lucinde,*" in *Friedrich Schlegel* (New York: Twayne, 1970), 85; M. Kay, "Women and Individualism: A Re-examination of Schlegel's 'Lucinde' and Gutzkow's 'Wally die Zweiflerin,'" *Modern Language Review* (1975), 557.
2. For example, Barbara Becker-Cantarino, "'Feminismus' und 'Emanzipation'? Zum Geschlechterdizkurs der deutschen Romantik am Beispiel der *Lucinde* und ihrer Rezeption," in Hartwig Schultz, ed., *Salons der Romantik: Beitrage eines wiepersdorfer Colloquiums zu Theorie und Geschichte des Salons* (Berlin:

Walter de Gruyter, 1997): 21–44; Martha B. Helfer, "Gender Studies and Romanticism," in Dennis Mahoney, ed., *The Literature of German Romanticism* (Rochester: Camden House, 2004), 33; Richard Littlejohns, "The 'Bekenntnisse eines Ungeschickten': A Re-examination of Emancipatory Ideas in Friedrich Schlegel's 'Lucinde,'" *Modern Language Review* 72.3 (1977): 605–614; Elena Pnevmonidou, "Die Absage an das romantische Ich. Dorothea Schlegels *Florentin* als Umschrift von Friedrich Schlegel's *Lucinde*," *German Life and Letters* 58.3 (2005): 273, 275; Lisa C. Roetzel, "Feminizing Philosophy," in Jochen Schulte-Sasse, Haynes Horne, and Andreas Michel, eds., *Theory as Practice: A Critical Anthology of Early German Romantic Writings* (Minneapolis: University of Minnesota: 1997), 362; Michaela Schrage-Früh, "Subversive Weiblichkeit?: Die Frau als Muse, Geliebte und Künstlerin im Werk Friedrich Schlegels und Karoline von Günderrodes," *Subversive Romantik* (2004): 371–72.
3. See, for example, Schlegel, *Lucinde*, 47, and Schlegel's repeated claim that "Mysteries are feminine" (KFSA 2, 268 Nr. 127, 269 Nr. 137).
4. Eichner, "*Lucinde*," 85.
5. Martha B. Helfer, "The Male Muses of Romanticism: The Poetics of Gender in Novalis, E.T.A. Hoffmann, and Eichendorff," *The German Quarterly* 78.3 (2005): 299–319; Alice A. Kuzniar, "Hearing Women's Voices in *Heinrich von Ofterdingen*," *Publications of the Modern Language Association* 107:5 (1992): 1204–5; Grant Profant McAllister, Jr., *Kleist's Female Leading Characters and the Subversion of Idealist Discourse* (New York: Peter Lang, 2005); Catriona MacLeod, "The 'Third Sex' in an Age of Difference: Androgyny and Homosexuality in Winckelmann, Friedrich Schlegel, and Kleist," in *Outing Goethe and His Age*, ed. Alice A. Kuzniar (Stanford: Stanford UP, 1996), 194–214; Joachim Pfeiffer, "Friendship and Gender: The Aesthetic Construction of Subjectivity in Kleist," trans. Robert D. Tobin, in *Outing Goethe and His Age* (Stanford: Stanford UP, 1996), 215–227; Val Scullion and Marion Treby, "Sexual Politics in the Narratives of E.T.A. Hoffmann," *Journal of Gender Studies* 22.3 (2013): 297–308.
6. For example, Ernst Brandes, *Ueber die Weiber* (Leipzig: Weidmanns Erben und Reich, 1787); Wilhelm von Humboldt, "Über den Geschlechtsunterschied und dessen Einfluß auf die organische Natur," *Die Horen* 2 (1795): 99–132; Wilhelmine Karoline Wobeser, *Elisa, oder das Weib, wie es seyn sollte* (Leipzig: Heinrich Gräff, 1795).
7. Schlegel, "On Philosophy. To Dorothea," in Ernst Behler, ed., *Friedrich Schlegel—Kritische Ausgabe seiner Werke* (Munich: F. Schöningh, 1958–2002), 8, 42, 54. All references to Schlegel's work are to this edition, hereafter, KFSA. All translations in this chapter are my own, except citations from Schlegel's novel *Lucinde*, which follow Peter Firchow's translations in *Lucinde and the Fragments* (Minneapolis: University of Minnesota, 1971).
8. Schlegel, KFSA 8, 43.

9. Schlegel, KFSA 8, 44.
10. Schlegel, KFSA 8,45.
11. Schlegel, KFSA 8,45.
12. Schlegel, KFSA 8, 44, KFSA 2, 269–70, Nrs. 127, 128, 270, 137.
13. Schlegel, KFSA 7, 59.
14. Schlegel, KFSA 2, 268 Nr. 127.
15. Schlegel, KFSA 8, 46–47; KFSA 2, 258, Nr. 19, 270 #137; *Lucinde*, 108.
16. For example, Humboldt, "Über den Geschlechtsunterschied"; Friedrich von Schiller, "Würde der Frauen" (1796).
17. Schlegel, KFSA 8, 41.
18. Becker-Cantarino, "'Feminismus' und 'Emanzipation'?" 29; Sara Friedrichsmeyer, *The Androgyne in Early German Romanticism: Friedrich Schlegel, Novalis, and the Metaphysics of Love* (Bern: Lange, 1983), 2; Pnevmonidou, "Absage," 279.
19. Roetzel, "Feminizing Philosophy," 369.
20. Schlegel, *Lucinde*, 49.
21. Schlegel, *Lucinde*, 47; see also 43.
22. Schlegel, *Lucinde*, 47.
23. Schlegel, *Lucinde*, 46.
24. Schlegel, *Lucinde*, 102.
25. Novalis, *Schriften. Zweite, nach den Handschriften ergänzte, erweiterte und verbesserte Auflage in vier Bänden*, ed. Paul Kluckhohn and Richard Samuel (Stuttgart: W. Kohlhammer, 1960–), vol. III: 262, #117.
26. Novalis, *Schriften* I, 311–312.
27. Novalis, *Schriften* I, 277, 279.
28. Alice Kuzniar, "Labor Pains: Romantic Theories of Creativity and Gender," in Richard Block and Peter Fenves, eds., *"The Spirit of Poesy": Essays on Jewish and German Literature and Thought in Honor of Géza von Molnár* (Evanston: Northwestern UP, 2000), 81. See also Helfer, "Male Muses," 307.
29. Kuzniar, "Labor Pains," 79. Kuzniar notes the roles of the characters Zulima, Mathilde, Ginnistan, and Fable in this respect; the unnamed princess in a story told to Henry by the merchants provides another example of a woman transferring the power of song to a male character.
30. Kuzniar, "Labor Pains," 80–81.
31. Kuzniar, "Labor Pains," 79.
32. Novalis, *Schriften* I, 135 s.3.
33. Novalis, *Schriften* I, 277.
34. Novalis, *Schriften* I, 288.
35. Novalis, *Schriften* I, 277.
36. Schlegel, *Lucinde*, 116–17.
37. Novalis, *Schriften* I, 322.
38. See endnote 4.
39. Friedrichsmeyer, *Androgyne*, 146.

40. Schlegel, *Lucinde*, 101.
41. Schlegel, *Lucinde*, 112.
42. Becker-Cantarino, "'Feminismus' und 'Emanzipation'?," 21–44; Friedrichsmeyer, *Androgyne*, 158; Helfer, "Gender Studies and Romanticism," 33; Schrage-Früh, "Subversive Weiblichkeit?." 371–72.
43. Schlegel, KFSA 8, 43; *Lucinde*, 59–60, 74–75.
44. Novalis, *Schriften* III, 568 Nr. 92; see also II, 610, Nr. 404. See Schrage-Früh, "Subversive Weiblichkeit?," 369.
45. Novalis, *Schriften* II, 275, Nr. 576.
46. Becker-Cantarino, "'Feminismus' und 'Emanzipation'?" 35; Friedrichsmeyer, *Androgyne*, 104–105, 158; Pnevmonidou, "Absage," 273–75; Roetzel, "Feminizing Philosophy," 370.
47. Littlejohns, "Bekenntnisse eines Ungeschickten," 613.
48. Friedrichsmeyer, *Androgyne*, 104.
49. Becker-Cantarino, "'Feminismus' und 'Emanzipation'?" 32, 35; Friedrichsmeyer, *Androgyne*, 62, 83, 159; Theresa M. Kelley, "Women, Gender, and Literary Criticism," in Marshall Brown, ed., *The Cambridge History of Literary Criticism* (Cambridge: Cambridge UP, 2000), 325; Kuzniar, "Hearing Women's Voices," 1205; Littlejohns, "Bekenntnisse eines Ungeschickten," 606; Schrage-Früh, "Subversive Weiblichkeit?," 377–78.
50. Friedrichsmeyer, "The Subversive Androgyne," in Marianne Burkhard and Edith Waldstein, eds., *Women in German Yearbook 3* (Lanham: UP of America, 1987), 69; Kay, "Women and Individualism," 552.
51. Friedrichsmeyer, *Androgyne*, 159; Elisabeth Krimmer, "Abortive *Bildung*: Women Writers, Male Bonds, and Would-Be Fathers," in Marjanne Goozé, ed., *Challenging Separate Spheres: Female* Bildung *in Eighteenth- and Nineteenth Century Germany* (Oxford: Lang, 2007), 235; Schrage-Früh, "Subversive Weiblichkeit?" 369–71.
52. Schlegel, *Lucinde*, 107.
53. Schlegel, KFSA 2, 258, Nr. 19.
54. Novalis, *Schriften* III, 569, Nr. 97.
55. Pnevmonidou, "Absage," 276.
56. Novalis, *Schriften* I:157, 6. See Helfer, "Male Muses," 304–5.
57. Helfer, "Gender Studies and Romanticism," 239.
58. Helfer, "Male Muses," 306; Krimmer, "Abortive *Bildung*," 237; Pnevmonidou, "Absage," 276; Schrage-Früh, "Subversive Weiblichkeit?" 375–76.
59. Novalis, *Schriften* III: 692, #702.
60. Friedrichsmeyer, *Androgyne*, 84.
61. Littlejohns, "Bekenntnisse eines Ungeschickten," 606.
62. Becker-Cantarino, "'Feminismus' und 'Emanzipation'?" 35.
63. Becker-Cantarino "'Feminismus' und 'Emanzipation'?", 29; Littlejohns, "Bekenntnisse eines Ungeschickten," 606; Schrage-Früh, "Subversive Weiblichkeit?," 369, 375.

64. Becker-Cantarino, "'Feminismus' und 'Emanzipation'?," 28, 42–43; Schrage-Früh, "Subversive Weiblichkeit?," 366.
65. Becker-Cantarino, "'Feminismus' und 'Emanzipation'?," 35.
66. Helfer, "Gender Studies and Romanticism," 33.
67. See, for example, Schlegel's equation of masculinity with both fertilizing and overcoming in his claim that: "Mysteries are, as already mentioned, feminine; orgies want to conquer or fertilize everything around them in the joyful exuberance of masculine power." Schlegel, KFSA 2, 269, Nr. 137.
68. See, for example, Schlegel, KFSA 18, 144, 145; Johann Wilhelm Ritter, *Fragmente aus dem Nachlasse eines jungen Physikers: Ein Taschenbuch fur Freunde der Natur* (Heidelberg: Mohr & Zimmer, 1810), vol. 2, 45, Nr. 434.
69. Novalis, *Schriften* III, 87–88, 255, Nr. 81.
70. Novalis, *Schriften* III, 264, Nr. 126.
71. Novalis, *Schriften* III, 262, Nr. 117; see also 255, Nr. 81, 264, Nr. 126.
72. Schlegel, KFSA 8, 46.
73. Novalis, *Schriften* III, 651, Nr. 564.
74. Novalis, *Schriften* II, 260, Nr. 511.
75. Novalis, *Schriften* III, 262, Nr. 117.
76. Novalis, *Schriften* II, 104, Nr. 1, 412, Nr. 1, 455, Nr. 95; Schlegel, KFSA 2, 201, Nr. 222.
77. Novalis, *Schriften* I, 88–90, III, 314, Nr. 398; Schlegel, KFSA 2, 182–83, Nr. 116, 185, Nr. 125.
78. Novalis, *Schriften* I, 82; Schlegel, KFSA 2, 270, Nr. 137.
79. Novalis, *Schriften* I:104; see also 284, 287–88; Schlegel, *Lucinde*, 49.
80. Novalis, *Schriften* II:545, Nr. 105, III: 390, Nr. 654.
81. Novalis, *Schriften* III: 686, Nr. 671.
82. Schlegel, KFSA 2, 258, Nr. 19, 267, Nr. 116.
83. Novalis, *Schriften* III:520, I:84; Schlegel, KFSA 8, 54.
84. Novalis, *Schriften* I:96, II:524–55 #13; Schlegel, KFSA 2, 267, Nr. 111.
85. Gisela Dischner, "Die Guenderrode," in *Bettine von Arnim: Eine weibliche Sozialbiographie aus dem 19. Jahrhundert* (Berlin: Wagenbach, 1977), 75; Roetzel, "Feminizing Philosophy," 362–63, 370.
86. Novalis, *Schriften* II:, 672, 522, Nr. 3, 523, Nr. 8, 427, Nr. 32–33, 463, Nr. 114.
87. Novalis, *Schriften* III:685–86, Nr. 671; see also II: 439, Nr. 68.
88. For example, Schlegel, KFSA 2: 42; 152, Nr. 42; 363f.
89. Schlegel KFSA 2, 267, Nr.128; Novalis, *Schriften* II:617, #17.
90. Novalis, *Schriften* II:275, #577, 261, #519.
91. Schlegel, KFSA 2, 42.
92. Helfer, "Male Muses," 300. See also Kuzniar, "Hearing Women's Voices," 1196.
93. Roetzel, "Feminizing Philosophy," 361–62.
94. Novalis, *Schriften* II:417 #14, III:559 #30; Schlegel, KFSA 2,286.

95. J.G. Fichte, "First Introduction to the *Wissenschaftslehre*," in *Introductions to the Wissenschaftslehre and Other Writings (1797–1800)*, ed. and trans. Daniel Breazeale (Indianapolis: Hackett, 1994), 9–11.
96. Schlegel, KFSA 2:72; KFSA 18:521, Nr. 22. See also Novalis, *Schriften* II: 546, #111.
97. Novalis, *Schriften* III: 430, #820.
98. Novalis, *Schriften* II:421, #21.
99. May Mergenthaler, "Die Frühromantik als Projekt vollendeter Mitteilung zwischen den Geschlechtern: Friedrich Schlegel und Dorothea Veit im Gespräch über Friedrich Richters Romane," *The German Quarterly* 81.3 (2008): 306–7; Lisa C. Roetzel, "Positionality and the Male Philosopher: Friedrich Schlegel's 'Ueber die Philosophie. An Dorothea,'" *Monatshefte* 91.2 (1999): 188, 193, 199.
100. Helfer, "Male Muses," 300. See also MacLeod, "Third Sex," 207; Pfeiffer, "Friendship and Gender"; Schrage-Früh, "Subversive Weiblichkeit?," 373.
101. Helfer, "Male Muses," 301.
102. Helfer, "Gender Studies and Romanticism," 243; "Male Muses," 301, 304.
103. Novalis, *Schriften* I: 271, 276.
104. Helfer, "Male Muses," 303.
105. Helfer, "Male Muses," 303.
106. Helfer, "Male Muses," 308.
107. Helfer, "Male Muses," 305.
108. Helfer, "Male Muses," 308.
109. Becker-Cantarino, "'Feminismus' und 'Emanzipation?'" 25; Gabriele Dürbeck, "'Sibylle,' 'Pythia' oder 'Dame Lucifer.' Zur Idealisierung und Marginalisierung von Autorinnen der Romantik in der Literaturgeschichtsschreibung des 19. Jahrhunderts," *Zeitschrift für Germanistik* 2 (2000): 258; Helfer, "Gender Studies and Romanticism," 229.
110. Roetzel, "Feminizing Philosophy," 365.
111. Helfer, "Gender Studies and Romanticism," 240.
112. Helfer, "Gender Studies and Romanticism," 242; Mergenthaler, "Frühromantik als Projekt," 316.
113. Roetzel, "Feminizing Philosophy," 376.
114. Pnevmonidou, "Absage," 273; Liliane Weissberg, "Schreiben als Selbstentwurf. Zu den Schriften Rahel Varnhagens und Dorothea Schlegels," *Zeitschrift für Religions- und Geistesgeschichte* 47.3 (1995): 244.
115. Helfer, "Dorothea Veit Schlegel's *Florentin*," 150; Krimmer, "Abortive *Bildung*," 247; Pnevmonidou, "Absage," 271–92.
116. Helfer, "Gender Studies and Romanticism," 241.
117. Juliane's father's remarks about her splendid but unflattering wedding attire ("it is not about the beauty of the clothing, but its appropriateness") and her mother's claim that Juliane will remain in her arms after marrying Eduard

also indicate that Veit-Schlegel means to highlight marriage's social and cultural role (*Florentin*, 118).
118. Veit-Schlegel, *Florentin*, 38.
119. Helfer, "Dorothea Veit-Schlegel's *Florentin*," 156; Johnson, "Dorothea Veit's *Florentin*," 43, 55; Pnevmonidou, "Absage," 275, 281–83.
120. Veit-Schlegel, *Florentin*: 72, 74.
121. Florentin defends himself to Juliane for this action, in the process revealing the narcissism that characterized his relationship to his wife and her pregnancy, crying: "Was she not a hard-hearted, faithless, unnatural murderer? She most unmercifully murdered me, me!" (Veit-Schlegel, *Florentin*, 74–75). Florentin also does not give his wife's name, resisting Juliane's questioning and complaining "Do not ask me about those sort of contingencies [...] they do not belong to me in the remotest way" (81).
122. Pnevmonidou, "Absage," 280.
123. Pnevmonidou, "Absage," 281.
124. Johnson, "Dorothea Veit's *Florentin*," 53.
125. Veit-Schlegel, *Florentin*, 15.
126. Veit-Schlegel, *Florentin*: 12, 16, 41–43, 46, 51–52.
127. Veit-Schlegel, *Florentin*, 145–47; see also 96–100.
128. Helfer, "Dorothea Veit-Schlegel's *Florentin*," 156; Johnson, "Dorothea Veit's *Florentin*," 41–42.
129. Veit-Schlegel, *Florentin*, 94.
130. Helfer, "Dorothea Veit-Schlegel's *Florentin*," 152; Johnson, "Dorothea Veit's *Florentin*," 43, 52; Kelley, "Women, Gender, and Literary Criticism," 327; Pnevmonidou, "Absage," 288.
131. Veit-Schlegel, *Florentin*, 17, 26–27; see also 13, 77, 80, 82–85, 139–40, 116.
132. Liesl Allingham, "Revolutionizing Domesticity: Potentialities of Female Self-Definition in Dorothea Schlegel's *Florentin* (1801)," *Women in German Yearbook* 27 (2011): 14–15; Helfer, "Dorothea Veit Schlegel's *Florentin*: Constructing a Feminist Romantic Aesthetic," *German Quarterly* 69.2 (1996): 156; Laurie Johnson, "Dorothea Veit's *Florentin* and the Early Romantic Model of Alterity," *Monatshefte* 97.1 (2005): 42, 43.
133. Veit-Schlegel, *Florentin*, 10.
134. Veit-Schlegel, *Florentin*, 153.
135. Veit-Schlegel may indicate that different types of *Bildung* are suited to different women. For example, Clementina maintains that Juliane and another girl, Therese, should follow opposite paths in their development (*Florentin*, 138). See Allingham, "Revolutionizing Domesticity," 15–16, 19.
136. Veit-Schlegel, *Florentin*, 35–38, 86–95, 101–105.
137. Krimmer, "Dorothea Schlegel's *Florentin*," in *In the Company of Men: Cross-Dressed Women Around 1800* (Detroit: Wayne State UP, 2003), 185. See also Allingham, "Revolutionizing Domesticity"; Helfer, "Dorothea Veit Schlegel's *Florentin*," 155.

138. Veit-Schlegel, *Florentin*, 61–62.
139. Veit-Schlegel, *Florentin*, 18–19.
140. Veit-Schlegel, *Florentin*, 129.
141. Veit-Schlegel, *Florentin*, 18–19, 108f.
142. Allingham, "Revolutionizing Domesticity."
143. Karoline von Günderrode, *Sämtliche Werke und ausgewählte Studien. Historisch-Kritische Ausgabe*, ed. Walther Morgenthaler (Basel: Stroemfeld/Roter Stern, 1990–1991), vol. I: 325.
144. Günderrode, *Sämtliche Werke* I: 68.
145. Joachim Heimerl, "Dem Tode verfallen: Die Ballade 'Piedro' im Kontext des literarischen Werks der Karoline von Günderrode," *Wirkendes Wort* 53.3 (2003): 408; Karin Obermeier, "Karoline von Günderrode (1780–1806)," in *Women Writers in German-Speaking Countries. A Bio-Bibliographical Critical Sourcebook*, ed. Elke P. Frederiksen and Elizabeth G. Ametsbichler, 180–88 (Westport, CT: Greenwood Press, 1988), 183.
146. Günderrode, *Sämtliche Werke* I: 33, 32.
147. Günderrode, *Sämtliche Werke* I: 446–47. Similarly, in her prose poem "An Apocalyptic Fragment" Günderrode describes cycles of existence as individual forms are absorbed into the whole and born again (I: 53).
148. *Anziehung* ("attraction" or "affinity") and *Gesezen* [sic] *der Verwandschaft* ("laws of affinity" or "laws of relationship") (Günderrode, *Sämtliche Werke* I: 446–47).
149. Novalis, *Schriften* II:427, #32.
150. Günderrode, *Sämtliche Werke* I: 447. Unlike Novalis and Schlegel, Günderrode is ambivalent about whether this is the purpose of existence or just a natural fact, and about whether the ideal end-point will ever be reached (448).
151. Günderrode, *Sämtliche Werke* I: 449.
152. Anna C. Ezekiel, "Introduction to *Hildgund*," in Günderrode, *Poetic Fragments*, trans. Anna C. Ezekiel (Albany: SUNY Press, 2016), 39–55.
153. See Liesl Allingham, "Countermemory in Karoline von Günderrode's 'Darthula nach Ossian': A Female Warrior, Her Unruly Breast, and the Construction of Her Myth," *Goethe Yearbook* 21 (July 2014): 39–56.
154. For example, Karin Obermeier, "'Ach diese Rolle wird mir allzu schwer': Gender and Cultural Identity in Karoline von Günderrode's Drama 'Udohla,'" in *Thalia's Daughters: German Women Dramatists from the Eighteenth Century to the Present*, ed. Susan Cocalis, Ferrel Rose, Karin Obermeier (Tübingen: Francke, 1996), 100.
155. Günderrode, letter to Gunda Brentano, Aug 29 1801, *Der Schatten eines Traumes. Gedichte, Prosa, Briefe, Zeugniss von Zeitgenossen*, ed. Christa Wolf (Munich: Deutscher Taschenbuch Verlag, 1997 [1979]), 160.

# 22

## Romantic Philosophy as Anthropology

### Carl Niekerk

The roots of Romantic philosophy as anthropology go back at least to the 1770s, a period that Jonathan Israel has characterized as the era of a "radical breakthrough"; it was also the era during which, simultaneously, the term "anthropology" entered the vocabulary of the major European languages.[1] Israel is thinking in particular of the anonymous publication of the *Philosophical and Political History of the Establishments & the Commerce of the Europeans in the two Indies* [*Histoire philosophique et politique des Établissements & du Commerce des Européens dans les deux Indes*] under the editorship of Guillaume-Thomas Raynal, commonly known as the "abbé Raynal" (1713–1796), a philosophical bestseller first published in 1770 in six volumes and republished in revised editions in 1774, 1780, and 1820.[2] By presenting itself as a "philosophical and political history" the book's title invokes "philosophy" as a tool for understanding the world, including the development of other, non-European societies and the people who inhabit these. And Raynal is not the only text to use the term "philosophy" in such a manner around 1770. Slightly earlier, between 1768 and 1770, Cornelis de Pauw (1739–1799) had published his *Philosophical Investigations on the Americans or Memoirs of Interest to serve the History of Humankind* [*Recherches philosophiques sur les Américains ou Mémoires intéressantes pour servir à l'histoire de l'espèce humaine*], a text that was reprinted several times as well and that also,

---

C. Niekerk (✉)
University of Illinois at Urbana-Champaign, Champaign, IL, USA
e-mail: niekerk@illinois.edu

© The Author(s) 2020
E. Millán Brusslan (ed.), *The Palgrave Handbook of German Romantic Philosophy*, Palgrave Handbooks in German Idealism, https://doi.org/10.1007/978-3-030-53567-4_22

already in its title, suggests the merits of a philosophical approach for the understanding of a specific society.[3] These texts by Raynal and de Pauw were highly influential among their contemporaries, and well into the early nineteenth century, and part of the early history of anthropological thinking, to be completely forgotten thereafter. Both texts are mainly studied today because of their criticism of colonialism, although the extent of that criticism is also questioned.

In the following I want to pursue the nexus suggested by Raynal and de Pauw between philosophy, anthropology, and globalization. I am interested in the reception of this link during the late Enlightenment and the Romantic era, and in particular in the transformation of the radical political ambitions articulated by Raynal and de Pauw—visible, for instance, in their anti-colonialism. What does the term "philosophical" ["philosophique"] tell us about the perspective from which de Pauw's and Raynal's texts were written? Both texts respond to Georges-Louis Leclerc, Comte de Buffon's *Natural History, in General and Particular* [*Histoire naturelle, générale et particulière*] (1749–1789) and in particular volumes 2 and 3 (1749) in which Buffon focused on the natural history of mankind and set out some broad principles to understand humans and their activities as part of natural history. Buffon not only argued for the unity of humankind claiming that all humans could be traced back to one common root, but also claimed that biological and cultural differences were the result primarily of the effects of climate and geography.[4] With that he enabled a new understanding of natural history and anthropology that no longer had to rely on archaic and outdated religious notions or a fantastic view of the non-European world, but that focused on what it saw as empirical reality. Raynal and de Pauw seek to apply Buffon's insights to colonial society; they present their texts as critiques of colonialism, without however arguing for the need of its abolishment, and both use the reconstruction of the history of European colonialism as a tool to come to a description and better understanding of the peoples and cultures that are colonized by the Europeans. By doing so, they set into motion a wave of publications that sought to understand biological and cultural differences philosophically—away from the religious paradigm that had long dominated this type of literature. In the following I will first discuss the German debate on the philosophical premises that enable these new views of other cultures and their ramifications for Germans' perspectives on their own culture, and then I will focus on three early German Romantic texts (by Achim von Arnim, Friedrich Schlegel, and Alexander von Humboldt) that can be considered exemplary for Romanticism's philosophical response to the anthropological challenge.

The philosophical perspective of Raynal and de Pauw is linked to their texts' global perspective. Both authors were trained by the Catholic church, and even though the first two editions of Raynal's book (1770 and 1774) were published anonymously and the author's name of the *Recherches philosophique* was indicated only as "Mr. de P\*\*\*," it was fairly soon known who the authors were. Adding the term "philosophique" to the titles was a clear indication of the fact that neither author intended to give a Christian perspective on the conquest of the non-European world as an imposition of Western values onto barbaric territories. In fact, both texts are quite critical of the church in their accounts of the interaction between the European and non-European world; the behavior of the church is one of the points of concern in both texts. Both authors, like Buffon before them, intentionally abstain from questions that could be considered controversial from a religious point of view—questions, for instance, concerning the constitution and origins of the planets, minerals, vegetables, and animals (for the attentive reader, however, their views on these issues were quite clear). They instead present an image of humankind that sought to understand differences through causal relations and relied on specific descriptions and comparison without referring back to metaphysical explanations in line with the *Encyclopédie*'s article "PHILOSOPHE" that had been published shortly before, in 1765.[5] By explicitly advertising their publications as "philosophical," Raynal and de Pauw linked their texts to a tradition of French radical thinking (the so-called philosophes or parti philosophique), a group within the *Académie française* that understood itself as materialist and progressive, and considered the "devote party" ["parti dévot"] as its opponent.[6]

Raynal's and de Pauw's texts were radical both in an epistemological and political sense. Calling on philosophy as an ally, these texts advocated a view of nature that was descriptive, conceptualized as open, and certainly not the expression of a static hierarchy (as Linnaeus had argued), or the result of a sequence of prearranged events. Such views had political implications because the static structure of society (as God-given, with the king and the church at the top of the hierarchy) was called into questions as well. By the time of the French Revolution both were hailed as its intellectual predecessors, even though the two authors distanced themselves fairly quickly from revolutionary events in France. Both texts, in conjunction with a popular new German translation of Buffon's *Histoire naturelle* that started publication in 1771,[7] also triggered a series of critical responses in German speaking lands. Using the terminology of Jonathan Israel, one could say that the radical designs of de Pauw and Raynal provoked a moderate political backlash, first, among philosophers who on the one hand believed in the merits of Enlightenment thinking, but on the other were concerned about the kind of consequences such thought might have on the stability of society. This backlash becomes more pronounced and in fact starts to dominate in the work of thinkers belonging to the Romantic School of the nineteenth century, picking up on certain ambiguities that were already present in anthropological discourse from its very beginning. In the following, my intention is to reconstruct the reception of philosophy as anthropology as Buffon, Raynal, and de Pauw had proposed it—philosophically inclined natural historians who were seeking to develop a branch of knowledge and who wanted to theorize knowledge of man and humankind on the basis of what was known about humankind's global variety. To some extent the Romantics' critical reception of this earlier generation of anthropologically oriented philosophers focuses upon "race," but, as the following will show, it is increasingly the German Romantics who were also quite interested in notions of "culture." Kant and Herder are transitional figures who play a key role in facilitating the Romantic backlash against radical Enlightenment philosophical anthropology.

It was Immanuel Kant (1724–1804) with his publications on "race" in the 1770s and 1780s who started the counter-attack against Raynal and de Pauw by seeking to put limits on the claims made in the name of philosophy (and redefining the role of philosophy in the process). As John Zammito has pointed out, in the 1770s Kant goes through a transition: after initially conceiving of himself as an anthropologist—there exists a portrait of Kant from 1768 holding a book entitled *Anthropology or Man understood as Part of Nature* [*Anthropologie oder die Naturkenntnis des Menschen*][8]—Kant turned to the rescue of philosophy from psychological and empiricist reductionism through a critical project focusing on a transcendental conceptualization of the mind.[9] Nevertheless Kant also continued to pursue anthropological issues (he taught, for instance, a successful course on pragmatic anthropology). This continued interest in anthropology is visible, for instance, in the essay *On the Different Human Races* [*Von den verschiedenen Racen der Menschen*], originally published as an announcement advertising his lectures on physical geography in 1775, and reprinted, in a somewhat extended version, in 1777 as a chapter in J.J. Engel's periodical *The Philosopher for the World* [*Der Philosoph für die Welt*]. While starting out with a reference to Buffon—he is the clear authority, and Kant endorses his rule that animals belong to one "species" ["Gattung" / "espèce"] if they can produce fertile offspring with each other—Kant fairly quickly goes on to introduce the concept of "race" to refer to those characteristics of humans that remain stable for a long time, also when the people in question are transplanted to other parts of the earth and produce "always hybrid offspring" ["jederzeit halbschlächtige Junge"] when mating with representatives of a different race.[10] Kant does acknowledge that "*air* and *sun*"

["*Luft* und *Sonne*"], a clear reference to Buffon's theory of climate, may be at the roots of race, but they do not prevent certain qualities from becoming permanent.[11] This investment in the concept of "race" puts Kant at odds with the general direction underlying the works of Buffon and Johann Friedrich Blumenbach, whose anthropological dissertation explaining human diversity, *On the Natural Variety of Humankind* [*De generis humani varietate nativa*], was published the same year as Kant's essay. Buffon and Blumenbach stress the flexibility of biological characteristics like skin color, and they prefer to speak of "varieties" ["variétés" / "Varietäten" or "Spielarten"] instead of "races."[12]

Kant's *Von den verschiedenen Racen der Menschen* argues for a concept of "race" as a fundamental category for understanding human diversity, but it also assigns a very specific role to philosophy. Already before his critical project—the *Critique of Pure Reason* [*Critik der reinen Vernunft*] was first published in 1781—Kant wanted to establish the relevance of what philosophy is and what it does, also in the context of the (among the reading public very popular) anthropological debates of the time. In the case of the debate on humankind's biological variations, philosophy is supposed to supply adequate concepts to help natural history become more accurate. But in doing so, Kant in a careful strategy of self-promotion also claims to speak in the name of and on behalf of the Enlightenment in its entirety,[13] while in reality promoting a moderate brand of Enlightenment that makes sure that its emancipatory ambitions do not have too great an impact on society's structures. And his strategy works. Christoph Girtanner in 1796 proposes introducing Kant's terminology as the standard idiom into natural history, and Blumenbach indeed follows suit and, after avoiding the term for a long time, starts using "race" from the fifth edition of his *Handbuch der Naturgeschichte* (1797) as a systematic category to describe humankind's variety of humankind to be used in those cases in which certain physical traits have become stable across the generations.[14]

Kant is not the only one to use developments in natural history and anthropology as a catalyst to rethink his philosophical view of humankind. His contemporary, former student, and later rival, Johann Gottfried Herder (1744–1803), also picks up on the anthropological trend, but Herder's position is more complex than Kant's. Herder is seen by many as an advocate of cultural relativism and a critic of imperialism, something that is often traced back to a statement in his essay *Another Philosophy on the History of the Development of Humankind* [*Auch eine Philosophie der Geschichte zur Bildung der Menschheit*] from 1774, in which Herder speaks out against comparing nations: "fundamentally all comparison turns deficient [...] every nation has its center of happiness" ["im Grunde also wird alle Vergleichung mißlich [...] jede Nation hat ihren Mittelpunkt der Glückseligkeit in sich"], a statement that however, as we will see in the following, needs to be taken with caution.[15] Herder develops his system of thought further in his *Ideas concerning the Philosophy of the History of Humankind* [*Ideen zur Philosophie der Geschichte der Menschheit*] (1784–1791) which closely follows Buffon's model. For Herder, like for Buffon, humans are part of one species, but subject to change; he sees them as having adapted to climate everywhere they live.[16] On the one hand, Herder follows Buffon's view that cultural difference is a product of climate and geography—combining identity and difference, universalism and relativism in his views on humankind. He disapproves of Kant's introduction of the concept "race" into anthropology: he sees no reason to speak of "races" because they suggest different roots ("eine Verschiedenheit der Abstammung") for dissimilar groups of humans (255). He gives Buffon's theories a clearer political turn, for instance by disapproving of Europeans colonial ambitions and their tendency to act like "demanding, violent, overly mighty despots" ["fodernde, gewalttätige, übermächtige Despoten"] in the countries they have occupied (259–60). One can read this as a cultural argument against colonial abuse: because Europeans are not rooted in the climate, geography, and culture of the countries they occupy, they do not belong there.

On the other hand, however, Herder's texts show that this cultural argument can also easily be turned against certain groups in society, in particular groups whose culture is not tied to a specific territory (shaped by climate and geography). In a section on "Foreign peoples in Europe" ["Fremde Völker in Europa"] (699), Herder refers to Jews as "a parasitical plant that attached itself to almost all European nations and drew in more or less of their sap" ["parasitische Pflanze, die sich beinah allen Europäischen Nationen angehängt und mehr oder minder von ihrem Saft an sich gezogen"] (702). Similarly, Herder refers to "Gypsies" ("Zigeuner"; Sinti/Roma), who in a European context are associated with mobility as well, as a "rejected Indian caste" ["[e]ine verworfne Indische Kaste"] (703) that since its expulsion has led a mobile life (cf. 493). Like Kant, Herder in his texts too adds a normative dimension: his texts speak to a desire among Germans for a cultural and national identity that the early German Romantics find quite appealing. As we saw, Herder's thinking is often associated with an openness for cultural difference, an ability to accept alterity without resorting to overarching notions of rationality that brand the notions of other cultures as irrational.[17] This is not incorrect. His statement about Jews and Gypsies show, however, that Herder's concept of alterity is closely tied to a notion of territoriality (as was the case with Buffon and Blumenbach, but neither of those used this notion to advocate excluding certain peoples and their cultures). Herder conceives of cultures as sedentary, because they are linked to climate and geography. There is no space for mobility in his theories.[18]

The texts by Kant and Herder from the 1770s and 1780s that I have discussed thus far set the stage and formulate the parameters for Romantic philosophy and its engagement with the emerging discipline of anthropology at the time. Kant and Herder were important for Romantic philosophy, but it is a highly ambiguous legacy the Romantics inherit from Enlightenment anthropology—an ambiguity that is mirrored in our image today of German Romanticism itself. Romanticism is in possession of a notion of alterity and an interest in the otherness of non-Western cultures; its concept of alterity is, following Buffon and Herder, closely tied to territory, based on the idea that different territories develop their own specific cultures and that these cultures should be respected. Romanticism, however, is also the era in which nationalism was born, a movement that ties culture to territory as well (in this case understood as "the nation"). It is in nationalism, with its racial and cultural components, that the link between territory and culture becomes problematic. In the following I will examine three Romantic texts (by Achim von Arnim, Friedrich Schlegel, and Alexander von Humboldt) in order to investigate the different constellations in which territory and alterity can be thought together. My point is that Romantic thinking offers a range of options of thinking through the links between culture, territory, and otherness. While traditionally German Romanticism is seen as fostering a sense of otherness because it breaks with what it sees as the Enlightenment's outdated universalism, Romanticism's reaction to the Enlightenment is not only more complex, but also multifaceted. In many respects Romantic texts mirror an ambiguity already present in Enlightenment anthropology.

Achim von Arnim (1781–1831) belonged to the second Romantic, the so-called Heidelberg school, and was known, among other things, for *The Youth's Magic Horn* [*Des Knaben Wunderhorn*] (1806–1808), a three-volume collection of (heavily redacted) German folk songs he edited together with his friend Clemens Brentano and that came to be associated with German Romanticism's nationalistic turn. Arnim was also known for the many novellas he wrote; one of these novellas is "Gentry by Entailment"[19] ["Die Majorats-Herren"] (1820)—the story of an illegitimately born child, referred to throughout the novella as the "Majoratsherr," secretly adopted by an older nobleman and his young wife, so that the estate will remain in their family, and of their biological daughter, Esther, born around the same time, and adopted and raised by a Jewish merchant as part of a secret arrangement with the nobleman. The novella starts in what was for Romantic poetics a rather programmatic way, with the narrative "wir"/"we" leafing through the images of an old calendar and reminiscing about how "rich and full" ["reich erfüllt"] the world was before the French Revolution.[20]

It would be wrong, though, to think that in "Die Majorats-Herren" this old pre-revolutionary world is idealized; Arnim's point is rather that in earlier times divisions were clearer, and this goes in particular for the role of Jews in German society who are contrasted with its old nobility to which the "Majoratsherr" (supposedly) belongs. In the words of his cousin, also referred to as the lieutenant, who takes care of him after he returns from a long stay abroad, and who lives in a house looking out over the "Judengasse" and does frequent business with Jews, Jews live "crowded together like ants; an eternal haggling, squabbling, and celebrating of ceremonies; and they always make trouble with their little food; sometimes it is forbidden, sometimes required, and sometimes they cannot make fire; in short the devil always gets his way with them" ["zusammengedrängt, wie die Ameisen; das ist ein ewig Schachern und Zänken, und Ceremonieenmachen, und immer haben sie soviel Plackerei mit ihrem bißchen Essen; bald ist es ihnen verboten, bald ist es ihnen befohlen, bald sollen sie kein Feuer anmachen; kurz, der Teufel ist bei ihnen immer los"] (113–14). A particularly bad example of such stereotyping of Jews in the text is Esther's stepmother, Vasthi, who has a "nose like an eagle" ["Nase wie ein Adler"], whose speech sounds like the "horrid cawing of ravens" ["ein fürchterliches Rabenkrächze"], and who speaks a "most contorted Jewish dialect" ["verzerrtesten Judendialect"] (122), and who, motivated by financial gain, eventually kills her stepdaughter Esther. It is not just the Jews who are blamed for Germany's sorry state. The "Majoratsherr" harbors an unsavory fascination with Esther (whom he assumes is Jewish), but, although he realizes what is going on, is ultimately not able to help her for lack of want and initiative. His cousin, who speaks Hebrew (to have a tactical advantage in his commercial dealings with Jews), and who owns books on Jewish history and culture (124) is also seen in a negative light.

Arnim's "Die Majorats-Herren" is clearly meant as a response to Gotthold Ephraim Lessing's drama *Nathan der Weise* (1779), which is mentioned in the text once (128) and deals with an adoption as well: the wise Jew Nathan adopts the Christian daughter of one of his friends, after he has lost his own wife and sons in a fire set by Christian mercenaries—making Lessing's text into exemplary for Enlightenment tolerance. The adoption that takes place in "Die Majorats-Herren" is primarily depicted as a financial transaction: Esther's biological father, the nobleman, has an interest in her being out of the way since that will allow him to claim his inheritance, and her adoptive father has an interest in the adoption because in exchange he receives large sums of money from her biological father. When Esther at one point is referred to as a "child stolen from Christians" ["geraubtes Christenkind"] (128), that is therefore, according to the logic of the novella, not accurate.

The portrayal of Jews in "Die Majorats-Herren" certainly has something to do with racism—Jews are portrayed as by nature devious. But there is a cultural dimension to the argument against Jews as well: the novella depicts Jews as not really belonging to German culture and undermining that culture. German culture is portrayed as in decline, for which the French Revolution is blamed, but also, and more importantly, the materialism of Jews in German society who profit from the new rights they have received as a result of the French occupation and its aftermath. At the end of the story the principle of noble estates inherited through primogeniture ["die Lehnsmajorate"] has been abolished and Jews are liberated from their narrow alley ["aus der engen Gasse befreit"]; Vasthi buys the estate for a trifle ["Kleinigkeit"], and pays for this by selling some of the paintings in it, to turn the "Majoratshaus" into a salmiak factory (146–47).

"Die Majorats-Herren" illustrates something about the nature of German Romantics' interest in other cultures; in an exemplary way it makes clear that an interest in alterity which is less rational than that of Raynal and de Pauw and professes to be more open to the otherness of other cultures does not necessarily lead to more tolerance or understanding (one could interpret the sixty-year-old cousin who reads books on Jewish history and culture as a personification of an earlier, Enlightened age that was naïve about Jewish culture and easily abused). Achim von Arnim was a member of the Christian-German Table Society ["Christlich-Teutsche Tischgesellschaft"], a conservative and nationalist group for which anti-Semitism was foundational (and that was meant as a counterforce to popular salons in Berlin run by Jewish women like Henriette Herz, Sara Levy, and Rahel Varnhagen).[21] The question to ask, however, is whether this anti-Semitism is incidental—specific to this literary text only and not linked to any overarching discourses—or inherent to the Romantic program? To answer that question, we need to look beyond literature, and we indeed need to consider how German Romanticism continues the specific brand of philosophical discourse we found in Raynal, de Pauw, Kant, and Herder—an anthropological conceptualization of philosophy.

The kind of philosophical histories of humankind that thinkers like Buffon, de Pauw, Raynal, and Herder wrote can be found among Romantic authors and intellectuals as well and shed some light on the thinking behind the attitudes articulated in Arnim's text. One example is Friedrich Schlegel's *Philosophy of History in eighteen Lectures* [*Philosophie der Geschichte. In achtzehn Vorlesungen*] (1829). It is noteworthy how exactly Schlegel frames his interest in the philosophy of history in a way that is very different from that of his Enlightenment predecessors. This is clear, for instance, from the opening sentence of his text: "The closest object and first task of philosophy is to reinstate in humans its lost mirror image of God; to the extent, namely/that is to say, that this concerns science and its entire area" ["Der nächste Gegenstand und die erste Aufgabe der Philosophie ist die Wiederherstellung des verlornen göttlichen Ebenbildes im Menschen; soweit dies nämlich die Wissenschaft und ihr ganzes Gebiet angehet"].[22] Philosophy, in the view of Friedrich Schlegel in the 1820s, during what has been called Schlegel's "conservative phase,"[23] the final stage of his intellectual development, is meant to restore the divine in humanity, in particular where science is concerned. While Enlightenment thinkers sought to emancipate philosophy from theology and radical Enlightenment thinkers like Raynal and de Pauw used their philosophical program to question the effect of religion(s) on society, Schlegel, in the later period of his thought, in contrast seeks to collapse the differences between philosophy and theology.

While Enlightenment anthropology engaged in a serious way with the precise relations between humans and apes, Schlegel in his first lecture categorically rejects the view that human beings are nothing but "an ennobled or somewhat better trained ape" ["ein veredelter oder etwas besser abgerichteter Affe"], an assumption that, according to Schlegel, neither cultural nor natural history supports, and he proceeds to argue that humans have far more in common with other animals (cow, sheep, camel, horse, etc.) (28). In line with this, Schlegel distances himself explicitly not only from Rousseau's thesis that humans initially lived in a state of nature, but also from the idea that it would be desirable to bring humankind back to such a state of nature (36–37). It is rather so that humans at times "turn wild and degenerate" ["verwildern und entarten"[24]] from a condition of civilization, as revolutions show: "Every revolution is a temporary epoch of barbarization" ["Jede Revolution ist eine vorübergehende Epoche der Verwilderung"] (36).

Schlegel then proceeds to reread the pre-history of humankind (its "Urgeschichte") as a conflict between those who seek God, love peace, and live according to patriarchal simplicity and custom on the one hand and, on the other hand, a "giant tribe" ["Riesenstamm"] of violent, strong, criminally arrogant people "who see themselves as sons of the gods" ["vermeintliche Göttersöhne"] (40). This leads Schlegel to distinguish between a noble tribe of God seekers and those who seek merely nature and its power (41). In essence this is the difference between "religion and irreligion" ["Religion und Irreligion"], a division that is still valid according to Schlegel also among his contemporaries (41). Schlegel does want his theory of humankind's early history to be understood as factual and historically accurate, but argues that this can be established by studying "poetry" ["die Poesie"], with which in this context he means sagas and the oldest available historical accounts which, even if they are poetically embellished, are nevertheless expressions of a historical truth (43). By making "poetry" into a conduit to culture, Schlegel returns to his early thoughts on the centrality of an aesthetic approach to reality in order to make sense of life.[25] More specifically in the new context, he is interested in the biblical story of Cain and Abel, but also Indian sagas that are referred to, but not discussed in detail. Humankind's divine mission is visible in "the word that is innate or imparted to humans" ["das dem Menschen eingeborne oder ihm verliehene Wort"], picking up on the first verses of the Gospel of John that "in the beginning was the word"; the "word" epitomizes for Schlegel the essence of what it means to be human, and can be studied in many different forms in "language and writing, holy transmission and historical saga, poetry, art, and science" ["Sprache und Schrift, heilige Überlieferung und historische Sage, Dichtung, Kunst und Wissenschaft"] with the help of what Schlegel terms "the ethnographical method" ["die ethnograpische Methode"] (50).

Consistent within this framework of his philosophical history, Schlegel focuses on the ca. fifteen "cultured countries" ["Kulturländer"], all belonging to Asia and Europe and mirroring how civilization developed from southeastern Asia to north-western Europe (55). He legitimates this through the "pyramid of languages" ["Sprachenpyramide"] he develops later in his lectures: the oldest languages (like Chinese) work with one-syllable sounds and basic words; a second group, consisting of the noblest languages (Indian-Persian, Greek-Latin, and Gothic-Germanic) have two-syllable roots and their basic structure ["Grundstruktur"] is characterized by an advanced grammar; a third group, mainly consisting of Semitic languages like Hebrew and Arabic, is characterized by three-syllable root-words, but does not have an advanced grammar, tends toward monotony, and is not capable of "poetic diversity" ["poetische Mannigfaltigkeit"] or advanced scientific expression (140–41).[26]

Through this genealogical view, Schlegel operationalizes a cultural argument that already can be found in Herder. His way of proceeding is hierarchical in two ways: (1) he distinguishes between areas of the world with and without culture and (2) within the cultured world he identifies a middle group characterized by an ideal cultural development that needs to be distinguished from both more primitive cultures (the Chinese) and cultures whose languages have become too complex to be fully functional (Hebrew, Arabic). Schlegel does not want to exclude the possibility that Hebrew, once more research has been done, might be close to the "Indian-Greek family of languages" ["indisch-griechische Sprachfamilie"], but also points in this context to the mixing of peoples that makes it harder to identify specific language types (142); later in his text he again highlights the Hebrews as an example of this (151). Schlegel clearly wants to accommodate Hebrew (and with it, the early Christians) as central to European culture, but simultaneously argues that the Jews later lost touch with this heritage, symbolized by Jerusalem and the symbolically important temple of Solomon that were of central importance to the crusaders (150). In interpreting this material, Schlegel repeats the importance of the notion of humanity as the mirror image of God (153, 164) and criticizes Enlightenment thinkers who emphasize the perfectibility of humans, but ignore their corruptibility (154–55). He who believes in reason alone will be engaged in an eternal struggle with himself (158); materialism and the doctrine of atoms are expressions of a misguided reason (162). It is important to understand the concept of man as the mirror image of God as the natural beginning of religion, not a "random symbol or a mere allegory invented by poets" ["ein bloß willkürliches Symbol, oder ein bloßes Dichtergleichnis"] (164), which, without a doubt, is meant as a critique not only of Enlightenment thinking, but also of some Romantic thinkers who took religion to be more spiritual and less institutional, including, perhaps, his younger self.

For Schlegel, the "primacy of the current European spiritual mindset" ["Vorrang der jetzigen europäischen Geistesbildung"]—which Schlegel takes to be Christian or, to be more specific, Catholic—is demonstrated by the "facts of world history or cultural certainty" ["weltgeschichtliche Fakta, oder Kulturtatsachen"] that this mindset not only dominates other parts of the world in Schlegel's time but also ruled in most periods of the past (160). The success of Christianity, in other words, proves not only its superiority but also its truth. Instead of using philosophical anthropology to criticize European colonialism, as Raynal, de Pauw, and Blumenbach had done, Schlegel uses European colonial successes as an indicator of European and Christian cultural superiority. He concludes his lectures with a defense of a monarchy (nineteenth-century Austria) on a Christian (Catholic) basis (410).

In Schlegel's view, philosophy as anthropology has the task to provide humankind guidance, meaning that it is to remind humankind of its spiritual needs (of which only the Catholic church can take care). Romantic philosophy, as Schlegel conceives of it in the final stage of his intellectual development, allies itself not so much with the natural sciences—although Schlegel likes to think of his language studies as part of science—but rather with the written word. Other, non-European cultures are of interest to Schlegel only to the extent that their writings can be situated in a genealogy in which Schlegel's concept of Christianity is central (it is not only the starting, but also the end point). In this, the later Schlegel defends an unabashed Euro-centrism, which is certainly at odds with the views he held in his early Romantic phase of thought. The normative framework developed by Schlegel after his conversion to Catholicism in 1808 is quite different from that of Buffon and his followers who accepted the rationality of all cultures, by understanding them as (rational) responses to climate and geography. While for these Enlightenment thinkers all peoples have their own brand of culture (even if some of these may be more developed than others), Schlegel distinguishes between those with and without culture.

Within European society the conflict between those with and without culture returns in Schlegel's text as a conflict between those believing in humans as the mirror image of God and those adhering to science and materialism. What is more, to Schlegel "poetry," understood in the broadest possible sense, is meant to guide humans back to the only true religion, away from a rational and materialist world view. This is in line with the early German Romantics' search for a "new mythology" that was meant to compensate for rationalist fallacies (and was also popular among later Romantics).[27] Schlegel, in his *Philosophie der Geschichte*, recognizes the legitimacy of philosophy, of what he calls "poetry," and of theology as separate disciplines which each in their own way mediate humankind's cultural knowledge (while anthropology and ethnology appear to be subsumed under philosophy). And yet, in his lectures, Schlegel also does much to collapse the separate identities of these disciplines: in the end, "poetry" and philosophy have a subservient role to theology; they are meant to confirm the truth of Schlegel's brand of theology. These are ideas that take us very far away from the far more critical attitude toward any form of ideological certainty of the young Schlegel who helped formulate the program of early Romanticism, but that, as we saw, do also build on concepts that play already a key role in Schlegel's early thinking (in particular "poetry," the idea of a "new mythology," and the role of aesthetics in making sense of the world).

There is no anti-Semitism in Schlegel's *Philosophie der Geschichte* that resembles the anti-Semitism we found in Arnim's "Die Majorats-Herren." (The fact that Schlegel was married to one of Moses Mendelssohn's daughters, Dorothea, who was born as Brendel Mendelssohn, may have something to do with this.[28]) And yet, some of the attitudes that inform Arnim's novella are remarkably similar to issues Schlegel raises in his lectures. Both share an aversion against the French Revolution, which turns into more than an argument against the revolution itself—the emancipatory and egalitarian agenda of the revolution is seen as endangering the essence of what it means to be German. For both thinkers Germany and the German intellectual and cultural tradition are central. Both Schlegel and Arnim utilize exclusionary mechanisms along the lines of an "us–against–them" dynamic, in which the concept of "culture" plays a key role: history is seen as a conflict between those with and those without culture. The past in Arnim's novella is as much of an artificial construction as the (highly subjective) cultural genealogy offered in Schlegel's lectures—both have little to do with a factual reconstruction of times past. While, in contrast to Arnim's text, there is no open racism in Schlegel's lectures, it is quite clear that Schlegel's cultural argument could easily be given a racist dimension (and in fact in Arnim's text cultural inferiority has a clear racial dimension as well—for instance if one thinks of his portrayal of Vashti). In particular Schlegel's already discussed observation that humankind at times can "turn wild and degenerate" ["verwildern und entarten"] (36) is to be interrogated for the biological imagery it uses.

Does this mean that the legacy of German Romanticism consists solely of a history of ethnocentrism, nationalism, and intolerance? No, it doesn't. There is a continuation of a mode of contemplation of the globe and its nature and habitation that is reminiscent of Buffon, Blumenbach, and Georg Forster and that can be found, for instance, in the writings of Alexander von Humboldt (1769–1859), who had studied with Blumenbach at the University of Göttingen. Take for instance the following passage from his popular *Views of Nature* [*Ansichten der Natur*], first held as public lectures in Berlin in 1806, then published in 1808, and republished in 1826 and 1860, and based on his travels in South America (1799–1804)—a project that through the range of geography covered does not lend itself for the kind of national fervor we found in Arnim and Schlegel. After having compared the spread of humanity with that of plant coverage, Humboldt argues that "knowledge of the natural characteristics of different areas of the world is connected with the history of humankind, and with its culture, in the closest possible way. [...] the direction of this culture, the character of the people, the peoples' dark or cheerful mood depend to a large extent on climatological factors" ["die Kenntnis von dem Naturcharakter verschiedener Weltgegenden ist mit der Geschichte des Menschengeschlechts, und mit der seiner Kultur aufs innigste verknüpft. [...] so hängt doch die Richtung derselben [Kultur], so hängen Volkscharakter, düstere oder heitere Stimmung der Menschheit, großenteils von klimatischen Verhältnissen ab"].[29] Humboldt's move to connect geography with culture does suggest an interest in explaining not only humankind's biology, but also its culture as the result of cause and effect—the principle of causality—and in ways very similar to those proposed by Enlightenment anthropologist Buffon.

## 22 Romantic Philosophy as Anthropology

And yet, that is not the whole story. Already in the very first lines of the text, Humboldt writes of the "lively senses" ["regsamen Sinne"] with which humans investigate nature, and the "phantasy" ["Phantasie"] used by humankind to measure wide spaces—terms that emphasize the subjective character/disposition of humankind's appreciation of nature, its emotional impact and multiplicity; he writes of "manifold impressions" ["vielfache Eindrücke"] (1).[30] Humboldt returns to the topic at the very end of the essay, when he laments the fact that Nordic peoples are not able to enjoy the richness of tropical nature and its wide variety (especially in areas with mountains, where one finds the products of different climates closely together). It is impossible to reproduce tropical nature successfully in green houses; at best they offer a sickly and bleak mirror image (46). However, here too human creativity may be able to help out: "in the creations of our language, in the glowing phantasy of the poet, in the figurative art of painters, a rich source of replacement is opened. From it the imagination creates lively images of an exotic nature" ["in der Ausbildung unserer Sprache, in der glühenden Phantasie des Dichters, in der darstellenden Kunst der Maler, ist eine reiche Quelle des Ersatzes geöffnet. Aus ihr schöpft die Einbildungskraft die lebendigen Bilder einer exotischen Natur"] (46). Clearly, Humboldt stays within the limits of the territorial understanding of alterity: for Humboldt too, culture is linked to climate and geography. What Schlegel called "poetry"—a kind of cultural condensation of humankind's creative forces—has a clear function for Humboldt as well, but a very different one from Schlegel. Humboldt is interested in mobility; in his view it is a loss that those living in the North cannot partake in the nature of the tropics. One of the functions of art is to compensate for this—to bridge the distance and substitute for a mobility that is not available. Humboldt sees this function as something positive. The aesthetic functions as a bridge, not only between North and South, but also between science and imagination. Culture does not separate peoples, as it does for Herder for instance, but it connects them by appealing to a sense of curiosity common to all humans.

To the second volume of the *Ansichten der Natur* Humboldt added a fictional story, "The Life Force or the Genius of Rhodes" ["Die Lebenskraft oder der Rhodische Genius"],[31] an addition meant to illustrate the links between philosophy, art, and nature. The people of ancient Syracuse adore one of the paintings among the city's possessions, "The Genius of Rhodes," and speculate about its possible meanings, until one day another, very similar painting is brought to town depicting a slightly different scene, but with the same figures. A philosopher, Epicharmus, a student of Pythagoras who is interested in explaining the forces of nature, is asked to explain both paintings, something he does promptly. He interprets the original painting—young men and women stretching their arms toward each other, with the genius holding a torch and a butterfly on his shoulder floating in their middle—as an illustration of a synthetic power, the "force of life" ["*Lebenskraft*"] (198), while the newer painting offers in his view an "image of death" ["*Bild des Todes*"] (198)—the genius stands with his head dropped, the butterfly has disappeared, the torch is burned out, and the young people are tangled up and, so we are given to understand, about to engage in intercourse.

Here too we find mobility and curiosity as basic characteristics of human interaction: part of the paintings' puzzle is that they both have been moved from their place of origin (Rhodes) to Syracuse, as a result of which their original meaning is no longer known. In the paintings, nature is depicted as in development, in line with natural history since Buffon; development can mean improvement or decline, and humans are capable of both. The story emphasizes commonality—it considers all humans part of nature, and also assumes they share basic traits. The story allows for a certain hermeneutic playfulness: before Epicharmus explains the original painting's meaning, citizens of Syracuse engage in a game of competing interpretations (191). The story does justice to the Romantic notion that our way of making sense of the world is fundamentally aesthetic, as expressed in Schlegel's notion of "poetry." Humboldt's text is clearly meant to be programmatic in the way in which it configures art and philosophy in relation to nature: philosophy needs art—the mediation that art offers—in order to understand nature; all three interact with one another, but maintain their own identity rather than being collapsed. Here too, imagination plays a key role; it is through human imagination that philosophical concepts are connected to empirical reality (nature). The text combines basic components of Romantic philosophy and aesthetics, but maintains a cosmopolitan impulse that is lost in many other Romantic texts.

Humboldt is an integral part of the German Romantic Movement, and his work is not free of the problematic side of German Romanticism that I have profiled. While Humboldt spoke out against colonial abuse by the West and slavery,[32] he nevertheless assumed a civilatory mission for Europeans in South America, and his works were later used to legitimate Germany's nationalist and colonialist ambitions.[33] Without a doubt, he saw the relationship between Europe and South America as one of "authority, hierarchy, alienation, dependency" and "Eurocentrism."[34] In his conversations with Thomas Jefferson, whose residence in Washington Humboldt passed on his way back to Europe from his trip to South America, he was happy to share his knowledge of Mexico's geography and nature, with the purpose of facilitating the United States' taking possession of contested areas.[35] By focusing primarily on landscapes and on the people living in those landscapes as absent or as a secondary concern, Humboldt does repeat old colonial narrative strategies. To categorize Humboldt's texts as "Romantic" is correct within a European framework and is helpful in understanding why he saw South America the way he did, but it ignores that the territories described were in the process of liberating themselves from Europe, and thus, at the very least, gives a very different meaning to what "Romantic" means when applied to them.[36] To his credit, Humboldt (and his assistant Bonpland) did speak to Spanish American intellectuals, and in divulging their knowledge functioned as transcultural mediators; one can add to this that Humboldt's work often functioned as inspiration for South American intellectuals, seeking to free themselves from the continent's colonial past.[37]

When thinking of texts like those by Arnim, Schlegel, and Humboldt that I have discussed here as expressions of a Romantic view of cultural diversity, it is important to be aware, that many of the philosophical ideas with which the early German Romantics approach other cultures have roots in pre-Romantic thinking. The notion of (biological and cultural) decline is not particular to German Romanticism alone, but already has roots in Enlightenment anthropology and the temporalization of natural history it set into motion. Also, the term "race" entered public discourse during the late Enlightenment, and one of the major Enlightenment thinkers, Immanuel Kant, played a major role in its introduction. The connection linking territory, culture, and alterity is inherited from Enlightenment anthropology as well (Humboldt in this respect is quite indebted to Blumenbach and Buffon). German Romanticism, however, also reinforced these ideas—something that explains at least in part why they have come to be identified with the legacy of German Romanticism. To some extent the Romantic response to the Enlightenment is motivated by the idea that radical Enlightenment thinking would go too far in endangering society's institutions; German Romanticism seeks to counter this radicalism, politically and philosophically.

There is without a doubt an intolerant side to German Romanticism; and this strand of intolerance should be of concern to us, but it may also help us understand the phenomenon of intolerance in German history. We tend to think of the history of intolerance as a history of racism, and indeed Arnim's text "Die Majorats-Herren" uses biological imagery to point to the inferiority of some of its characters. But often the argument for one's own nation's superiority (also) uses culture. Schlegel uses a separation between countries with culture ("Kulturländer") and those without as a means to construct a linear genealogy which has German culture as an endpoint (and quite possibly also highpoint). Sometimes notions of "race" and "culture" supplement each other, as is the case in "Die Majorats-Herren," in which Germany's cultural decline is linked to the infiltration by Jews who are portrayed as racially inferior.

If one looks at the actual reception history of German Romanticism, one can find arguments both for and against the thesis that Romanticism fosters an interest in otherness. Romanticism has been read as a source of nationalism, but also of anti-colonial movements and as fostering an interest in other cultures; it contributed to Nazi ideology, but also fostered an interest in environmentalism; it inspired the music of Wagner and Mahler, the films of Hans-Jürgen Syberberg and Werner Herzog, and the literary works of authors as diverse as Ernst Jünger, Hermann Hesse, and Christa Wolf. When examining specifically the legacy of Romanticism for German culture's and intellectual history's conceptualization of cultures seen as "other," this means that scholars face the difficult task of thinking of an interest in alterity and an emphasis on one's own identity (one's own "nation") as inextricably linked—as two sides of the same coin, of the same movement. The anti-Semitism that one can find articulated in Herder's *Ideen* and a number of texts by the German Romantics is not incidental, but tied to the question of how these thinkers conceptualize other cultures more generally. It is therefore a simplification to emphasize Herder's and the Romantics' anti-colonialism and cultural relativism without addressing their dislike of cultures perceived as mobile (such as the Jews and the Gypsies); both of these are related and closely intertwined.

Romanticism has left us with a highly ambiguous and richly varied legacy—a legacy that comes in many shapes and forms. To some extent this was by design; Romantic thinking was intended as a thinking in fragments, and it was meant to question our sense of certainty about the reality surrounding us. It may well be that the very multiplicity of Romanticism, the diversity of impulses lurking within the term "Romanticism," and the many shapes it has taken, which so affected its reception, are precisely what makes its study worthwhile. If anything, Romantic philosophy as anthropology makes it clear that there is not, and never was, one main trajectory for German culture, but rather that it lent itself to be taken in many different directions. Romanticism's perception of other cultures consisted of a number of simultaneous and related, but also varied, impulses, some of which seek to mobilize other cultures in the service of German culture and the German nation, while others aim for a better understanding of other (non-European) cultures on their own terms.[38] Romantic thinking can be deeply racist and anti-Semitic, but also progressively anti-colonial. A guiding thread in the Romantic discussions around race and culture is the link between culture and territory and the fear of mobility, links that at times still determine our thinking today. German Romanticism remains a relevant source for our thinking on those discussions today.

# Notes

1. Cf. Jonathan I. Israel, *Democratic Enlightenment: Philosophy, Revolution, and Human Rights 1750–1790* (Oxford: Oxford University Press, 2011):648–83. Regarding the pan-European popularity of the term "anthropology" in the late eighteenth century, see Han F. Vermeulen, *Before Boas: The Genesis of Ethnography and Ethnology in the German Enlightenment* (Lincoln, NE / London, UK: University of Nebraska Press, 2015), 362, who points out that between 1770 and 1800 forty-three books were printed using a form of "anthropology" in their titles.
2. Anon., *Histoire philosophique et politique des établissements et du commerce des Européens dans les deux Indes* (Amsterdam, 1770), no author or publisher listed. A bibliography of the forty-nine editions of Raynal's *Histoire des deux Indes* published between 1770 and 1843 can be found at http://www.abbe-raynal.org/histoire-des-deux-indes.html.
3. Mr. de P***, *Recherches philosophiques sur les Américains ou Mémoires intéressants pour servir l'Histoire de l'Espèce humaine*, 2 vols. (Berlin: George Jacques Decker, 1768, 1769); a third volume, including a defense of the previous volumes by the author, appeared in 1770.
4. [Georges-Louis Leclerc de] Buffon / [Louis Jean-Marie] Daubenton, *Histoire naturelle générale et particulière*, vol. 3 (Paris: Imprimerie royale, 1749), 530. The methodological importance of Buffon for the natural sciences, and in particular of the first three volumes of his *Histoire naturelle*, is often overlooked today, but is emphasized by older scholar like Ernst Cassirer in his *Die Philosophie der Aufklärung* (Hamburg: Felix Meiner, 1998), 102–07. See also Wolf Lepenies, *Das Ende der Naturgeschichte. Wandel kultureller Selbstverständlichkeiten in den Wissenschaften des 18. und 19. Jahrhunderts* (Muenich/Vienna: Hanser, 1976), 58–62, 71–72, and 75.
5. See Simón Gallegos Gabilondo, *Les mondes du voyageur. Une épistémologie de l'exploration (XVIe—XVIIIe siècle)* (Paris: Éditions de la Sorbonne, 2018), 232; the author discusses Buffon as the model for this type of philosophical approach. The *Encyclopédie*'s article "PHILOSOPHE" from 1765, authored by César Chesneau Dumarsais, speaks of the need to break the obstacles that religion has put in the way of reason ("ils ont brisé les entraves où la foi mettoit leur raison") to instead look for causes and live according to the insights gained; in: *Encyclopédie ou dictionnaire raisonné des sciences, des arts et des métiers*, vol. 12 (Neufchatel: Samuel Fauche, 1765), 509–11, here 509.
6. This distinction can be traced back to Melchior Grimm who reported on this division in his *Correspondance littéraire, philosophique et critique*, 2nd. ed., vol. 1 (Paris: F. Buisson, 1812), 490 (dated May 1771); see also Jonathan Israel, *Democratic Enlightenment*, 67–68, and https://fr.wikipedia.org/wiki/Parti_philosophique.

7. *Herrn von Buffons allgemeine Naturgeschichte. Eine freije mit einigen Zusätzen vermehrte Übersetzung nach der neuesten französ: Außgabe von 1769*. 7 vols. (Berlin: Joachim Pauli Buchhändler, 1771–1774).
8. John H. Zammito, *Kant, Herder, and the Birth of Anthropology* (Chicago and London: University of Chicago Press, 2002), 292–93.
9. See Zammito, for instance, *op. cit.*, 178–220, 278.
10. Kant, *Von den verschiedenen Racen der Menschen zur Ankündigung der Vorlesungen der physischen Geographie im Sommerhalbenjahre 1775* (Königsberg: Hartung, 1775), 2–3; Kant refers to Buffon, *Histoire naturelle*, vol. 4 (1753), 385–86.
11. Kant, 8.
12. See my essay "Buffon, Blumenbach, Lichtenberg, and the Origins of Modern Anthropology," in: *Johann Friedrich Blumenbach: Race and Natural History, 1750–1850*, edited by Nicolaas Rupke and Gerhard Lauer (Oxon, UK / New York: Routledge, 2019): 27–52, here, 37 and 39.
13. See Steffen Martus, *Aufklärung. Das deutsche Jahrhundert—ein Epochenbild* (Berlin: Rowohlt, 2014), 13 and 844.
14. As Robert Bernasconi has pointed out, the section of the 1797 edition of Blumenbach's *Handbuch der Naturgeschichte* that introduces the concept of "race" contains a footnote that can be read as endorsement by Blumenbach of Kant's thoughts on the matter: "This difference between races and varieties was first determined precisely by Prof. Kant in the Teutscher Merkur 1788, 1 B, 48" ["Diesen Unterschied zwischen Rassen und Spielarten hat zuerst Hr. Prof. Kant genau bestimmt, im teutschen Mercur 1788. 1. B. S. 48"] (Blumenbach, *Handbuch der Naturgeschichte*, 5th ed. [Göttingen: Johann Christian Dieterich, 1797]: 23; see Bernasconi, "Kant and Blumenbach's *Polyps*: A Neglected Chapter in the History of the Concept of Race," in: *The German Invention of Race*, ed., Sara Eigen and Mark Larrimore [Albany: SUNY Press, 2006]: 73–90, here 84]. In his corrections to the same edition of his *Handbuch*, Blumenbach adds to his note the following comment (overlooked by Bernasconi): "see regarding this matter in detail Mr. Privy Council Girtanner on the Kantian Principle and Natural History 1796. 8" ["s. hiervon ausführlich Hrn. Geh. Hoft. Girtanner über das Kantische Princip für die Naturgeschichte. Göttingen, 1796. 8"] (24); Blumenbach refers here to Christoph G. Girtanner, *Über das Kantische Prinzip für Naturgeschichte. Ein Versuch diese Wissenschaft philosophisch zu behandeln* (Göttingen: Vandenhoek und Ruprecht, 1796). This example shows that Kant's anthropological thinking only gradually gained in acceptance by the scientific community, and only after his three critiques had established his reputation.
15. Johann Gottfried Herder, *Auch eine Philosophie der Geschichte zur Bildung der Menschheit, Werke in zehn Bänden*, vol. 4, ed, Jürgen Brummack and Martin Bollacher (Frankfurt a.M.: Deutscher Klassiker Verlag, 1994):10–107, here, 38–39. Chunjie Zhang points to the central role of this statement in litera-

## 22  Romantic Philosophy as Anthropology  531

ture arguing for Herder's cultural relativism (*Transculturality and German Discourse in the Age of European Colonialism* [Evanston, IL: Northwestern University Press, 2017], 119–20), but, quite correctly, also points to the many inconsistencies in Herder's thinking about relativism 120; see also endnotes 5 and 6, at 213).

16. Herder, *Ideen zur Philosophie der Geschichte der Menschheit, Werke in zehn Bänden*, ed. Martin Bollacher, vol. 6 (Frankfurt a.M.: Deutscher Klassiker Verlag, 1989), 251, 256. Parenthetical page references in the following refer to this text.
17. See in this context John K. Noyes's argument that Herder's thought accepts reason as universal (something that makes humans human) that however can only exist as a plurality and manifests itself in many different ways (*Herder: Aesthetics against Imperialism* [Toronto Buffalo / London: University of Toronto Press, 2015], 301–02).
18. See Sankar Muthu who points to the juxtaposition of sedentary and nomadic cultures in Herder's work in *Enlightenment against Empire* (Princeton/Oxford: Princeton University Press, 2003), 238–39, 243–44. See my essay "The Romantics and other Cultures," in: *The Cambridge Companion to German Romanticism*, ed. Nicholas Saul (Cambridge: Cambridge University Press, 2009): 147–62, in particular the section on Jews and Gypsies as outsiders in Romantic culture (152–56), for a further elaboration of this point.
19. I take this title from the translation by Alan Brown (London, UK: Atlas Press, 1990). All translations from Arnim's text in the following are my own.
20. Achim von Arnim, "Die Majorats-Herren," *Werke in sechs Bänden*, vol. 4, ed. Renate Moering (Frankfurt a.M.: Deutscher Klassiker Verlag, 1992):107–47, here 107. Parenthetical references in the text in the following refer to this edition.
21. See "The Romantics and other Cultures" 155; Heinz Härtl, "Romantischer Antisemitismus. Arnim und die 'Tischgesellschaft,'" in *Weimarer Beiträge* 33 (1987):1159–73, and Stefan Nienhaus, *Geschichte der deutschen Tischgesellschaft* (Tübingen: Niemeyer, 2003). A concise summary of the development of Romantic anti-Semitism can be found in Detlef Kremer, Romantik, 3rd. ed. (Stuttgart / Weimar, J.B. Metzler, 2007), 14–15.
22. Friedrich Schlegel, *Philosophie der Geschichte. In achtzehn Vorlesungen gehalten zu Wien im Jahre 1828*. Edited by Jean-Jacques Anstett (Muenich / Paderborn / Vienna / Zuerich: Ferdinand Schöningh / Thomas-Verlag, 1971), 3. Parenthetical page references in the following refer to this text.
23. Elizabeth Millán distinguishes between Schlegel's "classical" phase characterized by his "Objektivitätswut" (1793–96), a romantic phase (Fall 1796–1808), and a "conservative" phase (1808–1829) in *Friedrich Schlegel and the Emergence of Romantic Philosophy* (Albany: SUNY Press, 2007), 10–11.
24. Note that Schlegel here uses the term "entarten"—a term that would have a long political reception well into the Third Reich—while Blumenbach, for

instance, uses the terms "verarten" and "ausarten"; see "Buffon, Blumenbach, Lichtenberg, and the Origins of Modern Anthropology" (see endnote 12), 38, 41.

25. "Poetry" ["Poesie"] plays a central role in Schlegel's early thinking; poetry allows for an intuition of the infinite in a finite form, and in fact it makes art central to society (see Manfred Frank, *Einführung in die frühromantische Ästhetik* [Frankfurt a.M.: Suhrkamp, 1989], 291–92); it creates a social community, and the term is linked to humans' purposeful acting (as in the Greek term *poiesis*) (see Matthias Löwe, "Universalpoesie," in *Friedrich Schlegel Handbuch. Leben—Werk—Wirkung*, edited by Johannes Endres [Stuttgart: J.B. Metzler, 2017], 331–33, here 331 and 333.

26. Schlegel builds these theories on earlier linguistic work in his (influential) book *On the Language and Wisdom of the Indians* [*Über die Sprache und Weisheit der Indier*] from 1808, where he argues for Sanskrit as the root of old Persian, Greek, Latin, and ultimately also the Germanic languages, thus excluding large parts of the Orient from his Germanic genealogy (see "The Romantics and other Cultures," 151).

27. The term "new mythology" ["neue Mythologie"] first appears in the so-called *Oldest Systematic Program of German Idealism* [*Das älteste Systemprogramm des deutschen Idealismus*] (1796/1797?), a text that seeks an aesthetic legitimation of life out of a critique of the "Machinenstaat" (see Manfred Frank, *Der kommende Gott. Vorlesungen über die neue Mythologie* [Frankfurt a.M.: Suhrkamp, 1982], 153ff, esp. 162 and 194). Long before the *Ältestes Systemprogramm* Herder had already been arguing for a rehabilitation of "myth" in his *Vom neueren Gebrauch der Mythologie* from 1767 (ibid. 124); Schlegel contributed to the debate through his *Rede über die Mythologie* from 1800 (205–09). While Schlegel envisions a universal mythology beyond national borders, he simultaneously, according to Frank, considers suspect what is "*esoteric, not generally communicable*" ["das *Esoterische, das nicht allgemein Mitteilbare*"], which he associates with the Enlightenment which has fragmented ["zersplittert"] humankind (ibid. 209).

28. Also late in life, after his turn to Catholicism, in a series of articles from 1815 and 1816 Friedrich Schlegel defended the freedom to practice Judaism and civil rights for Jews, understanding Jews as a religiously defined community, in the expectation however that eventually Judaism and Protestantism would merge into Catholicism; see Jeffrey S. Librett, *The Rhetoric of Cultural Dialogue: Jews and Germans from Moses Mendelssohn to Richard Wagner and Beyond* (Stanford: Stanford University Press, 2000), 219–20, 350–51.

29. Alexander von Humboldt, "Ideen zu einer Physiognomik der Gewächse," in *Ansichten der Natur, mit wissenschaftlichen Erläuterungen*, vol. 2 (Stuttgart / Tübingen: J.G. Cotta, 1826): 1–47, here 19 (see also 9–10). Parenthetical references in the text in the following refer to this edition. An earlier version of this text was published in volume 1 of the first edition of *Ansichten der*

*Natur* (Tübingen: J.G. Cotta, 1808): 157–204. A bibliography of Alexander von Humboldt's writings, including digital copies of the different editions of *Ansichten der Natur*, can be found at http://www.avhumboldt.de/?page_id=5.

30. Concerning the *Ansichten der Natur,* Mary Louise Pratt writes of an "interweaving of visual and emotive language with classificatory and technical language"; see *Imperial Eyes: Travel Writing and Transculturation* (London / New York: Routledge, 1992), 121.
31. "Die Lebenskraft oder der Rhodische Genius. Eine Erzählung," in *Ansichten der Natur*, vol. 2 [1826]:187–200. Parenthetical references in the text in the following refer to this edition. The text was originally published in *Die Horen*, vol. 1, no. 5, 1795:90–96. In the third edition of *Ansichten der Natur* Humboldt added comments meant to clarify the scientific issues raised by the story; cf. *Ansichten der Natur, mit wissenschaftlichen Erläuterungen*, vol. 2 (Stuttgart / Augsburg: J.G. Cotta, 1860): 222–25.
32. See Andrea Wulf, *The Invention of Nature: Alexander von Humboldt's New World* (New York: Knopf, 2016), 53, 106–08.
33. See "The Romantics and other Cultures," *op. cit.*, 149.
34. Pratt, *Imperial Eyes, op. cit.*, 197.
35. See Wulf, *The Invention of Nature, op. cit.,* 102–03.
36. See Pratt, *Imperial Eyes, op. cit.*, 137–38, 140; on Humboldt and Romantic ideology see also 115, 121, and 124.
37. See Pratt, *Imperial Eyes, op. cit.,* 182, 188, and 197.
38. While I welcome attempts to come to a pluralistic understanding of German Romanticism such as Rüdiger Görner's "pluralectic" view of Romanticism, it would be wrong, in my view, to see Alexander von Humboldt's *Kosmos* (1845–1862) as a kind of culmination point of a Romantic interest in a pluralist view of other cultures (for which the Romantic interest in India and Novalis are supposed to serve as examples). Görner simultaneously argues that in *Kosmos* Humboldt is interested in these worlds in their interplay with the German world (cf. *Die Pluralektik der Romantik. Studien zu einer epochalen Denk- und Darstellungsform* [Vienna / Cologne / Weimar: Böhlau, 2010], 44). Precisely the trend to think of "other" cultures in relation to German culture explains some of the problems with German Romanticism, as I hope to have shown above.

# 23

# From the Pantheism Panic to Modern Anxiety: Friedrich Schelling's Invention of the Philosophy of "Angst"

Jeffrey S. Librett

*The greatest part of humanity turns away from the things hidden within, just as they turn away from the depths of life in general, and are afraid to gaze into the abysses of that past, which is still all too present within them*
—Schelling, *Ages of the World* (207–8; 3–4)

What follows is an attempt to expose what is at stake in the theme of anxiety—*Angst*—along with certain affective states or mood states thematized in close association with it (such as pain, loathing, and sadness) in Schelling's writings, *Philosophical Investigations of the Essence of Human Freedom and Related Matters* from 1809 (hereafter *Freedom*), and *Ages of the World* from 1815 (hereafter *Ages*).[1] The role of anxiety as a theme in Schelling is crucially important both as an element of his originality vis-à-vis the philosophical tradition that precedes him, and as an element of his powerful and enduring impact on the subsequent tradition. For Schelling is both one of the first modern philosophers—perhaps *the* first—to make anxiety central to his thinking, and the point of departure for the significant later theoretical treatments of anxiety, beginning with his admiring and critical student Kierkegaard especially (but even earlier, and in a different direction, with Schopenhauer), extending through Heidegger, Freud, and their followers and critics.[2] Before

---

J. S. Librett (✉)
University of Oregon, Eugene, OR, USA
e-mail: jlibrett@uoregon.edu

© The Author(s) 2020
E. Millán Brusslan (ed.), *The Palgrave Handbook of German Romantic Philosophy*, Palgrave Handbooks in German Idealism, https://doi.org/10.1007/978-3-030-53567-4_23

outlining my argument, it is necessary to say a few words about the larger context in which Schelling broaches the topic of anxiety. Why would anxiety suddenly become a crucial focus of philosophical discourse in the early nineteenth century?

To sketch briefly an answer to this question as a frame for the detailed textual examination that follows, I will draw on work by Odo Marquard, a student of Joachim Ritter, on the role of nature in romantic philosophy, as an aesthetically centered philosophy, that is, one intent on hovering between the possible and the real.[3] According to the narrower strand of this thought with which I will connect here, for Marquard—and in this view he is not alone—the discourse of the philosophy of history (*Geschichtsphilosophie*) as it arises in the Enlightenment—a teleological narrative of history as the realization of human freedom and the installation of human rights—encounters in the French Revolutionary Terror, in the Kantian "antinomies" of pure reason, and in many other ways what appears increasingly as an insurmountable obstacle to the program of human self-emancipation: nature itself. The romantic cult of nature—which Marquard reads as a kind of massive "reaction formation"—is the result. For if nature in some sense appears always to overpower the human attempt to articulate the world and to realize freedom in a rational form, then the task of human salvation in a quasi- or partially secularized age sees itself faced with a troubling question. Namely: how can the power of nature be managed—outside of the rational (technical and ethical) domination of nature, which confronts insuperable limits—so as to render it nonthreatening? Marquard's hypothesis is that the first answer the German Romantics and Idealists provide, which was already broached in Kant's *Critique of Judgment* (1790), is an aesthetic one, specifically the aesthetics of genius—as treated for example at the end of Schelling's *System of Transcendental Idealism* from 1800, and as elaborated in his *Philosophy of Art* from 1804 to 1805 (but the aesthetics of genius is quasi-ubiquitous in the period). Subsequently, as may appear at first surprising: to the degree that this aesthetic solution starts to seem inadequate, a medical-therapeutic solution is attempted. In this sequence of proposed solutions to the dangers of nature, Marquard traces the striking continuity from Schelling all the way to Freud.[4] As he shows, already in the age and work of Schelling, we see the beginnings of a long period of transition—perhaps persisting up to today—in which aesthetics fraternizes with medico-therapeutic discourses, and vice versa, and in which the medico-therapeutic discourses tend to supplant the aesthetic ones with which they intermingle. As divergent as these discourses are, the task of each, beginning with the romantic turn, as Marquard claims and begins to explore, is to make nature unthreatening (even if by aesthetically celebrating or enjoying its threatening character, as in the sublime and the uncanny), to enable us to imagine we can save ourselves from nature while remaining within it. But how do we get to the art of healing from the art of genius?

The question of how the genius accesses his creative power can lead us to the reasons for, and the point of passage. The genius accesses his power—which rivals that of nature, and thus models for all an (exceptional) escape from nature's power—by imitating nature's creativity. But if, as the genius-aesthetic requires, the genius is supposed to go expressively beyond the mimetic representation of historically given social reality by imitating the creative power of nature (where imitation takes on a magically apotropaic force), nature will have to be in some sense present and available to the genius, as the origin of his origination.[5] But since, as conscious historical beings, we exist—that is, our consciousnesses exist—not only objectively within nature but subjectively at some distance from nature; nature, as an origin with which we might fuse in an identity (and not just, as Hegel will maintain, art itself as medium of presentation of the Absolute), is over—it exists only in the past.[6] (One can think of a text like Schiller's "On Naive and Sentimental Poetry" or "The Gods of Greece" as an illustration of this reflection.) If nature is *past* for our *consciousness*, however, nature may still be *present* as *unconscious*.[7] And indeed it accords perfectly with this reconstruction of the logic of Romanticism's "natural philosophy of art" (384) that Schelling invents the unconscious as the site of nature (and is followed in this by other early German Romantics such as his student Carus).[8] But the art of the genius nonetheless turns out eventually to seem regressive and therefore inadequate, both insofar as it can only *unconsciously* access what is forever in the *past*, and insofar as it cannot ultimately prevent the destructive aspects of nature from exercising their deleterious effects on society and on the individual (and eventually on the genius him- or herself). Genius—always quixotic—is not only finite but borders on madness, and however sublime madness may be, unfortunately it is also useless as a form of protection. Hence, it is not surprising that later romantic philosophy (in the mature Schelling and again, e.g., in Schopenhauer) represents nature no longer primarily as a living organism but as a threatening chaos. The aesthetic solution is dissolving.

According to Marquard's most important suggestion, at least for a genealogy of anxiety in modern Western thought, the main way in which Western thought tries to address this problem is to have the art of genius exceed itself, and leave itself behind, transforming itself into (or replacing itself with) the art of healing (*Heilkunst*): the negativity of nature is henceforth to be experienced, and potentially survived, in the care of a medical doctor (387).[9]

Schelling and other romantic thinkers were, as is well known, in communication with medical scientists of their day, in connection with the nature-philosophical side of their activities and interests, and Carus was himself a medical doctor. In light of Marquard's schematically suggestive considerations, which I can only minimally adumbrate here, one can see that what connects Romanticism to modernism in the specific path that leads from Schelling to Freud is much more than the continuous elaboration of a notion of the unconscious in close connection with (and in some cases as identical with) the foundations of nature, but a larger project, within which this elaboration takes shape. This project is the task of managing the overpowering effects of a partially destructive nature in a world where God's existence is no longer assured, where the authority of historical revelations is increasingly questioned by their modern interpretation as mere historical documents of human cultural imagination (beginning roughly with Spinoza), and where the (partially) secularizing philosophy of history in its Enlightenment form has come to seem a utopian dream, or at any rate both superficial and precipitous. The situation is now one in which the fragile human being appears to itself increasingly as autonomous (and self-responsible) vis-à-vis a God of uncertain status, but also as both *within* nature and somehow separated *from* nature, yet despite our separation exposed to an indefinite fear of nature's dangers. In such a situation, it begins to be comprehensible that the theme of anxiety (perhaps still midway between the aesthetic and the medico-scientific solutions) will become an urgent concern for philosophical discourse.[10] Precisely this occurrence is what I wish to expose here in Schelling.

Now, the more *specific* discursive situation out of which Schelling's writings emerge, and in which nature appears as a threatening materiality as the upshot of an ostensibly failed Enlightenment philosophy of history, is the pantheism controversy. After sketching the start of this controversy, and then indicating the senses in which Moses Mendelssohn's contribution to the controversy forms an important point of departure for Schelling's contribution in *Freedom* and *Ages*, I turn first to the *Freedom* text. I start by outlining the contours of Schelling's project, an attempt to split the difference between naturalism—the affirmation of an unconscious nature as foundation—and Christian theology. I then show how the theme of anxiety functions in his argument, at the problematic—read: impossible—point of articulation between nature and divinity, the site of human freedom, where Schelling attempts but fails to conjure away the dangerous excess of nature. I proceed to examine *Ages*, in which Schelling repeats the project of *Freedom* on a larger scale, and where he develops the motif of anxiety more extensively. In tracing the motif of anxiety in *Ages*, I try to expose the functions and sense of anxiety on several levels, the levels of "negativity" per se (one dimension of God's "nature"), of God's "nature" as a whole, and of God's free act of creation (both within material created nature and—most strikingly—within God himself as creator). Because both *Freedom* and *Ages* develop a broadly panentheistic position, anxiety in both texts can be said to be the anxiety of God, but what emerges from tracking the references to anxiety in both texts is that in *Freedom* anxiety appears primarily as a natural and especially human affair, whereas in *Ages*, Schelling much more explicitly makes God himself subject to anxiety, and even to a "divine madness" in an unheard-of sense. I discuss briefly in conclusion the implications of this "divine madness"—a kind of sustained divine panic attack in which the Absolute appears as an aesthetic genius (or *poète maudit avant la lettre*).

# 1 The Pantheism Panic: The Danger of a Deterministic Nature

As is well-known, the pantheism controversy began when Friedrich Heinrich Jacobi, a counter-Enlightenment gadfly (whose anti-Judaism played no small role in his polemical interventions), provoked Moses Mendelssohn, a major representative of the late German Enlightenment and the first major Jewish-German participant in (relatively) secular discourse, into a debate over the significance and legacy of the Enlightenment.[11] Jacobi accomplished this feat by publicly impugning G.E. Lessing, a representative of the late Enlightenment who was both more important (e.g. more generically wide-ranging, and a brilliant internal critic of Lutheran dogmatism) and much more religio-socially acceptable than Mendelssohn "the Jew" (whom Lessing had enabled to participate in public discourse in the first place). Jacobi besmirched Lessing's reputation shortly after Lessing's death, by claiming that before dying Lessing had privately confessed to Jacobi that he had always been a secret Spinozist. At the time this meant being an atheist, materialist, and determinist, all very bad things, scandalous and naughty in the extreme. Thus, Jacobi launched the pantheism controversy by suggesting that the Enlightenment discourse was ultimately atheist, materialist, and determinist, and by associating these positions further with being not only Jewish (as was Spinoza), hence faithless (i.e. adherent to the dead letter of the law, rather than to the living spirit of faith and mercy), but a faithless Jew, one so faithless that even the (by definition) faithless Jews had excommunicated him.[12] Jacobi went on, moreover, to argue that Spinoza's philosophy represented nothing less than the culmination of reason, the implication being that autonomous reason must be abjured—rather than critically self-delimited, as Kant much more judiciously and rigorously argued—to make room for (Christian) faith. The discussion that ensued constitutes the pantheism controversy, which included important contributions by Mendelssohn himself, Herder, Kant, Fichte, Schelling, and Hegel (all of whom Jacobi attacked at different points), as well as many others, up through Kierkegaard and even Heidegger (in his two lecture courses on Schelling's "Freedom"-lectures, the second of which includes, and not by chance, a long excursus on Kierkegaard, Schelling's student). Notably for our purposes, Jacobi at one point characterized Fichte's thought as an inverted Spinozism, and as "nihilistic," in one of the inaugural usages of that term.[13]

From the very beginning of his career, Schelling was well aware of this debate, and indeed from his earliest published writings we can see him trying to mediate between Jacobi and Spinoza, that is, between a personalistic God and the claims of freedom, on the one hand, and an appreciation for both rationality and the materiality of nature, on the other hand. Likewise, Schelling's project, as soon as he had managed to gain some critical perspective on Fichte, was to mediate between Fichte's subjective Idealism (which Schelling understood to be effacing nature while making excessive claims for the sovereign independence of the absolute Ego) and Spinoza's materialism (whose geometrical rationalism, he found, resulted in the inadequate conception of nature as a "dead" mechanism). In some contexts, Schelling formulated this ideal-real opposition as one between Leibniz and Spinoza.[14] His aim was to provide the unifying chiasmus: at once an account of nature that showed its always already organic and spiritual character, and conversely an account of spirit that showed its embeddedness in material nature, as well as the clarification of how these two accounts fit within a single larger system. In sum, he wanted to show—in partial displacement of the phonologocentric Pauline motif that still, to some extent, governed his thinking—that the letter (of nature) lives and that the spirit lives *in* the letter. As I'll indicate below at several points, this displacement supported a certain "tolerant" dimension of his relationship to Judaic sources and ideas, both Biblical and Kabbalistic, within the context of his nonetheless increasingly "Christian" thought.[15]

While few scholars would claim that Schelling ever definitively achieved his systematic aims, what remains interesting about his thought is what happens along the way, and especially the persuasive power—and influence on the subsequent philosophical tradition—of his simultaneous insistence on the acknowledgment of the materiality and finitude of human existence—to which anxiety is fundamental—and on the importance of a continuing commitment to human reason and freedom within the context of this material, natural existence, despite the fact that the latter poses enduring limits to the capacity of the mind to master and determine its own origins.

## 2 Toward the *Freedom* Lectures: Moses Mendelssohn as Implicit Point of Departure

Within Schelling's general approach to the pantheism controversy, an approach that gave its enduring direction to his philosophical project despite the frequently derided "protean" character of his writings, the *Freedom* lectures constitute an important contribution. This is first of all the case insofar as Schelling answers here the accusation, which by this point had frequently been leveled against his *Naturphilosophie*, that it would efface the possibility of human freedom.[16] It is specifically in the context of this confrontation of the human with its freedom, which as we'll see is always for Schelling a freedom for good or evil, that anxiety will play, in *Freedom*, its crucial role.

In the service of his desire to do justice, by way of a panentheistic solution, both to pantheistic and to theistic traditions, to necessity and to freedom (and responsibility), Schelling takes off implicitly from three suggestions that Moses Mendelssohn had made in his main written response to Jacobi's provocative claims that Lessing had been a closeted Spinozist, *Morgenstunden: oder Vorlesungen über das Dasein Gottes* (1785). Firstly, in his attempt to mitigate the scandal of Spinozism, Mendelssohn argued there that Spinoza is not an atheist, but an *acosmist*, meaning that Spinoza presents a view of the world as it was when it was still within God, prior to the act of creation as such. Then secondly, having claimed that in Spinoza there is a world separate from God, even if an *uncreated* world, he goes on to question our capacity to distinguish between an uncreated and a created one. He does so by pointing to the inevitably metaphorical, indeed catachrestic character of any language purporting to determine whether creation occurs within God or beyond him, or whether the world is "inside" or "outside" of God. In short, Mendelssohn argued that the figural (and hence improper, only relatively or partially adequate) character of the inside-outside, form-content distinction—at the very least with reference to the attempt to determine the relationship between God and world, Absolute and relative, substance and modifications, creator and created—makes any particular doctrine based on this figure doctrinaire and dogmatic, because overweening, overly ambitious.[17] This argument, which functioned to render undecidable the difference between theism and pantheism, constituted a crucial element in his strategic defense of Lessing's "purified" Spinozism, and thereby of his attempt to redeem, so to speak, Enlightenment *tout court*.

Concerning the first point, Schelling can be seen to pick up where Mendelssohn left off here, and to go beyond him—granted that, needless to say, Mendelssohn is not the only thinker he's responding to here—by developing a panentheistic view of nature according to which nature is both inside and outside of God, both God and not quite God at once, each in a different sense.[18] In *Ages*, he will on the other hand distinguish explicitly between the creation as mere possibility within God's nature, and creation actualized (see below).

Concerning the second point, that is, Mendelssohn's emphasis on the figurality of language: Schelling will acknowledge this concern, but at the same time embrace metaphorical language, as well as anthropomorphism, in accordance with his view of human existence (including language) as an existence that retains a degree of opacity due to its enduring inscription in the materiality of nature.[19]

Thirdly, Mendelssohn was arguing in *Morgenstunden* that a certain pantheism—which he called "purified" pantheism—was not a-moral (whereas Jacobi, following a host of anti-Spinozists before him, had branded pantheism as unethical due to the deterministic aspect of Spinoza's *Ethics*). In a similar vein, albeit in an entirely different (post-Kantian and post-Fichtean) philosophical idiom, Schelling argues here precisely for the compatibility of a certain "dynamic" (i.e. no longer mechanistic and immobile) pantheism with human freedom and responsibility. Human freedom, on his account, becomes the radical freedom to choose or not to choose to accept one's situatedness within the totality of a spiritualized nature. To see how this looks in more detail, and what place *anxiety* occupies within Schelling's conception, we have to retrace—very selectively, given limits of space—the main elements of his theory of the dialectics of divine nature in their narrative unfolding.

## 3 Dialectics of Ground and Existence: From the Divine Nature to Human Freedom

Schelling begins to develop his position in *Freedom* by invoking the logical relation between antecedent and consequent, and applying this by way of natural philosophy to the structure of the self-revelation of God in and as creation. In natural philosophy, he says, one distinguishes, within the being (*Wesen*), between that which is the (antecedent) ground (*Grund*) or basis

(*Basis*) of that being's existence (*Existenz*), on the one hand, and its existence itself, on the other hand.

This opposition is applicable to the relation between God and nature for the following line of reasoning. Since, according to traditional conceptions, nothing can exist either *before* God or entirely *outside* of God, Schelling writes, God must have the ground of his existence *within* himself. As the Absolute, God must be self-grounding. The ground of God cannot be separated from God, Schelling continues, but yet it must differ from (the rest of) him, that is, from his existence *per se*, in order to be precisely the *ground* of this existence. It is this ground or foundation of God that Schelling now calls "nature" (and sometimes "the beginning nature" [or "initial nature" in Hayden-Roy's translation, *die anfängliche Natur*]) (360; 240).[20]

Three analogies—one drawn from natural science as Schelling conceived it, another drawn from the anthropomorphic sphere of human affective experience, and the third drawn from the philosophical discourse on faculties of knowledge—serve as his principal concretizations for the ground-existence conceptualization of the nature-God relation. (The manifestly analogical form of his thought here illustrates, let it be said here in passing, his acknowledgment of a necessarily rhetorical-poetical dimension in philosophical discourse, in line with the wish for a mythology of reason expressed in the famous fragment known as *Das älteste Systemprogramm des deutschen Idealismus*, of his youth.) First, ground is to existence as gravity (qua principle of materiality, darkness, and abyssal descent) is to light (qua principle of spirit, illumination, and ascent). Second, ground is to existence as "longing" (*Sehnsucht*) is to fulfillment, which Schelling phrases as the desire of the divinity for its own self-revelation, construing this desire as the "longing of the eternal One to give birth to oneself" [*die Sehnsucht, die das ewige Eine empfindet, sich selbst zu gebären*] (359; 238) On this (metaphorical-anthropomorphic) level, ground is to existence as the longing of the anthropomorphic God for its own birth is to that birth itself. This longing is, as the figure implies, a self-anticipatory longing, mixing together the image of the mother with that of the future child, but it is also the divided self-anticipation of a unity. Schelling's figure contradicts or complicates within itself the notion of giving-birth, since birth here would be not separation (as usually conceived), but the *overcoming* of separation, between mother and child. In turn, however, the figure also simplifies or resolves this complication, assuming that the "eternal One" qua child born would absorb the dark ground of the maternal origin into itself, and that conversely, the "mother" here disappears into her "child." (For the human being, this type of birth does not occur, however long the labor of longing lasts.) These two analogies, then, remain crucial to Schelling's conception of the ground-existence relationship, and he develops them throughout this text. Before seeing how he does so, however, it is necessary to consider a third analogy, this one taken from the facultative language he inherits through Kant and Fichte, which overdetermines this ground-existence couple as an opposition between will (*Wille*) and understanding (*Verstand*) (359ff; 238ff). Because the ground or will *anticipates* or *prefigures* the existence of God, or understanding in the most emphatic and elevated sense, the will is evidently here the *not-yet* of understanding. Accordingly, Schelling defines it as feeling (or intuiting) and as unconscious ("nicht ein bewußter, sondern ein ahnender Wille," 359; 238). And in turn, because for Schelling the will only achieves itself, or arrives at itself, when it becomes understanding, the ground (or the will) is also the mere self-anticipation of the will, its not-yet. The will is the not-yet of the not-yet of the understanding.[21] For the created world (i.e. the world in which we live), therefore, the ground is always underground, and indeed abyssal, but ever threatening to break through the surface: "immer liegt noch im Grunde das Regellose, als könnte es einmal wieder durchbrechen" (359;238). The quasi-invisible persistence of this ungraspable ("unergreifliche" [360; 238]) ground remains the condition of all creaturely reality. And it retains the character of a threatening danger. But conversely, the existence of God (as light, the eternal One, and understanding) conditions its ground, both because the structure is the structure of a dialectical process, and because within this structure God's ground belongs to God's existence as its ground.

What, then, is the position and essential structure of the *human* within this interplay of divine ground and existence? To arrive at the human, we have to trace in outline the process of creation per se. The first step in the process of creation out of this initial (and enduring) tension between ground and existence is that God discovers himself, conceives (of) himself, and represents himself to himself, as pure understanding, which Schelling now also calls the "word" (i.e. *logos*), and expresses this "word." The "word," as the (self)response of God to the longing of the ground, mediates between this blind longing and the clear light of understanding. Such mediation, the speaking of God's word, initiates creation per se, through the penetration of darkness by light (for the word is light), and the partial unification (of darkness with light) in or as the world itself (while they are always already unified only in God per se). But within creation (as both process and result), which is the unfolding of the dark ground of God's "nature" and its (plantlike) growth toward his light (or toward God's existence as light), there remains always a tension between darkness and light, the downward pull of materiality and the upward pull of spirit, which is also a pull toward differentiation and reunification of the initially undifferentiated. The divine understanding draws out and "awakens" (361; 240) from within the dark ground of nature the *diverse forces* it latently contains, the forces that ultimately constitute, Schelling writes, the compound substances or *bodies* of the created. At the same time, the divine understanding draws out from the ground also the *unifying force* that is likewise immanently latent within it, the unifying force that ultimately constitutes the *soul* of each created being. A hierarchy of beings in nature results, in which, the more internally differentiated and complexly unified the creature, the more light it contains, the more perfect (*vollkommen*) its soul is, and the higher it stands in the hierarchy of creation (361; 240).

By way of this conceptual and metaphorical rewriting of the Old Testament creation myth, as overdetermined both by the New Testament motif of the origination of creation with the *logos*, and by his previously developed thoughts on the philosophy of nature, Schelling arrives at the characterization of the human being, in its freedom for good and evil. He broaches this characterization of the human first by determining the dark principle in the creature as its "Eigenwille"—its self-willed aspect or particular will—as opposed to what he now calls the "Universalwille"—the universal will—represented by the principle of light, or understanding. In the human, this self-will, at the "most inward, and deepest point of the original darkness" (363; 241), is "transfigured" (*verklärt*) (363; 241) into light, so that the two wills (particular and universal)—"the deepest abyss and the highest heaven, both centers" (363; 241)—are unified. This is also the place where "in the highest differentiation of the force the innermost center opens up [or 'breaks open,' or 'ascends and consumes itself,' depending on how one interprets the polysemous word, 'aufgehen,' which Schelling uses here to maximum effect]" [*in der höchsten Scheidung der Kräfte das allerinnerste Zentrum aufgeht*] (362; 241). Hence, the particular and the universal remain separate within their unity in humans, who constitute the first spiritual being in nature, whereas in God particular and universal are inseparable. The separability of the two principles in humans (as radically distinguished from their inseparability in God), the very site of human freedom as the possibility of good and evil, is the condition of God's revelation (because God cannot reveal himself to an entity lacking in freedom).

While the capacity to participate in the universal spirit raises the humans above nature, thereby giving humans freedom, it also enables them to choose to fall back behind themselves. Evil—the choice of this fall—is egotism: the conflation of one's own particular will *with* the universal will, and the refusal to subordinate one's particular will *to* it.[22] Indeed, in evil, one elevates ground (as particular will, self-will, or self-hood [*Selbstheit*]) *above* existence (the universal will of God), placing longing above understanding, as if the former could simply *be* the latter, in a kind of deluded wish-fulfillment, or introjection of an ideal, "from which ruin follows, within himself and outside of him" [*woraus Zerrüttung in ihm selbst und außer ihm erfolgt*] (366; 243). A "false life, a life of the lie" (366; 244) arises.

This fall, however, is paradoxical. Evil is not the mere persistence of the dark ground within, but the very *denial* of the persistence of this dark ground—the attempt to posit oneself as pure universal spirit (or to usurp the place of pure spirit), the refusal to accept one's natural, embodied irrationality (i.e. one's situatedness within a nature that is outside of God as his ground, and inside of God as proper to his existence). To become a transparent signifier of the divine signification is *not*, for Schelling, to shed one's materiality as such a signifier.[23] Accordingly, Schelling explicitly denies "that finitude for itself is evil" (370; 247). But on the one hand the denial of one's belonging to the dark ground here is paradoxically, at the same time, an excessive insistence on what this denial refuses, namely egotism. Evil arises when the human creature flees his creatureliness into his creatureliness. What egotism does best is to universalize itself, that is, to claim to be beyond its own particularity. And on the other hand, to affirm one's belonging to the ground is again to deny it, because the fundamental impulse of the dark ground, its very longing for the light, involves a tendency toward self-denial and self-disavowal. Hence, one must also say that evil arises when the human being enters into his creatureliness only to find him- or herself fleeing it. And here—along the precipitous verge of this (doubly) paradoxical structure—is where *anxiety* enters the scene.

## 4   Anxiety in the Experience of Freedom

Anxiety enters explicitly when Schelling is explaining the structure of good and evil in the human being. Schelling emphasizes the contradictory character (within the human) of the (properly divine) tendency toward universality, freedom, and unity, on the one hand, and the (creaturely) tendency toward particularity, unfreedom, and multiplicity or inequality (*Ungleichheit*), on the other hand. Within this tension, the human has an unavoidable tendency to insist on (denying) the creaturely, he writes, as when:

> a mysterious voice [*eine geheime Stimme*] seemingly calls a man seized by dizziness [*Schwindel*] on a high and precipitous pinnacle to plunge down, or as in the ancient myth the irresistible song of the sirens rang out from the depths in order to draw mariners sailing through down into the whirlpool. The combination of a general/universal will with a particular will in the human being [*Menschen*]

seems to be a contradiction which would be difficult if not impossible to unify. The "anxiety ('fear' in Hayden-Roy's translation, which is not quite right) of life itself" [*die Angst des Lebens selbst*] drives the human being out of the center in which he was created; for this center is, as the purest essence of all will, for every particular will a consuming fire; in order to be able to live within it, the human being must die to all ownhood [*aller Eigenheit absterben*] for which reason he must always necessarily attempt to step out of it and into the periphery, in order to seek rest there for his selfhood. (381–2; 256)

To begin to unpack the sense and structure of anxiety in this very dense passage, it is first of all necessary to note that the phrase, the "anxiety of life" (*Angst des Lebens*), is a genitive formulation that ambiguously combines the subjective with the objective genitive. According to the subjective genitive, life is what is anxious here, the life within the human, or human life. But according to the simultaneously implied objective genitive, life is the *object* of anxiety, that is, life is what appears here as indeterminately threatening, as well as threateningly indeterminate (which, in German, would be "*un-bestimmt*").[24] Hence, in the "anxiety of life," life fears life, feels unsettled and constrained by life, and experiences the unbearable, irresistible, and yet impossible temptation to flee life itself, a panicky temptation no doubt, since there is nowhere life can go to get away from itself, except into death.[25] The "self" of "life itself" is not one.

Indeed, these interpretive considerations help explain why Schelling invokes the sound-image of a "voice" (*Stimme*) calling the subject-object of anxiety into its own death, envisaged as a plummeting from the heights into the depths, where it would still fail to escape itself, since the depths constitute precisely the figure of the dark ground, where the reality of life resides, the abyssal origin from which, as life, it continually ascends.[26] We see here that anxiety draws us away from ourselves and back toward ourselves at once. The voice (or *Stimme*) that seems to promise to determine (*bestimmen*, as one would say in German) life, to give it a destiny (*Bestimmung*) through which it could escape its unbearable—dizzying or vertiginous—indeterminacy (*Unbestimmtheit*) and disorientation, its distance from the pure will and understanding of God (source of all orientation), draws it instead back into the indeterminate abyss of its own origination.[27]

What can the human being do, then, in response to this anxiety? How can s/he resist, escape, or withstand it? In order to escape the anxiety that "drives the human being out of the center in which he was created" (381–2; 256), or to escape the fall into evil that Schelling also characterizes as "stepping out of (the center) into the periphery" (381–2; 256), Schelling says here that s/he would have to "die to all ownhood" (381–2; 256). Otherwise, s/he will continue to burn in the "consuming fire" of anxiety—the affect that corresponds to being in the center, or the "purest essence of all will" (381–2; 256), that is, the presence of the universal will there in conflict with the particular will. But what does it mean here to "die to all ownhood"? To clarify this crucial question, let us consider the human being's position.

Life in the "center" is life in a dual center, as we saw above (363; 241), that is, the center of the most abyssal ground of the darkness of longing (which is the longing of darkness) and the center of the highest existence of the transcendent will and understanding of God. The human circle is elliptical. Remaining in the center therefore means accepting and assuming finitude, and the separateness of one's particular will from, as well as its subordination to, a universal will that remains unattainable, even as it continues to represent one's most proper self and life.[28] To die to all ownhood, or propriety, the condition of the possibility of escaping the flames of anxiety, rigorously implies renouncing, disavowing, or disidentifying with, both the ownhood implied by belonging to the ground (or having a body and an unconscious), and the propriety of the unity with the divine (the identification with universality) to which all ("grounded") human beings aspire. But such a renunciation would imply precisely *not* remaining in the (double) center; it would imply attempting to escape the human condition, living beyond the tension between ground and existence that is constitutive of all life, and thus identifying one's particularity with the pure universal spirit (365–6; 243) by claiming to place oneself beyond their contradictory unity: evil (and anxiety) once again. And yet, to affirm one's "split subjectivity" (as we might say today), one's life as finite longing, it is necessary to expose oneself to the continuous temptation to identify oneself with the Absolute once more. For the longing of finite humanity is defined as longing to be one with God, and this always entails the danger of putting oneself in God's place (by virtue of the structure of identification with which our own age will wrestle again, e.g., in psychoanalytic theory and practice). Either way—dying to all ownhood or not dying to all ownhood—one falls into evil and/or anxiety, which start to blend into each other at this point in the argument.

It is due to this ineluctability of the "anxiety of life itself," which "drives the human being out of the center," then, that Schelling can speak of the "universal necessity of sin and of death as the real dying off of ownhood, through which all human will must go as through a fire in order to be purified" (381–2; 256).[29] The fire of (un)grounded (non)existence in the split center is hence also here the fire of sin and especially the fire of death itself, as the anxiously self-sustaining tension between the mutually negating principles of longing and understanding, irrational and rational, body and mind, and (as perhaps we might add in a secularizing mode) nature and culture. Anxiety of evil, or evil and anxiety (each always bound up with the other) is for Schelling here "fundamental" to human life itself, as a life that is properly improper, continuously leaving itself behind even when it insists most vehemently (or even piously) on being itself, and continuously failing to escape itself even when it struggles to do so in order to attain to a position outside of itself from which it would no longer (need to) strive to leave itself behind.[30]

But if anxiety "*drives* the human being out of the center" (my emphasis), and if the human "must always necessarily attempt to step out of [the center]" into evil, then how is s/he free? In what consists the freedom of the human in the context of necessity? Where is it situated? And how can this freedom resist the necessity of evil, so as to act in accordance with the good? To account for this freedom, Schelling develops further in his own terms the notion of the human as an "intelligible essence" that he finds broached in Kant's ethics: "The intelligible essence [*Das intelligible Wesen*] of each thing, and above all [*vorzüglich*] of the human, is according to [Idealism] outside of all causal nexus [*Kausalzusammenhang*] as also outside of, or above, all time" (384; 258). Conceptually and metaphysically, this "intelligible essence" precedes temporally and causally determined existence, so that "the free act follows immediately out of the intelligible in the human [*aus dem Intelligiblen des Menschen*]" (384; 258). Each act, as a good or an evil one, follows from the human's "inner nature" (384; 258), for "free is that which acts only according to the laws of its own essence" (384; 258). Schelling thus tries to unify freedom with necessity through the notion of acting in accordance with one's own nature, on the presupposition that one's "own nature" is not pre-given empirically but rather self-chosen outside of all time: "the essence of the human is essentially his own deed" (384; 259).[31] This act of self-constitution "precedes" but also pervades consciousness (386; 259–60), as it occurs outside of time and for all time, although it presents itself, within consciousness, to the moral conscience as a feeling of self-responsibility. To the degree that we succumb to evil, then, this capitulation is our own act—which Schelling calls our "original sin." But equally, to the degree that we act for the good—toward which he says we are also drawn by an "inner voice" (389; 262)—and affirm the necessary (for in the good, the "spirit and heart, bound only through their own law, freely [*freiwillig*] affirm what is necessary" [391; 264])—this affirmation of necessity (here, the necessity of our being bound to the longing for existence) is also our own deed.

But does this attempted reconciliation of freedom with necessity actually supply us with an account of the human condition that renders transparent the possibility of escaping evil, and along with evil, the phenomenon of anxiety, as the affective equivalent of the departure and alienation from our own condition, the (un)grounded (non)existence of our originary splitting? One may certainly doubt it (as Heidegger did), insofar as even the *affirmation* of necessity, hence of our place in the ground—our belonging to which entails an attempt to get *beyond* it—is always also a *negation* of this necessity.[32] And even if affirmation of necessity is affirmation of the necessity of evil, does such an affirmation simply transcend what it affirms? If "radical evil" is a name in Schelling for this ineluctable partial negation of the human condition inherent in that condition, then whence the possibility of the good?

The difficulty Schelling encounters at this level perhaps explains why he has recourse toward the end of his text to a narrative solution the formulation of which entails, it seems unwittingly, a relativization of radical evil, and thus a contradiction of his initially announced intention *not* to deny the reality of evil. That is, toward the end of the text, he describes what precedes and what proceeds upon the opening up of the ground-existence couple in (or as) the process of divine revelation qua creation. Prior to the ground-existence couple, there is a pre-origin in what Schelling calls variously now the *Urgrund* (primal ground), the *Ungrund* (nonground), and *absolute Indifferenz* (absolute indifference): that is, the "nonbeing" (*Nichtsein*) of all opposites, prior a fortiori also to the duality of good and evil.[33] This nonground then divides itself into ground and existence (from which the possibilities of evil and good follow) "only in order that" [*nur damit*] the two may "become one through love" (407–8; 278). Schelling now designates the reunification of ground and existence through the action of divine love, the reunification that is the *telos* of all creation, as "absolute Identity." In the context of this designation, however, he determines evil as an *Unwesen*—a non-being or non-essence—that only has reality in opposition to love, not "in itself" [*an sich*] (409; 277–8). The "absolute Identity" that is metaphysically prior to evil ultimately, moreover, excludes it (409; 279). Thus, on the level of the metaphysical totality, through the mystery of love, Schelling "explains" (or rather surreptitiously dispenses with the problem of) the escape from the evil of anxiety or the anxiety of evil—(self)assertion as (self)negation—that was not properly conceivable on the level of Schelling's description of the human condition per se.

The point of digging into some of the unresolved tensions that surround Schelling's articulation of the "anxiety of life" in *Freedom* is not to suggest that Schelling's introduction of this concept into modern philosophy is somehow a failure. All the less so, as—to quote David Martyn, "nothing succeeds like failure."[34] Rather, the unresolved character of aspects of Schelling's thematization of anxiety is precisely what induces his followers—from Kierkegaard to

Heidegger to Freud to Lacan, just to name a few of the most prominent—to sustain, renew, and displace Schelling's initial articulation of the theme. More proximately, these difficulties help us see more clearly what problems Schelling is trying to resolve in his later efforts, notably the *Ages*, to whose more detailed and extensive mobilization of the anxiety-motif we turn for the remainder of the present chapter. In *Ages*, as we'll see (at least the fragment of it published in 1815), Schelling no longer appeals to the *Ungrund*, nor to absolute identity as telos, and he situates pure freedom in God as such, beyond being, in the attempt to account for the entrance of freedom into creation. Anxiety, however, not only remains an important motif there, but it is ultimately extended to God's own experience in creation. If that text, too, remains a fragment, its import for subsequent philosophical and also psychoanalytic thought is crucial, not least for the prominence it grants to anxiety.

## 5 From the Anxiety of Nature to the Anxious God in *Ages*

The never completed *Ages of the World* project repeats, on an even larger conceptual scale and with displaced conceptual elements, the undertaking of *Freedom*: the attempt to conceptualize in a dynamic or vitalistic mode the contradictory unity of necessity and freedom, real and ideal, nature and God. In this text, Schelling restates the original tension not as one between ground and existence, but as one between negativity—the force of contraction (which Schelling also characterizes as the "wrath" of God)—and positivity—the force of expansion (which he characterizes as God's "love").[35] These two forces, or "potencies," in their antagonistic relation with their unity, constitute the "divine nature" or the necessitated aspect of God. The reason why these two forces or potencies maintain an antagonistic relation with their unity is simply this: that in their unity they would disappear as distinct forces striving for Being. To the divine nature, God's free aspect, or God as such, is opposed. Schelling understands this free aspect further here as the "will that wills nothing," that is, the pure freedom to will or not to will, which is the freedom of God qua beyond being (à la negative theology). In this metaphysical context, the original negativity or force of contraction, in its tension with the positivity or expansive force that it attempts to suppress and withdraw into darkness, constitutes the (inwardly doubled) beginning of nature qua life, which however ontologically precedes creation.

Allow me to sketch here very schematically the structure of the text as a whole, so that I can then focus on the passages concerning anxiety (where I'll indicate in each case the situation of the passage within the structure of Schelling's narrative argument). The *Ages* manuscript traces first of all the process of the "divine nature" or "eternal nature" in terms of the striving to come into being of each term in the original tension (pure negativity and pure positivity), as supplemented by the unity of these terms, a unity to which however they can never attain in this first stage because they here still resist it as representing their own disappearance. These three terms, which also represent the bases of what will become nature, spirit, and soul, respectively, struggle initially with and against each other until they encounter, at a certain distance, the pure freedom of God, or God as freedom. At this point (which is not a temporal point but the very beginning of temporality) they advance to a second ontological level. Their internecine conflict is appeased on this level (although not entirely overcome) as the three potencies freely choose (having absorbed into themselves, as it were, some of God's freedom) to become a totality [*All*]: they consent to form a hierarchical simultaneity or architectonic structure in which negativity is at the bottom, positivity above that, and the soul on the uppermost floor. From this stage, they advance further to a third developmental stage where they unfold into the concrete possibilities of the natural world (negativity), and of the spiritual world (positivity). Schelling describes this unfolding as a kind of divine dream vision in which God sees what the world can become if he decides to create it. (This is where Schelling describes the state of the world prior to creation, as when Mendelssohn characterized Spinoza's concept of nature.) At this stage, the unity of negativity and positivity functions as the universal "soul," which mediates the communication of these first two potencies with God qua pure freedom. On a fourth level, finally, Schelling traces the actual creation itself, as God's free act of self-revelation. On each of these ontotheological levels and developmental stages (the second and fourth most explicitly), which we have only sketched here in the broadest terms, anxiety plays a key role.

## 6 Anxiety Within the Negativity of the Divine Nature

The first level on which anxiety enters explicitly is that on which the negative pole or potency—as "possible substratum for (external nature)" (according to the useful if imperfect synoptic table of contents that Karl Schelling, the philosopher's son, provided in the edition of 1861)—struggles to contain within itself its opposite, the positivity that it suppresses and tries to draw into the darkness. Schelling introduces the anxiety of negativity explicitly on this second level of the process, because negativity first clearly separates itself from positivity on this level, but the description of the anxiety of negativity given here would also apply to negativity at the more inchoate origin, prior to negativity's "acceptance" of its separate existence as the "ground" (244; 31) of positivity. Schelling tells us that this situation of negativity—which by its very nature attempts to suppress its immanent other, positivity—constitutes "a life of loathing and anxiety, since it does not know whether to turn inward or outward and so falls prey to an unintentional rotating movement" [*ein Leben der Widerwärtigkeit und der Angst, da sie nicht aus noch ein weiß und ebenfalls einen unwillkürlichen umdrehenden Bewegung anheimfällt*] (246; 32). Two comments on Schelling's wording are necessary, in order to unfold the connotations and structure of anxiety here.

First, the expression "nicht aus noch ein weiß" renders anxiety concretely comprehensible in terms of everyday human experiences of disorientation and panic, insofar as the expression—as does not appear in Jason Wirth's otherwise mostly fabulous translation—is an idiom in everyday speech, meaning figurally "doesn't know which way to go." As there is not yet, for (contractive) negativity, an instance that would successfully unify it with (expansive) positivity, the life of the subjectivity that is (the self-anticipation of) nature finds and feels itself in radical ambivalence and disarray. The phrase, "nicht aus noch ein weiß," is further appropriate to the situation it describes in that it literally corresponds, of course (as Wirth's translation does reflect), to the tension between contractive and expansive forces, pulling in and pushing out, a state in which the border between inside and outside is constantly and infinitely transgressing itself in both directions at once.[36] Thus, the play on "nicht aus noch ein weiß" evokes figuratively the disorientation of anxiety and literally the contradiction between contraction and expansion that plausibly characterizes such an anxiety. This interplay of figural and literal characterizes, as I've indicated, Schelling's style in general, which shares with German early Romantic Thought in general its openness to the interpenetrations of literary and philosophical language.

Secondly, it is important to consider why, through the word, *Widerwärtigkeit*, "anxiety" is linked to "loathing" (or "disagreeableness, loathesomeness, offensiveness, nuisance, bother; adversity, accident, calamity") here.[37] What work does the word *Widerwärtigkeit* accomplish in Schellng's text?[38] *Widerwärtigkeit* accords well with, and even translates or explicates "anxiety" here, because it bespeaks the sense in which the two aspects of the first potency—its predominant negativity and the positivity it both contains and suppresses in the struggle against it—are mutually at odds, as if they "loathed" each other. Anxiety in this sense contains an aspect of self-divided self-loathing. Further, in the contradiction or *Widerspruch* of this state, Schelling adds through Boehme's term an aspect of temporal expectation, since in the discomfiture of *Wider-wärtigkeit* the two sides of the first potency expect or await the reconciliation—*Widerwärtigkeit* contains not just *wider* (against) but also *warten* (awaiting)—that does not arrive.

As these remarks on the connotations of "nicht aus noch ein weiß" and "Widerwärtigkeit" help us to see, at this level in Schelling's narrative account of the structure of the becoming of God—a level ontologically prior to creation per se, and where we are still just dealing with the "first potency as a possible substratum for (external nature)"—there is no effective mediation between the contractive and expansive forces (within contraction itself), between "no" and "yes" (within the "no"). "Loathing and anxiety" serves as the compound name for this (absent) mediation, mediation without mediation, or radical ambivalence, and it will continue to do so, while its specific site develops and shifts.

## 7   Anxiety in Nature's Regressive Flight from God's Freedom

When the three potencies of "eternal nature" (i.e. the "divine nature") encounter God's freedom, albeit from a distance, the effect of this encounter, as I've indicated, is a partial pacification of the potencies' conflictual striving-to-be. The "pain, anxiety, loathing of the past life, come undone… through that crisis or setting into mutual opposition of the forces" (275; 55). But this undoing is only partial, and the three potencies persist in struggle, to the degree that the influence of God's freedom is still a mediated one. In the following passage, Schelling considers the ongoing struggle of "eternal nature," which perpetuates the struggle at the outset of the entire process, again in terms of "loathing and anxiety." The passage does not simply repeat what we have already seen, however, since here Schelling makes explicit and justifies (at least to some extent) three aspects of the conceptualization of the "loathing and anxiety" of "eternal nature" that remained implicit in the previously considered one: the figure of anthropomorphism for states of (non)being prior to creation; the tenet that all human existence in the absence of God is essentially an existence of "loathing and anxiety"; and the sense in which these states are actually states within God.

To begin with the first point: Schelling writes here that "eternal nature" as a whole, in its (non)relation to God qua freedom, can be understood in terms of the metaphor of human experience. However, this anthropomorphic metaphor, he claims, is something more than a metaphor, in the sense of an improper expression, because the human represents a higher level of the realization of precisely this conflictual structure, in which the unity of the contradiction remains separate from the contradictory terms and so has not yet managed to achieve their synthesis. "Eternal nature" can be understood anthropomorphically, that is, because the human constitutes the level of creation on which the transition from necessity to freedom will have to be achieved; the human constitutes a kind of realization of what "eternal nature" anticipates, as we saw also in *Freedom*, but here the realization only occurs through God's intervention, since here all freedom comes from God. Discussing specifically the way in which at this stage God as such, or the "divine spirit," relates to the (constantly regressing) totality of his "eternal nature," Schelling writes:

> Hence if one wanted (as is only right) to seek a human comparison for the relationship between the divine spirit and nature, it would be this. The eternal nature is the same in God as what in the person is their nature, provided that under "nature" one thinks that which consists of body, soul, and spirit. If abandoned to itself, this nature of the person, like the eternal nature, is a life of loathing and anxiety [*ein Leben der Widerwärtigkeit und Angst*], a fire that incessantly consumes and unremittingly produces itself anew. This nature also needs reconciliation, the means for which do not lie *within* itself but outside and beyond it. Only through the spirit of God ... can the nature of the person be born again, that is, escape the old life and posit it as something past and transition into a new life. That which is beyond being [*das Überseyende*] does not relate to nature therefore ... as the human spirit or soul relates to the human body. Rather, it relates to nature as that divine spirit, which does not belong to the human, relates to the entirety of the nature of the human. It serves as a Guide to life—as it was already called in the ancient Mysteries. (265; 46)

As this passage makes clear, the human serves in Schelling as an appropriate model for the "eternal nature" not just because the internal *structure* of the human, comprising body, soul, and spirit, is also that of "eternal nature," but because the human *experience* of this structure is the same as its *experience* in (or by) "eternal nature," namely a "loathing and anxiety" the only solution for which is God as source of freedom. Nature is the mirror-image of what it anticipates: loathing and anxiety.

Finally, despite the fact that this passage emphasizes the distinction between God's spirit *per se* (as pure freedom, will that wills nothing, and as beyond being) and his "eternal nature," it is important to track also the sense in which, because "eternal nature" is *God's* "eternal nature," it is *God himself* who experiences "loathing and anxiety" here. In this sense, God in Schelling is very different from God in Spinoza. Spinoza emphasizes that God's perfection places him beyond all desire, need, lack, or suffering of any kind. In contrast, Schelling's God, both on the level of necessity and, as we shall see, on the level of his free act of creation, is a radically anxious God.

## 8 Anxiety in the Free Act of Creation

In order to continue to trace how this vision of an anxious God develops in Schelling's thought here, we need to consider the recurrence of the motif of anxiety on the level of the actual creation of the world, first in the world's material dimension as nature in the narrow sense, and then finally within God's experience of his own creative act as such, where Schelling expands on God's suffering more extensively.[39]

How, then, is anxiety present in the actual creation of material nature? In accordance with Schelling's general principle that each renewed beginning, each new stage of development, corresponds to the assertion of the contracting force, or negativity, God's free act in the realization of the hitherto merely possible world begins with "no," the negation of this world in its possibility, and then emerges as "yes," moving from "wrath" to "love," or from the functioning of God as father to his functioning as son, in accordance with Schelling's singular interpretation of these traditional Christian motifs. The negative force coming from God as freedom induces the three potencies within the eternal nature of the possible world to flee apart once again, he writes, in a "mutual intolerance and revulsion" [*gegenseitige Unleidlichkeit und der Widerwille*] (319, 89). This mutual negativity of the three potencies comes about because the negativity of God's act affects even the positive and reconciling potencies of spirit and soul, respectively. The "no" of God introduces negativity into them and/or evokes the negativity they already contain, such that they each turn their negativity against the other two terms in the triad. One might say that they "contract" negativity. This striving apart (and against each other) of the basic dimensions or potencies of existence represents further, not just their absorption of negativity, but also their struggle against their effacement, since their unification under the force of negativity would entail as always their disappearance as separate tendencies. Here again—in this initial moment of creation—anxiety, loathing, and bitterness (the latter having been associated in Boehme with anxiety [see note 25]), enter the scene of Schelling's narrative, and strikingly as "the interior (or core) of all life":

> Here is the first source of bitterness [*der erste Quell der Bitterkeit*] which is—indeed, must be—the interior of all life, and which immediately erupts whenever it is not soothed. For love is coerced into hatred and the silent and gentle spirit cannot act, but rather is oppressed by the enmity [*Feindseligkeit*] in which all of the forces are transposed by the necessity of life. From here comes the profound discontent [*Unmuth*] that lies in all life and without which there is no actuality [*keine Wirklichkeit*]. This is the poison of life that needs to be overcome, yet without which life would pass away. (319, 89)

Schelling calls this renewed tension between, and rhythmic alternation of, contraction and expansion, the "orgasm of all forces" [*Orgasmus aller Kräfte*] as well as the "beating heart of the Godhead" [*das schlagende Herz der Gottheit*] (320; 90), two further figural expressions for this tension as, on the one hand, both end and beginning of life (orgasm) and on the other hand, the process of life itself (the beating heart). Both of these images concretize radical contradiction: "the first existence is contradiction itself and, inversely only in contradiction can the first reality exist... All life must pass through the fire of contradiction. Contradiction is the innermost driving force of life [*Widerspruch ist des Lebens Triebwerk und Innerstes*]" (321; 90). As a result, the "multiplicity in nature" [*Mannichfaltigkeit in der Natur*] can "only become in discontent [*nur im Unmuth werden*], and just as anxiety is the fundamental feeling of every living creature, so, too, everything that lives is only conceived and born in violent struggle" [*und wie Angst die Grundempfindung jedes lebenden Geschöpfs, so ist alles, was lebt, nur im heftigen Streit empfangen und geboren*]" (322, 91).[40] Indeed, even products of *inorganic* nature are for Schelling "manifestly the children of anxiety, of terror, indeed of despair [*offenbar Kinder der Angst, des Schreckens, ja der Verzweiflung*]" (322; 91). Illustrating this principle with the "first basis of the future human"—by which he seems to refer ambiguously to the sexual act, envisioned as a kind of primal scene, and/or to the birth-trauma *avant la lettre*—Schelling continues: "And so we also see in the only case in which we, to some extent, are permitted to be witnesses of an original creation, that the first foundation of the future human is only formed in deadly struggle, terrifying discontent, and anxiety that often extends to despair [*in tödtlichem Streit, schrecklichem Unmuth, und oft bis zur Verzweiflung gehender Angst ausgebildet wird*]. If this happens in individuals and in the small, could it be any different in the large, in the creation of the first parts of the world system?" (322–3; 91–2).

Finally, in contrast to the pathologizing approach to anxiety that tends to predominate in our own age, and anticipating (i.e. laying the foundations for) the existentialist approach to anxiety, which stressed its positive importance and universality, Schelling emphasizes here that this "rotating drive [*Umtrieb*]" (323; 92)—the dizzy drivenness of anxiety—is not accidental but essential, "active in the first creation." Anxiety is constitutive, not contingent, that is, "not, as prevailing opinion now has it, forces that only later externally and accidentally supplemented what came to be" [*nicht aber, wie jetzte die herrschende Meinung ist, erst zu dem Gewordenen äußerlich zufällig hinzugekommene Kräfte sind*] (323; 92). In this internal negativity precisely consists the "selfhood" [*Selbstheit*] or "ownness" [*Eigenheit*] of what is, in virtue of which each singular "thing seeks to withdraw itself from the universal center and eccentrically seeks its own center of gravity and point of rest" "[*sich dem allgemeinen Centrum zu entziehen und excentrisch seinen eignen Schwer- und Ruhepunkt sucht*]" (324; 92). The echoes of the necessity of anxiety and of "evil" to all natural existence from the *Freedom* text are clearly still audible, albeit amplified and further differentiated here.

## 9  Anxiety as a Creative Madness in God

What happens with this anxiety and struggle when we pass from creation as viewed from the standpoint of nature to creation as viewed from the standpoint of God's own experience, under the heading (again in Karl Schelling's formulation) of the "relationship of this activation [i.e the actual creation of the natural and spiritual worlds] to that which has Being itself [*zum Seyenden selbst*] ( = to the pure Godhead)" (198; 101)? Here, in what is perhaps the most astonishing and provocative development within Schelling's text, God himself, as creator, will be said to undergo a radical suffering of anxiety that attains the dimensions of madness. To approach this claim, Schelling writes of this pure Godhead that its "interior, no less than its exterior, must suffer and be lacerated by contradiction [*leiden und von Widerspruch zerrissen seyn muß*], as in powerful and lawless movements [*heftigen und gesetzlosen Bewegungen*] of an organic being its interior suffers too [*auch sein Inneres mit leidet*]" (335; 101). In the discussion that follows this opening, Schelling unfolds the suffering of the Godhead, which attends his creative process, in terms of pain, anxiety, and madness. Throughout this discussion, on the one hand, the emphasis on the suffering, or "Leiden," of God places Schelling's discourse at a provocative distance from the privilege of activity that most often attends presentations of the divinity as pure act in the Western metaphysical tradition, especially when, as here, it is not a matter of Christ as such but of the paternal figure of the creator-God. But on the other hand, the "suffering" of God is not simply passive here either, but a painful passage through the contradiction of passive and active, because what suffers here is pure freedom or spontaneity. To establish this perspective, however, Schelling is first of all at pains to stress and justify God's suffering:

> Pain [*Schmerz*] is something universal and necessary in all life, the unavoidable transition point to freedom. We recall the pains-of-development [*Entwicklungsschmerzen*] of the human life in the physical as well as the moral sense. We will not shun presenting even that primordial being (the first possibility of the externally manifest God) in the state of suffering [*im leidenden Zustand*] that comes from growth. Suffering is universal [*Leiden ist allgemein*], not only with respect to humanity, but also with respect to the creator. It is the path to glory. God leads human nature down no other path than that down which God Himself must pass. Participation in everything blind, dark, and suffering [*Leidenden*] of God's nature is necessary in order to elevate God to the highest consciousness. Every single being must get to know their own depths and this is impossible without suffering [*Leiden*]. All pain comes only from Being [*von dem Seyn*], and because all that lives [*alles Lebendige*] must first enclose itself in Being [*sich erst in das Seyn einschließen muß*], and break out of its darkness to transfiguration [*Verklärung*], so too must the in-itself divine essence [*das an sich göttliche Wesen*] in its revelation first take on nature and to this degree suffer [*leiden*], before it celebrates the triumph of its liberation. (335; 101)

Since the creation is itself the passage from necessity to freedom, from passivity to spontaneity, it is a passage through their contradiction, in which the pure freedom of God encounters his "eternal nature" in *realizing* that very nature, while the "eternal nature" of God conversely encounters God *qua* freedom. And since passage through contradiction is painful, disharmonious, the passage of creation involves radical "pain" and "suffering." But here "suffering," or *Leiden*, is not pure passivity, but rather passivity imbued with activity, activity in the process of its own passage into and out of passivity. This suffering is a passage through contradiction affectively experienced by no less than God himself as pain.

Schelling begins to describe this pain, which attends the increasing self-activation of the freedom of God and the increasing awakening of activity within nature itself, by contrasting it both to the "clairvoyance" [*Hellsehens*] of the pure Godhead (i.e. his condition prior to any encounter with his own nature), and also to the blissful dreams of God (as which he experienced the mere possible forms of the pre-created world). Unlike these states, the pain of God in creation is a divine nightmare, or what Freud will call an "anxiety-dream" [*Angsttraum*]. "Soon with increasing conflict these births of the night pass through his interiority like wild fantasies, in which he first feels all the terrors of his own essence" (336).[41]

Schelling determines this painful experience further now explicitly as anxiety: "Anxiety [*Angst*] is the governing affect that corresponds to the conflict of directions in Being, since it does not know whether to go in or out" (336; 101). Once again, in this context, the anxious affect is described in terms of the structure of a conflict in which the dark, negative will of necessity tries to assimilate to itself and assimilate itself to the spirit of God himself, but grasps only an intermediate phantom, "an intermediary between the utter night of consciousness and rational spirit" [*ein Mittleres zwischen völliger Nacht des Bewußtseyns und besonnenem Geist*] (337; 102), an intermediary between nature's possibility and the actuality of God qua radical freedom. But this divine anxiety or panic attack is anything but unproductive. From out of this struggle, the rationally structured world arises: "everything that e.g. in the world-structure is rational and ordered" [*alles… was z. B. in dem Weltbau Verständiges und Geordnetes ist*] (337; 102). Here, then, anxiety—as the anxiety of God in the process of creation—is understood as a painful process of the interpenetration of necessity and freedom, darkness and light, negativity and positivity, that gives rise to forms of order.

But Schelling goes one step further. Indeed, he goes on to elaborate the analogy between this creative process and the (human) artistic process as traditionally conceived, an elaboration with which he closes the main body of the text of Part I of *Ages*, the only part he completed. In this elaboration, Schelling emphasizes that all "creativity" [*Schaffen*] must arise out of a dark ground, a "blind force" [*eine blinde Kraft*], serving as the recipient of an "inspiration" [*Eingebung*]: "All conscious creation [*Alles bewußte Schaffen*] presupposes an unconscious creation [*ein bewußtloses*], and is only unfolding [*Entfaltung*], and articulation [*Auseinandersetzung*] of the latter" (337; 102). He then goes on to cite as evidence for his claims ancient traditions concerning Dionysos and related gods, which speak of "divine and sacred madness" [*göttlichen und heiligen Wahnsinn*] (337; 102). At once building on his earlier dealings with mythology and foreshadowing the later *Philosophy of Mythology*, he interprets these traditions here as an accurate characterization of creation—both as the creation of the world and as every subsequent act of creativity—in which the opacity of natural materiality and passivity encounters, and interpenetrates with, the transparent light of supernatural spirit. But here, the "divine madness" is the madness of God himself.[42] Thus, the panthers and tigers pulling the carriage of Dionysos are for Schelling images of this vertiginous verging of the natural world on the divine world (i.e. of necessity on freedom), as are also the images of self-castration, the dismemberment of gods, insane dances, and deafening music in pagan cultural mythologies.[43] And the psychopathology of everyday creativity never ends, across the entire history of creation, for "this self-lacerating madness is even now the innermost core of all things, only mastered and as it were legitimated or affirmed by the light of a higher understanding, the actual force of nature and of all of its productions" (338; 103).

And so Schelling ends the main body of his text (prior to a supplementary discussion of the Spinoza controversy, consideration of which I omit here) with a discussion of the relations between madness and the understanding (as *Verstand*), pointing unwittingly ahead, perhaps by a kind of inspired madness, to the modern "therapeutic" discourses that, according to Odo Marquard, will take up the relay. According to the typology he develops, there are three main structures. Those without madness, he says, are just stupid or dull, in effect dead—the understanding without madness is not even understanding. Those who possess madness but do not master it, in contrast, are simply mad. Finally, those who master their madness with the understanding, as Schelling no doubt hopes he is doing, are the creative spirits capable of bringing forth great works. (338–9; 103–4). As we have seen, however, this madness is closely akin to, constantly in communication with, indeed identical with anxiety, a theme on which Kierkegaard, Heidegger, Freud, Lacan, and many others will creatively—madly?—expand in influential ways, in the unfolding and displacements of Schelling's introduction of the theme into modern philosophy through his provocative presentation, in *Ages*, of the becoming of the anxious God in his creative self-revelation.

To conclude: if, as Odo Marquard argues, the period of German Romantic Philosophy and Idealism is driven by a generalized and indefinite fear of an overpowering nature, in Schelling, this motif—becoming explicit as the theme of anxiety—is subject to a number of specific variations, so many attempts to master this indefinite fear conceptually. First, in *Freedom*, nature as life induces "anxiety" in itself, which culminates in the collision between necessity and freedom (or nature and God), a collision humans experience in its full, dizzying measure as an inescapable "evil." Then, in *Ages*, not only nature and humanity, but also God *per se* (as pure freedom), in the eternal moment of his creative self-actualization, experiences extreme anxiety. Each of the moments or levels of anxiety's occurrence repeats and mirrors the others, in a harmony of dissonance from moment to moment. The very model *for* creative artistic genius, that is, the creator-God himself, proves to be (modelled upon) a creative genius and, like the genius, turns out to be threatened by the ever-present possibility of madness. The aestheticization of nature here fuses with an already historically belated recourse to salvation by the Christian God, but the fusion ends with God on the verge of a nervous breakdown, the dizzy verge where the art of healing is already hovering, preparing to replace aesthetic salvation (even as aesthetic notions from the age of Romanticism will continue to inform therapeutic discourses in various ways down to our own day). God's analyst, or at least the analyst of "his majesty the baby"—who may turn out to be another artist—is waiting in the wings.

## Notes

1. Friedrich Wilhelm Joseph von Schelling, *Schellings sämmtliche Werke* (Stuttgart, Augsburg: J.G. Cotta, 1775–1854), ed. K. F. A. Schelling. The English translations from which I cite, but which I take the liberty to alter here and there in accord with my own interpretations of the original texts, are: "Philosophical Investigations into the Essence of Human Freedom and Related Matters," trans. Priscilla Hayden-Roy, in Ernst Behler, ed., *Philosophy of German Idealism* (New York: Continuum, 1987), 217–84; and Friedrich Wilhelm Joseph Schelling, *The Ages of the World*, trans. Jason M. Wirth (Albany: SUNY, 2000). I do not consider the two first versions of *The Ages of the World* here, only the 1815 version. I provide references parenthetically in the body of the text, first to the German original, then to the English edition used. Page references to the German edition of the *Freedom* lectures are in volume VII, references to the German edition of *Ages of the World* are in volume VIII, of *Schellings sämmtliche Werke*.
2. The current essay is part of a book in preparation provisionally titled *Anxiety's Modes: Phenomenology, Psychoanalysis, Neuroscience*, in which I examine anxiety-theories from Kierkegaard to Heidegger, from Freud to Lacan, and in some contemporary neuroscientists. The analysis of Schelling serves as prologue to that sequence. For two excellent essays on anxiety in Schelling and Kierkegaard, see Jochem Hennigfeld, "Angst—Freiheit—System. Schellings Freiheitsbegriff und Kierkegaards *Der Begriff Angst*," and Axel Hutter, "Das Unvordenkliche der menschlichen Freiheit: zur Deutung der Angst bei Schelling und Kierkegaard," both in Jochem Hennigfeld and Jon Stewart, eds., *Kierkegaard und Schelling: Freiheit, Angst und Wirklichkeit* (Berlin: De Gruyter, 2003), 103–115 and 117–32, respectively.
3. I draw in particular on "Über einige Beziehungen zwischen Ästhetik und Therapeutik in der Philosophie des neunzehnten Jahrhunderts," "Idealismus

und Theodizee," and "Wie irrational kann Geschichtsphilosophie sein?" most especially the first of these, in *Schwierigkeiten mit der Geschichtsphilosophie* (Frankfurt: Suhrkamp, 1973), 85–106, 52–65, and 66–82, respectively, and Odo Marquard, "Zur Bedeutung der Theorie des Unbewußten für eine Theorie der nicht mehr schönen Kunst," in H. R. Jauß, ed., *Die nicht mehr schönen Künste. Grenzphänomene des Ästhetischen* (Munich: Wilhelm Fink, 1968), 375–92.

4. Another illustration of this trajectory from aesthetics to therapeutics would be the continuities and displacements involved in the movement from F. Schiller's "Spieltrieb" (play drive) to D. W. Winnicott's theory of play.

5. For important essays that examine the significance of the *loss* of a natural origin for the philosophy and poetry of German both around 1800 and subsequently, through Heidegger, see Philippe Lacoue-Labarthe, *L'imitation des modernes: typographies II* (Paris: Galilée, 1986).

6. In "Zur Bedeutung der Theorie des Unbewußten," Marquard follows Hegel's dictum that, with the romantics, art has become a thing of the past, but reads the history of art from that point forward as diverging from the art of the beautiful in order to recognize the consequences of its divergence from the purpose of having a salutary effect and function. To his account, one would have to add reflections on the fact that, with the development of both *l'art pour l'art*, which seals art's uselessness, and its opponent, "engagement," the romantic-age anxieties about the force of nature persist precisely in the sense of endangerment that pervades art-discourse and art-production in both directions. Further, reality and artifice replace nature and spirit in the later discussion as the guiding conceptual polarity, and God plays an ever more minimal or implicit role.

7. Note that the section of *Ages* we retain as a relatively finished manuscript (in three versions) is called "The Past," and describes the creation, nature's process of emergence from God, as an eternal past.

8. Marquard traces the lineage of instruction and influence from Schelling to Freud in "Über einige Beziehungen," 87–89, and in "Zur Bedeutung der Theorie des Unbewußten," 376–9 not only conceptually but also historically, in terms of passages of thought from student to teacher. The lineage runs in a relatively unbroken, if zig-zaggy (hence also in classical terms "not beautiful") line from Schelling to Freud. Andrew Bowie also points out the manifold conceptual affinities between Schelling and Freud (as well as Lacan) in *Schelling and Modern European Philosophy: an Introduction* (London and New York: Routledge, 1993). And of course Slavoj Zizek has worked out extensively the echoes of Schelling, most especially of *Freedom* and *Ages*, in Lacan, producing a detailed Lacanian reading of these texts, in *The Abyss of Freedom/The Ages of the World*, which includes a translation of the 1813 draft of Ages by Judith Norman (Ann Arbor: U of Michigan, 1997) and in *The Indivisible Remainder: an Essay on Schelling and Related Matters* (London and

New York, Verso, 1996). While Zizek's reading of Schelling as an allegory of Lacanian truths is to a great degree both illuminating and persuasive, his approach ignores interesting historical questions about the path leading from Schelling to psychoanalysis, as well as many aspects of the debates in which Schelling was embedded. Zizek focuses most of the attention he devotes to Schelling's philosophical context on Hegel, whose differences with Schelling he minimizes in interesting ways, although he is not the only scholar who questions whether or not Schelling's critique of Hegel is adequate or fair. Of the many who wonder about whether or not Schelling does hermeneutic justice to Hegel, one interesting recent example would be Terry Pinkard, who questions Schelling's Hegel-interpretation by questioning Kierkegaard's, on the assumption that Kierkegaard's Hegel-critique follows along the lines of Schelling's, in *German Philosophy 1760–1860* (Cambridge: Cambridge UP, 2002), 347–8.

9. In fact, in "Zur Bedeutung der Theorie des Unbewußten," Marquard argues that there are two main ways in which the aesthetic discourse attempts to deal with this problem. The first, he says, is the shift and expansion of aesthetics from an aesthetics of the beautiful to an aesthetics of the nonbeautiful (the sublime, the tragic, the ironic, the horrible, the ugly, etc.). This expansion already begins in the eighteenth century, but leaves both the "beautiful" and all "fine art" ("*schöne Kunst*" means both)—farther and farther behind as time goes on. As indicated above, one might also consider the aestheticist direction, in which art claims that nature imitates art itself: this would be a version of the autonomy thesis of idealism in a different form, and another ruse to escape the dangers of nature, although already at the end of Huysmans' *À rebours*, this doesn't work out very well, as Des Esseintes becomes ill. See also Marquard's essay on "Idealismus und Theodizee." I leave this rich topic of the arts of the nonbeautiful and the artificial aside for another piece of my current project in the genealogy of anxiety, which will consider Kafka's work as an exploration of what art becomes after the (partial) fall of its autonomy: the theme(s) and appropriate form(s) of aesthetic heteronomy. On the therapeutic supplementation of aesthetics, some discussion of Foucault's biopolitics would be useful, although it would lead too far afield here. One reason why Foucault seems not to note the replacement of aesthetic "genius" discourse with therapeutic ones in *The History of Madness* is that in that book he still embraces the "genius" discourse (in Hölderlin, Nietzsche, Van Gogh, etc.) as an attractive escape from the suppression of madness by reason; another reason is that Foucault at this stage, and even more in his later lectures, avoids as much as possible engaging with philosophical discourse in its canonical texts.

10. While he takes us to this brink, Marquard does not, as far as I am aware, discuss "anxiety" and its theories per se, not even in his lectures on existentialism, nor—oddly—does he discuss Freud's essay on "The Uncanny." This essay would perfectly illustrate, in a relatively late stage of its development (where

medicalization identifies itself in turn with its aesthetic forerunner), his notion of a medico-therapeutic displacement of the aesthetic. For Freud's "Uncanny" essay not only treats the aesthetics of anxiety from a medical-psychiatric point of view, but in so doing, as I argue elsewhere, conversely aestheticizes psychoanalysis, or develops an aesthetics of psychoanalysis. Moreover, Marquard's thesis on a continuity from Schelling to Freud is supported by the fact that, in "The Uncanny," one of the dictionary articles on the "uncanny" that Freud uses gives him the phrase from none other than Schelling that the uncanny is "that which was supposed to remain hidden but has been revealed," a definition that Freud uses as one basis for his development there of the "return of the repressed." These remarks do not, of course, constitute a criticism of Marquard, but rather provide further evidence for the soundness and potential of his philosophico-historical reflections.

11. I treat the pantheism controversy at length in *The Rhetoric of Cultural Dialogue: Jews and Germans from Moses Mendelssohn to Richard Wagner and Beyond* (Stanford: Stanford UP, 2000), in *Orientalism and the Figure of the Jew* (New York: Fordham UP, 2015), and with specific focus on Jacobi in "Humanist Antiformalism as a Theopolitics of Race: F. H. Jacobi on Friend and Enemy," in *Eighteenth-Century Studies*, 32.2 (1998–99): 233–245. On Spinoza's anti-teleological critique of anthropomorphism, the pantheism controversy, and Spinoza's effect on Romanticism (as distinguished from the Idealism and Kant, Fichte, and Hegel) and (post)modernism, see in this volume, Michael Mack, "Spinoza and Romanticism."

12. Of course, the fact of Spinoza's excommunication could also be used against Jacobi within an anti-Jewish philosophical discourse, to suggest that "Benedict's" thought was compatible with Christianity, even if "Baruch's" background constituted a philosophical liability.

13. For Fichte's response, see "Zu 'Jacobi an Fichte'," in *Fichtes Werke,* ed. Immanuel Hermann Fichte, vol. XI (Berlin: Walter de Gruyter and Co, 1971), 390–4. Jacobi's conceptualization of nothing and negativity, which guides his branding of Fichte as a "nihilist," receives an extensive response in Schelling's discussions of "negativity" and non-being in *Ages* especially.

14. See *Freedom*, 355–6, where he characterizes Leibnizian thought as giving us only the idealist "soul" of philosophy, while Spinoza's realism gives us only its "body," his own project aiming rather to establish the mediation between these two.

15. Anticipatorily, it makes sense to cite one example from *Freedom* here, where Schelling establishes the analogy: nature is to the human as Jewish (or Old Testament) is to Christian (New Testament). This analogy gives greater credit to the Old Testament than normative Pauline supersessionism, because for Schelling the ground of nature is always *necessary* to the spirituality of the human, not just a failed attempt to attain it. In addition, Schelling's extended discussion of the importance of the Old Testament in *Ages* (269–74; 49–53)

likewise supports such a reading of Schelling's gesture with respect to the Judaic predecessor-figure, especially since Schelling explicitly contests there the exclusive application of *figura*-doctrine to the reading of the Old Testament. This aspect of Schelling's text perhaps helps explain why a number of important modern German-Jewish thinkers, Franz Rosenzweig and Ernst Bloch amongst them, gravitated toward his works and adopted his influence. See Jürgen Habermas, "The German Idealism of the Jewish Philosophers," and "Ernst Bloch: a Marxist Schelling," in *Philosophical-Political Profiles*, trans. Frederick G. Lawrence Cambridge, MA and London: MIT, 1983), 21–44 and 61–78, respectively, as well as Habermas' dissertation (rarely mentioned), *Das Absolute und die Geschichte. Von der Zwiespältigkeit in Schellings Denken* (Dissertation der Rheinischen Friedrich Wlhelms-Universität, 1954), which forms the basis of his remarkable essay on Schelling in the German edition of *Theorie und Praxis*. On these matters, see the subtle and informative article by Paul Franks, "Inner Anti-Semitism or Kabbalistic Legacy? German Idealism's Relationship to Judaism," *Yearbook of German Idealism*, Volume VII, *Faith and Reason*, eds. Fred Rush, Jürgen Stolzenberg and Paul Franks (2010): 254–279.

16. This accusation had most recently been articulated by Friedrich Schlegel who was now entering his neo-Catholic and reactionary phase. See the useful overview in Horst Fuhrmans' introduction to F. W. J. Schelling, *Über das Wesen der menschliche Freiheit* (Stuttgart: Reclam, 1964), on this point 34.
17. I trace these arguments in Jeffrey S. Librett, *The Rhetoric of Cultural Dialogue: Jews and Germans from Moses Mendelssohn to Richard Wagner and Beyond* (Stanford: Stanford UP, 2000), 89ff.
18. For Schelling's polemic against Jacobi—including Jacobi's equation of reason with Spinozistic determinism, his irrationalism, his desire to return instead to historical revelation in its opacity as object of blind faith, and his revival of old animosities (notably, between Christians and Jews), see *Freedom* (409–16; 279–84).
19. On the question of language in Schelling, cf. Daniel Whistler, *Schelling's Theory of Symbolic Language: Forming the System of Identity* (Oxford: Oxford U Press, 2013); Marcia Sá Cavalcante Schuback, "The Work of Experience: Schelling on Thinking beyond Image and Concept," and Peter Warnek, "Reading Schelling after Heidegger: the Freedom of Cryptic Dialogue," both in Jason M. Wirth, *Schelling Now: Contemporary Readings* (Bloomington and Indianapolis: Indiana U Press, 2005), 66–83 and 163–83, respectively.
20. In the *Ages*, he puns more openly and insistently on the word "nature" (which can mean, of course, both "essence"—as opposed to "existence" or "appearance"—and "nature"—as opposed to "spirit" or "culture" or "artifice"), in speaking of the "divine nature" in both senses of "nature" at once.
21. Note that the anticipation-fulfillment model of the Pauline Jewish-Christian relation inheres here in the structure of the ground-existence or nature-God

unity. As I suggested in note 15 above, Schelling's mobilization of the anticipation-fulfillment model gives necessity in a strong sense to anticipatoriness, which is necessity itself in that it is needed to anticipate freedom, a necessity that anticipatoriness otherwise seems to lack in Pauline thought, becoming there invariably an obstacle of resentment triumphantly declared superfluous. Necessity is in Schelling necessary to freedom, not a mere contingent delay or inhibition of its arrival, and by implication, Judaism also regains an importance to Christianity that it often lacks in Pauline tradition. Whether the positive reception of Jewish thought (including Old Testament texts as well as Kabbala), however ambivalent, in Schelling's text has anything to do with the emergence of "anxiety" in his text, as if there might be a specific relation between "anxiety" and Judaism (given, e.g., Schelling's stress on the Old Testament's introduction of a contradictory duality of unity and multiplicity in God), is a complex question worth treatment I cannot provide here. One crucial point of reference for expansive treatment, which I address elsewhere, is Kierkegaard's position that "Judaism lies in anxiety," *The Concept of Anxiety*, 103ff.
22. Heidegger will re-formulate and displace this thought, as the substantialization of the subject, and the failure to grasp oneself as being-in-the-world.
23. Schelling says that self-hood is transformed into light "so daß er zwar (als Eigenwille) im Grund noch bleibt (weil immer ein Grund sein muß)—so wie im durchsichtigen Körper die zur Identität mit dem Licht erhobne Materie deshalb nicht aufhört Materie (finstres Prinzip) zu sein—aber bloß als Träger und gleichsam Behälter des höhern Prinzips des Lichts" (364–5; 242–3). This passage illustrates importantly again Schelling's displacement of the Pauline "dead letter" motif.
24. In the ensuing tradition, Kierkegaard will position anxiety in relation to sin, and determine anxiety itself as "freedom's actuality as the possibility of possibility"; Heidegger will argue that the "subject-object" of anxiety is existence (*Dasein*); Freud will say in sum that the object of anxiety is a libidinal excess occasioned by a separation reminiscent of birth, and Melanie Klein will see the object of anxiety as the death-drive or negativity, which as we'll see recapitulates what in *Ages* is the principle of "contraction," the displacement of what was dark "ground" in *Freedom*; and Lacan will argue that it is the "objet a." The connection between anxiety and birth that will become so important in Freud (through Otto Rank's influence) is prominently present already in Schelling, given that anxiety participates in the longing of the self (of God) to be born, and to give birth to itself through creation as such.
25. From a philological and philosophico-historical point of view, it is important to note here that "Angstqualität" ("the anxious quality") constitutes in Jakob Boehme's writings, which were of great importance for Schelling at this point, the third of the seven "source spirits" (*Quellgeister*) that contribute to the birth-process of creation. This third element can be seen as an attempted

synthesis of the first two, *Begierde* und *Bewegnis*. Cyril O'Regan (*Gnostic Apocalypse: Jacob Boehme's Haunted Narrative* [Albany: SUNY Press, 2002], 42) interpretively translates the seven spirits as: "imploding form," "directionless movement," "angst," "fire," "love," "meaning-giving movement of word," and "perfection of form." The first three qualities, as well as the last three, represent triadic groupings, and the fourth, "fire," mediates the passage from the first triad to the second. Robert F. Brown (*The Later Philosophy of Schelling: the Influence of Boehme on the Works of 1809–1815* [London: Associated University Presses, 1977]) also summarizes the seven qualities usefully: "The first (acrid) quality is the power of attraction and coagulation, the self-centeredness that produces rigidity… The second (sweet) quality is the characteristic of fluidity… The third (bitter) quality is the interpenetration of the first two, the rudimentary conjunction of form and flexibility, which makes possible motion. … The fourth (heat) is the source of organic life, the power of movement that is… vital. The fifth (love) is the power of realizing harmony among the first four qualities. … The sixth (sound) is the power of expression or realized form… The seventh (body) is the concrete result of the other six, the actual production of differentiated forms of beings" (41). A detailed exploration of the correspondences between Boehme's complex doctrine of the qualities and Schelling's thought, or even of the relationship between the "Angstqualität" in Boehme and anxiety in Schelling, certainly worthwhile (and a task Brown's wonderfully useful study nonetheless does not carry out), is beyond the scope of the present essay.

26. The word, "Schwindel," for "dizziness" in the passage under consideration can also mean, in other contexts, "hoax" or "swindle." Since it would be a hoax or swindle to pass one's particularity off as universality, there is an aspect of evil, and of the anxiety that cannot distinguish itself from evil, that is a swindle. In light of this implicit presence of the connotation of "swindle" in the background of the dizziness of anxiety, it is striking that, in a long note toward the end of *Freedom,* Schelling quotes Friedrich Schlegel as saying he wished the "unmanly pantheistic swindle" [*der unmännliche pantheistische Schwindel*] (409n; 279n) would stop—unless Schlegel should be understood as saying that he wants the "unmanly pantheistic dizziness" to stop, which is also a possible translation—and expresses his agreement with Schlegel, although not in the sense in which Schlegel intends. (The verbal echo disappears in Hayden-Roy's translation completely.) Schelling says, for example, that Jacobi's equation of Spinozism with reason belongs to the swindle, and at the same time, it is an equation that is indeed dizzying, since if Spinozism amounted to reason, any reasonable person would want to assent to it. Whether the suggestion of the possibility of a mutual substitutability of "swindle" for "dizziness" in the translation (or interpretation) of these passages is itself a swindle, or simply somewhat dizzying, is undecidable. On the passage of the signifier

"Schwindel" from Kant to Schelling to Kierkegaard, see Axel Hutter, "Das Unvordenkliche der menschlichen Freiheit" (122ff).

27. For the relevant philosophical background on the interwoven and ever-expanding thematic connotations of "voice" and "destiny" (*Stimme* and *Bestimmung*) see above all Johann Gottlieb Fichte, *Die Bestimmung des Menschen*, from 1800 *(Fichtes Werke,* ed. Immanuel Hermann Fichte, vol. II [Berlin: Walter de Gruyter and Co, 1971], 167–319). Concerning the philosophical foreground (i.e., Schelling's own posthumous destiny): the "innere Stimme" calling one into the "fall" into one's own "Eigenheit" in Schelling will be transformed, translated, or displaced by Heidegger in *Being and Time* into the "voice" of conscience calling one into one's "ownmost" potentiality to be, as one's own-most being guilty, which means "being the ground of a nothingness" (*Grundsein einer Nichtigkeit*), whereas in Schelling here it is the voice tempting one to choose the "false" self-hood of universalizing one's particularity, the egotism of evil or the evil of egotism.

28. Jacques Derrida alerted us, across the length of his prolific writing career, to the fragility of the "proper," in language and in reality, both in terms of the difficulty of attaining or determining it, and in terms of the quasi-unavoidable tendency of thought and experience to attempt just this.

29. It is noteworthy that Mendelssohn's word for the "purified" Spinozism—*geläutert*—reappears displaced in this position in Schelling's thought, as if to suggest that the purification, if there is to be one, must be situated here where the subject "dies to all ownhood" only through evil and death themselves, and not by way of a rational correction that would enable these things to be avoided.

30. To the affect (or mood) of anxiety—as attendant upon and expressive of the situation of being caught between the particular and universal will (or ground and existence), terms that will not completely coincide but toward the coinciding of which the particular will keeps pushing—Schelling adds the affect (or mood) of melancholy and sadness. The sadness comes, he says, from not being able to master the ground within ourselves: "This is the sadness [*Traurigkeit*] that clings to all finite life, and if even in God there is an at least relatively independent condition, then there is in him also a source of sadness, which however never comes to realization, but only serves the eternal joy of its overcoming. Hence the veil of melancholy [*der Schleier der Schwermut*] that is spread over all of nature, the deep indestructible melancholy [*Melancholie*] of all life. Joy must have sorrow [*Leid*], sorrow be transfigured into joy" (399; 270–1). Perhaps one can say that sadness comes from our mourning over the impossibility of mastering what causes our anxiety. On the doctrine of affects in the *Stuttgart Lectures*, where melancholy functions as the lowest, or most materially natural of feelings, see Brown, *The Later Philosophy of Schelling*, 172–186.

31. Note the similarity of the form of this utterance to the form—as well as the contrast of its content with the content—of Heidegger's displaced repetition as "the essence of the human lies in its existence," and to Sartre's displacement of Heidegger's thesis as "existence precedes essence."
32. On Heidegger's sense that in Schelling freedom is primarily freedom for evil, see Warnek, "Reading Schelling after Heidegger," 172ff.
33. The fact that Schelling takes the term, *Ungrund*, from Boehme is of importance and interest, but of course it does not yet tell us exactly why, in systematic conceptual terms, he needs to do so in this context. For a useful explication of the notion of *Ungrund* in Schelling, see Cem Kömürcü, "The Non-existence of the Absolute: Schelling's Treatise on Human Freedom," in S.J. McGrath and Joseph Carew, eds., *Rethinking German Idealism* (London: Macmillan Publishers, 2016), 99–120.
34. David Martyn, *Sublime Failures: the Ethics of Kant and Sade* (Detroit: Wayne State UP, 2003), 136 passim. Heidegger agrees, as Warnek discusses on various levels in "Reading Schelling after Heidegger." Zizek (*The Indivisible Remainder*, 7) likewise emphasizes that it is in Schelling's failures that his greatest insights and breakthroughs are situated.
35. For the notion of the contractive force, Schelling is drawing here, through the mediation of Jakob Boehme, but also through his direct knowledge of the Jewish mystical tradition, on the Kabbalistic notion of *Zimzum*, as the original contraction of God that enabled the possibility of creation. See Christoph Schulte, "*Zimzum* in the Works of Schelling," *Iyyun: The Jerusalem Philosophical Quarterly* 41 (January 1992): 21–40; Christoph Schulte, "Kabbala in der deutschen Romantik. Zur Einleitung," in Eveline Goodman-Thau, Gerd Mattenklott, and Christoph Schulte, eds., *Kabbala und Romantik* (Tübingen: Max Niemeyer, 1994), 1–22. Roughly a century later, these positive and negative forces will reappear (further secularized and psychologized) in Freud, *Beyond the Pleasure Principle*, as eros and thanatos.
36. When Freud says, as he does repeatedly, that the ego (*Ich*) is the "actual/authentic site of anxiety" (*die eigentliche Angststätte*), he will be positing the ego-anxiety or anxiety-ego in similar terms, mutatis mutandis, since the ego is defined as an overdetermined limit—between reality and id (*Es*), between reality and superego (*Überich*), between superego and id—tasked in each case with an ongoing, that is, endless or impossible mediation. (Sigmund Freud, "Hemmung, Symptom, und Angst," A. Mitscherlich et al, eds., *Studienausgabe*, vol VI [Frankfurt: Fischer, 1971], 280.)
37. *Cassell's English and German Dictionary* (New York: Funk and Wagnalls Company, 1958), 566.
38. In terms of the background "sources": as I have indicated above, Boehme had characterized anxiety as the third of the fundamental "qualities," or "sources," situated in the position of the contradictory interpenetration of the first two, *Begierde* and *Bewegnis*, which O'Regan summarizes as "imploding form" and

"directionless movement," respectively, and to which Schelling's first two potencies here roughly correspond. In the passage we are considering, more specifically, when Schelling conjoins "Widerwärtigkeit und ... Angst," in a gesture that moreover he will elsewhere repeat, he is alluding to the presence of this conjunction in Boehme's account of creation in *Aurora, oder Morgenröte im Aufgang*, from 1612 (*Aurora oder Morgenröte im Aufgang* [e-artnow, 2018]), where Boehme writes that "the creatures will live in great anxiety and loathing and will not be able to bear themselves through one body, but through two" ("die Kreaturen werden in großer Angst und Widerwärtigkeit leben und sich nicht werden können durch einen Leib gebären, sondern durch zweene") (Ch. 18, line 110, p. 192). In turn, as Schelling no doubt was aware, Boehme is alluding to Psalm 138, "Mein ganzes Herz erhebet dich," in the German translation of which we find the line "In Angst und Widerwärtigkeit wird mir allzeit dein Antlitz leuchten" ("In anxiety and loathing your visage will ever light my way.") While this standard German translation is hardly a literal one, the Hebrew term that "Angst" translates is "tsarah," in verse seven, meaning something more like "trouble" in the sense of dire "straits." The use of "Angst" for "straits" is strikingly apt, insofar as the etymology of "Angst" and "anxiety" goes back to Latin *angere*, "to choke or distress" (OED), and so implies a constriction or narrowing of the chest, throat, and lungs, as when an expansive movement would be constrained by a contractive one, precisely the situation when, in Schelling's terms here, the contractive movement of negation acts in contradiction to the expansive movement of positivity. The imagery of constriction contained in both "Angst" and "tsarah" in turn accords well with the "birth" imagery that pervades Schelling's accounts of divine becoming as creative self-revelation in both *Freedom* and *Ages*, as it already pervades Boehme's accounts of creation, to which Schelling is among other things trying to give a rigorous philosophical form. Indeed, Schelling goes back to the Hebrew for "created"—"bara"—and develops a fanciful etymological connection between that term and the German word "gebären"—to bear, to give birth to—later in the text (332; 99).

39. Because Schelling says almost nothing about the actual creation of the spirit world, bowing to the "limits of human powers," we omit discussion of the role of anxiety on this level.
40. In the context of this discussion of creation, anxiety is again figured as a rotation around one's axis ("likewise move about their own axes [*sich ebenfalls um ihre eigne Axe bewegen*]" (322; 91), and articulated again in terms of the image of not knowing whether one should be going out or going in, which he characterizes further as an "inner revulsion [*inneren Widerwillens*]" (323; 92).
41. Inexplicably, Jason Wirth's translation omits this line.
42. For Kierkegaard's commentary on this development in Schelling, see *The Concept of Anxiety: a Simple Psychologically Orienting Deliberation on the*

*Dogmatic Issue of Hereditary Sin*, ed. and trans. Reidar Thomte, in collaboration with Albert B. Anderson (Princeton: Princeton UP, 1980), 59n.

43. Indeed, Schelling does not hesitate to claim that "nothing is more similar to that inner madness than music," because it embodies the potencies of contraction and expansion so purely by contracting and expanding the tonal space between the different tones of which it is composed, becoming itself "a turning wheel … that departing from One point, through all of its excesses again and again runs back into the beginning" (338; 103). Music spins out dizzyingly the rotating anxiety of the beginning of all things. Schopenhauer will pick up on this analysis, transmitting it through Wagner and Nietzsche to modernist discourse.

# 24

## Romanticism and Pessimism

Frederick Beiser

Nowadays we tend to think of Romanticism and pessimism as completely different intellectual movements. They are assigned very different points of origin and time spans: Romanticism begins in the late eighteenth century and it dwindles by the middle of the nineteenth century, but pessimism does not start until the 1860s and it lasts until the beginning of the First World War. More importantly, these movements appear to be ideologically opposed. Romanticism, at least as first expressed by the early German Romantics (Schelling, Schleiermacher, Novalis, Hölderlin and Friedrich Schlegel), was deeply optimistic: it assumed that we human beings, through constant striving, could at least approach, even if we could never attain, the ideals of the good life. Life was for the romantic a wonderful adventure, where we could recreate, if we only tried hard enough, the beauty and harmony that had once been given to us in childhood. Such idealism is utterly opposed to the central thesis of pessimism: that life is not worth living, that it would be better if we had never been born. That thesis, in just that stark and harsh formulation, is explicit in all the German pessimists, in Schopenhauer, Eduard von Hartmann, Philipp Mainländer, Julius Bahnsen and the young Friedrich Nietzsche. The pessimists hold to this thesis because they are convinced that life is so filled with suffering and sorrow that no one in their right mind would want to live their lives over again. The early German Romantics were never naïve or blind

---

F. Beiser (✉)
Syracuse University, Syracuse, NY, USA
e-mail: fbeiser@syr.edu

© The Author(s) 2020
E. Millán Brusslan (ed.), *The Palgrave Handbook of German Romantic Philosophy*, Palgrave Handbooks in German Idealism, https://doi.org/10.1007/978-3-030-53567-4_24

to the facts of sorrow and suffering; but they believed that we could still make the world a better place through moral effort and striving. Although we have lost the unity with self, others, and nature which was once given to us, the early German Romantics believed we could still attempt to recreate it through our own efforts. The pessimists, by contrast, tell us that there is little point in striving to improve the world; the sorrow and suffering clings to existence itself; the only hope for redemption lies in escape from this life in aesthetic contemplation or asceticism.

Such, at any rate, would be my initial and tentative way of describing the relations between Romanticism and pessimism. But, as so often in the history of ideas, this very broad characterization comes unstuck when we describe the relations between particular thinkers allegedly illustrative of these broad movements. "The prince of the romantics" was Friedrich Wilhelm Joseph Schelling; and the father of pessimism was Arthur Schopenhauer. When, however, we examine their ideas in more detail, we see a surprising and striking similarity between them. Indeed, the affinity seems so great that some scholars have said that Schopenhauer's philosophy is little more than a restatement of Schelling's. Not only are Schopenhauer's basic principles the same as Schelling's, these scholars claim, but his pessimistic attitude toward life already appears in Schelling. On this view, then, pessimism was the sickly child of Romanticism.

This view of the relationship between Schelling and Schopenhauer has been remarkably persistent and pervasive. Two of the first reviews of Schopenhauer's *Die Welt als Wille und Vorstellung*—a short anonymous one and a long substantial one by no less than Johann Friedrich Herbart—noted the striking similarity between Schelling's and Schopenhauer's philosophy.[1] Both reviewers were puzzled by Schopenhauer's sharp polemics against Schelling, given that his ideas showed an obvious dependence on him. In 1859 the neo-Kantian philosopher Ludwig Noack, in a long study of Schelling and Romanticism,[2] reaffirmed the thesis of Schopenhauer's first reviewers. Noack maintained that there was nothing new or original in Schopenhauer's philosophy, whose entire content could be derived from Schelling's writings. Schopenhauer's philosophy was just Schelling's, though in a slightly different jargon. The reason that Schopenhauer lambasted Schelling, Noack explained, was partly to disguise his lack of originality, and partly to vent his anger and envy at Schelling's genius and success.

The same interpretation of Schopenhauer appears ten years later—some fifty years after the original reviews—in a remarkable book by Eduard von Hartmann: *Schelling's Positive Philosophie als Einheit von Hegel und*

*Schopenhauer*.[3] That no less than Hartmann was the author of this book is a very interesting and important fact for us because he was one of the central figures of German pessimism. The pessimism controversy, which dominated German intellectual life from the 1870s until the First World War, centered around Hartmann's *Philosophie des Unbewussten*, which was first published in 1869. In his Schelling tract Hartmann suggests that much of the inspiration for Schopenhauer's metaphysics and pessimism came from the late Schelling. Hartmann pointed out three basic similarities between Schelling and Schopenhauer: (1) both affirm the dualism between intuition and concept against Hegel; (2) both stress the primacy of the will, making it the ultimate reality; and (3) both maintain that life is filled with sorrow and suffering. Unlike Noack, however, Hartmann does not belittle Schopenhauer's originality, and he points out some important differences between them. Nevertheless, he holds that the similarities in their doctrines are so profound that Schopenhauer was perhaps influenced by Schelling. He notes that Schopenhauer had read Schelling's *Untersuchungen über das Wesen der menschlichen Freiheit*, which had appeared only a few years before the gestation of his own philosophy.[4]

The similarities between Schopenhauer's and Schelling's philosophy are not likely to appear so strange and striking once we put aside our later ideas of intellectual history and focus instead on Schopenhauer's intellectual development. Although pessimism became an intellectual movement only in the 1860s, Schopenhauer wrote his great masterpiece, *Die Welt als Wille und Vorstellung*, from 1812 to 1818, years when Romanticism was in full bloom. It is one of the bizarre accidents of intellectual history that Schopenhauer's book, which sank like a stone when it was first published in 1819, became something of a cult classic by the 1860s. Schopenhauer scholars have often noted his great debts to the early German Romantics, especially to Tieck and Wackenroder as well as to Schelling.[5] Some leading themes of his philosophy were common property of the German Romantics, viz., the organic concept of nature, the role of genius in art, the power of art in grasping truth and in giving value to life.

Because of Schopenhauer's debts to Romanticism, one might be tempted to describe the later vogue for his ideas as a recrudescence, or even continuation, of Romanticism. But I would like to argue in this chapter that we should resist this temptation. The more closely we examine the parallels between Schopenhauer and Schelling—the more we place them in their intellectual context—the more we find that Schopenhauer and Schelling are ultimately at odds with one another. My original intuitions and description of the antithesis between Romanticism and pessimism—so I will argue—are fundamentally correct. They only need more explanation. So my central thesis is this: we go seriously astray if we think that pessimism is little more than sad and bad Romanticism. Pessimism and Romanticism are antithetical worldviews, just as our first intuitions would have it.

# 1 The Historical Dimension

The question about Schelling's influence on Schopenhauer is rather complex. It has a historical and a logical dimension. The historical dimension concerns what Schopenhauer as a matter of fact learned from Schelling, in what respects he stood under his influence. The logical dimension concerns the similarities or dissimilarities in their doctrine, both in their meaning and their motivation. These are quite independent variables. Even if we could show that Schopenhauer was influenced by Schelling in important respects, it would not follow that their doctrines would be logically identical or exactly alike. And even if we could show that Schopenhauer was not influenced at all by Schelling, it would not follow that their doctrines are logically different. The issue becomes even more complicated because Schopenhauer, who read avidly everything written about himself, knew the charges about his lack of originally and he dismissed them brusquely and contemptuously. But then the question arises: Should we believe him? Should we take him at his word? Some of his early critics did not, claiming that Schopenhauer's disavowals were entirely defensive and disingenuous.

To cut through these issues, I propose first to consider the historical dimension of the question. In other words, I want to examine the facts of the case, that is, *what* did Schopenhauer read of Schelling, *when* did he read him and *what evidence*, if any, is there that he was influenced by him? Having treated the historical dimension, I will then move on to the logical one, comparing two of Schelling's and Schopenhauer's doctrines and placing them in their proper context. We shall find that, despite broad similarities, there were in fact deep differences between these philosophers—differences so great that they make it implausible to claim that Schopenhauer simply recast Schelling's ideas in a different terminology.

We know for a fact that the young Schopenhauer was a careful reader of almost all of Schelling's writings. Schopenhauer's first notebooks, which were written from 1812 to 1817, the crucial formative years for his philosophy, have many references to Schelling.[6] Almost all these references—it is worthy to note—are highly critical. There is one doctrine of Schelling in which Schopenhauer shows particular interest: the thesis of the identity of the ideal and the real.[7] Schopenhauer thinks that there is much truth to this thesis, though he does not think that Schelling has formulated it properly.[8] Here is one point—so I would argue—where Schelling might well have had an influence on Schopenhauer. Schopenhauer's own theory of the world as both will and representation makes perfect sense when we regard it as his own version of Schelling's thesis.

Besides Schopenhauer's notebooks, there are also the *Studienhefte*,[9] which are critical commentaries on the writings of particular philosophers (viz., Kant, Fichte, Fries, Jacobi). There are several critical discussions of many of Schelling's writings—*Die Weltseele, Bruno, Philosophie und Religion, System des transcendentalen Idealismus, Ideen zur Philosophie der Natur*—all of which Schopenhauer studied with great care. Schopenhauer also read Schelling's *Philosophische Schriften*—a compilation of his early writings—and the *Studienheft* devoted to it shows that he read *Untersuchungen über das Wesen der menschlichen Freiheit*, the text which is often cited to show most clearly his dependence on Schelling.[10] The contents of these *Studienhefte* are scattered and sundry—a *mélange* of critical comments and conspecti—and so they are very difficult to summarize. They are, however, very interesting in one light: they show that Schopenhauer took his Schelling very seriously; that he examined his doctrines carefully, that he weighed their pros and cons, and he took each case on its merits. Schopenhauer's many dismissive comments about Schelling might make it seem as if he were not willing to give Schelling's ideas a fair hearing; but the *Studienhefte* belie this impression. While it is fair to say that Schopenhauer's contempt for Hegel was so great that he could not give his philosophy anything approaching an objective assessment, the same cannot be said for his treatment of Schelling.

How Schopenhauer treated Schelling in his *Studienhefte* was one thing, how he treated him in his published writings was quite another. In his published writings Schopenhauer usually throws Schelling together with Fichte and Hegel as practitioners of sophistry and "*Scheinphilosophie*". His main objection to Schelling, and indeed Fichte and Hegel, is methodological. These philosophers follow Kant's definition of philosophy as a science of concepts, so that for them philosophy consists in analyzing and assembling abstractions that have no clear reference to anything given in experience.[11] Their philosophy lacks content because it does not derive concepts from experience but takes them up just as they are found in ordinary language. Schelling in particular is accused of pushing this a priori methodology too far, because he attempts to prove a priori what really should be given in experience.[12]

It is interesting and instructive to note what Schopenhauer has to say to rebut the charges that he had secretly followed Schelling. He takes up this complaint at the end of his 'Fragmente zur Geschichte der Philosophie' in the *Parerga*.[13] Schopenhauer examines especially the charge that his doctrine of the primacy of the will—that is, that the will is the thing-in-itself—already appears in Schelling's *Untersuchungen über das Wesen der menschlichen Freiheit*. Schopenhauer is happy to concede that he was not the first to advance this thesis—the same idea goes as far back as Clemens Alexandrinus—but he insists that he was the first to see its grounds and consequences, to examine its full meaning and import. Only he who has seen all this, he insists, is the proper founder of a doctrine; as it appears in Schelling, however, this doctrine appears vaguely and only suggestively, so that it is *"ein bloßer Vorspuk meiner Lehre"*.

It is completely unfair of Schopenhauer to claim that Schelling's doctrine is a mere vague anticipation of his own. Schelling knew full well the grounds and consequences of his thesis, to which he gives a very different meaning than Schopenhauer. Their statements about the primacy of the will appear in very different contexts, so that they ultimately do *not* mean the same thing by it. Yet, though this point is off the mark, Schopenhauer does give an interesting explanation for how Schelling and he came to espouse such similar doctrines.[14] Both began from Kant's theory of freedom, Schopenhauer explains, according to which the will is one noumenon or thing-in-itself. Both took the Kantian theory beyond its limits, however, by claiming that the will is not *one* thing-in-itself but *the* thing-in-itself. According to Schopenhauer, then, Schelling and he began from the same *Grundgedanke*—that the thing-in-itself is the will—and so they arrived at very similar theories. There is much to be said for Schopenhauer's geneaology, given that Schelling himself gives the same account of the origins of his view.[15] If Schopenhauer had limited himself to giving this geneaology, that would have been sufficient to defend his own originality; there was no need for him to claim that Schelling did not understand the full meaning or grounds of the Kantian doctrine.

All told, the historical sources provide no compelling evidence that Schopenhauer was influenced by Schelling in any particular point of doctrine. There is no smoking gun in the *Nachlaß* or published writings where Schopenhauer expressly declares his debts to Schelling. There is also no reason to exclude, however, that Schelling did have an influence on Schopenhauer. The evidence gives plenty of grounds for thinking that Schopenhauer *could have been* influenced by Schelling; but it gives no evidence for anything stronger than that.[16] We also have to keep in mind that, for many romantic doctrines, there were other sources for Schopenhauer than Schelling. Many of Schopenhauer's ideas were the common *Gedankengut* of the romantic generation. His organic concept of nature could well have had for its source Johann

Friedrich Blumenbach, who was his professor at Göttingen; and his belief in the value of art could have come solely from Wackenroder, whom he had read as a young man.[17]

There are, however, two Schellingian doctrines in particular that are uncannily similar to Schopenhauer's, so much so that they are held to have been important influences upon him. We now have to consider each of these doctrines.

## 2 The Logical Dimension

One of these doctrines is Schelling's metaphysics of the will, which seems suspiciously like Schopenhauer's own doctrine. Both Schopenhauer and Schelling regard the will as the ultimate reality, as the originator and source of all things. Schelling's first full statement of the doctrine appears in his *Untersuchungen über das Wesen der menschlichen Freiheit*. There he declares:

> *Es giebt in der letzen und höchsten Instanz gar kein anderes Seyn als Wollen. Wollen ist Urseyn, und auf dieses allein passen alle Prädicate desselben: Grundlosigkeit, Ewigkeit, Unabhängigkeit der Zeit, Selbstbejahung. Die ganze Philosophie strebt nur dahin, diesen Ausdruck zu finden.*[18]

This statement was often cited as evidence for Schelling's affinity with Schopenhauer, as one reason for thinking that they have the same metaphysics.

*Prima facie* this statement is very much Schopenhauer's position too. He also holds, as we have seen, that the will is the thing-in-itself, which is at least part of what Schelling means by *Urseyn*. But beyond this general point—this one *Grundgedanke*, as it were—the two thinkers part company. The main difference between them concerns the ontological status that they attribute to the will. For Schelling, the will must be the attribute of something, of some substance, which is the absolute or indifference point.[19] The Absolute is for Schelling simply a philosophical expression for what in more popular language is called God. Furthermore, his reflections on the primal act of will appear in a specific theological context: the attempt to address the old conundrum of the problem of evil. Evil, we learn, is the product of this primal act of will, the will of God to reveal himself in the world. For Schopenhauer, however, the will is not the property of anything; it is nothing more than a blind urge, a restless striving, which does not inhere in any independent or self-sufficient substance or Absolute. The Absolute is for Schopenhauer only a euphemism for God, whose existence he emphatically and explicitly denies.

The entire theological context of Schelling's theory of the will is for him only so much antiquated rubbish. For Schopenhauer, there is no such thing as the problem of evil in the traditional sense, given that the very existence of evil proves the *non-existence* of God.

This difference between Schopenhauer and Schelling is fundamental, affecting the very spirit of their worldviews. Throughout his philosophical development Schelling never abandoned the attempt to explain and rationalize theological doctrine. Understanding and justifying, interpreting and rationalizing, the ideas of the Christian tradition was for him the very purpose of philosophy.[20] Schopenhauer, however, wanted to separate philosophy from religion, which he saw as only an allegorical version of the truth.[21] While he was happy to explain and justify many religious doctrines, one stood beneath rational justification: the belief in the existence of God. This belief—whether in its theistic or pantheistic form—was for Schopenhauer a relic of earlier non-enlightened ages, which philosophy should now finally disavow. No one saw more clearly Schopenhauer's historical importance in this respect than the young Nietzsche who deemed Schopenhauer "the first admitted and unbending atheist that we Germans have had".[22]

As basic and pervasive as this difference is, it was overlooked by Schopenhauer's first reviewers and by Ludwig Noack. To his credit, it was noticed by Hartmann, who claimed that Schelling's and Schopenhauer's opposing attitudes toward the Christian heritage was one of the central differences between them.[23] Strangely, however, Hartmann was not willing to admit the full force of this difference. He continued to call Schopenhauer's theory a version of "pantheism", which he defined in rather narrow terms as monism.[24] Yet it is very misleading—I would insist—to call Schopenhauer's philosophy a form of "pantheism". There are too many religious associations attached to that term, all of which would have been repudiated by Schopenhauer himself, who never regarded his will as deserving the slightest reverence.

Beside the very different ontological status they ascribe to the will, Schelling's and Schopenhauer's account of the will differs in another important respect—indeed, they differ so drastically that it is hard to see how they were ever conflated. Schopenhauer had claimed that the will is the dominant power in the mind, and that it uses the intellect only for its purposes. There is indeed a radical voluntarism in Schopenhauer's philosophy, according to which whatever the will desires is good just because it wills it.[25] Although Schopenhauer too has a theory of ideas, these ideas seem to have no independent validity or regulative force over the will; they are not laws that constrain it but simply products of its energy. There is no such radical voluntarism in Schelling, however, who remained still very much an idealist. Although his later philosophy gives ultimate power to the will as the source of the *existence* of things, it bestows no such power upon it over the realm of *essences*, which have an eternal and autonomous validity. Both Schopenhauer and Schelling assume that, if only for the purpose of analysis, we can distinguish the will in itself from any particular goals; their will, as such, is only a blind striving, a subconscious urge, which has no specific ends. Schelling insists, however, that if the will is to be complete—if it is to be an actual will—it must have ends or purposes.[26] A will that is not a will for something is for Schelling a mere abstraction. When the will is complete, striving for specific ends, it submits or conforms to certain ideas of reason, which then serve as limits or restraints upon it.

The other doctrine of Schelling's philosophy that shows a great affinity with Schopenhauer is its pessimism. While Schelling never uses the term "pessimism", it seems to describe well his general worldview. Indeed, in its bleakness and blackness, Schelling's portrait of life in his later writings competes with Schopenhauer's. His primal will is no less the source of suffering and evil than that of Schopenhauer. The will, Schelling teaches, is by its very nature a striving, which is motivated by need or deficiency. The feeling of that need or deficiency is pain; so, as long as there is striving—and it never stops—there will also be pain.[27] No less than Schopenhauer, then, Schelling describes life in general as a never-ending tale of suffering and woe: "*Schmerz ist etwas Allgemeines und Nothwendiges in allem Leben…Aller Schmerz kommt nur vom Sein.*" [28] The life of every creature is a '*Schmerzensweg*" because that creature grows and develops only through conflict, which is the source of suffering. What the will wants in its striving is really *not* to will, to be free of its willing, which it feels as a great burden; but the more it strives for will-lessness, Schelling warns us, the more elusive that goal becomes.[29]

There is "a shroud of melancholy" hanging over all nature, "a deep indestructible sadness" affecting all life, Schelling writes, because the will always has to strive against some obstacle, something which it cannot overcome without destroying itself.[30] Because life emerges only out of conflict, and because it never knows the outcome of its struggles, the pervasive feeling in life is anxiety (*Angst*).[31] This means that "the basic stuff of all life and existence is horror."[32] Not only does Schelling think that human life is filled with pain and sorrow; he also points out that it is felt as worthless and pointless. Every finite human being finds itself subject to the moral law but unable to execute its requirements. Because it cannot do what it knows it ought—act for the sake of the law and not only according to it—the human being then feels itself worthless; it recognizes "*das Nichts, den Unwerth seines ganzen Daseins*".[33]

All these features of Schelling's bleak view of life were brought out by Hartmann,[34] who saw them as the precursor of Schopenhauer's later pessimism. Hartmann did not go on to specify, however, any differences in Schelling's and Schopenhauer's views of life. Schelling, in his opinion, was just as much a pessimist as Schopenhauer. It comes as little surprise, then, that Hartmann incorporated Schelling's dark view of life into his own pessimism, which is indebted to Schelling just as much as it is to Schopenhauer.

Although Hartmann was right to point out these affinities between Schelling and Schopenhauer's worldviews, he went too far in conflating them and in turning Schelling into a pessimist *avant la lettre*. All of Schelling's statements about the negative side of life are valid for only one part of his general theory of history. According to that theory, life consists in a movement from primal unity, to alienation, and then to the overcoming of alienation in a return to primal unity. This is also a movement from unity, to difference, to unity-in-difference; or, as Schelling sometimes puts it, from being-in-itself, to being-for-itself, to being-in-and-for-itself.[35] There is a profound optimism behind this theory of history because the moment of alienation or difference is always overcome in the return to unity and wholeness. Although the moment of negativity is indeed essential and inevitable, it is only the necessary means to higher self-awareness and freedom. And while the new unity is again affected by alienation or difference, that difference too is overcome on a still higher level, so that there is a constant growth of spirit. This theory of history is a familiar to all students of German idealism; it first appears in Kant and Schiller, but then again in the early German Romantics. Schelling was no exception. Although his later philosophy gives this theory a theosophic cast, he reaffirms and reapplies it constantly in his last works.[36]

The crucial point to see here is that Schelling's bleak statements about the sorrow and suffering of life apply only to the second stage of his theory of history, the stage of alienation or difference where spirit loses its primal unity. That loss is difficult and painful, a terrible trauma, to be sure, but it is also one that spirit has to experience on its way to greater self-consciousness and self-realization. Schelling never doubts that this sorrow and suffering will be overcome in a final, triumphant stage where spirit overcomes its alienation and returns to its original spiritual unity and wholeness.

Schelling's philosophy of history therefore leaves open the possibility of progress, of achieving the good life again after having lost it. We only have to contrast it with Schopenhauer's theory of history to see the profound difference between him and Schelling. Schopenhauer regards history as one damn cycle after another, as a long repetitious tale about the same terrible old thing.[37] There is no progress in history according to Schopenhauer. Although he does believe in the possibility of redemption, of achieving some measure of the good life for a few rare and isolated human beings, that redemption comes not from acting but from retreating entirely from history into the realm of aesthetic and religious contemplation.

Finally, then, we can see two fundamental differences between Schelling's and Schopenhauer's philosophy. Schelling affirms and Schopenhauer denies the existence of the Absolute or God; and Schelling affirms and Schopenhauer denies the possibility of progress in history. These are basic differences not only between Schopenhauer and Schelling, I would argue, but between Romanticism and pessimism in general, which have fundamentally opposing views about the value of life. When Schelling affirmed the existence of God, and when he upheld progress in history, he made it possible for evil to be overcome and for goodness to prevail on earth and heaven. When, *per contra*, Schopenhauer denied the existence of God, and when he disputed progress in history, he undercut that very possibility. Evil and suffering are for Schopenhauer insurmountable realities which no amount of human striving will ever diminish. These competing attitudes toward evil are decisive, I would suggest, in making for an optimistic or pessimistic worldview. Pessimism is not, then, just bad or sad Romanticism; it is, in these two basic respects, the very antithesis of Romanticism. Such is the lesson we learn—so I hope to have showed—when we compare Schelling, the eternal romantic, with Schopenhauer, the grumpy grandpa of pessimism.

## Notes

1. The anonymous review appeared under the title 'Freie Mittheilungen eines Literaturfreundes' in *Literarisches Wochenblatt,* Band IV, No. 30 (October 1819), 234–6. Herbart's review appeared in *Hermes* 3. Stück (1820), 131–149, reprinted in *Johann Friedrich Herbart, Sämtliche Werke*, eds. Karl Kehrbach and Otto Flügel (Langensalza: Hermann Beyer & Söhne, 1887–1912), XII, 56–75.
2. Ludwig Noack, *Schelling und die Philosophie der Romantik. Ein Beitrag zur Culturgeschichte des deutschen Geistes* (Berlin: Mittler, 1859), 2 vols. On Schopenhauer, see II, 360–75.
3. Eduard von Hartmann, *Schelling's positive Philosophie als Einheit von Hegel und Schopenhauer* (Berlin: Otto Loewenstein, 1869).
4. Ibid, 24n**.
5. See especially Arthur Hübscher, *The Philosophy of Schopenhauer in its Intellectual Context*, translated by Joachim Baer and David Cartwright (Lewiston: Edwin Mellen Press, 1989), 34–85.

6. Arthur Schopenhauer, *Der handschriftliche Nachlaß*, ed. Arthur Hübscher (Frankfurt am Main: Verlag von Waldemar Kramer, 1966–8), I, 28, 35, 46, 78, 79, 135, 142, 168, 191n, 201, 361–362.
7. Ibid, I, 28, 35, 201, 361–2.
8. See Schopenhauer's critique of the theory in 'Lehre vom Idealen und Realen', *Parerga, Werke* IV, 37–40.
9. *Der handschriftliche Nachlaß*, II, 304–340.
10. Ibid, II, 313–15.
11. See Schopenhauer's objection in 'Ueber Philosophie und ihre Methode', in *Paralipomena*, in Schopenhauer, *Sämtliche Werke*, ed. Wolfgang von Lohneyesen (Darmstadt: Wissenschaftliche Buchgesellschaft, 1989), V 15.
12. See Schopenhauer, 'Den Intellekt betreffende Gedanken', in *Paralipomena, Werke* V, 73.
13. *Werke* IV, 165–170.
14. Schopenhauer, *Parerga, Werke* IV, 166.
15. Schelling, *Untersuchungen über das Wesen der menschlichen Freiheit, Sämtliche Werke*, ed. K.F.A. Schelling (Stuttgart: Cotta: 1856–61) I/7, 352. (The Roman numeral indicates an 'Abtheilung', the Arabic numeral a volume number).
16. In his article 'Schopenhauer und Schelling. Aufzeichnungen über den Begriff der Entzweiung des Willens', in *Schopenhauer und die Schopenhauer-Schule*, eds. Fabio Ciraci, Domenico Fazio and Matthias Koβler (Würzbürg: Königshausen & Neumann, 2009), 73–87, Sandro Barbera argues that Schopenhauer was especially influenced by Schelling's idea of polarity and the conflict of the basic forces of nature. He writes that Schelling's idea "must have influenced Schopenhauer" (85). Yet, as if to underline the uncertainty, Barbera also notes the important differences between Schopenhauer's concept and Schelling's. We can say at best here that Schelling's idea was the stimulus for Schopenhauer's own thinking.
17. On Schopenhauer and Blumenbach, see David Cartwright, *Schopenhauer, A Biography* (Cambridge: Cambridge University Press, 2010), 142–3; on Schopenhauer and Wackenroder, see Hübscher, *Philosophy of Schopenhauer*, 38–48.
18. Schelling, *Werke* I/7, 350. Cf. Schelling's statements from the *Philosophie der Offenbarung*: "*Freiheit ist unser Höchstes, unsere Gottheit, diese wollen wir als letzte Ursache aller Dinge*" II/3, 256. Cf. II/3, 206, 207.
19. See Schelling, *Untersuchungen über das Wesen der menschlichen Freiheit, Werke*, I/7, 406, 409, 412. See also Schelling, *Die Philosophie der Offenbarung, Werke* II/3, 218, 222, 234, 236.
20. See, for example, Schelling's polemic against Eschenmeyer in the opening sections of *Philosophie und Religion, Werke* I/6, 16–27.
21. For Schopenhauer's views on the relationship between philosophy and religion, see his 'Über das metaphysische Bedürfnis', in *Die Welt als Wille und Vorstellung, Werke* II, 212–217.

22. Friedrich Nietzsche, *Die Fröhliche Wissenschaft*, §357, in *Sämtliche Werke, Kritische Studienausgabe*, eds. G. Colli and M. Montinari (Berlin: de Gruyter, 1967–77), III, 599.
23. Hartmann, *Schelling's positive Philosophie*, 34–5.
24. Ibid, 25, 50.
25. See Schopenhauer, §63 of *Die Welt als Wille und Vorstellung, Werke* I, 480.
26. *Untersuchungen über das Wesen der menschlichen Freiheit, Werke* I/7, 359.
27. See Schelling, *Philosophie der Mythologie, Werke* II/1, 472–3.
28. *Die Weltalter, Werke* I/8, 335.
29. See Schelling, *Die Weltalter, Werke* I/8, 235–6.
30. *Untersuchungen über das Wesen der menschlichen Freiheit, Werke* I/7, 399.
31. *Die Weltalter, Werke* I/8, 336.
32. Ibid, 339. Cf. *Philosophie der Offenbarung, Werke* II/3, 226.
33. *Philosophie der Mythologie, Werke* II/1, 556.
34. Hartmann, *Schelling's Positive Philosophie*, 26–7.
35. Schelling, *Philosophie der Offenbarung, Werke* II/3, 253.
36. See especially the section 'Freiheit, Sittlichkeit und Seligkeit: Endabsicht und Anfang der Geschichte', in *Philosophie und Religion, Werke* I/6, 50–9. Schelling applies the same theory of history throughout his *Die Weltalter* and *Philosophie der Offenbarung*.
37. See Kapitel 38, 'Über Geschichte', of *Die Welt als Wille und Vorstellung, Werke* II, 563–573.

# 25

# Romanticism as Modernism: Richard Wagner's "Artwork of the Future"

Günter Zöller

This chapter argues for German Romanticism's preparatory and anticipatory relation to modernism by drawing on the works of the composer, writer and theater practitioner, Richard Wagner (1813–1883). Section 1 addresses the special status of music, especially Austro-German music, in European Romanticism. Section 2 places Romanticism in general and musical Romanticism in particular into the wider context of the early modern debate about the respective merits and demerits of ancient and modern art and culture. Section 3 introduces Wagner as an innovative theoretician and practitioner of Romantic-era music theater. Section 4 presents Wagner's main operatic works as manifestations of a modernism in romantic guise. Throughout the focus is on Wagner's critical reception of ancient, classical theater and modern, romantic opera. In methodological terms, the chapter seeks to provide a comparative and contrastive morphology of Romanticism in order to exhibit the latter's affinities with modern art in general and with modern music theater in particular.

## 1 Romanticism and Music

Not unlike "being" in Aristotle, "Romanticism" is said in multiple ways. In particular, the term and concept "Romanticism" has varied considerably in its meaning and use across time and space. Originating in the designation for a

G. Zöller (✉)
University of Munich, Munich, Germany
e-mail: zoeller@lmu.de

form of poetry from the Middle Ages ("romances"), so labeled retrospectively, "Romanticism" subsequently became associated with the aesthetic forms and norms of a culture different from classical, Greco-Roman antiquity, and embraced as an alternative to the latter's retake in various waves of classicism and neo-classicism. By the late eighteenth century, "romantic" had become the opposite of "classic" and Romanticism the counterculture to classicism. The rivalry between the two principal modes of cultural orientation typically involved a dialectical relation, with Romanticism functioning as a rebellious countermovement to the perceived strictures of classicism, and (neo-) classicism calling for a return to the conservative concern for order and form.

Historically, the romantic revolution spread across Europe in the late eighteenth and the early nineteenth century, stretching from early beginnings ("proto-Romanticism") through an almost classical culmination ("high Romanticism") to subsequent developments ("late Romanticism") and even revivals toward the end of the nineteenth century ("neo-Romanticism"). The main countries of the emerging and maturing Romantic Movement were France, Germany, England, Scotland and Italy. The main arts involved in European Romanticism were poetry in the wider sense, including lyric poetry and literary prose works, especially novels, as well as drama, but also the visual arts, especially painting and drawing, and music.

In the case of literature and the visual arts, Romanticism typically turned on the revision, rejection or replacement of a previous classical art form, to be found either in classical antiquity or in the latter's various revivals since the Northern and the Italian Renaissance. In the latter case, Romanticism often arose in the context of a national tradition and by recourse to a national history or mythology. By contrast, in music Romanticism arose in opposition not to classical antiquity, from which practically no musical works had survived, but in opposition to more immediately preceding musical styles and manners, especially the European baroque style of the seventeenth and the first half of the eighteenth century, chiefly characterized by a pathos and formality that musical Romanticism sought to oppose, or rather counterbalance, with the sonic cult of personal feeling and individual expression.

In the singular case of music—of music as a high art, as opposed to popular music past and present—the emerging Romanticism stood in close proximity and thorough continuity with a recent new style in music joining expressiveness and poise, which came to constitute the "classical style"[1] in music, as epitomized in the works of the so-called Viennese school or Viennese classicism (Haydn, Mozart, Beethoven).[2] In fact, certain aspects and entire work complexes of those classical composers—the prime example being Beethoven—can be rightfully regarded as romantic, or at least proto-romantic, in character. Inversely, the romantic composers immediately following the Viennese masters could be considered to belong to a comprehensively conceived core of classical music. Accordingly, musical Romanticism encompasses a classical and a post- or even anti-classical stance and, moreover, includes genuinely romantic as well as pseudo- and even anti-romantic musical characters and features.

In terms of musical genres and forms, Romanticism, when taken to include even the more narrowly classical composers of the Austro-German tradition, chiefly Beethoven, spanned the entire spectrum, ranging from the symphony and the solo concerto through chamber music and instrumental solo works to vocal and stage works. In more general, socio-cultural terms, Romanticism in (Austro-German) music marked the shift from the ceremonial and representational role of music in courtly culture and princely settings in early modern Europe to bourgeois music making and music listening in middle-class homes and public concert halls, a development that began in the later eighteenth century and burgeoned in the nineteenth century. In politico-economic terms, Romanticism in music involved the gradual change with regard to the operatic art form from being a site of ostentatious expense and conspicuous consumption to being subject to economic commercialization and social democratization—a development that reached its full form only over the course of the twentieth century.[3]

A particularly striking area of music writing and music making under conditions of Romanticism was the historical development of opera from the baroque period, in which the operatic art form first arose, through the nineteenth century, in which it reached its apogee. After its invention in humanist efforts to revive and recreate ancient Greek and Roman tragedy around 1600 (Claudio Monteverdi), opera had undergone a rapid growth and spread throughout the seventeenth and the early eighteenth century.[4] Originally centered in Italy, especially Venice and Naples, the operatic form found further development in France and the German-speaking lands, with classical French opera (*tragédie lyrique*) representing an alternative type to the Italian twin typology of comic and serious opera (*opera buffa, opera seria*) and opera in the German lands largely following the Italian precedents, often with Italian composers, singers and players active throughout Europe.

In terms of dramatic content and with regard to the textbooks (libretti) underlying the compositions, the operatic art form of the extended Baroque period, from Monteverdi's *Orfeo* (1607) through Mozart's late contribution to the tradition, *The Clemency of Titus* (1791), was deeply indebted to Greek mythology and Roman history. By contrast, romantic opera manifested a distinct preference for topics from the more recent past or from locally specific mythical or historical events, in effect replacing the internationalism of earlier, Baroque opera with nationally specific operatic works. Moreover, while the earlier opera tradition mostly worked with a fixed set of published libretti, set to music numerous times over many decades, romantic opera tended to be based on textbooks specifically written for a given compositional project, even if the plot in question derived from earlier sources.

By the early nineteenth-century post-baroque, romantic opera came to exist in distinct, nationally differentiated formats: Italian *bel canto* opera on serious, heroic subjects (Vincenzo Bellini, *The Puritans*, 1835); Italian *opera buffa* on comical bourgeois subjects (Gioachino Rossini, *The Barber of Seville*, 1816); French comic opera (*opéra comique*) involving middle-class characters and spoken dialogue (François-Adrien Boieldieu, *The White Lady*, 1825); French *grand opéra* on heroic historical subjects executed on a large scale and in grand style (Giacomo Meyerbeer, *The Huguenots*, 1836; *The Prophet*, 1849) and German light opera (*Singspiel, Spieloper*), with spoken dialogue and popular action (Carl Maria von Weber, *The Freeshooter*, 1821; Heinrich Marschner, *Hans Heiling*, 1833; Albert Lortzing, *Undine*, 1845). In musical terms, all these developments, with the exception of colossal *grand opéra*, tended to cherish cantability over complexity and sonority over construction.

The change from Baroque opera to the simplified and popularized forms of opera that spread in the Age of Romanticism had been prepared by the reforms of the operatic genre at the hands of Christoph Willibald Gluck (1714–1787) and Luigi Cherubini (1760–1842). Working both in the Italian and in the French tradition, Gluck aimed to reduce the theatrical trappings of baroque opera to classical poise and purity even in the rendition of passion and pathos. Cherubini, in his efforts to straddle the gap between the Italian emphasis on melody and the French focus on harmony, transposed the political fervor of the French Revolution into the expressiveness of an operatic drama populated with heroes and heroines rendered as real human beings and with ordinary human beings becoming heroes and heroines.

Wagner's emerging operatic work presupposed all those developments and further continued the romantic turn in music in general and in the operatic art form in particular. By the time Wagner emerged on the musical theater scene in the second third of the nineteenth century, the center of specifically operatic innovation and generally artistic advancement had shifted from Italy and the German-speaking lands, chiefly Mozart's Vienna, to Paris—that "capital of the nineteenth century" (W. Benjamin). Wagner's aesthetic fascination with grandiosity and monumentality, coupled with his penchant toward intricate details and fine features, owed as much to Beethoven's large-scaled but minutely executed symphonic works as to *grand opéra* at the hands of its primary practitioner, Meyerbeer, and the latter's introduction of mass spectacles and scenic extravagance into opera, coupled with more intimate scenes and private situations. To be sure, rather than acknowledging his aesthetic and artistic debt to Meyerbeer's successful innovations in romantic opera, Wagner attacked him (along with the neo-classical romantic composer, Felix Mendelssohn Bartholdy [1809–1847]) with aesthetically coded antisemitic slander (*Judaism in Music*, 1850, 2nd rev. ed. 1869).[5]

## 2 Ancients and Moderns

Romanticism's general reorientation of the arts from the emulation of classical antiquity to the fascination with later periods of history belongs to a larger cultural context that both preceded and succeeded the Romantic era. Considered in a broader perspective that stretches backward to the seventeenth and early eighteenth century and forward into the later nineteenth and early twentieth century, European Romanticism forms parts of a larger debate about the aesthetic, scientific, social and political merits of the recent past and the present in comparison with earlier periods in general and with classical antiquity in particular. The debate originated in France as a learned dispute about the aesthetic and artistic significance of classical authors for the writing of current literary works, chiefly lyric poetry and drama.

In the debate, termed "the quarrel between the ancients and the moderns," the "ancients" were not the classical authors themselves but their admirers and emulators, who advocated the "imitation of the ancients" in current aesthetic endeavors. By contrast, the "moderns" maintained the need to adapt aesthetic theory and practice to the circumstances and exigencies of the contemporary world, marked by the new scientific worldview, Christian religion in its newly arisen confessional varieties and the emerging monarchically ruled sovereign territorial state. The debate soon widened to encompass the general contrastive comparison of the ancient and the modern world. In the process, the horizon of the debate shifted from more narrowly aesthetic and artistic issues to social and political concerns. In particular, ancient Rome's republican constitution as a civic society instituted and maintained in the interest of the common good (*res publica*, commonwealth) became the center of attention of historically informed philosophical thinking about ancient and modern modes of political rule, chiefly so in Montesquieu's monumental comparative study of socio-civic life across space and time, *The Spirit of the Laws* (1748).

Against the broader backdrop of the quarrel between the ancients and the modern, the Romantic era takes on a wider socio-cultural significance. The romantic alternative to classical antiquity and its neo-classical revivals is no longer limited to the aesthetic espousal of post-classical, essentially medieval mythology and history. In addition to turning back to a romanticized pre-modern past, Romanticism reflects specifically modern concerns with a world that is no longer, as had been the case in the classical and the medieval world, governed by traditional order but marked by increasing individuality and novel forms of sociality. Even where Romanticism seems to seek the solidity and security of a pre-modern culture and society, as in its nostalgia for the Middle Ages and the countryside, it is the absence of such solidity and security in modern life that drives the imaginary longing for it. Moreover, not a few of the German Romantics, rather than turning to a mythical or historical past, squarely address themselves to the aesthetic and political challenges of the contemporary, essentially modern world. This holds especially for the early German Romantics (Hardenberg-Novalis, Fr. Schlegel), who formulate their aesthetics and poetics under the formative influence of contemporary critical philosophy (Kant, Fichte).

The ambiguous position of Romanticism between pre-modern nostalgia and proto-modern progressivism finds an apt expression in the call for a "new mythology," to be found in the romantic classicist, Friedrich Hölderlin (1770–1843), and the classicist romantic, Friedrich Schlegel (1772–1829), alike.[6] In seeking to invent and implement a contemporary set of basic beliefs and functioning fictions, the romantic—or rather, the modern—mythologists recognize the continued need for shared assumptions and common convictions in the face of modern, liberalized but also fragmented life. To be sure, the modern mythology remains more a plan and a project than an actual achievement. Where the undertaking finds a measure of success, as in the late hymnic poetry of Hölderlin with its daring fusion of pagan and Christian religious figures, it runs the risk of turning into a private mythology not easily to be shared by a larger public.

But the modernism implicit in European Romanticism, especially in German early Romanticism, is not limited to creatively confronting the classical past with the current present. Romantic modernism also encompasses a progressive orientation toward the future—a future to be shaped and brought about by human artistic and social efforts. By the late eighteenth century and the early nineteenth century, the binary opposition underlying the confrontation of antiquity and modernity has been integrated into a tripartite scheme that expands the past and the present by including the future. The philosophy of history so articulated is chiefly due to Kant and his idealist successors (Fichte, Schelling, Hegel). From a romantic perspective, the philosophical (re-)construction of ancient as well as modern history involves a radical reassessment of modernity in that the latter now is divided between an earlier and still incomplete or even deficient form of modernity, viz., the present, and a completed and perfected form of modernity yet to be brought about, viz., the future.

The first philosopher to introduce the future as the appropriate area of ameliorative action on an individual as well as social, even global scale is Fichte,[7] eventually to be followed by the Hegelians on the left of the political spectrum, chiefly Ludwig Feuerbach and Karl Marx. In the aesthetic realm, the dual modernity of a still deficient present, on the one side, and a perfected future, on the other side, typically plays out as the eventual sublated ("dialectical") retrieval of a lost primary phase or earlier era by means of which the still lacking present is reformed and redeemed. A particularly striking example of the dialectical development of human nature and culture, as perceived in modernist Romanticism, is the Kantian-inspired account of world history as the regaining of a lost paradise only after the traversal of the entire history of the world, advanced by the patriotic poet and political publicist, Heinrich von Kleist (*On the Marionette Theater*, 1810).

The integration of the binary opposition between antiquity and modernity into the triple sequence of past, present and future provides the yearning and longing that is outright definitional of Romanticism with a twofold orientation: to some remote past and to some distant future. Moreover, in the romantic imagination the opposite ends of the world-historical spectrum tend to merge, making it difficult to distinguish the nostalgic retrieval of some past from the eager anticipation of some future—and vice versa. With regard to Romanticism's anticipatory and preparatory identity with modernism, the intertwining of endings and beginnings brings with it the uneasy relationship of the romantics to the present, in which things are forever suspended between their pristine origin and their perfect end. Accordingly, from a romantic perspective, "modern" may denote both a regretful loss and an expected gain. As a modernist, the romantic sees the future in the present; as a romantic, the modernist misses the future in the present.

As far as music in the Austro-German tradition is concerned, the forward-looking, modernist dimension of apparently backward-bent Romanticism is ideally illustrated by the works of Robert Schumann (1810–1856). In his cyclically arranged pieces for solo piano (e.g., *Kreisleriana*, *Phantasy Pieces*) and his orchestral compositions, chiefly his four symphonies, Schumann infuses music with a longing and urging that is at once retrospective—"romance" being a favorite work title of his—and progressive, engaged in self-abandonment and self-transcendence. The further development of Romanticism in Austro-German music later in the nineteenth century turns on the parallel formation of two (informal, non-institutional) schools of composition, one headed by the piano virtuoso turned composer, Franz Liszt (1811–1886), and labeled "new German school," the other spearheaded by the more conservatively inclined Johannes Brahms (1833–1897), who yet proved to be a secret cofounder of musical modernism—"Brahms the progressive" in the words of Arnold Schoenberg.[8]

While Liszt seeks to advance musical Romanticism with formal innovations such as the "symphonic poem" and with daring musical means, chiefly involving harmonics, Brahms clads his version of musical progress into classical forms and traditional genres, such as the symphony and the string quartet. The aesthetic difference between the rivaling camps is epitomized by the opposition of Lisztean "program music," based on some extra-musical notion such as a mythical or historic person or a locale (e.g., *Orpheus, After Reading Dante, The Bells of Geneva*), and "absolute music," free of extra-musical content and essentially involving "sonically moved forms," as described and prescribed by Eduard Hanslick in his seminal treatise *On the Musically Beautiful* (1854).[9]

## 3 Drama and Music

As a composer of operatic works, based on textbooks (libretti) and informed by the dramatic developments of detailed plots involving multiple characters and their complex actions and interactions, Wagner partakes in the turn to programmatic music championed by the new German school. Moreover, like his predecessor of sorts, Meyerbeer, and his near contemporary and musical rival, Giuseppe Verdi (1813–1901), Wagner is a composer of stage works only, with the exception of minor, mostly early, purely orchestral works and some works for solo piano. Moreover, after some early operas based on works of world literature (Gozzi, Shakespeare), all of Wagner's further stage works, from *Rienzi* (1842) to *Parsifal* (1882), are based on textbooks written by himself. In addition, Wagner's entire musical career is tied to the theater, initially through conducting posts at a number of opera houses (Magdeburg, Riga, Dresden) and eventually through the long-term planning, preparation and realization of his own theater, with regular summer performances of his own works only, in the Franconian provincial town of Bayreuth.

His beginnings in the romantic opera tradition and his adherence to the program-based composition style of the new German school notwithstanding, Wagner's work is marked by a radical departure from established musical forms and ingrained aesthetic norms. Wagner soon comes to regard opera, especially its most recent monumental manifestation as French spectacular opera (*grand opéra*), as aesthetically flawed and musically failed. In particular, Wagner objects to the traditional opera aesthetics, still preserved in romantic opera, of granting primacy to the musical (orchestral as well as vocal) element in opera, to the detriment of the scenic action accompanied by the composed music. On Wagner's critical assessment, as presented in great detail in his main work on the past, present and future of the operatic art form, *Opera and Drama* (1851), traditional opera tends to consider the music as originally independent from the scenic action and treat it as an art by itself ("absolute melody," "absolute music," "absolute instrumental music").[10]

By contrast, Wagner sets out to create operatic works from their origin in action ("drama"). For Wagner music is to be a means to drama—the main means, but still only a means to an extra-musical end, which consists in the comprehensive scenic rendition of the drama that is human existence in general and human individual existence in a social context in particular.[11] In its comprehensive, humanist ambition, opera, as reconceived by Wagner, is linked more closely to ancient drama, especially Attic tragedy, than to romantic opera. Wagner himself establishes the connection, citing the works of Aeschylus and Sophocles and explicitly referring to the former's *Oresteia* (*Agamemnon*, *The Libation Bearers*, *The Eumenides*) and the latter's Theben plays, *Oedipus the King* and *Antigone*.[12] To be sure, in line with his general project of modernizing traditional opera, Wagner refrains from recycling Greeks myths, as had been the custom in the operatic tradition from Monteverdi (*Orfeo*, 1607) through Rameau (*Hyppolite et Aricie*, 1733) and Gluck (*Alceste*, 1767) to Mozart (*Idomeneo*, 1781) and Cherubini (*Medea*, 1797).

His pointed modernization of traditional opera notwithstanding, Wagner still agrees with the essentially tragic outlook of classical drama, to be found in the (preserved) works of Aeschylus and Sophocles, which have the human being go under in pursuit of some real or perceived required action that turns out to involve a disastrous transgression.[13] It deserves mention that Wagner's constructive engagement with Attic tragedy antedates by two decades Nietzsche's philological cast defense of Wagnerian opera as the modern rebirth of ancient drama (*The Birth of Tragedy*, 1872).[14] More closely considered, it is Wagner's earlier sustained reflection on the relationship of (modern) opera to (ancient) drama, rather than Nietzsche's learned but contested reconstruction of Attic tragedy as an ancient foreform of opera, that inaugurates late and post-romantic opera's claim to inheriting the humanist scope and the tragic vision of ancient drama. To be sure, Wagner's successors in that regard will return to ancient mythology in their efforts to forge a genuinely modern form of opera, as attested to by that genre's chief practitioners in the continued Austro-German tradition, from Richard Strauss (*Electra*, 1909) through Carl Orff (*Antigonae*, 1949) to Hans Werner Henze (*The Bassarids*, 1966) and Aribert Reimann (*Medea*, 2010).

A further feature that sets off Wagner's creative engagement with ancient drama from Nietzsche's more professorial perspective on the topic is the social, even political focus of Wagner's retake on Attic tragedy. While acknowledging the ritualistic and religious origins of ancient drama in cult and service, Wagner clearly perceives the civic dimensions inherent in the development and the deployment of ancient drama as a tragically refined mirror of the exigencies of life in the *polis*.[15] To be sure, in his daring appropriation of classical drama for modern opera, Wagner does not simply continue the ancient poetics and politics of human tragic existence. As a composer-thinker steeped in early nineteenth-century philosophical and political debates, Wagner develops not into an inventive neo-classicist, as Berlioz would with his colossal opera project, "The Trojans" (1856–1858), but into a progressive modernist inspired by ancient and by modern culture and society alike.

Wagner's singular position in the history of romantically modern, or modernly romantic, art in general and operatic art in particular is not the least due to the theoretical, even philosophical background that sustains his work for the music theater. While being primarily a seasoned practitioner and radical reformer of the operatic art form, Wagner's practical work is prepared and propelled by an extensive body of theoretical writings of his that attest both to Wagner's voracious readings in literature and philosophy and to his sustained attempts at articulating and advancing the theory and practice of modern operatic theater. Wagner's writings, which comprise several book publications and dozens of essays and articles, supplemented by hundreds of theoretically oriented letters or parts of letters, were written over the span of almost half a century.[16] They form an integral part of his artistic *œuvre*. Wagner himself eventually gathered most of those previously published pieces in the edition of his *Collected Writings and Poetic Works*, the latter term (*Dichtungen*) denoting the textbooks for his operatic works, which he considered literary works of their own, to be valued independent of the musical scores which were set to them.

While Wagner's writings have found some consideration in scholarly publications on Wagner's musical works, for which they provide an important self-interpretation, Wagner has rarely been considered and treated as a theoretician, much less a philosophical thinker, in his own right. In part, this neglect is due to the mode and manner of Wagner's theoretical writings, which tend to be written in a heavy-handed and belabored style. In their outward appearance, Wagner's prose works exhibit neither the scholarly trappings of academic publications nor the ease and fluidity of journalistic or popular prose. Moreover, Wagner's theoretical *œuvre* is vast and varied, thereby posing special demands on its comprehension and assessment.

A further factor in the underappreciation of Wagner the theoretician and thinker, as opposed to Wagner the composer and dramatist, is the disciplinary orientation of most of his scholarly readers and academic interpreters, who typically approach him from the specific perspectives of musicology, theater studies, literary theory, or cultural studies. To the extent that those readings and interpretations treat Wagner as a thinker, they chiefly refer to the theoretical assumptions and assertions implied by his artistic work—the textbooks and the compositions of his operatic *corpus*. Where they consider his theoretical writings, they tend to treat their author as a dilettante thinker and regard his work as largely derivative of earlier authors.

Taking Wagner seriously as a thinker in his own right—and as a philosophical thinker at that—requires a distinctly philosophical perspective on his work and one that is informed by the general outlook and the doctrinal specifics that form the background of his theoretical efforts. This background against which Wagner's writings have to be assessed is classical German philosophy in its vast extent from the critical works of Kant through the writings of his followers in German Idealism, especially Hegel, to the latter's aftermath in the left or Young Hegelians, chiefly Feuerbach, and on to Hegel's self-styled opponent on a grand scale, Schopenhauer.[17] Wagner refers, directly or indirectly, to all these authors, with whom he was familiar, if not through his own study of their texts, then through his interchanges with intellectuals among his friends.

To be sure, Wagner's philosophical debt specifically to Schopenhauer has long been recognized.[18] But this has often happened at the expense, even at the exclusion, of recognizing the earlier and lasting influence exercised on Wagner's thinking and writing by the idealists and post-idealists, especially Hegel and Feuerbach. In particular, even after discovering and reading Schopenhauer's main work, *The World as Will and Representation*, which culminates in an ethics of individual salvation through resignation, in the mid-1850s, Wagner retains his commitment to the social and even political dimension of human ethical existence that he inherited from Hegel and Feuerbach.[19] Moreover, an attitude of tragic resignation in response to the potentially catastrophic condition of human existence in general and that of modern existence in particular is to be found in Wagner's reflections already prior to his acquaintance with Schopenhauer's pronounced pessimism.[20]

The overall character of Wagner's theoretical writings from the late 1840s through the early 1880s is that of sustained politico-philosophical thinking about human social existence under conditions of modernity. In particular, Wagner's is a modernity that is equally marked by present deficiencies as by future potentialities and that is, accordingly, received and regarded by disaffection and by hope, by diffidence and by confidence alike. As an intrinsically modern and specifically political thinker moving away from the past, facing the present and advancing toward the future, Wagner belongs to an entire group of mid-nineteenth-century thinkers that face the challenges of modernity with a vision focused on freedom, while addressing social concerns. The chief members of this group are John Stuart Mill, who combines individual liberalism and social utilitarianism, and Karl Marx, who joins egalitarian socialism with classless communism.[21]

To be sure, unlike in the cases of Mill and Marx, Wagner's politically dimensioned thinking is not presented as political philosophy or political economy. Instead, Wagner's socio-political thinking is part and parcel of his sustained reflection on the forms and norms of art, especially operatic art, under conditions of modernity. Yet even with its pronounced aesthetic and artistic focus, Wagner's thinking remains eminently political. The radical changes Wagner envisions and enacts in (operatic) art are borne from a profound concern for a life liberated from alienation and estrangement and returned to human essence or essential humanity, and they are geared toward the eventual realization of such a life on a general social scale.

## 4 Modernism as Romanticism

Its thematic unity notwithstanding, Wagner's theoretical work exhibits a clear chronology and a distinct development. Wagner's career as a published writer begins in the late 1840s in the context of his involvement with the Dresden uprising during Europe's revolutionary double year 1848/49. In the German lands, the revolutionary activities, which ultimately fail, center around the call for political freedom (parliamentary system) and political unity (nationalism). After the military defeat of the Dresden uprising in May 1849, Wagner, at that point the local music director, who has been involved in the street fighting, becomes a wanted fugitive throughout Germany and flees to neighboring Switzerland, where he remains for a decade, before benefiting from an amnesty and being able to return to Germany. While in Switzerland, Wagner lays the theoretical foundations as well as prepares and begins the actual execution of all his main musical works, from *Tristan and Isolde* (1865) through *The*

*Mastersingers of Nurnberg* (1868) to the four-part *Ring of the Nibelung* (1876) and *Parsifal* (1882).[22]

In the context of the revolutionary double year 1848/49 Wagner writes and, in part, publishes a number of shorter pamphlets and longer essays that connect the attempted political revolution to a larger cultural revolution, to be effectuated through the arts in general and through operatic art in particular. The philosophical tenor of these writing, chiefly among them *Art and Revolution* (1849) and *The Artwork of the Future* (1850), is that of a call for freeing human beings from the alienation characteristic of modern society in order to realize their truly human, humanist potential—an aesthetico-political program inspired by Feuerbach's earlier critique of alienated consciousness in matters of religion and resembling Marx's contemporary transformation of the limited critique of religion into the comprehensive critique of politics and economics. Rather than advocating overt political revolution, Wagner proposes an "aesthetic education of the human being" that transposes the moral improvement envisioned by Schiller's eponymous work from 1795 into the realm of civico-political betterment.

The more overtly revolutionary and somewhat sketchy writings from 1849 and 1850 find a more settled and more detailed continuation in Wagner's two publications from 1851, his aesthetico-political *chef d'œuvre*, *Opera and Drama*, and his self-defense as a social reformer-artist, *A Communication to My Friends*. In his Zurich writings Wagner frequently cites ancient drama, especially Attic tragedy, as the main literary source for the aesthetic, political, and philosophical inspiration behind his project of a specifically modern drama under the guise of radically reformed romantic opera ("music drama").[23] But he is equally explicit on the need to replace the general outlook as well the particular features of earlier dramatic forms, including early modern neo-classical drama in France (Corneille, Racine) and Germany (Goethe), along with their operatic variants (Rameau, Gluck), with an aesthetics, a poetics and a politics that match modern conditions.[24]

In particular, Wagner plans to replace the chorus, as the consolidated voice of the people, in ancient drama, with the orchestra, as the instrumental reflection on the scenic action, in modern (operatic) drama.[25] Moreover, he conceives the illustrative and interpretive orchestral accompaniment of scenic singing and acting as a continuous melodic stream ("unending melody"[26]), thus abandoning the traditional parceling and fragmenting of an opera into distinct musical units ("numbers opera"). Most importantly, drawing on a famous recorded pronouncement by Napoleon to Goethe, when the two met in Erfurt in 1808, Wagner has "fate," as the inscrutable numinous force behind the unfolding of ancient drama, be replaced by "politics," as the equally unforeseeable but humanly made motor behind modern drama.[27]

Further features of Wagner's (music) drama of the future, as first planned in his Zurich writings and actually executed in subsequent years, were: the idea of a festival dedicated exclusively to the periodic performance of his future theater works; the associated conception of a theater that no longer replicates the hierarchical social order (parquet, boxes, galleries) but reflects the egalitarian aesthetic community to be created by the artwork of the future; and the concerted effort to coordinate the specific contributions of the individual arts involved in musical theater (singing, instrumental music making, dancing, costume design, stage design) to form an aesthetically integrated, multi- and intermedial artwork ("comprehensive work of art").[28]

The Bayreuth Festival Theater eventually erected, based on plans for an unrealized Munich theater purloined by Wagner from his Dresden-years' friend, the architect Gottfried Semper, is a simple, comparatively inexpensive but large-scale utilitarian structure, with an unadorned brick outer shell, a timber construction on the inside and the seats all arranged in one steeply ascending triangle. The proto-modern practical design of the Bayreuth Theater proved influential for the democratized theater architecture of the twentieth century, as evidenced early on in Munich's Prince Regent Theater (1901). Another innovation, which remains unique to Bayreuth's festival theater architecture though, is the covered orchestral pit that serves the dual purpose of having the orchestral sound appear magically mixed, as though coming out of nowhere, and of doing away with the disillusioning visual gap between the theatrical scene and the audience hall, not to mention the unseemly sight of the orchestra members physically producing their individual contributions to the creation an imaginary collective soundscape. Bayreuth also proved a pioneer in introducing such modern theater practices as darkening the auditorium during playing time, refraining from scenic applause, and not entering or exiting the auditorium during a performance.

From its earliest conception Wagner destined the Bayreuth Festival Theater for the first performance and subsequent repeat performances of one work, *The Ring of Nibelung*—a work planned and executed since the late 1840s, initially announced under the title *Siegfried's Death*, and subsequently extended to include three preceding installments leading up to Siegfried's rise and demise, thus constituting a fourfold cycle composed of *The Rhinegold*, *The Valkyrie*, *Siegfried* and *Twilight of the Gods*. After the work's first complete performance at Bayreuth in 1876—the first two parts of the tetralogy had seen separate earlier premieres in Munich (1869 and 1870, respectively), where also *Tristan and Isolde* and *The Mastersingers of Nurnberg* had received their first public performances—the Festival was opened up to include Wagner's earlier operatic works, starting with *The Flying Dutchman* (1843). Eventually, the Bayreuth repertoire came to include Wagner's last complete stage work, *Parsifal* (1882), which, for the duration of 20 years, was intentionally reserved for stage performances in Bayreuth only, on the basis some Europe-wide copyright regulation.

The modernism that marks Wagner's theater reforms culminates in the transformation of traditional opera, including romantic opera, into a distinctly modern music theater. Wagner's musical modernism, which is in essence a hyper-Romanticism that surpasses Romanticism by pushing it to extremes, chiefly resides in the expressive character of his music, designed to convey intense feelings (rather than abstract thoughts, as conventional illustrative program music would have it). In Wagner, music no longer accompanies scenic action, but discloses the latter's inner workings at an intensely affective and deeply emotional level. In particular, orchestral music in Wagner's mature stage works provides hermeneutic clues under the guise of musical motives (*Leitmotive*) to the dramatic action—clues that undergo continuing transformation and reconfiguration, thus functioning as the orchestral under- and inside of the drama that unfolds on the stage. In the literature Wagner's novel treatment of music in opera is often traced to Schopenhauer's account of music as a universally intelligible, yet untranslatable inner language. But Wagner's attributing to the (post-romantic, proto-modern) orchestra a "linguistic capacity" with regard to the "unspeakable" clearly predates his acquaintance with Schopenhauer.[29] Moreover, Wagner chiefly credits Beethoven, especially the Beethoven of the symphonies and most of all Beethoven's Ninth Symphony, with introducing into (romantic) music highly individualized expressiveness in the context of large-scale musical works.[30]

Their musical and theatrical modernism notwithstanding, *The Ring of the Nibelung* as well as Wagner's earlier and later mature operatic works eschew modern plots and contemporary settings. Yet in drawing on medieval myths—and, in the exceptional case of *The Mastersingers*, on an early modern historical figure and an associated historical institution, viz., the cobbler-poet Hans Sachs and Nurnberg's guild of singer-artisans—Wagner is not abandoning his aesthetic as well as political focus on the modern condition. The choice of mythological plots and characters, instead of the recourse to current fads and fashions,[31] serves Wagner's overall intention of reorienting the alienated modern individual to a liberated existence in line with a timelessly true humanity. Moreover, by resorting to Germanic and Celtic, rather than Greek or Roman mythology, Wagner seeks to avoid the historical aesthetic ballast that has accrued to the stories of Oedipus and Orestes, of Antigone and Medea, and other mythological figures, through their previous neo-classical renderings.

Viewed against the backdrop of his programmatic and preparatory writings, the central story of the *Ring*, Wagner's core creation, turns on the carefully prepared but ultimately failed attempt to bring about a genuinely free individual, Siegfried, unencumbered by past pacts, restrictive rules, and constraining conditions. It attests to the preponderance of Wagner's creative genius and tragic worldview over his theoretical ambitions and philosophical programmatics that, unlike in the case of Nietzsche's *Zarathustra*, the *Ring* is not a work advocating and enacting some superhuman *posthistoire*.

In line with his essentially tragic outlook on the modern world, Wagner features in his mature works the factual impossibility of genuine freedom in a world ruled by all-too-human Gods, rather than by godly human beings. The same balanced outlook, which matches highly idealist aspirations for some remote future with a deeply realist immersion into the imperfect present, also characterizes Wagner's final and finest work, *Parsifal*, which draws on religion in general and on redemption in particular as dramatic tropes for addressing the actual ailments as well as the perfectionist potentials of modern life. Musically, Wagner's *opus ultimum* looks ahead even farther beyond Romanticism and into modernity than the *Ring* does, or *Tristan and Isolde* for that matter. In particular, *Parsifal*'s modernity resides in its radical reduction of external action in favor of inner transformations, in the addition of declamation and exclamation to song and chant, in the staggered spatial deployment of choral forces, in the intense portrayal of extreme anguish and utter despair and in the overall reduction of extroverted music theater to the austere atmosphere of an introverted scenic oratorio.

The modernity of Wagner's mature works, from *Tristan and Isolde* through the *Ring* cycle to *Parsifal*, was first perceived by Nietzsche, who linked Wagner with Baudelaire, another artist situated at the juncture between Romanticism and modernism and an early enthusiastic admirer of Wagner's (*Richard Wagner and Tannhäuser in Paris*, 1861), who shared the latter's ambivalent relation to the modern condition, which both of them despised as much as embraced in their romantically modern and modernly romantic works.[32] Somewhat later than Nietzsche, G. B. Shaw also detected Wagner's modernism and located it, not in the dimension of aesthetics and arts, but in the sphere of politics and economics by reading the *Ring* as an allegory on high modern industrial capitalism, with the eponymous ring of the work standing for that most modern politico-economic power tool, viz., the stock certificate (*The Perfect Wagnerite*, 1898).

In the twentieth century, Wagner's modernist potential made him an inspiration to avant-garde composers in the Austro-German tradition, such as the early Richard Strauss (*Salome*, 1905) and the early Arnold Schoenberg (*Expectation*, 1909). But Wagner's sustained self-differentiation from previous Romanticism and his allied (proto-)modernism also became the object of denial and contestation—aesthetically so, when composers such as Hans Pfitzner (1869–1949) (*Palestrina*, 1917) claimed him for their neo-romantic brand of an alternative, more limited and to that extent anti-modern modernism, and politically so through his capture for nationalist, racist, and fascist political purposes. It was only due to the increasingly creative character and experimental approach of stage directing in European theater in general (*Regietheater*) and in German opera theater in particular, during the second half of the twentieth century, that Wagner re-emerged as a composer of significant intellectual stature and of a considerable, though controversial political vision—a vision invested in a body of work, some ten operatic masterpieces, designed for a present that is not to look backward in a romantic way but forward in a modern way.

# Notes

1. See Charles Rosen, *The Classical Style. Haydn, Mozart, Beethoven*. Expanded edition (New York/London: W. W. Norton, 1998).
2. On the difficult differentiation between the classical and the romantic in music, see *Metzler Musik Chronik. Vom frühen Mittelalter bis zur Gegenwart*, ed. Arnold Feil (Stuttgart: J. B. Metzler, 1993), 371–373.
3. On the early origins of opera's commercialization, see Beth L. Glixon and Jonathan E. Glixon, *Inventing the Business of Opera: The Impresario and His World in Seventeenth-Century Venice* (Oxford: Oxford University Press, 2006) and Ellen Rosand, *Opera in Seventeenth-Century Venice: The Creation of a Genre* (Berkeley and Los Angeles: University of California Press, 2007).
4. For a concise account of the origin and development of opera, see Donald Jay Grout and Hermine Weigel Williams, *A Short History of Opera* (New York: Columbia University Press, 1988).
5. For a comprehensive documentation of Wagner's antisemitic tract, see Jens Malte Fischer, *Richard Wagners "Judentum in der Musik." Eine kritische Dokumentation als Beitrag zur Geschichte des Antisemitismus* (Frankfurt/M.: Insel, 2000).
6. See Anon., "Das älteste Systemprogramm des deutschen Idealismus," in Friedrich Hölderlin, *Sämtliche Werke*, ed. Friedrich Beißner, 15 vols. (Stuttgart: Cotta and Kohlhammer, 1943–1985), 4:297 and Friedrich

Schlegel, "Rede über die Mythologie," in *Kritische Friedrich Schlegel Ausgabe*, ed. Ernst Behler *et al.* (Paderborn/Munich/Darmstadt: Schöningh, 1958ff.), 2:311–322.

7. On Fichte's entire philosophy as a philosophy of the future, see Günter Zöller, *Fichte lesen* (Stuttgart-Bad Cannstatt, 2013).
8. See Arnold Schoenberg, "Brahms the Progressive," in Arnold Schoenberg, *Style and Idea* (New York: Philosophical Library, 1950), 52–101.
9. See Eduard Hanslick, *On the Musically Beautiful: A Contribution Towards the Revision of the Aesthetics of Music*, transl. Geoffrey Payzant (Indianapolis: Hackett, 1986).
10. On Wagner's non-Hegelian understanding of the term "absolute" in the sense of "severed" or "dissociated," hence equivalent to Hegel's use of the term "abstract," see Richard Wagner, *Oper und Drama*, ed. Klaus Kropfinger (Stuttgart: Reclam, 1994), 76f., 81, 84, 90–92, 117, 334f..
11. See Richard Wagner, *Oper und Drama*, ed. Klaus Kropfinger (Stuttgart: Reclam, 1994), 19f. and 108.
12. See Richard Wagner, *Oper und Drama*, ed. Klaus Kropfinger (Stuttgart: Reclam, 1994), 189–200.
13. For Wagner's autobiographical account of his early fascination with the *Oresteia* of Aischylus, especially the *Agamemnon* and the *Eumenides*, see Richard Wagner, *Mein Leben*, 2 vols. (Munich: Bruckmann, 1911), 1:407. On the parallelism between the *Ring* and the *Oresteia*, see Herfried Münkler, "Mythos und Politik—Aischylos' 'Orestie' und Wagners 'Ring'," *Leviathan* 15 (1987), 562–580 and Daniel H. Foster, *Wagner's "Ring" Cycle and the Greeks* (Cambridge: Cambridge University Press, 2010).
14. On the larger context of Nietzsche's reading of Wagner through Greek tragedy, see Günter Zöller, "Die Philosophie im tragischen Zeitalter der Deutschen. Nietzsches Antikenprojekt," in *Die Philosophie des Tragischen. Schopenhauer—Schelling—Nietzsche*, ed.. Lore Hühn and Philipp Schwab (Berlin/New York: de Gruyter, 2011), 453–472.
15. On Wagner's civic-political reading of Attic tragedy, see Richard Wagner, *Oper und Drama*, ed. Klaus Kropfinger (Stuttgart: Reclam, 1994), 76f. and 189–200. On the political profile of Attic tragedy in general, see Christian Meier, *Die politische Kunst der griechischen Tragödie* (Munich: C. H. Beck, 1988).
16. See the bibliographical details in Peter Jost, "Die Ausgaben und Schriften," in *Wagner-Handbuch*, ed. Laurenz Lütteken (Kassel: J. B. Metzler, 2012), 154–158.
17. For a succinct account of the continuous development and the overall unity of nineteenth-century philosophy, see Günter Zöller, *Die Philosophie des 19. Jahrhunderts. Von Kant bis Nietzsche* (Munich: C. H. Beck, 2018).
18. See Bryan Magee, *Wagner and Philosophy* (London: Penguin, 2001) and Julian Young, *The Philosophies of Richard Wagner* (Lanham/London: Rowman & Littlefield 2016).

19. On Wagner's philosophical position between Feuerbach and Schopenhauer, see Udo Bermbach, "'Die beste Philosophie ist, gar keine Philosophie zu haben'. Richard Wagner und die Philosophie," in Udo Bermbach., *Opernsplitter. Aufsätze. Essays* (Würzburg: Königshausen. & Neumann: 2005), 295–305. On Wagner's relation to Hegel, see Günter Zöller, "World-Drama. Wagner's Hegelian Heritage," forthcoming in *Wagner in Context*, ed. David Trippett (Cambridge: Cambridge University Press).

20. For documentary details on this point, see Günter Zöller, "Schopenhauer," in *Wagner und Nietzsche. Kultur—Werk—Wirkung. Ein Handbuch*, ed. Stefan Lorenz Sorgner, H. James Birx and Nikolaus Knoepffler (Reinbek: Rowohlt, 2008), 35–372. For a comparative account of Wagner's and Nietzsche's relation to Schopenhauer, see Günter Zöller, "Liebe, Lust und Leid. Die Auseinandersetzung mit Arthur Schopenhauer bei Richard Wagner und Friedrich Nietzsche," in *Grenzen der Rationalität. Kolloquien 2005–2009 des Nietzsche-Forums München*, ed. Beatrix Vogel and Nikolaus Gerdes (Regensburg: Roderer, 2010), 367–384.

21. For a sustained reading of Wagner as an aesthetic thinker with a political intent, see Udo Bermbach, *Der Wahn des Gesamtkunstwerks. Richard Wagners politisch-ästhetische Utopie*. Second, revised and expanded edition (Stuttgart/Weimar: J. B. Metzler, 2004).

22. For a discussion of Wagner's writings after the Zurich years, with special regard to their extended focus on the relation of art and politics to religion, see Günter Zöller, "'Wahnspiel'. Staat, Religion und Kunst in Richard Wagners Münchner Meta-Politik," in *Richard Wagner in München*, ed. Sebastian Bolz and Hartmut Schick (Munich: Allitera, 2015), 103–116 and Günter Zöller, "Zur Kunst wird hier die Religion. Richard Wagners *Parsifal* zwischen Vergangenheit und Zukunft," in: Richard Wagner, *Parsifal*. Bavarian State Opera. Season 2017/18 (Munich: Bavarian State Opera Publications, 2018), 70–89.

23. On Wagner's guarded use of the term, "music drama," see Richard Wagner, "Über die Benennung 'Musikdrama'," in *Dichtungen und Schriften. Jubiläumsausgabe in zehn Bänden*, ed. Dieter Borchmeyer (Frankfurt/M.: Insel, 1983), 9:302–307.

24. On Wagner's self-distancing from Greek culture in general and from Greek tragic art in particular, see Günter Zöller, "'[...] wir wollen nicht wieder Griechen werden'. Richard Wagners Kunstwerk der Zukunft jenseits von Antike und Moderne," *wagnerspectrum* 28 (2018), 37–61.

25. See Richard Wagner, *Oper und Drama*, ed. Klaus Kropfinger (Stuttgart: Reclam, 1994), 349.

26. For Wagner late coinage of the term, see Richard Wagner, "Zukunftsmusik," in *Dichtungen und Schriften. Jubiläumsausgabe in zehn Bänden*, ed. Dieter Borchmeyer (Frankfurt/M.: Insel, 1983), 8:93.

27. See Richard Wagner, *Oper und Drama*, ed. Klaus Kropfinger (Stuttgart: Reclam, 1994), 187.
28. For Wagner's use of the term "comprehensive work of art," which occurs only occasionally in writings, see "Das Kunstwerk der Zukunft," in *Dichtungen und Schriften. Jubiläumsausgabe in zehn Bänden*, ed. Dieter Borchmeyer (Frankfurt/M.: Insel, 1983), 6:28 and Richard Wagner, "Die Kunst und die Revolution," in Richard Wagner, *Dichtungen und Schriften. Jubiläumsausgabe in zehn Bänden*, ed. Dieter Borchmeyer (Frankfurt/M.: Insel, 1983), 5:296. On the general project of the unification of the plural arts into art-in-the-singular, see Nicholas Vazsonyi, "The Play's the Thing: Schiller, Wagner, and *Gesamtkunstwerk*," in *The Total Work of Art: Foundations, Articulations, and Inspirations,* ed. Margaret Menninger and Anthony Steinhoff (New York: Berghahn, 2016), 21–38.
29. See Richard Wagner, *Oper und Drama*, ed. Klaus Kropfinger (Stuttgart: Reclam, 1994), 329.
30. On Wagner's Beethoven interpretation in its historical and systematic context, see Günter Zöller, "The Musically Sublime. Richard Wagner's Post-Kantian Philosophy of Modern Music," in *Das Leben der Vernunft. Beiträge zur Philosophie Immanuel Kants*, ed. Dieter Hüning, Stefan Klingner and Carsten Olk (Berlin/Boston: de Gruyter, 2013), 635–660.
31. On Wagner's critique of presentist, defective modernity as mere "fashion," see Richard Wagner, "Das Kunstwerk der Zukunft," in *Dichtungen und Schriften. Jubiläumsausgabe in zehn Bänden*, ed. Dieter Borchmeyer (Frankfurt/M.: Insel, 1983), 6:22–26.
32. For Nietzsche's linking of Wagner with Baudelaire, see Friedrich Nietzsche, *Werke. Kritische Gesamtausgabe*, ed. Giorgio Colli and Mazzino Montinari (Berlin/New York: de Gruyter, 1967-), 11: 601.

# 26

# Between Appropriation and Transmission: The Romantic Thread in Heidegger's Existential Notion of Understanding

## Pol Vandevelde

Martin Heidegger's place in the reception and transmission of the ideas of early German Romanticism is both clear and complex. What is clear is that he read and commented on Friedrich Schlegel, Schleiermacher, and Novalis. Otto Pöggeler was among the first to note the various mentions of the early German Romantics by Heidegger,[1] which can now be counted, thanks to the *Heidegger concordance*.[2] Heidegger quotes Novalis in 14 of his works, Schlegel in 6, and Schleiermacher in 20.[3] Despite showing sympathy for some of their views, Heidegger remains largely critical and is sometimes dismissive of the movement, alleging that Romanticism is still confined to a strong subjectivism and only manages to offer a "transfiguration" (*Verklärung*) of reality, which promises more than it delivers. It is only a "popularization" of metaphysics,[4] which, he says, "vivifies" what we see around us and gives the impression that "something new seems to arise."[5] This is why he wants to preserve Hölderlin from Romanticism: "We should ascribe Hölderlin's poetry neither to 'romanticism' nor to 'classicism.'"[6]

The complexity of Heidegger's position is that he was both a recipient of these views and a relay in their transmission to other philosophers. In his own reception of Romanticism, he was influenced by Wilhelm Dilthey, who

---

I want to thank Trevor Gullion for his editorial help.

---

P. Vandevelde (✉)
Marquette University, Milwaukee, WI, USA
e-mail: pol.vandevelde@marquette.edu

© The Author(s) 2020
E. Millán Brusslan (ed.), *The Palgrave Handbook of German Romantic Philosophy*, Palgrave Handbooks in German Idealism, https://doi.org/10.1007/978-3-030-53567-4_26

himself carried the heritage of the romantics, especially Schleiermacher. Heidegger received this influence of Dilthey in the early 1920s at the same time that he was practicing Husserl's phenomenology. There had been exchanges between Husserl and Dilthey that led to a mutual influence. Dilthey acknowledged his debt to phenomenology and his works prompted Husserl, after the *Logical Investigations,* to take a greater interest in historical questions. Besides receiving the romantic ideas in these different ways, Heidegger was himself a relay of those ideas. In Germany, his student Hans-Georg Gadamer took over the heritage of Dilthey and Romanticism through the mediation of Heidegger's philosophy, which led to a recasting of the romantic enterprise of hermeneutics into a "philosophical hermeneutics." In France, Jacques Derrida and others developed insights regarding the role of literature, which were close to those of the romantics and mediated by Heidegger's effort to "overcome metaphysics." This reception gave the early romantics a postmodern look.[7] Thus, what started as romantic hermeneutics was transformed into a historical discipline by Dilthey, which informed Husserl's phenomenology in its turn toward history and the lifeworld. This became a "hermeneutic phenomenology" in Heidegger, before becoming a "philosophical hermeneutics" in Gadamer and a "deconstruction" in Derrida.

Within such a complex web of interrelationships, especially when it comes to original thinkers such as Heidegger and the early German romantics, any attempt to find direct influences—relying on an efficient causality between minds—would miss the very originality of these thinkers, which was precisely one of recasting the tradition they had inherited. As Heidegger points out, "only the one who is great and open can be truly influenced."[8] Because of this thick tangle of relationships, some commentators may deny any real and significant influence of the romantics on Heidegger. Andrew Bowie, for example, writes that Heidegger "never seriously ... pays any attention to the Romantic ideas."[9] By contrast, others may see an obvious proximity between them. Hannah Arendt, for example, considers that "Heidegger is in fact (let us hope) the last romantic—as it were, a gigantic gifted Friedrich Schlegel or Adam Müller."[10]

To raise the question of influence may even seem ironic in the case of the romantics who held that a work—theirs included—should not be treated as a well-delineated whole, but as a fragment that needs to be completed by interpretation. The task of interpretation is precisely to "characterize" the work (in Schlegel's words), to understand it "better" (for Schleiermacher), or to bring it to its second power through interpretation (for Novalis). It was in the spirit of a "symphilosophy" that the Schlegel brothers, Friedrich and August, as well as Schleiermacher, Novalis, and some others contributed anonymous pieces to the review *Athenaeum*, which was published from 1798 to 1800. Heidegger shared their views about the independence of the work from its writer and offered his own recasting of the major figures of Western philosophy.

If the question of direct filiation between Heidegger and the romantics is a dubious one, it would also be unproductive to select particular themes and topics in their works and then proceed to compare and contrast them. In a sense, anything can be compared to anything if we take a retrospective stance and look for antecedents of Heidegger's views. We would then overlook the fact that it is because we have Heidegger's works, first, that we can, in a second step, look for predecessors in the romantics.

Between a search for a direct filiation and a comparative approach, I attempt to show how some of the romantic ideas fill an explanatory gap in the very development of Heidegger's views. They help explain how the early Heidegger, who was very much immersed in the philosophy of life and phenomenology of religion, significantly reformulated this project into an analytic of existence devoted to the question of Being in *Being and Time*, and why the "existentialist" Heidegger of 1927 "turned," as it is said, toward a "history of being" in the 1930s. Instead of speaking of an "early Heidegger," followed by a "Heidegger I," who turned into a "Heidegger II," we may find in some of the romantic ideas the common thread that connects the different changes of direction in a singular and original "Heidegger." In doing so we will also see how the efforts of the romantics inscribe the Heideggerean project in a movement of thought that attempted to provide an alternative to a certain modernity.

I focus on the question of understanding, which is central in both the romantics and Heidegger, and see three points of contact between them, which can be supported by textual evidence: (1) understanding (*Verstehen*) as an ontological historical condition; (2) understanding as the element in which work, author, and interpreter find their identity; and (3) understanding as a carving out of the world into specific entities.

# 1 Understanding as an Ontological Historical Condition

When Heidegger places "understanding" (*Verstehen*) among the key components of human existence—what he calls an "existential" of Dasein—he transforms a central concept of "romantic hermeneutics" into an ontological category. In a sense, Schleiermacher had shown Heidegger the way to do this in his *Discourse on Religion*, especially the second one, on which Heidegger commented in 1918/1919.[11] In this work, Schleiermacher argues that religion is not a matter of doctrine but of life. As such, religion is, in Heidegger's words, "a way of thinking" (*Denkungsart*) and "a manner of behaving" (*Handlungsweise*), for which "feeling" (*Gefühl*) is central.[12] As Schleiermacher states, "intuition without feeling is nothing and can have neither the proper origin nor the proper force; feeling without intuition is also nothing; both are therefore something only when and because they are originally one and unseparated."[13] Understanding is thus not merely a matter of consciousness nor is it a mere technique. It is rather an attitude or a mode of Being, anchored in life with its existential import.

At the time he commented on Schleiermacher, Heidegger was very much interested in the philosophy of life and also studied Dilthey, giving several lectures on his work in Cassel in 1925.[14] Under the influence of Schleiermacher and his hermeneutics, Dilthey was looking for a way to account for the "coherence of a life" (*Zusammenhang des Lebens*). Life is not just a series of actions, movements, and events, in the form of a mechanistic process or biological development, which could be "explained" by natural sciences, but rather has an "internal connectedness" or "coherence" that consists in being lived in the transitive sense. This can only be "understood" (instead of "explained") and requires a particular discipline (the human sciences). Heidegger embraces this distinction between understanding and explanation, and differentiates in *Being and Time* the ontology of things (with its categories of readiness-to-hand and presence-at-hand) and the ontology of human beings (with its own set of "existential components" or "existentialia"). He also takes from Dilthey this notion of living life transitively, what he calls the "enactment" or "actualization" (*Vollzug*) of life. Life is not just what is lived as a set of events befalling us. Rather, it is what we ourselves "enact," "realize," or "actualize" in the transitive sense through our behavior.[15] This "enactment" as taking my life upon myself is precisely what understanding does, especially in the process of understanding oneself and the things around us. We can "understand" how life can be enacted by me as mine (my own, *Eigentlichkeit*) or by the They (and not mine, not my own, *Uneigentlichkeit*). This is a central distinction in *Being and Time*. It is not so much a question about authenticity, as the term is generally translated, because there is no self before the act of taking one's life upon oneself, that is, before we "enact" our life.

At the same time that Heidegger takes from Schleiermacher and Dilthey the existential and historical character of life and understanding, he is also fascinated by Saint Paul, about whom he lectured in 1919/1920. He finds in some of Paul's letters a connection between understanding and a specific historical situation in which we may have access to a form of temporality other than the present. For Paul and the early Christians, life is to be understood in anticipation of the second coming of Christ (the *Parousia*), which Paul expected to take place during his lifetime. As Heidegger writes, "Christian experience lives time itself ('to live' understood as *verbum transitivum*)."[16] This life lived in historical time can be "enacted" in another temporality when we realize in the *kairos* that we can choose it, which means for Saint Paul to prepare ourselves for the second coming.[17]

The moment of choice in *Being and Time* is what Heidegger calls "a moment of vision" that occurs when anticipating our death and choosing our life as our own. As in Saint Paul, our life can be "seized" in a moment, "in the enactment of life [*im Vollzug des lebens*]."[18] This kind of understanding for Heidegger is not a matter of principles or generalizations out of various instantiations, rather understanding itself is "a form of enactment" (*vollzugsmässig*) and motivated by or arising from the given "situation" (*aus der Situation*).[19] Heidegger discovers in Saint Paul the ontological weight of the activity of understanding that Schleiermacher and Dilthey had elaborated. Understanding is the way our historical situatedness is lived and it is within this historically situated understanding that the world and things appear as they "are." The question of the Being of things thus cannot be separated from the understanding human beings have of themselves.

This is how Heidegger transforms Schleiermacher's and Dilthey's notion of "understanding" into an "existential" component of human existence. This understanding comes with a "situatednes" (*Befindlichkeit*), which manifests itself through moods (*Stimmungen*)—this is how life can be seized and "enacted." One of these moods is particularly important for Heidegger, namely anxiety. It is a "fundamental mood" (*Grundstimmung*) and one that brings understanding to a halt. In anxiety, Heidegger says, the "insignificability" (*Unbedeutsamkeit*) of the world becomes apparent.[20] Although it is disturbing (we lose the "familiarity" of the world, we have a sense of "uncanniness [*Unheimlichkeit*]," of "not-being-at-home [*Nicht-zuhause-sein*]"[21]), it is also liberating as it gives us a lucidity in a moment of vision (Saint Paul's *Kairos*) about whether our life is "enacted" by us (lived as our own, in the sense of *Eigentlichkeit*) or not on our own terms (*Uneigentlichkeit*).

Heidegger can then reformulate the question of Being in a phenomenological hermeneutics, which links the "is" (when we say that something "is") with the "as" (when something is understood "as" something). "When we say: being 'has meaning' this means: it has become accessible in its being."[22] Instead of an idealistic move, it is a radical historicizing of the question of Being. Understanding itself is a "happening" (*Geschehen*) or an event. In a

1943–1944 course on Heraclitus, Heidegger reminds us that the word "being" itself points to a certain temporality: "When the thinker thinks beings [*das Seiende*] he understands this participial word not in the substantive sense but in the verbal sense."[23] Asking the question of Being is thus not wondering "whether beings are a stone or a bone or a donkey or a triangle, but the question asked by the thinker, 'what are beings?' only has the meaning: what is the being of beings [*was ist das Sein des Seiende?*], what is that in which and through which something is 'being' ['*seiend*' *ist*]? What characterizes in general the 'being' [*das* '*Seiend*'] as such?"[24] Because understanding is historical due to the fact that "existence" itself is a "happening" (*Geschehen*), Being itself is history in the sense of what Heidegger calls in the 1930s a "history of being." What Dilthey characterizes as the historical nature of life is recast by Heidegger as an existential temporality. "There is only a history from out of a present," Heidegger claims.[25]

Besides this first point of contact between Heidegger and the romantics regarding the status of understanding as an ontological historical condition, understanding is also at the basis of interpretation in the narrow sense, through which we connect with others and their works.

## 2 Understanding as the Element in Which Work, Author, and Interpreter Find Their Identity

As is commonly said, Heidegger transformed phenomenology into hermeneutics. Against the view that there are perennial problems of philosophy to which philosophers offer their particular solutions, Heidegger argues that powerful philosophers, in fact, invent new vocabularies, formulate new perspectives, and in the process give form to new issues and problems. Understanding authors in a genuine manner cannot just consist in stating their beliefs or doctrines, precisely because we would have to assume that we know what their issues and problems are before interpreting them. Understanding aims at recovering the moment of "production" in thought, at grasping how philosophers "produced" those beliefs or doctrine. This productive aspect of thought can only be accounted for if it is "enacted" by interpretation, and this means that authors need to be recast into the framework of the interpreters. This is how Heidegger re-interpreted Plato, Aristotle, Kant, Nietzsche, Hegel, and others, often against established scholarship and under Schleiermacher's motto of "understanding better," which Heidegger adopts.

He writes: "An interpretation ... goes beyond what is to be interpreted. It must understand the author better than he understood himself."[26] Of his interpretation of Kant he famously said that it is "'historically' incorrect, granted! But it contributes to history" [*'historisch' unrichtig, gewiß, aber sie ist 'geschichtlich'*].[27] There is thus, on Heidegger's reading of it, a necessary violence involved in interpretation because it is supposed to render the "enactment" aspect of that object. In *Being and Time*, this violence comes from the fact that interpretation is a "project."[28] As such, it does not repeat or duplicate the object to be interpreted, as if from a neutral ground, but always involves the interpreter for the sake of whom the interpretation is done. As a project, interpretation has a "fore-structure," which Heidegger breaks down in three components. First, because interpretation is always situated in a specific context with its presuppositions and assumptions it has a "fore-having" (*Vorhabe*); second, interpretation always takes a particular perspective or angle and has something in view when interpreting—it has a "fore-sight" (*Vorsicht*); and, third, interpretation always moves in a particular conceptual framework, which may not be the same as the one of the object interpreted—it has a "preconception" (*Vorgriff*).[29]

Although Heidegger significantly transforms the romantic notion of understanding, this notion was for the early German Romantics themselves not merely a technical activity but, as we saw, essentially an attitude. This attitude is motivated by a non-understanding. Non-understanding—or misunderstanding as a form of non-understanding—is not just a negative notion as an absence. For Schleiermacher the theologian, it is the motivation for understanding as an existential experience of a lack, for example not understanding passages from the Bible, which as a living word needs us to unfold. If the very motivation of hermeneutics is existential, interpretation itself is also existential in the sense that the work will be understood by being made part of the life of the interpreters. The work needs to be continued. We have here the two key aspects of romantic hermeneutics: non-understanding as a starting point of interpretation and, correlatively, the work as a fragment, incomplete before being interpreted.

The notion of fragment has become a cliché of Romanticism as the name for the infinity of interpretation, for the striving for an unreachable Absolute, or for the delight in incompleteness. This notion of fragment is sometimes associated with the fascination the early German Romantics have for ruins and the nostalgia for what has been lost. Yet, what is fascinating about ruins, for example, is not so much the ruins as such, as a sign of what has been lost (of an absence), but rather what the ruins allow us to see: the inner structure of an edifice or the remnants of how a past life was organized.[30] When seen "romantically," that is to say, "understood," ruins in fact make present and bring the past back to life, but in another incarnation. The same holds true for texts, and Schlegel sometimes describes critique as what turns the work into ruin, but with a positive goal. The critic ideally "will only divide the whole [of the work] into elements [*Glieder*] and masses and pieces, but never dismantle it in its original components [*Bestandteile*], which are dead in relation to the work because they are no longer unities of the same kind as comprised in the whole."[31] This is what completing the work means. It is not bringing it to a final stage but perfecting it in the ontological sense of intensifying its life. This is done by treating it as a fragment—fragmenting it—in order to free it from any established understanding or canon.

Any work, even a long one, such as Goethe's *Wilhelm Meister*, which was considered as the ideal of the romantic work, can only find its efficacy (readership, influence, etc.) when readers or interpreters lend it a life and complete it as a (provisional) whole. As the future of the work depends on interpretation, the fragment is, positively, an invitation or incitement to be continued (in an unending process). Thus, when envisaged from its reached efficacy, that is, the future of the work, the work is unfinished as a fragment. This is how, Schlegel argues, ideal critics "will complete the work, rejuvenate it, configure it anew."[32]

This view of the work as a fragment can be qualified as polemic and irenic (from the Greek *irenē*, "peace"). The polemic aspect is due to the provocation of questioning both the metaphysical notion of the work (as a well-delineated entity that is now supposed to have porous boundaries) and the self-identity of the author (to the extent that the boundary between author and interpreter becomes blurred). This polemic aspect can be seen as postmodern and is a clear antecedent to Derrida's notion of graft—to interpret is to graft a new text onto an existing one. However, even when Derrida uses the motive of the hedgehog,[33] to which Schlegel compares the fragment—the hedgehog, Schlegel says, only has one idea[34]—Derrida abandons the very ideal of completing the work and instead focuses on an anonymous process of a *différance*, which makes the subject an effect of language and eliminates the counterpart of the letter—of the "signifier"—which the romantics call the "spirit." There is no "outside-of-the-text" [*il n'y a pas de hors-texte*],[35] according to the Derridean slogan, and thus no need to reconcile letter and spirit, as romantic hermeneutics dedicated itself to doing. However, there is an alternative to this postmodern take on the polemic aspect of furthering the work by completing it. The polemic aspect can also be seen as part of a "symphilosophy" between author and interpreter in the form of a dialogue in which dissent (in the sense of non-understanding ) is what gives traction to the back and forth of the discussion. Gadamer's hermeneutics is based on this model of the dialogue.

Besides being polemic, the fragment is also irenic. Interpretation is called for by the text as giving it life, as sustaining its spirit when its letters may appear dead. Interpretation is thus productive in the sense that interpretation gives the work a new lease on life, breathes new life in it, and keeps it relevant for a new readership.[36] Novalis attests to this productivity or "poetics" of interpretation when he considers the reader as a "broadened author."[37]

For describing this furthering of the work, the early German Romantics characterize interpretation as a potentialization in that it actualizes the potentiality of the work. They use two senses of potency—the metaphysical Aristotelian sense of potentiality and the mathematical sense of power. Against Aristotle's understanding of potency, the potentialities of the work were not pre-determined by a corresponding actuality that would logically precede the potentialities themselves, as is the case in Aristotle's mature oak tree that logically precedes the potentiality included in the acorn.[38] There is no *telos* in the potentiality. Interpretation is also and at the same time a maximization of the power of the work in the sense of bringing it to its second power, in the mathematical sense. Schlegel uses the formula "all critique = $x^2$"[39] and explains: "The true critique is to be the author at the second power [*die wahre Kritik ein Autor in der 2t Potenz*],"[40] in the sense that the critique enhances the author, as it were, and makes the author "ideal" as the model this particular text requires. These two senses of potency can be illustrated by Schlegel's review of Goethe's novel *Wilhelm Meister*, which he calls his *Übermeister*, written in one word. As Antoine Berman shows, it is a commentary "on" *Wilhelm Meister*, but also a way of bringing this novel beyond its context of origin by granting it a new life.[41] As such a "raising," the critique maximizes the power this novel can have, bringing it to its second power.

Novalis complements the raising of the work to the second power with another mathematical operation, which he calls a "logarithmicization." His famous notion of "romanticization" includes the two operations: a "qualitative potentialization" by interpretation, which elevates the work, makes it more relevant and vibrant, and, afterward, a logarithmicization, which consists in reformulating the second power of the work (provided by interpretation) in terms that make familiar and intelligible what the potentiality is. Interpretation has to make clear, in other words, how the raising to the second power was accomplished and give a logarithm of the operation. Novalis writes: "This operation [of romanticization] for what is higher, unknown, mystical, infinite is logarithmicized through this association. It takes on an ordinary form of expression … Raising and lowering by turns."[42] The Interpretation is thus invasive and violent as a fragmentation but also, as a logarithmicization, "completing" the original work through this "lowering" of the second power.

This is how a "characterization" of a work functions, which is Schlegel's term of choice for interpretation.

The word "characteristic" [*Charakteristik*][43] names the task of finding the specificity of the work, given the space and time of its creation, and understanding the work through its author within its context. Criticism, Schlegel tells us, is a "divinatory critique" [*divinatorische Kritik*] that aims at characterizing the "ideal" of the work.[44] In this sense, "all critique is divinatory. To complete a project is about the same as completing a fragment."[45] We have here again an effort to account for both the universality of the work (as understandable by all and part of a culture or tradition) and the individuality of the work (as bound to its historical situation).

It is in this context that Schleiermacher's romantic motto of "understanding better" has to be situated. As he states, "the highest perfection of interpretation consists in understanding an author better than he could answer for himself"[46] or, in another formulation, "one must understand as well as and better than the author."[47] Interpreters, in their act of understanding, have to account for the text (in a grammatical interpretation) and for the author (in a technical or psychological interpretation). "Since we have no direct knowledge of what was in the author's mind, we must try to become aware of many things of which he himself may have been unconscious, except insofar as he reflects on his own work and becomes his own reader."[48]

Gadamer takes issue with Schleiermacher's notion of "understanding better" when he transforms romantic hermeneutics into a philosophical hermeneutics through the mediation of Dilthey and Heidegger. Gadamer considers the "understanding better" as a "meliorative" in the sense that it adds to what a previous understanding did and carries the work over and beyond the present state of understanding. Against this meliorative understanding, Gadamer argues that "we understand in a different way, if we understand at all."[49] However, "understanding better" need not be reduced to a "meliorative" understanding, as Gadamer suggests, but can be grasped as bringing the work to its second power and recasting it into a different context, as the romantics propose.

As the early German Romantics show, in order to reach the stage of the "better," one needs to place oneself in an attitude of non-understanding, as the starting point of interpretation. It is a decision or attitude by interpreters to make themselves vulnerable toward the text by allowing themselves to be questioned by the text itself. Schlegel was annoyed by common criticisms that many of the romantic writings were obscure. There was even a joke circulating at the time: "If there is something we do not understand, a Schlegel wrote it."[50] Schlegel directly addressed this criticism in an apology for "incomprehensibility" (*Über Unverständlichkeit*). He argues for the fruitfulness of a certain incomprehensibility when it puts the reader or the interpreter in an attitude in which they can be solicited by the work, instead of attempting to take control of the work by leading it where they feel secure. Incomprehensibility is thus an attitude of vulnerability that allows the work to reveal itself in its power or potentiality. Schlegel writes: "But is incomprehensibility really something so unmitigatedly contemptible and evil? … verily, it would fare badly with you if, as you demand, the whole world were ever to become wholly comprehensible in earnest. And isn't this entire, unending world constructed by the understanding out of incomprehensibility or chaos?"[51]

Like the two sides of a fragment—a product of a fragmentation and as invitation to be completed—understanding and non-understanding are not two different stages of a single process, but rather two poles between which interpreters can navigate. Instead of a linear intellectual process of moving from non-understanding to understanding—in the meliorative sense of understanding better—it is a movement back and forth. Schlegel speaks of a "progressive incomprehensibility" (*Progressive Unverständlichkeit*).[52] Each of the two poles of understanding and non-understanding can take a positive or negative valence. While a positive understanding, we can speculate, is one that is successful, a negative understanding is one that stays at the surface of the work and only states "what the matter actually is, where it stands and must stand in the world."[53]

Schlegel also speaks of "a merely negative and a positive non-understanding."[54] A negative non-understanding is merely a failure to understand. More interesting is the positive non-understanding. It is an attitude of accepting to be disconcerted by the work or solicited by it. This is violent because it forces the work to break open. Schlegel writes: "When understanding and non-understanding touch each other there is an electric shock. This is called polemic."[55] Some interpretations are able to render a work incomprehensible compared to how it had been received until then and, by doing so, liberate the work and make it alive again. For example, consider Patrice Chéreau and Pierre Boulez's production of Wagner's *Ring Cycle* for its 100th anniversary at Bayreuth in 1976. They situated the old German myth back into the industrial revolution, pitting the industrialists against the proletariat and "updating" the mythology, as it were. This production literally freed Wagner's work from the canon by making it incomprehensible—this is the polemic aspect: it is not the *Ring* as we knew it—and allowed the work to continue living. This continued life is obviously not necessarily progress but only a new pull exerted in the tension or the polarization between understanding and non-understanding. What matters in this pendulum movement is the movement itself and thus its dynamics. There is no final stage that can be reached for a work to be understood. Non-understanding can thus be intensified and cultivated, precisely for the sake of doing justice to the work to be interpreted so that there is a methodological fruitfulness in incomprehensibility. It maintains the work in the dynamic state of a fragment.

The attitude of non-understanding in the romantic sense is very much present in Heidegger. In *Being and Time*, this state of non-understanding was caused by anxiety, in which we face the "insignificability" of the world. The positive aspect is that we are freed from all entanglement in the world, when things are "merciless" because they offer no respite, relief, comfort, or taste.[56] Once a particular concretion of world has dissolved, with its set of things (objects of concerns) and other people (objects of solicitude), a new concretion may arise, to which individuals would give their consent, taking it as their own. In this "resolution" on the basis of a non-understanding, an authentic understanding may be reached.

We find these moments of non-understanding in later works as well. A work of art, for example, can rupture the familiarity of the world. Although Heidegger mocks the "transfiguration" (*Verklärung*) of the romantics, as if they were merely adding a coat of varnish on reality to make it glimmer, he borrows from them the view that a work of art may cause a thrust (*Stoss*) in our world and interrupt its familiarity. This is done positively because the work is not conveying messages to us, but only brings us some lucidity about the way we live our life. Through a work of art, things may look strange, no longer objects of use but instead, like the shoes of van Gogh, useless, while positively revealing the "reliability" that was at the basis of their use and thus at the basis of their being things. We also have the different strategies Heidegger uses to interpret previous philosophers in a non-canonic way in order to make them relevant against a philological desiccation of their views or an academic burial in the history of ideas or the history of the problem.

Besides the existential historical aspect and the "interpretive" aspect, there is a third aspect of understanding that connects Heidegger and the early German Romantics: the productive power of disclosure.

## 3 Understanding as a Carving Out of the World into Specific Entities

In *Being and Time*, as we saw, Heidegger clearly saw understanding as the threshold of intelligibility. Existence as disclosure (*Erschlossenheit*) frees entities so that they can only be approached from the perspective of the understanding of Being and thus "be" when understood. His question was: "Is this connection between being and understanding of being so fundamental that what holds of being also holds of the understanding of being, that being is identical to its disclosure?"[57]

This view is eminently romantic and may be the most daring contribution of the early German Romantics and Heidegger. They envisage a moment of production or *Dichtung* in our relationship to things. In the same way that we are connected to things and in overlap with them, and not merely a mind or a consciousness, things themselves are not neat, clearly delineated entities outside our body and psyche, but give themselves to us, responding to our projects, as it were. By questioning the very foundation of our philosophical world view, Heidegger and the romantics offer an alternative to the different brands of empiricism and idealism: we know who we are as minds and we know that the world is made of things, facts, states of affairs, and the like. Yet, when we take our historical situation into consideration, we can surmise an event of disclosure that opens the possibility for the kind of understanding of the world and of ourselves that we have, which is different from the world of ancient Greece or modernity, for example. If there is a moment of disclosure in our world, if it "happens" and is "produced," and thus "historical," there is a constant "becoming" in things and ourselves. It is no coincidence that Plato was for both the early German Romantics and Heidegger one of their key dialogue partners. Plato is a "romantic philosopher," Schlegel tells us,[58] and he elaborated the project to translate Plato's works with Schleiermacher, who ended up doing all of the work. We find the same place of pride for Plato in Heidegger, who laments how Plato was misunderstood and quotes Hölderlin with approval: "I believe that in the end we will say: holy Plato, forgive us! We have … heavily sinned against you."[59]

What both the romantics, especially Schlegel, and Heidegger find in Plato is at least twofold. First, they see in his philosophy a confirmation of their view about the inability of what is sensible or material to impose its own intelligibility on us. There is in things and the world a native fluidity or incompleteness. Understanding cannot thus take direct hold of them, but can only provide a framework within which they gain stability vis-à-vis what matters to us and appears in such a guise. Second, the romantics and Heidegger also find in Plato a thinker who saw the need for such an understanding to be of a productive nature. Understanding is active and needs to find the means—dialogue or symphilosophy—to accompany the revelation of reality. As Schlegel says, Plato's philosophy is a *Mischung*, an interconnection of all possible genres of prose: history, rhetoric, criticism, the law.[60] He is the "Shakespeare of Greek prose"[61] who "made use of every genre of art and science available at that time for that purpose."[62] For Heidegger, the productive role of understanding is due to the connection Plato sees between what things are and the comportment of human beings. He praises Plato for recognizing a degree of Being in things. There can be "more being" (understood as a present participle) depending on how we behave toward things.

Both the early German Romantics and Heidegger call this productive aspect of understanding *Dichtung* (poetry) or *Poesie*, understood in the broad sense of an invention of meaning and a configuration of reality, whether this configuration is literary or scientific.[63] Schlegel and Novalis speak of a "transcendental" poetry, which would reconcile not only philosophy and literature but even these two disciplines with the sciences. For Heidegger, "poetry is nothing but the elementary emergence into words, the becoming uncovered of existence as being in the world. For the others who before it were blind, the world first becomes visible by what is thus spoken."[64] For the romantics and Heidegger, thinking is itself *Dichtung*—configuration and invention so that there is a poetics of knowledge or a poetics of truth. Truth is "invented" in the sense of the German word *Erfinden* ("to invent"), which is neither a mere discovery of what is already fully articulated nor a mere fabrication of what did not exist before. As Paul Ricoeur recommends, "one has to return to the beautiful [French] word *inventer* ["to invent"] in its twofold meaning, which entails at the same time to discover and to create."[65]

The invention of meaning has two sides: one pertaining to consciousness and the other to the object or reality. If we envisage meaning as a process through an invention, consciousness is no longer a self-contained directedness toward an independent object, but rather what belongs to the flesh of the object, as it were, or what overlaps with the object. Consciousness is understanding. Correlatively, the object is no longer a clearly delineated entity, waiting to be taken as object by an act of consciousness. The object or reality becomes a project to be completed. We find these two views in the romantics. "The world is incomplete [*unvollendet*]," Schlegel tells us,[66] as well as the human being, who is "an infinite animal" (*ein unendliches Thier*[67]) or "a constant becoming."[68] In *Being and Time*, consciousness is reformulated as a being-in-the-world and, accordingly, as a "situated understanding" that opens a realm of intelligibility (*Bedeutsamkeit*). The "object" is precisely what is carved out in this intelligibility through our "projects" so that "stuff," literally, materializes (enters into presence) by making sense ("being ready-to-hand" or "present-at-hand") as a specific "something." Only within human projects can a chair or an electron "be."

If what things are—a chair or an electron—is in response to our projects, inquiring into the Being of things is inquiring not only into the fact that they are, but also into the historical and cultural conditions that allow things to take the *eidos*, the appearance or the essence they happen to have for us now. The two models of the invention of meaning offered by German Romanticism and Heidegger, respectively, thus represent a remarkable effort to articulate the two ontological sides of: (1) consciousness as being interpretive; and (2) the object as what "materializes" because it "makes sense." For the early German Romantics, there is a *Kunstpoesie* (artistic poetry) because there is a *Naturpoesie* (a poetry of nature). According to Schlegel, there is an "unformed and unconscious poetry which stirs in the plant, radiates in light, laughs in a child, shimmers in the bloom of youth, glows in the loving heart of women."[69] Both the poetry of nature and the art of poetry are the two poles of a general translatability of the world. "The true beginning," Novalis says, "is poetry of nature. The end is the second beginning and is artistic poetry."[70] This is how, Schlegel writes in his *Transcendentalphilosophie*, "human beings poetize the world, as it were. It is just that they do not quite know it."[71] Invention belongs to the means we use to make sense of the reality around us and reality is of the order of what is understood. This explains the need for a "romanticization" of the world: "The world must be romanticized … Romanticization is nothing but a qualitative potentialization … To the extent that I confer a higher meaning to what is common, a secret aspect to what is habitual, the dignity of the unknown to what is known, the appearance of infinity to the finite, I romanticize it."[72] This is how *Dichtung* or *Poesie* in the broad sense of a configuration of reality works.

Novalis offers a nice example of what the *Dichtung* of science consists of. He distinguishes six different manners in which a stone can be classified: "A stone can be treated: 1. in relation to its subjective origin—or its determination in our faculty of representation …; 2. in relation to its objective origin or formation …; 3. in relation to the time of the planets …; 4. in relation to the space of our earthly body. Mineralogical geography …; 5. in relation to its connection with the other natural bodies or its political nature…; 6. in relation to our private goals."[73] This alternative mode of classification is polemic—challenging an established one—and irenic—asking for a bridge between alternative modes of classification across disciplines, such as mineralogy and politics, a connection that is still problematic today, for example with regard to the impact of mining on the environment. This classification is poetic both in the sense of productive of meaning and configurative: it situates stones in another framework of reference, allowing them to reveal themselves differently.

In line with the "romanticization" of the early German Romantics, Heidegger summarizes his project of poetry as an invention of meaning when he claims that "poetry makes beings more being [*Die Dichtung macht das*

*Seiende Seiender*]."[74] As for the early German Romantics, to say that things are poetized is to reject the transitive view that, first, we would have things at our disposal and, then, these same things would be configured or presented in their mystery by poetry. As stated in *Contributions to Philosophy*, "plant, animal, rock and sea and sky become being [*seiend werden*]."[75] It is important to see "being" as a present participle as it points to a movement in being: things, such as a plant or a rock, "become being." What appears as a stone or a plant is a stage of the thing in its unfolding and this stage is a configuration or preservation—an understanding. Science itself is for Heidegger a form of *Dichtung*, of production or a poetics. The laws of gravitation or of motion are also "inventions": Newton had to invent a manner of formulating that which he saw. Heidegger writes: "It is only from a world that 'the' sun and 'the' wind come to appearance and are only what they are to the extent that they are poetized from 'this' 'world.'"[76] What he calls the "*Dichten* of astronomy and meteorology" pertains to modern natural explanation on the mode of "calculation and planning."[77]

Heidegger uses the word *Wesen*, which normally means "essence," in the sense of the old German verb *wesen*, "to unfold" to name the "becoming" of things within the configuration (*Dichtung*) by human beings. In his reading of Plato, in particular the cave myth, when the prisoner turns to the light, *pros mallon onta tetrammenos*, Heidegger understands the expression *mallon onta* literally: the prisoner is turned toward what is "more being" (*seiender* or *mehr seiend*) as opposed to his world, which is "less being" (*weniger seiend*). Thus, for Plato, Heidegger says, "even beings have degrees!" (*das Seiende hat ebenfalls Grade!*).[78] He also notes Plato's use of *alesthetera*, "truer," and writes: "What is most striking is the talk of unconcealment in the comparative. Unconcealment can be more or less unconcealment."[79] This means that an entity (*Seiende*) and the movement of being (*seiend*) should not be confused: "Being and being [*Seiend und seiend*] are not without further ado the same [*dasselbe*]."[80] When we say that something is, the "is" is in fact a stage, as it were, at which the thing "stands." There can be "a more in being" (*ein Mehr an seiendem*)[81] or a less in being (*weniger*): "Beings differentiate themselves in more or less being."[82]

It is precisely because of this lack in things, of their deficit in Being that human beings have to be *Dichter* and *Mit-dichter*, poets and co-poets. By their understanding, they contribute to the very being of things in configuring and preserving them. They can augment the Being of things, making them "more being," or lead to an "abandonment of being," as Heidegger believes technology tends to do. Because there is a moment of "*seiend*" in *Seiende*—a moment of Being, as a participle, in beings—we cannot simply equate beings with things as well-delineated entities. This was already the case in *Being and Time*.

There is a process involved in the very Being of a tree, namely a temporal process in at least two senses. First, there is a present as indicated by the verbal form—the present participle—but also, second, there is another subtending temporality that encompasses the being-present of the tree. Heidegger expresses this other temporality in the *Contributions* as a "becoming," which points to an event or a happening in the tree's very presence. Poetry renders beings with more Being, not because it gives them an increase in relevance, beauty, effability, and so on, but precisely because poetry reveals their singularity (instead of classifying them under universal categories) and shows what is variant (instead of what is invariant). Poetry makes us sensitive to the "becoming" or what the romantics call the "power" of things. *Energeia* means entering effectuation, *en-ergon*, and this is how Heidegger characterizes the work of art in his lecture "The Origin of the Work of Art" as the "setting-into-work of the truth," the *ins-Werk-setzen*, which is a translation of *en-ergon*.

Yet, the early German Romantics as well as Heidegger want to keep their distance from any form of idealism and preserve a moment of givenness for things. There is at the heart of things a power or a force that asks to be transposed and makes of the world a moment between fluidity and stability. The fluidity is the potentiality inhabiting things and allowing them to be transformed, to become otherwise. The stability is precisely this possibility of exchange. The romantics would reject the "deconstructionist" consequences drawn by Jacques Derrida—another inheritor of Romanticism—namely, that everything is an interpretation, that there is nothing outside of the text, and that the subject is a function of language.[83] Because things are in a state of becoming through the many stages or configurations in a process of development, this becoming requires from understanding an attitude of benevolence. Knowledge is affective. We recall Schleiermacher's insistence on the connection between understanding and feeling. The German Romantics even claimed that what is called "love" governs the poetics of knowledge.

If the object needs love to be understood, it is because it is not mere matter. Schlegel goes so far as to consider an object as a "counter-subject" (*Gegen-ich*), a "you" (*ein Du*). Things, he writes, "are not non-ego outside the ego; not merely a dead, dull, empty, sensible reflection of the ego, which limits the ego in an unintelligible manner, but … a living, potent counter-ego, a thou."[84] The object can thus reveal something of itself if we approach it in the right attitude. In Schlegel's words, "the sense immediately shines, the *thou* speaks at the moment the essence *in its totality is understood by the ego*, addresses the ego and *manifests to him the essence of its existence.*"[85] Rejecting Aristotle's view that matter is potentiality (as what explains the possibility for change), Schlegel sees matter as "an intermediate thing between form and power, a transition of power to form" or, he says, "matter is nothing else than dissolved power or dissolved form."[86] Because matter is this point of dissolution, matter seems to be like a residue that points to an "infinite multiplicity" (*unendliche Mannigfaltigkeit*)[87] of an object. Things "materialize" when we approach them in an attitude of letting them be. Schlegel writes:

> This immediate perception of sense [*Sinn*], the meaning [*Bedeutung*], which is the basis of the proper understanding, is a proper connection of separate but similar spirits, a loving becoming-one of the *ego* with what the object of the ego is, the thou. And to the extent that we can very well call "*love*" this *perception and grasping* of the ego of the object, this marriage of the *perceiving ego* and the perceived spirit, we can formulate the proposition, *Without love there is no sense; the sense, the understanding rely on love.*[88]

We find analogous formulations in Schleiermacher: "In order to intuit the world and to have religion, man must first have found humanity, and he finds it only in love and through love."[89]

While these kinds of formulations used by the early German Romantics may have irritated Heidegger because they sound too subjectivistic, he too saw the need for a "feeling" to keep understanding anchored and prevent it from imposing its arbitrariness on things and the world. In *Being and Time*, the general characterization of human existence is "care" (*Sorge*) as being concerned about things and in solicitude for other human beings. In the Zollikon seminars, as pointed out by Cavalcante Schuback, Heidegger considers love as a form of *Sorge*. He writes: "Correctly understood (i.e., in a fundamental-ontological sense), care is never distinguishable from 'love' but is the name of the ecstatico-temporal constitution of the fundamental characteristic of Da-sein, that is, the understanding of being."[90] In the conclusion of his lecture course *Fundamental Problems of Phenomenology* of 1919/20, he writes: "Understanding lies in love [*in der Liebe ist Verstehen*]."[91] To understand is to love in the sense that, as Heidegger explains in *Besinnung*, "love" is "the will that the beloved be in the sense that it finds its essence and unfolds in it [*Liebe ist der Wille, daB das Geliebte sei, indem es zu seinem Wesen finde und in ihm wese*]." Philosophy is "a love for wisdom" (*Die Liebe zur Weisheit*) and as such "loves" Being. "This, that being 'be,' is the beloved of philosophy."[92] With regard to things, while it could appear that *Being and Time* only addresses things as ready-to-hand or present-at-hand, Heidegger later comes to consider a thing, such as a jug, as a "gathering" of a world in which what he calls the "fourfold," namely: mortals, gods, earth, and sky, gather, and this gathering requires from us a "step back" and an attitude of "letting be."[93]

## 4 Concluding Remarks

The three points of contact I have highlighted between Heidegger and the early German Romantics illustrate almost performatively how understanding in fact works. It works existentially as part of a philosophy of life; it is the element in which we connect with others and their works through interpretation, as Heidegger connects with the romantics, and it is the flesh of things around us, which are "our quasi-companion," as another inheritor of the romantics, Merleau-Ponty, calls them.[94] It is through such a thick and complex understanding that the early German Romantics continue to live, not as a body of doctrine, but as what has been taken over and carried forward, in our case by Heidegger. Heidegger brought out the potentiality and power of some of the romantic ideas, allowing us to understand them "better" in the sense of granting them their future. Conversely, the early German Romantics allow us to understand Heidegger "better," by giving us the thread—the "connectedness," *Zusammenhang*—that ties together the early Heidegger's philosophy of life, the fundamental ontology of *Being and Time*, and the late turn to poetry.

## Notes

1. See, among Pöggeler's works, *Heidegger und die hermeneutische Philosophie* (Freiburg: Karl Alber. 1983).
2. *The Heidegger Concordance*, by François Jaran and Christophe Perrin (London: Bloomsbury, 2013).
3. Among recent sources, see Ian Alexander Moore, "Homesickness, Interdisciplinarity, and the Absolute: Heidegger's Relation to Schlegel and Novalis," in *A Companion to Early German Romantic Philosophy*, ed. Elizabeth Millán and Judith Norman (Leiden: Brill, 2018), 280–310.
4. *Beiträge zur Philosophie (vom Ereignis)*, GA 65, ed. Friedrich-Wilhelm von Herrmann (Frankfurt am Main: Klostermann, 1989), 496; English translation: *Contributions to Philosophy*, trans. Parvis Emad and Kenneth Maly (Bloomington, IN: Indiana University Press, 1999), 349.
5. GA 65, 497; *Contributions*, 349.
6. *Hölderlins Hymne "Andenken,"* GA 52, ed. Curd Ochwadt (Frankfurt am Main: Klostermann,1982), 84.
7. As, for example, in Philippe Lacoue-Labarthe and Jean-Luc Nancy, *L'absolu littéraire: Théorie de la littérature dans le romantisme allemand* (Paris: Éditions du Seuil,1978).
8. *Hölderlins Hymnen Germanien und Der Rhein*, GA 39, ed. Susanne Ziegler (Frankfurt am Main: Klostermann, 1980), 85.

9. Andrew Bowie, *From Romanticism to Critical Theory: The Philosophy of German Literary Theory* (New York: Routledge, 1996), 167.
10. "What is Existential Philosophy," in *Essays in Understanding 1930–1954. Formation, Exile, and Totalitarianism*, ed. Jerome Kohm (New York: Schocken Books, 1994), 163–187 (p. 187). See also Pöggeler, *Heidegger und die hermeneutische Philosophie*, 31.
11. *Phänomenologie des religiösen Lebens*, GA 60, ed. Matthias Jung, Thomas Regehly, and Claudius Strube (Frankfurt am Main: Klostermann); English translation, *The Phenomenology of Religious Life*, trans. Matthias Fritsch and Jennifer Anna Gosetti-Ferencei (Bloomington, IN: Indiana University Press, 2004).
12. *Phänomenolgie des religiösen Lebens*, 319. In Schleiermacher's words, "religion's essence is neither thinking nor acting, but intuition and feeling" (*On Religion: Speeches to its Cultural Despisers*, trans. Richard Crouter (Cambridge: Cambridge University Press, 1996), 22).
13. *On Religion*, 31–32.
14. "Wilhelm Diltheys Forschungsarbeit und der gegenwärtige Kampf um eine historische Weltanschauung (16.–21. April 1925)," in *Vorträge*, Part 1 *1915–1932*, GA 80.1, ed. Günther Neumann (Frankfurt am Main: Klostermann, 2016), 103–158.
15. On Heidegger's use of "enactment" (*Vollzug*), see Hans-Georg Gadamer, *Hermeneutics between History and Philosophy, The Selected Writings of Hans-Georg Gadamer*, Volume 1, ed. and trans. Pol Vandevelde and Arun Iyer (London: Bloomsbury, 2016), 115.
16. GA 60, 82; *The Phenomenology of Religious Life*, 57.
17. Theodore Kisiel considers that "kairology" is part of "the *most* essential, but largely unspoken, core of BT itself" (*The Genesis of Heidegger's Being and Time* (Berkeley: The University of California Press, 1993), 152). On the connection between the early Heidegger and early Christianity, see also Dermot Moran, "Choosing a Hero: Heidegger's Conception of Authentic Life in Relation to Early Christianity," in *A Companion to Heidegger's Phenomenology of Religious Life*, ed. Andrzej Wiercinski and Sean McGrath (Amsterdam: Rodopi, 2010), 349–375.
18. GA 60, 116–117; *The Phenomenology of Religious Life*, 83. Heidegger explains: "Enactment and enacting [*Vollzug und Vollziehen*] are an event [*Geschehen*]. Connections of lived experiences [*Erlebniszusammenhänge*] enact themselves" (GA 59, 147).
19. GA 60, 111; *The Phenomenology of Religious Life*, 78.
20. *Sein und Zeit*, (Tübingen: Niemeyer, 15th. ed., 1984), 273; *Being and Time*, trans. John Macquarrie and Edward Robinson (New York: Harper and Row, 1962), 317.
21. *Sein und Zeit*, 188; *Being and Time*, 233.
22. *Sein und Zeit* 324; *Being and Time*, 371.

23. *Heraklit*, GA 55, ed. Mandfred Frings (Frankfurt am Main: Klostermann 1987), 55.
24. GA 55, 55.
25. GA 60, 125; *The Phenomenology of Religious Life*, 89. Translation modified.
26. *Sein und Wahrheit. 1. Die Grundfrage der Philosophie 2. Vom Wesen der Wahrheit*, GA 37/37, ed. Hartmut Tietjen (Frankfurt am Main: Klostermann, 2001), 167. Although he speaks of poetry, it arguably holds true for all texts.
27. GA 65, 253.
28. *Sein und Zeit*, 311; *Being and Time*, 359.
29. *Sein und Zeit*, 150; *Being and Time*, 191.
30. See Werner Hamacher, *Premises: Essays on Philosophy and Literature from Kant to Celan*. (Cambridge, MA: Harvard University Press, 1996), 244–5.
31. KFSA 2, 140.
32. KFSA 2, 140.
33. Jacques Derrida, *Was ist Dichtung? Qu'est-ce que la poésie? What is Poetry?* (Berlin: Blinkmann und Bose, 1990).
34. KFSA 2, 197, n. 206.
35. "Afterword," in Jacques Derrida, *Limited Inc*, ed. Gerald Graff (Evanston, IL: Northwestern University Press, 1988), 111–160 (p. 136).
36. This aspect was eminently brought to the fore by Walter Benjamin in "Der Begriff der Kunstkritik in der deutschen Romantik," ed. Uwe Steinmer (Frankfurt am Main: Suhrkamp, 2008).
37. Novalis, *Schriften*, vol. II, *Das philosophsiche Werk* I, ed. Richard Samuel (Stuttgart: Kohlhammer, 1960), 470.
38. As Aristotle says, "to every potentiality of this kind actuality [*energeia*] is prior, both in the notion and in the essence [*logō kai tē ousia*]" (*Metaphysics* IX, 1049b10, trans. Hugh Tredennick. Loeb Library. Cambridge, MA: Harvard University Press, 1980, 454. Translation modified).
39. *Philosophische Lehrjahre (1796–1806)*, ed. Ernst Behler, KFSA 18 (München/Paderborn/Wien: Ferdinand Schöningh; Zürich: Thomas-Verlag 1963), 55, n. 362.
40. KFSA 18, 106, n. 927.
41. Antoine Berman, *The Experience of the Foreign: Culture and Translation in Romantic Germany*, trans. S. Heyvaert (Albany, NY: State University of New York Press), 1992), 107–8.

    For a reading of Schlegel's review of *Wilhelm Meister*, see Elizabeth Millán, *Friedrich Schlegel and the Emergence of Romantic Philosophy* (New York: SUNY, 2007), 50–58.
42. Novalis, *Schriften II*, 545, n. 105; English translation: *Philosophical Writings*, ed. and trans. Margaret Mahony Stoljar (Albany, NY: State University of New York Press, 1997), 60, n. 66. Translation modified.
43. See Frederick Beiser, *The Romantic Imperative: The Concept of Early German Romanticism* (Cambridge, MA: Harvard University Press, 2003), 23.

44. KFSA 2, 183.
45. KFSA 18 49, n. 308.
46. *Hermeneutik und Kritik,* ed. Manfred Frank (Frankfurt a.M.: Suhrkamp, 1977), 325; English translation: *Hermeneutics: The Handwritten Manuscripts,* trans. James Duke and Jack Forstman (Atlanta, GA: Scholars Press, 1986), 69.
47. *Hermeneutik und Kritik,* 94.
48. *Hermeneutics,* 112.
49. *Truth and Method,* 2nd ed., translation revised by Joel Weinsheimer and Donald Marshall (New York: Continuum, 1998), 297. Manfred Frank interprets Schleiermacher's "understanding better" on Gadamerian lines, claiming that "understanding 'better' cannot mean understanding more truly or correctly but only differently and more richly" (Frank 1997, 40). While Frank is right in protecting Schleiermacher from a psychological interpretation, there is another alternative than an "understanding differently." In other words, the fact that "better" is indeed not to be understood merely psychologically as meliorative does not entail that the alternative to the meliorative is a mere Gadamerian "otherwise."
50. Hans Eichner, "Einleitung," in Schlegel *KFSA* II, xii-lxxii. (p. xcviii).
51. KFSA 2, 370; "On Incomprehensibility (1800)," in J.M. Bernstein (ed.), *Classic and Romantic German Aesthetics* (Cambridge: Cambridge University Press, 2003), 297–307 (p. 305).
52. KFSA 19, 216. See Bärbel Frischmann, *Vom transzendentalem zum frühromantischen Idealismus: J.G. Fichte und Fr. Schlegel* (Paderborn: Ferdinand Schöningh, 2005), 355.
53. KFSA 18, 140.
54. KFSA 18, 129, n. 89.
55. KFSA 2, 401.
56. *Sein und Zeit,* 393; *Being and Time,* 343.
57. *Vom Wesen der menschlichen Freiheit. Einleitung in die Philosophie,* GA 31, ed. Hartmut Tietjen (Frankfurt am Main: Klostermann, 1982), 124.
58. KFSA 18, 284, n. 1055.
59. GA 52, 177.
60. KFSA 11, 112–13.
61. KFSA 16, 160, n. 883.
62. KFSA 11, 125.
63. See Beiser, *The Romantic Imperative,* 15.
64. *Die Grundprobleme der Phänomenologie,* GA 24, ed. Friedrich-Wilhelm von Herrmann (Frankfurt am Main: Klostermann, 1989. 2nd ed. ), 244.
65. Paul Ricoeur, *La métaphore vive* (Paris: Les Editions du Seuil, 1975), 387–88.
66. KFSA 18 421, n. 1222; *KFSA* 12, 42.
67. KFSA 18, 453, n. 234.
68. KFSA 12, 42.
69. KFSA 2, 285.

70. Novalis, *Schriften II*, 536, n. 50; *Philosophical Writings*, 57, n. 44. Translation modified.
71. KFSA 12, 105.
72. Novalis, *Schriften II*, 545, n. 105; *Philosophical Writings*, 60, n. 66. Translation modified.
73. Novalis, *Notes for a Romantic Encyclopaedia: Das allgemeine Brouillon*, ed. and trans. David W. Wood (Albany, NY: State University of New York Press, 2007), 209–210, n. 67.
74. *Vom Wesen der Wahrheit. Zu Platons Höhlengleichnis und Theätet*, GA 34, ed. Hermann Mörchen (Frankfurt am Main: Klostermann, 1988), 64.
75. GA 65, 293; *Contributions to Philosophy*, 207.
76. GA 52, 40.
77. GA 52, 40.
78. GA 34, 33.
79. *Sein und Wahrheit. 1. Die Grundfrage der Philosophie 2. Vom Wesen der Wahrheit*, GA 36/37, ed. Hartmut Tietjen (Franfurt am Main: Klostermann, 2001), 137.
80. GA 34, 33.
81. GA 34, 33.
82. GA 34, 33.
83. *Margins of Philosophy*, trans. Alan Bass (Chicago: The University Press of Chicago, 1982), 15.
84. KFSA 12, 337.
85. KFSA 12, 350.
86. KFSA 12, 376.
87. KFSA 12, 376.
88. KFSA 12, 350–51; See Frischmann, *Vom transzendentalem zum frühromantischen Idealismus*, 2005, 281; Ernst Behler and Ursula Struc-Oppenberg, "Einleitung," in Schlegel KFSA 8, xv–ccxxxii. (p. cxxxiv).
89. Schleiermacher, *On Religion*, 38.
90. *Zollikon Seminars. Protocols—Conversations—Letters*, ed. Medard Boss, trans. Franz Mayr and Richard Askay (Evanston, IL: Northwestern University Press, 2001), 190.

    Marcia sá Cavalcante Schuback list the different works in which Heidegger mentions love in "Heideggerian Love" (See *Phenomenology of Eros*, eds. Jonna Bornemar and Marcia Sá Cavalcante Schuback (Huddinge: Södertörns högskola, 2012), 129–152 (p. 138). https://www.diva-portal.org/smash/get/diva2:524777/FULLTEXT01.pdf accessed 11/14/2018).
91. *Grundprobleme der Phänomenologie (1919/20)*, GA 58, ed. Hand-Helmuth Gander (Frankfurt am Main: Klostermann, 1993), 168. He also notes: "Love as *motivation* ground of phenomenological understanding. Necessarily co-given in its enactment sense [*Vollzugssinn*]" (GA 58, 185).

92. *Besinnung*, GA 66, ed. F.-W. von Herrmann (Frankfurt am Main: Klostermann, 1997), 63. See Schuback, 151.
93. In the "Letter on Humanism" Heidegger writes: "To embrace a thing or a person in its essence means to love it, to favor it. Thought in a more original way such favoring (*Mögen*) means to bestow essence as a gift." He equates this favoring or loving with a letting be (*Basic Writings*, ed. David Farrell Krell (San Francisco: HarperSanFrancisco, 1993), 213–165 (p. 220).
94. *The Visible and the Invisible*, trans. Alphonso Lingis (Evanston, IL: Northwestern University Press, 1968), 180–81.

# 27

# Sensibility, Reflection, and Play: Early German Romanticism and Its Legacy in Contemporary Continental Philosophy

Elaine P. Miller

In his recent article "Aesthetic 'Sense' in Kant and Nancy," Charles Shepherdson asks whether aesthetic experience has a unique or privileged role in making evident the connection between the body and language, and traces a lineage of contemporary French philosophy that takes Kant's third *Critique* as its point of departure in developing this question. In particular, Shepherdson considers the relation of the two senses of "sense" in the context of aesthetic experience, namely, bodily sense perception, on the one hand, and linguistic meaning or communicability, on the other.[1] In this chapter, I will argue that this connection between the body and language was made salient much earlier by German Romanticism, which took Kant's mostly transcendental, a priori sense of taste and transformed it into a material aesthetics. As Novalis articulated it, German Romanticism took the body, and by extension all of material reality, to be thought "precipitated" and "crystallized" in space."[2] This bodily expressibility transformed Kant's theory of aesthetic ideas into an ontological account, one in which body and language, rather than imagination and understanding, play.

I will argue that the concept of reflection in Kant, which, according to Walter Benjamin, became the foundation of early German Romantic

E. P. Miller (✉)
Miami University, Oxford, OH, USA
e-mail: millerep@miamioh.edu

© The Author(s) 2020
E. Millán Brusslan (ed.), *The Palgrave Handbook of German Romantic Philosophy*, Palgrave Handbooks in German Idealism, https://doi.org/10.1007/978-3-030-53567-4_27

Philosophy, can be connected to this bodily aesthetics of taste by virtue of its quality of conceptual indetermination, hovering in infinite playfulness. This indeterminacy takes a different form in early German Romanticism than in Kant, however. Whereas for Kant, judgments of taste appear to be about nature or artworks, but actually concern a relation of the subject to itself in a kind of intellectual sensation, for Novalis and Friedrich Schlegel, reflective aesthetic judgment refers not only to the feeling of imagination and understanding playing indeterminately and harmoniously, but also fundamentally, to a living connection to the natural world and to the Absolute, one that makes one "forget one's narrow self."[3] As Benjamin puts it, the move in early German Romanticism is from the "thinking of the ego," in a Fichtean sense, toward a "thinking of thought," where "subject" and "object" lose their oppositional stance and become relative determinations of the medium of reflection.[4] To reflect is to consume one's insular self, namely, to take in the world while also connecting oneself to the same world, as well as to infinite other selves as equally reflections of that world.

Benjamin's consideration of the concept of reflection draws on Friedrich Schlegel and Novalis in exploring the romantic appropriation of Kant's reflective judgment and in devising a different kind of "concept," the constellation, where reflection is not restricted to the activity of a subject. In his doctoral dissertation, "The Concept of Criticism in German Romanticism," Benjamin shifts the consideration of reflection from the subject as the arbiter of taste to the artwork as a phenomenon capable of revealing new ways of relating to the world and to others.

Although the term "reflection" seems to denote a uniquely mental process, in Novalis and Schlegel and also in Benjamin, it has an irreducibly ontological significance; as Benjamin notes, "Novalis tries to interpret the whole of terrestrial existence as the reflection of spirits in themselves, and to interpret man within this earthly life as partly the dispelling and 'breaking-through of that primitive reflection.'"[5] Reflection was posited by the early German Romantics as an activity that can effect a mediation between a world that is so familiar that it seems objectively real and another world that shakes certainty in that reality, bringing the two together in a shared sense of the Absolute.

In contrast to the metaphysical interpretation of reflection, but equally taking up the disequilibrium emphasized by both the early German Romantics and Benjamin, Jacques Rancière deploys the concept of "play" from Friedrich Schiller's expansion of Kant's concept of aesthetic reflective judgment into what Schiller called the "play impulse," to denote the fundamental operation of art's critical relationship to politics or the distribution of the sensible, a distance that allows for something unprecedented to emerge. Rancière reads Kant's "disinterestedness" as a decisive break between artistic intention and received meaning. Such a break between cause and effect separates the two senses of "sense" by unmooring aesthetic effects on the audience, or the "sensorium of enjoyment," from what Rancière calls the "sensorium of its fabrication." That is to say that art may be taken up in a way that opens up a new world for the viewer, one that is, if not unconnected to that of the artist, nonetheless fundamentally different from it. This apprehension is not an individual interpretation on the part of the spectator, however, but rather represents the unfolding of a fundamentally new and objective possibility in the way humans sensorily apprehend the world. This shift results in a conflict between the old and new regimes of sense, which Rancière calls a dissensus, leading to an analogous move, philosophically speaking, away from the subject and toward the "objective" structures by which the world is apprehended. The philosopher in turn can articulate a conceptual frame manifesting this tension between two sensory worlds, giving others a lens through which to perceive their interconnections and differences, as well as articulating the democratic possibilities made visible for those who have previously been excluded from them. This documented shift in focus allows for the perception and dissemination of perspectives heretofore covered over by the dominant distribution of the sensible. Rancière thus articulates a politically shifting version of the Kantian *sensus communis*. I will argue that both Benjamin and Rancière deploy German Romanticism for political ends. As Benjamin argues in a latter essay, for art to have a genuine political impact it must be created in such a way as to make subordination to an ideological position impossible.[6]

In order to put this legacy into context, I will begin by looking back to Kant's analytic of aesthetic judgment, which puts nature into play with something that exceeds it. Reflective judgment, of which aesthetic judgment is one type, takes a presentation of nature or a material artwork as its point of departure, but ultimately involves a subject's relation to itself. However, in Kant's aesthetic idea, a result of the productive activity of nature in genius, a multiplicity of fragments gesture toward a greater whole, which Kant calls an indeterminate ideality, bridging the gap between subject and object. The fragmentary nature of these aesthetic ideas does not decrease the significance they hold as material entities that reach toward a greater totality.

I will focus on the fragmentary style of writing of early German Romanticism, which puts into action the aesthetic idea as a poetico-philosophical performance of the relationship between nature and thinking.[7] Gasché argues that the German Romantic philosophers practiced the genre of the fragment as a way of enacting the Kantian claim that a regulative idea can never be presented in totality, and that imagination, through the aesthetic idea, works over and transforms the material of nature into something different that surpasses nature.⁸ Because these representations constantly multiply their features, no definite concept is capable of fully comprehending them.

I will consider the Kantian aesthetic idea and romantic fragment as bits of nature, like seeds, that give rise to ideas.⁹ In consuming these ideas, what arises is not a simple unity of subject with itself or the subject with an object, but a materiality that cannot be completely digested, one that serves as the term of a further reflection, an infinite series that, for Kant, served as a symbol of morality and for the early German Romantics a passage to the Absolute. In integrating nature and the body in an objective, rather than a purely subjective sense, early German Romanticism transformed Kant's vision of the unity of freedom and necessity from an ideal to a real unity, and shifted the emphasis from (a passage to) morality to the political.

## 1  Kant on Aesthetic Ideas and Beauty as a Symbol of Morality

Kant's comments on aesthetic ideas form part of his justification of judgments of beauty to legitimate their claim to universal validity for everyone and their grounding in an a priori principle.[10] As Shepherdson notes, a judgment of beauty is necessarily based on sense perception and thus has a bodily dimension, but it also, in its claim to universal validity, rests on a universal communicability based not on a determinate concept but on the conditions for facilitating cognition or "sense"-making.[11] Both dimensions of "sense" are relevant to aesthetic ideas. Kant describes genius, the natural power that works through the human artist, as the capacity to exhibit aesthetic ideas, where an aesthetic idea is a "presentation of the imagination which prompts much thought, but to which no determinate thought whatsoever…can be adequate."[12] The aesthetic idea, like the fragment, evokes one or a "multiplicity of partial presentations"[13] without being reducible to the sum total of them.

The aesthetic idea goes much further than metaphoricity, however. Kant writes that the aesthetic idea is capable of "restructuring experience" even to a point where it surpasses nature.[14] It can add "much content" to an existing concept, or even fill in for one where there is none available. Finally, it is able to express what is ineffable in a mental state accompanying a given artistic presentation in such a way as to make it universally communicable, whether through poetic language, visual art, or a teleological judgment. Teleological judgment does not simply refer to judgments specifically about the purposiveness of nature, but also to the possibility of fitting discrete natural laws into a systematic whole. Kant writes that the aesthetic idea "reveals a new rule that could not have been inferred from any earlier principles or examples."[15] As such, it is capable not only of evoking new thoughts, but also of creating new concepts. Kant names the animating principle in the mind capable of creating aesthetic ideas *Geist,* or Spirit, a "purposive momentum" that strengthens the cognitive powers.

"Sense" thus refers to the ability to communicate not only through concepts, but also through a new lexicon that is still in the process of being developed. The aesthetic idea adds to a concept, quickening our cognitive powers in a way that "connects language, which otherwise would be mere letters, with spirit."[16] Even beyond this capacity to enhance and augment language, aesthetic ideas, Kant claims, point beyond nature to an indeterminate supersensible realm, one that is at the origin of all human capacity to judge *per se.*

Kant extols the imagination as a productive cognitive power, a new role for it here. At first, he writes, what the imagination does is to entertain us when experience "strikes us as overly routine." However, he soon goes on to claim that it also has another role, namely, that it can "restructure experience." The imagination effects this restructuring by moving analogically, when considering empirical nature, from known concepts of the understanding to others that either are unknown or for which there are not yet concepts. For example, a scientist might move from observation of known phenomena to the description and explanation of newly discovered entities or effects. Such a process is not limited to empirical phenomena; he writes that we may "also follow principles which reside higher up," namely within reason, a process that allows us to feel a freedom from the law of the imagination and a capacity to move into something that surpasses nature. This is not simply a description of the creation of art or a new scientific theory, although these are Kant's paradigm examples. In opening up toward this unknown area, reason may be compelled to "think more than what can be apprehended and made distinct in the presentation" or even in ordinary language. A new concept or concepts may slowly come into being. Cognition is not simply the attachment of a concept to an intuition, but it is also the discovery of a concept from the production of imaginative new applications of an intuition. The aesthetic idea is truly the counterpart of the rational idea, which posits supersensibly without hope of being actualized in experience. The aesthetic idea begins with the empirical, and moves from there to posit a new, indeterminate universal. As I will argue later in this chapter, the potential refiguring of conceptual categories arguably entails a shift in what Rancière calls the "distribution of the sensible," and what Benjamin calls the historical transformation of the mode of human sense perception.[17]

In the Dialectic of Aesthetic Judgment, Kant considers the "Antinomy of Taste," the apparent contradictions one can get into when one wants to argue both that a judgment of taste cannot be based on concepts, and at the same time that it is possible to argue about judgments of taste. This dispute is significant because if we take one side or the other, we are left with incompatible visions of cognition as it relates to aesthetic criticism. If we argue that judgments of taste are not based on concepts at all, we are left with nothing but individual, subjective feelings about what is beautiful. If we argue that judgments of taste *are* based on concepts, we seem to be left with formulae for judging art that are immutable, and the impossibility of anything new that is not already conceptually determined to come into being. The contradiction disappears, he argues, if we say that a concept does underlie the judgment of taste, but it is a concept that "does not allow us to cognize and prove anything concerning the object, because it is intrinsically indeterminable and inadequate for cognition." It is a concept, but an indeterminate one in that it is valid for everyone, or universal. Therefore, the basis that is shared by everyone must be one that links humans together, and Kant refers to it as the "supersensible substrate of humanity."[18]

Calling this indeterminate concept a supersensible substrate of humanity, or even, as he does later, a supersensible substrate of appearances, is a surprise move this late in the critique. Up until this point, Kant had insisted only that the judgment of taste rested on an indeterminate concept, but since only imagination and understanding were involved in the intellectual pleasure given rise to by their harmonious interplay, there was no question of a supersensible dimension. By invoking a supersensible substrate of humanity or of appearances, Kant refers to aesthetic *ideas* that refer to intuitions for which adequate concepts can never be found.[19] With aesthetic ideas "the understanding with its concepts never reaches the *entire* inner intuition that the imagination has and connects with a given presentation."[20] The aesthetic idea gives rise to multiple fragments that move up toward something that surpasses any determinate concept. These fragments are not broken bits of a previous whole, but bits that point to a totality that can never be fully presented: they are "that whole itself *in actualitas*—the only way in which the supersensible substrate occurs, or becomes present."[21] This is what Kant means by saying that the totality is "supersensible"; it is present as a fragment, or seed, but it will never be a fully sensible present.

Kant calls this indeterminate supersensible to which the art of genius refers the "supersensible substrate (unattainable by any concept of the understanding) of all the powers" of the genius. The subjective standard for the aesthetic purposiveness in fine art that lays claim to everyone's necessary liking "can be supplied only by that which is merely nature in the subject but which cannot be encompassed by rules or concepts." Such a standard is supplied by "that by reference to which we are to make all our cognitive powers harmonize," which is, in turn "the ultimate purpose" given to us by the intelligible element of our nature.[22]

This reference to an ultimate purpose also informs the section that Kant entitles "Beauty as a Symbol of Morality," which follows the solution to the Antinomy of Taste. Here he writes that due to the limitations of human cognition, our ultimate purpose can never be given to us purely intelligibly. Instead, establishing the reality of any kind of concept requires intuitions. There are two types of concepts, pure concepts of the understanding, and rational concepts or ideas; only the former give rise to and order sensible experience. The ideas of reason go beyond the bounds of possible experience and name entities for which we have concepts but no intuitions, such as freedom, immortality, and God. These rational concepts still need to be established as real, argues Kant, and they can be so established, although not objectively, through a reference to practical reason *via* examples of beauty. In the case of establishing concepts of the understanding, the imagination schematizes intuitions in such a way as to make sensible content adequate to the understanding, "but if anyone goes as far as to demand that we establish the objective reality of the rational concepts (i.e., the ideas) for the sake of theoretical cognition, this is impossible."[23] Here Kant introduces the concept of hypotyposis, which is nothing more than the process of making a concept sensible. There are two types of hypotyposis, schematic and symbolic. Schematic hypotyposis concerns our experience, and, accordingly, is organized according to a concept provided by the understanding, and thus is demonstrative and straightforward. But when no such concept exists in the understanding because the concept goes beyond reason's limitations, Kant argues that through art, another kind of hypotyposis can obtain. This kind of hypotyposis, or making a concept sensible, is "symbolic" rather than schematic:[24]

Symbolic presentation is a kind of intuitive presentation that uses an analogy to convey a meaning that otherwise could not be expressed in conceptual language. Kant writes that symbolic exhibition "applies the mere rule by which it [symbolic hypotyposis] reflects on" a given intuition "to an entirely different object, of which the former object is only the symbol."[25] For example, the word "foundation," although used to mean the underlying basis of an argument or system," also means the lowest lying weight bearing part of a building, where "foundation" in the former sense draws on the latter by analogy.

From this incontrovertible argument (given that without it, we would lose a large portion of our shared language), Kant makes the broader argument that the beautiful is the symbol of the morally good.[26] The judgment that connects beauty and morality emerges from a third supersensible substrate that is neither purely that of nature nor purely subjective, but a "possible harmony" of the two joined into a unity "in an unknown manner."[27] This supersensible substrate that combines subject and object is effectively limited to the subjective realm for Kant, since it is only evoked in a judgment of taste, which he has previously specified to be merely subjective.[28]

## 2   Schlegel and Novalis

The idea that art can indirectly symbolize the morally good, briefly alluded to by Kant, gets taken up forcefully by the early German Romantics, in particular by Friedrich von Hardenberg (Novalis). Kneller asks why Kant insists on "the complete inability of imagination in free play to portray moral Ideas," given its creative role in reflective judgments of this type, and argues that for Kant, portraits of humans could make visible moral attributes such as goodness of soul, and even that secular teleological possibilities for humans such as a peaceful, universal, moral community might be embodied in a concrete artistic vision.[29] While I think there is more evidence against this position than for it in Kant's critical work on art, I do think a version of this interpretation is present in German Romanticism. However, Novalis and Friedrich Schlegel retained the Kantian injunction against any determinate totalizing presentation in the aesthetic symbolization of the morally good. In other words, artworks might suggest a moral vision, but they could never completely and determinately present it, which is one of the reasons the fragment is such an important medium of romantic philosophy. Even for Kant, in discussing morality in the context of aesthetics, "moral" refers more broadly to the indeterminate supersensible rather than to any specific moral judgment; beauty, when it functions as a "symbol of morality," evokes "something that is neither nature nor freedom and yet is linked with the basis of freedom."[30] Thus, Schlegel and Novalis, while involved much more directly than Kant in the actual production of art, reinforce the Kantian interpretation of the relation of beauty and morality.

Kant argues that the feeling occasioned by the harmonious play of faculties in the judgment of taste is a feeling of *life*: this is not simply a subjective interior feeling, but also an opening to the life of the other, to the one who created the work, and also to the lives of all others. We can see this expansive notion of connective life both in Kant's reference to nature as the source of genius and in his discussion of the *sensus communis* that guarantees universal communicability of judgments of taste. Both Schlegel and Novalis adopt the Kantian emphasis on life, but whereas in Kant, "life" infuses spiritual achievement but is otherwise disembodied, in Schlegel and in particular in Novalis "life" refers not only to human feeling and achievement but also to all of nature, including, of course, the human body. Thus, "feeling" is transformed into "reflection," a subjective/objective sense of "sense," where the mind reflects something outside of it in order to come to an understanding of its own nature and that of the Absolute.

Following Kant, the first important facet of romantic reflection is nature. In Kant, the concept of nature has three primary meanings. First, it is the determined, mechanically structured, realm of appearances that can be known only in the way in which it appears to a very particular kind of human cognition. Second, it is the sphere of inclinations, to be ignored and avoided by moral reasoning. Finally, in the *Critique of Judgment*, nature is both what gives rise to quintessential judgments of taste and sublimity, but also a means for what turns out to be a purely subjective experience. In judgments of teleology and nature, nature as a whole is a subjectively presupposed totality that is never knowable as such. This dual project of idealistic conceptualization of the whole of nature, combined with skepticism toward the possibility of knowing it in its totality, informs the German Romantic project.

Novalis describes nature as both independent and self-modifying,[31] characteristics that Kant argued we must attribute to the organism, although we mistakenly assume these features to constitute its objective nature beyond our own subjective grasp of it. Novalis focuses on the dynamic changeability of nature, which means that humans training their vision toward the Absolute, can nevertheless grasp it only a fragment at a time. Poetry and investigation of nature work together to harmonize this (ultimately unbridgeable) gap. Even the physicists, Novalis writes, consider matter and energy to be working together in harmony, making scientific research analogous to the evolving relationship between nature and morality.[32] What this means, I think, is that, like Kant, Novalis recognizes that science is always directed by the theoretical presuppositions of human minds. In more contemporary terms, we might say that all observation is theory-laden. The systematic image we project of nature, however grounded it may be in experiment and repeated observation, does not derive from but rather informs our investigation of it. Novalis uses the term "moral" in Kant's broadest sense, as an idea of reason, specifically the *a priori* idea of the totality of nature that is ultimately supersensible, or beyond the grasp of empirical investigation. He writes that nature is intrinsically dynamic and never remains the same; beyond this self-transformation, however, as people "perceive, understand and imagine it," nature changes in a different way, that is, "it becomes more moral"[33] for our theoretical vision. Whether nature gives rise to mind, or mind gives rise to nature, a conclusion that we cannot determine, both exist in a perpetual dynamic reciprocal effectiveness.[34] The aim, which can be pursued only in a fragmentary and often contradictory way, is the "creation of a purely spiritual world" involving the gradual "dissolution of nature altogether," an aim that is never fully attained.

The second important facet of romantic reflection or reflective judgment (which I am drawing together) lies in aesthetic presentation. In Kant, what separates the art of genius from other artworks is the feeling of life expressed in the artwork, but this feeling is neither biological nor psychological, neither individual nor emotive. It is affective in the sense of an energetic transmission from nature ineffably to genius and from genius in a universal voice to its audience. For Novalis, this "feeling of life" has a more metaphysical status. Benjamin explains this relation in his analysis of romantic reflection, arguing that it emphasizes "not an infinitude of endless advance, but an infinitude of connectedness" (126).[35] The knitting together of nature and poetry or art, following Goethe in modifying Kant's conclusions, is not limited to the subjective realm, but rather concerns a relation of self to natural world and to the objective intersubjective world of language and institutions.

It might seem surprising at first to say that the German Romantics espoused an infinitude of connectedness, to the extent that this phrase connotes communicability and systematic coherence. In addition to writing primarily in fragments, Novalis wove a fairy tale into his *Bildungsroman*, and his *Lehrlinge zu Sais* presented his views in an impressionistic form. Schlegel, for his part, celebrated incomprehensibility in a famous essay.[36] The literary form favored by Schlegel and Novalis reflects their fundamental conviction that nature cannot be fully grasped as a totality, whether in terms of empirical investigation or in terms of theoretical articulation. Novalis considered fragments to be like seeds that would bear fruit in the reader, however, and, as Dalia Nassar points out, Schlegel's aim was to create a system of fragments which, like an organism, is living and growing, aided in large part by the multifaceted ways in which it is received.[37]

To call a fragment a seed rather than a shard or an atom is to emphasize its intentional interpretive open-endedness, its metamorphosis and bodily growth. Both Novalis and Schlegel focused on living, growing nature, rather than upon a subjective feeling of life or the formal structure of the organism. Every living thing is "the seed of everything," and to the extent that we do not recognize this and identify ourselves only with what is enclosed in our individual body, we "remain forever a fragment."[38] Beauty is none other than "what reminds us of nature and thereby stimulates a sense of the infinite fullness of life. Nature is organic, and whatever is most sublimely beautiful is therefore always vegetal, and the same is true of morality and love."[39]

In Fragment 13 of his *Logological Fragments I*, Novalis contrasts the "scholastic" thinker with the "crude, intuitive poet" or "alchemist." The former "builds his universe out of logical atoms," thereby destroying all living nature.[40] The latter vivifies nature, but at the expense of laws. One starts from parts and tries to build to the Absolute, while the other assumes the Absolute but cannot articulate it. While the first is a "head without hands," the latter is a set of "hands without head." Both hands and head are needed, and, because they lack one or the other, both of these kinds of thinker, just as both of these pictures of nature, mechanistic and spiritual, are fundamentally one-sided. Their limitation is due to a "weakness of the productive imagination—which at the moment of transition" from thinking to being "could not remain suspended in contemplation of itself."[41]

The romantic philosopher artist, then, cultivates the productive imagination in order to strengthen the Kantian account of the reflective judgment in its role as a transition and unifying link between theoretical and practical philosophy. According to Nuzzo, this romantic account of the oscillation of the productive imagination transforms and takes the place of the Kantian reflective judgment as "an in-between in which thinking's and consciousness' movement between" the empirical and the Absolute can occur.[42] The productive imagination was interpreted by post-Kantian German philosophers to be an original unity prior to the distinction between concepts and intuitions, the source of both aesthetic ideas and new concepts. For Fichte, the productive imagination was at the origin of all of psychic life, and thus the unifying force of the "I." The imagination "hovers" (*schwebt*) between the I and not-I, the empirical and the Absolute, and this hovering is the condition both of intuition, and, ultimately, of reality itself.[43] In Novalis' work, as in other accounts influenced by Fichte, the productive imagination is a unifying power emphasized as a way of overcoming Kant's dualism. It binds nature to human freedom, when sufficiently strong. Notably, in the fragment from Novalis' *Fichte Studies* foregrounded by Manfred Frank, Novalis describes the relationship between nature and self as a kind of double mirroring or reflection. When we look into a mirror, our reflection is reversed, so that we see not ourselves, but an inverse image of ourselves, the subjective mirrored in the objective. By re-reflecting the reflection, that is, "romanticizing," through art's mediation with nature, humans can best come to self-understanding.[44]

Let us look at this passage in greater detail. First of all, Novalis speaks of orienting oneself according to an original schema. Here, I think he refers to Kant's essay "What Does it Mean to Orient Oneself in Thinking?"[45] In this essay Kant considers the phenomenon of proprioception, by means of which, through orienting ourselves in our bodies, that is, knowing where various parts of our body are in relation to each other without having to look at them, we are also able to orient ourselves in the sensible (and ultimately supersensible) world. Kant draws our attention to the origin of the concept of orientation, literally based on the meaning of "orient" as "East," the direction of the rising sun. If I see the sun in the East, I can find West, South, and North as well. For such an orientation, however, Kant says, I must not only be able to perceive differences on the horizon, but also within my own body. Such a proprioception is not conceptual; although we might alternatively be able to chart, say, the position of constellations in the sky or the arrangement of furniture in a familiar room by measuring and mapping them. "Orientation," as Kant discusses it here, is based on a *feeling* of our subjective (bodily) outline, our parts in spatial relation to each other. What is notable here is that this feeling of orientation takes not only the mind, but also the physical body and even the horizon of nature into account.

For Novalis, the schema always goes beyond our bodily self to the whole of nature. The Fichtean subject initially looks at itself as reflected in what it intuits as not-I, and thereby thinks it knows itself. However, Novalis' point, considered after reading Fichte, is that when we purport to "know" ourselves in a mirror, even one provided by nature, what we see is actually a reverse of what we are, not a faithful reproduction, a "not-I" that cannot be further determined or known. In order to fully understand subjectivity, and perhaps the entire subjective structure of the "I" or Fichtean Absolute, humans must re-reflect nature back to themselves through the activity of poeticizing. To poeticize is to render nature mysterious, as well as the mysterious natural. This process can be thought of as a kind of oscillation between opposites. The productive imagination occupies a place that hovers between the finite and the infinite and between nature and mind.[46]

The phrase "remain suspended" recalls the feeling of life associated with the Kantian reflective judgment, its lingering and hovering in indeterminate play. In the *Fichte Studies,* Novalis writes that "*Harmony* is the condition of [the I's] activity—*of* [*its*] *oscillating,* between opposites."[47] Novalis takes this oscillation to be a fundamental ontological principle at the origin of both nature and thought, and not just a subjective power, however: "All being, being in general, is nothing but being free—*oscillating* between extremes that necessarily are to be united and necessarily are to be separated."[48] He adds: "Should there be a still higher sphere, it would be the sphere between being and not-being—The oscillating between the two.—Something inexpressible, and here we have the *concept of life*."[49] The result of this oscillation is that neither a unified, systematic picture of nature nor one of the self is ever possible, even if that is the aim.[50]

Schlegel describes this oscillation poetically as both the "warp and woof of everflowing creation," and the play of the definite and indefinite relations in human life. He writes that: "Nature itself wills the eternal cycle of eternally repeated experiments; and nature also wills that every individual should be perfect in himself, unique and new, a true image of supreme, indivisible individuality."[51] Schlegel emphasizes play and irony as the metaphysical condition of life. Nature carries out its oppositions with "incredible humor" and "roguish meaning," while working toward a "final shape and perfection."[52] Human sensuality, including sexual relations between masculine and feminine are considered as natural, yet provisional antitheses,[53] plays in this same way toward the infinite and away from it. It is essential to note that for the early German Romantics this play does not move unidirectionally and teleologically toward a perfect end. Instead, "with eternally immutable symmetry," nature and human activity "both strive in opposite directions toward the infinite and away from it," creating shapes and then destroying them, resulting in the natural activity of life and death, and the human dialectic between desire and satiety.[54]

Following this non-fixed route, there exists a third way between the scholar and the poet, that of the "artist, who is at once tool and genius" and who knows that both sides "must be united in a common principle."[55] The common principle is a "living reflection," which "with careful tending afterwards extends of itself into an infinite formed spiritual universe—the kernel or germ of an all-encompassing organism." It is the beginning of a "true self-penetration of the spirit" that never ends.[56] The artist reflects the fact that: "All reality radiates from this light-point of oscillation—everything is contained in it—object and subject have their being through it, not it through them."[57] Life connects to productive imagination through the oscillating principle of being, and art, too, stems from, continues, and reflects this process.

Such a discussion of the productive imagination has its roots in Kant, but goes much further than Kant would allow. Recall that in his discussion of the genius whose work produces aesthetic ideas in the mind of the audience, Kant describes the imagination as "very mighty" in its role as a productive cognitive power, able to create "another nature out of the material that actual nature gives it."[58] While for Kant the "other nature" is a subjectively and potentially linguistically rich imaginative panorama, one which presents "the concept's implications and its kinship with other concepts" and "prompts the imagination to spread over a multitude of kindred presentations that arouse more thought than can be expressed in a concept," for Novalis and Friedrich Schlegel, poets are able to actually transform material nature into spiritual nature, and this is their natural end, understood in an Aristotelian sense as their potency. Schlegel writes, "Just as a child is only a thing which wants to become a human being, so a poem is only a product of nature which wants to become a work of art."[59]

For Schlegel, romantic poetry is privileged among the arts because it acknowledges its own finitude and eternally dynamic striving and changing nature. While other poetry considers itself "finished" and "capable of being fully analyzed," romantic poetry is "still in a state of becoming" and "that is its true nature." Its fundamental and essential incompleteness is more reflective of nature for being so. Romantic poetry, for this reason, can, more than any other aesthetic form, "hover at the midpoint between the portrayed and the portrayer, free of all real and ideal self-interest, on the wings of poetic reflection, and can raise that reflection again and again to a higher power, can multiply it in an endless succession of mirrors."[60]

We see here that the language of reflection is not purely inward or subjective, but that it follows the oscillating rhythms of nature. What the poet does is to intensify this rhythm in order to bring it into full view. The transformation of nature may be described as a perfection of it, but this perfecting transformation is essentially incomplete, always striving higher. Reflection in the romantic sense takes up the dual sense of reflective judgment as the effect of both aesthetic experience and the judgment of nature as teleological, described by Kant as "merely subjective," and presents them as the essence of nature and of the human as the one who interprets and works upon nature to make it into something higher yet essentially connected to its origin. Schlegel compares this activity to the role of sociability in human life, which takes a mere biological being-together and transforms it into a political community in which love and friendship bind people together. Schlegel calls this "openness," or a place "where everyone can enter without resort to violence."[61]

The activity of writing poetry and reading a text and of trying to interpret it philosophically, especially when it is fragmentary, thus mirrors the oscillating rhythm of Being and non-Being. Taking up the "seed" of the fragment requires the active participation of the reader, practicing in reading the oscillating rhythm of reflective judgment, which is also the rhythm of expansion and contraction in nature.[62] Schlegel writes that "A human being should be like a work of art which, though openly exhibited and freely accessible, can nevertheless be enjoyed and understood only by those who bring feeling and study to it."[63] As Lacoue-Labarthe and Nancy express it, the romantic activity of reflection is not simply a reflection of thinking on thinking, or thought thinking itself, as in Fichte, but expands to "literature producing itself as it produces its own theory,"[64] or, in Benjamin's word, criticism. The production of literature adds to reflection a material element that is an essential part of early German Romanticism.

## 3     Walter Benjamin on Critique and Reflection

For Benjamin, early German Romanticism also has political import, not as a "fact" of "literary history,"[65] but as a result of its reimagining of the Kantian concept of critique as the active practice of criticism. Far from consisting of passing judgment on artworks in a kind of high court, the romantic practice of criticism, on Benjamin's reading, strives to complete the work by perfecting the good and obliterating anything of insignificance in a kind of purification process.[66] Through philosophical critique, an artwork, such as a photograph, a play, or a film, may make new sensory and conceptual possibilities evident which have social and political ramifications. In other words, art has the capacity to open up potencies that have been covered over, including envisioning other views of the social and political world, and the possibility of nature opening up toward freedom.

Benjamin focuses initially on the romantic concept of reflection, inherited in its formal structure from Fichte but transformed by Novalis and Schlegel into what they call an infinitely productive form of thinking. As we saw earlier, for Fichte, reflection is thinking that takes itself as its object, and as such is the pure form of knowledge. Thinking belongs only to the "I," for Fichte, although this "I" is the subjective structure of all Being. Although inspired by this vision, Schlegel and Novalis, as we have seen, change the emphasis. On their interpretation, reflection becomes, not an overarching self-like structure of Being conceived as thinking thinking itself, but rather a multiplicity of self-like beings. Everything that is, whether subject or object, has the structure of thought; as Benjamin expresses it, thinking-oneself "is proper to everything, for everything is a self."[67] The difference between these two views is that the first accords to the unity of Being the structure of reflection, whereas the latter visualizes each individual thing as a participant in the structure of the whole by virtue of its own reflective nature, without giving a definite description of the Absolute itself. According to this vision, reflection activates not only the structure of consciousness, but also that of all Being.[68] In human consciousness, reflection is a self-conscious analytical thinking, producing shards of intuitive vision crafted as linguistic fragments, which in juxtaposition with other reflections, potentially produce insight into the whole. As Schlegel expresses it in a fragment, the human being is "nature creatively looking back at itself."[69]

Frank argues against a common misperception that early German Romanticism has to do solely with the self's infinite relation to itself. Unlike the German Idealists, Frank argues, the early German Romantics did not believe that consciousness is a self-sufficient phenomenon capable of making its own nature and the presuppositions that it brings to bear on the world comprehensible to itself.[70] Novalis and Schlegel are ontological realists who believe that reflection requires both nature and a reflecting consciousness. The foundation of the self for the early German Romantics, on Frank's reading, is a puzzle, which cannot be deciphered by reflection alone. The Absolute itself is transcendent to reflection; therefore, philosophy requires art to complete it.[71] Because of the essential finitude of human knowledge, the process of striving for the Absolute will never end, and there will always be a part of human consciousness that is not conceptualizable. Benjamin argues that art, too, is a product of reflection, understood in the broader metaphysical sense.

Although reflection formally and dynamically structures Being, it requires criticism to give it content. If reflection breaks things down in the sense of ana-lysis or loosening up, criticism can be thought of as a kind of filling-in. Benjamin calls this content-building a kind of "elevation to consciousness." Kant's affirmation of the possibility of thinking an intellectual intuition, combined with his conviction that this could never actually happen in empirical life, led to the fervent romantic search for this possibility. Reflection is an infinite process, in which each subsequent reflection can reflect on the one that preceded it. Through this free action, "the form is taken up as content into a new form, the form of knowing."[72] The infinitely many stages of reflection build upon each other as each subsequent one takes the former as its content. Nature can be uncovered in interconnecting bits and pieces but never entirely. As this gradual building up of reflection on reflection proceeds, contemporaneously something disintegrates, namely, the "I" that reflects. Benjamin's claim is that in its place, the early German Romantics reinterpret the nucleus of reflection as aesthetic form or the idea of art.[73]

Thus, this activity is not simply a filling out or substantiation, but with each reflection, "a disintegration in this original form takes place."[74] From the point of view of "circumscribed thinking," reflection progressively turns into "formless thinking, which directs itself upon the absolute."[75] However, from the point of view of what Schiller would call formative thinking, and using

Schillerian language, Benjamin also writes that "reflection does not take its course into an empty infinity, but is in itself substantial and filled."[76] The content of this filled infinite, as Schlegel expresses it, is a "'thou'—not as in life, as something opposing yet similar to the 'I'...but in an '*ur*-I'" of infinitely filled reflection.[77] Benjamin seems to be primarily interested in the relationship between the sensuous and the ideal. Reflection that is "unfilled" would be abstract, a kind of empty fantasy. Filled reflection engages the world but in service of the ideal.

The written idea is produced in fragments, but must be taken up by readers and made their "own," not in a radically individualistic but rather in an intersubjective sense. Criticism is the activity by which "food" is made "body." Novalis describes this process as "romanticizing" or "qualitative potentiation" where the empirical "I" progressively becomes identified with a higher "I," although it never reaches this point completely. The important distinction between the philosophy of Schlegel and Novalis, on the one hand, and that of Kant and Fichte, on the other, lies in the claim that the midpoint between ordinary reflection and the Absolute lies in art, not in the interiority of the human subject.[78] Through criticism, art becomes embodied reflection that unites Being and thinking beyond the individual "I..

In *The Origin of German Tragic Drama,* Benjamin pursues a topic that he considered to have resonances with the romantic depiction of the infinite cosmic rhythm of reflection and disintegration.[79] Benjamin's examination of Baroque drama begins with an Epistemo-Critical Prologue that performs the structure of reflection and criticism that he discusses in his dissertation on the German Romantics. He begins by discussing the formal structure of philosophical texts, contrasting attempts at constructing a philosophical system with the medieval doctrine or esoteric essay. The nineteenth century, he writes, was overly determined by the concept of system as a "syncretism which weaves a spider's web between separate kinds of knowledge in an attempt to ensnare the truth as if it were something which came flying in from outside."[80] Philosophy's object should not so much be the acquisition of knowledge as the representation of truth, in Benjamin's view, so that if it is to remain "true to the law of its own form" then attention to the exercise of this form is crucial.[81] This articulation follows the formal structure of romantic reflection, which progresses by branching out, yet which never loses sight of its own finitude. He describes it in the following way: "...by pursuing different levels of meaning in its examination of one single object it receives both the incentive to begin again and the justification for its irregular rhythm."[82] The irregular rhythm of reflection responds to the fact that, as

Schlegel writes, philosophy always begins *in medias res*. Reflecting this conviction, Benjamin writes that *Ursprung*, or origin, does not describe the process by which a given existent comes into being, but rather, "that which emerges from the process of becoming and disappearance."[83]

Benjamin compares a true philosophical doctrine or treatise to mosaics, which "preserve their majesty despite their fragmentation into capricious particles."[84] Unlike, say, a model that is fit together with multiple pieces in a specific series of steps, none of which is dispensable to the whole, a mosaic's pieces hold together only loosely, and point to a whole rather than determinately constituting it. Here we can see again an emphasis on the fragment; Benjamin writes that "the value of fragments of thought is all the greater the less direct their relationship to the underlying idea."[85] Another important aspect of a mosaic is that the fragments that constitute it may be rescued from their place in existing configurations, and redeemed by being reorganized into different patterns. Perhaps to emphasize their transcendent nature, Benjamin comes to call these ideas constellations. He writes that ideas are to objects as constellations are to stars. This means that they are neither the concept of stars nor their laws, nor do they contribute to knowledge of them in any way.[86] Ideas are timeless and by virtue of belonging to them, phenomena are subdivided and redeemed.[87] Like the Kantian reflective judgment, their unity is indeterminate and yet cohesive in a singular, rather than universally repeatable manner, in the way that, say, Orion relates to the stars that make it up.

Benjamin indeed uses Kantian language to describe the relationship between "concepts" and "ideas." While concepts organize our human knowledge of the empirical world, ideas express truth. Through their mediating role, concepts allow empirical phenomena to participate in the existence of ideas, yet phenomena are not for that reason incorporated into ideas.[88] The "great philosophies of the world," such as Plato's theory of ideas or Hegel's dialectic, remain valid as attempts to describe the world, even though the conceptual frameworks through which this attempt was instantiated have been outstripped.[89] The philosopher lies between the artist and the scientist; she shares with the scientist a desire to get beyond the empirical, and with the artist, an interest in the task of representation.[90] This middle path resembles the path that both Novalis and Schlegel developed to blend philosophy, poetry, and science.

## 4    Rancière on Play and the Fragment

Lying between Kant, Novalis, and Schlegel, Friedrich Schiller's work has only recently received the attention that it is due. Schiller's work also forms part of what would become the early German Romantic move to blend aesthetics into the very fabric of philosophy. In *Letters on Aesthetic Education* Schiller argues that the education of the human will only be fully realized if it includes not only attention to reason and morality, but also to beauty. Schiller's theories have been taken up by Jacques Rancière as part of a project that could be described as an inquiry into the ways in which sense perception can be shaped to political ends, In the *Letters*, Schiller expounds on the romantic feeling of life in all senses. For Schiller, there are two contrary forces within the human being and within nature, one of which he calls the sensuous impulse, which proceeds from physical existence, works on existence, and occupies the realm of what is changeable or in time. This impulse unfolds successively, and, when it is present, limits form. The contrary formative impulse, by contrast, strives to set what is limited at liberty but at the same time to maintain what most essentially is, most notably the human self, throughout every change. These forces are at odds, according to Schiller, but one is not to dominate over the other, and so a third force is required to bring them into dynamic equilibrium. Both impulses and "energies" require restriction. According to Schiller, "Humans can never learn really to conform to the idea of humanity and to be in the full sense of the word a human, so long as they satisfy only one of these two impulses exclusively or only alternately."[91] The highest human moments are situations in which one feels both of these impulses simultaneously, affording a "complete intuition" of humanity, and awakening a new impulse, the play impulse, which aims at the "extinction of time within time."[92] Arguably the play impulse, which expands upon Kant's reflective judgment, inspired the romantic discussion of oscillation. The object of the play impulse is a living, beautiful shape.[93] Schiller writes that, "[t]he human plays only when they are in the full sense of the word human, and they are only wholly human when they are playing,"[94] simultaneously at rest (melting) and in extreme movement.[95] Beauty transports us into the intermediate condition between matter and form.[96] The condition of the human spirit before any determination is an unlimited capacity for being determined (through the impressions of the senses),[97] what Schiller calls an *empty infinity.*

For Schiller, and subsequently for Novalis and Schlegel, the *feeling* of the play impulse just is a pure feeling of *life,* which includes the participation of the sensuous impulse, not just the mind. The feeling passes from sensation to thought through a middle disposition in which sensuousness and reason are active simultaneously. This middle disposition, in which our nature is constrained neither physically nor morally, yet is active in both ways, is called the *aesthetic*.[98]

Humans receive determination by means of sensation, but also aesthetically. Schiller writes that there are two different kinds of indeterminacy, one that is "mere indeterminacy," the condition of an empty mind, and the latter aesthetic indeterminacy. While mere indeterminacy is unlimited because it has no reality at all, aesthetic indeterminacy has no limits because it "combines all reality."[99] When the mind perceives, it limits itself in determination, but when it is aesthetically engaged, it reflects.[100] What Schiller means by "reflection" is that an "infinite inner abundance" fills the mind without resting in any determined form, very similar to the Kantian reflective judgment. While mere indeterminacy is an empty infinity, aesthetic freedom is a "filled infinity."[101] The task of the human is to "annihilate" the determinations of their condition while at the same time preserving them[102] by replacing them with aesthetic determinations.

In the aesthetic condition, humans, in Schiller's words, are rendered "ciphers," that is, both of and foreign to nature. The aesthetic disposition of the mind is a cipher, but also a condition of the highest reality, according to Schiller. It brings forth an infinite state characterized by the absence of all limits and the sum total of all powers. The infinity de-individualizes humans, but thereby renders it possible for them *"on the part of Nature"* to make of themselves what they choose and what they ought to be. Beauty is thereby a "second creator."[103]

Rancière is interested in German Romanticism, both in the Romanticism of Schiller and of Friedrich Schlegel, for what he calls its "de-figuration," its disruption of the coherence of plot and of the old distinction of art from what it mimics, that is, reality. Romantic fragmentation exemplifies the apotheosis of the aesthetic regime, whose logic rejects the representative model of construction in favor of "an originary power of art initially distributed between two extremes: a pure creative activity thenceforward thought to be without rules or models, and the pure passivity of the expressive power inscribed on the very surface of things, independently of every desire to signify or create."[104] The multiplication of levels of meaning found in the infinite reflective nature of poetic activity and in the genre of the philosophical fragment is echoed, in Rancière's mind, in the logic of filmmaking.

In *The Politics of Aesthetics*, Rancière traces his understanding of aesthetics to Kant, as historicized by Foucault: what he means by the distribution of the sensible is "the system of *a priori* forms determining what presents itself to sense experience."[105] In other words, the distribution of the sensible is a form of historical *a priori* that shifts according to political and economic change. He describes particular historical forms of sensibility as aesthetic communities.

An aesthetic community or *sensus communis* has a threefold significance: (1) it indicates a certain combination of sense data, one that renders the sensible intelligible and unintelligible in very specific ways; (2) it indicates the possibility of *differing* communities of sense; and (3) it indicates the possibility of a conflict arising between two or more regimes of sense, two sensory worlds, a possibility that he names *dissensus*. The philosopher can provide a conceptual framework to the tensions between two sensory worlds. Rancière argues that whereas art prior to the literary writing of the German Romantics promoted a concordance or correspondence between the two meanings of "sense" as the complex of sensory signs or materiality through which poetry emerges, and "sense" as the complex of understanding and thinking through which the artwork is felt and understood, in the literary writing of early German Romanticism the two were often prised apart in order for a new understanding of the world to appear.

In the old idea of *sensus communis*, still present in Kant, there exists a continuity between the community addressed by the artwork and the universality of human nature. In his revised understanding of *sensus communis*, inspired by Schiller, Rancière juxtaposes this old, continuous idea of *sensus communis* to aesthetic efficiency, which effects a break in the sensory logic, "a break in a relation between sense and sense—between what is seen and what is thought, or what is thought and what is felt." At the same time, he still traces aesthetic efficiency to Kant's account in the third *Critique*. Produced by the very break of any determined link between cause and effect, the free play evoked by the beautiful is the product of a "disconnected community" between two sensoria: the sensorium of the work's fabrication and the sensorium of its enjoyment. Its ontology is one of *dissensus*, a fictional ontology, a play of "aesthetic ideas" that potentially has the capacity to disrupt our ordinary way of seeing things, an effect that is eminently political, in Rancière's view, because it may give voice to the voiceless and make invisible structures perpetuating injustice visible or provide access to a more liberating understanding of being. Such disruptions are indeterminate in Kant's sense, because they may happen at any time or place, and cannot be calculated in advance.

Rancière traces the romantic definition of the human as a creator who transforms nature, articulating it as part of the "aesthetic regime," where, historically, starting with Kant, the emphasis in the analysis of art shifts from ways of doing (mimesis of nature) to "ways of sensible being" or the self-presentation of the beauty of nature or of art.[106] Rancière refers to Hegel, who argued that the origin of art "resides in the act of the child who skims stones, transforming the surface of the water, that of 'natural' appearances, into a surface for the manifestation of his lone will."[107] This definition of artistic activity appears to make it solely a human phenomenon, but he adds that "this child, who skims stones, is also a child whose artistic ability is born of the pure contingency of proximate noises, of the mixed noises of artless nature and material life."[108] This mixing of nature and art marks the aesthetic regime, which blurs the distinction between those things that belong to art, and those that belong to nature or ordinary life.[109] Rancière is interested in the aesthetic regime for its linkage of two things: the articulation of a specific genre of human experience henceforth designated as "aesthetic," and the promise, correlative with it, of a new, social humanity to come.[110]

For Rancière, the designation of this stage is the true sense of "modernity."[111] He contrasts the aesthetic regime of historicity to that of the mimetic regime. Within the mimetic regime, art is evaluated by the degree to which the sensible work adequately corresponds to the Idea or object that it presents. Prior to the mimetic regime, as art gradually freed itself from its subservience to religion, it began to be evaluated according to how adequately it depicted the object of its representation.[112] In the aesthetic regime, by contrast, a specific realm is opened up, that of the artwork, which gains its identity neither by conforming to an idea nor by representing its subject well. The artwork now has a specific ontological status, separated from non-art. The temporality specific to the aesthetic regime of the arts is a "co-presence" of the "heterogeneous temporalities" of the sensuous, which is always in time, and the aesthetic, in which the annulment of time takes place within time, following Schiller. This annulment of time enacts "power of a form of thought that has become foreign to itself" in contrast to the time of nature.[113] In this regime, again following Schiller, a double movement and double speech is enacted, transmitting the suffering, protest, and struggle of humans, but at the same time expressing the "song of the earth," forces of chaos that resist the human will of transformation. Somewhere between these two lies "the hope of a people which is still missing."[114]

What Rancière reimagines, beginning with Kant's account of the free play of the understanding and imagination in the judgment of taste and continuing with Schiller's discussion of the play impulse, is a decisive break between two sensoria: that of the artwork (pleasure) and that of the world. Although it might seem that this break, signified in Kant through the word "disinterest," cuts art off from any social and political significance, Ranciere argues that the

## 27 Sensibility, Reflection, and Play: Early German Romanticism...

contrary is true. Art's distance from the world, its very bracketing of any use or even attachment to the real existence of the work, prohibits it from being absorbed in the world even while it remains firmly situated there. What this means is that, amid a given distribution of the sensible that renders certain things visible or audible, and others invisible or inaudible, the artwork refuses to participate. Because of its distance, an artwork may intervene in the world with an as yet unheard voice, one of a people yet to come. This is the very vision of art developed by the early German Romantics, even if the radical politics of democracy Rancière envisions does not coincide with that of Novalis or Schlegel.

He describes the art of romantic poetics as an abandonment of the poetics of action, character, and knowledge exemplified by Aristotle's *Poetics,* in favor of a "poetics of signs." This poetics of signs has a threefold "variable signifying power." First, in the fragment, a single sign, even in isolation can present the whole, just as a single organism can present the whole of nature in a Kantian sense. Second, signs from different regimes, be it those of nature, social life, or art, are put in correspondence through resonant or dissonant relationships. Third, he singles out the "power of reflection" also foregrounded by Benjamin, that multiplies the levels of meaning of the poem.[115]

Such a poetics has political implications in several senses, according to Rancière. First, by breaking down the barriers between art and the spectator's life, art embodies a "promise of community," of a specific common space. Aesthetic education aims at the transformation of the task of humans away from domination of nature through the understanding toward the appreciation of freedom as reflected in human transformation of nature. He refers to the "Oldest System program of German Idealism," written by either Hegel, Hölderlin, or Schelling in their youth, which outlines a program to "render ideas sensible, to turn them into a replacement for ancient mythology; in other words, into a living tissue of experiences and common beliefs in which both the elite and the people share."[116] He argues that this program defined not only an aesthetic, but also a political revolution, transposed by Marx into a new identification of the aesthetic human as the producer.[117]

Second, specific to the aesthetic regime is the refusal of use or social role, what Rancière calls "the politics of resistant form."[118] In such a politics, art carries promise because it does not have a social function; here we can hear echoes of Adorno's aesthetic theory, and indeed this theory has a connection, through the influence of Benjamin, to the early German Romantics.

## 5 Conclusion

For both Benjamin and Rancière, what makes early German Romanticism so fruitful a resource for the politics of art lies in the "playful" relation between sensibility and conceptualizability. What Benjamin calls the historical transformation in the mode of perception,[119] the ways in which human perception is conditioned by both nature but also by social and political events, is echoed in Rancière's articulation of the historically shifting distribution of the sensible. While Marx is a natural place of commonality between the two thinkers, Rancière's account of the genealogy of the concept of aesthetic revolution—initiated by the German Romantics and Idealists inspired by Kant's third *Critique,* and developed through Marx and the Frankfurt school—shows that the beginning goes back further in history. Indeed, Benjamin traces the meaning of his mysterious term "aura" to Novalis' articulation of a reflexive perception in which nature, gazed on by the human, looks back with a prehistoric eye. The dialectical interplay between nature and human, sensible and supersensible, sense 1 and sense 2, initiated in the fragment but ultimately carried to fruition only in the minds and projects of future individuals and communities who nurture the seed and in turn pass it on to others, can be seen in a passage from the *Athenäum* that Rancière cites:

> A project is the subjective embryo of a developing object. A perfect project should be at once completely subjective and completely objective, should be an indivisible and living individual. In its origin: completely subjective and original, only possible in precisely this sense; in its character: completely objective, physically and morally necessary. The feeling for projects—which one might call fragments of the future—is distinguishable from the feeling for fragments of the past only by its direction, progressive in the former, regressive in the latter. What is essential is to be able to idealize and realize objects immediately and simultaneously to complete them and in part carry them out within oneself. Since transcendental is precisely whatever relates to the joining and separating of the ideal and the real, one might very well say that the feeling for fragments and projects is the transcendental element of the historical spirit.[120]

In this passage, which is a fragment, the unnamed author draws together the most important themes of early German Romanticism, not only in its own time, but as it informs contemporary continental philosophy: overcoming an absolute distinction between subjective and objective, attention to affect and beauty, and eschewing totalizing approaches to knowledge, morality, and aesthetics. The "feeling for fragments and projects," which is perhaps the most distinctive difference of the early German Romantics from Kant, whom they nonetheless follow in spirit, comes forward in the romantic emphasis on sensibility, reflection, and play.

## Notes

1. Charles Shepherdson, "Aesthetic "Sense" in Kant and Nancy," *New Literary History* 48:2, (Spring 2017):197–221.
2. Novalis, *Notes for a Romantic Encyclopedia: Das Allgemeine Brouillon,* trans. David Wood (Albany: State University of New York Press, 2007), #942, 167.
3. Novalis, *Philosophical Writings*, trans. and ed. Margaret Mahoney Stoljar (Albany: State University of New York Press, 1997), #25, 54.
4. Walter Benjamin, "The Concept of Criticism in German Romanticism," *Selected Writings* Volume 1, 116–200. (Cambridge: Harvard University Press, 1996), 129.
5. Benjamin, "The Concept of Criticism in Early German Philosophy," 121.
6. Walter Benjamin, "The Work of Art in the Age of its Technological Reproducibility," Second Version. *Selected Writings* Volume 3 (Cambridge, MA: Harvard University Press, 2002), 101–133.
7. Rodolphe Gasché, "Ideality in Fragmentation," Foreword to Friedrich Schlegel, *Philosophical Fragments,* trans. Peter Firchow (Minneapolis: University of Minnesota Press, 1991), vii-xxxii.
8. Immanuel Kant, *Critique of Judgment,* trans. Werner Pluhar (Indianapolis: Hackett Publishing, 1987), 314. All page numbers refer to the German *Akademie* edition, as given in the margins of this text.
9. This is the way in which Novalis described his own fragments.
10. Kant, *Critique of Judgment,* Deduction of Aesthetic Judgments, 141–209.
11. Shepherdson, "Aesthetic "Sense" in Kant and Nancy," 1.
12. Kant, *Critique of Judgment,* 315.
13. Ibid, 316.
14. Ibid, 314.
15. Ibid, 317.
16. Ibid, 316.
17. See Jaques Rancière, *The Politics of Aesthetics: The Distribution of the Sensible,* trans. Gabriel Rockhill (London and New York: Continuum, 2004), and Walter Benjamin, "The Work of Art in the Age of its Technological Reproducibility."
18. Kant, *Critique of Judgment,* 340.
19. Ibid, 342.
20. Ibid, 343, my emphasis.
21. Gasché, "Ideality in Fragmentation," xii.

22. Kant, *Critique of Judgment*, 344.
23. Ibid, 351.
24. Ibid, 353.
25. Ibid, 352.
26. Ibid, 353.
27. Ibid.
28. Ibid, 204.
29. Kneller, *Kant and the Power of Imagination* (Cambridge: Cambridge University Press, 2009), 55–57.
30. Kant, *Critique of Judgment*, 354.
31. Novalis, *Philosophical Writings*, 122.
32. Ibid, 122.
33. Ibid, 157.
34. Ibid, 165.
35. Walter Benjamin, "The Concept of Criticism in German Romanticism," 126. To be considered in greater detail in the following section.
36. Novalis, *Henry von Ofterdingen*, trans. Palmer Hilty (Prospect Heights, IL: Waveland Press, 1964) and Friedrich Schlegel, "On Incomprehensibility," in *Lucinde and the Fragments*, trans. Peter Firchow (Minneapolis: University of Minneapolis Press, 1971), 259–271.
37. Dalia Nassar, *The Romantic Absolute: Being and Knowing in Early German Romantic Philosophy, 1795–1804* (Chicago: The University of Chicago Press, 2014), 131–32.
38. Friedrich Schlegel, *Lucinde*, in *Lucinde and the Fragments*, trans. Peter Firchow (Minneapolis: University of Minneapolis Press, 1971), 118.
39. Ibid, 86.
40. Novalis, *Philosophical Writings*, 49.
41. Ibid, 50.
42. Nuzzo, "The Productive Imagination in Hegel and Classical German Philosophy," 68.
43. See Angelica Nuzzo, "The Productive Imagination in Hegel and Classical German Philosophy," in *Productive Imagination: Its History, Meaning, and Significance,* ed. Saulius Geniusas and Dmitri Nikulin (London: Rowman and Littlefield, 2018), 66.
44. Kneller argues that this is the meaning of "romanticizing" as "setting right," in Kneller 2017, 131.
45. Immanuel Kant, "What is Orientation in Thinking?" in *Kant's Political Writings*, trans. H.B. Nisbet (Cambridge: Cambridge University Press, 1970).
46. Jennifer Ann Bates, *Hegel's Theory of Imagination* (Albany: State University of New York Press, 2004), 5.
47. Novalis, *Fichte Studies,* trans. Jane Kneller (Cambridge: Cambridge University Press, 2003), Nr. 555, 164.
48. Ibid, 164.

49. Novalis, *Fichte Studies*, Nr. 3, 6.
50. As Jane Kneller also argues, in *Kant and the Power of Imagination*, 123.
51. Friedrich Schlegel, *Lucinde*, 120.
52. Ibid.
53. Although Schlegel's descriptions of physical and spiritual love at times seem reductively heteronormative, as Tobin shows, the characters in *Lucinde* take on roles that transcend the bounds of their gender. See "The Emancipation of the Flesh: The Legacy of Romanticism in the Homosexual Rights Movement," *Romanticism on the Net*, July 27, 2005.
54. Friedrich Schlegel, *Lucinde*, 120.
55. Novalis, *Logological Fragments 1*, in *Philosophical Writings*, 50.
56. Ibid.
57. Ibid, 50–51.
58. Kant, *Critique of Judgment*, 314.
59. Friedrich Schlegel, *Critical Fragment* Nr. 21 in KFSA 2, 149/*Philosophical Fragments*, 2.
60. Friedrich Schlegel, *Athenaeum Fragment* Nr. 116 in KFSA 2, 182–83/*Philosophical Fragments*, 31–32.
61. Friedrich Schlegel, *Athenaeum Fragment* Nr. 336 in KFSA 223–25/ *Philosophical Fragments*, 66–69.
62. See Elaine P. Miller, *The Vegetative Soul: From Philosophy of Nature to Philosophy in the Feminine* (Albany: State University of New York Press, 2002).
63. Friedrich Schlegel, *Athenaeum Fragment* Nr. 336 in KFSA 223–25/ *Philosophical Fragments*, 66–69.
64. Lacoue-Labarthe and Jean-Luc Nancy, *The Literary Absolute: The Theory of Literature in German Romanticism*, trans. Phillip Barnard and Cheryl Lester (Albany: State University of New York Press, 1988), 12.
65. Benjamin, "The Concept of Criticism in German Romanticism", 117.
66. Ibid, 178.
67. Ibid, 128.
68. As Walter Benjamin puts it, "For Fichte, consciousness is 'I [*Ich*], for the romantics, it is 'itself' [*Selbst*]." "The Concept of Criticism in German Romanticism," 128.
69. Schlegel, *Ideas Fragment* Nr. 28, in KFSA 2, 258/ *Philosophical Fragments*, 96.
70. Manfred Frank, *The Philosophical Foundation of Early German Romanticism*, trans. Elizabeth Millan-Zaibert (Albany: State University of New York Press, 2004), 178.
71. Ibid, 178.
72. Benjamin, "The Concept of Criticism in German Romanticism," 121.
73. Ibid, 135.
74. Ibid, 129.
75. Ibid.
76. Ibid.

77. Friedrich Schlegel, *Vorlesungen,* as cited in Benjamin, "The Concept of Criticism in German Romanticism," 131.
78. Benjamin, "The Concept of Criticism in German Romanticism," 134.
79. As he states in a letter to Gershom Scholem from March 5, 1924. In *The Correspondence of Walter Benjamin 1910–1940* (Chicago: University of Chicago Press, 1994), 238.
80. Benjamin, *The Origin of German Tragic Drama,* trans. John Osborne (New York: Verso, 1998), 28.
81. Ibid, 28.
82. Ibid, 28.
83. Ibid, 43.
84. Ibid, 28.
85. Ibid, 29.
86. Ibid, 34.
87. Ibid.
88. Ibid.
89. Ibid, 32.
90. Ibid.
91. Friedrich Schiller, *Letters on the Aesthetic Education of Man,* trans. Reginald Snell (New Haven: Angelico Press, 2014), 58.
92. Ibid, 59.
93. Ibid, 60.
94. Ibid, 63.
95. Ibid, 64.
96. Ibid, 69.
97. Ibid, 72.
98. Ibid, 78.
99. Ibid.
100. Ibid, 79.
101. Ibid.
102. Ibid, 77.
103. Ibid, 80.
104. Jacques Rancière, *Film Fables,* trans. Emiliana Battista (New York: Berg Press, 2001), 8.
105. Jacques Rancière, *The Politics of Aesthetics,* trans. Gabriel Rockhill (London and New York: Bloomsbury Revelations, 2004).
106. Jacques Rancière, *Aesthetics and Its Discontents*, trans. Steven Corcoran (Cambridge: Polity Press, 2009), 11.
107. Ibid, 12.
108. Ibid.
109. Ibid, 5.
110. Ibid, 14.
111. Ibid, 24.

112. Ibid, 29.
113. Ibid, 23.
114. Jacques Rancière, *Aesthetic Separation, Aesthetic Community: Scenes from the Aesthetic Regime of Art*, http://www.artandresearch.org.uk/v2n1/ranciere.html#_ftnref1.
115. Jacques Rancière, *Flim Fables*, 160.
116. Rancière, *Aesthetics and its Discontents*, 37.
117. Ibid, 38.
118. Ibid, 39.
119. "Benjamin, The Work of Art in the Age of its Technological Reproducibility, 23.
120. Cited in Rancière, *Mute Speech: Literature, Critical Theory, and Politics* (New York: Columbia University Press, trans. James Swenson, 2014), 77.

# 28

## 'The Concept of Critique': Between Early German Romanticism and Early Critical Theory

### Nathan Ross

Among the philosophical schools of the twentieth century, there is arguably none that shows a greater affinity to the methods and insights of the early German Romantics than early Frankfurt School of critical theory. This is because one of the founding members of critical theory, Walter Benjamin, started his philosophical career as a scholar of early German Romanticism, before going on to influence the development of critical theory. His work on German Romanticism is worth considering in its own right both as a scholarly interpretation of early German Romanticism and as a work that imparts vital themes to his own philosophy, as well as to subsequent critical theorists.

There are many core themes that connect these two schools of thought: the emphasis on art and particularly literature as modes of disclosing truth; a critique of the Enlightenment as offering an incomplete realization of its program of human liberation; a notion of critique not as the mere weighing and rejecting of various ideas, but also as the unfolding of the inner truth of an object ('immanent critique');[1] a progressive politics that focuses on education and critique as ways of developing human consciousness; a method of writing and thinking that makes use of fragments and essays rather than systematic writings in order to express the complex ways in which philosophical arguments condition and enrich each other.

---

N. Ross (✉)
Adelphi University, Garden City, NY, USA
e-mail: nross@adelphi.edu

In what follows, I will focus especially on the meaning of the notion of critique in early critical theory, and its origin in early German Romanticism. What does it mean to be critical? What lessons does early German Romanticism have for early critical theory? How do the early German Romantics and the critical theorists understand art criticism? And what deeper philosophical implications about the nature of knowledge and political critique can we glean from this philosophy of art criticism? These themes make up the center of Benjamin's treatment of early German Romanticism, but they also stand at the very center of Benjamin's own philosophical project, and of the common interests that tie Benjamin to critical theory in general. The chapter thus begins with a reading of Benjamin's dissertation, then traces this influence into Benjamin's subsequent works, and concludes with a brief consideration of how Adorno's philosophy of art owes essential insights to this relationship.[2]

# 1 Benjamin's Problem-Historical Approach

Although Benjamin's dissertation, *On the Concept of Art Criticism in German Romanticism*, reads as a work of secondary literature, it also serves to define many of the central features of his own later, groundbreaking work as a critic.[3] The early German Romantics redefine criticism in such a way that it is not so much something that we do to art, the judgment of the work according to the pleasure of the subject, but rather something that art does to itself with our participation, the "self-judgment of the work". This distinction represents a crucial discovery for Benjamin because it marks criticism as a form of knowledge that redeems its subject from a merely instrumental mode of assimilating objects to its own demands. This move to distinguish a romantic version of critique from an enlightenment notion gives us a key clue as to how the critical theorists think about critique: to use a phrase from Adorno, critique saves things from the "curse of being useful". But at the same time, it also helps us to think about the romantic emphasis on art and poetry in a way that points beyond the traditional categories of aesthetics (enjoyment, beauty), and toward categories of first philosophy (subject-object relation, truth content), thus leading toward a more inherently philosophical reading of the early German Romantics.

Benjamin specifies that his study represents not so much a contribution to the history of philosophy as to the "history of problems": it is concerned more with revealing the romantic contributions to defining *criticism* as a mode of knowledge, than with defining German Romanticism as a moment in the development of the history of philosophy.[4] Benjamin turning to the philosophies of Friedrich Schlegel, Novalis, and Friedrich Hölderlin[5] develops an *ontology of art* and an *epistemology of art criticism* that would continue to guide his own practice as a critic of art, culture, and literature. Some readers of this text have questioned whether Benjamin had access to texts that provided a rich enough understanding of early German Romanticism. I believe it is most fruitful to consider his study not merely as a somewhat outdated attempt at historical scholarship, nor merely in terms of Benjamin's own pre-existing "affinity" for the early German Romantics, but rather in terms of what he learns from his encounter with the romantics for the development of his own critical practice.[6] In particular, Benjamin's reading emphasizes the romantic rejection of the "economic" model of criticism—the critic as an arbiter of taste for various goods in the marketplace—in order to show how criticism offers an immanent knowledge of art as a medium of reflection. The main purpose of criticism, in the romantics as well as Benjamin, is to use a process of immanent reflection to redeem cultural products from their status as commodities. The German Romantics of Benjamin's study anticipate the "retreat of the beautiful"[7] as a fateful phenomenon of modern art, developing a critical practice focused not on the selection of objects of enjoyment, but rather the cultivation of subjectivity through reflection on the work. Benjamin's most important contribution to the scholarship of early German Romanticism is beyond doubt his discovery of *the principle of sobriety* as the ideal disposition and the cognitive ideal of their philosophy of art. While this discovery is based on a cogent reading of this theme in the works of Schlegel and Hölderlin, which distinguishes them from the theory of genius in Kant, as well as from the older theory of poetic inspiration in Plato, it ends up articulating a critical posture toward art that would infuse Benjamin's later works. Sobriety, we will see, represents the great discovery of the romantic theory of art, because it is not merely a mood, or an absence of intoxication, but a revolutionary way of integrating theory and experience.

## 2    Romantic Object Knowledge

Benjamin formulates what is distinctive in Schlegel's method of critique as follows:

> With this the basic principle of Romantic object-knowledge is given: that everything that is in the absolute, everything real, thinks... The germ cell of all knowledge is thus a process of reflection in a thinking being through which it

gains knowledge of itself… Where there is no self-knowledge, there is no knowledge.⁸

In the romantic theory of knowledge, an object is only known insofar as it is understood as knowing itself, possessing its own awareness. Such knowledge considers nature not as an object, but as a subject, as a set of relations that embody subjective understanding in their own relationality. (This theory of knowledge must have a great affinity for the young Benjamin as it bears a strong relation to his own conception of nature as a series of mimetic relations, or as a creation that contains its own linguistic content.) To engage in an experiment on nature is to bring nature into a context where its own self-understanding communicates itself to the awareness of the observer. This knowledge takes place in what Benjamin terms a "medium of reflection", because rather than an active-passive relationship between subject (knower) and object (known), there is a medial relationship, in which the awareness of the observer becomes involved in the awareness of nature.

As mystical as this notion of natural cognition might seem, it forms the basis for an ontology that breaks down the subject-object dichotomy and explains how knowledge can be true both to its content matter and to an infinite state of becoming. Benjamin seems most concerned with showing how this ontology allows the early German Romantics to gain a particularly fruitful understanding of how we cognize art: "Art is a determination of the medium of reflection—probably the most fruitful one that it has received. Criticism of art is knowledge of the object in this medium of reflection".⁹ Even if we question the view that all natural objects, and nature as a system of relations, have their own self-awareness, it should be more clear that every product of culture is both an object (something given to awareness with fixed properties) and a subject (a creation of human thought and awareness, in which thought and awareness play a constitutive role). Thus, the early German Romantics consider the act of criticism as a way of activating the reflection proper to the work of art, bringing out not the way that the artist understands the work, but the way that the work reflects or embodies awareness in its objective structure. They consider criticism not so much as an act of judgment, in which the subject classifies the work and submits it to the standards of taste, but more as an experiment upon the work. "Criticism is, as it were, an experiment on the artwork, one through which the latter's own reflection is awakened".¹⁰ To write critically is to write in a way that enters into the work, that communicates an experience of the structure and thought content of the work.

Benjamin notes that the real radicality of this notion of criticism consists in the way that it suspends the moment of judgment: judgment is the power of the subject to apply values or standards to the work, such as the notions of beauty, taste, or perfection.[11] In viewing art as a medium of reflection, the early German Romantics no longer relate the work to a general standard of judgment, but see it as advancing its own self-concept, which the critic serves to elucidate. "Insofar as it judges the artwork, this occurs in the latter's self-judgment… In it, a necessary moment in all judgment, the negative, is completely curtailed".[12] Benjamin summarizes the crucial social result in this notion of criticism as "the complete positivity of criticism, in which the romantic concept of criticism is radically distinguished from the modern concept, which sees criticism as a court of judgment".[13] This distinction between the romantic model of criticism and the modern concept enables the early German Romantics to see the function of aesthetic culture in the most expansive terms, not merely as a matter of pleasure or the refinement of one's taste, but as serving to educate and develop subjectivity. Benjamin describes a crucial epochal shift in the basic goal of aesthetic theory:

> The concept of beauty has to retreat from the romantic conception of art altogether, not only because, in the rationalist conception, this concept is implicated with that of rules, but above all because as an object of delight, of pleasure, of taste, beauty seemed incompatible with the austere sobriety that, according to the new conception, defines the essence of art.[14]

While there is a romantic side even to Kant's aesthetic theory, in that he balances the analytic of the beautiful with that of the sublime, as two very different modes of aesthetic appreciation, Schlegel's romantic theory transforms the very way that we understand the nature and function of aesthetic experience. The early German Romantics replace the goal of refined pleasure, the cultivation of tasteful enjoyment by the task of immanent analysis, with the engagement of the work on its terms and education of one's own self-awareness through engagement with the work. Indeed, it should be clear that this "retreat of the beautiful" has great importance for the later work of Benjamin, as well as for Adorno, and perhaps serves as the most adequate way to understand what they each see at stake in the rise of modern art forms.[15] In Benjamin's later *Artwork* essay, the romantic thesis on the retreat of the beautiful develops into his influential thesis on the decline of the "aura" of artworks that call for isolated contemplation in favor of those new disenchanted artistic forms that call forth a direct link between enjoyment and awareness of the work's method of production.[16] In Adorno's *Aesthetic Theory*, this thesis on the retreat of the beautiful leads to the demand to consider the function of art as a matter of truth content rather than the pleasure of the spectator.[17] In his lectures on aesthetics, Adorno gives a thorough critique of the view that art is there to please us, and he paints a caricature of the aesthete as someone who lingers on the surface of artworks out of fear of being injured by them.[18] This core principle of Adorno's thought has to be traced back to Benjamin's work on the romantic concept of critique, which Adorno held in especially high esteem among his friend's work.[19]

## 3    Romantic Art Criticism

Benjamin prepares the way for his own critical practice in the way that he distinguishes the romantic conception of art-criticism from a more prevalent, modern notion of criticism. With the rise of a cultural marketplace in the modern era, in which consumers can choose between a profusion of products too great to allow comprehensive experimental knowledge, the critic is called on to play an economic role by distinguishing the good from the bad and thus allowing us only to spend time and money on those that pass muster. The critic thus acts as arbiter between the consumer and the marketplace filled with products meant as means of enjoyment. This economic conception of the critic matches not only the way most consumers see the purpose of the film or literary critic, but aligns with the dominant trend of modern aesthetic theory, from Hume to Kant's *Critique of Judgment*. In these theories the purpose of art is to produce a particular kind of pleasure and the purpose of theory is to act as a tribunal for deciding what makes a work beautiful, what makes a spectator tasteful, what makes an artist's work worthy of aesthetic experience, and more broadly, what role theory can play in delimiting such a field of experience. Benjamin is drawn into the romantic theory of Schlegel and Novalis not only by rejection of the economic conception of the role of the critic, but also by the way that they use this rejection as a means of developing an alternative theory of critical experience. Benjamin sees in the early German Romantics a *redemption* of the notion of criticism and the task of the critic, so that criticism: (1) does not play the role of a theory of taste; (2) does not allow us to choose from a profusion of objects those which will please us; and (3) does not serve as a subjective guide to our own reaction to the works. The early German Romantics redeem criticism for Benjamin by seeing it as a mode of knowledge that allows us to enter into works of art, to activate the work's own subjectivity rather than making those works instruments of our own subjectivity. At the same time, by freeing criticism from its economic function, the early German Romantics make criticism into a force for gaining knowledge of the self and society, knowledge that is redemptive. The ideal of immanent critique informs Benjamin's enterprise, even in his later, overtly political phase, because its initial impulse is informed by a resistance to the commodification of cultural products in the theory of aesthetic judgment.

The notion of redemption plays a crucial role throughout Benjamin's work, from his early essay on language to his late "Theses on the Philosophy of History": the former is concerned with a redemption of language from its debasement to a utilitarian context, in which words merely serve to express human intentions, rather than to name the nature of things;[20] the latter work seeks to redeem history by giving voice to the hopes and suffering of those who are left behind by the historical movement of progress.[21] In both works, as different as they might be, a common notion of redemption emerges, unifying Benjamin's early language mysticism and his later work as a Marxist critic: to redeem something is to bring it out of its instrumental context, or to free it from its reified character as a means or a commodity. In this sense, many things call for redemption: nature, words, the labor process, historical events. Redemption is thus a form of knowledge that considers things not as commodities or as information, but as subjectivities, as moments of consciousness. While this act of redemption is most properly a subject of ethical philosophy, as a philosophy that concerns itself with the encounter between subjectivities in the practical sphere, it also provides a method for approaching and criticizing culture. Humans are cultural beings to the extent that they produce things that communicate their relation to the world, from words to works of art. These cultural products have an ambivalent status throughout Benjamin's philosophy, because they serve both as a medium of knowledge and as a medium of reification.[22] Criticism is the mode of knowledge proper to these cultural products, and in his work on the romantic notion of criticism, he seeks to distinguish that mode of criticism that does not reify works of art as products of human enjoyment, but that knows them as mediums of reflection.

It might seem that we lose a great deal that we expect from aesthetics if the romantics banish the negative moment in judgment: would it not lead to an aesthetic critique in which there is no distinction, no discernment, no scale of values, no way of rejecting inferior works? Does it not lead to a pernicious kind of aesthetic relativism, in which all products demand the same respect and attention? Benjamin demonstrates that the romantic response to this problem consists in their notion of the "uncriticizability of bad works". "If a work can be criticized, then it is a work of art: otherwise it is not".[23] To put it another way, their notion of the medium of reflection does not apply to all things equally, but is constituted by the objective structure of the work. It is not that all works are equally good and none are bad or inferior, but rather the act of judging the good and the bad in relation to the feeling of the spectator is replaced by an engagement that seeks out those works that deepen the self-awareness of the critic, while passing over, or ironically pushing to the margins, those works that are not reflective in their structure. Rather than a judgment according to a standard of taste or discernment in terms of the grade of pleasure, there is an activity of reflection that ranges from the ironic to the infinitely sober.

Indeed, the act of criticism is more about discovering the limits in a work than about a blind immersion in that work: every work embodies its own awareness within its structure, but in order to know this internal structure of awareness, the work has to be taken beyond itself, submitted to an act of criticism that dissolves it within what Benjamin calls the "medium of art".[24] It is obviously fictional to think of any "thing", whether a product of nature or of human artifice, as capable of reflection on its own qua thing. In the romantic conception of reflection that Benjamin explicates, reflection always takes place in a medium, in a relation of interaction between subject and object. Every "thing" in nature or art has a form that can only be known within a continuity of forms. By dissolving the work within this continuity of forms, we see it as part of a process that takes place between subject and object.

The romantic notion of criticism pays special attention to the notion of form, and yet it completely alters the meaning of the notion of form from its meaning in enlightenment theories from Baumgarten to Kant. Benjamin writes: "The Romantics, unlike the Enlightenment, did not conceive of form as a rule for judging the beauty of art… Every form as such counts as a peculiar modification of the medium of reflection … the critic will hit upon their connectedness as moments within the medium of reflection".[25] And: "Form is the objective expression of the reflection proper to the work, the reflection that constitutes its essence".[26] To consider a form as pleasing or not pleasing involves placing the objective form in relation to some teleology that is in the subject. Thus, despite his attention to aesthetic form, Kant's aesthetics subjectivizes the distinctively aesthetic element of art, because his interpretation of form makes it aesthetically meaningful insofar as it touches off a "free play of the cognitive faculties", and thus robs aesthetic experience of its status as a form of determinant knowledge.[27] By contrast, the early German Romantics understand form as meaningful in the way that it brings the subject into the process of art. Forms are to be ranked, qualified, valued, and placed in dynamic relation with each other to the degree that they allow the subject to discover patterns of reflection in them. For Benjamin, this means that the

German Romantics tended to prefer literature as epitome of art, because of how language can encapsulate and reflect on other experiences, and to prefer prose as the sublation of poetry, because of its sobriety and its ability to comment on and contain reflections in an unbounded way.[28] He writes:

> Art is the continuum of forms and the novel is the comprehensible manifestation of this continuum… The idea of poetry is prose. … Prose is the creative ground of poetic forms, all of which are mediated in it and dissolved as though in their canonical creative ground.[29]

## 4     Romantic Sobriety

One of Benjamin's greatest and most original contributions to the interpretation of early German Romanticism consists of his discovery of sobriety as the cognitive ideal and essential mood of the arts. Just as prose is the sublation of poetry in romantic criticism, sobriety is the frame of mind that penetrates and stands above the manic comportment often equated with poetic creativity. Benjamin cites a series of passages in Schlegel, Novalis, and even draws connection to crucial reflections of Hölderlin,[30] in which they celebrate the value of sobriety as the prosaic frame of mind that does the most to promote aesthetic creativity. As Benjamin notes, the early German Romantics hereby reverse a long tradition in philosophy, going back at least to Plato, of associating the poetic frame of mind with drunkenness, cognitive lack of clarity, and mania. Plato associates the poet with the manic just as he denies the mimetic artist the cognitive clarity to interpret the meaning of their most inspired creations. What is at stake in this debate over mania versus sobriety is not so much a moral condemnation of intoxication or a kind of instrumental prescription for how best to write poetry, but ultimately nothing less than the status of the art as a form of knowledge. Insofar as we associate the creation of the work with mania, and distinguish poetry from the prose that explains it, criticism as a form of knowledge is always external to the work. Socrates proclaims in Plato's *Apology* that he found great poets least able to interpret the meaning of their works because they wrote them in a state of divine inspiration. Kant preserves this view of the relation between the poet and the work in more prosaic terms with his theory of genius: creation of artistic beauty happens according to a quasi-natural process, by which a lack of understanding is actually constitutive of the creation of great art. To say that one is a genius is precisely to say that a lack of formal knowledge is constitutive of the formal perfection of their work. This conception of genius or divine inspiration serves to reinforce a division of labor between philosophy and art. It is precisely this division of labor in aesthetic and cognitive matters that Benjamin seeks to challenge in his discovery of the sobriety of art within romantic theory. By dissolving the work of poetry in a medium of reflection, seeing prose as the ground of poetry and sobriety as the truth of inspiration, the early German Romantics allow the critical comportment to arise out of the work, as part of what constitutes its specifically aesthetic character, and they understand the experience of the work as a process of immanent critique, and art as a medial form of knowledge. As Benjamin points out: "Criticism is far less the judgment of the work than its consummation".[31] In romantic theory, criticism even takes a kind of ontological and epistemic precedence over the works, since the works themselves are only activated in their truth as parts of a medium of reflection through the critical awareness that dissolves them into this medium. In the poetry of the future, it seems that the early German Romantics hope for a poetry that transitions into prose in order to reflect itself, a literary criticism that is itself a work of art.

The key to understanding the romantic notion of sobriety might be teased out of an important Hölderlin text:

> There are degrees of enthusiasm. Beginning with merriness, which is probably the lowest, right up to the enthusiasm of the general, who in the midst of battle mightily maintains his genius, there is an infinite ladder. To ascend and descend this ladder, is the vocation and bliss of the poet.
>
> That is the measure of enthusiasm that is given to every individual, that the one still maintains his consciousness to the necessary degree in a greater, the other only in a weaker fire. There where sobriety leaves is the limit of your enthusiasm. The great poet is never removed from himself, he may elevate his self as high as he wishes.[32]

We see that Hölderlin defines sobriety in a constitutive relation with enthusiasm, not in opposition to it.[33] He measures sobriety precisely by the degree of enthusiasm that it can bear, by the ability to "maintain consciousness to the necessary degree", to move up and down amid various emotional states as if on a ladder. He places poetry in a special relationship to this measure of sobriety. This passage offers us insight not only into Hölderlin, but also into the way that Benjamin deploys the notion of sobriety:[34] it is not that early German Romantics prescribe prose as a remedy to poetry, but they see it as the more intensive mode of writing that is able to slip in and out of its intoxication with linguistic revelry in order to gain clarity. Prose is the truth of poetry because it can contain and comment on poetry. This interpretation seems supported by the ontology of the medium of reflection, in which works are dissolved in order to find their inherent cognitive content.

This highly original and cogent discovery of the principle of sobriety in romantic theory tells us something about Benjamin's own conception of art criticism. In his elevating of sobriety above genius, Benjamin values the spirit that is not so taken in by the creative process that it fails to reflect on all of the different ways in which the work could be understood. In the romantic conception, the artist is creative precisely to the degree that she can move from creation to commentary, from poetry to prose, in a seamless manner. In the most programmatically crucial work of Benjamin's later, political phase, *The Artwork in the Age of its Technical Reproduction* (1935), Benjamin activates this principle of the sobriety of art as an antidote against the fascist tendencies of his age. He engages in a critique of the "aura" of art, as that aesthetic feature by which the arts present the "nearness of distance" in such a way as to captivate and intoxicate the subject. His critique of aura is bound up not only with his hope for a new, technological medium of aesthetic experience, but also with the romantic insight into the "retreat of the beautiful" in place of art as a medium of reflection. In the epilogue of the *The Artwork in the Age of its Technical Reproduction* essay, he makes a distinction between two opposite possibilities confronting aesthetic experience in the age of fascism: society must choose between the politicization of art and the aesthetization of war (fascism).[35] Either art opens up a space of critical distance within everyday experience, making us more aware of possibilities to transform society, or as in the case of fascism, society itself gets aestheticized in a way that stifles reflection. It is with this gesture that the romantic principle of sobriety becomes politically fruitful in Benjamin's aesthetic thought. He reads the relation of theory and aesthetic experience as not merely a matter of aesthetic theory, or of the academic division of labor, but also as a core choice of the political direction of society. In a key section of the *Artwork* essay, Benjamin makes precisely the immanence between reflection and enjoyment (which is just what he means by sobriey) into the feature that marks the distinction between progressive art and art which serves as ideology.[36] If the creation and critique of aesthetic forms is not able to unify critical sobriety with the sensible experience of being carried along by the artwork, then he argues that what results is something like the fascist spectacle, what he calls the aesthetization of politics. In the *Artwork* essay, he sees it as one of the qualities of fascism to substitute "mere" aesthetic feeling in a context that requires reflection. Although this interpretation of fascism as an anti-critical form of aesthetics requires more explanation than is possible here, the point that is worth highlighting in the present context is that his earlier notion of romantic sobriety provides him with the perfect point of contrast. The early German Romantic philosophers provide Benjamin with a way of thinking about art and art criticism in terms of immanent criticism, sobriety, and reflection that aligns with his later notion of modern art as an antidote to fascist spectacle.

## 5 Translation as Mode of Critique

Benjamin's reading of the concept of critique in his early work is clearly one that cuts across problems of knowledge, politics, and aesthetics. The early German Romantics help Benjamin to pose the question of how art helps to make us into critical subjects. As Benjamin continued to develop his own critical method, and to refine his reflections on literature, knowledge, and politics, the problem of translation came increasingly to the fore, and in this too, he was influenced by the early German Romantics. Benjamin was an experienced translator of the works of Baudelaire and Proust, just as some of the key figures in early German Romanticism were influential translators. Not only are their translations of such high literary quality that they are still read today, but they also left a mark on the very theory of translation. Thinking deeply about translation in *On the Task of the Translator* allows Benjamin to pose the question yet again of how language and artistic form relate to the discovery of truth.

Benjamin considers translation as a challenge to language itself. It is not merely a matter of understanding the original and then communicating it correctly, but more a matter of introducing freedom into one's own language through the act of translation. In developing this view, Benjamin cites the early German Romantics as the most important forerunners to his own view of translation:

> They (the Romantics) more than any others were gifted with an insight into the life of literary works—an insight for which translation provides the highest testimony. To be sure, they hardly recognized translation in this sense, but devoted their entire attention to criticism—another if lesser factor in the continued life of works.[37]

Benjamin here understands translation to be a further intensification of the concept of critique, that I discussed in Sect. 4. Just as a true critique is one that grasps the work as a medium of reflection, the translation is nourished by the "life" of the literary work. What does Benjamin mean by the life of literary works? They have life in a dual sense: because artworks live on after their creation and gain in meaning and because languages themselves have life, that is, a tendency to grow, take on new words, or give new meanings to old words in order to convey different experiences. Just as artworks have a history of interpretation and reception that adds new layers of meaning that belong to them, languages also have a history, which entails a complex movement of forgetting, growth, and decay. Translation of literary works is for Benjamin one of the most powerful ways in which languages grow through contact with foreign life so as to gain the power to express different experiences. The successful translation is not the one that tames the foreign language by making it fit within the language of translation, but rather the one that challenges the language of translation to say what it could not say before. Although in the above citation, Benjamin seems to say that the early German Romantics hardly recognized the role of challenge as a possibility for translation, that is, the push to help the text say what it could not say before its translation, it is in fact one of the early German Romantics, who gives Benjamin the best example of such literary translation: Hölderlin's German translations of Sophocles and Pindar. These translations were considered to be products of mental instability in Hölderlin's own time because they did not seem to conform to the standard uses of the German language, and yet they have come over time to be recognized as exemplary translations in both their poetic quality and their grasp of ancient Greek poetics. Benjamin regards this kind of translation as the best example of the achievement of the translator: "It is the task of the translator to release in his own language that pure language which is exiled among alien tongues, to liberate the language imprisoned in the work in his recreation of that work".[38] The translator is someone who is trying both to know the original through the medium of another language and to find the resources or expressive possibilities in their own language that have been lost or exiled in a foreign language. As Eduardo Mendieta writes, for the critical theorists, the language of philosophy is not so much a "house of being", but an incessant foray into foreign language.[39]

The problem of translation reveals a deeper dynamic of Benjamin's thinking and his debt to the early German Romantics: a debt concerning the role of language in capturing truth. In his very earliest writing on language from 1916, Benjamin thinks of the multiplicity of languages and the translation from one to another as a result of the fallen state of mankind, having lost the language that would truly translate the nature of things. But after his work on the early German Romantics, he sees translation, along with it the multitude of languages, as a key to pursuing and capturing truth. For the early German Romantics, the truth of a work resides not in its original Being but in its life process, in the historical process of responding to the work, much like what

Gadamer calls its *Wirkungsgeschichte*. The truth lies not in mere faithfulness to the original, but in a deeper, mutually transformative response to its expressive potential.

## 6 Conclusion

In this chapter, I have focused on Benjamin's *Concept of Critique* as offering a crucial point of contact between early critical theory and early German Romanticism. However, more work would need to be done to trace the influence of this work on Benjamin's subsequent development and on critical theory in general. To what extent did Benjamin continue to develop the notion of art criticism treated here? And how did his "one true student",[40] Adorno, adopt key insights from this phase into his own philosophy?

It might first seem as if by the time of his key work, *The Origin of German Tragic Drama*, Benjamin had developed a very different notion of criticism. While he had understood the romantic conception of critique as one that gives life to the object, making the object appear as a subject, in this later work Benjamin articulates critique in a somewhat inverse sense as "mortification" of the work. He formulates this point perhaps most clearly in a letter from this phase: "My definition is: criticism is the mortification of the works. Not the intensification of consciousness in them (that is Romantic!), but their colonization by knowledge".[41]

His notion of "mortification" resembles the central movement of his translation essay: the translator does not achieve a truly literary effect by making a "dead" work speak in a living language, as the cliché might have it, but rather by infecting the living, familiar language with what is uncanny and unfamiliar in the language from which the work is translated. This insight has to be applied more fundamentally as an understanding of what it means to be critical: to be critical is *not* to make the work relevant, to translate a work of literature into a context that would make it easy to absorb into our current set of concerns. Rather, to be critical is to allow our current set of concerns to be invaded by some possibility of expression that has been killed off by the course of history. The critic "mortifies" the work by attending to what is dead in it, but as a lost possibility that illuminates the present.

Benjamin's re-articulation of criticism as mortification might seem at first to represent a break with the romantic concept of critique, as he seems to phrase it in opposition to his earlier notion. Yet it is noteworthy that he formulates it so explicitly as a reversal of his earlier conception of the romantic medium of reflection precisely because it deepens the set of negations and commitments that he had articulated in his work on German Romanticism. He had been interested in the way in which the romantic theory represents a break with the modern conception of the critic as someone who assigns an instrumental value to the object. The early German Romantics make art into something that has its own, internal awareness precisely because they want consciousness to be transformed by the work's nascent subjectivity, rather than letting the work be subsumed to the needs of the marketplace. Benjamin's conception of mortification involves a deepening of this very move away from the instrumental value of the work. The romantic conception of critique makes the *mere* object into a subject-object that has its own voice; Benjamin's conception of critique as mortification makes the object *dead*, not in the sense of making it back into a mere object, but by insisting that what is true within it has not been allowed to survive. It is thus just as he is turning toward the Baroque notion of allegory that he discovers a deeper meaning in the romantic philosophy of the fragment, a subject he addresses in his chapter on Schlegel.[42] Rather than looking at the artwork as a series of symbols that reflect our present, he proposes in his *Trauerspiel* book to regard the work's truth content as a series of broken pieces that reveal the constitutive role of suffering, loss, and forgetting in human history. This theme of fragmentation represents another point of continuity with the early German Romantics.

It is this notion of criticism as a way of finding truth content in the artwork that exercises a crucial influence on Adorno. In his massive posthumous work, *Aesthetic Theory*, Adorno develops a wide-ranging and fragmentary theory of modern art, according to which the artwork is a site of a particular mode of aesthetic truth content. In Adorno's account, artworks embody riddles that have to be deciphered by philosophical criticism. The truth content of artworks is not simply a philosophical message in another form, but a flip side of philosophy that is only open to a mimetic, open-ended form of experience. As Susan Buck-Morss argues in her incisive study, it was Benjamin who led Adorno beyond the hermeneutics of Dilthey, the phenomenology of Husserl, and the neo-Kantianism prevalent at the time by giving him a method for reading truth within the objective, unintentional expressions of culture.[43] As a culmination of this impetus, Adorno's *Aesthetic Theory* measures the function of art in terms of its ability to present truth content in its objective structure. Adorno's work on aesthetics revolves around the difficult idea that art entails a distinctive mode of truth in how it challenges and refigures experience, issuing challenges both to mere enjoyment and to conceptual understanding. This project represents a direct extension of Benjamin's notion of art as intentionless truth, which itself emerges out of Benjamin's interpretation of art criticism in German Romanticism.

## Notes

1. For a contemporary discussion of immanent critique within critical theory, see the work of Rahel Jaeggi, *Critique of Forms of Life*, trans. Ciarin Cronin (Cambridge: Harvard University Press, 2019), 177.
2. I would like to thank Tim Mehigan for his invitation to the conference "Romantic Hermeneutics" in September 2018. Interacting with the scholars at this conference, including Elizabeth Millán, helped me to develop many of the thoughts contained in this essay. I have been working on the relation between early German Romanticism and critical theory over several years, and some of the passages contained in this essay have been reworked from the fourth chapter of my book, *The Philosophy and Politics of Aesthetic Experience* (New York: Palgrave, 2017). The introduction to this book provides a more general discussion of common themes that I found between early German Romanticism and critical theory.
3. It is, of course, possible to criticize Benjamin's essay purely as a work of secondary literature and find many limitations, both in the scope of Benjamin's knowledge of German Romanticism, and in the way that he sometimes draws overly strong conclusions based on limited textual evidence. Such an approach may be found in Winfried Menninghaus, "Walter Benjamin's Exposition of the Romantic Theory of Reflection" in *Walter Benjamin and Romanticism*, ed. Beatrice Hansen and Andrew Benjamin (London: Continuum, 2002). It is obvious that Benjamin did not have access to the range of texts that we have today. However, this limitation-focussed approach rests on ignoring several of the key features of Benjamin's essay, such as his intentionally loose definition of the romantic school to include Hölderlin, and it also often interprets romantic concept formation in an overly rigid and one-sided way. For more on this, see note 31. It seems more helpful to read Benjamin's essay not merely as an interpretation of Schlegel and Novalis, but more broadly as an effort to define the notion criticism in a forward-looking way. This is in keeping with Benjamin's own methodological distinction between *Problemgeschichte* and *Geschichte der Philosophie*.
4. Rodolphe Gasché, defines, I think correctly, what is at stake in this methodological distinction and thus the interpretive horizon against which Benjamin's essay has to be considered: "It is a matter of analyzing 'their own most proper intentions'. In other words, a philosophical analysis, that is, an analysis regarded from an historic-problematic has to focus on what, from a philosophical perspective, are the most proper intentions of the Romantics concepts… Obviously, an interpretation of this kind may have to stretch the meaning of their concepts well beyond what the Romantics themselves may have intended them to say in order to bring out their philosophical inten-

tions". Gasché, "The Sober Absolute" in *Walter Benjamin and Romanticism, op. cit.,* 53.

5. The poet and theorist Friedrich Hölderlin is not generally considered a member of the romantic circle that formed in Jena around 1800, but Benjamin's frequent references to Hölderlin in his study assimilate him to their school after the fact. "One spirit moves into the wider circle, not into the center—a spirit who cannot be comprehended merely in his quality as a 'poet' in the modern sense of the word (however high this must be reckoned)… this spirit is Hölderlin, and the thesis that establishes his relationship to the Romantic school is the principle of the sobriety of art". See *Benjamin Selected Writings 1,* 175/*Kunstkritik,* 97. Benjamin was well ahead of his age in recognizing Hölderlin's significance not merely as a poet, but as a theoretical writer who made contributions to the development of post-Kantian debates, a position that was not widespread in philosophy until the work of Dieter Henrich from the 1970's. For an account of the way that Benjamin maintained an interest in Hölderlin throughout various phases of his development, see Beatrice Hansen, "Dichtermut and Blödigkeit: Two Poems by Friedrich Hölderlin interpreted by Walter Benjamin" in *Walter Benjamin and Romanticism, op. cit.,* 143–144.

6. The context of this dissertation within Benjamin's intellectual development has to be reconsidered along these lines. It is argued by Menninghaus, and repeated by Rudolph Gasché, that Benjamin had very limited grasp of the problems of post-Kantian philosophy, and of the texts of the early German Romantics, but that he actually "got it right" in some general sense because he was already predisposed to a romantic way of thinking due to his notion of language, as formulated in his 1916 essay *On Language.* (See Rudolph Gasché, "The Sober Absolute" in *Walter Benjamin and the Romantics, op. cit.,* 51.) But this approach ignores the fact that Benjamin's views on language and mimesis actually changed as a result of his encounter with the early German Romantics. While the early language essay considers the mimetic feature of (human) language as an effort to preserve the original divine language of things, his later essay on translation actually argues that translation produces the truth precisely by adapting the original into a new medium. This essential Benjaminian insight about the truth-producing nature of mimesis seems to derive precisely from his encounter with the early German Romantics. So the question should not be why Benjamin had an inherent affinity to the early German Romantics, but what he learned from them and how they influenced his philosophical development.

7. *Benjamin Selected Writings* 1, 177/*Kunstkritik,* 100. Although Benjamin develops this thesis on the retreat of the beautiful out of his reading of the romantics, it has vital implications for his later thought, especially in his essay, *On the Artwork in the Age of its Technical Reproducibility,* where his famous thesis on the liquidation of aura in modern art involves a critique "beautiful

semblance". See his text "The Significance of Beautiful Semblance" in *Benjamin Selected Writings 3*, 137–138. Indeed, this thesis also has vital implications for Adorno's conception of modern art in *Aesthetic Theory*. See Ross Wilson, "Aesthetics" in *Theodor Adorno: Key Concepts*, ed. Deborah Cook, (Stocksfeld: Acumen, 2008), 153. Wilson gives an account of the impact of Benjamin's reading of Schlegel on Adorno.
8. *Benjamin Selected Writings* 1, 144–146/*Kunstkritik*, 51–53.
9. Ibid., 149/57.
10. Ibid., 151/58.
11. Rebecca Comay's interpretation leads her to claim: "Abandoning its traditional legislating and legitimizing role, Romantic criticism instead comes to realize it as an inexhaustible process of supplementation of the individual work through repetitive recycling of prior texts" in "Benjamin and the Ambiguities of Romanticism," *The Cambridge Companion to Walter Benjamin*, ed. David Ferris (Cambridge: Cambridge University Press, 2004), 140. This interpretation seems to assimilate Benjamin's German Romantics to the deconstructive method: it hinges on conflating the method of immanent reflection with "repetition and recycling" of texts.
12. *Benjamin Selected Writings 1*, 151–152/*Kunstkritik*, 58.
13. Ibid. 152/58.
14. Ibid. 177/100.
15. *Benjamin Selected Writings 3*, 137. In a much later text that he wrote as part of his famous, *On the Artwork in the Age of Technological Reproducibility*, he reiterates this thesis on the retreat of the beautiful: "The significance of beautiful semblance is rooted in an age of perception that is now nearing its end". See also note 22 of the second version of the *Artwork* essay. While Benjamin and Adorno disagreed about the direction of modern art, it is safe to say that Benjamin's thesis on the retreat of the beautiful had a great influence on Adorno: for a discussion of the centrality of this theme in Adorno's work see Jay Bernstein's, "The Demand of Ugliness: Picasso's Bodies"in *Art and Aesthetics after Adorno*, ed. Jay Bernstein (Berkeley: UC Press, 2010), 209.
16. "The progressive reaction (to a work) is characterized by the direct, intimate fusion of visual and emotional enjoyment with the orientation of the expert". *Benjamin Selected Works 3*, 116.
17. "Art is directed toward truth, it is not itself immediate truth; to this extent truth is its content. By its relation to truth, art is knowledge; art itself knows truth in that truth emerges through it. As knowledge, however, art is neither discursive nor is its truth the reflection of an object,". Theodor Adorno, *Aesthetische Theorie* (Frankfurt: Suhrkamp, 2003), 418.
18. Theodor W. Adorno, *Ästhetik (1958/59)* (Frankfurt: Suhrkamp, 2009), 270–271.
19. See Susan Buck-Morss, *The Origin of Negative Dialectics* (New York: The Free Press, 1977), 21.

20. "On Language as such and the Language of Man" in *Benjamin Selected Writings 1*, 62–74. He writes that it is the "the bourgeois conception of language" which considers the words as a means of communications between humans. To this he opposes another purpose of language, bound up with the redemption of things: "God's creation is complete when things receive their names from man," *Benjamin Selected Writings 1*, 65.
21. *Benjamin Selected Works 4* and also in Walter Benjamin, *Illuminations*, ed. Hannah Arendt (New York: Schocken, 1968), 253–264.
22. See Ibid., seventh thesis. Here he writes famously that all products of culture are also products of barbarism.
23. *Benjamin Selected Works 1*, 160/*Kunstkritik*, 73.
24. "The individual work should be dissolved in the medium of art". *Benjamin Selected Works 1*, 153/*Kunstkritik*, 60.
25. Ibid. 158/71.
26. Ibid. 156/70.
27. Hans-Georg Gadamer develops his argument on the "subjectivization of aesthetics by Kant" in *Truth and Method*. Hans Georg Gadamer, *Wahrheit und Methode, Heremeneutik 1* (Tubingen: Mohr, 1990), 48–87. It seems possible to reconstruct Gadamer's argument about the subjectivity of Kant's aesthetics by looking at Benjamin's work on the German Romantics: if anything, Gadamer's thesis is enriched by a deeper knowledge of the aesthetic tradition immediately after Kant.
28. This logic of dissolution, progression and sublation between art-forms in the Romantic theory places them in a kind of unacknowledged proximity to the aesthetic philosophy of Hegel, who also thought of all other arts as "sublated" into poetry, and poetry as sublated into prose. (See Comay, "Benjamin and the ambiguities of Romanticism" in *The Cambridge Companion to Walter Benjamin, op. cit.,* 142).
29. *Benjamin Selected Works 1*, 173–174/*Kunstkritik*, 95–96.
30. It is on this point that Benjamin assimilates Hölderlin to the Romantic school: "One spirit moves into the wider circle, not into the center… the thesis that establishes his relationship to the Romantic school is the principle of the sobriety of art". Ibid. 175/97.
31. Ibid. 153/60.
32. Anthologized as "Seven Maxims" in Freidrich Hölderlin, *Essays and Letters*, ed. Jeremy Adler and Charlie Louth (London: Penguin, 2009), 240. The text is referred to as "*Reflexion*" in German. See Vol. 14 in Friedrich Hölderlin, *Sämtliche Werke*, ed. D. Sattler (Frankfurt: Roter Stern, 1979).
33. In the context of an extremely critical essay on Benjamin, Menninghaus argues that Benjamin overemphasizes sobriety and prose in his reading by pointing to passages in which Schlegel and Novalis write of the ecstatic nature of the aesthetic. Winfried Menninghaus, "Walter Benjamin's Exposition of the Romantic Theory of Reflection" in *Walter Benjamin and Romanticism*, ed.

Beatrice Hansen and Andrew Benjamin (London: Continuum, 2002), 35–36. This criticism is incorrect because first, it fails to acknowledge that Benjamin considers Hölderlin, even more than Schlegel, as the originator of the notion of sobriety, and more importantly, because its rests on the argument that sobriety is a concept defined merely in opposition enthusiasm, or that prose is defined merely as the lack of poetry. But the true romantic argument is that prose is the truth of poetry not because it negates it, but because it includes it within a medium of reflection.

34. Benjamin could not have known this text at the time: however, there are many poems of Hölderlin that express similar notions about measure and sobriety, especially *"Brod und Wein"*. For a strong account of various passages in which Hölderlin deploys the notion of sobriety, see Beatrice Hansen, "Dichtermut and Blödigkeit: Two Poems by Friedrich Hölderlin interpreted by Walter Benjamin" in *Walter Benjamin and Romanticism*, 147–148. She writes: "As the antidote to Platonic *mania*, sobriety was the structure that ruled the law of reflection, conceived of as a dialectic between sober self-limitation and ecstatic self-extension".
35. *Benjamin Selected Writings 3,* 122.
36. In section 15 of the second version of the essay, he compares the progressive reaction of the masses to a Chaplin film to the reactionary attitude that the public demonstrates to avant garde painting. He writes: "The progressive attitude is characterized by an immediate, intimate fusion of pleasure—pleasure in seeing and experiencing—with the orientation of an expert". *Benjamin Selected Writings 3,* 116. Here Benjamin analyzes not merely how some arts, such as film, are more subject to simultaneous experience by a mass of spectators, but also the way in which "expertise", i.e. a knowledge of the laws of aesthetic creation, can be more of less immanent to the immediate experience of the work. Photography and film embody the structure of sobriety in their very form, because of the way that they combine sensuous, immediate experience with a quasi-scientific dissection of the material of daily experience.
37. Ibid. 258.
38. Ibid. 261.
39. Eduardo Mendieta, "The Jargon of Ontology and the Critique of Language: Benjamin, Adorno and Philosophy's Mother Tongue" in *The Aesthetic Ground of Critical Theory*, ed. Nathan Ross (Lanham: Rowman and Littlefield, 2016): 47–63.
40. Benjamin himself referred to Adorno in this manner. See Howard Eiland and Michael Jennings, *Walter Benjamin: A Critical Life* (Cambridge: Harvard University Press, 2014), 359.
41. Benjamin, *Selected Works* 1, 389. An almost identical formulation appears in the *Trauerspiel* text: "Mortification of the works: not then—as the Romantics have it—awakening of the consciousness in living works, but the settling of

consciousness in dead ones". Walter Benjamin, *The Origin of German Tragic Drama* (New York: Verso, 1998), 182.
42. "It is not possible to conceive of a starker contrast to the artistic symbol, the plastic symbol, the image of organic totality, than this amorphous fragment, which is seen in the form of allegorical script. In it, the Baroque reveals itself to be the sovereign opposite of classism, as which only Romanticism has hitherto been acknowledged. And we should not resist finding the features which are common to both of them". Benjamin, *Origin,* 176.
43. Susan Buck-Morss, *The Origin of Negative Dialectics* (New York: The Free Press, 1977), 21.

# 29

# Romanticism, Anarchism, and Critical Theory

## Fred Rush

When one surveys the main statements within Critical Theory of its relations to other advanced forms of social and political critique from the Left, it is striking that there is no treatment of anarchism in either its classical nineteenth-century or its later syndicalist forms that is comparable in insight to Critical Theory's various analyses of socialism.[1] There is at best judgment rendered *en passant*, almost always guarded. Typical is Adorno's remark, delivered in the last paper published during his lifetime, that the "return" of anarchism is "that of a specter [*die eines Gespensts*]".[2] The image, as is usual for Adorno, is diagnostic. He has in mind those he took to be undisciplined university students, whose "anarchism" he thought to be theoretically undigested, really little more than a word. Provisioned with this phantasm of a concept, their political activity could amount to nothing; it was mere reflex action. True, this is not a judgment concerning anarchism *per se*, but it is not exactly an endorsement of it either. Or, if an endorsement, it is an obscure one, relying as it does on unpacking the allusion to Marx and Engels' opening sentence of the *Manifesto*.[3] One might expect Marcuse to be more tolerant of anarchism given his connection, deserved or undeserved, with the New Left. And so he seems, writing in a more historical vein that the anarcho-socialist Charles Fourier "comes closer than any other utopian socialist to elucidating the dependence of freedom on non-repressive sublimation".[4] Fourier certainly cannot be faulted for a tepid

---

F. Rush (✉)
University of Notre Dame, Notre Dame, IN, USA
e-mail: rush.12@nd.edu

© The Author(s) 2020
E. Millán Brusslan (ed.), *The Palgrave Handbook of German Romantic Philosophy*, Palgrave Handbooks in German Idealism, https://doi.org/10.1007/978-3-030-53567-4_29

approach to social and political progress; the countercultural credentials of the *phalanstère* are incontestable and must have impressed Marcuse positively.[5] A brighter thought, then, but the point remains that neither Adorno nor Marcuse develops anything resembling an articulated account of anarchism from the perspective of Critical Theory.

Critical Theory's lack of engagement with anarchism might seem especially surprising given the role anarchists played in the German revolutions of 1918–1919. The Bavarian Soviet that succeeded the socialist People's State of Bavaria was founded and administered by anarchists, among them the playwright, satirist, and pamphleteer Erich Mühsam and the philosopher, novelist, and literary critic Gustav Landauer. Munich was the center of the revolt, a city to which Horkheimer moves in 1919 in order to begin his university studies, at which time he reads a great deal of both socialist and anarchist theory. Walter Benjamin lived in Munich from 1915 to 1917, during which time he met Landauer.[6] Benjamin had already sampled anarchism with Gershom Scholem, whom he befriended during their time as members of the *Jugendbewegung*.[7] For his part, Marcuse was located in Berlin, also a center of revolutionary activity. It is uncertain whether he was a member of the Spartacus Group, but his sympathy for it is well documented. Nor is it subject to doubt that the murders of the leaders of the Group, Karl Liebknecht and Rosa Luxemburg, affected him deeply.

Horkheimer and Marcuse reacted to the failed revolutions and the inauguration of the Weimar Republic rather oddly, with intense bookishness. It takes special discernment to radicalize oneself through the study of Kant's third *Critique*, German Romanticism, and Hegelian dialectics as bodies of martyrs only lately have been fished out of the Landwehrkanal and retrieved from the mass grave outside Stadelheim Prison. It is not enough, however, to mark the intellectual abstraction of these men as a cause of their lack of engagement with anarchism. No doubt this was due in part to the real dangers of being publically politically Left, and especially of being so as Jewish intellectuals. Munich, after all, was a hotbed for all manner of radical politics of the time, of the Left and the Right. The proto-fascist *Freikorps* patrolled the streets looking for people to harass, arrest, or kill.[8] Berlin also knew such dangers. A fuller answer to why early Critical Theory bypassed anarchism and reacted to the failed socialist revolutions by retrenching in academic matters also has to take into consideration the fractious state of Left political theory of the times. Anarchism and communism suffered a schism after the disbanding of the First International of course, but by 1918, that was old news. More pressing was the question of why oppressed workers had not taken control of European society, as Marx had envisioned, especially after the German defeat in the war.

A sharp divide within socialism ensued between dialectical materialism and forms of Marxism that reincorporate aspects of Idealist social thought. Critical theorists were decidedly of the second church, which stressed deeper theoretical engagement with issues of ideology. But classical anarchism appeared to offer no systematic account of collective self-deception and, therefore, no prognosis as to how it might be resisted. Coordinate to this failure, anarchists also tended to treat revolution as an achievable optimal state in which there would be no further need for ongoing political criticism. Not only might one object to this theoretically, but it also seemed contrary to the historical record. It was, simply, falsely utopian.

Given the missed opportunities, one must broach the issue of the kinship of Critical Theory and anarchism reconstructively. One such reconstruction focuses on a strand of early twentieth-century anarchism that couples a reassessment of revolutionary potential with a deep analysis of culture beyond economics. One then looks for overlap with similar trends in early Critical Theory. The overlap might be adventitious or stem from a common historical source. The anarchist who best fits the bill is Landauer. The critical theorists who share several of Landauer's philosophical tendencies are Benjamin and Adorno. The common historical lineage is early German Romanticism. What triangulates the views is what I will call *productive anachronism*.

## 1    Landauer: Revolution, Time, Utopia

It is perhaps best to think of anarchism as a form of practical engagement, not a social theory. Anarchism shares with certain strands of liberalism and socialism an emphasis on free development of human capacities, and the expressive self-knowledge that both motivates and results from such exercise. Whatever impedes such development blocks individual and group function. Any such impediment, therefore, requires the most stringent justification. If unjustifiable, a structure that materially contributes to the impediment must be dismantled and society reformed to that extent. Classical anarchism holds that modern forms of the political state are such impediments and are to be judged by the most uncompromising standards. Anarchism's stance against the modern state is but one of its anti-authoritarian aspects. It is worth recalling that Bakunin's incendiary pamphlet was titled *God and the State* and that the rallying cry of the Blanquists was "neither God nor master" (*ni Dieu, ni maître*).[9] Anarchism treats the state and organized religion as of a piece.

Anarchism's conceptualization of the place of revolution in political practice is its calling card. But, as noted, for the most part classical anarchism leaves unanalyzed the phenomenon of ideology or similar structures of social pathology. As also noted, this is bound to make anarchism appear naïve in the eyes of the critical theorist. Proudhon and Bakunin are, indeed, all but nativist when it comes to such matters; once debilitating authoritarian structures are removed, humans will revert to their benign natures without residual effects, the scales will simply fall away and one will be left with unsullied individuals operating freely. Moreover, on account of this social-psychological "primitivism", classical anarchism lacks a theory of counter- or pseudo-revolution.[10] Partisans of the so-called humanist wing of socialism dispense the epithet "vulgar Marxism" to tag crudely causal views of social change. One might be tempted to coin a variant of the tag to describe forms of anarchism that suppose that removal of institutional barriers alone will correct the internal self-regard of agents. Early twentieth-century anarchists, however, were not quite so trusting, and this provides a potential bridge between anarchism and early Critical Theory. Landauer develops an account of continuing critique and of the place of individuality in sociality that is much less accepting of the idea of a final palliation consisting in the mere removal of institutional structure.

Landauer holds that revolution and ideology must be considered in concert and in the context of a general theory of historical time. He contrasts two aspects of historical time: "topia [*Topie*]" and "utopia [*Utopie*]".[11] The key to the contrast is the concept "place [τόπος]". Places are relatively fixed, concrete *locations*. "Location" as it is used here is especially to be distinguished from the idea of spatial expanse. A location is specified by what is present there; "space" is a more abstract term that refers to geometric boundedness. To Landauer's way of thinking, the idea of place also has a temporal dimension; a location is both a "there" and a "then".[12] One wouldn't say *fin de siècle* Paris was a space (although it displaced whatever space it did), but one would say that it was a place. It was a discrete habitation at a particular time in history. The topian aspect of historical time is placed-time, that is, life in reasonably settled form. In such a form, human individuality and community have regularized practices that are continuity-preserving and, by and large, unquestioned. Landauer does not condescend to such normalized communities. Humans must inhabit places; topias provide necessary sustenance and allow one to be rooted in accepted practices. But part of the point in coining the neologism "topia" by dropping the "u" from "utopia" is to register that this aspect of historical temporality, and the more settled form of practical engagement it makes possible, is, appearances notwithstanding, secondary to a more basic aspect, that is, the utopian. This reversal—the idea that what is utopian is basic and that which is not is derivative—is a cornerstone of Landauer's thought.

One might assume this to be a kind of Platonism, but that would be mistaken. The Platonist's lionizing of invariance could not be further from Landauer's conception of the utopian aspect of historical time. All history for Landauer is fundamentally "a becoming [*ein Werden*]"; settled locations do not limn the fundamental temporal structure of history.[13] Landauer argues that there is a tendency to resist stasis, which characterizes human existence. This tendency has its expression in what he calls "illusion [*Wahn*]", which he conceives as an ordinarily covert impulse that is, nonetheless, omnipresent in history in virtue of the constitution of historical agents.[14] Gaining theoretical purchase on the impulse is tricky from Landauer's perspective. Stable discursive structures like theories are apt to distort the phenomenon or cause it to disappear altogether, unless one introduces modifications that reflect more process-oriented and open-ended systematicity. This explains why Landauer considers art to better express the drive. In deploying the term "Wahn", Landauer of course does not mean to imply that the drive is delusional or foolish. The term refers, rather, to a particular exercise of imagination. Forms of imagination, like forms of any other cognitive process, may be constrained by regularities present in individual cases of topia. That is, forms of imagination, as well as imaginative content, are socialized. *Wahn* is imagination untethered from normalcy and is, for this reason, ecstatic, that is, it stands outside of constraint.

Landauer has in mind a continuous process of imagination-based resistance. Most of the time—that is, in topias—this is recessive, bounded by the status quo and adjusting itself to satisfy everyday human creativity. Humans often do not pause to reflect pointedly on whether their dissatisfactions with the world are being addressed or even what those dissatisfactions are. Under such conditions, resistance to the world as it is registers mildly—in daydreams, fictions, games, or just musing about what might be possible. But, at other times, the impulse is more explicitly present. At such times, there is active and tenacious questioning of given standards. And rarely, imagining ways things might be otherwise wells up and overtakes the everyday to the point that the given form of life is no longer taken to be viable and resistance transforms into action for radical change. Revolution for Landauer is nothing more than this entire process and, because the process is uninterrupted, revolution is continual. Put another way, what is utopian for Landauer is not a specific place that is realized as optimal, or any other sort of place; rather, it is the continued interrogative, critical, and imaginative power of humans. Revolutions, that is, periods of action that break radically from convention, are but parts of that whole. Revolutions considered as discrete events are rebound effects that are consequent on trying but not being able to discharge pent-up imaginative responsiveness to given unsatisfactory states of affairs. The ebb and flow of resisting topia just *is* history, that is, history *as such* is revolutionary. Seen from another angle, topias are the places they are not because there is a complete lack of utopia in them. They are the places they are because the utopian impulse is, for the time being, quieted. This is not at all to say that what one more commonly calls revolutions are not of interest to Landauer. He holds that such outbreaks are cataclysmic and self-ampliative, situations in which the revolutionary impulse "condenses [*dichtet*]", breaks from external governance, and persists by spiraling deeper and deeper into its own structure, becoming for a time all-consuming.[15] Revolutions end through dissipation, not by achieving final ends. The utopian aspect of time exhausts its energy and reverts back to its implicit status. After a time, the cycle repeats. By Landauer's lights, then, revolutions do not aim to replace one specific *order* with another and, for that reason, are not necessarily progressive.[16] What they accomplish is their instantiation, that is, that they *be*.

The second component of Landauer's account of revolution specifies what critical procedures might best alert historical agents to their utopian vocation. It is important to note at the outset that Landauer's preferred way to engage critical imagination is not by means of detailed argumentation. Although he does not spell out why this is so, it is clear from the foregoing why he might think standard forms of philosophical engagement are inadequate to the task of making utopian thought more express. Topias are characterized by stability, and argumentation can be an excellent tool for articulating such a structure in its own terms. It analyzes the structure into its basic components, constructs premises therefrom, and investigates the structure and its implications inferentially. In order to do this argumentation requires that a structure be relatively fixed in order to secure the needed premises. When it comes to stepping out of the structure sufficiently to critique its core elements, it is precisely these premises that are placed in question. This leaves argumentation with little critical punch, given the shifting nature of the structure it purports to detail. Of course, no critique steps entirely outside of the structure it targets, but that is not the point. If there is significant dissolution of the set terms for agreement and disagreement, argumentation loses a great deal of scope and cannot present itself as a basic mode of criticism. In view of the potential danger that arguments tend to replicate the status quo ante and restrict social imagination, Landauer opts instead to deploy imaginary constructs that contrast severely with more intellectually conservative ways of thinking of social structures and their relation to history. An example of just the sort of schema Landauer takes to be potentially productive for anarchic social renewal is present in Novalis' *Christianity, or Europe* (1799), which is discussed below in section 3 of this chapter. Before turning to it, it is worthwhile to situate Landauer's understanding of what form of social imagination might best function in a more historically proximate theoretical context: Ferdinand Tönnies's distinction between "community [*Gemeinschaft*]" and "society [*Gesellschaft*]".[17]

Community is a form of social organization typified by direct, personal interaction—often, but not exclusively, work—in which small-scale fraternal or guild organization plays a decisive role in reflecting back to community members their solidarity.[18] The word "normative" is thrown around nowadays to refer to any constraint that can be internalized by agents as providing a measure for conduct, but it is misleading to categorize social constraint in communities as normative. Such constraint does not obtain due to inculcation of a *rule*. In communities, social constraint is typically expressed in terms of exemplarity and practices of social identification. Structuring human interaction primarily in terms of rules causes agents to regard themselves as significant to the extent that their conduct conforms to abstract generalities. They thereby value themselves in terms of regularity and constrain their self-understanding to the existing roles they fulfill. Societies, accordingly, enforce strict division of labor and role separation, both of which undermine human diversity. Community better serves development of diverse human capacities without requiring individuals to think of discrete social roles as defining them. This may leave the impression that communities cannot nurture individuals with strong senses of subjective vocation. But it is mistaken to conclude that community is devoid of individuality. It *is* the case that communities lack the type of individuality that modern societies encourage: the atomistic individual for whom maximizing return on subjective preference is a be-all and end-all.

For Landauer, one develops a greater relation to oneself by acting or working among others, where there is inherent meaningfulness of one's product through one's cooperative contribution to oneself and others. He calls this "daily activity [*Werktätigkeit*]".[19] This is not a technical term of Landauer's invention, but he intends an emphatic sense of "active [*tätig*]" with philosophical roots in Fichte and Goethe.[20] The "act [*Tat*]" in this tradition is understood as an aboriginal and autonomous form of human sentience. Because Landauer stresses the drive *within one* to know one's hopes, desires, and beliefs for what they are in order to gainfully contrast them with the standing order of things, such subjective activities are part of *Werktätigkeit*. Landauer alleges that this form of social tie was present in medieval Europe and persists in modernity only at the margins.

Thinking of ways things might be radically otherwise requires exercises of imagination. But, as already mentioned, imagination typically is constrained as to both its form and content by historically available materials and regimens. This boundedness is easy to miss if one takes it that imagination is typically free, that it is the human capacity that cannot be so dominated. But the idea that the imagination is free by default is an illusion; accordingly, use of imagination that is properly critical will check itself against such limitations. Since historical conditions are constantly changing, circumspection on this count will be continual. Any utopian thought worth its salt will carry within it *as utopian* this hesitancy concerning form and focus. How best to model this tentative yet idealizing form of thought? The early German Romantics forwarded a number of procedures. Novalis proposed what he called "romantization [*Romantizierung*]", a discursive technique in which one pushes what is familiar toward strangeness by divesting it of its common predicates and what is strange toward the familiar by investing it with the same.[21] The Jena Romantics held such procedures to be indicative of thinking experienced in its fundamental form and, therefore, of subjectivity itself. This purportedly enables a unique form of sociality in which imaginative intercourse is the basic relation. Landauer's juxtaposition of topia and utopia, which inverts the order of precedence between the here-and-now and the what-might-be, is a similar procedure. One expects that "utopia" will refer to an exceptional, perhaps impossible, state. Topias would then be unexceptional, perhaps the only possible states. And, in a way, that is correct. Topias are the only possible *states*, because states require fixity. Utopia is a no-state, a "no-place". Rather, it is a current that runs through all forms of human agency.

Recall that Landauer deploys what he takes to be exemplary set-pieces to display the slippage between utopia and topia, that is, the degree to which a given topia fails to live up to the utopian impulse that gave rise to it. The unhinging of utopia from topia occurs because utopian impulses outrun the places they have created. This is somewhat akin to what Hegel holds is the case with *Geist*, a term Landauer sometimes uses to gloss utopia. What sort of article might Landauer have in mind here? It would consist in an exemplar that is concentrated enough and different enough from the run-of-the-mill to provide the necessary unmistakable contrast, an imaginative idealization of uncommon power.

One usually thinks of anachronism as a species of error, rendering as it does the unfamiliar in terms of the familiar by reading the present back into the past. Suppose one holds that history is a narrative structure retrospectively constructed by means of the following heuristic: understand as significant those aspects of the past that have issued in the stability of the present. This form of selection perforce leaves out much, and crucially it may leave out those aspects of the past that were cast aside as worthless in their own times (or in times subsequent). It would not *have to* do so of course; the picture on offer does not rule out that those features held to be significant in the present might have been unrecognized in the past as significant for *that* present. But historical evidence is dependent on past preservation, and being selected for preservation may depend in turn on being regarded as important, either now or for posterity. The point is that things may be considered worthless because they do not fit in with majority tastes, and things may not so fit in on account of their being implicitly or explicitly critical of that taste. One ordinarily thinks of anachronism as running from the present to the past, but it can operate in reverse, from the past into the present. *Productive anachronism* involves the removal of an item or event from the narrative continuum of the past and the insertion of it, out of time, in the present. Inserting the overlooked past in the present accentuates a lack of fit with a present that understands itself to rest unproblematically on the past. The aim is to increase critical impact; that is the sense in which the anachronism is productive. Juxtaposition of something so out of joint with the present may cause one to reconstruct the conditions under which the thing expresses what turned out to be a suppressed imaginative vision. Such reconstruction would have to circumvent the usual conditions on historical reconstruction, which take the past to be sufficiently settled as to its content so that the content may be conceptually refined.

Productive anachronism is one of Landauer's preferred forms of idealization, one that he holds is less apt to be assimilated to standard modes of imaginative responsiveness than others that are more straightforwardly discursive. He is intensely attracted to the idea that historical eddies and backwaters may be tapped for critical purposes and fashions a view of the nature of history and temporality in support of the attraction.[22] The idea that official history shunts ephemera that may register lost potential was no oddity in Central European thought of the time, nor was speculative reconstruction of the conditions under which such material might be retrieved. Jung, Klages, Heidegger, and others feature versions of the thought and, as we shall see, so do Benjamin and Adorno. This is, again, a romantic inheritance: one might consider Novalis's, Schlegel's, Hölderlin's, and Schelling's calls for "new mythology" to be exercises in such retrieved exemplarity.[23] For Landauer productive anachronisms both initiate introspective rooting out of social pathology within one's own character and insert in the present, alongside authoritarian forms of governance, historically anti-canonical social alternatives.[24]

## 2  Benjamin and Messianic Anti-history

Standard accounts of how one deepens historical understanding hold that one does so by providing more in the way of relevant context. A modification, stemming from R. G. Collingwood's idea of re-enactment, is that one also tries to use the added context to enhance one's understanding of the world from the point of view of the historically situated agent.[25] This involves establishing continuity, both within the contemporaneous historical domain and from that domain to the present. Adjust as one might for the specificity of the historical object, one cannot help but project continuity with the present onto it. Benjamin suggests that, while this may be a presupposition of normal modes of historical understanding, such understanding cannot be revolutionary. The overriding demand for continuity inhibits the deepest and most unsettling ways of treating the past as a present source for possibility. Understanding the past, present, and future as paratactic—that is, as radically non-assimilated in terms of one another—is Benjamin's prescription for both individual and social remediation and forms the crux of his conception of "dialectic at a standstill [*Dialektik im Stillstand*]" or, what is more or less the same thing, dialectical "images [*Bilder*]".[26] Carefully crafted juxtaposition of a chosen item plucked out of its historical place and time with items in the present introduces needed tension in the present in terms of its past. As with Landauer, the items are chosen because the present has written them out of its own history. Much of this marginalizing will have occurred in the past, that is, in the present of the item sought to be resuscitated. Accordingly, the first step in selecting the item is to isolate its non-dominated form, and this requires decontextualizing it from those relations, both synchronic and diachronic, that have served to sideline it. This radical decontextualization permits one to lift the item from its past and transplant it in the present with singular effect. Because the item has been made to shed the very context that would make it continuous with the present, it presents itself in the present as alien, as out-of-sync. It is not of the past of *this* present. One is, in essence, showing the item to be of another possible past from the perspective of this present and, thus, as of the actual past of another possible present. Were the item to have "won out" in the past, the present would be different. This opens the possibility of an equally radical recontextualization of the present in terms of what it might have otherwise. It is crucial from Benjamin's perspective that this challenge be issued by *sheer* juxtaposition. The two components are unconnected; they merely co-instantiate. He insists on this because of the coordinate concern that any relatedness between the present and past will tempt assimilation one to the other, reestablishing historical continuity, thereby sacrificing critical purchase. Confronting the present with its forgotten past, accordingly, cannot dictate to the present a set of recontextualizing relations. All it can do is disturb complacency. This non-assimilating tension is the key to Benjamin's conceptions of both dialectic and revolution.

One could do worse than to consider Benjamin's idea of the dialectical image in terms of reification. When Marx introduces the idea of commodity fetishism—the basis for Lukács' treatment of reification—he cautions that in order to make this power of commodity comprehensible "we must take refuge in the misty realm of the religious world [*wir müssen in die Nebelregion der religiösen Welt flüchten*]".[27] Marx means to stress that the predominance of exchange-value sunders the product from producer, rendering the product a new sort of object. Such objects, stranded from practical value, confront one as if they transcend practicality as such, as if their nature were divorced from making—a reverse animism. Benjamin stresses this religious dimension.[28] To overcome commodification, all but closed around itself and seemingly unavoidable, one might confront commodity structure with dead commodity, such as Benjamin liked to extract from the Parisian arcades. It is especially hard to assimilate one's corpse precisely because it is both you and not you. Instead, one undergoes a "shock experience [*Chockerlebnis*]".[29] The implications for historical time, he thinks, are significant. What he calls "now-time [*Jetztzeit*]"[30] is placed side-by-side with "the present [*die Gegenwart*]". The latter is a conception of "now" that homogenizes time qualitatively as the advancing movement of same interval to (next) same interval. "The present", that is, sustains temporal continuity by means of increment-sameness.[31] The former is "messianic"; it is the "now" conceived as a continual point of potential break in sequence. It is as if a "shard [*Scherbe*]" of eternity—of timelessness—were driven into the temporal sequence.[32]

The kinship with Landauer is evident. The contrast between topia and utopia also calls for a radical isolation of past from present. One must dislodge what is past from the standard run of history in order that it have critical potential. One must see it as both not-present and present simultaneously. In that way lies the future. When it collects itself into a revolutionary moment, the utopian impulse all but sunders itself from the assimilated past. Landauer hopes that humanity is poised for yet another such moment. Consider in this light Benjamin on Klee's *Angelus Novus* (1920):

> There is an image [*Bild*] by Klee called *Angelus Novus*. In it an angel is presented [*dargestellt*] looking as if he were about to move away from something upon which he is gazing. His eyes are wide open, his mouth ajar, and his wings spread.

> The angel of history must look like that. He has turned his face towards the past. Where a chain of events appears [*erscheint*] before *us*, *he* sees there one single catastrophe that incessantly piles rubble upon rubble, hurling it in front of his feet [*sie ihm vor die Füße schleudert*]. The angel would like perhaps to linger, awaken the dead, and conjoin what has been smashed to pieces. But a storm is blowing from paradise that is caught up in his wings and is so strong that the angel can no longer close them. The storm drives [*treibt*] him inexorably into the future, to which he turns his back, while the pile of rubble before him grows skyward. *This* storm is what we call progress [*Fortschritt*].[33]

Think of the angel as a divine witness, sent hurtling backward by the gale of primordial catastrophe. The winds originated long ago, perhaps at the inception of time itself, and continue unabated over the expanse of all that has been. The angel is helpless against them, its wings pinned open by their force. The angel is turned toward the catastrophe and thus toward the past; its back faces the future. It regards with stunned horror the trail of wreckage. It is not that the past is one thing and the wreckage is another; the past is nothing but the unfolding of catastrophe. If one were being strict, there has been only one event—catastrophe. By implication, catastrophe is the fabric of historical time, its quality. The future is precisely not a domain upon which one may project possibilities relative to present actuality, for the present is nothing more than forced-backward catastrophic movement and, for that reason, is captive to the ever expanding past. The angel may wish to bend down and reconnect the fragments of existence, to stop catastrophe, to turn around to fly toward the future under its own power, but that is impossible. To piece together the fragments would be to annul time itself.

This is a dialectical image, an image of progress. All progress amounts to is banked retrogression. Breaking the hold of catastrophe would require introduction of an element ulterior to existence—not merely something that does not yet exist, but something that is contrary to existence, cannot exist at all. This is contradiction in the sense that bothered medieval European logicians. From a contradiction anything follows (including further contradiction), and if anything follows, then there is nothing that binds the world together. Armageddon. Truly divine intercession could only be incomprehensible from the standpoint of one situated within existence. That divinity would have to interpose itself on the catastrophe in a form that is existentially impossible and yet active in that realm. It would have to be, that is, messianic. The thought Benjamin is entertaining here is apparently darker than Landauer's. Is this a matter of difference or of degree? For Landauer, history being utopian does not mean at all that it is progressive or that revolutionary moments are frequent. For the most part, history is repressive *even though* it is utopian. For Benjamin, the primordial catastrophe, the entirety of the past, piles wreckage at the angel's feet and stunts its actions. But the angel is *there*, protecting as best it can. Perhaps it is more accurate to see Benjamin and Landauer as two expressions of a single thought. Radical criticism must be circumspect, willing to face the enormity of what is presented to it and suspicious that it is ever finished its task. Would Landauer deny this gloss of the romantic desideratum of infinite deferral?[34] It seems unlikely, given the stress he lays on critical introspection. But radical criticism must also be a form of hope, for there have been utopian forms of ideology lodged in history that one can expropriate under the right conditions. Would Benjamin deny this? It seems unlikely, given his views on historical redemption.

## 3 Novalis and Productive Anachronism

Aspects of Landauer's and Benjamin's conceptions of historical time, revolution, and the dialectical function of images stem from romantic doctrines having to do with the centrality of inverse reflective practices. This is patent in the case of Benjamin, the topic of whose dissertation was the aesthetics of the Jena Circle, but it is present in Landauer as well. Even more pervasive is the common concern spanning anarchism, Critical Theory, and early German Romanticism to limn religious thought in order to check perceived encroachments of instrumental reason, rationalization, and reification.

Consider Novalis' pamphlet *Christianity, or Europe* as an example of productive anachronism.[35] The tract is sometimes taken to be a paean to a medieval unity that never was, but it is a good deal more than that. The essay considers what Novalis and other early German Romantics found to be a link between advances in the theory of the physical sciences and untoward results in the breakdown of the Holy Roman Empire. Roughly speaking, although there is further subdivision present in the essay, Novalis partitions the history of his subject matter into three epochs. The first is a time in the European Middle Ages where the Roman Church provided a fully harmonized form of life, in which the paternalistic constraint Christianity placed upon scientific knowledge was calibrated carefully to answer to the capacity of the faithful to incorporate such knowledge in a way that did not compromise its harmony with faith.[36] Novalis is vague about timeframe; he identifies large-scale war as the point of breakdown of this period, so one might take the Hundred Years' War (c. 1337–1453) as its *terminus ad quem*. Of course, no one would agree that medieval Europe from the fifth through the fourteenth centuries was an impeccable system of Christian joy, but that is not at issue. Novalis is positing an ideal, not entering a factual report—a prelapsarian world that miraculously evanesces in the Middle Ages. His conception of this structure as an overarching "high guild [*hohe Zunft*]" to which each belongs is a way to rotate imaginatively the corporate structure of the Church toward a more democratic and local model of artisanal production. A second phase sees the structure dissipate under the dual advances of natural science and the advent of the nation state.[37] The sciences reduce the world to what is measurable and considered apart from supernatural origin. Although Novalis might have gone so far as to think of the thoroughgoing materialism of La Mettrie or Helvétius as the logical conclusion of this period (he does allude to the *philosophes* as a group), he seems to have in mind for this role deism's idea of a "watchmaker god", that is, a being that creates the world and then steps back from it in an act of benign indifference. This reduction finds a political correlate in nationalistic wars of commercial opportunity, the Hundred Years' War already mentioned and, one might presume, the Thirty Years' War (c. 1618–48), which exceeded even it in religious spleen and indiscriminate carnage. The development that such hostilities track is of course the Reformation. Here the main actor is Luther, whose impact was progressive, but at a cost. Rebellion against the corrupt Church was correct, but the deinstitutionalization of Christianity that followed and the insistence on the ultimate superiority of internalized religious experience over rite and practice exposed faith to political colonization in the form of religion-specific nations that were more or less subject to the whims of kings.[38]

Out of this springs the possibility of a third epoch, in which religion again will take the lead. The conditions that Novalis identifies as progressive are indebted to Lutheran notions of subjectivity, that is, the philosophical positions of Lessing, Kant, Fichte, and Schelling.[39] He proposes that his own time is on the cusp of realizing a new, more advanced unity of knowledge and faith and prepared to establish an international moral and political order of near perfection.[40] "True anarchy [*wahrhafte Anarchie*]" is the creative element of such religious activity.[41] He appears to be of two minds concerning the continuing role of Christianity in establishing such a utopia, or even in thinking about it. He seems to consider the term "Christianity" to be a term of art neutral with regard to religious doctrine, indicating rather the required relation between the faithful and their faith, that is, a "joyous" one in which one experiences one's freedom directly.[42] Within the space of a few sentences, however, he asserts that Christian *doctrine* is uniquely tuned to the required experience. A heady brew, and much must be taken on credit as there is not an argument to be seen, although there is a (rudimentary) form of historical dialectic.

This idealized Middle Ages might well count for Benjamin as an extended dialectical image or for Landauer as utopian thought. This is not because Novalis discusses specific social and political aims that appeal to critical theorists or anarchists. Rather, the pamphlet is relevant in that it is an entry in the genre of conjectural history, remarkable in that it mythologizes actual history, that is, it does not operate with already-mythic materials provided by Abrahamic religions that characterize many narratives in this genre. From Benjamin's perspective, however, Novalis' conjecture proves half-short of bold. He complains in his dissertation that the Jena Romantics have a teleological agenda—a symbolic and, therefore, progressive conception of how human knowledge converges on "the Absolute". And it must be said, Novalis' essay reads this way. As we saw, for Benjamin the required form of utopian thinking is to posit something on the order of a paradox, something that is not only exceptional when judged against the run-of-the-mill, but something of another order altogether, something that explodes the domain of possible experience. Benjamin concludes in his *Trauerspielbuch* that symbolic representation of utopia must give way to allegory, a form of discourse in which there is no reference whatsoever to what constitutes utopia, merely a hermeneutic gloss on what might do so. Landauer's reaction to early German Romantic idealizations is considerably more tolerant. He does not press the iconoclastic point so severely; scenarios like the one *Christianity, or Europe* forwards are not, for him, insufficiently skeptical concerning the very prospect of human realization of utopia. Landauer faults not the idealization, but the idealizer. The early German Romantics did not demand enough of themselves to put their program into action. To be sure, being insufficiently motivated also results in putting forward an insufficient vision, and this comes close to Benjamin's complaint in substance if not in form. These misgivings aside, Benjamin and Landauer agree that the early German Romantics were serious utopian thinkers, whose efforts are a promising point of departure from which to begin again.

# 4 Coda: Adorno's Share

Adorno, whose jabs at the student movement began this chapter, developed his thought in close quarters with Benjamin. An adequate account of his romantic-anarchist debt is not possible here, but consider the following excerpt from his inaugural lecture at the Institute for Social Research in 1931:

> [T]he idea of science is research; that of philosophy is interpretation [*Deutung*]. In this remains the great, perhaps the perpetual paradox: philosophy, ever and always with the claim of truth, must proceed interpretatively without ever possessing a sure key to interpretation: nothing more is given to it than fleeting, disappearing traces [*flüchtige, verschwindende Hinweise*] within the ciphers [*Rätselfiguren*] of what is and their wondrous entwining. The history of philosophy is nothing other than the history of such entwining. That is why it reaches so few 'results', why it must always begin anew, and why it cannot do without the slightest thread that the dim and distant past [*Vorzeit*] has spun, which might complete the literature that transforms the ciphers into text.[43]

And this from his signature work, published twenty years later:

> The only philosophy that can be responsibly practiced in the face of despair would be the attempt to contemplate all things as they would present themselves from the standpoint of redemption [*vom Standpunkt der Erlösung aus sich darstellten*]. Knowledge [*Erkenntnis*] has no light but that shed on the world by redemption: all else is reconstruction, remains a bit of technique. Perspectives must be produced that both displace [*sich versetzt*] and estrange [*verfremdet*] the world, reveal [*offenbart*] it to be, with its rifts and crevices [*Risse und Schründe*], as indigent and distorted [*bedürftig und entstellt*] as it will appear one day in the messianic light [*in Messianischen Lichte daliegen wird*]. To gain such perspectives without willfulness or violence [[*o*]*hne Willkür und Gewalt*], entirely from the felt contact with objects [*aus der Fühling mit den Gegenständen heraus*]—this alone is the task of thought.[44]

The stamp of Benjamin on both passages is unmistakable and, with it, the influx of ideas from early German Romanticism and the form of anarchism important to Benjamin and Landauer. The task of philosophy, its "present relevance", is to rescue the critical potential of the systematically overlooked, items that appear only fleetingly given the onrush of what occludes them. Against the background of traditional modes of explanation, they appear as occult trace-effects of culture, presenting themselves to understanding as riddle-like "figures". Even more redolent of Romanticism, thought must estrange the world in order to denature it, but doing so requires thinking of objects as multivalent sources of felt meaning, not merely as observational posits. Only redeeming bits of the past as the bits they are is justifiable. The critical theorist, that is, stands in for Klee's angel.

Adorno eventually parted company with Benjamin when it came to dialectical method, unable to accept the claim that the motor of the utopian impulse must be construed as revelation withheld. He held Benjamin's position to be perilously close to fascist notions of naïve insight and communal immersion. But reliance on religious modes of thought to offer critical resistance to consumerism, the contention that philosophical systematics requires non-closure around given concepts, the idea that fragmentary philosophical writing best conveys one's subjectivity, and the use of the past to upset and temper the present all token an ongoing indebtedness to Romanticism in early Critical Theory that lasts well into the 1960s. That Adorno and others in the Frankfurt School would dismiss its neo-romantic cousin, anarchism, with a swipe at undergraduate students is unfortunate. Anarchism may have seemed to Adorno like a specter, but closer attention to it and its connections to Critical Theory might have revealed that, in the end, Novalis was correct: "[w]here there are no gods, specters rule".[45]

# Notes

1. Citation to Novalis is to *Schriften*, ed. P. Kluckhohn and R. Samuel (Stuttgart: Kohlhammer, 1960 ff.) [=NS], by volume number, followed by page number. Parallel citation to: *The Early Political Writings of the German Romantics*, ed. & trans. F. Beiser (Cambridge: Cambridge University Press, 1996) [=EW] or to *Philosophical Writings*, trans. & ed. M. M. Stoljar (Albany: SUNY Press, 1997) [=PW]. Citation to Benjamin is to *Gesammelte Schriften*, ed. R. Tiedemann and H. Schweppenhäuser (Frankfurt a/M: Suhrkamp, 1974 ff.) [=BGS], by volume number, followed by page number. Parallel citation to: *Selected Writings*, ed. & trans. M. Bullock, H. Eiland & M. Jennings (Cambridge, MA: Harvard Belknap, 1996–2003) [=BSW], by volume number, followed by page number or to *The Arcades Project*, ed. & trans. H. Eiland & K. McLaughlin (Cambridge, MA: Harvard Belknap, 2002) [=A]. Citation to Landauer is to *Ausgewählte Schriften*, ed. S. Wolf (Hessen: Verlag Edition AV, 2008 ff.) [=LAS], by volume number, followed by page number. I have modified translations where necessary.
2. 'Resignation' [1969], *Gesammelte Schriften*, ed. R. Tiedemann (Frankfurt/M: Suhrkamp, 1977), 10.2: 797/*Critical Models*, trans. H. Pickford (New York: Columbia University Press, 1998), 292.
3. Marx and Engels write that communism is a specter haunting Europe ([*e*]*in Gespenst geht um Europa—ein Gespenst des Kommunismus*). 'Manifest der kommunistichen Partei', in: *Marx-Engels-Werke*. Berlin: Dietz, 1962), 4: 461/'Manifesto of the Communist Party', in: *Later Political Writings*, ed./trans. T. Carver (Cambridge: Cambridge University Press, 1996), 1. In saying this, they are concerned to point out that Europe is dealing with a bogeyman

version of communism, conjured up in order to hunt down. Marx and Engels offer the *Manifesto* as a flesh-and-blood corrective.
4. *Eros and Civilization* (Boston: Beacon, 1966), 218.
5. A neologism that Fourier coins by combining the Greek φάλαγξ with the French *monastère*. The term refers to an architectural form allegedly best suited to eliciting the 'passionate mutuality' required for freely chosen communal cooperation. Phalansteries are perhaps the most abiding legacy of Fourier; several utopian communities in Europe and the United States featured such structures.
6. It is difficult to tell precisely what role Landauer's thought played in Benjamin's formation. The most exhaustive biography of Benjamin mentions Landauer only once in passing. See Howard Eiland and Michael Jennings, *Walter Benjamin: A Critical Life* (Cambridge, MA: Harvard Belknap, 2014), 122. Benjamin seems to have heard of Landauer through Scholem, who reports Benjamin's interest in Landauer and freely characterizes his own shared political concern with Benjamin (in the seminal year 1919) as 'theokratischer Anarchismus'. See *Walter Benjamin—die Geschichte einer Freundschaft* (Frankfurt/M: Suhrkamp, 1975), 19–20, 22, 108. Benjamin's own preferred term to describe his political position at this time was 'nihilism'. See Benjamin to Scholem, 16. IX. 1924, Walter Benjamin, *Briefe*, ed. G. Scholem and T. W. Adorno (Frankfurt/M: Suhrkamp, 1993), 1: 355. Benjamin associates the term with Friedrich Schlegel, one might assume, on the basis of Schlegel's conceptual proximity to F. H. Jacobi.
7. The background of early Critical Theory and of early twentieth-century philosophy and social science more generally in the vibrant and complex intellectual life of German Jewish culture is a subject too demanding to treat here. A good overview is Jack Jacobs, *The Frankfurt School, Jewish Lives, and Antisemitism* (Cambridge: Cambridge University Press, 2015), chapter 1.
8. It is sometimes assumed that Hitler, also present in Munich at this time, was a member of the *Freikorps*. Not so; he was assigned to a regular army unit.
9. It does not follow from this that anarchism forbids religion as such, either as a manner of individual conscience or as a group practice. Pacifistic anarchism can be explicitly religious (e.g. Tolstoy).
10. See E. J. Hobsbawm, *Primitive Rebels: Studies in Archaic Forms of Social Movement in the 19th and 20th Centuries* (New York: Norton, 1959), 74–92.
11. *Die Revolution*, LAS, 13: 56.
12. In other words, Landauer is deploying the idea of place in order to circumvent what he takes to be spatial conceptions of time, according to which time is essentially quantitatively incremental. Not thinking of time on the order of space was a mainstay of German/Central European philosophy of the time. Heidegger is the most famous representative of this line. See the discussion of a similar concern in Benjamin, below § 2.
13. LAS 13: 66–7.

14. LAS 13: 73. The idea of impulse (*Impuls*), or drive (*Trieb*), is of central importance to Landauer, placing him in a historical line with figures like Schiller, Schelling, Schopenhauer, and Nietzsche. Landauer also considers Eckhart, Spinoza, and Leibniz to be predecessors in this regard. Detailing the various conceptions of drives in this literature is an extremely complex matter to which I cannot hope to do justice here.
15. This must be distinguished from the line running through Blanqui, Bakunin, and Sorel according to which revolution is *sui generis* on account of its relation to 'creative' violence. Landauer expressed compassion for violent revolutionaries, but was himself a pacifist.
16. Cf. John Dunn, *Modern Revolutions: An Introduction to the Analysis of a Political Phenomenon* (Cambridge: Cambridge University Press, 1972), 18.
17. It is unclear whether Landauer read *Gemeinschaft und Gesellschaft*. I have not encountered mention of it in his work, nor is such knowledge noted in any of the several biographies of Landauer, the most recent of which (Tilman Leder, *Die Politik eines "Antipolitikers"* (Hessen: Verlag Edition, 2014)) is exhaustive to a fault. It is hard to imagine, however, that Landauer was completely unaware of Tönnies's views and would not have found them congenial. The second edition of the book appeared in 1912 and became an intellectual sensation, a virtual handbook for neo-Romantics.
18. See *Aufruf zum Sozialismus*, LAS 11: 138–40; 'Volk und Land: Dreißig sozialistische Thesen', LAS 3.1: 109–22. Landauer's appeal to *Bünde* as primary forms of collective is another point of connection with Tönnies.
19. LAS 13: 90–1.
20. That is, in Fichte's conception of the *Tathandlung* and in Faust's translation of λόγος as 'Tat' (John 1:1). See *Wissenschaftslehre*, in *Fichtes sämmtliche Werke*, ed. H. Fichte (Berlin: de Gruyter, 1971), I: 468 [Zweite Einleitung § 5] and *Faust, Erster Teil*, 1224–37.
21. NS 2: 384/PW 60 [Fr. 37/66]. Friedrich Schlegel offered a theory of irony with much the same effect.
22. Fritz Mauthner's *Beiträge zur Sprachkritik* (1901–3) was a lasting influence on Landauer's development of these ideas. See *Skepsis und Mystik. Versuche im Anschluß and Mauthners Sprachkritik*, LAS 7: 42–7, 64–8; see also ibid. 148–68, 191–201, 206–7. Landauer is following Mauthner when he writes that the realization that human action vastly outstrips its record in history mandates treating all history as more or less contemporaneous and, accordingly, contemporary. Landauer changes the idea in part, offering a tripartite scheme of history in terms of how contemporary it is. Only the last historical epoch—what Landauer calls *die eigene Geschichte*—is philosophically pertinent. See LAS 13: 69, 71 ff. This is the history of Christianity. The idea that Christianity demarcates modern thought is common to Schlegel, Novalis, and Hegel, but its proximate source is likely the theologian-sociologist Ernst Troeltsch, although Landauer does not name him as a source.

Landauer may also take from Troeltsch the idea that the most pertinent strain of Christianity is medieval Roman Catholicism and that modern life has incrementally marginalized its valuable social resources.

23. See Manfred Frank, *Der kommende Gott* (Frankfurt/M: Suhrkamp, 1982) for a detailed consideration of the idea and its history.
24. This introspective, even solitary, dimension in Landauer is very strong. He finds precedent not only in the usual European sources, but also in Emerson. 'Ein paar Worte über Anarchismus', LAS 2: 224.
25. R. G. Collingwood, *The Idea of History* (Oxford: Clarendon Press, 1946), chap. V, § 3. I have in mind the so-called Cambridge School, for example, John Dunn, Peter Laslett, J. G. A. Pocock, and Quentin Skinner.
26. See *Passagen-Werk*, BGS V.1: 576–7, 595/A 462, 475 [¶¶ N2a.3, N10a.3].
27. *Marx-Engels Werke*, 23: 86/ *The Marx-Engels Reader*, 2d ed., ed. R. Tucker (New York: Norton, 1978), 321.
28. See, for instance, the early fragment 'Kapitalismus als Religion' BGS VI: 100–2.
29. See 'Über einige Motive bei Baudelaire', BGS I.2: 653/SW 4: 343; see also 'Über den Begriff der Geschichte', BGS I.2: 703/SW 4: 396 [§ XVII].
30. 'Über den Begriff', BGS I.2: 703/SW 4: 396 [§ XVIII]; see also ibid., BGS I.2: 702/SW 4: 396 [§ XVI]; *Passagen-Werk*, BGS V.1: 490–1/A 388–9 [¶ K1.2]. It is sometimes supposed that Benjamin is coining a neologism here; he is not. In ordinary German *Jetztzeit* means 'nowadays'. Benjamin is merely repurposing the word. Cf. Adorno's use of *Vorzeit*, discussed below.
31. Cf. note 12, above.
32. Benjamin rejects the Hegelian proposition that discursive contradiction is the motor of dialectic. Of course, Hegel's final account of conceptuality denies that concepts are arrived at merely by subsuming particulars. The point remains, however, that dialectical progression at many, if not most, of its points deals 'on the ground' with the understanding's mode of conceptuality, not reason's. Dialectics at a standstill is, in essence, an attempt at dialectical ἐποχή, that is, a dialectical suspension of dialectic.
33. 'Über den Begriff', BGS I.2: 697–8/SW 4: 392 [§ IX]. This is not the place to discuss the several layers of meaning present in this passage. Suffice it to say that some of the vocabulary draws from philosophical terminology utilized in German idealism and Romanticism and that several terms have multiple connotations. Benjamin owned the Klee print, which Scholem inherited upon his death. It now resides in the permanent collection of the National Museum of Israel.
34. Cf. Landauer's reaction to Bloch's *Geist der Utopie*, which he considered beneath contempt. The main reason for this was what Landauer called the book's 'charlatan' conception of utopia. The basic issue between them, it seems, is that Bloch in this book considers utopia on the order of a Kantian regulative ideal, whose fulfillment entails its 'extinction' as he puts it, that is,

violation of its essential function as a principle requiring one to 'go further'. Bloch makes the point in an odd ontological register ill-suited to the Kantian thought and bordering on the paradoxical, that is, that realizing a utopia would mean it never would have been. I take it the main point is that fulfillment contradicts the semantics of Kantian regulative posits. Landauer, like Benjamin, views this as weak tea: the idea that utopia means 'not yet' is compatible with utopia meaning 'closer than before', indeed, 'infinitesimally close to'. That is, near convergence on truth is built into the Kantian idea (it is its lifeblood). That is too tepid and optimistic an idea for Landauer (and Benjamin).

35. The title is tricky to render. "Or [*oder*]" can be read as disjunctive, explicative, or both. I have inserted a comma in the title not present in the original German, in order to express my view that it is the explicative sense that is primary.
36. NS 3: 508–09/EW 62–3; cf. Landauer's comment on the essay at LAS 13: 70.
37. NS 3: 511–6/EW 65–71.
38. NS 3: 511/EW 65–6.
39. NS 3: 521–2/EW 75–6.
40. NS 3: 523–4/EW 77–9.
41. NS 3: 517/EW 72.
42. NS 3: 523–4/EW 78.
43. 'Die Aktualität de Philosophie', in: *Gesammelte Schriften*, 1: 334 /'The Actuality of Philosophy', trans. B. Snow *Telos* 31 [1977]: 126.
44. *Minima Moralia*, 21st ed. (Frankfurt/M: Suhrkamp, 1993), 333–4/*Minima Moralia*, tr. E. F. N. Jephcott (London: Verso, 1978), 247 [¶ 153]. The passage is rich in philosophical allusion: to Kant (*Erkenntnis, Willkür*), to Schelling (*darstellen, offenbaren*), to the Jena Romantics (*Fühling*), even to Heidegger (!) (*Riß*).
45. *Wo keine Götter sind, walten Gespenster.* NS 3: 517/EW 75. Thanks to Amy Allen, Raymond Geuss, Alex Honneth, Tom McCarthy, Brian O'Connor, and audiences at Dartmouth College and University College Dublin for helping me try to clarify the main ideas.

# 30

## Conclusion: Romantic Currents of Thought: An Open Ending

Elizabeth Millán Brusslan

As I mentioned in the introduction to this volume, the revival I noted in 2005 has only intensified in recent years. Several of the contributors to this volume have fueled the return to Romanticism. Fred Beiser has provided influential philosophical analyses of crucial ideas that shaped the period, investigating, for example, the meaning of German idealism, the relation between the *Aufklärung* and *Frühromantik*, and the nature of romantic *Poesie*.[1] Jacqueline Mariña has brought the thought of Schleiermacher into sharper focus both with her, *Transformation of the Self in the Thought of Friedrich Schleiermacher*, and the *Cambridge Companion to Fr. Schleiermacher*, which has essays by Frank, Beiser, and Bowie, all of which discuss the romantic dimensions of Schleiermacher's thought.[2] Robert Richards brought the early German Romantics into scientific circles with his, *The Romantic Conception of Life*, a major contribution to the field, which redeemed the scientific dimensions of romantic thought, with a narrative that successfully weaves together a compelling story of the path from Romanticism to Darwin.[3] Jocelyn Holland's, *German Romanticism and Science: The Procreative Poetics of Goethe, Novalis, and Ritter*, further develops the line of research that highlights the close connection between German Romanticism and the natural sciences.[4] Leif Weatherby's, *Transplanting the Metaphysical Organ: German Romanticism between Leibniz and Mark*, is another excellent contribution to the line of scholarship connecting early German Romanticism and the natural sciences.

E. Millán Brusslan (✉)
Department of Philosophy, DePaul University, Chicago, IL, USA

© The Author(s) 2020
E. Millán Brusslan (ed.), *The Palgrave Handbook of German Romantic Philosophy*, Palgrave Handbooks in German Idealism, https://doi.org/10.1007/978-3-030-53567-4_30

Weatherby focusses on the term "organ" and uses that term to conduct a focused discussion of life and metaphysical processes from Kant to Marx, with a special focus on the work of the German Romantics.[5]

A striking feature of much recent work in the field of German Romantic philosophy are the new lines of inquiry that are being opened. Jane Kneller's, *Kant and the Power of Imagination*, brings the early German Romantics, especially the work of Novalis and Hölderlin, into a productive dialogue with Kant. In her path-breaking volume, Kneller presents an account of Novalis' Kantianism and Kantian Romanticism, liberating Novalis from the traditional historical narrative according to which the early German Romantics are derivative thinkers.[6] In a similar liberatory vein, Fred Rush, in *Irony and Idealism: Rereading Schlegel, Hegel, and Kierkegaard*, presents an innovative and detailed account of irony, idealism, and Romanticism, bringing Hegel, Schlegel, and Kierkegaard into a conversation that illuminates aspects of the philosophical developments from the 1790s to the 1850s that are often left in the shadows.[7] Pol Vandevelde's, *Heidegger and Romanticism*, creates a richer context in which to understand the early German Romantics, Heidegger, and hermeneutics.[8]

New connections between romantic conceptions of nature and issues of gender have also been uncovered in the recent literature. Elaine Miller's, *The Vegetative Soul: From Philosophy of Nature to Subjectivity in the Feminine*, is a contribution that situates the postmodern critique of subjectivity in the concept of nature developed by the German Idealists and early German Romantics. Miller makes an original contribution to the problem of feminine subject formation by the convincing connection she draws between French feminist thought and the analysis of nature (as read through Goethe, Hölderlin, Hegel, and Nietzsche).

Alison Stone has also done important work to connect the work of the early German Romantics to issues about nature and gender and the relation between early German Romanticism and German Idealism. Her recent book, *Nature, Ethics, and Gender in German Romanticism and Idealism*, demonstrates just how relevant early German Romanticism is to contemporary environmental and social justice issues.[9] Dalia Nassar's, *The Romantic Absolute. Being and Knowing in Early German Romantic Philosophy*, 1795–1804, further contributes to the on-going debate around the relation between early German Romanticism and German Idealism, with a focus on three thinkers (Schlegel, Novalis, and Schelling) and their views of the Absolute.[10]

In addition to many excellent monographs that explore the romantic dimensions of early German Romanticism, several edited collections indicate that there is strong interest in the philosophical contributions of the early German Romantics. *The New Light of Early German Romanticism—Its*

*Innovations, Consequences and Contemporary Relevance (Das neue Licht der Frühromantik—Innovative philosophische Leistungen der Frühromantik, ihre Folgen und ihre Aktualität)*, that I co-edited with Bärbel Frischmann, brings together voices from the United States and Europe to discuss romantic contributions to science, poetry, religion, politics, and philosophy.[11] Nassar's edited collection, *The Relevance of Romanticism. Essays on German Romantic Philosophy*, is another volume that nicely highlights just how contemporary the concerns of the German Romantics remain.[12] Recently, Judith Norman and I co-edited, *Brill's Companion to German Romantic Philosophy*, a volume that highlights romantic contributions to religion, language, myth, *Bildung*, and irony.[13] Such collections have helped create a vibrant dialogue between early German Romanticism and the main currents of German philosophy. The trend of countenancing the contributions of the early German Romantics is evident in the second edition of Karl Ameriks' important, *Cambridge Companion to German Idealism*, which has even more material on the early German Romantics than the first edition contained.[14]

Manfred Frank's work has opened a lively debate concerning whether the early German Romantics are realists or idealists.[15] Rüdiger Bubner also produced works which shed philosophical light on the contributions of the early German Romantics. While Frank has focused more on Hölderlin, Novalis, Schlegel, and the work done in the pages of *Das Philosophisches Journal*, Bubner's work uncovers some of the connections between Schlegel, Hegel, and Goethe. Dieter Henrich's work on Hölderlin was path-breaking, and his *Konstellationsarbeit* has brought to light fascinating new connections between the leading thinkers of the period. The lines of scholarship opened by their work are still being developed and continue to shape the field of work in German Romanticism.

Translation work has been a key element in the growing appreciation of German Romantic philosophy. Kneller opened the field of early German Romanticism to a much broader audience with her translation of Novalis', *Fichte Studies*.[16] David Wood's excellent translation of Novalis, *Notes for a Romantic Encyclopaedia*, helped open new paths in the study of Novalis.[17] My 2004 translation of Manfred Frank's, *The Philosophical Foundations of Early-German Romanticism*, brought Frank's work to Anglophone readers, creating a richer context for the work of Schlegel, Novalis, Schelling, and Hölderlin to be read and understood.[18] Anna Ezekiel's translation of Karoline von Günderrode was long overdue and will help facilitate scholarship on the work of the women of early German Romanticism.[19] The role of women in early German Romanticism and their contributions is certainly an area that will see growth in the coming years.

All of this scholarship on the philosophical dimensions of *Frühromantik* can be seen as evidence for Schlegel's claim in Athenäum Fragment Nr. 116 that "Romantic poetry is a progressive, universal poetry...[it] is still in the state of becoming; that, in fact, is its real essence: that is should forever be becoming and never perfected."[20] In the work of the early German Romantics, we find a revolt against limits, an embrace of infinite longing and striving. Indeed, there is a romantic refusal of finitude, of closed systems, final words. As Martha Helfer indicates in the preface to her excellent collection, *Rereading Romanticism*, "[g]iven its programmatic mutability, Romantic discourse demands to be continuously reread."[21] To this insightful claim, I would add that the writings of the early German Romantics not only demand to be continuously re-read, but also *deserve* to be read and re-read by poets, scientists, and philosophers.

# Notes

1. See esp., *German Idealism: The Struggle against Subjectivism, 1791–1801* (Cambridge, MA: Harvard University Press, 2002) and *The Romantic Imperative: The Concept of Early German Romanticism* (Cambridge, MA: Harvard University Press, 2003).
2. See Jaqueline Mariña, *Transformation of the Self in the Thought of Fr. Schleiermacher* (Oxford: Oxford University Press, 2008) and *The Cambridge Companion to Schleiermacher* (Cambridge: Cambridge University Press, 2005).
3. Robert Richards, *The Romantic Conception of Life* (University of Chicago Press, 2002).
4. Jocelyn Holland, *German Romanticism and Science: The Procreative Poetics of Goethe, Novalis, and Ritter* (New York: Routledge, 2009).
5. Leif Weatherby, *Transplanting the Metaphysical Organ: German Romanticism between Leibniz and Marx* (New York: Fordham University Press, 2016).
6. Jane Kneller, *Kant and the Power of Imagination* (Cambridge University Press, 2007).
7. Fred Rush, *Irony and Idealism. Rereading Schlegel, Hegel, and Kierkegaard* (Oxford: Oxford University Press, 2016).
8. Pol Vandevelde, *Heidegger and the Romantics: The Literary Invention of Meaning* (New York: Routledge, 2012).
9. Alison Stone, *Nature, Ethics, and Gender in German Romanticism and Idealism* (London: Rowman and Littlefield, 2018).
10. Dalia Nassar, *The Romantic Absolute. Being and Knowing in Early German Romantic Philosophy, 1795–1804* (Chicago: University of Chicago Press, 2014).

## 30 Conclusion: Romantic Currents of Thought: An Open Ending

11. Bärbel Frischmann and Elizabeth Millán, eds., *The New Light of Early German Romanticism—Its Innovations, Consequences and Contemporary Relevance (Das neue Licht der Frühromantik—Innovative philosophische Leistungen der Frühromantik, ihre Folgen und ihre Aktualität)* (Paderborn: Schöningh Verlag, 2008).
12. Dalia Nassar, ed., *The Relevance of Romanticism* (Oxford: Oxford University Press, 2014).
13. Elizabeth Millán Brusslan and Judith Norman, eds., *Brill's Companion to German Romantic Philosophy* (Leiden: Brill, 2019).
14. Karl Ameriks, ed., *The Cambridge Companion to German Idealism*, Second Edition, (Cambridge: Cambridge University Press, 2017).
15. See Manfred Frank, *Unendliche Annäherung. Die Anfänge der philosophischen Frühromantik* (Frankfurt am Main: Suhrkamp, 1997). Part of this has been translated into English as *The Philosophical Foundations of early German Romanticism*, trans. Elizabeth Millán (Albany: SUNY Press, 2004). See also, *Auswege aus dem Deutschen Idealismus* (Frankfurt am Main: Suhrkamp, 2007).
16. Jane Kneller, ed./trans., *Fichte Studies* (Cambridge: Cambridge University Press, 2003).
17. David W. Wood, ed./trans., *Novalis. Notes for a Romantic Encyclopaedia/Das Allgemeine Brouillon* (Albany: SUNY Press, 2007).
18. Albany: SUNY Press, 2004.
19. Anna Ezekiel, ed./trans., *Karoline von Günderrode. Poetic Fragments* (Albany: SUNY Press, 2017).
20. KFSA 2, 182, Nr. 116/Firchow, 31–32.
21. See Martha B. Helfer, *Rereading Romanticism* (Amsterdam: Rodopi, 2000).

# Index[1]

## A

Absolute, The, 6, 9, 11, 29, 32, 35, 38n20, 38n27, 39n40, 45, 52, 66, 70–72, 74, 81, 82, 88, 89, 95, 96, 100, 104–108, 114, 115, 142, 148, 150, 152, 212, 214, 238, 250n18, 255, 257–261, 264–266, 267n5, 272, 274, 276–279, 281, 283, 288, 291n43, 296n119, 315n44, 322, 341n10, 392, 401, 402, 405, 421, 423, 425–428, 431, 432, 434, 436–440, 443, 452, 475, 480, 537, 539–541, 543, 548, 550, 551, 579, 583, 604n10, 613, 632, 634, 639, 641, 645–647, 654, 663, 697, 706

Adorno, Theodor, 15, 205, 653, 662, 665, 666, 674, 675, 678n7, 678n15, 678n17, 680n40, 683–685, 691, 697–699

Aenesidemus, 142, 143

Alexandrinus, Clemens, 578

Alienation, 44, 488, 550, 582, 598, 599

Allegory, 111, 277, 436, 452, 479, 489, 522, 564n8, 602, 675

Ameriks, Karl, 116n10, 229n59, 707

Anarchism, 12, 15, 223n5, 683–699

Aphorism, 19, 272–280, 282–288, 290n17, 290n32, 291n34, 293n67, 399, 402, 420n49, 425

Aristotle, 41, 258, 396n22, 416, 449, 587, 612, 615, 623, 627n38, 653

Arnim, Bettina von, 123, 125, 126, 129–130, 201n65, 493

Arnim, Ludwig Achim von, 13, 130, 201n65, 512, 517–519, 523, 524, 527

Asceticism, 162, 574

*Atheismusstreit*, 5, 42–44

*Athenäum* (journal), 4, 36n2, 97, 417n6, 654

---

[1] Note: Page numbers followed by 'n' refer to notes.

## B

Badiou, Alain, 423, 424
Bahnsen, Julius, 573
Beauty, 29, 32, 127, 158, 161, 162, 164, 166, 168–171, 175n42, 182, 190–194, 243, 244, 246, 257, 369, 375, 381, 452, 478, 507n117, 573, 623, 634–638, 641, 649, 650, 652, 654, 662, 665, 668, 669
Beck, J. S., 237, 417n1
Beethoven, Ludwig van, 588–590, 601
Behler, Ernst, 153n1, 257, 267n1, 298, 301, 304, 307, 308, 310, 311, 417n6, 464n1, 503n7, 562n1
Being, 5, 6, 8, 12, 51–53, 66, 96, 101–107, 109, 111–114, 123, 148, 277, 283, 286, 288, 299, 385, 406, 407, 424, 428, 432, 437, 451, 453, 457–464, 551, 558–560, 609–612, 618, 620, 622–624, 644–647, 673
Beiser, Frederick, 13, 14, 38n27, 72–74, 154n3, 159, 160, 229n59, 277, 282, 291n43, 444n14, 453, 705
Benjamin, Walter, 14, 15, 212, 298–301, 305–307, 310, 314n33, 315n48, 319, 320, 452, 466n17, 590, 627n36, 631–633, 635, 640, 645–648, 653, 654, 661–675, 676n3, 676n4, 677n5, 677n6, 677–678n7, 678n11, 678n15, 679n27, 679n30, 679–680n33, 680n34, 680n36, 680n40, 680–681n41, 684, 685, 691–695, 697, 698, 700n6, 700n12, 702n32, 702n33, 703n34
Berlin, Isaiah, 72
*Bildung*, 121, 124, 125, 127, 131n1, 132n6, 150, 170, 178, 180, 208, 241, 383, 385–391, 449, 457, 483, 490, 497, 498, 508n135, 707

Biology, 10, 343n33, 347–369, 450, 451, 454, 456, 462, 467n33, 524
Blumenbach, Johann Friedrich, 370n9, 386, 396n21, 396n22, 400, 455–457, 468n33, 515, 516, 522, 524, 527, 530n14, 531n24, 578–579
Blumenberg, Hana, 464n3
Breazeale, Daniel, 36n6, 58n9, 58n10, 59n14, 59n16, 59n19, 59n20, 60n22, 250n12, 507n95
Bubner, Rüdiger, 707

## C

Carus, Carl Gustav, 10, 11, 347–369, 463, 537, 538
Cassirer, Ernst, 529n4
Cervantes, Miguel de, 2, 241, 305
Christ/Christianity, 205, 218, 436–438, 440, 522, 523, 559, 565n12, 567n21, 611, 626n17, 695–697, 701–702n22
Classicism, 7, 125, 157, 177–184, 192–195, 198n29, 377, 384, 394, 588, 607
Coleridge, Samuel Taylor, 67, 76, 80, 88–91, 347, 465n4
Community, 3, 7, 35, 87, 119, 226n23, 265, 306, 319, 341n10, 429, 438, 530n14, 532n25, 532n28, 600, 638, 644, 651, 654, 686, 689, 700n5
Copernican Revolution, 29, 384
Critical theory, 2, 12, 15, 24, 182, 198n26, 301, 661–675, 683–699
Critique
    literary, 8, 233–248
    philosophical, 9, 20, 233–248, 276, 645

# Index

## D

Darwin, Charles, 11, 348, 363, 365–369, 468n33, 705
de Staël, Madame, 41, 131n1, 132n6, 136n22, 140n71
Descartes, Rene, 41, 70, 71, 74, 75, 78, 80–82, 84, 86, 89, 220, 381
Dialectic, 50, 56, 81, 82, 86, 120, 217, 324, 542–546, 593, 636, 643, 648, 680n34, 684, 693, 696, 702n32
Diderot, Denis, 83, 200n62

## E

Eschenmayer, Carl, 417n1
Evolutionary theory, 364–365, 367–369
Ezekiel, Anna, 12, 13, 447n63, 707

## F

Fatalism, 65, 67–69, 72, 88
Feeling, 27, 31–35, 95, 101, 103, 108–115, 158, 161–163, 165, 166, 175n39, 175n42, 182, 188–194, 201n65, 216, 218, 258, 273, 276, 311, 324, 327, 331, 334, 349, 359, 377, 379, 390, 405, 424, 425, 462, 483, 487, 489, 544, 549, 557, 569n30, 581, 588, 601, 610, 623, 624, 626n12, 632, 636, 638–640, 642, 645, 649, 654, 668, 671
Fichte, Johann Gottlieb, ix, 2, 5–8, 20, 21, 23, 26, 27, 29–31, 36n4, 37n9, 38n31, 41–48, 50–52, 56, 58n11, 59n16, 59n20, 60n22, 61n36, 66, 68–75, 82, 86, 87, 89, 96, 97, 99, 100, 103–106, 109–111, 113, 114, 116n10, 129, 141–153, 182, 196n6, 198n26, 205–222, 233–240, 242, 247, 291n43, 312n1, 321, 330, 341n10, 344n44, 380, 382, 383, 394, 399, 401, 402, 405, 418n10, 459, 490, 492, 498, 540, 544, 565n11, 565n13, 569n27, 577, 592, 593, 641, 642, 645, 647, 689, 696
*Tathandlung*, 27, 69, 99, 382, 701n20
*Wissenschaftslehre*, 5, 20, 23, 36n4, 42, 43, 46, 52, 56, 97, 99, 103, 141–143, 145, 146, 149, 152, 154–155n14, 214, 233, 236–240, 242, 247
Formalism, 468n33
Foucault, Michel, 211, 451, 461, 464, 564n9, 650
Foundationalism, 7, 66, 70, 89, 234, 295n106
anti-foundationalism, 66, 255
Fourier, Charles, 683, 700n5
Fragments, 2, 8, 9, 84, 104, 105, 107, 121, 190, 213–215, 226n25, 227n37, 239–242, 244, 247, 248, 255–266, 267n1, 268n17, 271–288, 303, 307, 308, 315n44, 322, 325, 329, 399, 405, 408, 410, 412–414, 425, 427, 484, 489, 528, 543, 551, 608, 613–618, 633, 634, 636, 638–641, 644, 646–654, 661, 675, 681n42, 694
and aphorisms, 272–276, 278–280, 284–286
Frank, Manfred, 36n4, 38n27, 66, 72, 97, 104, 214, 253n71, 278, 401, 403, 417n6, 532n25, 532n27, 628n49, 641, 646, 707
French Revolution, 3, 43, 44, 125, 174n33, 241, 312n1, 383, 384, 513, 518, 519, 523, 590

Freud, Sigmund, 13, 320, 322, 329, 341n11, 535, 536, 538, 551, 560, 561, 562n2, 563n8, 564–565n10, 567n24, 570n35, 570n36
Friedrich, Caspar David, 320, 321, 357–360
Friedrichsmeyer, Sara, 481, 483

G

Gasché, Rodolphe, 314n33, 633, 676–677n4, 677n6
*Geisteswissenschaften*, 8, 205–222
Gender, 12, 120, 127, 410, 443, 448n63, 475–492, 494, 497–502, 706
Geneaology, 578
Generation, 10, 11, 27, 28, 42, 100, 130, 179, 180, 195, 196n6, 201n65, 241, 310, 353, 362, 399–417, 451, 452, 468n33, 514, 515, 578
Genre, 84, 120, 141, 191, 243, 244, 248, 271, 273, 283, 286, 297, 299, 300, 387, 400, 404–407, 415, 423, 425, 430, 444n4, 452, 461, 464n3, 589, 590, 594, 596, 619, 633, 650, 652, 697
God, 5, 6, 13, 33, 38n27, 42, 44, 48, 50, 51, 59n16, 61n44, 62n54, 70, 72–74, 77, 78, 80, 84, 87–89, 91, 95, 102, 103, 108–110, 114, 169, 179, 181, 186, 187, 202n81, 207, 214, 218–222, 238, 263, 285, 288, 405, 432, 435, 436, 440, 461, 481, 520, 522, 523, 538–548, 551–552, 554–556, 558–562, 563n6, 563n7, 567n21, 567n24, 569n30, 570n35, 579, 580, 583, 602, 624, 637, 679n20

Goethe, Johann Wolfgang von, 10, 11, 41, 43, 51, 60n26, 75, 79, 80, 89, 123–125, 130, 136n28, 140n71, 149, 150, 157, 158, 178–181, 183, 189, 194, 195, 196n6, 199n33, 201n65, 229n59, 241–243, 263, 281, 282, 297–312, 347, 348, 350, 352, 357–365, 367, 368, 369n1, 369n3, 372n43, 372–373n44, 375–394, 408, 411, 419n31, 422, 430–432, 439, 467n33, 599, 614, 615, 640, 689, 706, 707
*Augenmensch*, 376
*Colour Theory*, 375
*Elective Affinities*, 377, 379, 383, 432
"The Experiment as Mediator between Object and Subject," 430
*Faust*, 123, 311, 380, 382, 383, 385, 439, 447n60
friendship with Schiller, 383–385
and metaphysics, 378–383, 392
*On Morphology*, 385, 394, 396n22
*The Sorrows of Young Werther*, 377
*Wilhelm Meister's Apprenticeship*, 10, 149, 150, 299, 301–305, 308, 310, 312, 313n11, 315n46, 383, 387, 388, 390, 391
Gottsched, Johann Christoph, 178, 240, 241, 244
Gunderröde, Karoline von, 12, 13, 141, 201n65, 422, 440–443, 447n63, 476, 493, 494, 498–502, 503n2, 707

H

Haller, Albrecht von, 450, 454, 455, 457, 468n33
Hamann, Johann Georg, 41, 183

Hardenberg, Friedrich von, *see* Novalis
Hartmann, Eduard von, 573–575, 580, 582
Hegel, G. W. F., ix, 6, 41, 51, 68–70, 74, 75, 81, 82, 86, 87, 90, 91, 96, 104, 105, 114, 141, 178, 196n6, 207, 215, 222n2, 248, 288, 295n109, 298, 303, 306, 311, 312, 315n48, 325, 342n16, 343n33, 380, 381, 394, 405, 430, 432, 461, 463, 537, 540, 563n6, 564n8, 565n11, 575, 577, 592, 597, 604n10, 612, 648, 652, 653, 679n28, 690, 701n22, 702n32, 706, 707
  *Phenomenology of Spirit*, 311
Heidegger, Martin, 12–14, 205, 206, 214, 423, 535, 540, 550, 551, 561, 562n2, 563n5, 567n22, 567n24, 569n27, 570n31, 570n32, 570n34, 607–625, 691, 700n12, 706
Heine, Heinrich, 79, 128, 384
Helfer, Martha, 154n3, 469n49, 491–493, 495, 503n2, 708
Henrich, Dieter, 96, 144–146, 154–155n14, 312n1, 341n10, 677n5, 707
Herder, Johann Gottfried, 5, 7, 8, 13, 41, 79, 80, 89, 123, 177–195, 382, 456, 457, 461, 514–517, 519, 521, 525, 528, 530–531n15, 531n17, 540
  *Humanität*, 181, 183–187, 192–195, 199n37
  *On the Cognition and Sensation of the Human Soul*, 189
  *Sculpture*, 8, 187–193, 197n21, 200n62, 201n71
Hermeneutics, 5, 8, 20, 119, 201n65, 205–222, 229n59, 244–246, 526, 564n8, 601, 608, 610–614, 616, 675, 676n2, 697, 706

Herz, Henriette, 6, 123, 125–127, 129, 136n22, 140n70, 493, 519
Herz, Marcus, 122, 126
Herzog, Werner, 10, 320, 321, 323–331, 334–336, 338–340, 341n7, 341n11, 528
Hoffmann, E. T. A., 328, 411, 477, 481
Hölderlin, Friedrich, 6, 88, 89, 96, 97, 104–106, 108, 141, 178, 180, 195, 201n65, 282, 329, 341n10, 405, 430, 432, 439, 440, 564n9, 592, 607, 619, 653, 663, 669, 670, 673, 676n3, 677n5, 679n30, 680n33, 680n34, 691, 706, 707
Holland, Jocelyn, 11, 430, 452, 459, 465n10, 705
Hollingdale, R. J., 273, 274
Horkheimer, Max, 15, 684
Humboldt, Alexander von, 13, 41, 127, 128, 180, 205, 223n4, 358, 359, 364, 365, 369, 370n9, 411, 456, 512, 517, 524–527, 532–533n29, 533n38
Humboldt, Wilhelm von, 41, 126, 178, 180, 189, 194, 195, 209, 211, 221, 223n4, 225n13, 225n15, 387
Husserl, Edmund, 107, 608, 675
Hypotyposis, 637

Idealism
  Fichte's, 97, 103
  German, ix, x, 2, 66–69, 72, 82, 233, 405, 430, 450, 453, 454, 582, 597, 702n33, 705
  Kant's, 29, 41, 70, 89, 96, 248, 451
  magical, 296n116, 428

Imagination, 32–36, 39n40, 77, 88–91, 103, 147, 169, 191, 275, 303, 320, 322, 323, 332, 335, 400, 402, 403, 427–429, 443, 464, 487, 525, 526, 538, 593, 631–633, 635–638, 641–644, 652, 687–690
Infinite, 4, 35, 45, 49, 51, 53, 72, 78, 80, 82, 86, 96, 103, 107, 110, 112, 113, 145, 146, 150, 151, 206, 226n28, 227n37, 255, 259, 262, 264, 278, 300, 306–309, 311, 364, 387, 410, 427, 431, 433, 434, 436, 439, 452, 455, 464, 481, 532n25, 615, 632, 634, 641–643, 646, 647, 650, 664, 670, 695, 708
Intellectual intuition, 99, 106, 110, 212, 382, 646
Irony
  romantic irony, 8, 9, 66, 255–266, 326, 335, 404, 406–407
  Socratic irony, 258, 283

J

Jacobi, Friedrich Heinrich, 2, 5, 6, 41–56, 65, 67–69, 71, 72, 74–76, 82, 88, 89, 97, 100–105, 108, 109, 111, 115, 183, 341n10, 539–542, 565n11, 565n12, 565n13, 566n18, 568n26, 577, 700n6
Jean Paul, 125, 178, 183, 194, 195, 441
Jena, 3, 4, 10, 20, 21, 23, 95, 97, 100, 125, 137n33, 188, 211, 215, 218, 226n23, 247, 249n2, 276, 341n10, 349, 376, 383, 387, 439, 452, 465n4, 467n33, 498, 677n5, 690, 695, 697

K

Kant, Immanuel, ix, 2, 19–36, 41, 68, 95, 142, 180, 208, 233, 276, 312n1, 341n10, 347, 376, 399, 424, 451, 514, 577, 592, 612, 631, 663, 684
Kielmeyer, Carl Friedrich von, 370n9, 400, 414, 415, 456, 457
Kierkegaard, Soren, 13, 535, 540, 550, 561, 562n2, 564n8, 567n21, 567n24, 569n26, 571n42, 706
Kleist, Heinrich von, 129, 317–319, 334, 339, 340n2, 378, 477, 593
Klopstock, Friedrich Gottlieb, 41, 180, 194
Kneller, Jane, 5, 214, 229n59, 401, 638, 706, 707
Kuzniar, Alice, 308, 480, 504n29

L

Lacoue-Labarthe, Philippe, 289n1, 292n58, 311, 315n44, 315n49, 452, 645
Landauer, Gustav, 15, 684–695, 697, 698, 700n6, 700n12, 701n14, 701n15, 701n17, 701–702n22, 702n24, 702–703n34
Leibniz, Gottfried Wilhelm, 70, 86, 208, 381, 540, 701n14
Lenoir, Timothy, 467n33, 468n33, 470n55
Lessing, Gotthold Ephraim, 41, 100, 123, 189, 199n33, 200n62, 243, 244, 518, 539, 541, 696
Levin, Rahel, 125, 127
Lichtenberg, Georg C., 274, 469n43
Liebknecht, Karl, 684
Life
  aesthetic life, 158, 444n14, 532n27, 574
  ethical life, 389

moral life, 55, 162–164, 168
philosophy of life, 12, 14, 609, 610, 625
Liszt, Franz, 594
Literary form, 3, 8, 245, 271–273, 275, 276, 280, 306, 310, 415, 427, 640
Longing, 87, 134n13, 136n24, 499, 543–546, 548, 549, 567n24, 592, 593, 708
Love, 23, 36n5, 86–89, 130, 165, 166, 169, 214, 218, 275, 329, 335, 337, 343n29, 347, 349, 353, 375, 376, 381, 388, 404, 424, 478, 480, 481, 483–485, 487, 488, 494, 495, 497–500, 520, 550, 551, 556, 557, 568n25, 623, 624, 629n90, 630n93, 641, 644, 657n53
Lovejoy, A. O., 1
Lukacs, Georg, 298, 311, 315n46, 693
Luxemburg, Rosa, 684
Lyotard, Jean-François, 205, 276

## M

MacIntyre, Aladair, 219–222
Mainländer, Philipp, 573
Marcuse, Herbert, 15, 683, 684
Mathematics, 33, 234, 262, 263, 280, 349, 429
Mayr, Ernst, 348, 367
Mendelssohn, Moses, 45, 62n57, 75, 124, 523, 538, 539, 541–542
Mendelssohn-Bartholdy, Leah, 123
Messner, Reinhold, 323–325, 327–339, 342n24, 343n26, 343n27, 343–344n36
Millán, Elizabeth, 153n1, 229n59, 253n71, 372n40, 531n23, 676n2
Modernism, 2, 6, 12, 14, 66, 84, 91, 538, 587–603

Modernity, 65–88, 205, 322, 323, 342n12, 375, 376, 448n65, 592, 593, 598, 602, 606n31, 609, 619, 652, 689
postmodernity, 6, 72, 78, 79, 84, 91, 608, 614, 706
Morality, 7, 11, 15, 21–23, 33, 37n7, 50, 77, 89, 158–161, 166–168, 171, 172, 276, 286, 368, 390, 425, 438, 634–639, 641, 649, 654
Moritz, Karl Philipp, 198n29, 332, 343n25, 434, 437
Morson, Gary, 272, 273, 275
Mühsam, Erich, 684
Müller, Adam, 129, 608
Müller-Sievers, Helmut, 343n33
Mysticism, 89, 196n4, 279, 423, 483, 667
Mythology, 180, 187, 191, 312, 405, 406, 425, 432–438, 440, 443, 448n63, 532n27, 543, 560, 561, 588, 589, 592, 595, 601, 617, 653
new mythology, 11, 406, 422, 434, 435, 437, 438, 440, 443, 447n63, 523, 532n27, 592, 691

## N

Nancy, Jean-Luc, 289n1, 292n58, 311, 315n44, 315n49, 452, 625n7, 631, 645
Nassar, Dalia, 396n23, 640, 706, 707
Nationalism, 13, 140n68, 218, 223n5, 517, 524, 528, 598
Nature
alienation from nature, 488
appreciation of nature, 80, 295n115, 525, 540, 653
beauty of nature, 652
forces of nature, 456, 457, 525, 584n16

Nature (*cont.*)
  Hegel's philosophy of nature, 41, 68, 104, 105, 114, 207, 315n48
  laws of nature, 69, 74, 454
  poetry of nature, 260, 621
  rational nature, 55, 167
  sciences of nature, 10, 24, 33, 70, 83, 207, 209, 211, 212, 295n115, 341n10, 400, 434, 522, 529n4, 610, 705
  *Naturphilosophie*, 349, 417n1, 427, 439, 447n63, 451, 456, 457, 461–464, 467n33, 468n36, 470n55, 470n58, 541
Nazis, 66, 67
Newton, Isaac, 348, 375, 378, 379, 439, 453–455, 468n33, 622
Nietzsche, Friedrich, 9, 271–288, 311, 322, 330, 564n9, 572n43, 573, 580, 595, 596, 602, 604n14, 605n20, 606n32, 612, 701n14, 706
Nihilism, 3, 41–56, 100, 700n6
Noack, Ludwig, 574, 575, 580
Norman, Judith, 563n8, 707
Novalis, 3, 5, 19–24, 48, 84, 96, 97, 141, 178, 205–222, 234, 255, 256, 271, 297–312, 322, 347, 399, 421, 453, 475, 607, 631, 638, 663, 688, 706
  and Copernican turn, 29, 186
  *Europe or Christianity*, 421, 437
  Hegel's critique of, 312
  Heidegger and, 214, 607, 609, 620, 691
  *Heinrich von Ofterdingen*, 10, 300, 301, 308–310, 312, 411, 415, 437, 480, 481, 483, 484, 491, 495, 496
  Hölderlin and, 6, 88, 89, 96, 97, 108, 141, 178, 201n65, 282, 341n10, 439, 663, 669, 676n3, 707

O
Oken, Lorenz, 10, 348–350, 352, 356, 361, 362, 368, 370n11, 372n44, 461–463

P
Pantheism, 13, 42, 65, 67, 68, 71–74, 76, 82, 88, 89, 535–562, 580
Paradox, 52, 89, 256, 258–260, 265, 266, 328, 697, 698
Paradoxical, 34, 90, 146, 424, 425, 433, 444n10, 546, 703n34
Peace, 184, 330, 349, 520, 614
Pessimism, 12–14, 220, 573–583, 597
Pippin, Robert, 75, 86
Plato, 21, 28, 29, 54, 55, 62n57, 174n32, 209, 244, 245, 278, 391, 612, 619, 620, 622, 648, 663, 669
Platonic, 11, 62n57, 245, 276, 391, 680n34
Platonism, 29, 248, 391–392, 687
Poetry
  ancient poetry, 303
  *Dialogue on Poetry*, 434
  modern poetry, 3, 195
  and myth, 95, 340, 532n27, 545, 546, 617, 622, 707
  and philosophy, 3, 90, 91, 348, 426, 523
  poetry of nature, 260, 621
  romantic poetry, 6, 11, 12, 76, 88, 90, 91, 241, 256, 259, 260, 279, 280, 292n58, 387, 421, 422, 443n4, 449, 450, 458, 460, 644, 708
Poiesis, 141, 399, 404–407, 430–433, 532n25
Progress, 13, 19, 25, 35, 54, 70, 82, 122, 125, 130, 174n33, 185, 220, 287, 302, 383, 500, 582, 583, 594, 617, 647, 667, 684, 694

## R

Ranciere, Jacques, 15, 632, 633, 635, 649–654
Reinhold, Karl, 20–24, 26, 36n6, 37n9, 41, 44, 51, 57n4, 61n36, 96, 97, 99, 142, 143, 154n3, 194, 211, 222n2, 233–239, 247, 250n11, 250n18, 341n10, 376
Religion
　Hölderlin and, 6, 89, 96, 108, 178
　and humanism, 435
　Schelling and, 96, 178, 202n91, 580, 696
Respect, 9, 22, 48, 60n26, 66, 106, 124, 148, 153, 165, 166, 198n26, 235, 238, 241, 242, 277, 279–283, 285, 288, 291n43, 315n48, 334, 335, 337, 382, 453, 456, 468n33, 504n29, 517, 527, 559, 566n15, 576, 580, 583, 667
Revolution, 15, 29, 48, 81, 127, 185, 208, 220, 297, 384, 385, 520, 523, 524, 588, 599, 617, 653, 654, 684–691, 693, 695, 701n15
Richards, Robert, 10, 79, 229n59, 467–468n33, 705
Ritter, Johann Wilhelm, 12, 399, 408–410, 422, 430, 431, 445n22, 456, 458–460, 477, 481
Rohmer, Eric, 317–319, 339, 340n2
Romantic subjectivity, 153
Rorty, Richard, 205, 283
Rousseau, Jean-Jacques, 60n35, 174n33, 452, 520

## S

Salon, 5–7, 67, 119–131, 222, 519
Schelling, Caroline von, 247, 341n10, 493
Schelling, Friedrich von, 340, 399, 403, 405, 407, 417n1, 456–459, 461, 463, 467n33, 468n35, 468n36, 469n40, 498, 535–562
Schiller, Friedrich von, 5, 7, 15, 41, 121, 127, 134n14, 135n21, 157–172, 179, 183, 194, 195, 198n27, 203n94, 208, 211, 229n59, 303, 315n48, 342n17, 383–385, 390, 392, 394, 537, 563n4, 582, 599, 632, 646, 649–652, 701n14
　*Aesthetic Letters*, 159, 160, 166–168, 170–172, 383, 384
　form drive, 167, 168
　*Lucinde*, 10, 140n73, 141, 149–151, 250n22, 267n7, 268n14, 268n19, 268n21, 289n14, 299–301, 305, 310, 404–406, 418n22, 477, 479, 481–485, 494–496, 502n1, 503n2, 503n7, 656n38, 657n53
　"On Grace and Dignity," 159–168, 171, 173n9, 173n10, 174n29
　sense drive, 167, 168, 171
Schlegel, August Wilhelm, 188, 189, 195, 247, 341n10
Schlegel, Dorothea Mendelssohn, 3, 7, 13, 131, 132n5, 137n35, 247, 309, 507n99
Schlegel, Friedrich, 4, 7, 9–13, 15, 20, 21, 30, 35, 36n5, 41, 43, 69, 84, 108, 127, 137n33, 140n73, 142, 178, 182, 194, 198n26, 201n71, 211, 226n23, 239, 241, 249n2, 255–257, 267n1, 277, 282, 295n115, 298–301, 306, 310, 312n5, 322, 329, 335, 338, 341n10, 343n33, 348, 387, 426, 427, 434, 464n1, 476, 477, 494, 495, 512, 517, 519, 520, 532n28, 566n16, 568n26, 592, 607, 608, 632, 638, 644, 650, 663, 700n6
　*Concept of Irony*, 259
　and incomprehensibility, 3, 256, 257, 489, 616–618, 640

Schlegel, Friedrich (*cont.*)
  influence on Heidegger, 608
  *Meister* essay, 312n1,
    313n12, 313n16
Schlegel Schelling, Caroline, *see*
  Schelling, Caroline von
Schleiermacher, Friedrich, 3, 6, 8, 20,
    95–98, 103, 105, 108–115,
    121–123, 127, 129–131, 132n3,
    134n14, 134–135n16, 135n17,
    135n21, 137n32, 178, 180,
    196n6, 201n65, 202n91,
    205–222, 234, 244–247, 249n2,
    256, 282, 396n27, 477, 481,
    573, 607, 608, 610–613, 616,
    619, 623, 624, 626n12,
    628n49, 705
*Schmerz*, 559
Schmid, Carl Christian Erhard, 96
Scholem, Gershom, 684,
    700n6, 702n33
Schopenhauer, Arthur, 574–583,
    584n16, 584n21, 597, 601,
    605n19, 701n14
Science, 1–3, 6, 8–12, 22, 24, 31, 33,
    35, 45–49, 51, 52, 54, 57n4, 66,
    69, 70, 73, 74, 78–81, 83, 84,
    86, 110, 151, 154n3, 190,
    201n71, 206–215, 217, 219,
    223n6, 235–237, 240, 245,
    249n8, 250n18, 261–265, 287,
    295n115, 311, 330, 339,
    341n10, 347–349, 352, 354,
    357, 358, 365, 368, 379, 382,
    400, 402, 403, 421–443, 450,
    451, 453, 454, 461, 488,
    520–523, 525, 529n4, 543, 577,
    610, 619–622, 639, 648, 695,
    696, 698, 700n7, 705, 707
Seyhan, Azade, 469n49
Shakespeare, William, 2, 181, 196n6,
    199n33, 241, 302, 594, 619
Shepherdson, Charles, 631, 634

Skepticism, 57n4, 182, 214, 234, 278,
    280, 639
Sociability, 20, 36, 120–124, 126, 131,
    134n14, 137n32, 137n35,
    217, 644
Socrates, 54–56, 209, 257, 258, 669
Sophocles, 595, 673
Spinoza, Baruch, 4–6, 29, 37n8, 42,
    45, 46, 57n4, 65–91, 100, 101,
    286, 367, 378, 394, 434, 435,
    538–542, 552, 556, 561,
    565n11, 565n12,
    565n14, 701n14
  *natura naturans*, 73
  *natura naturata*, 73
Steigerwald, Joan, 468n33
Stone, Alison, 334, 338, 706
Striving, 4, 9, 32, 39n40, 150, 153,
    178, 185, 244, 255–257,
    259–261, 263, 265, 267n5, 280,
    293n58, 296n119, 387, 389, 390,
    551, 552, 556, 573, 574, 579,
    581, 583, 613, 644, 646, 708
*Sturm und Drang*, 57n4, 178, 381,
    382, 385
Sublime, 43, 162, 320, 323–330, 332,
    337–339, 342n17, 377, 394,
    478, 537, 564n9, 665
Suffering, 24, 54, 165, 275, 335, 354,
    371n30, 479, 556, 558, 559,
    573–575, 581–583, 652,
    667, 675
Symbol, 59n16, 67, 136n24, 209, 393,
    435, 436, 447n56, 452, 481,
    522, 634–638, 675, 681n42
Symbolic, 379, 436, 438, 452,
    637, 697
System
  Kant's system, 26, 142
  Schelling's system, 536
  systematic philosophy, 42–43,
    284, 287
  system building, 286

## Index

### T

Tieck, Ludwig, 301, 305, 325, 328, 329, 331, 341n10, 342n17, 411, 575

Translation, 15, 115n1, 135n20, 137n35, 183, 210, 214, 225n14, 225n15, 244, 245, 268n17, 319, 320, 343n26, 395n12, 401, 437, 440, 463, 464n1, 493, 503n7, 513, 531n19, 543, 547, 553, 562n1, 563n8, 568n26, 571n38, 571n41, 623, 628n49, 672–674, 677n6, 699n1, 707
  hermeneutics and, 214, 244, 245

*Tugendbund*, 6, 119, 126, 127, 129

### U

University of Berlin, 8, 206–211, 218, 219, 221, 225n13, 225n15, 229n59

### V

Varnhagen, Karl August von, 122, 123, 127, 128

Varnhagen, Rahel, 7, 123, 126–127, 133n9, 136n22, 140n73, 493, 519

Veit, Dorothea, *see* Schlegel, Dorothea Mendelssohn

Vocation, 308, 309, 351, 477, 485, 486, 488, 489, 492, 495, 497, 500–502, 670, 688, 689

Voltaire, 60n35

### W

Wackenroder, Wilhelm Heinrich, 3, 575, 579

Wagner, Richard, 12, 14, 318, 340n2, 528, 572n43, 587–603, 617

Weatherby, Leif, 12, 416, 445n17, 705, 706

Wilhelmy-Dollinger, Petra, 120, 122, 130, 132n6, 134n13, 136n24, 136n26, 137n35, 140n70

Will, 544

Winckelmann, Johann Joachim, 188, 189, 200n62, 315n48

Wit, 140n68, 260, 266, 274, 279–281, 293n67

Wolf, Caspar Friedrich, 454

Wordsworth, William, 324, 347

### Z

Zammito, John, 514

Ziolkowski, Theodore, 3–4, 410

Zizek, Slavoj, 74, 75, 86, 563–564n8

Printed in the United States
By Bookmasters